EXPERT ACCOUNTING EVIDENCE

EXPERT ACCOUNTING EVIDENCE

A Guide for Litigation Support

Gervase MacGregor
BDO Stoy Hayward
and
Ian Hobbs
Littlejohn Frazer

Legal Editors:
Herbert Smith

with a contribution from
Tony Levitt
RGL International

Accountancy Books
Gloucester House
399 Silbury Boulevard
Central Milton Keynes
MK9 2HL
Tel: 0171 920 8991
E-mail: abgbooks@icaew.co.uk
Website: www.icaew.co.uk/books.htm

ISBN 1 85355 800 1

British Library Cataloguing-in-Publication Data

A catalogue record for this book is available from the British Library.

Throughout this book the male pronoun has been used to cover references to both the male and female.

Typeset by RefineCatch Limited, Bungay, Suffolk
Printed in Great Britain by MPG Books Limited, Bodmin, Cornwall

Contents

Part 2 – The practice of the expert witness

Part 5 – Regulatory matters

Appendices

Foreword

Litigation has become a substantially more sophisticated process over the last few years. The nature of the expert support available to the lawyers of the parties has been one of the causes. This has opened up to examination in the course of litigation issues which would have been unexplored in the days when I was in practice and a trial judge. The parties have, as a result, become increasingly dependent on expert assistance from other professions as well as lawyers. The assistance is required to evaluate the merits and value of a claim, the steps which are necessary to prepare the case for trial and at trial and the form of the expert evidence. The range of experts offering to provide this assistance is continually expanding, but undoubtedly accountants have been in the forefront in providing this support. Regularly, it is accountants who are the leading members of a party's litigation team.

This expanded role can only be properly performed by accountants if they have a thorough understanding of the litigation process and what is required of experts. The Academy of Experts and the Expert Witnesses Institute have been set up to promote the necessary understanding and proper professional standards. But those bodies do not diminish the need for a book which will provide for accountants, who become involved in the litigation process, the knowledge which they need to be able to provide expert services of the required quality.

That is what this book does admirably. It explains in clear and simple language everything of which the expert accountant should be aware in order to be an effective expert. It includes excellent examples of many of the topics covered which illustrate the information contained in the text. It also cites selectively previous decisions of the courts which are likely to be of particular interest to accountants. It manages within a relatively compact volume to cover an amazing range of subjects. It will provide a valuable addition to any firm of accountants' library. I can anticipate an accountant who is called upon to give advice or evidence at short notice turning to this book with relief to check that his or her recollection of some aspect of the legal process is accurate.

I welcome the publication of this book and congratulate the authors on a job well done. I do so, because while I welcome the greater involvement of accountants in the court process, this welcome is conditional. It is conditional on the involvement being constructive. It can only be constructive if the involvement is knowledgeable and proportionate. Unfortunately, sometimes it is not and this is all too often due to ignorance or a lack of professionalism for which this book provides the remedy. The authors rightly stress the need to keep costs under control and echo the messages which are contained in my report on *Access to Justice*. The primary duty which experts owe is to the courts.

The Right Honourable The Lord Woolf
The Master of the Rolls

Preface and acknowledgements

> 'When an expert witness is called my hopes are always high that I am about to reach an oasis of truth in a desert of half truths, evasions and downright lies. Often my hopes are realised, but sometimes I fear they are dashed to the ground.'

So said Lord Justice Murray at the annual conference of what was then the British Academy of Experts in 1991. Accountants are frequently asked to provide expert assistance in litigation and will be only too well aware, either from personal experience or from professional reading, that accountants themselves are not immune from suit.

Much litigation results in the award of damages and, even though most cases are settled before they come to trial, assessment of the likely level of damages is usually an integral part of settlement negotiations. Accountants are used to dealing with numbers, and their expert advice may be sought both on the numbers and on accounting issues generally in a surprisingly wide range of civil and criminal proceedings.

At first blush it would seem surprising that expert evidence from an accountant would be needed in connection with a trial, at the Old Bailey, of directors of a company accused of arson and manslaughter, but the motive for the arson, which resulted in the death of a fireman, was alleged to be financial, and accountants were retained by the Crown and the defence to provide expert assistance to the court on the financial state of the business immediately before the trial.

If an accountant is to act as an expert, and to write reports with a view to giving evidence, it is important that he should understand the legal process and the part he plays in it, and this book has been written with a view to explaining to accountants what their responsibilities are and how to go about fulfilling them. It is not a legal textbook although, as we understand it and with considerable help from Herbert Smith particularly, there are no legal howlers.

The book has been written to assist accountants in understanding:

- the legal process in England to the extent that they are likely to be involved with it as experts;
- the role of the expert.

The role of the expert is illustrated by reference to the various types of litigation in which their services may be required and by illustrations, from reported cases and otherwise, of what can happen if things go well and what can happen if, unfortunately, things do not go quite so well.

Litigation in England is adversarial and, when matters come to trial, there are winners and losers. For a case to come to trial at all, both sides must think that they have a reasonable chance of winning. The expert's job is to assist the court on technical matters and to that extent Lord Woolf's proposal, in *Access to Justice*, that there should be one court-appointed expert would seem a logical consequence of the function of the expert. However, the reported cases, and many more unreported ones, demonstrate that two experts in the same profession can hold, legitimately, very different views on the same subject, whether it be liability in the case of, say, accountants' negligence, or on quantum in other cases. The experts retained by each side may, therefore, hold very different views of the consequences of the same set of facts, and it is for the court to decide which expert evidence is preferred. The best that the expert can hope for is that his opinion will be preferred to that of the expert on the other side. At worst, the ill-prepared or dishonest expert will be identified as such by the court, and to the world at large.

We hope that this book will assist accountants wishing to act as experts to decide on whether that is something they really want to do, and whether they are equipped to do it. We hope that it will assist accountants in carrying out their work and, particularly, in understanding their role as part of the team.

The book has not been designed to be read from cover to cover. Those who do decide to do that will find some necessary duplication. We expect people to read chapters of particular interest to them and hope that what they find will be helpful.

We have had a great deal of help from those within our respective firms and from lawyers ranging from assistant solicitors to Queen's Council. We have also been helped enormously over the years by receiving instructions to practise what we preach, and this book could not have been written without the help and suggestions given, over many years, by those instructing us, by counsel and by the courts.

We would particularly like to thank the following:

Tony Levitt, RGL International; David Natali, Mary-Emma Smith and many other members of Herbert Smith; The Right Honourable The Lord Woolf, Master of the Rolls; Edmund Lawson QC; John Ellison, KPMG; Ian Cherry, A I Cherry; Richard Pearson, Pannell Kerr Forster; Rodney Nelson-Jones,

Field Fisher Waterhouse; James Stanbury, RGL International; Lynn Graham, Legal Aid Board; Maggie Rae, Mischon de Reya; John Kendall, Allen & Overy; Brian Spiro, Simons Muirhead & Burton; Peter Danial, Wayne Anthony, David Templeman and Kate Pipe, BDO Stoy Hayward.

Gervase MacGregor
Ian Hobbs
August 1998

Table of cases

Table of abbreviations

AC	Law Reports, Appeal Cases, 1891–current
All ER	All England Law Reports, 1936–current
App.Cas.	Law Reports, Appeal Cases, 1875–1890
BCC	British Company Cases, 1983–current
BCLC	Butterworths Company Law Cases
CA	Court of Appeal
Ch	Law Reports, Chancery Division, 1891–current
Ch D	Law Reports, Chancery Division, 1875–1890
CLR	Commonwealth Law Reports, 1903–current (Australia)
CLY	Current Law Year Book
Cr.App.R	Criminal Appeal Reports, 1908–current
Crim. LR	Criminal Law Review, 1954–current
Dougl.	Douglas' Reports, King's Bench, 1778–1785
EG	Estates Gazette, 1858–current
EGCS	Estates Gazette Case Summaries
Fam	Law Reports, Family Division, 1972–current
FCR	Family Court Reporter
FLR	Family Law Reports, 1980–current
FSR	Fleet Street Reports, 1963–current
ICR	Industrial Cases Reports, 1972–current
KB	Law Reports, King's Bench Division, 1900–1952
KIR	Knight's Industrial Reports
Lloyd's Rep.	Lloyd's Reports, 1951–current
LR	Law Reports, from 1865
Med.LR	Medical Law Reports
NY	New York Reports
NZLR	New Zealand Law Reports, 1883–current

PIQR	Personal Injuries and Quantum Reports
PN	Professional Negligence
QB	Law Reports, Queen's Bench Division, 1891–1900; 1952–current
QBD	Law Reports, Queen's Bench Division, 1875–1890
RPC	Reports of Patent Cases, 1884–current
SC	Court of Session Cases (Scotland), 1906–current
STC	Simon's Tax Cases
TLR	The Times Law Reports, 1884–1952
WLR	Weekly Law Reports, 1953–current

Table of statutes

Arbitration Act 1996	14.2, 14.2.4
s1	14.2.4
s33(1)(a)	14.2.1
Banking Act 1987	
s39	26.5.13
Broadcasting Act 1990	
s166	23.2
Civil Evidence Act 1968	12.3.2
Civil Evidence Act 1972	
s3	2.5
(1) (3)	2.7
Civil Evidence Act 1995	2.8.4, 12.2.6
s1(1)	2.8
s4(2)	2.8, 2.8.4
s10	21.4.1
Companies Act 1929	29.1
Companies Act 1948	30.2
s332	31.5.1
Companies Act 1985	26.2, 26.5.13, 34.1, 34.9
s151	26.5.5
ss155, 156	30.3.1
s173	30.3.1
(3)(b)	30.4
s226	26.3
s232	26.5.5
ss233, 234, 234A	26.3
s263	26.5.12
s390(2)	26.5.8
ss431–433	34.3

Table of rules and regulations

Part 1
The accountant and the legal process

Chapter 1
The legal framework

1.1 Introduction

Litigation is something that everybody fancies they know a bit about. Any readers of detective books will be thoroughly aware of the detection and forensic processes. Rumpole has exposed large numbers of people to such principles of English justice as the presumption of innocence, the cynicism of barristers and the unreasonableness of judges.

For those who do not read, or maybe supplement their reading, the television courtroom drama has shown a wide audience in-depth presentations of criminal trials in the USA (*Murder One*), and rhetorical flourishes and clever cross-examination by lawyers in civil and criminal cases (*Kavanagh QC*); those of a slightly older generation will remember the cinema-verité of *Crown Court*.

Literature and drama concentrate, quite rightly, on the high points of litigation, in order to keep the audience's interest. What they do not do is expose people to the legal system as a whole; however, television can overcome even this, at least as far as a trial is concerned, as the live proceedings of the OJ Simpson and Louise Woodward trials demonstrate.

But litigation is wider than a trial – trials are just the conclusion of months of legal preparation. This first chapter attempts to set out the framework of the English legal system and the part the expert accountant plays in the proceedings, and to act as an introduction to the book.

1.2 Facts and proof

One of the obligations imposed by law is that a person bringing an action in a tribunal against another person must prove his case on the balance of probabilities. A person proves his case by adducing evidence (mainly oral evidence but also documentary and real evidence) and opinion. Furthermore, the vast majority of litigants use an advocate to present that evidence to the tribunal through the oral examination of witnesses. The advocate also argues the litigant's case before the tribunal.

The party against whom the case is brought, the defendant, is entitled to test this evidence. Again, he uses an advocate, who tests the evidence by cross-questioning the witnesses; likewise, his advocate argues his case.

Defendants are not required to present any evidence in their own defence, however, if they do, and they usually do, they will do this through the presentation of evidence and the process of examination and cross-questioning is mirrored.

At the end of the presentation of the evidence and the speeches by the advocates, findings of fact are made, either by the judge as in most civil trials, or by the jury as in most criminal trials. The successful bringer of the action in a civil action, the plaintiff, will have proved his case on the balance of probabilities; in a successful criminal action, it will be the successful prosecutor who has proved his case against the defendant beyond reasonable doubt.

Facts, and the proof of facts, are therefore all important in English law.

1.3 Findings of law

In contrast to findings of fact, courts also make findings of law. This is always carried out by a judge. A finding of law is a statement of what the law is in a particular area. English law is primarily a judge-made legal system, that is, findings of law by one court are binding on courts in cases later on.

This judge-made law develops through a series of precedents, which are applied in identical or similar situations through time. Parliament makes law, through Acts of Parliament, but it is the judiciary which interprets legislation. Furthermore, judges in superior courts have the power to overrule decisions of inferior courts, thus, the House of Lords can overrule a decision of the Court of Appeal but the opposite cannot happen. There are many philosophical and constitutional reasons for giving this power to judges, but on a practical level it is impossible to legislate for every eventuality which might arise; legislation, by its nature, must be drawn relatively widely.

Part of the advocate's role is to address the judge on points of law, referring to precedents and making submissions on what the law is.

1.4 Experts

Expert witnesses play a very strange role in this process, giving opinion evidence. It is worth setting out what experts are not, in the light of the above characters.

First of all, experts are not advocates, that is, they do not argue and present a litigant's case. However, there is a view that one role of the expert is to advance a litigant's case. Even if they do not perform this function in the witness box, they are certainly capable of carrying it out before a trial.

Second, experts are not factual witnesses, they are opinion witnesses, that is, on a given set of facts they will give evidence on what conclusions can be drawn from those facts. However, experts do give factual evidence in cases. Sometimes they are the only person able to adduce certain factual evidence.

Third, the expert is not judge or jury, that is, the court does not allow the expert to make binding findings on facts or on law. However, an expert can give evidence on ultimate issues and sometimes his evidence will be so compelling that a court will almost certainly accept it.

1.5 Accountants and accounting experts

Many criminal prosecutions and most commercial litigation involve money. Money is the motive for large numbers of crimes; civil proceedings are normally undertaken for financial reasons. It is fair to say that money is at the centre of most litigation in this country.

Therefore, it is natural that accountants have a role in much litigation; indeed, on this money construction of the basis for litigation, it is surprising that the accountant does not play more of a central role in more cases.

However, there is a fundamental problem in the current status of experts, particularly expert accountants, and it is this. Because accountants can play such a fundamental role in litigation, and because their final report may include a mixture of pure opinion evidence, accounting evidence which is the result of computational analysis, and a recitation of the facts (disputed or not) of the case, it is difficult for courts and for opponents to work out what it is they are saying which is admissible as expert evidence. Indeed, it may be that case law is insufficiently developed for this problem to be adequately resolved in most litigation.

Thus, there is often pressure on expert accountants to include in their reports much information which may be of little use to the court or the litigation as a whole as expert evidence, but which appears to advance one side's case overall.

On the other hand, there is probably much that an accountant can carry out in trial preparation which does not form part of his final report, but which is extremely useful for trial preparation. One thinks of, for example, cross-examination strategies, assistance with pleadings and discovery and the general commercial knowledge which a properly experienced accountant can bring to any business situation. This role of the accountant is more akin to that of a member of his instructing solicitor's team.

However, any accountant who gets involved in litigation should not forget that he may have to give independent evidence at trial, and he cannot afford to get so involved in a case that he loses his objectivity. Nor must he have such a poor knowledge of the legal system that he does not appreciate when his instructing solicitors or counsel are trying to get him to say things in his report which will come to haunt him at trial.

1.6 The framework of this book

This book attempts to teach accountants the nature of expert evidence, how best to give expert evidence and the basics of the English legal system, with an emphasis on their role within it.

Part 1 looks at the nature of expert evidence and what makes for good expert evidence. It then looks at the two particular areas of giving expert evidence, in court and in a report. Chapter 5, looking at evidence in court, considers what it is that advocates are attempting to do when they stand up to address the court and question witnesses.

Part 1 also has a chapter discussing Lord Woolf's proposals, with an emphasis on how the role of the expert may change in the future.

Part 2 is entitled 'the practice of the expert witness' and looks at how the accountant should organise his practice. It also gives practical help on understanding two extremely important areas for any expert who wishes to be successful profitably as well as professionally – costs and legal aid.

There are also two complementary chapters, setting out how a solicitor should use the expert and how an expert should use his instructing solicitor.

Part 3 looks at civil litigation. It first of all describes civil procedure, and then considers the various areas of civil litigation which the accountant is likely to come across in practice. These range from straightforward damages claims in personal injury cases, through libel to tracing claims. It also looks at how damages are calculated, the most common task for any expert accountant in civil proceedings. Additionally, there is a chapter on alternative modes of settling civil disputes, which are likely to increase in importance with time.

Part 4 looks at the related matters of criminal law, insolvency and fraud. In this section there is an emphasis on insolvency and its determination. As damages are of fundamental importance to any accountant in civil proceedings, so insolvency plays a similar role in criminal proceedings as it is on this aspect that the accountant can expect to give evidence in the criminal courts.

Finally, Part 5 deals with the specialised area of disciplinary and regulatory proceedings.

Chapter 2
Expert accounting evidence

2.1 Introduction

It is a general principle of English law that witnesses in proceedings may generally only give factual evidence.

Judges make findings of fact in civil trials, juries make findings of fact in criminal trials. Witnesses merely give evidence, and the judge or jury must decide whether they believe them.

The role of the expert cuts across all of this. Experts give opinion evidence (but they may also give factual evidence). Experts also, it must be said, make findings which are a judge's responsibility to make.

The role of the expert will, if current developments (such as envisaged in the Woolf Report) continue, become even greater.

There are many types of expert – handwriting experts, chemists, psychologists – indeed as many types of experts as there are professions. However, it is doubtful if any has the potential to play a more extensive role in court proceedings than the accountant. Why should this be the case? The simple answer is that figures are at the heart of most civil proceedings, figures in the form of damages and financial records, their calculation and interpretation.

In criminal cases, accountants have a central role to play in fraud. But they are also used in murder trials (money as a motive for murder), drugs trials (establishing or tracing the proceeds of crime) and any other trial where help is needed with the figure work.

The pinnacle of an expert's part in a case may well be when he steps into the witness box; however, he will often have played a central role prior to the case going to court, assisting in drafting the pleadings and advising on discovery, on merits or on settlement.

The purpose of this chapter is to look at the nature of the expert accountant's evidence.

2.2 What is expert evidence?

Expert evidence is the giving of an expert opinion. Munkman describes this as follows:

> 'An expert opinion consists of a conclusion, drawn from facts, which may or may not be true, by inferences, which may or may not be sound.'

2.3 The nature of expert evidence

Experts have been used in courts since medieval times, but undertook their modern role in the eighteenth century. In the case of *Folkes* v *Chadd* [1782] 3 Dougl. 157, it was alleged by the plaintiff that a sea bank which had been erected for the purpose of preventing the overflowing of the sea had caused the decay of a harbour. An engineer called by the defence said that, in his opinion, the bank was not the cause. Lord Mansfield made the following statements in his judgment:

> 'It is objected that Mr Smeaton is going to speak, not as to facts, but as to opinion. That opinion, however, is deduced from facts which are not disputed . . . Mr Smeaton understands the construction of harbours, the causes of their destruction and how remedied . . . The cause of the decay . . . [of the harbour] is . . . a matter of science, and still more so, whether the removal of the bank can be beneficial. Of this, such men as Mr Smeaton alone can judge. Therefore, we are of the opinion that his judgment, formed on facts, was very proper evidence.'

All of the hallmarks of expert evidence are set out in this judgment:

(a) Mr Smeaton was an expert (he understood the construction of harbours, their destruction and how remedied);
(b) one of the issues before the court (causation) was one on which the court needed assistance;
(c) Mr Smeaton's evidence was based on facts; and
(d) the court believed Mr Smeaton, that is, he was credible.

2.4 The limits of expert evidence

A cursory glance at Lord Mansfield's judgment may indicate that the court had abrogated its decision-making role to Mr Smeaton. This is not the case because, even if unchallenged, courts do not necessarily have to accept the opinion of an expert. As Lord President Copper said in *Davie* v *Edinburgh Corporation* [1953] SC 34:

> 'Expert witnesses, however skilled or eminent, can give no more than evidence. They cannot usurp the functions of the jury or Judge sitting as jury . . . The scientific opinion evidence, if intelligible, convincing and tested, becomes a factor (and often an important factor) for consideration along with the whole other evidence in the case . . . '

2.5 The statutory basis for the use of expert evidence

In civil trials, expert evidence is allowed by virtue of s3 of the Civil Evidence Act 1972:

> '3(1) . . . where a person is called as a witness in any civil proceedings, his opinion on any relevant matter on which he is qualified to give expert evidence shall be admissible in evidence.'

In criminal proceedings, the common law position of expert evidence, as set out in *Chadd*, still holds. However, the ability to adduce expert evidence is recognised by s81 of the Police and Criminal Evidence Act 1984:

> '81(1) Crown Court Rules may make provision for–
>
> (a) requiring any party to proceedings before the court to disclose to the other party or parties any expert evidence which he proposes to adduce in the proceedings . . . '

2.6 The different types of expert evidence and expert accounting evidence

Hodgkinson distinguishes five types of expert evidence, as follows:

1 expert evidence of opinion, upon facts adduced before the court;
2 expert evidence to explain technical subjects or the meaning of technical words;
3 evidence of fact, given by an expert, the observation, comprehension and description of which require expertise;
4 evidence of fact, given by an expert, which does not require expertise for its observation, comprehension and description, but which is a necessary preliminary to the giving of evidence in the other four categories;
5 admissible hearsay of a specialist nature.

Hodgkinson uses these categories as a basis for considering the manner in which expert evidence can be adduced, and indeed whether it is expert evidence. This analysis is also useful for looking at the different types of expert evidence which an accountant may give.

In category 1 is what one may term pure expert accounting evidence. It is easiest to look at it in terms of a negligence case. The auditor did not carry out the following test – this is an established fact. In my opinion he should have carried out that test.

In category 2 would come the explanation of, for example, the term 'goodwill' in a set of financial statements.

In category 3 one finds a very large amount of expert evidence. A company accounts for work in progress in a certain way. An accountant is needed to explain what this means.

Category 4 is that type of evidence, not strictly expert evidence but factual evidence, that every accountant will give. For example, in a damages claim, he will give evidence on what the profit shown by a set of accounts is, where he uses that profit in assessing quantum.

Category 5 is the work of others in the expert's field of expertise. This is considered separately below.

The above analysis gives a useful introduction to what an accountant can and cannot say in court. Consider the following case studies.

2.6.1 A fraudulent misrepresentation case

The case involves a dispute over a purchase and sale agreement. The consideration for the purchase of a company is to be based on a multiple of earnings as shown by the last accounts. It is warranted that the accounts of the seller have been drawn up in accordance with generally accepted accounting policies (GAAP), consistently applied.

The purchaser has alleged in the statement of claim that the earnings shown by the accounts were overstated. He alleges further that the accounts were not drawn up in accordance with GAAP. He further alleges that the director-shareholders of the target company knew this, and deliberately and dishonestly misstated the profits. He calls expert accounting evidence. The expert accounting evidence and the category of that evidence is as shown in Figure 2.1.

Figure 2.1

Evidence given	*Category of evidence*
The disputed accounts show the following profits and other items.	This is factual, or what would be called category 4 evidence.
The purchase and sale agreement contains a clause which states that the accounts were to be drawn up in accordance with GAAP.	This is a fact – however, bear in mind that the legal effect of this clause, and any breach of the clause, are not matters for the accountant.
GAAP means the following.	The accountant is giving expert evidence on what is a technical accounting term, that is, GAAP. This is category 2 evidence.

The accounts did not comply with GAAP for the following reasons, for example, the accounts did not make a write-down for obsolete stock.	This is factual, category 4 evidence; however, the accountant may also be explaining technical accounting terms.
In my opinion, a provision should have been made for obsolete stock.	This is category 1 expert evidence. Notice, however, that this is based not just on facts, but also on the accountant's understanding of what GAAP is.
In my opinion, the directors knew that such a provision should have been made because they had a series of reports from their financial controller stating that a large amount of stock had not been sold for many years, no longer had a market and should be written off.	What is this type of evidence? The existence of the reports may be factual, but what is this factual evidence a preliminary to? Whether the directors knew or not on the basis of these reports is evidence of the directors' state of mind – hardly a subject for expert evidence. However, see **2.7** below on 'the ultimate issue'.
In my opinion, the only conclusion which can be drawn from this is that the directors deliberately misstated the accounts, that they did it dishonestly and that they misrepresented the earnings of the company fraudulently.	This is not evidence of any kind, it is a summing-up of the case. The accountant is basing his opinion on a mass of facts and other opinions. Again, see **2.7** below.

This type of case is one in which accountants are commonly asked to give evidence. However, the accountant needs to be very wary of circumstances where he is asked to make interpretations of documents with a view to giving evidence of motive or state of mind, rather than accountancy.

2.6.2 A fraud case

A director is charged with the theft of money from a company which has gone into liquidation. The prosecution have produced a number of cheques from debtors of the company payable to the director, statements from the company's bank account showing that such cheques were not received by the company, witness statements from these debtors confirming that the director asked that cheques to pay the company's debts were made out to him and the defendant's own bank account showing the receipt of these monies. The accounting records are extremely disorganised. An expert accountant is instructed to review the accounting records of both the company and all of the director's financial affairs with a view to providing evidence to support the director's defence that such monies were used solely by him to pay the company's wages bills. The accountant is also asked to agree or otherwise financial schedules produced by the prosecution.

The expert accounting evidence and the category of that evidence is as shown in Figure 2.2.

Figure 2.2

Evidence given	*Category of evidence*
An analysis of all receipts into the director's own bank accounts, analysed between amounts received from debtors of the company and from personal sources.	Factual, either category 3 or category 4.
An analysis of all payments from the director's own bank accounts, analysed between amounts paid to the company's employees and amounts for personal purposes.	Factual, either category 3 or category 4.
A comparison of the total of the receipts from the company's debtors and the total of payments to the company's employees, with the comment that the totals agree.	Factual, either category 3 or category 4.
An analysis of the company's wages records for individual employees showing that the amounts they received from the director were equivalent to amounts received from the company, and that receipts from the director only started when receipts from the company ceased.	Factual, either category 3 or category 4.
An analysis of individual receipts from debtors and payments to employees showing that individual amounts received were credited and amounts paid from those receipts debited on the same day.	Factual, either category 3 or category 4.

This is an extreme example, but should be looked at regardless of the merits of the charge brought or any other work that the accountant may be asked to carry out in the case.

The surprising thing about the evidence is that none of it could be construed as opinion evidence, in that the accountant reaches no conclusions on the basis of the facts. The 'expert' is solely being used to introduce into evidence certain unused material, for example the accounting records, and his analyses. Whether the evidence is category 3 or category 4 depends to a certain extent on the ease of obtaining it. A good example of category 3 type evidence is given by Stone:

> '[Expert witnesses] . . . may report facts which are inaccessible to lay witnesses, eg, the alcohol content of the deceased's stomach.'

In the above example there is a clear implication that the accounting records are not capable of easy analysis because of their disorganised state. An analysis of the director's bank account should be a more straightforward matter. The presentation of the figurework in the analyses is something which could be done by any reasonably numerate person. The explanation of the provenance of the figures from, particularly, the accounts, is something an accountant would do.

2.6.3 A personal injury case

A very successful self-employed writer is run down by a motor car and suffers extensive injuries, including limited brain damage. Following the accident he is no longer able to write. Medical evidence to be called on his behalf suggests that his inability to write is a direct result of the injuries suffered, particularly the brain damage.

An accountant is instructed to prepare a loss of income claim.

The expert accounting evidence and the category of that evidence is as shown in Figure 2.3.

Figure 2.3

Evidence given	*Category of evidence*
The accounts of the writer, showing his profits, for the last, say, six years up to the date of the accident.	Factual, category 4 evidence.

An extrapolation of the above profits up until a date when, the accountant has been instructed, the writer would have retired from writing. Additionally, the accountant has justified that the writer would have continued to earn royalties from book sales on the basis of: (a) increasing sales to the date of the accident; (b) confirmation from the writer's publisher that he was a very popular writer; (c) a draft contract offering the writer a 10 book contract.	Expert evidence category 1 – the accountant is making a forecast of future income from past accounts (a very common accounting technique, though not restricted to accountants) and is saying in effect that, in his expert opinion, the forecast is reasonable given the confirmatory evidence.
Tax is applied to each year of profits.	Category 3 factual evidence – the calculation of tax is a matter of fact, requiring assistance from an expert for its comprehension. Note the two assumptions on which this is based, first that the court will accept the accountant's calculations of loss of income and, second, that tax rates in the future will not change.
Interest is applied to the lost profits prior to the date of trial, to the date of trial.	Calculation of interest is a matter for the court, however, many accountants will show the calculation using an assumed rate of interest to aid the court in its own calculations – not strictly evidence at all.
Profits after the date of trial are discounted back to the date of trial.	Again, more properly a matter for the court. The accountant needs to make an assumption as to the discount rate which is used, and may be required to explain why this is appropriate.

The critical part of the accountant's evidence in a case like this is the calculation of the loss after the date of the accident and his reasons why this figure is reasonable. This type of exercise is one which is typical accounting opinion evidence. Whether the calculation is reasonable and, in particular, whether the confirmatory evidence used is reasonable are matters for the court.

Consider the position of the expert accountant called by the defence. He may question the reasonableness of the reliance on certain information. He may, for example, question its relevance. The draft contract may, for example, have been in respect of a type of book different to that normally written by the writer, and in a field where he had no previous sales. He may also bring other information into the equation by, for example, showing that since the writer's accident, the particular field in which the writer specialised is no longer in great demand. The accountant on either side may bring into consideration a large amount of third party information to justify his expert opinion. This aspect of accounting evidence is considered in more detail below.

2.6.4 An audit negligence case

Taking the fraudulent misrepresentation case, assume that the auditors to the target company are also being sued for their failure to spot the overstatements in the accounts.

An expert accountant is instructed by the purchasers. His evidence is as shown in Figure 2.4.

Figure 2.4

Evidence given	*Category of evidence*
The disputed accounts show the following profits and other items.	This is factual, category 4 evidence.
The accounts are accompanied by an audit certificate, saying that the accounts show a true and fair view.	This is factual, category 4 evidence.
The accounts did not make a write-down for obsolete stock.	This is factual, category 4 evidence; however, the accountant may also be explaining technical accounting terms.
In my opinion, a provision should have been made for obsolete stock, because the effect of that provision is material to the accounts.	This is category 1 expert evidence. Notice, however, that it is based not just on facts, but also on the accountant's view of materiality. The accountant will also give his category 1 opinion on what materiality is in the context of the accounts, and explain the technical accounting term materiality.
In my opinion, the accounts do not show a true and fair view, and therefore the audit certificate is wrong.	Category 1 opinion evidence.

The audit work carried out on stock by the auditors was as follows.	Category 3 factual evidence, requiring the accountant to explain what was carried out.
The auditors did not carry out the following work on stock.	Category 3 factual evidence.
In my opinion, a reasonably careful auditor should have carried out these tests.	Category 1 opinion evidence; however, phrases such as 'reasonably careful', 'a proper audit', 'a competent auditor' or 'it is standard audit practice' may properly be findings for the court.
In my opinion, the audit was carried out negligently and the auditors are liable for the losses sustained by the purchasers.	This is summing-up. The finding of negligence by the auditors and the finding of liability to the purchasers are matters for the court.

2.7 The ultimate issue

As noted above, s3(1) of the Civil Evidence Act 1972 includes the following:

> ' . . . his opinion on any relevant matter on which he is qualified to give expert evidence shall be admissible in evidence.'

Subsection 3(3) states that 'relevant matter' includes an issue in the proceedings. It is therefore recognised by statute that experts can give evidence on matters which are for the court to decide. However, as has been seen above, the expert cannot usurp the role of the court and, therefore, the court is not bound to accept what an expert says. Secondly, s3(1) states that an expert can give evidence where he is qualified to give such evidence, not where he is not. There are cases where the determination of issues is clearly based on expert evidence.

Example

'Is emigration a method of avoiding capital gains tax?'
'Yes.'
'Would any reasonably competent accountant have advised emigration in these circumstances?'
'Yes.'

However, there are many other cases where other issues are brought into play. Consider the evidence given in the fraudulent misrepresentation case at **2.6.1** above:

> 'In my opinion the directors knew that such a provision should have been made because they had a series of reports from their financial controller stating that a large amount of stock had not been sold for many years, no longer had a market, and should be written off.'

This was objected to because whether the directors knew or not on the basis of these reports is evidence of the directors' state of mind, and not an issue for an accountant. There may have been many other areas, including non-accounting areas, on which the court would hear evidence and which would lead it to make a finding about what was in the directors' minds.

However, the accountant should be able to give evidence on the following lines:

> 'In my opinion the directors should have known, on the basis of these reports, that a large amount of stock should have been written off.'

Example

'In my opinion, the only conclusion which can be drawn from this is that the directors deliberately misstated the accounts, that they did it dishonestly, and that they misrepresented the earnings of the company fraudulently.'

This was objected to because the accountant based his opinion on a mass of facts and other opinions.

However, the accountant should be able to give evidence on the following lines:

> 'In my opinion the accounts were deliberately misstated. The reports should have told them that stock was overstated. I have seen nothing which would be a reasonable justification for not writing this stock off.'

2.8 The expert and hearsay

Hearsay is a fact which has not been perceived by a witness, but has been told to him by another person. In criminal trials, there is a rule that hearsay, that is the former statements of a person, may not be given in evidence if the purpose of the evidence would be to assert the truth of the matters contained in the former standards. In civil trials, the rule against hearsay evidence has been removed by s1(1) of the Civil Evidence Act 1995 (which came into force on 31 January 1997).

In civil trials, although hearsay evidence is admissible, the fact that it is hearsay means that this is a relevant consideration which the court needs to take into account when deciding the weight to be attached to the evidence. Subsection 4(2) of the CEA lists out a number of matters which the court has to have regard to, for example, whether it would have been reasonable and practicable for the maker of the original statement to have been called, whether the evidence is multiple hearsay, whether the statement was made contemporaneously with the occurrence or existence of the matters stated or whether any person involved would have had a motive to conceal or misrepresent matters.

When an expert is giving evidence based on his experience and his training, this involves him accepting hearsay information. This is clear when an accountant gives evidence in the following terms:

> 'In my opinion, this transaction should be accounted for in the following way . . . I say this because, in my experience, this is the way in which this transaction is invariably treated, and I have never seen it treated in a contrary way.'

There are three areas where an expert uses hearsay in his evidence, being specific material used, an expert's experience of similar situations and an expert's general experience. However, it must be noted that the cases on this subject pre-date the implementation of s1 of the CEA, and how the rules will affect expert evidence in civil trials is not clear. This aspect is dealt with in the concluding section of this chapter, but it must be noted that the case law on similar situations may be out of date as a result of the CEA.

2.8.1 Specific material

Once the primary facts on which his opinion is based are proved, he is entitled to draw on the work of others in his field of expertise as part of the process of arriving at his conclusion (*R* v *Abadom*, 76 Cr.App.R 48 CA).

The Court of Appeal in that case recognised that part of an expert's experience is based on his knowledge and evaluation of unpublished material. Experts are allowed to draw on such material provided that it is referred to in their evidence.

2.8.2 Experience of similar situations

In *English Exporters (London) Ltd* v *Eldonwall Ltd* [1973] 1 Ch. 415, it was held that an expert valuer:

> '. . . may express the opinions he has formed as to values even though substantial contribution to the formation of those opinions have been made by matters of which he had no first-hand knowledge . . .'

If he had knowledge of particular transactions he could use such transactions as the basis of his opinion. However, he could not give evidence of a particular transaction itself if he had no personal knowledge of it:

> '. . . it seems to me quite another matter when it is asserted that a valuer may give factual evidence of transactions of which he has no direct knowledge, whether per se or whether in the guise of giving reasons for his opinion as to value. It is one thing to say "From my general experience of recent transactions comparable with this one, I think the proper rent should be £x": it is another thing to say "Because I have been told by someone else that the premises next door have an area of x square feet and were recently let on such-and-such terms for £y a year, I say the rent of these premises should be £z a year".'

The effect of this last statement seems to be that it provides a limit to the specialist hearsay which an expert may use. If something is within an expert's own experience, then he can refer to it; if he has been told it by a fellow professional, he cannot, because the court is denied the opportunity of hearing the other professional being cross-examined. If we consider the position of an accountant, this can be illustrated as in Figure 2.5.

Figure 2.5

Question	*Evidence*	*Admissible?*
What would be the normal gross profit one would expect in this particular industry?	In my experience of the accounts of companies in this particular industry, the gross profit which one would expect is x per cent.	Yes – however, if the expert is cross-examined the evidence may not be. See three possible questions below.
On what is your experience based?	I asked a number of partners in my office who deal with clients in this sector and they told me that x per cent was the average.	No – reliance on others, who are not giving evidence.
On what is your experience based?	I myself act for a number of clients in this sector and the average is x per cent.	Yes.
On what is your experience based?	My firm acts for a number of clients in this sector. As part of the preparation of my report, I reviewed their accounts, and the average gross profit was x per cent.	Yes.

However, the comments made above need to be considered in the light of the CEA, as noted in the next section.

2.9.3 General experience

There is a further aspect in which the expert gives evidence based on specialist hearsay, and that is in relation to general information which has, over time, contributed to his expertise. The *English Exporters* case deals with this issue as well:

> 'Textbooks, journals, reports of auctions and other dealings, and information obtained from his professional brethren and others, some related to particular transactions and some more general and indefinite, will all have contributed their share . . . the opinion that the expert expresses is none the worse because it is in part derived from matters of which he could give no direct evidence . . . the less reliable the knowledge that he has . . . the more his experience will tell him that he should be ready to make some discount from the weight that he gives it in contributing . . . No question of giving hearsay evidence arises in such cases; the witness states his opinion from his general experience.'

For expert accountants the role that general experience plays is ambiguous. On the one hand, it could give rise to an answer to a question on accounting for a particular transaction, as follows:

> 'In all my years as an accountant I have never seen this particular transaction accounted for in any other way.'

On the other hand, it could extend to areas which are not strictly accountancy, but which are within the accountant's wider business experience, as follows:

> 'In my experience, when a board of directors is faced with a letter from the bank notifying them that facilities were about to be withdrawn, they take that letter very seriously indeed.'

> 'It is the Inland Revenue's invariable practice to refuse such an election once the time limit has passed. I have never seen a situation to indicate otherwise.'

The way courts treat such evidence depends on specific circumstances, not least the overall experience of the expert.

2.8.4 Effect of the CEA

As noted above, experts have always been allowed by the courts to give certain types of hearsay evidence, other types of hearsay evidence being inadmissible. The CEA now allows as admissible all hearsay evidence (but the court will decide what weight to attach to it).

A question which arises, therefore, is how is the expert's evidence changed by the CEA. Not surprisingly, there are no cases on this, given the short time the new rules have been in force. However, one can speculate that there will be two effects:

(a) the hearsay evidence which experts have always been able to give will now be covered by the new rules, or at least judges will have regard to the matters set out in s4(2);
(b) experts may now be able to give any type of hearsay evidence, notwithstanding the restrictions noted above arising from the *English Exporters* case.

Where the expert is likely to be affected most is in the second type of hearsay noted above, the experience of similar situations. The effects of the CEA may be to make admissible evidence where an expert does refer to what he was told by others. However, in such a situation it would surely be beholden on the expert to carry out some verification work himself. Therefore, using the example above, if an expert has asked his fellow partners what the average gross profit in a section is, he should check the actual accounts to ensure that what he is being told is correct.

However, until there is a decided case on this aspect of expert evidence, the position of the expert is uncertain.

2.9 References

Hodgkinson, T. (1990) *Expert Evidence: Law and Practice*, Sweet & Maxwell.

Munkman, J. (1991) *The Technique of Advocacy*, Butterworths.

Stone, M. (1988) *Cross-examination in Criminal Trials*, Butterworths.

Chapter 3
The quality of expert accounting evidence

3.1 Introduction

This chapter considers the way the courts assess expert evidence and the value judges place on it. The chapter primarily looks at the Cresswell Code for experts. Other chapters deal with the way in which an expert comports himself in the witness box and the manner in which reports should be written. This chapter is much more of an analysis of the way in which an expert should approach his work, the key word being 'independence'.

3.2 The Cresswell Code

The court will view expert evidence, in part, on the extent to which the expert has complied with his duties and responsibilities to the court. These were stated by Cresswell J in 'The Ikarian Reefer' (*National Justice Compania Naviera SA* v *Prudential Assurance Co.* [1993] 2 Lloyd's Rep. 68) and are reproduced in the notes to Order 38 paragraph 38/4/2 of the White Book (Rules of the Supreme Court).

3.2.1 Independence of production

> '1. Expert evidence presented to the Court should be, and should be seen to be, the independent product of the expert uninfluenced as to form or content by the exigencies of litigation.' (*Whitehouse* v *Jordan* [1981] 1 WLR 246 at p.256, per Lord Wilberforce)

The *Whitehouse* v *Jordan* rule comes from the following part of Lord Wilberforce's judgment:

> 'One final word. I have to say I feel some concern as to the manner in which part of the expert evidence called for the plaintiff came to be organised. This matter was discussed in the Court of Appeal and commented on by Lord Denning M.R. [1980] 1 All ER 650, 655. While some degree of consultation between experts and legal advisers is entirely proper, it is necessary that expert evidence presented to the Court should be, and should be seen to be, the independent product of the expert, uninfluenced as to the form or content by the exigencies of litigation. To the extent that it is not, the evidence is likely to be not only incorrect, but self-defeating.'

The comment by Lord Denning in the lower court (*Whitehouse* v *Jordan* [1980] 1 All ER 650) was even more scathing:

3.2.4 Proper research and limitation of scope

'5. If an expert's opinion is not properly researched because he considers that insufficient data is available, then this must be stated with an indication that the opinion is no more than a provisional one (Re J. sup.). In cases where an expert witness who has prepared a report could not assert that the report contained the truth, the whole truth and nothing but the truth without some qualification, that qualification should be stated in the report (Derby & Co. Ltd and Others v Weldon and Others (No. 9), The Times, November 9, 1990, per Lord Justice Staughton).'

It is not the fault of the accountant if there is inadequate information to enable him to reach a final conclusion. Indeed, in many cases the accountant knows that there will be a lack of information, such as where accounting records are not available, or where there is inadequate historical information to enable the accountant to make a forecast which is reasonable in all respects. Any limitations on the information available to the accountant should be clearly spelt out in the report.

Where the accountant is at fault is where he fails to mention this, giving any reader of his report the impression that he has all the information he needs in order to reach his opinion. He also needs to make this clear in oral evidence.

However, there is a further aspect to this. Because of the way litigation is conducted it is inevitable that further evidence will come to light which may change his opinion. In this respect, the conclusions of most expert accountant reports are provisional. This is dealt with in the next rule.

3.2.5 Changing of opinion

'6. If, after exchange of reports, an expert witness changes his view on a material matter having read the other side's expert's report or for any other reason, such change of view should be communicated (through legal representatives) to the other side without delay and when appropriate to the Court.'

3.2.6 Documents used by the expert

'7. Where expert evidence refers to photographs, plans, calculations, analyses, measurements, survey reports or other similar documents, these must be provided to the opposite party at the same time as the exchange of reports (see 15.5 of the Guide to Commercial Court Practice).'

This particular rule is considered in more detail in Chapter 4 concerning the preparation of the expert report. However, at the very least it means that there is a duty on the expert to make it clear what information he has reviewed for the purposes of his report, what information he has used and to ensure that his solicitors have copies of such documents for disclosure to the other side.

3.3 Criticism of the Cresswell Code

The Cresswell Code has received a lot of publicity, especially among expert accountants, to the extent that it is almost a statement of good practice for experts. However, there is some doubt over whether every part of the Code reflects the law or the practice of litigation. A critique of the Code by Anthony Speaight QC appeared in the *New Law Journal* (Expert Witness Supplement, July 26 1996, p.1,000).

Speaight makes the following comments on the responsibilities of expert witnesses as set out in the 'Ikarian Reefer':

> 'Expert evidence presented to the court should be, and should be seen to be, the independent product of the expert uninfluenced as to form and content by the exigencies of litigation.'

The form of an expert report is always going to be influenced by the exigencies of litigation because expert reports contain matters which would not be seen in other reports. Furthermore, the report is directed to matters at issue in the case on which the expert can give evidence.

As far as the content is concerned, again Speaight sees influence because the lawyers will pose questions to be answered in expert reports. Speaight makes the distinction between a lawyer having involvement in a report where he extends the posing of a question and where he distorts an answer. However, he goes further and says that he sees nothing wrong in asking for a conclusion to be withdrawn if that conclusion is not related to a matter at issue in the case. He gives the example of an obstetrician pulling too hard on forceps where the expert report refers to negligence by the doctor in carrying out a subsequent Caesarean section. If the latter is not pleaded, the lawyer can justifiably ask for it to be removed on the grounds that a litigant is under no obligation to improve his opponent's case.

> 'An expert witness should provide independent assistance to the court by way of objective unbiased opinion in relation to matters within his expertise. An expert witness in the High Court should never assume the role of an advocate.'

Speaight considers that there is a distinction between unbiased opinion (a proposition he supports) and independent assistance. This arises from the role of the expert out of court giving advice to one side. Indeed, he refers to the *Polivitte* case quoted in this section of the Code as authority for this, where Garland J stated:

> 'I have almost considered the role of the expert to be two-fold: first, to advance the case of the party calling him, so far as it can properly be advanced on the basis of the information available to the expert in the professional exercise of his skill and experience and secondly, to assist the Court, which does not possess the relevant skill and experience, in determining where the truth lies.'

All accounting experts should be aware of this distinction.

> 'An expert witness should state the facts or assumption upon which his opinion is based. He should not omit to consider material facts which could detract from his concluded opinion.'

Speaight agrees with this to the extent that it relates to matters on which the expert has been asked. This appears to be an extension of the criticism of rule 1 and really means that, if an expert has not been asked about his opinion on a matter, he should not give it.

> 'An expert witness should make it clear when a particular question or issue falls outside his expertise.'

Speaight agrees with this.

> 'If an expert's opinion is not properly researched because he considers that insufficient data are available, then this must be stated with an indication that the opinion is no more than a provisional one. In cases where an expert witness who has prepared a report could not assert that the report contained the truth, the whole truth and nothing but the truth without some qualification, that qualification should be stated in the report.'

Speaight quotes in full the remarks of Staughton LJ in *Derby & Co.* v *Weldon (No. 9)* which, he says, give a more realistic nuance:

> 'I do not think that an expert witness, or any other witness, obliges himself to volunteer his views on every issue in the whole case when he takes an oath to tell the whole truth. What he does oblige himself to do is to tell the whole truth about those matters which he is asked about.'

> 'If, after exchange of reports, an expert witness changes his view on a material matter having read the other side's expert's report or for any other reason, such change of view should be communicated (through legal representatives) to the other side without delay and when appropriate to the Court.'

This is the part of the Code with which Speaight has most difficulty because he does not feel that it is current practice. For a start, Speaight has never heard of such a communication being made. Second, it goes against the obligation to disclose after service. Furthermore, the expert may not be called by his side. Speaight states that there is no need to make such a disclosure.

> 'Where expert evidence refers to photographs, plans, calculations, analyses, measurements, survey reports or other similar documents, these must be provided to the opposite party at the same time as exchange of reports.'

Speaight agrees with this.

Overall, Speaight's criticism of Cresswell can be summarised as follows:

(a) by their very nature expert reports are the product of litigation;
(b) experts are not required to answer questions which they have not been asked to address;
(c) experts assist both the court and their client;
(d) there is no duty to disclose a change of opinion between the service of the report and trial.

Two of these criticisms require clarification. In respect of (b), it is often wholly unrealistic to frame a question to an expert accountant in a very narrow way, because it almost invariably means asking the expert to take on board certain assumptions which may not be valid. Take the following example.

Example

An expert is asked what is the loss of profits of a company as a result of an alleged act of negligence on the basis that the act caused a loss of customers. In these circumstances is the accountant expected to work on the basis that the assumption is correct without carrying out any investigation himself? What if, as a result of his work, he comes across evidence that there are other factors which could have caused a loss of custom? There must be a time when the expert says to his client that his quantum calculations will be invalid if the issue of causation is not addressed.

There is, therefore, a real conflict in certain areas between Speaight and Cresswell. Furthermore, the expert accountant who closes his mind to questions related to his evidence on which he could give evidence may have a difficult time in the witness box.

As far as (c) is concerned, experts, especially expert accountants, have a very difficult role in distinguishing between supporting a case outside court and being wholly independent inside.

What Speaight has done in this article is air some of the major difficulties which experts face and which can impinge upon the quality of their evidence.

3.4 Independence

A great deal of Chapter 7 deals with the investigation and avoidance of conflicts of interest. There are two points which should be discussed here. First, can someone who has a connection with a party to the action, other than because of the proceedings themselves, be an expert witness.

Second, because an expert witness becomes involved in matters other than the simple drafting of an expert report, does he necessarily become a non-independent witness.

3.4.1 Connection with a party

The rules of evidence discussed in this book are concerned, primarily, with expert witnesses, not independent expert witnesses. The fact that an expert is not independent is no bar to calling that person as a witness. Indeed, the notes to Order 38 rules 37 to 39 (dealing with expert evidence) state:

> 'The rules of this Order apply generally to independent experts, to so-called "in house" experts and to the parties themselves, their employees or former employees whose expert evidence is intended to be adduced at the trial or hearing (Shell Pensions Trust Ltd v Pell Frischmann and Partners [1986] 2 All ER 911).'

Whether an expert witness is independent or not will affect the weight given by the court to his evidence. However, the independence that the court is concerned with is the independence of the expert in the way in which he has gone about producing his expert evidence.

It therefore follows that, if an employed accountant gave expert accounting evidence on behalf of his employer, and the court was satisfied that he had complied with the Cresswell Code, then his position as employee should not affect the decision of the court in deciding whether or not to accept his evidence.

What, therefore, is the position of the accountant in public practice who has a conflict of interest of the type identified in Chapter 7? The answer must be that, as long as he approaches his work in an independent manner (as set out in the Cresswell Code) his conflict should make no difference to his evidence.

This is graphically demonstrated by the rule that, as with a witness of fact, there is no property in an expert witness. The case of *Harmony Shipping Co. SA* v *Saudi-Europe Line* [1979] 1 WLR 1380 concerned proceedings where a handwriting expert was consulted by both sides on whether a document was a forgery. His first instruction was from the plaintiff. His advice was that the document was probably a forgery. As this did not help the plaintiff's case, the expert was not used. Some time later, the defendant instructed the expert. He had forgotten his previous advice to the plaintiff, and he gave the same opinion as before. When he realised that he had already had an involvement in the case, he told his client, the defendant, that he could no longer act. The expert's practice was never to accept instructions from both sides in a case.

The defendant subpoenaed the expert to give evidence and was successful. Lord Denning stated:

> '. . . the Court is entitled, in order to ascertain the truth, to have the actual facts which he has observed adduced before it and to have his independent opinion on those facts.'

(Interestingly, Lord Denning also said that a contract by which a witness bound himself not to give evidence would be contrary to public policy and therefore void. This raises doubts about the effectiveness of lawyers asking for tenders for expert accounting services from a number of firms and getting their confirmation that, if a firm is unsuccessful in winning the tender, it will refuse to accept instructions from the other side.)

For most conflicts, the reasons that instructions are not accepted are three-fold:

(a) to avoid a difficult cross-examination intended to demonstrate a lack of independence;
(b) to avoid embarrassment to clients or to the firm;
(c) to avoid being asked questions in cross-examination on questions of fact concerning his involvement with his client.

3.4.2 Involvement of the expert in other aspects of the litigation

Expert accountants are inevitably brought into so many other aspects of the litigation that they are effectively part of the 'legal team'. Examples are as follows:

- carrying out an investigation which gives rise to the litigation;
- assisting with drafting pleadings;
- commenting on the merits of a case;
- assisting at the interview of witnesses;
- attendance at settlement negotiations;
- helping counsel with cross-examination.

There is of course a contradiction between these roles, where the accountant appears to be owing a duty to his client and is acting to help him win his case or settle on the best possible terms, and the giving of expert evidence where the accountant owes his first duty to the court, and is required to give unbiased evidence regardless of the benefit or harm it does to his client's case.

There is no reason why an accountant cannot carry out the former tasks and still approach his work for his expert evidence in a thoroughly unbiased manner. However, when an accountant becomes too involved in his client's case, he may find this difficult.

3.5 Expertise

There are very many accountants who are able to give expert accounting evidence and often little difference between the expertise of two accountants in any one case. For example, take the personal injury case in Chapter 2 at **2.7.3**. The accountants instructed to give evidence may have broadly similar expertise. The court may find little in the way of different expertise to enable it, on that basis alone, to prefer the opinion of one expert over another.

Consider where their expertise may, on the face of it, be different and where this may be relevant.

One may have been an accountant for more years, but does that give him a greater level of expertise? Not necessarily.

One may appear regularly as an expert witness, the other may be an accountant who normally carries out general practice work. Is the former to be preferred? Again, not necessarily. It may enable him to write a more structured report and appear more confident in the witness box, but these matters will be taken into account under the other heads dealt with in this chapter. On the other hand the court may prefer the evidence of someone who practices as an accountant, rather than just an expert accountant!

One accountant may have clients who are writers or who are publishers. Is his evidence to be preferred? Again, not necessarily. The principles of accountancy apply to any business, and an accountant with no experience of acting for writers may have just as much ability to research the manner in which a writer earns his living as someone who acts for a writer.

However, there are certain areas where particular accounting specialisms should affect the weight placed by a court on evidence. For example, evidence on certain aspects of tax can only be given by tax specialists. One accountant may have dealt with offshore tax planning once or twice in his career, but a court would take more notice of an expert on the other side who regularly advises clients on offshore tax planning. The court, in a bank audit negligence case, would also be more likely to accept the evidence of someone who audited banks, rather than someone who attempted to apply auditing theory to a bank audit but had never before carried out such an audit.

3.6 Previous opinions

> ***Example***
>
> Consider the position of the expert accountant giving evidence on a leasing contract, and how it should be accounted for under SSAP 21. In his opinion, the SSAP should be interpreted in a particular way with respect to this particular contract, the contract should be accounted for as follows, and the following disclosures made. Unknown to everyone in the court other than the accountant, in an earlier case, unrelated to this one, but with a hire purchase contract drafted in broadly the same terms, he gave a different interpretation.

It goes without saying that each interpretation favours the client instructing the accountant. What is the value of the evidence in the later case? On the face of it, of little value. The accountant may feel that there are sufficient differences between the two contracts to allow different interpretations. The accountant may have changed his mind (perhaps because of his experience in the earlier case). Whatever the reason, this is something which should be explored on cross-examination because his evidence in the earlier case may cast doubt upon his opinion expressed in the present case (*British Hartford Fairmont Syndicate Ltd* v *Jackson* [1932] 49 RPC 495).

However, how does the court find out about this? The short answer is, it normally does not.

Contrast this position with the way experts are dealt with in the USA. Under Rule 26 of the Federal Rules of Civil Procedure, being the general provisions governing discovery, the expert witness has to give a list of all publications authored within the previous 10 years, and a listing of all other cases in which the witness has testified as an expert at trial or by deposition in the preceding four years. (Deposition is the taking of oral evidence prior to the trial, and includes cross-examination.)

Given that transcripts are taken of all evidence, an expert witness in a US court is liable to have the value of his testimony brought into question where he expresses contrary views on similar facts in different cases. He will also be in difficulty where his views in any article or book differ from those being given in evidence.

In English litigation it is becoming far more common for legal advisers to carry out searches on prior cases where an expert has given evidence. However, these searches are limited to judgments rather than the transcripts of the evidence. Any questions in cross-examination are only likely where a judge refers to the opinion given by an expert. Furthermore, many English cases are not reported, and it is difficult to get copies of the judgments.

Where an expert is criticised by a judge in strong terms for the quality of his evidence, for example being called evasive, then if this becomes widely known it may give an expert severe difficulties in getting a court to accept his evidence in future proceedings.

3.7 Other matters

In addition to compliance with the Code, the court will also take note of a number of other matters when assessing the weight to be attributed to expert accountancy evidence. These have a lot to do with the manner in which expert accounting evidence is presented, both in the written report and orally. These aspects are dealt with in detail in Chapters 4 and 5 concerning report writing and giving oral evidence. However, they can be summarised as follows:

(a) a clear written style which is jargon-free;
(b) a clear succinct style of answering questions, which avoids the use of jargon and does not seek to patronise the court;
(c) an implicit understanding in both reports and oral evidence of the duties and responsibilities of being an expert.

In the case of *Loveday* v *Renton (No. 2)* [1992] 1 Med.LR 117, Stuart Smith LJ gave guidance on the way expert evidence was assessed by the court. This case predated *Ikarian Reefer* and is in many respects a more practical explanation of the role of the expert and how the court will assess the quality of his evidence. The *Loveday* trial lasted 65 days and concerned injuries to young children allegedly as the result of the administration of whooping cough vaccine. The evidence during the trial consisted almost entirely of expert evidence of a highly technical nature. One of the parties to the action had produced a library of 50 files containing the literature on the subject. The judgment itself was 300 pages of transcripts and evidence. Not surprisingly, the judge had the opportunity to assess over an extended length of time the quality of the experts giving evidence. In commenting on the expert, the judge said the following:

> 'The court has to evaluate the witness and the soundness of his opinion. Most importantly this involves an examination of the reasons given for his opinions and the extent to which they are supported by evidence. The judge also has to decide what weight to attach to a witness's opinion by examining the internal consistency and logic of his evidence; the care with which he has considered the subject and presented his evidence; his precision and accuracy of thought as demonstrated by his answers; how he responds to searching and informed cross-examination and in particular the extent to which a witness faces up to and accepts the logic of a proposition put in cross-examination or is prepared to concede points that are seen to be correct; the extent to which a witness has conceived an opinion and is

> reluctant to re-examine it in the light of later evidence, or demonstrates a flexibility of mind which may involve changing or modifying opinions previously held; whether or not a witness is biased or lacks independence.
>
> There is one further aspect of a witness's evidence that is often important; that is his demeanour in the witness-box. As in most cases where the court is evaluating expert evidence, I have placed less weight on this factor in reaching my assessment. But it is not wholly unimportant; and particularly in those instances where criticisms have been made of a witness, on the grounds of bias or lack of independence, which in my view are not justified, the witness's demeanour has been a factor that I have taken into account.'

So, as well as complying with the Cresswell Code, the expert has to ensure that his written work and his oral evidence meet certain high standards. These requirements are dealt with in Chapters 4 and 5.

3.8 Consequences of non-compliance with the Cresswell Code

Where an expert does not comply with the Code, he risks his evidence being ignored by the court. This is graphically illustrated by the comments of R Reed QC, sitting as a deputy High Court judge, in *Re Oakframe Ltd* [1996] BCC 67. That case was a directors' disqualification action. The defence had filed two affidavits from accountants. The Official Receiver applied to the court to have the two affidavits struck out under Order 41 rule 6 on the grounds that they were irrelevant or oppressive.

The judge first of all referred to the Cresswell Code and then turned to the affidavits.

In respect of the first affidavit he said the following at p.72:

> 'The difficulty, when one looks at the report annexed to the affidavit overall is that it does not state clearly the basis on which the expert is purporting to draw expert opinions. It does not identify what the expert opinions are supposed to be, or [to] what issues they are supposed to go. I respectfully suggest it had not been thought through by reference to any consideration of what might usefully be the role of an expert in this particular case.
>
> In my judgment, the vast bulk of this report, and hence the affidavit of which it forms the only substantive part, is irrelevant in that it is advocacy, hearsay evidence, and comment. It is not what can properly be regarded as being a proper expert's report for the purpose of this litigation, aimed at specific matters on which expert opinion could properly be sought and on which expert opinion would properly be admitted.'

The second report was similarly criticised, and both affidavits were struck out.

The judge recognised that much of the work carried out by the accountants would be useful for the purpose of case preparation. However, this work was not the same as the material which could form part of expert evidence.

In *Oakframe*, the judge criticised those instructing the accountants for not appreciating the true role of the expert and for not realising the circumstances in which expert evidence could be adduced or be of assistance. However, sometimes the expert himself is criticised. In the case of *ADT Ltd* v *BDO Binder Hamlyn* [1996] BCC 808, which involved allegations of audit negligence, May J said at p.874 of one of the expert accountants, a Mr Bray, that:

> 'Although Mr Bray eventually made concessions on this topic such that Binders by counsel admitted negligence, I record (since it contributed to my general judgment of Mr Bray's evidence) that I judged his evidence here to have been poor to the point of studied evasion.'

Evasiveness in an expert witness is a complete failure to comply with rule 2 of the Cresswell Code, and will inevitably lead to the court discounting much, if not all, of the expert evidence where it conflicts with the evidence of an expert for the other side.

Chapter 4
Report writing

> 'The Judge is not a rustic who has chosen to play a game of Three Card Trick. He is not fair game, nor is the truth.' (Mr Justice Laddie in *Cala Homes (South) Ltd* v *Alfred McAlpine Homes East Ltd (No 2)*, *The Independent*, October 30, 1995 (CS) ChD

4.1 Introduction

Such was Mr Justice Laddie's reaction to the evidence of an expert who had previously referred, in a published article on the role of the expert witness ('The Expert Witness: Partisan with a Conscience', *Journal of the Chartered Institute of Arbitrators*, August 1990), to a three card trickster deceiving the eye of an innocent rustic. As mentioned in Chapter 3, the expert should beware of inconsistencies between what he says in one case and what he has said previously in another or, perhaps more importantly, written for publication.

This chapter deals with expert reports and their:

- purpose;
- content;
- style; and
- status.

Most civil cases are settled before trial and, therefore, everything which the expert wants to say, within the confines of his instructions, must be contained in his report. He cannot leave his best points for the trial, because:

(a) under the rules of court his report will constitute his evidence in chief and he will not be allowed to explain or elaborate unless given the opportunity by counsel cross-examining him;
(b) he will probably not have a chance to have his say, not least because most civil cases settle before trial.

4.2 Purpose

As the role of the expert is to provide technical assistance to the court, it follows that the report should give, and should confine itself to giving, that technical assistance. The assistance should be restricted to technical matters arising from the pleaded issues, although the expert acting for the plaintiff may well have, and usually will have, considerable input into the way the technical issues are pleaded.

The expert acting for the defence may have some input into the way the technical issues are pleaded in defence, but his report should deal only with the plaintiff's pleaded case and the defendant's case in response (but see the discussion below).

It is important that the expert should always bear in mind the fundamental purpose for which he is retained and should assume, in spite of the statistical evidence to the contrary, that he will be required to answer for his report in court.

While the ultimate purpose should be borne in mind, the initial instructions to the expert may not go so far as to require him to prepare a report for exchange and with a view to giving evidence. All that may be required at the start is a preliminary opinion on the technical issues.

If, for example, the case is one concerning an accountant's professional negligence, the solicitor acting for the potential plaintiff may ask the expert for a preliminary opinion on whether the conduct of the accountant concerned fell below the standard reasonably to be expected of an accountant doing that type of work.

The preliminary opinion, if it is to be of any use, will have to be properly researched and the expert asked to act for a potential plaintiff will need access to relevant documents. If proceedings are commenced then the opinion may need modifying in the light of:

- the defence;
- discovery;
- exchange of witness statements.

At this stage the expert will have to firm up his opinion, because the next stage for him will be exchange of expert reports. If the other experts' views cause him to change his mind he should tell his instructing solicitors immediately.

However, see the discussion on whether this actually reflects current practice at **3.3**.

4.3 Content

The Academy of Experts has published a model form expert's report (which is contained in Appendix 1 to this book), but there is no legal requirement that the expert's report should follow that form. The model does, however, give a helpful guide to the usual content of a report by an expert accountant.

The introductory note refers to the scheme of the model form of report as follows:

> 'The **Model Form** is written in 5 distinct sections with suggested headings: notes are given.
>
> **The Front Sheet** – the *first visible sheet* should contain the items of keypoint information indicated by the model and should not be obscured by a cover. The first report prepared for disclosure should be entitled "Report" and not "First report".
>
> **The Contents Page** – may be omitted altogether in the case of a short report of say seven pages or less.
>
> **Section 1 Introduction** – deals with all the formal matters and chronology. The text is largely standard. Most of the material is transferred to appendices.
>
> **Section 2 The Background to the Dispute and the Issues**. This section of the report will normally include:
>
> (a) a list of the people who will be referred to in the report with a short uncontroversial description of their role.
> (b) the assumed or given factual background of the case.
> (c) the issues, set out clearly and numbered, which the expert will address.
>
> *No opinion* is expressed in this section.
>
> **Section 3 Description of the Technical Investigation or Enquiry** – this section is, again, factual only. The description should be given in itemised paragraphs with sub-headings.
>
> **Section 4 The Facts on which the Expert's Opinion is Based** – distinguishing those facts which he was told from those he observed for himself.
>
> **Section 5 The Expert's Conclusions** – with opinion and reasons in full on each issue in turn, set out clearly and numbered. In this section, there should only be such repetition of fact as is necessary for the exposition of the opinion.
>
> **Signing Block** – the report must be signed by the writer and dated at the end of the Conclusions.
>
> **Appendices** – each Appendix should be provided with a front sheet of the type indicated in the model.
>
> **Headers** – each continuation page of a section should be provided with a header on the left-hand side showing the number and short title of the section

> and a header at the right hand side with the information suggested by the model.
>
> **Presentation** – the practice is growing of the Court directing that a copy of experts' reports be made available on disc to the judge or official referee. Where practicable, therefore, reports should be typed in double spacing and prepared or readily transferable to WordPerfect 5.1. The report should be presented on A4 paper, already hole punched for use in a standard lever arch binder and in a format that can be copied readily on a photocopier with automatic feed.'

In practice, the expert may be given explicit instructions on the form and coverage of his report, but the expert should not accept instructions which are so restrictive as to prevent him expressing a fair opinion for the benefit of the court.

The instructing solicitor should instruct the expert on the issues about which his expert opinion is invited. If, having read the papers, it seems to the expert that the instructions are incomplete he should say so.

The content of the report will, of course, vary depending on the circumstances and the facts of the case but, in a typical accountant's negligence case, the content might be as set out below. Where an expert is called as a witness and his report has been disclosed in accordance with a direction under rule 37, his report may be put in evidence at the beginning of the expert's examination in chief or at a time directed by the court (RSC order 38 rule 43). In practice, the report will not usually be read out in court and the expert will merely be asked whether the contents of his report are true and whether he stands by the opinions in it. If he confirms that the report is true and that he stands by his opinion, the expert may immediately be at the mercy of cross-examination.

An expert report may be admissible in criminal proceedings whether or not the expert attends to give oral evidence. If the court grants leave, the report will be evidence of any fact or opinion which could have been given orally (s30(1) Criminal Justice Act 1988).

There may be arguments about admissibility in both civil and criminal proceedings. What is admissible is a matter for the trial judge.

Example

An application was made by a plaintiff at an interlocutory hearing that the trial judge should not be allowed to read an expert report prepared on behalf of the defence. It was argued that the report was not an expert report at all, but was more a skeleton argument or a draft judgment, and was such a pernicious document that the trial judge should not be allowed to read it.

The court took the view that it was for the trial judge to decide what was admissible and what was not and the application was rejected.

The plaintiff sought shortly thereafter to discontinue his action, but had to pay a substantial proportion of the defendant's costs in order to do so.

A typical report in an accountant's negligence case will have a cover sheet showing the names of the parties and the fact that it is an expert report by the writer. The cover should be dated.

The introduction may take the form of a letter to the instructing solicitors and might read as in the following example.

Example

In accordance with your instructions, I have considered, as an expert accountant, the technical accounting issues arising. My qualifications to act as an expert in this matter are contained in Appendix X.

Your client, Mr Smith, employed Jones & Co to advise him on the tax consequences of the sale of his company, Smith & Co Ltd. He claims that that advice was negligent and that as a result he has suffered losses which he puts at £400,000. Mr Smith is also claiming interest and costs.

The report which follows is based on the pleadings, the discovery documents, the witness statements and research at Companies House and elsewhere. I have not attempted to audit or verify in any way the documents produced to me.

In part 1 of the report I deal with my understanding of the background before going on, in part 2, to consider the relevant tax legislation and relevant professional standards. In part 3 I deal with the liability issues pleaded before going on, in part 4, to consider the question of loss.

For the reasons fully set out in the report it is my opinion that Jones & Co acted in accordance with the standards of their profession in providing the advice that they did, and that the tax liability suffered by Mr Smith arises as a consequence of the transaction undertaken and not because of anything which Jones & Co did or did not do.

Yours faithfully

While the detailed conclusions will be included within the body of the report and, usually, in summary form at the end, it is sensible to give the judge an early indication of the conclusion to be reached so that, in his pre-trial reading, the background and technical issues will be read bearing the conclusion in mind. The expert report is not a detective novel with the denouement on the last page. It should be constructed so that the conclusion is a logical consequence of what precedes it.

While it is the expert's opinion that is being sought, it is important to remember that it is his opinion as to whether the conduct complained of met the standard of the reasonably competent accountant doing that work which is required, rather than whether the conduct met his own standard.

4.4 Background

The background section of the report will be largely based on contemporary documents, supplemented, where necessary, by references to the witness statements. The background will usually be dealt with chronologically, starting at the beginning, going on to the end and then stopping. Usually, in accountants' cases at least, the authenticity of documents will not be in dispute, but if there is a dispute as to whether certain letters were received or read, then that dispute should be acknowledged, as should any dispute as to the facts. The nature of the dispute will usually be explicable by reference to the witness statements.

The appendices to the report will largely be copies of the contemporaneous documents. It is not necessary to include copies of the witness statements.

When the report is bound, it is usually sensible to bind the appendices separately so that the reader of the text can refer readily to the appendices without having to turn over the pages of the report. Having the documents in the appendices also means that it is unnecessary to make extensive quotes from the documents to be included in the report. It is now recommended that pages are sequentially numbered throughout, including the appendices.

The documents will be culled from both sides' discovery and, although the appendices will be sequentially numbered for cross-reference to the report, it will usually be helpful if they also show an indication of their original source by reference to the lists of documents produced on discovery. However, the expert should bear in mind that the appendices will also ultimately be paginated for the purposes of the trial bundle and it will usually be sensible for space to be left for this at the foot of the page in the centre.

4.5 Relevant legislation and professional standards

The second section of the report will contain references to the relevant legislation and to professional practice and, once again, copies of the relevant sections of the Taxes Act (or Companies Acts, etc.) and of the relevant professional guidance should be contained in the appendices and cross-referenced.

4.6 Liability

The third part of the report will deal, if appropriate, with liability issues by reference to the pleaded case, and it will usually be convenient to set out the relevant pleading before the expert expresses his opinion on the conduct of his client in connection with that allegation. Opinions should not be expressed on matters of law.

It will usually be sensible to draw an overall conclusion on liability at the end of the section, also summarising the key points giving rise to the expert's overall conclusion.

4.7 Loss

Quantum is best dealt with separately and it may be appropriate to calculate quantum on various alternative bases, to illustrate the expert's opinion of the financial consequences of different decisions on liability.

While it may be that quantum follows liability as night follows day, it might also be that, even if the accountant is frightfully negligent, his negligence has caused no loss. There may, in fact, be no loss at all let alone one which is attributable to anything which the defendant did or did not do.

4.8 Style

The question of style is a matter for the expert because it is his report – he is giving his opinions, and it is his reputation which is on the line.

Because the report is the report of an expert and not his firm, it is the authors' view that it should always be written in the first person and, indeed, should be written by the stated author. Some reports are written in the plural ('we') and signed in the name of the firm and such reports usually (and should) include details of the expert in the introduction. If, however, the report is not written by the expert, he faces dangers well illustrated by the following example, which is taken from the transcript of a recent cross-examination of an expert in the High Court.

Example

An expert accountant is being cross-examined about the content of his report. It contains a mistake in that the expert's opinion is based on a wrong assumption about whether a document was copied from a file. The questions and answers were as follows:

Counsel	. . . so they did not actually have a stock take attendance programme on their files?
A	That is correct. This is wrong, I apologise.
Judge	Why is it wrong?
A	I have said that the attendance programme . . .
Judge	No, how did you come to make such a mistake?
A	I don't know. The report was written for me, My Lord, by a team.
Counsel	The report was written for you?
A	No, no, no, sorry.
Counsel	What did you say?
Judge	That is what he did say.
A	The report was written by a team of people including myself and between us one of us must have made a mistake, and I am sorry.
Counsel	Is this a bit of the report that you wrote?
A	I almost certainly did not put pen to paper first of all for this paragraph. What I did was discuss the issues with my team, express to them my views, and they then drafted something for me to consider and re-draft.
Counsel	Are you at this stage able to remember which bits you did write?
A	The whole report is my opinion.
Counsel	That is not an answer to the question.
A	I am sorry, I did not write any of the report.
Counsel	Any of it?
A	Correct.
Judge	I think you want to add a 'but'.
A	But I came into the witness box aware of the papers in the case, and comfortable with the opinions expressed. The views that were first written go through many drafts, My Lord, and I make sure that I hold the view that I express. That was obviously an oversight, but it is a question of fact and it is not misleading in terms of opinion, I believe.

In many cases it will be inevitable that the expert will be assisted in gathering facts, and if such assistance has been obtained that fact should be stated, as should the qualifications, if not the name, of the assistant. If the expert has been assisted in his opinions he should state that also, but, in that case, the court might wonder why the expert is there at all, because it is his opinions which count, not the opinions of others.

In the authors' view the expert should, at the very least, write all of the paragraphs containing his opinion himself. It is also highly desirable that the background and technical sections should also be written by the expert, because it is essential that he is familiar with the facts and documents upon which his opinion is based and that he is confident that the documents he relies on fairly represent his understanding of the facts.

While style is a matter for the author, form is not, to the extent that paragraphs and pages should be numbered and the text should cross-refer to numbered appendices. The report should be on A4 paper (although appendices and, for example, Scott Schedules, may have to be on larger paper) and, for ease of reading, should be either one and a half or double spaced.

The rules of good writing apply to expert reports as they do to any other form of writing:

(a) short words are better than long ones;
(b) short sentences are better than long sentences;
(c) short paragraphs are better than long paragraphs;
(d) headings assist the reader's understanding, and serve as an introduction to a new topic;
(e) Latin should be left to the lawyers.

The author might do well to remember the recommended approach to the making of presentations by reference to the four 'Ps':

- position;
- problem;
- possibilities;
- proposal.

('Making your Case', Video Arts Ltd).

The author of an expert report has to consider the *position*, as set out in the pleadings, the discovery documents and the witness statements, has to consider the *problem* by reference to relevant legislation and professional standards, has to consider the *possibilities* (not least that the opinions of others may differ from his) and has to reach a *proposal* or conclusion, which is his opinion.

> 'It is necessary that expert evidence presented to the court should be, and should be seen to be, the independent product of the expert, uninfluenced as to form or content by the exigencies of litigation. To the extent that it is not, the evidence is likely to be not only incorrect but self-defeating.' (Lord Wilberforce in *Whitehouse* v *Jordan* [1981] 1 All ER 267 at 276)

4.9 Status

Until disclosed, an expert report is confidential to those commissioning it. The Court of Appeal in *Derby & Co.* v *Weldon (No. 9), The Times*, November 9, 1990 held that an expert's report prepared for the purposes of litigation is privileged until disclosed by the party commissioning it. It is for the solicitor to decide, in the light of the report, whether to disclose it and whether to call his expert. If he decides not to disclose the report then the court will not order disclosure.

The general rule is that statements made in the course of judicial proceedings enjoy absolute privilege, which means that no action in defamation can be taken in the light of them even if they are made maliciously. (See *Carter-Ruck on Libel and Slander* (5th edn) at p.22 and Lopes LJ in *Royal Aquarium* v *Summer and Winter Garden Society Limited* [1892] 1 QB 431.) Absolute privilege extends to all tribunals recognised by law which exercise 'functions equivalent to those of an established Court of Justice'. It does not extend to bodies exercising administrative functions (*O'Connor* v *Waldron* [1935] AC 76 per Lord Atkin).

4.10 Privilege

Letters and other communications passing between a party and his solicitors are privileged from production provided they are confidential and written to, or by, the solicitors in his professional capacity and for the purpose of legal advice.

Communications between a solicitor and a non-professional agent or third party which come into existence after litigation is contemplated or commenced and made with a view to such litigation, either for the purpose of obtaining or giving advice in regard to it or of obtaining or collecting evidence to be used in it, or obtaining information which may lead to the obtaining of such evidence, are privileged.

Documents embodying communications with a non-professional servant/agent/third party are only privileged if they come into existence for the purpose of obtaining legal advice in existing or anticipated proceedings.

Even if a party to proceedings decides not to disclose the report of the expert they have commissioned or indeed to call them to give evidence at trial, there is no property in a witness, which means that any person can be called, by a subpoena if necessary, to give evidence in judicial proceedings. It would therefore be possible, at least in theory, for a plaintiff to call a defendant's expert witness to give evidence, even though the defendant had decided not to call that witness. However, a plaintiff taking such a step would have no idea what the expert might say since his unserved report would not be discoverable.

In *Derby* v *Weldon* Lord Justice Staughton said:

> 'I do not think that an expert witness, or any other witness, obliges himself to volunteer his views on every issue in the whole case when he takes an oath to tell the whole truth. What he does oblige himself to do is to tell the whole truth about those matters which he is asked about.'

On the other hand, Mr Justice Cresswell said in 'The Ikarian Reefer':

> 'An expert witness should state the facts or assumption upon which his opinion is based. He should not omit to consider material facts which could detract from his concluded opinion.'

Lord Woolf in his *Access to Justice* recommendations states that the first responsibility of an expert witness is to the court. This duty overrides any obligation to the person from whom he has received instructions.

Following 'The Ikarian Reefer' and in the light of Lord Woolf's proposals, it is clearer than ever that the expert must express his honest opinion on the matters he is asked about. In connection with those matters he must leave nothing out.

Although draft reports will continue not to be disclosable, instructions to experts (including letters subsequent to the original instructions and a note of oral instructions) will be, if Lord Woolf's proposals are accepted. The expert's report will have to end with a declaration that it includes everything which the expert regards as being relevant to the opinion which he has expressed in his report, and that he has drawn to the attention of the court anything which would affect the validity of the opinion.

The expert whose report contains his honest opinion has nothing to fear from cross-examination, at least in terms of his integrity, although, if his opinions are based on an incomplete or inaccurate understanding of the facts or if he has missed some relevant law or practice, he may be vulnerable to attack as inexpert or incompetent.

While privilege from discovery will apply to evidence in criminal or civil proceedings and would apply to reports prepared with a view to giving evidence, an expert witness cannot claim immunity from a suit by his clients for advice given during preparation for a possible claim. It was held in *Palmer* v *Durnford Ford* [1992] QB 483 that an expert could be liable for advice given on the merits of the claim, particularly if proceedings had not been started. If, therefore, a whole case is built on erroneous preliminary advice given by an expert, the cost to the expert could be considerable. To that extent, the expert acting for the defendant is in a more comfortable position if he only becomes involved after the commencement of proceedings. If, however, he becomes involved at the 'letter before action' stage then he may be vulnerable. As Lord Goff put it in *Henderson* v *Merrett Syndicates Ltd* [1994] 3 All ER 506:

> '. . . if a person assumes responsibility to another in respect of certain services, there is no reason why he should not be liable for damages to that other in respect of economic loss which flows from the negligent performance of those services.'

4.11 Reference

Carter-Ruck, P. F. and Starte, H. (1997) *Carter-Ruck on Libel and Slander* (5th edn), Butterworths.

Chapter 5
Advocacy and the expert witness

5.1 Introduction

This chapter has two purposes. The first is to explain what advocates are trying to do when they stand up in court, with particular emphasis on the way they approach expert witnesses. The second is to explain what it is experts do when they are in the witness box.

5.2 Advocacy

Put simply, an advocate's role is to argue his client's case to help him win it. Whether he believes in his client's case is irrelevant; indeed, he should have no personal opinion on whether his client is right or not.

Broadly speaking, an advocate does this in a variety of ways. He makes an opening speech, setting out his case; he calls his witnesses with a view to adducing evidence that supports his case; he cross-examines the other side's witnesses with a view to minimising any harm which their evidence may do to his case; and he sums up his client's case after the evidence has finished.

5.3 Opening speech

Each side in a trial makes an opening speech. It is simply an outline of their case, the facts on which they will rely and the witnesses who, they hope, will adduce those facts. Opening speeches also deal with points of law which will be argued.

Counsel often prepare 'skeleton arguments', summaries of their opening speeches, which are disclosed to the other side in advance.

5.4 Evidence in chief

When counsel calls one of his own side's witnesses, he examines him 'in chief'.

The aim of the examination in chief is to get a witness to tell his story with as little prompting as possible. This can often be difficult for both witness and counsel. The witness may have made his written statement some time before trial, and will probably not have seen it since. Counsel, although he will have seen the statement recently – probably immediately before he starts his examination – and will have it to hand during the examination in chief, is not allowed to ask leading questions (although the court has a discretion to relax this rule so far as justice may require).

A leading question is one which suggests the answer, such as 'on the fifteenth of June last year were you watching the test match at Lords?'. On the other hand, 'can you tell the court what you were doing on the fifteenth of June last year?' is not a leading question.

Experts, especially accounting experts, are in a different position to other witnesses. They will probably have had a hand in the preparation of the case up to trial. They will be familiar with the pleadings, will have read the key witness statements and will probably have seen the skeleton arguments affecting their evidence. They should therefore know what is expected of them. Additionally, unlike with factual witnesses, experts and barristers are allowed to discuss a case, under paragraph 607 of the Bar Code of Conduct, amended by No. 5 effective from 25 October 1996.

Furthermore, experts are allowed to sit in court during the evidence of other witnesses and should therefore be able to gain an understanding of how their evidence fits into the proceedings.

Finally, given the extent to which expert reports are disclosed pre-trial, in civil trials at least there may be little need to carry out an extensive examination in chief. The judge will usually have read the expert's report prior to the expert being called and the report can be taken as his evidence. The examination in chief is likely to be restricted to asking the expert his name and address, asking him to confirm that this is his report, asking him whether there is anything he wishes to change in it, and then saying 'no further questions'. Experts are not normally asked to read their reports in the witness box.

However, there are a number of situations where the in chief is slightly longer. These include the following.

5.4.1 Confirmation of expertise

Counsel may wish the court to hear the witness's expertise. It reinforces far better than a written biography the witness's suitability for being called as an expert.

5.4.2 Amplification of key points

Counsel may wish to amplify the key points in the expert's report. Without leading, the barrister will ask the witness to talk about the documents he has seen, the substance of his calculations, and his findings as to quantum. This draws the court's attention to the key parts of the expert's evidence.

5.4.3 Changes to the expert's findings

A common question in chief is 'is this your report? . . . Do you wish to make any changes to it?'.

On the basis that the accountant does not want to change his report because he has uncovered a mistake in it, in what circumstances would an accountant want to change his findings?

An expert report is based on facts which may or may not be correct, makes assumptions which may or may not be correct and contains the expert's opinions on facts. It is the nature of litigation that as soon as the expert has signed his report, further evidence will come in which may result in him wanting to make certain amendments. This is often the case when the other side's expert report is received. However, it happens particularly during the trial. Up to trial, such matters can often be dealt with by way of a supplemental report, subject to the agreement of the court or the other side. It is less easy to do this when the trial is in progress.

If there are changes necessary, these should have been discussed by counsel in advance of the accountant being called.

5.4.4 Weak points

There are often weak points in an accountant's report, not necessarily due to anything the accountant has or has not done, but more often due to a lack of factual evidence. It is important that any weak points are raised during examination in chief rather than in cross-examination. The expert gets the opportunity to explain the weakness(es), how he dealt with them, any alternative explanations, and how he came to his conclusion in a relatively friendly environment. If the matter is raised in cross-examination, it may give the impression that it has been uncovered by the other side, affecting the expert's credibility.

Example

Munkman gives an illuminating example of this applied to a witness for the defence with previous convictions (not an expert!). In the Mr A Case, Sir John Simon KC was examining his own witness:

Sir John Simon	'I am sorry to have to ask you, Mr Newton, but I had better ask it here. Have you been convicted of forgery?'

Mr Newton	'Yes, I have, Sir John . . .'
Sir John Simon	'In the year 1907?'
Mr Newton	'I suppose that would be the year.'
Sir John Simon	'. . . and you served a sentence in respect of it?'
Mr Newton	'I did, yes.'

Far better that this is raised here than by opposing counsel, asking a number of questions about the witness's honesty and then asking him, if he is honest, how come he has a conviction for dishonesty.

5.4.5 Criminal cases

In criminal cases leave of the court to allow an expert report to be admissible in lieu of oral evidence is rarely given. As a result, the jury is not often shown the experts' reports, making an oral examination in chief inevitable.

5.5 Cross-examination

5.5.1 Aims of cross-examination

Cross-examination is the process by which the opposing barrister tests a witness's evidence. Did the witness really see that? Was it not a dark night? Could he not have mistaken it for something else?

By its nature, cross-examination is about asking leading questions, by which counsel hopes to undermine evidence given in chief. Munkman identifies four aims of cross-examination, being:

- to destroy the material parts of the evidence in chief;
- to weaken the evidence where it cannot be destroyed;
- to elicit new evidence helpful to the party cross-examining;
- to undermine the credibility of the witness.

Counsel has these aims with an expert witness as with a witness of fact. Before looking at these aspects in detail, it is necessary to raise an evidential point. If the other side disputes a witness's evidence then the witness must be challenged on that evidence. Munkman also refers to a rule of practice that an 'advocate in cross-examining must put to the witness the case he is going to set up, so far as it lies within the witness's knowledge'. The matter cannot be left to closing speeches. If the witness is not cross-examined on disputed evidence then the court will assume that the evidence is unchallenged and that the witness's account is accepted.

5.5.2 Destruction

This is a rare occurrence for any witness, but there are instances of experts suffering this fate. Counsel will show that, because of errors, lack of proper reasoning or lack of relevant experience, none of what the expert says can be relied upon.

This is a terrible fate for a witness. For the court, it is akin to watching a bloodsport. However, the end point is that one side has little in the way of expert evidence to support its case.

Destruction will come following the achievement of the three other aims.

5.5.3 Weakening

The most common aim of counsel in cross-examining experts is to weaken their evidence. This means attacking the facts on which the accountant has based his opinion and the strength of his logic. In essence, it is a far milder form of destruction, but with the realisation by counsel that he is unlikely to get the expert to resile completely from his opinions.

5.5.4 Eliciting new evidence

Eliciting new evidence is, for an expert, the mirror image of weakening the existing evidence. Counsel's objective is to put the expert in the position whereby, for example, a particular opinion that is helpful to the other side is just as reasonable, if not more reasonable, than his opinion which is helpful for his own side.

5.5.5 Undermining

Undermining an expert witness is normally the process of questioning the witness's expertise, experience or methods, whereby the court is put in doubt as to the validity of the expert's opinions.

5.5.6 Techniques of cross-examination

Munkman identifies two main techniques for cross-examination, being probing and insinuation (see Munkman p.65). He describes probing as the process of enquiring thoroughly into the details of a story to discover flaws. When applied to experts, this means probing them as to the facts relied upon, their reasoning and their assumptions. Insinuation is the process of building up a different version of the evidence, quietly leading the witness on (gentle insinuation) or driving him on (firm insinuation).

Barristers use a variety of questioning methods to cross-examine witnesses.

5.5.7 Pinning-out

Pinning-out is a favourite type of questioning, especially of experts. It involves asking a number of questions to which the barrister gets an agreement, until he asks his final question with which, based on his earlier answers, the expert can do nothing but agree, but with which, if asked at the start, the expert would have disagreed. This type of questioning is akin to leading the witness up the garden path. The witness is made to accept a series of relatively uncontroversial statements before the hammer blow. Evans gives an example in *Advocacy at the Bar* (p.154).

Example

The cross-examination is of a police officer by the defence. Counsel is trying to establish why no contemporaneous note has been taken of an interview at the police station with the defendant. However, as part of this, he wishes to establish that there was no good reason why one should not have been taken. (Bear in mind that this is pre-Police and Criminal Evidence Act rules.)

'Q You interviewed Sykes in a cell or a room?
A Detention room, sir.
Q Was there a table there?
A Yes, sir.
Q Chairs?
A Yes, sir.
Q Mr Sykes was sitting or standing while being questioned?
A Sitting, sir.
Q Were you sitting or standing yourself?
A Sitting.
Q Anyone else in the room with you apart from Mr Sykes?
A D/S Idle, sir.
Q It seems that you asked all the questions, correct?
A That's right, sir.
Q What was D/S Idle doing, just sitting there listening?
A Yes, sir.
Q Have you heard of a contemporaneous note, officer?
A Yes, sir.
Q Was there some reason why D/S Idle could not have taken one?
A . . .'

This sort of questioning undermines the credibility of the witness. However, with an expert it can also be used to good effect with the next approach, the use of the hypothetical.

5.5.8 Hypotheticals

Hypotheticals are questions based on a fact which has not been proven and perhaps may never be proven. In fact, hypotheticals may be completely unreasonable, but are used to start off a line of questions which ends with the expert giving evidence at variance to his stated opinion.

> ***Example***
>
> A hypothetical may start something like this:
>
> Q Let's work on the basis that these stock reports did not exist at the time the accounts were being finalised. Do you understand the situation I'm describing?
> A Yes.
>
> and end something like this:
>
> Q So the position is, there would be nothing to tell the directors that any of the stock was obsolete?
> A I suppose that would be correct.

The use of hypotheticals is a good way of weakening the expert's stated evidence. However, if a similar, but slightly more subtle, approach is used – the alternative reasonable assumption – the expert's own evidence can be weakened, and either new evidence elicited or the opposing expert's own opinion strengthened.

5.5.9 Alternative reasonable assumptions

Accountants base their opinions on assumptions which may or may not be right, but should be reasonable, i.e., they must not omit to consider material facts which could detract from their concluded opinion. One assumption may be more reasonable than the other, and that may be the one the expert has used. However, counsel could raise a line of questioning as follows.

> ***Example***
>
> Q Now, you have told the court that, in assessing the loss, you have used a gross profit of 50 per cent, correct?
> A Yes.
> Q And that you have based that figure on a review of the 20 other companies' accounts in this particular sector, is that correct?
> A Yes.
> Q It's correct, isn't it, that the range of gross profits for those 20 companies is between 42 per cent and 65 per cent?

A Yes.
Q So it could be that my client's company would have earned 65 per cent?
A Well, I suppose so.
Q Isn't it stronger than that, given that another company carrying out exactly the same business earned 65 per cent, isn't it entirely reasonable to assume that my client could also have made 65 per cent?
A Yes.
Q Thank you. Now, turning to the deductions you've made, let's look first at wages and salaries . . .
Q . . . and you've accepted that the deduction for wages and salaries could be 15 per cent and finally, you told the court that a gross profit of 65 per cent would be reasonable. I wonder if, taking those figures, you could make a calculation of the lost profit?

5.5.10 Lots of questions, multi-question questions, the same question and the surprise question

Each of the above examples illustrates another barrister's ruse – the short snappy question. Asking questions in such a way can often give the witness little time to think. A series of short questions, of itself, seems to demand a series of short answers, often 'yes'. These can be extremely offputting to a witness if he feels that the questioning is going in an uncomfortable direction.

An alternative to the short question is the long, involved, complicated question which appears to contain a number of questions. This is often poor technique by a barrister and confusing to the court, but because it is also confusing to the witness, it can put him off his stride.

Another trick is to ask the same question again and again. The blunt approach is to ask exactly the same question, but if a witness has already answered this then the court may say to counsel there is little point in going further. Much more subtle is to ask the question in a slightly different way. The question may be repeated once the expert has made a concession or over an extended period of time. The aim is to catch the expert out and weaken his evidence.

The surprise question is the one which comes out of the blue, and which the expert is not expecting. Expert witnesses generally know what it is that they have come to give evidence on, and will be troubled if a different question is asked to that which they are expecting. It is worth considering this one with the next questioning approach – doubting the witness's expertise.

5.5.11 Doubting the witness's expertise

Consider the case of *R* v *Rouse* (1914) 10 Cr.App.R 179, CCA. Sir Norman Birkett KC, who rarely prosecuted, was leading for the Crown in a notorious murder case. The prosecution's case was that the victim had been murdered in a car by the defendant, which, it was alleged, had then been set on fire. The defence was that the fire had started accidentally. The Crown's case was rested on the finding of a brass nut found loose on a petrol pipe. The defence claimed that the nut came loose in the fire. An expert engineer was called for the defence on the fusion of two bits of metal. Birkett's first question, and the subsequent cross-examination, were as follows:

'Q What is the coefficient of expansion of brass?
A I am afraid I cannot answer that question out of hand.
Q If you do not know, say so. What do I mean by the term?
A You want to know the expansion of the metal under heat.
Q I asked you what is the coefficient of the expansion of brass. Do you know what it means?
A Put that way I probably do not.
Q You are an engineer?
A I dare say I am.
Q Well you are not a doctor or a crime investigator or an amateur detective are you?
A No.
Q Are you an engineer?
A Yes.
Q What is the coefficient of the expansion of brass? Do you know?
A No, not put that way.'

The story goes that Birkett had no idea how to cross-examine an engineer, and just said the first thing that came into his head.

There are two points to be made about this. First, the expert is unlikely to have gone into court expecting to be asked the coefficient of the expansion of brass. If he had, he would probably have mugged up on the subject. The second point is that counsel challenged extremely effectively the witness's expertise. This was an engineer giving evidence on the fusion of metals, including brass, under heat. He did not know the coefficient of expansion of a metal, brass. Could the witness be relied upon at all? Birkett himself got the witness to doubt his own expertise:

'You are an engineer? I dare say I am.'

The court was left with the impression that the witness did not know the answer to a technical question he should have known, and was therefore not an expert.

Whether this is a fair impression, who knows (although apparently the witness's demeanour and the way he answered the questions did not help). In a case involving financial statements, it may be the equivalent of asking an expert accountant the title of FRS 1. It may be like asking an accountant when FRS 1 became effective. Whichever it is, it can be a very effective type of question.

Having said that, it is rare that an accountant gets asked such a precise technical question. The chances are that every accountant knows that FRS 1 is entitled *Cash Flow Statements* (and would probably correct counsel and say that, actually, it is FRS 1 (revised)). Such questions are only likely to increase the witness's credibility in the court. Asking an extremely detailed question, which may have little relevance to the case in hand, for example, 'can you summarise paragraph 2 of your Institute's guidance on ethical matters for members in business' will probably be held to be just that, irrelevant.

However, it is more common to be asked a question along the following lines:

> 'Mr X, given that we're looking at a company involved in manufacturing drain-pipes, could you tell the court how many of your clients do manufacture drainpipes?'

Or even, in the knowledge that many expert accountants do nothing but litigation accountancy:

> 'Mr X, when was the last time you signed an audit report?'

5.5.12 Questions outside the witness's expertise

Experts are often asked questions outside their expertise. The effect of this is as follows.

Experts know that their role is to help the court, and it is natural for them to try to answer each question. A question which is completely outside their expertise will not be answered. However, one which is partially outside their expertise, in that in some way they have had to consider the issue, may give them more trouble. Take the following example. An expert accountant is giving evidence on a net asset statement, based on the accounts of a company. What is the effect of the following question on him:

> 'And what do you consider the value of this plant and machinery was?'

The expert is not an expert valuer, so on the face of it, he cannot answer. However, he has included within his calculation of net assets values for plant and machinery. But these figures may not equate to the real value of the plant and machinery. If he says that he does not know, why has he used these figures in the first place? If he says that it is £x, the figure in the accounts, does this equate to the value? Will he be taken on some pinning-out exercise, perhaps being asked to value all sorts of other assets?

Counsel seems to have won either way, and of course he has unsettled the witness.

5.5.13 Doubting the witness's reasonableness

Another way of undermining the witness is to show that he holds an unreasonable position. This can be effectively achieved by using the alternative reasonable assumption approach. If the witness disagrees with the position at the end, then he may appear to be unreasonable. Furthermore, if a witness refuses to accept an alternative proposition or even a hypothetical, he may give the impression of unreasonableness.

5.5.14 The detailed analysis

Examples of detailed analysis have already been given above. For barristers cross-examining experts, it is an extremely effective way of finding out exactly what they have and have not done, what they have relied on and what detailed assumptions have been made. By its nature it can be time-consuming and laborious. It also needs an extremely patient and tenacious counsel, who has been well briefed by his own expert.

The reason it can be effective is because the construction of expert evidence is very much a bottom-up process, that is, an accountant starts with the raw accounting materials, records, working papers, correspondence, etc. and builds up a picture. Detailed analysis is a way of deconstructing the whole exercise. A good counsel will be able to prise out any inconsistencies or items missed.

5.5.15 Comment and hectoring

Comment is not questioning at all. At its worst it can be counsel making gratuitous insults to the witness. More often it is just a comment about the evidence just given. The point about comment is that, because it is not a question, the expert is left in difficulty as to what to do with it. There is no question to answer. He cannot comment back, yet he is left with a vague feeling that he should do something, but he cannot and is therefore troubled.

Where counsel makes a comment about the evidence, the court should really step in and ask him what his question is. However, counsel often try it and get away with it. It is particularly effective in criminal trials, where a jury is unlikely to know the niceties of court procedure.

Counsel often make comments which, on the face of it, are completely neutral. A good example is 'we'll come back to that later'.

This normally marks the end of a line of questioning, particularly if the expert has scored a strong point, and counsel has no intention of coming back to it later. The expert, however, does not know this, and is left with a vaguely disturbed feeling.

Hectoring really is designed to unsettle the witness, and the witness's counsel or the judge should step in.

Experts are particularly prone to this sort of attack because, first of all, they have to give explanations and, second, many of their answers cannot be in the form yes or no. Interrupting a witness in the middle of an answer with another question is extremely bad form, but again, it does unsettle the witness. Another technique – 'come on, Mr X, yes or no' – can also be used to frustrate him.

5.6 Re-examination

Re-examination is where the witness is again examined by counsel for the side which called him. The aim of re-examination is, quite simply, to repair the damage done by the cross-examination, and new topics cannot be introduced. Witnesses in cross-examination may make certain admissions unhelpful to their own side, and helpful to the other side. That is, of course, the objective of cross-examination. In re-examination, counsel will attempt to clarify or qualify these admissions.

Barristers have a dilemma in deciding whether to re-examine a witness. The dilemma is that if the witness has made a damaging admission and the witness is re-examined on that evidence, the court is reminded of it and the witness may confirm the admission or make the admission stronger.

The problem for counsel is that, as with the examination in chief, counsel may not lead the witness during re-examination.

To illustrate how a re-examination works, it is worth considering the concept of the fatal question. In cross-examination, barristers are wary of going one question too far and destroying a picture which they have built up. There is a classic fatal question in Richard Du Cann's *Art of the Advocate*.

Example

'A young man was once charged with having unlawful sexual intercourse with a girl under sixteen. The corroborative evidence supporting the girl's story came from a farmer who said he had seen a pair lying in a field.

He was asked:

Counsel	When you were a young man, did you ever take a girl for a walk in the evening?
Farmer	Aye, that I did.
Counsel	Did you ever sit and cuddle her on the grass in a field?
Farmer	Aye, that I did.
Counsel	And did you ever lean over and kiss her while she was lying back?
Farmer	Aye, that I did.
Counsel	Anybody in the next field, seeing that, might easily have thought you were having sexual intercourse with her?
Farmer	Aye, and they'd have been right, too.'

Re-examination can often be the process of asking that fatal question to get rid of a picture created in cross-examination, and can be seen using an example from Evans' *Advocacy at the Bar*.

Example

Two men were being tried for an attempted burglary in the middle of the night. A policeman had apparently discovered them and he had given evidence that he had approached within 12 feet of them without them noticing. The cross-examination was designed to show that the policeman must have been wrong as this was impossible:

'Q Sergeant, would you be kind enough to tell us how tall you are?
A Six foot three, sir.
Q And no weakling! Would you mind telling us your weight?
A Tip the scales at just under twenty-three stone, sir.
Q That night – wearing uniform, were you?
A Yes, sir.
Q Helmet?
A Yes, sir.
Q Greatcoat?
A Tunic, actually, sir.
Q Boots?
A Yes, sir.
Q Regulation issue boots, sergeant?
A Yes, sir.
Q What size were they?
A Size twelve, sir.
Q Yes, I see. Size twelve boots. Studded with hobnails, were they, like the normal regulation issue?
A (Pause) Yes, sir.
Q They had a small horseshoe of metal on each heel?
A Er, yes, sir.
Q And you say that you approached to within twelve feet of these men without their seeming to notice your arrival, sergeant?

A (Pause) Yes, sir.
Q In a totally empty square at two in the morning?
A (Pause) Yes, sir.
Q Nobody else around was there?
A No, sir.
Q Normal flagged pavements were there?
A (Pause) Yes, sir.
Q I mean, you didn't approach over a lawn or grass of some kind, did you?
A (Pause) No, sir.'

The barrister has made the point. What the policeman is describing appears highly unlikely. If there is a reasonable explanation, then, by continuing to ask questions, counsel is going to find out what it is, and weaken the point he has made.

Example

'Q Well, really, sergeant, can you suggest to the magistrates how you could possibly have got as close as you say you did without being heard by the defendants?
A On my bicycle, sir.'

If counsel for the defence had not asked the fatal question then the point would have been made. How could the sergeant have got so close? Could he be believed? This would be exactly the situation for re-examination, in order to reassert the witness's credibility. Evans suggests the following.

Example

Q You told us both in your evidence in chief and in cross examination that you approached to within twelve feet of these men and they did not appear to notice your arrival. Is that correct?
A Yes, sir.
Q Did you get that close to them?
A Did indeed, sir.
Q Did they look up?
A No, sir.
Q Later, did you have the opportunity of assessing whether they were of normal hearing?
A Oh, they could hear all right, sir.
Q Well, solve the mystery for us, sergeant. How did you do it?
A I was on my bicycle, sir.'

With an expert accountant, counsel is likely to want to re-examine on areas which have been weakened as a result of hypotheticals or the reasonable alternative assumption:

> 'Q Mr X, m'learned friend asked you to imagine a situation where the stock reports were not in existence. Do you remember what your evidence was on that.'

5.7 Closing speech

The closing speech is each side's summary of their case, having regard to the evidence which has now been given. The purpose is to persuade the court of the merits of the case by interweaving the story with appropriate evidence and discussion of the relevant law.

5.8 The expert accountant's conduct in court

How does the accountant deal with the process of giving evidence. From what has been said above, especially concerning cross-examination, he is at an extreme disadvantage. Barristers will use all sorts of ruses to trick him, the aim of opposing counsel will be to discredit him, and even his own counsel may wish to put him in a position where his evidence is stronger than he feels it should be.

However, there are a number of things which the accountant should remember. The first is, the accountant's duty as an expert witness is to the court, not to his own side. He is there to give his honest opinion. The second thing to remember is that he owes it to himself, to his firm and to his profession generally to give evidence in a way which does him credit. Like anything the accountant does in practice, giving expert evidence is an exercise in being professional.

The accountant should always bear in mind that, no matter how knowledgeable counsel appears to be about his area of expertise, he actually knows very little. Counsel's knowledge of accountancy is a minute proportion of that of any accountant. Counsel is only likely to be really comfortable when dealing with the small area he knows about. Step outside that and counsel is likely to be lost:

> 'I understand the point which is being made to me. On the basis of one interpretation of the SSAP, that is how this transaction could be accounted for. However, I do think that the terms of an exposure draft which had been issued six months before should be considered.'

Nobody apart from the experts in court may know what an exposure draft is, let alone any relevance it may have. This lack of knowledge applies to counsel on both sides.

This is both a problem and a benefit. On the one hand, the expert could speak over the court's head so it does not understand the evidence. On the other, the expert should bear in mind that counsel is unlikely to be able to sustain questioning on a particular area of accountancy for any length of time before he runs up against his knowledge limit.

Finally, the accountant should remain to some extent in control. This means no more than being in the frame of mind of feeling that he is not a tennis ball being hit backwards and forwards across the net. The issue of control is a precursor to feeling confident, and the confident witness is a far better witness than, say, the expert engineer who says 'I dare say so'.

How the expert should act in court is considered chronologically through the trial.

5.9 The expert pre-trial

It should go without saying that the expert should be thoroughly acquainted with his own report. After all, he signed it.

It is rare that an expert carries out all of the work himself in the preparation of his report. However, when he does, he will feel a great sense of control over the documents underlying his report and its contents. In this type of situation an expert will be thoroughly comfortable with the contents of his report and ready to answer any question on cross-examination. In order to prepare himself for the real thing he should indulge in a role-play with another accountant.

The expert should get one of his own partners to read the report with an extremely critical eye. He should tell his fellow partner where the weak points are. His fellow partner should then attack it, verbally, as strongly as possible.

The same goes for a report where the work, and perhaps some of the drafting, has been carried out by staff members, except that this time the process should be more rigorous, and the staff should join in.

The accountant should also expect his legal advisers and his own counsel to ask him difficult questions on the report.

None of this is meant as a softening-up exercise; what it should do is let the accountant know that this is as bad as the cross-examination can get. It should also be used as preparation for how to deal with the really difficult questions he is going to get in court.

The accountant should ensure that his legal team understands the report. Often, this can be done by asking them what they think it means. The draft skeleton argument will also contain counsel's interpretation of what the report says. The skeleton should be consistent with the accountant's own findings.

5.10 The expert in court

Ideally, an expert will sit in court from the opening speeches to the closing speeches, or to judgment, if it is not reserved. He gets a sense of the proceedings, the way the case is going and, importantly, the ebb and flow of evidence.

Sitting through a trial gives an expert a thorough understanding of how the importance of matters can increase and decrease during a trial. However, this happens only occasionally. Trials are expensive and adding an accountant to the team only increases that expense. Experts are in the lucky position of being allowed to sit in court during the whole proceedings and therefore they should take advantage of this. Even if an accountant is only required to be in court during his evidence, he should go to court before this for the following reasons.

First, he will soak up some of the atmosphere of the court. He will know which side of the judge the witness box is, where his own counsel and opposing counsel are sitting, and how the proceedings in that particular trial are going. Next, he will be able to take the opportunity to see how his own counsel examines someone in chief and, more importantly, how opposing counsel cross-examines. He will therefore get some sense of what his own ordeal will be like. He will also get an idea of what the judge is like.

One thing which an expert should try before court has started is to sit in the witness box. This is akin to a speaker standing on a rostrum in an empty lecture theatre before he speaks. He gets some sense of what the real experience will be if he imagines the court full of people.

If there is an expert on the other side, and the other side's evidence is given first, the expert will get first-hand experience of the cross-examination of an accountant, the reason being that the expert will be assisting in the questioning. This aspect is now considered.

5.11 Assisting counsel

Some counsel like a lot of help when cross-examining experts, others require none at all. If the trial involves particularly complicated accounting evidence, counsel may need a lot of input, first of all to ask the questions, and then to interpret the witness's replies. (It should be noted that accountants may also be asked to assist in the cross-examination of factual witnesses where there are financial issues involved in the factual witness's evidence.)

The accountant will already have mapped out a cross-examination strategy with counsel beforehand, but during the actual cross-examination, he will be feeding counsel written questions, or whispering them to him. This is normally done from the bench before or behind counsel, depending on whether counsel is a silk or a junior. However, it occasionally happens that counsel will ask the judge for permission for the expert to sit beside him because, essentially, the cross-examination is being carried out by the accountant.

Assisting in this way is often the most exciting part of an accountant's role. The witness is on oath, is giving answers which need to be understood and questions need to be fed to counsel in a way that he can understand.

However, there is one thing that the accountant must remember – and this goes for the examination of any witness – and that is, no matter how exciting the questioning becomes, the accountant must never show it. He should keep a blank expression all the time. He must on no account grin if a point goes his side's way. Reacting in this way is most unprofessional, and the judge is likely to notice.

5.12 Into the witness box

When the expert is called to give evidence, he will either be in court or waiting outside. He effectively starts giving evidence the moment he is in court and walks towards the box, because it is at that moment that the court sees him for the first time as a witness. He should walk with a slow measured tread, not rushing. When he gets into the box, he should take time to get comfortable, taking his report and calculator out of his briefcase in his own time.

First of all, he will be sworn in. He should already have practised saying the words so that he is comfortable with them and he should look towards the bench and say the words slowly, clearly and seriously to show that he realises exactly what he is saying, that is, that he will tell the truth, the whole truth and nothing but the truth. If the witness is swearing on the Bible he will have been handed this by the usher. He should say thank you then, and thank you when he hands it back. Witness boxes have seats and, especially in long cases, he may be invited to sit down. If not, and he feels like sitting down, he should ask the judge for permission.

One of the problems of giving evidence – reinforced by fictional trials on television – is that the witness seems to be having a conversation with whichever counsel is questioning him. The witness looks at the barrister as he gives his answer. Witnesses should avoid this. The evidence is to the judge, or the judge and jury. Witnesses also find that they feel less intimidated if they do not have to look at counsel when they are answering questions. Therefore, the expert should place himself in such a position so that he is facing the judge, and has to turn to look at counsel when a question is being asked. If the witness is sitting down, he should position his chair so that it is facing the bench.

After being sworn in, the expert's own counsel will stand and ask for the witness's name and business address. The examination in chief will then start, the contents of which will generally have been discussed before with counsel.

5.12.1 Addressing the judge

- High Court judges are referred to as 'My Lord' or 'My Lady'.
- Judges in the Central Criminal Court are referred to as 'My Lord' or 'My Lady'.
- Circuit judges and recorders are referred to as 'Your Honour.
- County court district judges are referred to as 'Sir' or 'Madam'.

Confusion often arises because of the following:

(a) High Court judges also sit in the Crown Court or the county court, where they will be referred to as 'My Lord' or 'My Lady';
(b) circuit judges sit in the Central Criminal Court where they will be referred to as 'My Lord' or 'My Lady';
(c) Retired High Court judges may sit as circuit judges;
(d) circuit judges with the honorary office of Recorder of Manchester or Recorder of Liverpool are referred to as 'My Lord' or 'My Lady'.

The witness can always check the way in which the judge in his particular case is to be addressed by looking at the list outside the court which will state, for example, 'His Honour Judge . . .'.

The witness should be wary of using these phrases too much, and there is certainly no need to preface each answer with such an address.

5.12.2 Answering questions

Whenever an expert answers a question he should bear in mind the following:

(a) any answer should be given to the judge, or the judge and jury, not to the counsel who asked the question;
(b) the witness should speak loudly;
(c) questions should not be answered if they are not understood, and the expert should tell the judge that he does not understand;
(d) questions outside the expertise field should not be answered;
(e) 'I don't know' should be used if the answer is not known;
(f) there is no harm in spending time thinking about the answer to a question, and any question should only be answered after some thought. An answer which is well thought-out is far more convincing than one which is made up along the way;
(g) be as brief as possible;
(h) using technical accounting terms is often unavoidable, but they should not be overused, or used when unnecessary. Normal language is by far the best language to use, and jargon should be avoided at all costs;
(i) avoid giving evidence which reads like this:

> '. . . and SSAP 1 basically says, and I'm paraphrasing here but I can explain in a bit more detail if you would like, it basically says that if you have an associated company, I suppose I should define that, that associated companies should be accounted for on an equity accounting basis, there's another term I'd better define, but that also the equity accounting basis shouldn't be used if, well there are a couple of reasons . . .'

This is hardly the way a letter would be written, but is the way that the transcript will appear and the transcript may be the only record of what the expert evidence has been;
(j) speak clearly and confidently;
(k) speak slowly;
(l) the judge will be taking notes of what the expert says – the golden rule is to watch the judge's pen;
(m) never be evasive, hostile or partial;
(n) never argue;
(o) be fair;
(p) correct any mistakes;
(q) finally, avoid humour and sparring with the barristers. A colleague of one of the authors once experienced the following piece of cross-examination:

> 'Q Mr X, I wonder if you would take those figures which we have discussed, and which I note you have carefully written down, add them up, multiply them by the gross percentage and tell us what the profit is.

A I am afraid I can't.
Q I beg your pardon?
A I am afraid I can't.
Q You can't. And why is that?
A Because I do not have a calculator with me.
Q You don't have a calculator with you. Well, that is surprising. I thought that accountants carried calculators with them at all times.
A I'm afraid, Mr Y, that's just another one of your wild assumptions.

(Laughter in court.)'

The colleague got away with it that time (and managed to get away with not having a calculator which should always be taken to court). However, this works very rarely.

5.13 Cross-examination

When the examination in chief has finished, the expert's own counsel will say something along the lines of 'Thank you, Mr X, I wonder if you could stay there, m'learned friend would like to ask you a few questions'.

The cross-examination is about to begin. The expert should know by now how to address the court. This section therefore deals with how the expert should deal with the various techniques which opposing counsel will use to weaken the expert's evidence and undermine his credibility. Three points first, though. The expert should never answer a question if he does not understand it. He should say to the judge that he does not understand the question, and would like it to be clarified.

Second, if he feels he has made an error, the expert should tell the judge, and ask to be allowed to correct the error:

> 'My Lord, in response to Mr Y's question a minute ago I gave an answer which I believe was incorrect. In response to a question . . . I said the following . . . That is not strictly the position and perhaps I could be allowed to correct what I said.'

Finally, the accountant should bear in mind that every question is an opportunity for him to confirm his evidence; cross-examination need not be the discrediting of his earlier evidence in chief.

5.13.1 Pinning-out

The expert has to be extremely wary of pinning-out because he will end up being put in a position he does not like. The way to spot pinning-out is that it consists of a number of, on the face of it, harmless questions, to which the answer is either yes or no, or very short. Of course, this questioning may be very fair, but often there is a logical fallacy or incorrect statement in one of the questions.

Example

Q Mr X, you are an accountant who has been in practice for 20 years?
A Yes.
Q And it's true, is it not, that you carried out an extremely detailed investigation into your client company's affairs?
A That's correct.
Q You have carried out a number of detailed analyses of the transactions which are the subject of the dispute in this case, correct?
A Correct.
Q It's true to say, is it not, that you have undertaken an extensive analysis of all of the papers in this trial to produce what is a most voluminous report.
A Yes.
Q And you have also looked at, again in some detail, the accounts of a number of companies which compete with your client?
A I have, yes.
Q If your analysis is, as you say, so complete, could you explain why no mention is made of the matters in the documents which you will find at trial bundle reference . . .

Counsel has asked the accountant a number of questions to which the easiest answer is yes. The problem for the accountant is that, at question 4, he has agreed that he has reviewed all of the papers in the case. Has he? He should know. The sources of information which he has relied on should be exhibited to his report. The correct answer to question 4 should have been:

> 'My Lord, the papers which I analysed are set out in Appendix I to my report. I cannot tell you whether there are other papers which I have not been shown.'

To sum up, pinning-out should signal itself by its mode of questioning. The accountant should be alert to the fallacious question and deal with it when it is asked.

5.13.2 Hypotheticals

Hypotheticals (and in the next section, the reasonable alternative assumption) will themselves signal the start of a pinning-out exercise. Therefore, as soon as the accountant hears 'Mr X can I ask you to assume for the moment . . .' or 'let's work on this basis . . .' he should be wary, and ask himself the question 'how reasonable is that proposition?'.

The earlier example on hypotheticals started as follows:

> 'Q Let's work on the basis that these stock reports did not exist at the time the

accounts were being finalised. Do you understand the situation I'm describing?
A Yes.'

There are two ways of dealing with this. The first is to answer all of the questions, but to keep in mind that this is a hypothetical situation. The expert can remind the court of this every now and then, and then when it comes to the final question, answer like this:

Example

Q So the position is, there would be nothing to tell the directors that any of the stock was obsolete?
A That is correct, on the basis that there were no stock reports. However, in reality the directors did have the stock reports and those stock reports did disclose that stock was materially overstated.

The expert gets the opportunity here to confirm his earlier evidence.

The other way of dealing with the hypothetical is to refuse to answer it. The problem with this is that the expert may appear intransigent, and could be criticised by the judge. He could also be seen to be arguing his own client's case, something an expert should never do. He could, however, say:

> 'My Lord, must I answer that question? It appears to have been put to me on the basis that the directors did not see the stock sheets. However, not only has the finance director responded in writing to the stock report, he admitted in evidence that he had read it and understood it.'

The accountant is asking the judge for help, quite properly, and the court will not want to see its time wasted on a wild goose chase.

5.13.3 Alternative reasonable assumptions

Alternative reasonable assumptions have to be answered. The one thing the accountant has to bear in mind is that he has, implicitly, disagreed with the appropriateness of using that assumption in using his own. Accountants base their opinions on assumptions which may or may not be right, but should be reasonable. One may be more reasonable than the other, and that may be the one the expert has used.

Example

Q Now, you have told the court that, in assessing the loss, you have used a gross profit of 50 per cent, correct?

A Yes.
Q And that you have based that figure on a review of the 20 other companies' accounts in this particular sector, is that correct?
A Yes.
Q It's correct, isn't it, that the range of gross profits for those 20 companies is between 42 per cent and 65 per cent?
A Yes.
Q So it could be that my client's company would have earned 65 per cent?
A It is, yes.
Q Isn't it stronger than that, given that another company carrying out exactly the same business earned 65 per cent, isn't it entirely reasonable to assume that my client could also have made 65 per cent?
A No. The company could have made a profit of 65 per cent, but I think that it is far more likely that it would have achieved 50 per cent. My Lord, I have already given the reasons in my report – would you like me to go through them again . . .
Q . . . and you've said the deduction for wages and salaries might have been 15 per cent and finally, you told the court that a gross profit of 65 per cent could be reasonable. I wonder if, taking those figures, you could make a calculation of the lost profit.
A Yes, I make the figure £250,000. However, I would like to make the point that I do not believe that the company would have made that level of profit. All of the work which I have carried out leads me to conclude that the profit would be less than that. In my opinion the profit would have been £100,000.

Again, the accountant uses the opportunity to restate his own evidence.

5.13.4 Lots of questions, multi-question questions, the same question and the surprise question

Just because a question is short, part of a series of short questions, and appears to demand short, snappy answers, this does not mean that that is how the accountant should answer it. Every question should be answered on its own merits, and that means thinking about it. By doing this, the expert can often slow down the rate of questioning.

The long involved complicated question should be easy to deal with. First of all, if a question does ramble, and is confusing, the chances are that counsel does not know what he is trying to ask. The expert, if he does not understand what a question means, should ask the judge if it could be clarified.

Where the question is multi-faceted, the response should be as follows:

> 'My Lord, Mr Y asked me five questions then. Do you mind if I take them one by one? Thank you. First, I was asked whether . . . and finally . . .'

An alternative is to finish with:

> '. . . and finally, My Lord, I am afraid that I cannot remember the fifth question. Perhaps it could be repeated to me.'

Counsel will probably have forgotten what he asked as well.

When asked the same question over and over again, the expert should avoid any thoughts that, just because he is being asked the same question, there is something wrong with his opinion. He should be firm. The judge will eventually step in and stop this line of attack. The accountant does need to watch for the same question couched in slightly different terms. He needs to analyse each question and ask himself, have I heard that one before?

The way to deal with surprise questions is to take time and think.

5.13.5 Doubting the witness's expertise

> 'Q What is the coefficient of expansion of brass?'

The coefficient of brass is two things. It is a number. However, it is also shorthand for an expression, being 'the amount by which a set quantity of brass will expand if the temperature is raised by a certain amount'.

Now, even an engineer could be forgiven for not remembering a specific number. But the concept of a coefficient of expansion should be apparent to many people, experts or not. What was the answer Birkett was looking for? He did not know. It was the first thing which came into his head (see **5.5.11**).

The point here is that many questions may equally demand a difficult answer as a simple answer.

Barristers are not in the position of being experts. They may know a little bit for the purposes of cross-examination, but they do not practice accountancy day in day out. They themselves, therefore, may be uncertain as to the question which they are asking, and completely disinterested by the answer. It is therefore necessary to deconstruct these technical type questions.

> 'What is FRS 1?'

FRS 1 is a number of things. It is:

- a financial reporting standard;
- the financial reporting standard dealing with cash flow statements;
- a summary of the standard;

- the complete text of the standard;
- the complete text of the standard and the appendices.

Which one does counsel want? If counsel had wanted a summary of the standard, he would probably have asked for it. No one knows the complete text off by heart, which leaves the first two options. Why has counsel asked the question? To see whether the expert knows what counsel has been told is a piece of technical accounting. He may not know the simplest of the five answers. Therefore, the expert can use the first answer:

> 'Actually, My Lord, I think counsel may be referring to FRS 1 (revised). It is an example of a financial reporting standard.'

If counsel wishes to cross-examine the expert in more detail, so be it. However, the accountant has answered the question entirely properly.

A more difficult question for many experts would be 'what is section 151 of the Companies Act?'.

Unless an issue in the case specifically deals with financial assistance, many accountants would not know the answer to this. It is not an accounting question, it is a legal question. However, there is a reasonable assumption that accountants have some passing knowledge of the Companies Acts, not least because they have been examined on them in the dim and distant past. The same would go for sections of the Taxes Acts. However, just because an accountant does not know the answer does not mean he is unqualified to give expert evidence. An answer like this would be acceptable:

> 'My Lord, I am not a lawyer, and I'm afraid I do not know the sections of the Companies Acts by heart. However, if counsel could remind me of the title of the section, then I am sure I could let the court know its relevance to my evidence.'

As noted above, counsel will often refer to the particulars of the case, and try to get the accountant to admit that he has no experience of something relevant and therefore is not qualified to give evidence:

> 'Mr X, given that we're looking at a company involved in manufacturing drainpipes, could you tell the court how many of your clients do manufacture drainpipes?'

For most industries, it should not matter at all if the accountant has never carried out the audit of a company within it. The answer to this question should be:

> 'My Lord, I have never audited a company which manufactures drainpipes. However, the principles of accountancy apply to any business.'

If appropriate, the accountant could continue like this:

> 'Having said that, I do have a number of clients involved in manufacturing – one, indeed, which manufactures plastic products. In all of those companies, the management accounting techniques, that is, the use of a standard costing system and monthly stocktakes, are extremely similar to those used by the plastic drainpipe manufacturer in this case.'

An accountant may be asked 'Mr X, when was the last time you signed an audit report?'. This is going to be a difficult question for expert accountants who have not signed an audit report for many years, and rightly so, in some cases. If an accountant is giving evidence on audit negligence but spent the last 10 years carrying out nothing but forensic accountancy, his evidence may carry little weight. A possible answer is:

> 'I have not carried out an audit for 10 years. However, I have reviewed the audit working papers of other firms of accountants many times in that period, in my role as a forensic accountant.'

However, even on paper this response is not very convincing. It may not, of course, matter. An accountant does not need to have carried out an audit to give evidence on loss of profits, or insolvency. In these circumstances, it would be relevant to speak to the judge in the following terms:

> 'I have not carried out an audit for the last 10 years. My Lord, may I ask a question? Is there a suggestion being made that, because I do not carry out audits, this in some way undermines my ability to give expert accounting evidence on the profits lost by the company in this case?'

The judge may say that it depends on where counsel's line of questioning is going. However, the seed is planted in the court's mind.

5.13.6 Questions outside the witness's expertise

The best way to deal with questions which lie outside the expert's field is to say that they are not within the witness's professional knowledge. For example, counsel may ask:

> 'And what do you consider the value of this plant and machinery was?'

To which the expert accountant may reply:

> 'If by value counsel means open market value, then I cannot answer that question because I am not an expert valuer; I am an expert accountant. If by value, counsel means net book value, that is, the amounts at which those assets are stated in the accounts, then their value is the amount which I have used in my calculation of net assets.'

If the expert is uncertain whether the question does fall within his expertise, then he should ask for clarification of any ambiguous terms. In the above example, the ambiguous term is 'value':

> 'Could I ask for clarification of what counsel means by value?'

5.13.7 Doubting the witness's reasonableness

This has been dealt with in considering hypotheticals and the reasonable alternative assumption.

5.13.8 The detailed analysis

This is probably the most difficult stage of any cross-examination. The accountant is required to give a full explanation of every step of his work, to respond to why he did or did not do something, and to get it completely right. Another old adage holds true – the barrister can get it wrong over and over again but one mistake by the expert can be fatal.

Responding to the detailed analysis can give problems where some of the actual work has been carried out by staff, or was carried out some time before the case is heard.

The accountant is going to be more ready to stand up to the detailed analysis if he has a thorough understanding of the work carried out. Therefore, he should make himself aware of any work carried out by other members of his staff and should re-acquaint himself with that work carried out some time before.

5.13.9 Comment and hectoring

The expert should ignore most comments. However, where he feels that counsel is making a point impugning him, he should speak to the judge:

> 'My Lord, before he asked me that last question, Mr Y made a comment to the effect that my firm has some interest in the outcome of this case. I wonder if you could ask him to explain that comment and find out whether I am expected to respond.'

Or:

> 'My Lord, could I ask the significance of that comment.'

The judge can then sort out with counsel what it is he is getting at.

Where the expert is being hectored he should wait for counsel to finish speaking and then reassert his position:

'My Lord, I cannot answer that question yes or no. Would you like me to continue with the answer I was giving when I was interrupted?'

5.14 Communication with the expert

When they are giving evidence, witnesses, including expert witnesses, are forbidden from discussing their evidence with anyone, including their own staff. Where evidence goes on for some time, for example, over days or over a weekend, the witness is in a fairly lonely position. He is aware that his own side will be discussing the case and his evidence (i.e., how he did as a witness in the context of the case and how his evidence came across), but he cannot join in, and he must resist any attempts to do so.

However, accountants are often asked to carry out tasks, such as further analysis or calculations, overnight. If the expert wishes to use his own staff to do some of this work, he should ask the permission of the judge.

5.15 Re-examination

Re-examination is often the most difficult time for an expert. He is aware that, if he is being re-examined, there may be admissions which he has made which need clarification. The expert needs to think about the questions being asked, and to relate them back to evidence given in cross-examination. He should also be aware that counsel is not allowed to lead him, and must be prepared to give full answers.

Example

Q Mr X, m'learned friend asked you to imagine a situation where the stock reports were not in existence. Do you remember what your evidence was on that?

A Yes.

Q You said, did you not, that there would be nothing to tell the directors that the stock was overstated?

A Yes. But I would like to make the point that I answered that question on the basis of a hypothesis, and I do not consider that hypothesis to be reasonable.

Q Because the stock reports were in existence, were they not?

A Yes, they were. And not only were they in existence, the evidence which I have seen shows quite clearly that the directors saw those reports. Indeed, I remember the managing director in his evidence confirming that he had seen the report.

Q And could you remind His Lordship what those stock reports said?

A Yes, I can. My Lord, the stock reports showed quite clearly that a large amount of the stock was obsolete and recommended that the stock should

	be written down. The amount of the write-down recommended was £350,000.
Q	Was any write-down made?
A	No, no provision was made. This meant that stock in the accounts was overstated by £350,000 and, subject to tax, that profits and net assets were overstated by £350,000.
Q	Thank you. No further questions, My Lord. My Lord that completes my re-examination. Unless Your Lordship has any questions, I wonder if the witness might be released?

Although it is possible for re-cross-examination, and further re-examination, to take place, this is extremely rare. Unless the judge has any questions, the expert's ordeal is over and he may either leave the court or go back and sit with his solicitor.

5.16 Questions from the judge

> 'Thank you Mr Y. Mr X, I wonder if I might detain you a few minutes longer. There are some points on which I would like your views, and one area which I would like clarified.'

Judges can ask questions at any time during a witness's evidence, not only at the end. English judges do ask questions on a regular basis, where they are unsure of the evidence. However, they can also ask questions which, seemingly have no relevance to the case in point. One of the authors has, in advance of his evidence, been asked questions on part of the Companies Act.

Judges are extremely courteous when they ask questions, and are genuinely trying to get the answer to something, rather than give an impression to the court the way counsel do. All the normal rules of speaking in court apply here.

5.17 After the witness's evidence

Regardless of any other tasks which the expert has after his evidence, such as assisting in cross-examination, there are three important things he must do. First, he should consider whether there are any important points which he has made which have gone unchallenged. Such points may form part of counsel's closing speech.

Second, he should get feedback on his performance. He can get this from his solicitor and barrister. Finally, he should also take time to read the transcript of his evidence. In the unlikely event that an error has been made in taking down his evidence, he should advise his solicitor. He should also read how he appears on paper.

5.18 References

Du Cann, R. (1993) *The Art of the Advocate*, Penguin.

Evans, K. (1992) *Advocacy at the Bar*, Blackstone Press.

Munkman, J. (1991) *The Technique of Advocacy*, Butterworths.

Chapter 6
The Woolf proposals

6.1 Introduction

Civil justice in this country is very complex. It is also expensive and time-consuming. Furthermore, as can be seen from Chapters 12 and 13 there exists a two-tier civil system with separate procedural rules.

The problems of civil justice led to the establishment by the Lord Chancellor in March 1994 of a team of enquiry into the civil court system under the leadership of Lord Woolf, who is now the Master of the Rolls.

Lord Woolf's terms of reference were to aim to produce a combined set of rules for the High Court and the county court to replace the Rules of the Supreme Court (RSC) and County Court Rules (CCR) and generally to review civil procedures with a view to simplifying the system and making access to justice (through the courts or by way of mediation) easier and cheaper for the parties involved.

Lord Woolf issued the enquiry team's interim findings in June 1995 and the final report (and Draft Civil Proceedings Rules) in July 1996. The Lord Chancellor announced his final decisions with regard to the significant changes to civil procedure proposed by Woolf on 20 October 1997, and the reforms will be implemented in March or April 1999.

Draft Civil Proceedings Rules were published in July 1998 which incorporate further changes brought about by the Rule Committee. The final version of the new Rules is expected in January 1999.

Lord Woolf's report is entitled *Access to Justice*; most practitioners and commentators refer to it as 'The Woolf Report'. The aim of this chapter is to outline the main proposals to reforming the system of civil justice, and to look in detail at the reforms to the use of expert evidence.

6.2 Reform of civil justice

Lord Woolf's main area of recommendation comes in case management, that is, the management by the court of the process of litigation. Woolf seeks to streamline the civil process, not through the formal unification of the High

Court and the county courts but by increasing those common areas between the two systems. Woolf's final report proposes a unified set of core civil rules to govern the main aspects common to all civil litigation. These rules are entitled the Civil Proceedings Rules (CPR).

6.2.1 Case management

Woolf's recommendations are based on the view that the existing civil legal systems, which are essentially adversarial in nature, can only be streamlined by the courts themselves taking control of the litigation process. In order to speed up the legal process and to save the costs of litigation the system requires that the courts take a more pro-active role in assigning cases to the most appropriate court, in allocating resources to those cases most worthy of public (and litigant's) costs, and in generally accelerating the legal process.

In order to achieve these central ambitions Woolf proposes that all civil cases be allocated to one of three 'tracks' according to the size of the case and other considerations such as public importance.

The three tracks proposed are:

- small claims track;
- fast track; and
- multi-track.

Cases will initially be allocated to one of the three tracks based on value. Woolf proposes that:

(a) the small claims limit be increased from £500 to £3,000 excluding personal injury claims (a proposal which has already been implemented);
(b) the fast track will encompass all claims other than personal injury claims valued between £3,000 and £10,000 and all personal injury claims up to £10,000; and
(c) all other claims be assigned to the multi-track.

The draft CPR provide that a court is to allocate a claim to the lowest track which is deemed appropriate given the circumstances of the case.

It is *envisaged* that the fast track will encompass the vast majority of contested litigation within the monetary band £3,000–£10,000 and that it will also deal with non-monetary claims such as injunctions, declarations and orders for specific performance. Fast track litigation will be tried by the county courts presided over by a district judge, and will have the following characteristics:

(a) court directions will be simple;
(b) actions should be tried (unless of course settled beforehand) within 20 to 30 weeks of filing the defence;
(c) trials will be restricted to a maximum of one day with a target of half a day per action;
(d) expert evidence will be provided in written form and, crucially for the accountant engaged in expert accountancy in claims of low value, it is proposed that in the majority of cases the current adversarial role of the expert be removed by the appointment of a single expert appointed by the parties, or by the court where necessary;
(e) legal costs in the fast track will be fixed, depending on the value of the case. There are three levels:
    (i) up to £5,000 in respect of straightforward cases;
    (ii) up to £5,000 with 'additional work factors' and straightforward up to £10,000;
    (iii) up to £10,000 plus 'additional work factors'.

Examples of additional work factors are the need for expert evidence, multiple defendants, etc. The decision as to which cost banding the case should fall into will be decided by the district judge at the paper review stage, time of allocation to the fast tracks and by reference to the circumstances of the case. Furthermore, these bands do not include the costs of interlocutory applications which will be awarded, assessed and paid at the time of the application.

The multi-track will encompass all other cases not allocated to one of the lower tracks.

It is proposed that six or eight weeks after the defence has been filed a case management conference will take place with the stated intentions of:

'(a) identifying, defining and limiting the issues between the parties;
(b) identifying in broad terms in relation to each contended issue:
    (i) the nature of the evidence to be adduced;
    (ii) those areas in which expert evidence will be required;
    (iii) those classes of documents which may need to be discovered;
(c) summarily disposing of hopeless or weak cases;
(d) seeking to narrow the areas of dispute on one or more issues;
(e) seeking agreement between the parties where possible;
(f) considering whether mediation (Alternative Dispute Resolution) would be appropriate in resolving any or all of the issues;
(g) achieving transparency of costs;
(h) giving directions as to the necessary steps to be taken to bring the action to trial, including directions as to the early trial of one or more issues;
(i) preparing a timetable for the trial; and
(j) fixing the next hearing, either as in most cases a pre-trial review or the trial itself.

> In many cases a pre-trial review will be fixed (to take place when all preparatory work other than final preparations are completed) about eight weeks before trial and conducted, wherever practicable, by the trial judge assigned to the case. The pre-trial review is seen as an important opportunity for the parties, their solicitors and trial advocates to meet in a forum designed to encourage settlement before the trial commences.
>
> Where settlement at the pre-trial review is not possible it is intended that at this hearing the trial agenda be fixed. The trial agenda is intended to include a statement of the issues to be tried, with a timetable breaking the trial down into stages allotting time at each stage to the respective parties.' (Butterworths *Civil Court Practice 1997*, pp. 5–6)

6.2.2 Discovery

Much discovery in civil litigation is completely unnecessary, delaying trials and involving high costs in the production of documents most of which hardly seem germane to the issues in the case. The current rule in discovery is that all relevant documents in a client's possession, custody or power should be disclosed and, unless privileged, made available for inspection. Relevance is based on what is called the *Peruvian Guano* test, that is, any document which contains information which may advance a party's case or damage the other's or lead to a train of enquiry with either of these consequences. (It should be noted that *Peruvian Guano* refers to the case giving rise to this rule – *The Compagnie Financiere et Commerciale du Pacifique* v *The Peruvian Guano Company* (1882) 11 QBD 55.)

Woolf replaces the term 'discovery' with 'disclosure'. The only documents which are disclosable by a party in fast track cases will be those on which it relies to support its contentions and those documents which to a material extent undermine its own case or support another party's case. This is called 'standard discovery'.

Extra disclosure in multi-track cases is by court order where the court is convinced that the disclosure is necessary, having had regard to the issues in the case, where the cost is not disproportionate to the benefit and the resources and circumstances of the parties.

There are other recommendations such as only having to disclose one version of a document and the nomination of an individual on behalf of each party who is responsible for collecting documents and drawing up lists of documents.

6.3 Commentary

As anyone who has been involved in litigation can confirm, the civil justice system is time-consuming and expensive. However, the reasons for this are less to do with the existing rules (for example, under the existing procedures it is possible with the current time limits to go from issue of writ to trial within a few months) than with the attitudes of those involved in litigation – the lawyers.

Most experts will have experienced at least once the situation where they have been instructed by a solicitor, asked that solicitor when the date for exchange is, only to be told that the time limit expired months before. Some unlucky accountants will have received instructions just a few days before a trial. Every expert will have seen deadlines and time limits routinely ignored by all sides in litigation, although this practice is not endorsed by the Law Society nor by the law firms themselves.

It is for these reasons that the Woolf Report is mainly about taking case management away from the lawyers and the clients, and putting it in the hands of the judges. It is almost as if case management is so important that the lawyers cannot be trusted with it.

How successful the reform of discovery will be must be open to doubt; this relies on the honesty and diligence of clients and their solicitors, and this will be unchanged by the new rules. Not surprisingly, many clients are terrified of the 'smoking gun', and the deliberate suppression of documents which harm a party's case was recognised by Lord Woolf as ' . . . not unknown in practice' (paragraph 45 chapter 12, Final Report). A new system moving towards less extensive discovery at the same time as conditional fee arrangements are being introduced puts a great deal of pressure on solicitors. However, something needs to be done about the use of discovery as a tactic in delaying litigation, in putting pressure on another party as a result of the costs involved in complying with orders and in conducting fishing expeditions.

These proposals should be good for expert accountants. It is hoped that, following the necessary change in the attitude of lawyers to time limits and management, experts will be instructed at a far earlier stage and their instructions will be focused on the relevant issues because of the sanctions which will be applied if a deadline is missed.

Furthermore, in cases where financial documents play an important role, the expert accountant should find he is being used more and more in advising on the disclosure of documents.

The worry is that these proposals will only take proper effect after a complete overhaul of attitudes to litigation, and that there will be a lag between this and implementation of the case management system; there is the possibility of a system in place imposing new techniques on an unprepared profession. If this does happen, then many solicitors will be even more at sea than they are now. The old system of getting extensions for the submission of expert's reports will still be in their minds, and they will instruct experts with only a very short time before a fixed court deadline.

6.4 The use of expert evidence

How then will Lord Woolf's proposals impact on the role of the expert accounting witness? Chapter 13 of the Final Report is entitled 'Expert Evidence'. Paragraph 1 reads as follows:

> 'It was a basic contention of my interim report that two of the major generators of unnecessary cost in civil litigation were uncontrolled discovery and expert evidence. No-one has seriously challenged that contention.'

Lord Woolf referred to a large litigation support industry which had grown up (in which most of the readers of this book will work!), generating a multi-million pound fee income, which went against all principles of proportionality and access to justice, and that its most damaging effect was the way it had created an ethos of what was acceptable which had filtered down to smaller cases. In particular, Lord Woolf criticised the way in which many experts had become partisan, instead of neutral fact-finders or opinion-givers. He also said that the English courts were becoming uncompetitive due to unacceptable cost and delay. Lord Woolf proposed a greater use of single, neutral experts jointly selected, or court-appointed experts.

Lord Woolf's proposals have been criticised by some in the legal profession because it has been felt that he is undermining the adversarial nature of our legal system. Certainly, the proposals regarding case management are designed to take certain responsibilities out of the hands of the parties and give them to the judiciary. But this, of itself, is not an attack on the adversarial system. However, taking over the use of experts has been seen as a move away from the adversarial system, probably because the court-appointed expert is a feature of the continental inquisitorial approach.

In paragraph 5 of chapter 13 Lord Woolf wrote:

> 'My detailed proposals on experts, however, have provoked more opposition than any of my other recommendations. Most respondents favour retaining the full-scale adversarial use of expert evidence, and resist proposals for wider use of single experts (whether court-appointed or jointly appointed by the parties) and for disclosure of communications between experts and their instructing lawyers.'

However, Lord Woolf said that the argument for the full, 'red-blooded' adversarial approach only works if the time and cost considerations are put aside. Furthermore:

(a) a party can achieve something other than a just result by taking advantage of the other side's lack of resources or ignorance of relevant facts or opinions, and expert evidence is one of the principal weapons used by litigators who take this view (paragraph 7, chapter 13, Final Report);
(b) the traditional English way of deciding between contentious expert issues is for a judge to decide, which is not necessarily the best way of achieving justice if the issues are technical or if the judge has no experience of the area, particularly as the judge's decision may be based on, for example, which expert is the more fluent or persuasive (paragraph 8).

Lord Woolf set out his new approach at paragraph 11 as being based on the premise that an expert is there to assist the court, and that there should be no expert evidence at all unless it will help the court. However, what he proposes is a flexible system to foster an approach which emphasises the impartial assistance to the court in a focused way.

Lord Woolf has 18 recommendations concerning expert evidence. Sixteen of these are considered below (the remainder concern doctors). They should all be considered in the light of case management and impartiality, rather than an abandonment of adversarial principles.

6.4.1 The flexible approach

1 *The calling of expert evidence should be subject to the complete control of the court.*

This is part of the case management system, and will include directing that no expert evidence be adduced without leave of the court, or no expert evidence of a particular type or on a particular issue be adduced.

6.4.2 Use of single experts

2 *The court should have discretion, with or without the agreement of the parties, to appoint an expert to report or give evidence to the court.*

The appointment of a single neutral expert will not necessarily mean that either side cannot call its own expert evidence, or cross-examine the court-appointed expert, if that were justified by the scale of the case. However, Lord Woolf believes that in certain areas, such as quantum, single experts will be acceptable. Acceptance of a single expert on liability issues is generally limited to cases where the amount in issue is very small, or where there is little scope for disagreement. He does not go so far as to specify particular areas of litigation where a single expert should or should not be used. In certain types of expertise, where there are several schools of thought or where knowledge is being extended, the full adversarial system with cross-examination of experts is likely to achieve a just result. However, Lord Woolf also makes the following recommendation.

3 *As a general principle, single experts should be used wherever the case (or the issue) is concerned with a substantially established area of knowledge and where it is not necessary for the court directly to sample a range of opinions.*

Lord Woolf considers that too often experts are in fact agreed, but that their reports only set out the extreme position.

As part of his general principle of access to justice, Lord Woolf abhors the ability of one party being able to adduce expert evidence just because he is able to pay for it. As part of the whole approach of encouraging the use of single experts Lord Woolf puts the onus on each party (and on the judge) to justify not following this recommendation.

4 *Parties and procedural judges should always consider whether a single expert could be appointed in a particular case (or to deal with a particular issue); and, if this is not considered appropriate, indicate why not.*

6.4.3 Use of expert assessors

5 *The court should have wide power to appoint assessors*

The use of expert assessors is a controversial proposal because of the fear that an assessor will usurp the role of the judge. However, Lord Woolf believes that the assessor's role would be to educate the judge where there are complex technical issues to enable him to reach an informed decision. In a particularly complex case, assessors could be appointed by each side. However, in some cases Lord Woolf sees no objection to appointing an independent expert as adjudicator.

6.4.4 Impartiality

In his efforts to ensure that experts are objective, and that their evidence will assist the court, Lord Woolf has a number of recommendations to ensure the impartiality of expert witnesses.

6 *Experts should be given clear guidance that, when preparing evidence or actually giving evidence to a court, their first responsibility is to the court and not to their client.*

This is a restatement of the common law rule, as set out in **3.2.1** (*Whitehouse* v *Jordan* [1981] 1 All ER 650).

7 *Any report prepared for the purposes of giving evidence to a court should be addressed to the court.*

This recommendation is intended to concentrate the mind of the expert as he writes his report.

8 *Such a report should end with a declaration that it includes everything which the expert regards as being relevant to the opinion which he has expressed in his report and that he has drawn to the attention of the court any matter which would affect the validity of that opinion.*

This recommendation and the next are designed to allay Lord Woolf's concerns about the disclosure of all relevant material. In particular, Lord Woolf is concerned that relevant opinions or factual evidence may be suppressed.

9 *Expert evidence should not be admissible unless all written instructions (including letters subsequent upon the original instructions) and a note of any oral instructions are included as an annex to the expert's report.*

Major problems arise when experts are working from different instructions, and even a single expert's report may be unclear or open to misinterpretation if the instructions are not known.

The Interim Report went even further, denying professional privilege to draft reports (as is the case in the USA). However, due to various difficulties envisaged in this proposal, not least the need to review drafts to identify changes and the reasons for them, this is not a recommendation in the Final Report.

6.4.5 Access to evidence: inequality of resources

10 *The court should have a wide power, which could be exercised before the start of proceedings, to order that an examination or tests should be carried out in relation to any matter in issue, and a report submitted to the court.*

The purpose behind this recommendation is to ensure that the imbalance between litigants with vastly different resources is, to some extent, corrected. The benefits of Lord Woolf's proposal can be seen in the case of a plaintiff, not qualifying for legal aid, suing a defendant backed by a large insurance company, but not knowing whether the case is worth pursuing because of insufficient resources to pay for a medical report, for example.

6.4.6 Narrowing the issues: experts' meetings

Lord Woolf has a number of recommendations concerning the much-maligned without prejudice meeting of experts. Although a good idea in theory, in practice both lawyers and experts have often circumvented the principle of experts' meetings by merely attending and not agreeing to anything. Such conduct appears to have been so ingrained in some practitioners that it risks becoming an old Spanish practice. Even where agreement is reached, it is almost invariably subject to instructing solicitor's agreement.

One of the authors considers that, in his career as an expert accountant, he has only ever experienced two useful experts' meetings. Having said that, one of those was so successful (with decisions made at the time without reference to solicitors) that it was reckoned to have saved weeks of court time, so they can work where there is intent on both sides.

The recommendations are as follows:

11 *If experts instructed by the parties meet at the direction of the court, it should be unprofessional conduct for an expert to be given or to accept instructions not to reach agreement. If the experts cannot reach agreement on an issue they should specify their reasons for being unable to do so.*

12 *Experts will be required to produce a report identifying areas agreed and areas in dispute.*

13 *Experts' meetings should normally be held in private. When the court directs a meeting, the parties should be able to apply for any special arrangements such as attendance by the parties' legal advisers.*

Lord Woolf envisages meetings properly conducted with clear agendas. If lawyers attend, it is only in the role of observer to ensure fair play and not to participate in the discussion. He expects any case of any substance to have such a meeting.

Furthermore, he expects that experts should communicate at the earliest possible date, as soon as possible after the submission of the defence. Indeed, Lord Woolf expects a high degree of co-operation.

14 *Where opposing experts are appointed they should adopt a co-operative approach. Wherever possible this should include a joint investigation and a single report, indicating areas of disagreement which cannot be resolved.*

6.4.7 Improving the quality of experts' reports

Expert reports, as well as being partisan, have the tendency to include irrelevant material, to stray beyond the field of expertise and to fail to address the real issues. Lord Woolf's recommendations to improve the quality of expert reports are as follows:

15 *Codes of practice providing guidance as to the practice in relation to experts should be drawn up jointly by the appropriate professional bodies representing the experts and the legal profession.*

16 *Training courses and published material should provide expert witnesses with a basic understanding of the legal system and their role within it, focusing on the expert's duty to the court, and enable them to present written and oral evidence effectively. Training should not be compulsory.*

Lord Woolf does not propose an exclusive system of accreditation because of the possibility of narrowing the field of available experts and the difficulty of finding an accredited expert in an unusual field. He also sees the need for improving guidance for solicitors in the way they instruct experts.

6.5 Commentary

There is little doubt that, if these recommendations are implemented, expert accountancy will change radically in a large number of cases. The majority of cases undertaken by expert accountants are concerned with quantum in personal injury cases. There will almost certainly be a narrowing of the number of experts likely to be instructed as lawyers seek to ensure that experts have received the proper training. Accountants who offer themselves as experts, particularly those with little experience of litigation, will be less ready to subject themselves to the rigours of Lord Woolf's requirements.

The vast majority of cases do not reach court. Therefore, most accountants are never subjected to the thorough scrutiny of their work through cross-examination. Where two experts are appointed, the proposed pre-trial procedure of experts' meetings, and the need to produce reports, will weed out the false assumptions, weak logic and bias which are features of many reports. In any case, the appointment of the single expert in many cases will ensure that properly qualified experts are used because of the obvious benefit that this has for both sides.

Because many accountants are capable of giving expert accounting evidence on the basis of experience, accreditation is a real possibility.

All of this is likely to mean fewer, better qualified experts involved in litigation work. However, this in many respects will follow a trend already apparent in the practice of expert accountancy. As with other fields of accountancy the number of expert practitioners has reduced as individuals specialise.

In many cases, the determining factor for a client or solicitor is cost, a development seen over the last few years in auditing. Fewer expert accountants may increase costs, but more solicitors better educated in the use of experts and more accountants experienced at carrying out expert work may reduce costs; and of course the use of single experts who are more focused in their instructions will also reduce costs. Lord Woolf may achieve his aims.

However, in respect of one area of the proposals it is entirely possible that the cost of experts will increase. The use of a court-appointed expert will not necessarily stop each side appointing its own expert. Given the disclosure proposals for instructions, there may be a tendency for lawyers to appoint two sets of accounting experts, one to give evidence and one to advise in a litigation support capacity. The instructions to the latter will still be protected by privilege. There may be a move to 'protect' the expert who will give evidence from the litigation process, with tightly drafted instructions and little exposure to the development of the case. The losing party will not have to pay for the costs of the behind-the-scenes accountants, but it is difficult to anticipate their effect on the legal process and Lord Woolf's proposals.

Lord Woolf's proposals are to be welcomed. However, in themselves they are not the end of the story for developments in the civil justice process. Expert accountants must keep abreast of the changes.

6.6 Reference

Greenslade, R. (ed.) (1997) *Butterworths Rules of Court – Civil Court Practice – 1997*, Butterworths.

Part 2
The practice of the expert witness

Chapter 7
Terms of engagement

7.1 Introduction

The life of an expert accountant is often like that of a soldier in war – long periods of boredom punctuated by short periods of anxiety and terror. In a case, the accountant has to be aware that he will rarely be controlling matters. What he does, when he does it and how much time he has will be directed by his solicitor, the barrister, the other side's legal advisers, the client, court orders, the judge, etc.

Given the extent to which the accountant can be pushed and pulled through the litigation process, it is important that he sets out his terms of reference at the earliest possible opportunity. He also needs to be aware that the detail of his terms of reference will almost certainly change with time and he must act accordingly. This chapter sets out how the accountant should go about accepting an appointment, framing his terms of reference and developing those terms as a case develops.

7.2 Conflicts of interest

7.2.1 The general position

Whenever an expert accountant receives potential instructions, it is important that he immediately ensures that he has no conflict in acting. There are a number of areas which could provide a conflict, either arising through relationships which the individual himself has, or which his firm has.

Conflicts normally, but not always, arise because of a relationship with one of the parties to a matter. Such relationships include the following:

(a) already acting for one of the parties to an action as expert;
(b) where one of the parties to an action is already a client;
(c) where one of the parties to an action has been a client;
(d) where the individual or the firm have already had an involvement in some of the issues in question or in the case;
(e) where the individual or the firm has an interest in the outcome of the action;

(f) a personal connection to one of the parties in the action, for example through blood ties or marriage.

Possible conflicts can therefore occur in a great many instances, and the accountant should attempt to discover them before accepting an engagement. Why is this the case? The Cresswell Code, referred to in Chapter 3, includes the following statement:

> 'An expert witness should provide independent assistance to the court by way of objective unbiased opinion in relation to matters within his expertise.'

If an expert is independent, objective and unbiased then surely it does not matter what ties he or his firm have with the action. That, of course, is certainly a view many accountants do take, choosing to see conflicts in only the most extreme cases. Therefore, where one firm or individual may see a conflict in a given set of circumstances, another may not.

It is therefore appropriate to try to understand what the term 'conflict of interest' means.

7.2.2 Rules of professional conduct

Unfortunately, there is little in the way of firm guidance for expert accountants on conflicts of interest. Reproduced in Appendix 5 is the ICAEW's statement 1.204 on conflicts of interest. The statement is split into two parts, one dealing with the conflict between a firm and its clients, the other dealing with the conflict between two clients.

In respect of the first type of conflict, the key phrase is:

> '. . . whether the perception of a reasonable observer at the time would be that the objectivity of the firm is likely to be impaired.'

In these circumstances, the firm should not accept the engagement.

In respect of the second type of conflict, the ICAEW statement says that there is nothing improper in a firm having two or more clients whose interests may be in conflict. However:

> '. . . the activities of the firm should be so managed as to avoid the work of the firm on behalf of one client adversely affecting that on behalf of another.'

However, it is only where the interests of one client would be materially prejudiced that a conflict should be declared. In other cases, the keys to managing an appointment are disclosure and Chinese walls.

The Institute's statement is not specifically drafted for expert accountants, to whom different and perhaps more stringent rules apply. The Academy of Experts includes within its Code of Practice the following statement:

> 'An expert should not accept instructions in any matter where there is an actual or potential conflict of interests. Notwithstanding this rule if full disclosure is made in writing the expert may in appropriate cases accept instructions when the client specifically acknowledges the disclosure.'

Other than in the case of conflicts between a client's and a firm's interests, these statements effectively put the onus for declaring a conflict on to the potential client or his solicitor. It is therefore helpful to consider the guidelines laid down for solicitors in relation to conflicts of interest, as set out in the Guide to the Professional Conduct of Solicitors 1996 (seventh edition). The position can be summarised as follows.

A solicitor must:

(a) refuse instructions to act for two or more clients where there is a conflict or a significant risk of a conflict between the interests of those clients;
(b) not accept instructions to act against a client where he has acquired relevant confidential information concerning the client during the course of acting;
(c) not continue to act for two or more current clients where a conflict of interests arises between those clients;
(d) not act where his own interests conflict with the interests of a client or potential client.

A conflict between the firm and a client can arise where, for example, a solicitor acts in a personal capacity, or where a partner or employee is interested, where the solicitor has a family interest or where he holds a directorship. A conflict may also exist where the solicitor or a related party holds an office. For example, there would be a conflict between a solicitor acting in respect of proceedings following a death where he or a partner was the coroner who investigated the death.

Conflicts with former clients will arise where the solicitor acquires relevant confidential information during the course of acting for that client, which he would be under a duty to disclose to his present client if material to his case. In this case the solicitor would not be able to act for his present client unless he has the consent of the former client. This could therefore be the case in matrimonial or partnership disputes.

The same rules apply where the interests of existing clients of a firm or solicitor conflict. The solicitor may not be allowed to act for either client, unless he gets the consent of the other client and does not have relevant knowledge:

> 'In this case the solicitor must usually cease to act for both clients. A solicitor may only continue to represent one client if not in possession of relevant confidential information concerning the other obtained whilst acting for the other. Even in such a case it would be prudent to confirm that the other party does not object.' (SPR, notes to 15.03)

One of the most important considerations for the solicitor, therefore, will be the acquisition of confidential information or knowledge.

The position is therefore that, when a potential conflict arises, the accountant must disclose the conflict to his instructing solicitor. Where the conflict is between the interests of his firm and those of the potential client, he should refuse to accept the appointment. Where the potential conflict is between two clients of his firm he may accept the appointment, depending on the circumstances of the conflict. The acquisition of knowledge as a result of prior association will always raise the issue of a conflict. Before individual conflicts are considered, it is necessary to examine the position of the expert who chooses to ignore a conflict of interests.

7.2.3 What is the effect of acting as expert where there is a conflict of interests?

The simple answer to this question is that the expert runs the risk of his evidence being undermined or held to be inadmissible because it is biased and not independent. Style and Hollander at p. 87 say:

> 'While his [i.e., the expert's] partiality is a factor which the court will take into account in adjudicating upon any conflict of evidence, he is not debarred simply because he is not independent.'

This could, of course, put his client in a weaker position in a case. Where the conflict has not previously been disclosed, then the accountant has breached accountancy ethics and runs the risk of being held liable for negligence.

This is an extreme situation. However, if there is a conflict of interest, disclosed or not, opposing counsel is likely to dwell on the matter in cross-examination as a way of undermining the expert's credibility.

7.3 Examples of potential conflicts of interest

7.3.1 Already acting for one of the parties to an action as expert

> ***Example***
>
> The expert has already been retained to act as expert for the plaintiff in an action. He is approached by the solicitor for the defendant and asked if he will act as the defence expert.

A clear conflict of interest, and the expert must decline the second appointment. Although as far as his report is concerned the accountant's opinion should be the same whichever side has retained him, in practice, the accountant will be unable, independently, to advise on, for example, the merits of a case, strengths and weaknesses, settlement negotiations, etc.

> ***Example***
>
> Another partner in the expert's firm has already been retained to act as expert for the plaintiff in an action. The expert is approached by the solicitor for the defendant and asked if he will act as the defence expert.

A conflict of interest but, technically, manageable under the ICAEW's statement 1.204 and the Academy of Expert's Code of Practice. However, most firms would, in practice, decline the second appointment because of the potential embarrassment of having two partners from the same firm giving different opinions on, for example, the interpretation of the same facts.

> ***Example***
>
> Another partner in a firm associated with the expert's firm has already been retained to act as expert for the plaintiff in an action. The expert is approached by the solicitor for the defendant and asked if he will act as the defence expert.

Firms of accountants ally themselves with other firms both nationally and internationally. These associations are not always firms, in the sense of being partnerships. There may be a limited financial relationship, for example agreements on referring work or sharing the costs of a secretariat. There may be some sort of overall quality control. There is of course a potential for conflict, but this is more likely to arise in the potential embarrassment of both member firms criticising the other's report. The credibility criticism in the witness box will apply, if it applies at all, to both firms. It is safer to decline such appointments.

7.3.2 One of the parties to an action is already a client

> ***Example***
>
> One of the firm's audit clients is a party to an action. That client approaches an expert in the firm to act as its expert witness in the action.

On the face of it, no conflict. Even if the expert was himself the audit partner for that client there is no conflict, however, it is advised that this latter situation is avoided. The problem which can arise here is that the expert/auditor could be cross-examined on matters within his knowledge as auditor, that is, on matters of fact, making his role somewhat ambiguous. His audit working papers may become discoverable.

For this reason, it is better to have two different partners and two different teams involved on an audit and on an expert witness assignment with a Chinese wall between the two. Information used by the expert team should come only from the client's discovery.

The potential exists for the firm itself to have a conflict where it has an interest in the outcome of the litigation. If a firm, acting as expert, is owed substantial audit fees and those fees are unlikely to be paid than on the winning of the action in which the firm acts as expert, there is a conflict because the objectivity of the accountant will be called into question. Lack of objectivity is a breach of accountancy ethics and will undermine the client's case (ICAEW *Members Handbook* 1.201).

> ***Example***
>
> One of the firm's audit clients is a party to an action. The other party to the action approaches an expert in the firm to act as its expert witness in the action.

Not a conflict, unless the audit client's interests may be materially prejudiced by the outcome of the case. The firm may have a conflict if the client is an important client of the firm, and that relationship may be put at risk as a result of the appointment as expert. There is also the issue of confidentiality of information received by the firm.

In practice, most firms would decline this appointment.

> ***Example***
>
> An associated firm's audit client is a party to an action. The other party to the action approaches an expert in the firm to act as its expert witness in the action.

Not a conflict, but there is the potential for conflict where the audit client is particularly large.

> ***Example***
>
> An expert is asked by one party to an action to act as its expert. The expert has already acted for that party as expert in an earlier action.

Not a conflict. This is a relatively common occurrence where experts are effectively 'retained' by clients to act as their experts in certain cases. For example, the client may be an insurance company regularly instructing the expert on personal injury cases. (In insurance cases, the insurer is not a party to the action, the insured is. However, the insurer will be the client of the expert, agreeing the instruction and being responsible for fees.)

> ***Example***
>
> An expert is asked by one party to an action to act as its expert. The expert has already acted against that party as expert in an earlier unrelated action.

Not necessarily a conflict. To continue the above example, there is no reason why an expert should not act for an insurance company in one personal injury case, and against that insurance company in a later case. Experts can also be instructed for and against the DTI in separate cases.

However, the nature of the accountant's dealings with the client in the earlier case may give rise to a conflict because of confidentiality. If acting in the earlier case, the expert may have become privy to confidential information which he will be unable to close his mind to in a later case where he is on the opposite side. Much will therefore depend on the work carried out by the expert in the earlier case.

> ***Example***
>
> An expert is asked by one party to an action to act as its expert. The expert has already acted against that party as expert in an earlier related action.

Likely to be a conflict, but this depends on the relationship between the two actions. If the two actions are part of a series of proceedings concerned with broadly the same issues, the expert will be conflicted out of the second actions. Confidentiality considerations are also likely to apply.

7.3.3 One of the parties to an action has been a client

> ***Example***
>
> One of the firm's former audit clients is a party to an action. That client approaches an expert in the firm to act as its expert witness in the action.

No conflict.

> ***Example***
>
> One of the firm's former audit clients is a party to an action. The other party to the action approaches an expert in the firm to act as its expert witness in the action.

Not a conflict, other than that arising from the issue of the confidentiality of information received by the firm. The circumstances in which the former audit client ceased to be a client of the firm may give rise to conflict issues, for example, if there was a fee dispute or a complaint over the quality of work.

> ***Example***
>
> An associated firm's former audit client is a party to an action. The other party to the action approaches an expert in the firm to act as its expert witness in the action.

Not a conflict.

7.3.4 The individual or the firm have already had an involvement in some of the issues in question

> ***Example***
>
> The firm has acted as auditor to a company. A director of that company has been charged with fraud arising from alleged false transactions entered into by the company, which the firm has missed in its audit procedures. An expert at the firm is asked to be an expert for one side in the prosecution.

A clear conflict. The likelihood is that, for whichever side the expert acts, he will be giving evidence in respect of transactions which his firm has previously audited. Whether or not the audit should have discovered the alleged falsity of the transactions is beside the point. In evidence, the expert may be held to be defending his own actions during the audit.

> ***Example***
>
> An associated firm has acted as auditor to a company. A director of that company has been charged with fraud arising from alleged false transactions entered into by the company, which the associated firm has missed in its audit procedures. An expert at the firm is asked to be an expert for one side in the prosecution.

This situation is more difficult because of the position of the associated firm. The expert may be criticising the associated firm, in which case there will be some embarrassment, or held to be defending the associated firm.

In practice, a firm would decline this appointment.

> ***Example***
>
> A company has been placed into liquidation. The firm has acted as liquidator. Proceedings have subsequently been taken against a director of the company. An expert in the firm is asked to act as expert in the proceedings.

There is likely to be a conflict here where the expert is asked to act for the defence. Whatever proceedings are brought may well be as a result of the liquidator's reports. The liquidator will probably be a witness of fact in the case.

There is less likely to be a conflict where the expert is instructed by the prosecution or plaintiff. However, the expert should bear in mind the possibility that his firm's actions as liquidator may be criticised by the defence. This situation should be manageable given effective Chinese walls.

> ***Example***
>
> A company has been placed into liquidation. The firm has represented an audit client at a creditors' meeting. Proceedings have subsequently been taken against a director of the company. An expert in the firm is asked to act as expert in the proceedings.

Despite the existence of the double relationship, that is, as auditor and as representative, there is unlikely to be a conflict in this situation.

> ***Example***
>
> A company has been placed into liquidation. The firm has previously been involved in a failed attempt to raise finance for the company. Proceedings have subsequently been taken against a director of the company. An expert in the firm is asked to act as expert in the proceedings.

Not necessarily a conflict. However, there is the possibility of the expert giving expert evidence on one side and another partner in the firm giving factual evidence for the other. The situation should be manageable given effective Chinese walls.

7.3.5 The expert has an interest in the outcome of the action

> ***Example***
>
> The expert's fees are contingent on the outcome of the case. If his side wins, he receives a bonus. If his side loses, he receives only half his time-costed fee.

A conflict. The expert has an interest in the outcome of the case and cannot be objective or independent. Experts should never take on assignments on a contingent fee basis.

> ***Example***
>
> The payment of substantial outstanding audit fees are dependent on the outcome of the case.

A conflict. The expert has an interest in the outcome of the case.

7.3.6 Personal connections

> ***Example***
>
> The expert is the brother of one of the parties to an action where he is expert.

Family ties are sufficient to call into question the expert's impartiality.

> ***Example***
>
> The expert is the non-executive director of a company and he is asked to act as that company's expert in an action.

Again, commercial ties such as directorships, partnerships and trusteeships are sufficient to call into question the expert's impartiality.

However, the rule should always be that, if there is a potential conflict, the expert, even if he decides that he can act, should disclose the matter to the solicitor.

7.4 Discovering conflicts of interest

Before accepting an appointment as expert, the accountant should always undertake a conflict of interest search. This will normally be limited to his own firm and those in his national association. However, where there are international aspects to the case, he should also make enquiries of selected offices in any international firms with which he is associated.

A common way to carry out a search is to look through the firm's list of jobs. This will not, however, necessarily pick up all possible conflicts. Individuals who are directors of client companies may not be listed. Furthermore, the job list may only give the name of, for example, a holding company in a group; one of the parties may be a subsidiary.

For this reason it is more appropriate to circulate all partners in a firm, either by memo or e-mail.

The contents of the search should include the parties to the action, their addresses where they are individuals and a brief note on the nature of the case. The reason for the latter is because there is always a problem in carrying out a conflict search that there may be an involvement with the case, but not necessarily with any of the parties.

The expert should also be aware that he may find out information during the life of a case, but after he has accepted appointment, which gives rise to a potential conflict.

7.5 Accepting the engagement

Subject to there being no conflicts, or any possible conflicts having been resolved, the accountant is now in a position to accept the engagement.

In accepting the engagement, the accountant must understand the issues in the case and the matters on which he will be required to give evidence. At this point he will also be able to determine whether he is suitably qualified to give evidence on those matters.

The best way to understand the issues involved at this stage is to read the pleadings and a copy of counsel's opinion recommending the use of an expert. In all but the simplest cases, he should also meet with the solicitor and counsel to discuss the case and the nature of the work he will be required to carry out.

Once terms have been agreed it is necessary to set these out in a letter of engagement to the solicitor. Even if the solicitor has previously written to the expert with instructions, the accountant should send a letter of engagement setting out his terms for acting.

In Appendix 6 are two standard letters of engagement, one for actions where the party on behalf of whom the accountant is being instructed is not legally aided, and one where the party is legally aided. The significance of this is explained below at **7.10**. The component parts of the letter of engagement are now discussed in detail.

7.6 To whom is the letter addressed?

Letters of engagement are normally addressed to the person giving the instructions, that is, the solicitor. The question is often asked, if it is the client of the solicitor that is undertaking the action, why is it not addressed to him? Two points can be made here. First, it is the solicitor who will be liaising with the accountant, instructing him, passing him documents to review and discussing his report. That is not what the client does.

The more important point concerns professional privilege. Where a lawyer communicates with a third party such as an expert, and where that communication is made with a view to existing or contemplated litigation, it is privileged and not disclosable to the other side in the litigation.

The position of the client communicating with the expert is more difficult. Where the client is acting as an agent of the solicitor, he is carrying out the lawyer's protected functions. Where the client is not acting as the solicitor's agent and communicating with an expert then the principle which protects communications between solicitor and client does not apply. Therefore, these communications may not be privileged.

Thus, unless the client is acting as agent of the solicitor, the instruction should be addressed to the solicitor. The seventh edition of the Guide to the Professional Conduct of Solicitors states that:

> 'A solicitor is personally responsible for paying the proper costs of any professional agent or other person whom he instructs on behalf of a client, whether or not the solicitor receives payment from the client, unless the solicitor and the person instructed make an express agreement to the contrary.' (SPR 20.01)

However, it is sometimes the case that a solicitor does not wish to be responsible for the expert's fees, and therefore wishes the letter to be addressed to the client. The reason for this is that, by signing a letter of instruction addressed to him, a solicitor may be giving an undertaking concerning the payment of his fees, and the only way he can give such an undertaking is to be put in funds by his client. Where this situation arises, and the solicitor does not wish to give such an undertaking, then the letter of engagement can be amended with a paragraph to the effect that the expert will not hold the solicitor liable for his fees. However, in these circumstances, the expert should ensure that a letter is obtained by the solicitor from the client where the client assumes responsibility for the expert's fees.

7.7 Background to the case

The first section of the letter of engagement, outlining the expert's understanding of the case sets out the expert's understanding of the facts. Obviously, this should coincide with the solicitor's understanding! This also acts as an introduction to the work the accountant will be asked to do.

7.8 Work phases

The letter is then broken down into four phases. Phase one is likely to be the most detailed, setting out in detail the work which it has been agreed between the expert and the legal advisers that he shall carry out.

It is important that, where the expert is expected to read documents such as the pleadings and witness statements, this work is set out clearly in the letter of engagement. Pleadings can run into hundreds of pages and the expert should not be expected to carry out this task for nothing.

It is also important to realise that a piece of litigation is a living creature. It can be expected to grow and develop. It is likely that the work set out in this section will not cover all of the work which the expert will be asked to carry out during the course of the litigation. It may be that some of the work in this section becomes no longer necessary. The contingency nature of the work, and the possibility of the need to carry out further work should also be mentioned in the letter of engagement.

The second phase of work is the production of an expert report, based on the work in phase one, suitable for introduction to the court. It may be the case that, at this stage, all the solicitor requires is a letter of advice dealing with the merits. If this is the case, then this should be written into the letter.

Phase three concerns the expert's work with regard to the other side's expert's report. First, the expert will review and provide a commentary or supplemental report on any expert report prepared by the other side. Second, the expert will attend without prejudice meetings with the other side's expert with a view to resolving any differences between them and, potentially, to enter into settlement negotiations.

Phase four concerns the appearance of the expert at court to give oral evidence and to provide other assistance. 'Other assistance' is likely to involve assisting counsel by providing useful 'ammunition' with which to cross-examine the other side's witnesses, particularly their own expert.

7.9 Fees

This section of the letter sets out the basis on which the expert will charge his fees, that is, on a time-costed basis. It is appropriate to give an estimate of fees for particular items of work; it is not appropriate to work for a fixed fee. If the expert has agreed a fixed fee, he runs two risks if further information comes to light which was not envisaged at the time of the original instructions.

First, if he ignores this information, because he will not be paid to review and consider it, he is restricting his scope and, potentially, leaving himself open to the criticism that he has not taken all factors into account when preparing his report.

If he does carry out further work, then he may be undertaking it at his own cost, with all the further risks that this entails.

It is appropriate for the expert to charge different hourly rates depending on the nature of the work involved. Some tasks may be extremely complex requiring and demanding high professional rates. If work is complex or difficult the expert should not forget the need to factor into any cost estimates the need to consult with other partners within his firm.

The expert should also be aware that litigation cases may extend over many years, during which time charge-out rates will go up, and he should reserve the right to increase rates in these circumstances.

The expert should reserve the right to bill on a regular basis, in advance of the production of any report. The solicitor will normally do this and, again, where cases last for some time, the accountant should not be in the position of having large amounts of unbilled work in progress or unpaid bills. It is not the expert's task to fund litigation.

The standard letter of engagement includes a paragraph which states that the basis of charging fees is not dependent on the outcome of the case. This is particularly important as it confirms that the expert is not retained on a contingency basis.

It is also advisable to state in the letter of engagement that, if the client is successful and recovers his costs on taxation, he will probably not recover all of his costs. If this does happen, the expert would nevertheless still expect to bill for the work carried out at the rates agreed.

7.10 Legally aided clients

The legal aid system is briefly covered in Chapter 8. If the client on whose behalf the expert accountant is instructed is likely to qualify for legal aid without making any contribution himself, the Legal Aid Board will therefore pay the expert accountant's costs.

Solicitors instructing accountants in legal aid cases are unlikely to want to take on the responsibility for the accountant's costs themselves. The solicitor may ask the accountant to enter into a contractual relationship whereby the solicitor gives the instructions, but confirms that he will not be responsible for the accountant's fees. Instead, the solicitor will pass on to the accountant what he receives from the Legal Aid Board following taxation or assessment This is the reason for the amended letter of engagement in Appendix 6. However, most experts will request that they are paid a specific fee.

Two points should be made about legally aided experts' fees. Such fees are, as far as the Legal Aid Board is concerned, a disbursement. The solicitor can make an application for prior authority to incur such expenditure from the Legal Aid Board on submission of the appropriate form (in civil cases the CLA31 and in criminal cases the CRIM10 – both forms reproduced at Appendix 7 and Appendix 8).

The effect of prior authority will be to guarantee payment up to a certain amount to the solicitor from the Legal Aid Board which will then be passed to the expert.

In order to grant prior authority for expert's fees, the Legal Aid Board will often require an opinion from counsel setting out the reasons for instructing an expert, and an estimate of fees to be incurred by the accountant. The exact nature of the information required in terms of fees depends on individual caseworkers at individual offices. However, it is becoming increasingly common for a fully costed breakdown of time to be spent by each fee-earner on each task to be needed.

On receipt of this, the Legal Aid Board can approve the whole amount, strike out certain amounts of work, reduce hourly rates or give maximum hourly rates. The whole process can take many weeks, and the expert accountant's fee for which prior authority is given may be somewhat reduced. However, as long as the work is carried out, that fee is not challengeable on taxation. Furthermore, when the case is concluded and has gone to taxation, it is always open to the expert to request that his final bill is costed at his normal charge-out rate and to state that the bill includes any work for which prior authority was not given, or for which prior authority was not applied.

This leads on to the second point, concerning 'unauthorised' fees. It is often the case that the Legal Aid Board is slow in granting prior authority, or that authority is not granted in full or that, because of the need to produce work in a short space of time, it is not practicable to apply for prior authority. Such work can always be carried out, subject to the risk the accountant takes that his fees will not be recoverable in full on taxation.

The Legal Aid Board is, these days, generally extremely prompt about paying bills once they have been submitted for payment. The accountant should ensure that he bills regularly, and that the solicitor pays the fees when he receives the money from the Legal Aid Board. Work for which prior authority is obtained should always be billed and paid.

Where the work is unauthorised, the expert can send in an application for a payment on account to the solicitor, and the Legal Aid Board may pay it. However, if the expert's bill is reduced on taxation, it will be the responsibility of the solicitor to repay the amount of the reduction. The accountant may therefore have to confirm that, where he has been paid on account and where a bill is subsequently reduced on taxation, he will repay to the solicitor the reduced amount.

In respect of any prior authorities granted, the accountant should always request that he receives a copy from the solicitor.

Chapter 8
Legal aid

8.1 Introduction

Legal aid is government funding for those who cannot afford to pay for legal advice, assistance and/or representation.

The State, through the provision of legal aid, funds an extremely large amount of litigation in England and Wales. It is inevitable that an expert accountant will be asked to undertake legal aid work at some stage of his career. Indeed, for some expert accountants, a large amount of their practice derives from legal aid work.

The first reaction of many accountants when asked to carry out a legally aided case is to refuse it. Legal aid has the reputation of being poorly paid, and what money is paid only arrives months or even years after the case has settled. In fact, this is not the case. The truth of the matter is that a large number of solicitors who derive a large amount of their work from legally aided clients are extremely disorganised and operate their practices on a basis which would make any work they carry out seem unprofitable.

This chapter gives an overview of the operation of the legal aid system, where the Legal Aid Board fits into the system, the other government bodies which have responsibility for the administration of legal aid, and how the accountant should manage his practice to deal with legally aided work.

Legal aid is a changing area for various reasons. One is that, increasingly, work is undertaken by franchised firms who meet certain standards of quality assurance and can make some of the decisions normally reserved to the area offices of the Legal Aid Board, as well as receiving differential rates of pay. Another is that the Board now undertakes civil legal aid means assessment and is introducing a new computerised information system (CIS). Finally, significant changes to the scope of legal aid, such as the removal of most money and damages claims from legal aid, are under consideration by the Lord Chancellor's Department and are likely to be implemented in the near future.

The first part of this chapter deals with legal aid's reputation.

8.2 The reputation of legal aid

One of the mainstays of the legal aid system is the legal advice and assistance scheme, also known as the green form scheme (Legal Advice and Assistance Regulations 1989). Any individual who passes the statutory means test (admittedly, set at very low levels) can walk into a solicitor's office which carries out legal aid work and get advice on a wide range of legal issues. There is no longer any system of contributions but the work done is not necessarily free to the client as the solicitor has a first charge on money/property recovered or preserved and will exercise this, subject to certain exemptions unless his costs are recovered from the other party, if any. It is only where the solicitor cannot recover his costs from the other party or through the charge that an application for payment at fixed rates is made to the Legal Aid Board. Such claims are then assessed prior to any payment.

Legal advice and assistance is given on matrimonial disputes, benefit enquiries, disputes with a landlord, problems with the council tax – indeed, practically anything so long as it constitutes a matter of English law. The scheme encompasses advice on both contentious and non-contentious matters. The only areas of work which are excluded from the scheme are advice on foreign law, representation at a court or tribunal, most conveyancing, and will-making (see the Legal Advice and Assistance (Scope) Regulations 1989). However, even some of these excluded areas are subject to exemptions in certain circumstances or for certain types of work.

The advice initially covers up to two hours' work in all cases other than matrimonial (i.e., divorce and judicial separation), where the limit is three hours if the work done includes the drafting of a petition. Legal advice and assistance often leads on to more substantive advice in the context of proceedings where a full legal aid certificate may be granted, although the costs limit for legal advice and assistance may be extended (i.e., increased) subject to a reasonableness test.

The practitioner (usually but not necessarily a solicitor) giving advice fills out a 'green form', which is both the application form and costs claim form, and is, if necessary, sent to the local legal aid area office for assessment for payment. Vast numbers of forms are sent to the Legal Aid Board for payment – currently 1.6 million per year. The rates payable for the work are set by regulations, and they are indeed low, and the average payment for each form is around £50.

It should be noted that the green form does not cover legal representation, for which a full legal aid certificate is required.

Given that the rates are so low, one would have thought that any solicitor would endeavour to get his green forms into the Legal Aid Board as quickly as possible, to ensure payment as quickly as possible. However, individual area offices receive completed green forms months, sometimes even years, after the advice has been completed. There are reports of green forms being received six years after they could have been sent. It is difficult to think of a more blatant example of bad practice management.

It is not as if the Legal Aid Board is slow in paying forms. Some years ago, the legal aid system had the reputation of being slow in paying bills. However, it now has published targets for performance and an effective system of paying claims, with two payment runs to legal aid practitioners a month. If the form has been completed correctly, there is no reason why a solicitor should not be remunerated as fast as, if not faster than, by a private client. However, the next problem for many solicitors is completing the forms correctly. Many legal aid forms are rejected and sent back to a solicitor for correction because of a failure to enter simple administrative matters, further delaying payment.

It is true that legal aid rates are, generally, far lower than private client rates. However, the manner in which solicitors operate their practices does not help them. This has an implication for expert accountants, because if the solicitor is inefficient then the accountant is going to suffer, thus confirming legal aid's reputation. The message is simple – if an accountant is going to undertake legal aid work, he needs to understand the legal aid system. Further information can be obtained from the Legal Aid Handbook, which contains the Board's targets, and its Annual Report, which contains a wealth of statistical information.

8.3 Types of legal aid

There is a bewildering array of types of legally aided advice. Each of them has different systems and different forms for obtaining payment. A basic summary is given in the Board's leaflet 'A practical guide to legal aid'. The systems are as follows.

8.3.1 Legal advice and assistance (green form)

This is discussed at **8.2** above. This is an area the expert accountant is unlikely to meet in practice; however, there is in principle no reason why a solicitor should not call on an expert accountant for advice under the green form scheme, given that he can incur disbursements. The solicitor would, however, need an extension to the initial costs limit and there is no system of payments on account.

8.3.2 Assistance by way of representation (ABWOR)

ABWOR is a type of advice and assistance but an approval is usually required from the Legal Aid Board, subject to a means and merits test. ABWOR is designed to pay a solicitor's costs incurred in preparing and representing a client in certain types of proceedings. These include criminal and civil proceedings in the magistrates' courts, hearings before Mental Health Review Tribunals, the Parole Board and prison disciplinary hearings. Again, accountants are unlikely to come across ABWOR in practice, but there is a system of payments on account.

8.3.3 Duty solicitor scheme

The duty solicitor scheme is a system of providing 24-hour representation for individuals held at police stations. The Police and Criminal Evidence Act 1984 gives accused persons the right to legal advice. The duty solicitor scheme gives effect to that right by ensuring that there will always be a solicitor available to advise the suspect being held. Such advice is given without regard to the person's financial circumstances and is a free service.

Expert accountants are most unlikely to come across this type of legal aid in practice.

8.3.4 Criminal legal aid

Any accountant involved in criminal litigation will come across the criminal legal aid scheme. Fraud trials being what they are – long and expensive with a substantial amount of preparation time – many defendants who do not initially qualify for legal aid, which is means-tested, may qualify prior to trial once their capital has been exhausted. Criminal legal aid is subject to a means test, a system of contributions and a merits test, based on the 'interests of justice'.

First, in the magistrates' court, legal aid is applied for on Form 1 to the magistrates' clerk or orally to the court but usually with Form 5 (a statement of means). There is some discretion in whether to grant legal aid in such cases, but three of the discretionary criteria which appear in s22(2) Legal Aid Act 1988 – that the defendant is likely to lose his liberty if convicted, that it is likely he will lose his livelihood if convicted and that the case involves the expert cross-examination of a prosecution witness – will nearly always be met in a fraud case.

Second, following committal or transfer to the Crown Court, there is a further application for legal aid in the Crown Court proceedings, unless a 'through' order was made by the magistrates' court covering work in the Crown Court.

8.3.5 Civil legal aid

Legal aid is available for all civil proceedings in the higher courts in England and Wales, other than in defamation actions, election petitions, most undefended divorces and certain actions concerned with the recovery of penalties and judgment summons. Even in defamation actions, legal aid is allowed in certain circumstances to defend a counterclaim, and it is also available in cases alleging malicious falsehood. It follows that, other than for defamation actions, for any civil case where an expert accountant is instructed, legal aid will be available, generally subject to the means test on financial eligibility and the merits test.

The merits test is particularly important, and aspects of it affect the ability of an accountant to carry out work under a civil legal aid certificate. For the purposes of granting legal aid the Legal Aid Board has to be satisfied that the applicant has reasonable grounds for taking, defending or being party to proceedings, and legal aid may be refused if, in the particular circumstances of the case, it appears unreasonable that legal aid should be granted. The main points are that there must be an issue of fact or law, which it is reasonable to submit to a court for a decision, that the applicant would undertake the case privately if he had the means, and that there is a reasonable prospect of success if the facts are proven.

The application for a legal aid certificate is made to the local area office of the Legal Aid Board. There is a system of financial contributions, and the Board has a statutory charge on money/property recovered or preserved where there is not a full recovery of costs from the other party (see **8.4.1** below).

In certain circumstances, emergency legal aid certificates can be granted for civil proceedings. These circumstances will apply where a person would qualify financially for legal aid, but that person cannot wait for the application to be processed, because of, for example, a deadline being approached. Therefore, emergency legal aid is awarded on the basis of the merits test *only*. Emergency legal aid certificates should, in due course, be converted into full legal aid certificates, i.e., once the applicant's means have been assessed. Certificates are limited in scope as to their duration and as to the amount of costs (including disbursements) which can be incurred.

8.4 Administration of legal aid

The administration of legal aid is another involved subject which is liable to change due to increased computerisation. The majority of the administration is carried out through 13 legal aid area offices. These are the area offices which, in general, consider applications for certificates and process claims for payment. Payment itself is administered by the Board's head office, based in

Gray's Inn Road in London. Legal aid funding, as far as the Legal Aid Board is concerned, is split into two elements, being the payment of legal aid itself, and the costs of administering the legal aid fund.

Therefore, when, for example, a green form is received, it will be processed by an area office and then instructions for payment sent to head office. When an application for civil legal aid is made, this will be sent to the area office and approval granted or refused by that area office.

However, where the application is made in respect of criminal legal aid for an appearance in the magistrates' courts, the application is processed not by an area office but by the court.

Means assessment for civil legal aid is now under the control of the Legal Aid Board. Civil legal aid means assessment was previously carried out by the Benefits Agency. Criminal means assessment is currently dealt with in the magistrates' courts by the magistrates' clerks.

Taxation of costs and payment of legal aid bills is similarly subject to controls by different bodies. Criminal legal aid bills in respect of the appearances in the magistrates' courts are taxed (technically the term is 'assessed') by area offices. Criminal legal aid bills in respect of the higher courts are assessed and paid by the courts themselves or the Central Taxing Unit, that is, they are paid out of funds not administered by the Legal Aid Board. Furthermore, work in the magistrates' courts which is undertaken in anticipation of Crown Court work is only payable by the Legal Aid Board where it is justified for the particular work to be done at that stage in the particular case (Legal Aid Board Costs Appeals Committee decision CRIMLA 30 reproduced as Note for Guidance 18–54, Legal Aid Handbook 1997/98).

In civil litigation, taxation works as follows.

Where proceedings have not been issued, any bill is assessed by the local area office. (Such bills can actually be extremely large, for example where a firm is advising a large group of potential plaintiffs in a class action such as medical negligence or product liability (Civil Legal Aid (General) Regulations 1989, Reg 105(2)).)

Where proceedings are issued, and there is an *inter partes* costs order issued, the bill will be taxed, for example by the Supreme Court Taxing Office in the case of High Court proceedings, or by a district judge in the case of county court proceedings.

Where there is no *inter partes* costs order, the area office must assess the bill if it is less than £500. Above £1,000 the bill will be taxed, and between £500 and £1,000 the solicitor can choose to have the bill taxed or assessed at his option. Prescribed, fixed rates are applied to the solicitor's costs in an increasing range of cases, but experts' fees are subject to discretion, although bandwidth fees are usually applied.

8.4.1 Statutory charge

In civil cases, one should also be aware of the statutory charge, because of the effect this has on whether proceedings should be commenced or continued.

The Legal Aid Board has a statutory charge over any property recovered or preserved in proceedings, either as a result of a judgment or settlement. The charge can arise even if proceedings have not been commenced. The charge is to enable the Legal Aid Board to have a claim over assets to enable it to recover costs it has paid out. For example, if the Legal Aid Board pays out taxed costs of £20,000 in respect of a plaintiff who is awarded damages of £30,000, and there are *inter partes* costs taxed and recovered at £15,000, then the plaintiff will have to pay out of his damages award the £5,000 difference between the amount paid out for costs and the amount recovered from the other side.

The statutory charge kicks in immediately on a payment of damages, so a legally aided successful party may, with the area office's agreement, receive the judgment sum immediately, less that amount paid to the Legal Aid Board.

How is it that a legal aid taxation can result in a higher amount than an *inter partes* taxation given that they will usually both be taxed on the same basis, that is, the standard basis? (See Chapter 9 for a discussion of taxation and what the standard basis is.) The reason is that certain taxed costs which are recoverable from the Legal Aid Board are not recoverable from the other side. These costs arise principally from work expended in relation to the granting of legal aid. Furthermore, work carried out on prior authority (see **8.5.1** below) may not be recoverable.

The successful litigant will also have to pay for any costs payable to the other side, although the liability of a legally aided person is limited to the amount which is reasonable in all the circumstances including the financial resources of all the parties and their conduct in connection with the dispute (s17 Legal Aid Act 1988).

The aim of the statutory charge is to ensure that no assisted person gains a financial benefit from the litigation until the Legal Aid Board has been reimbursed in full. In that sense, legal aid is a 'loan' rather than a 'gift'.

Clearly, the amount of any damages and the amount of costs are critical factors in deciding whether the Legal Aid Board should continue to fund civil cases. It will be apparent that a successful action could result in a minimal amount of money, if any, being obtained or preserved, once the costs not recovered from the other side are taken into account.

8.5 Expert accountants

The costs of experts are a disbursement of the solicitor. At the end of a case the solicitor will prepare a bill of costs setting out his own costs and disbursements incurred. The bill will be taxed by the court or assessed by the area office, and the taxed or assessed amount paid to the solicitor.

Technically, whenever a solicitor incurs a disbursement, he becomes liable to the provider of the disbursement for the cost of that disbursement. The fact that he does not get paid by the Legal Aid Board for the full amount, or within a reasonable period of time after the billing of the disbursement, may be irrelevant – the contract is between the provider of the disbursement and the solicitor, not the provider of the disbursement and the Legal Aid Board. The terms of the contract will determine the rights and liabilities as between the solicitor and the service provider.

Expert accountants' fees can be large, sometimes the largest item on a bill of costs. Not surprisingly, solicitors do not want to be responsible for an expert's fees, especially if they might not be fully recovered on taxation/assessment. Furthermore, in most cases, the client is unlikely to have the money himself to pay the expert's fees not agreed on taxation and, indeed, the regulations generally preclude 'topping up' by payments other than from the legal aid fund. Most solicitors will therefore, in accordance with Note 3 to Principle 21.11 of the Law Society's Guide to the Professional Conduct of Solicitors (1996), enter into an arrangement whereby they are not responsible for the expert's fees, but pass on what they receive in legal aid following taxation or assessment.

The accountant is therefore in a dilemma. A large job, on the face of it attractive, may mean work in progress tied up for many years. There are, however, three ways in which the accountant can minimise his exposure.

8.5.1 Prior authority

In advance of any disbursement being incurred, the solicitor can apply to the Legal Aid Board for prior authority for that expenditure. In civil cases, the application is made on form CLA31 (post-CIS, APP 6), in criminal cases on form CRIM10 (post-CIS, APP 7) (see Appendices 7 and 8).

The rule is that no question as to the propriety of any act in relation to which prior authority has been obtained can be raised on any taxation/assessment of costs. Therefore, if the Legal Aid Board gives prior authority to incur £100,000 of accounting fees, then that is what the accountant will get if the fees are actually incurred.

The only exception to this is where either the solicitor or the client knew that the purpose for which such authority was granted had failed, or become irrelevant or unnecessary, before the costs were incurred.

As noted above, disbursements which are subject to prior authority, although generally payable by the legal aid fund, have to be justified on taxation to be recovered from the other side. The granting of prior authority does not bind the taxation in an *inter partes* taxation. Therefore, a costs order, to the extent that it does not cover all of the expert's fees (whether subject to prior authority or not), will mean that the shortfall is recovered from the client by way of the statutory charge.

The expert would therefore be advised to include in his terms that his costs in respect of work subject to prior authority will not be repayable to the solicitor to the extent that his costs are not fully recovered on an *inter partes* taxation despite the prior authority. The accountant should not be put in the position of not recovering his fees in full, despite the plaintiff gaining a financial benefit from the litigation.

It should, however, be noted that the statutory charge applies to monies and/or property recovered or prepared by an assisted person. To the extent that the recovery/preservation is insufficient, there is no question of the Legal Aid Board making a claim against the accountant.

In summary, the accountant has no relationship with the Board and should address any queries, complaints or legal action to the instructing firm and not to the Legal Aid Board.

8.5.2 Payments on account

The rules allow for solicitors to make applications for payments on account of disbursements incurred or to be incurred in respect of civil cases under legal aid/ABWOR (Reg 101, Civil Legal Aid (General) Regulations 1989 and Reg 30A(1) Legal Advice and Assistance Regulations 1989) and, where prior authority has been obtained, criminal cases in the Crown Court. This includes accountants' fees.

Therefore, the accountant should always ensure that bills are regularly sent to the solicitor to enable him to apply for payment on account.

One matter should be noted. Where the work has received prior authority, the work will generally be paid in full on a legal aid taxation. Where, however, it is not subject to prior authority, the amounts billed may not be recovered in full on taxation. The solicitor may therefore be in the position of paying amounts of money to the accountant, on account of bills in respect of work which is not subject to a prior authority and some of which has to be paid back to the Legal Aid Board. The accountant should, if requested, enter into an undertaking that he will repay such amounts to the solicitor.

Where payments on account are claimed, they are generally paid within a very short period of time. The accountant should get the agreement of the solicitor that, when such claims are paid, the amounts are remitted immediately to the accountant.

8.5.3 Work carried out without prior authority

Just because work is carried out without prior authority does not mean it will not be recovered in full on taxation. However, the risk is that either the charge-out rates and/or the work carried out will be reduced. There is little that can be done in respect of the former. However, as far as the actual work is concerned, the accountant should always ensure that proper instruction is obtained from the solicitor, and that, if appropriate, this is backed up by an opinion from counsel that the work is necessary.

In respect of all work carried out, proper records of time spent should always be kept.

8.6 Future developments

Mention was made at the beginning of this chapter of future changes in legal aid. The proposed removal of legal aid for some money claims is likely to have a significant effect on experts. Solicitors for plaintiffs in such cases will have to take on cases on a conditional fee basis. Accountants (and any other experts) are forbidden from taking on work on a contingency fee basis. It is not clear how experts will be instructed in such cases. Solicitors will be unwilling to be at risk for their costs. However, the effect on experts will only be known with time.

Chapter 9
Costs orders and taxation of costs

9.1 Introduction

Litigation is an extremely expensive business. Not surprisingly, the successful litigant will expect to have his costs paid by the unsuccessful litigant; after all, if the unsuccessful litigant had not brought the case, or defended the case, the costs of both sides would have been saved.

The unsuccessful litigant, again not surprisingly, having lost the case is going to want to pay as little as possible of the other side's costs. Why should he pay for the other side's bill, just because the other side chose to use the most expensive lawyers in town? Why should he pay for the costs of exploring every blind alley and following every wild goose chase? The issues in the case were clear. If the other side wanted to provide their experts with copies of all the documents, no matter how relevant, why should he pay for it?

Who pays what is dependent on costs orders and taxation.

9.2 Payment of the other side's costs – the general principles

Under the English legal system, it is the courts in their discretion who have the full power to determine the extent to which costs are paid and by whom (RSC Order 62 rule 2(4)). These costs will include fees, charges, disbursements, expenses and remuneration (RSC Order 62 rule 1(4)). The general rule is that 'the costs follow the event' (RSC Order 62 rule 3(3)), i.e., the unsuccessful party must pay the successful party's costs, as well as his own. However, there are three circumstances where the losing party may not be liable to pay the other side's costs.

First, a defendant can take action during the litigation to protect himself against bearing these costs. There are two methods. Where the case involves a claim for a sum of money, in, for example, a personal injury claim, the defendant can make a 'payment into court'. This means that the defendant will pay a sum of money into court that he considers will cover any award of damages made by the judge in the event that the judge finds against him. It should be noted that the judge is never made aware of the fact that a payment into court has been made until the court has to decide the issue of costs. If the award is less than or equal to the payment made by the defendant, the costs arising after the date of the payment into court was made will be awarded against the plaintiff even though he was successful in his case. The principle behind this is a matter of public policy, as it is considered that the plaintiff should have accepted the payment offered by the defendant (if reasonable) and not have continued with the action. Furthermore, it is an attempt to settle the matter without having to continue with expensive, time-consuming litigation.

However, if the plaintiff beats the payment into court, even by a pound, the defendant is liable for all of the costs of the plaintiff as well as his own.

Where the subject of the claim is non-monetary (e.g., a claim for an injunction/specific performance, etc.), in certain circumstances the same effect can be achieved by a 'Calderbank letter' (RSC Order 22 rule 14) – a procedure first commenced by the Court of Appeal in *Calderbank* v *Calderbank* [1975] 3 All ER 333. This is a written offer from one party to the other and is made on a without prejudice basis. The letter making the offer is headed up 'without prejudice, save as to costs'. In the case of *Cutts* v *Head* [1984] 1 All ER 597 caution was expressed that Calderbank letters should not be used as a substitute for a payment into court where a payment into court under Order 22 rule 1 is appropriate, however, both can be used in conjunction. In *Singh* v *Parkfield Group PLC, The Times*, May 27, 1994 (affirmed by the Court of Appeal March 20 1996) it was held that an offer letter must be backed by a payment into court to achieve any protection against costs. Furthermore, there are certain types of case where there is a monetary claim but where a Calderbank letter can be used. For example, a Calderbank letter could be an offer setting out what a defendant thinks his contribution to damages should be where there are third parties or more than one defendant.

Second, it is possible for the court to make no order as to costs. The general principle of RSC Order 62 rule 3(2) is that:

> 'No party to any proceedings shall be entitled to recover any of the costs of those proceedings from any other party to them except under an order of the Court.'

Furthermore, RSC Order 62 rule 4 states that there is no order for costs in the following situations:

(a) appeal/application to appeal under s6(2) Pensions Appeal Tribunal Act 1943;
(b) appeal to Court of Appeal from county court under s56 Representation of the People Act 1983;
(c) certain probate actions.

Finally, throughout a piece of litigation there are likely to be a number of procedural applications, such as discovery, amendment of pleadings, submission of new evidence, such as proving facts in a notice to admit facts. In each one of these applications or actions there is a costs implication. It does not necessarily follow that the party who wins the litigation wins every application, or is responsible for the costs of every procedural action, as stated above. In many procedural matters a costs penalty is imposed on one party automatically. For example, under RSC Order 62 rule 5(6) costs of any application to extend time fixed by the rules or directions of the court shall be borne by the party making the time extension application (see also RSC Order 62 rule 5(7)).

One other matter should be raised. In complex litigation there may be a number of matters raised and litigants may be partially successful and partially unsuccessful. In these circumstances one party will obtain a fractional costs order, the percentage of recovery depending on the number and expense of unsuccessful issues raised by him. It is also possible, though far less common, for fractional costs orders to be made against each side, so each side to the litigation ends up paying a percentage of the other side's costs.

Other than as explained above, a successful party is rarely deprived of his rights to costs, however, in litigation no party has an automatic right to costs and any order is a matter for the judge's discretion (RSC Order 62 rule 3(2)). At the close of proceedings the judge may order for one party to pay the other party's costs with the proviso that 'such costs to be taxed, if not agreed'.

If the costs can be agreed between the sides, then that is an end of the matter. If not, however, then the costs are taxed.

The remainder of this chapter explains the terminology used and gives an overview of the general principles applied by the court in the taxation of costs.

9.3 Taxation of costs

Taxation is the judicial process by which the amount of legal costs and expenses that are to be paid are checked for reasonableness. In *Francis* v *Francis and Dickerson* [1955] 3 All ER 836 it was held that the correct view to be taken by the Taxing Master in considering whether something is reasonable is that of the 'sensible solicitor' considering what, in the light of his then knowledge, was reasonable in the interest of his client. The court may allow or disallow any item claimed in a bill, or may vary any figures claimed in respect of them. In this context the word taxing has nothing to do with income tax or indeed with any other tax. It derives from the Norman French word 'taxer', to determine.

The process is used in determining the legal costs and expenses to be paid in the following circumstances:

(a) successful litigants (*inter partes*), that is, costs payable by one litigant to another litigant under the terms of an order made by the court;
(b) in respect of work done on behalf of fee-paying clients where those persons are dissatisfied with the level of the charges being claimed; and
(c) solicitors, counsel and other legal representatives acting on behalf of litigants who are legally aided.

Taxation of costs for all divisions of the High Court in London is administered by the Supreme Court Taxing Office (SCTO). The individuals hearing the cases are known as taxing officers if the bills do not exceed £35,000 and exclude category (b) above, and Taxing Masters if the bills exceed this amount. Only a Taxing Master has jurisdiction to tax costs as between solicitor and client. Taxation in the county court is conducted by the district judge. Similarly, taxation of costs in district registries of the High Court are taxed in the relevant courts.

The taxation procedure begins at the SCTO where the clerk will allocate the case to a particular officer or Master dependent on the total value of the bill under a ballot system (White Book Notes 62/30/1).

The procedures involved when costs are to be taxed are predominately the area of the instructing solicitor who acts for the recovering party and he is responsible for initiating the procedure; however, it is essential that the expert has an understanding of the terms used and the process involved. There will of course be a direct impact on the expert in that there is the possibility that the bills rendered for his services are also subject to scrutiny and may be deemed unreasonable by the court and therefore reduced.

9.4 Order 62 Supreme Court practice

Taxation of costs is covered by Order 62 Parts III to VI of the Supreme Court, specifically regarding taxation practice, and the main points are:

(a) the meaning of costs (Order 62 Part I);
(b) entitlement to costs (Order 62 Part II);
(c) stage of proceedings at which costs to be taxed (Order 62 rule 8);
(d) basis of taxation (Order 62 rules 12, 14, 15, 16 and 18);
(e) procedure on taxation (Part V) – commencement of proceedings (Order 62 rule 29);
(f) application and procedures for a review (Order 62 Part VI):
    (i) by taxing officer (Order 62 rule 34);
    (ii) by judge (Order 62 rule 35);

(g) number of expert witnesses (Order 62 Appendix 2(16)). White Book Notes 62/A2/16 refer to the number of expert witnesses limited under Order 38 rule 4.

Each of these are discussed in detail below.

9.4.1 Meaning of costs

Costs as defined by Order 62 rule 1(4) can be split into three categories:

(a) disbursements – the expenses which a solicitor has to pay out in order to carry out his professional obligations to his client, such as counsel's fees, expert witness fees, court fees, etc.;
(b) solicitor's profit costs – the fees which a solicitor charges his own client;
(c) VAT associated with (a) and (b) above.

Order 62 rule 1(4) allows for incidental costs incurred prior to the proceedings to be included. Megarry VC considered the circumstances in which costs incurred prior to the commencement of proceedings could be allowed on taxation in *Re Gibson's Settlement Trusts*, which held that costs of disputes antecedent to proceedings which are in some degree relevant to them are allowed to be included on taxation. As always this will be allowed at the discretion of the court.

9.4.2 Entitlement to costs

The general principle is that no party to any proceedings shall be entitled to recover any of the costs of those proceedings from any party to those proceedings except under court order. The costs are at the discretion of the court and the court may, if it sees fit, make any order as to the costs of the proceedings. The usual order is that the costs shall follow the event, i.e., the losing party will pay the costs of the winning party.

9.4.3 Stages of proceedings at which costs to be taxed

The general rule is that the costs of any proceedings shall not be taxed until the conclusion of the 'cause or matter' in which the proceedings arise. However, if it appears to the court when making an order for costs that all or any part of the costs should be taxed at an earlier stage, it may order accordingly. The effect of this rule is that costs are not to be taxed until the conclusion of the proceedings irrespective of the stage of the proceedings at which the order is made unless the court expressly orders an earlier taxation. In such cases the court order will usually contain the words 'costs to be taxed/paid forthwith'. Such an order cannot be made against a legally aided party (RSC Order 62 rule 8(3)).

9.4.4 Bases of taxation – the standard and indemnity bases

Costs payable by one litigant to another litigant under the terms of a court order are payable either on a standard basis or on an indemnity basis. Taxation on the standard basis means that there is allowed a reasonable amount in respect of all costs reasonably incurred. Any doubts which the taxing officer may have as to whether the costs were reasonably incurred or were reasonable in amount is resolved in favour of the paying party.

The taxation of costs on an indemnity basis means that all costs are allowed except insofar as they are of an unreasonable amount or have been unreasonably incurred. Any doubts which the taxing officer may have as to whether the costs were reasonably incurred or were reasonable in amount shall be resolved in favour of the receiving party.

The overriding test to be applied on taxation of costs, whether on a standard or indemnity basis, is that of reasonableness. In a leading case (*Francis* v *Francis and Dickerson* [1956] p.87, [1955] 3 All ER 836, [1955] 3 WLR 973) it was held that (*per curiam*) the correct viewpoint to be taken by a taxing officer in considering whether any step was reasonable is that of a sensible solicitor considering what, in the light of his then knowledge, was reasonable in the interest of his client.

Obviously, any winning litigant will prefer to receive costs on an indemnity basis. In general terms, taxation on the standard basis will result in a recovery of between 65 per cent and 75 per cent. The indemnity basis will result in a costs recovery of about 10 per cent more. (Successful litigants rarely receive all their costs back.) However, in practice the indemnity basis is only ordered in exceptional cases, such as where the conduct of the losing party is wholly unmeritorious (*House of Spring Gardens* v *Waite* [1991] 1 QB 241) or oppressive (*Singh* v *The Observer* [1989] 2 All ER 751) or a contempt (*Midland Marts* v *Hobday* [1989] 1 WLR 1148).

9.4.5 Procedure for taxation – commencement of proceedings

Taxation proceedings are commenced on the production of the requisite document, usually the original judgment or order, plus a photocopy of the judgment/order being delivered to the SCTO of the High Court. At the same time, a statement containing particulars as set out at RSC Order 62 rule 29(7)(b)(i), a bill of costs (Order 62 rule 29(7)(c)) and any other papers required as set out in Order 62 rule 29(7)(d) need to be lodged at the SCTO unless the taxing officer otherwise orders. In addition, a deposit of half the taxing fee is due (currently 3.75 per cent of the total of the bill, rounded up to the nearest £100).

The primary obligation to commence the taxation process falls upon the party in whose favour the order for costs has been made, called 'the receiving party'. The receiving party must commence proceedings within three months of the sealing of the order, judgment, direction or its equivalent. Note that if the party receiving costs takes more than the three months to commence taxation, a Taxing Master or district judge has full discretion to disallow all or any part of costs of taxation (White Book Notes 62/28/3), as such is seen as a delay which may render a fair taxation impossible. If the receiving party fails to commence taxation within three months then, any other party, usually known as 'the paying party', to the litigation may with the leave of the taxing officer begin the taxation proceedings. Where the taxing officer has granted the paying party leave to commence proceedings, that party shall proceed as if they were the original party entitled to commence taxation proceedings.

It is essential that the requirements of rule 29 are strictly followed as failure to comply will result in a penalty and possibly return the bill to the bottom of the queue. This should not be ignored. Taxations can take months or years to complete. Therefore, it is essential for the expert witness to be in a position to provide a detailed account of his bills to the instructing solicitor to facilitate the taxation process. Indeed, practice directions provide that any account for substantial expenses must be accompanied by details showing the work done, the time spent, by whom and when, and the computation of the charge.

Two additional documents usually required on commencement are:

(a) a Statement of Parties which identifies each party in the action and gives their full details, including the solicitors acting (RSC Order 62 rule 29(7)(b)(i));
(b) unless the taxing officer otherwise orders, the bill of costs in a form complying with Order 62 Appendix 2 Part II and the SCTO Practice Direction No.2 of 1992;
(c) those documents as required and specified in RSC Order 62 rule 29(7)(d).

The Statement of Parties should include for each party the full postal address (although whether it is the party's personal address or their solicitor's depends on whether they acknowledged acting in person at the conclusion of the proceedings giving rise to the taxation proceedings), telephone number, fax number and DX address (only for the solicitor) and any office reference relevant to them or to the solicitor acting for them.

9.4.6 Application to taxing officer for review

Any party to the taxation proceedings who is dissatisfied with any decision of a taxing officer may apply to the taxing officer to review his decision, unless the decision was on a provisional taxation or a decision under Order 62 rule 28, i.e., in relation to misconduct of a party in taxation proceedings. An application for review must be made within 21 days of the taxing officer's original decision or within such other period as may be fixed by the taxing officer.

An application for review under this rule must be accompanied by a written statement specifying what points are being objected to and stating concisely the nature and grounds of the objection in each case. This written statement is referred to as 'the objections'. A copy of the written statement must be delivered to any party that was entitled to receive notice of the appointment for the original taxation proceedings. Failure to comply with this rule will delay the hearing of the objections.

Any party to whom a copy of the objections is delivered has the right to provide written answers to the objections, stating concisely the grounds on which he will oppose the objections. The answers in writing to the objections should be delivered to the taxing officer and a copy should be delivered to the party applying for review, normally within 21 days of delivery (or any other period as may be fixed by the taxing officer) of the written objections being sent to him.

Reviews under rule 33 are usually conducted by a Taxing Master even if the original decision was made by a taxing officer. Points that are raised in the objection will be reviewed on the basis of a re-hearing of the original decision on any particular item and the Taxing Master will hear the matter as though no previous decision on those points had been made. There is no right of subsequent review by a judge on points not raised in the objections (see White Book 62/33/1).

Rule 34 states that a review under rule 33 shall be carried out by the taxing officer who conducted the taxation except that, where the taxation was conducted by a principal or a senior executive officer, the review shall be conducted by a Taxing Master or registrar.

If at the end of the objections process the Taxing Master sees fit to award costs of the proceedings before him to any party, costs may be taxed by him and may be added to or deducted from any other sum payable to or by that party in respect of costs (RSC Order 62 rule 34(2)).

Any party may, normally within 14 days of the Taxing Master's review, request the taxing officer to state in the certificate or provide in writing the reasons for his decisions by reference to each of the points raised in the objections. A copy of the written statement annexed to the certificate will be sent to all parties involved in the taxation proceedings without charge.

9.4.7 Review by a judge

Any party who is dissatisfied with the decision of the Taxing Master on a review under rule 33 may apply, normally within 14 days of the Taxing Master's certificate being issued, in accordance with rule 34(4), to a judge for an order to review that decision either in whole or in part, provided that one of the parties to the taxation proceedings has requested that officer to state the reasons for his decision in accordance with rule 34(4).

Review by a judge is usually heard in chambers rather than in open court. It is usual for the judge to appoint assessors to assist him in his review; these are usually a Taxing Master and a practising solicitor.

Unless the judge otherwise directs, no further evidence shall be received on the hearing of an application under the rule, and no ground of objection shall be raised which was not raised on the review before the Taxing Master. Subject to those limitations, the judge at the review may exercise all such powers and discretion as are vested in the Taxing Master in relation to the subject matter of the application.

All parties are requested to have available at the hearing an estimate of their costs of the review. Such estimates should be exchanged no later than seven days before the hearing and three copies of the estimate should be made available to the court on the day.

9.4.8 Number of expert witnesses

The court may, at or before the trial of any action, order that the number of medical or other expert witnesses who may be called at the trial shall be limited as specified by the order (Order 38 rule 4). Whether or not an order is made under this rule, it is for the Taxing Master to determine whether the calling of any witness was reasonable. If the Taxing Master considers that the costs of an expert were unnecessary or unreasonable, then these costs will be disallowed.

9.5 The taxation hearing

In advance of the matter being fixed for hearing, there is a requirement that the paying party identify matters in issue. This requires the paying party to prepare a short document setting out succinctly the reason for disputing an item and, where a reduction is sought, should suggest a reduced figure.

A receiving party may, and invariably does, respond in answer.

No timetable is given for this procedure, however, the practice directions provide that points of dispute and any response should be given to the taxing officer at least seven days in advance of taxation.

In practice, the hearing is normally held in chambers and only the parties and their legal representatives have the right to be present. Any other person may be admitted only with the prior consent of the taxing officer or Taxing Master conducting the hearing (s67 Supreme Court Act 1981).

The taxing officer or Taxing Master will endeavour to keep the hearing as informal as possible. The taxing official is not concerned with, and will not enter into discussion about, the merits of the earlier proceedings. The taxing official is concerned with the history of the proceedings only in order to gain a full understanding of the case in order to allow the costs to be tested for reasonableness.

Having considered the evidence, both oral and written, and having heard the arguments, the taxing official will give his decision orally in respect of each item of dispute as and when it arises. The taxing official always delivers his decision at the hearing.

In general, the receiving party will be awarded the costs of the taxation proceedings including the taxing fee, which is discussed next. By Order 62 rule 27 note 1, the Master has the discretion to look to Calderbank letters written by the paying party on the issue of costs.

The SCTO charges a fee for the provision of the taxation of costs service known as the 'taxing fee'. The fee is payable by post to HM Paymaster General or by personal attendance, in accordance with the Supreme Court Fees Order 1980 (SI 1980 No 821) (as amended). In a taxation of costs payable by one litigant to another litigant under a court order, that is, *inter partes* costs, the fee is payable by the receiving party. A deposit or taxing fee due is payable on commencement of taxation proceedings, the balance being payable before the issue of the final certificate of taxation. The total fees are calculated at 7.5 per cent of the costs allowed for every £100 or part thereof rounded up to the nearest £100. The current rate is 7.5 per cent subject to a minimum fee of £25.

At the conclusion of the taxation proceedings the taxing officer will issue a certificate for the costs to be allowed by him. In the course of taxation he may also issue an interim certificate for any part of the costs which have been taxed, or for any part, the amount of which is not in dispute.

9.6 Practical aspects of taxation of costs

As mentioned above, taxation of costs is predominantly dealt with by the instructing solicitor. It is in the expert's interest to have an understanding of the mechanics of taxation.

When preparing a bill of costs, a solicitor will normally use a costs draftsman to prepare the bill. Costs draftsmen are either employed by the solicitor's firm, or external consultants who charge a fee, usually as a percentage of the bill as prepared for taxation or as an hourly rate. Bills of costs can be substantial documents setting out a costing of every single piece of work in the litigation. A costs draftsman must include within the bill the expert's own costs. To enable the costs draftsman to do this, or to enable the accountant to do this if he sends in his bill without reference to the costs draftsman, requires a lot of detailed analysis of the expert's time costs (see Practice Direction 2 of 1992, paragraph 1.12).

The expert should maintain a system of recording the time and costs incurred in the production of his expert evidence. It is essential that detailed notes are kept on what was done when and how long it took. This will facilitate the expert when required to provide a detailed bill. A detailed bill will be required by the instructing solicitor irrespective of whether costs are to be taxed or not. The system chosen by the expert can be as simple as a manual record on the front of a file where each time it is worked on a note is kept of the time spent and the work performed, or a sophisticated computerised time-recording package. Whichever method is chosen, the key is to ensure the records are kept up to date with sufficient details of the work performed.

Litigation can often be a long drawn-out process and the expert will not want to spend time going back over his records to provide details of the work performed over the last several months.

If an expert is dissatisfied with the original decision on taxation of his costs he can request the instructing solicitor to apply for authority (from the Legal Aid Board and/or the parties to the litigation whose costs have been taxed) to carry in objections or to apply to the court for review, on the grounds that he was dissatisfied with the decision made by the taxing officer in relation to the fees of the expert witness.

The Taxing Master has discretion to allow the expert to give evidence in support of his charges and to receive evidence in respect of market rates. The expert should ensure that the rates charged for his services are in line with the market rates for his profession and that he can justify in writing the rate used. The expert should maintain a record of the rates used in the past and rates used by competitors (*Cementation Construction Ltd* v *Keaveney* [1988] New LJ 242 D.C.).

If the expert is acting on behalf of a defendant who has been granted legal aid and has agreed in his engagement letter or terms of reference that his fees would be restricted on taxation, he has no right to be heard at the taxation hearing. It is the responsibility of the instructing solicitor to use his best endeavours to secure the allowances on taxation of a proper fee for his expert.

Finally, it should be noted that under a recent practice direction there is an abridged taxation procedure available in the commercial court from 1 October 1997. This procedure gives greater flexibility to parties to resolve differences prior to the taxation hearing. The procedure, which has a trial period of one year, involves a 'broad brush' approach to taxation. Full details are in 'Practice Direction (Commercial Court) Abridged Taxation of Costs Procedure' (*The Times*, 2 October 1997).

Chapter 10
Choosing and using the expert

'. . . you should never trust experts . . . they are required to have their strong wine diluted by a very large admixture of insipid common-sense. Many times have I seen the need for this.' (Lord Salisbury to Lord Lytton in 1877)

10.1 Introduction

This chapter deals with choosing an expert and using him.

The expert will rarely have the opportunity of putting himself forward for a particular assignment, but opportunities may arise following publicity given to a particular case, and where it is obvious from reading the published details that experts will be required.

More generally, experts advertise the availability of their services through directories (such as The Law Society's Directory of Expert Witnesses and in Chambers and Partners' Directory) and by advertising, usually in special editions of legal journals (such as the Expert Witness supplements in the *Solicitor's Journal*).

It is, of course, ultimately the client, usually with advice from his solicitor, who chooses the expert, because he is paying the bill.

Clients with experience of litigation, whether as regular plaintiffs or defendants, may have their own ideas about who they want to act for them, but, in the usual case, potential plaintiffs will seek advice from their own legal advisers and perhaps from their own accountants/auditors. The solicitors may, in turn, if they have not had previous experience of litigation involving the expertise required, consult counsel or insurers.

Sources of initial instruction are likely, in the case of most experienced experts, to be:

- solicitors;
- insurers;
- barristers;
- clients;
- directories;
- advertising.

Potential experts should recognise the criteria by which solicitors generally select experts. The criteria will include:

- experience;
- compatibility;
- resources;
- availability;
- cost;
- identity of other experts.

10.2 Experience

While the experience of the expert is critical as to whether he will be appointed, probably the single most important criterion for the solicitor is his previous experience of using that expert. If that has been a happy experience, particularly if the case had a happy outcome, then the solicitor will be pre-disposed to reappoint the expert should another opportunity arise. The expert will, of course, have to decline if the subject matter of the dispute is not within his expertise.

First impressions are very important and if, on the first occasion, the expert acts with integrity and applies his experience diligently and cost effectively to the problem in hand, he is, at the very least, likely to be considered by the solicitor the next time an opportunity arises.

Many firms of solicitors retain databases of approved experts, but more commonly solicitors searching for an expert ask around the office for recommendations. That is a particularly sensible way of approaching the problem because, of course, the appointment is a personal one. While it is easy to ring up a large firm of accountants and ask for the litigation support department, requesting an expert in a particular field, it may be just as simple, and far more effective, to call an individual of whom the firm has had previous experience and ask whether he has the necessary expertise and availability.

It might be thought that there is a catch-22, on the basis that you cannot be an expert until you are an expert, but everyone has to start somewhere. Status and experience of the matter in hand can be quite sufficient to outweigh any inexperience in the witness box. An expert must, in any event, have experience (and current experience at that) of the subject matter. If he is expressing opinions on audit practice he must carry out audits, if he is expressing opinions on the practice of the Inland Revenue then he should have experience of that practice, but not necessarily from working for the Inland Revenue. An expert expert is not much use to anyone.

The experience of the expert must be enquired into and a solicitor will normally request a copy of a CV. Before providing a CV it will be sensible for the expert to ask for broad details of the nature of the problem, so that he can include within the CV particulars of his experience in that area. An all-singing and all-dancing CV would either include insufficient or too much specific information.

The experience must be relevant to the matter in hand. For example, a manager in the litigation support department of a firm of accountants who qualified in 1992 would not be a suitable person to draft a report, let alone answer for it in the witness box, regarding audit practice and audit opinions in 1988.

The other side will do their research and, for example, an expert on auditing matters is likely to have his expertise challenged if it turns out that he is not authorised by his firm to sign audit opinions. If the expert has never had to express an audit opinion for himself he is ill-qualified to express his view on the audit opinions of others.

Experience as an expert is probably an advantage, because, with a bit of luck, the expert will understand his role, will have a broad understanding of the legal process, will understand what he is being asked to do, and will do it. He will also understand that it is not his job to come up with the answer his client wants but to express his honest opinion, on the basis of the facts as he understands them and reasonable assumptions.

There have been occasions when experts have gained reputations as being good 'defence' or good 'plaintiff' experts. While that reputation may be deserved, on the facts of the cases, the sensible expert will try to avoid being labelled as one or the other. One way of maintaining an independent approach to the work is to try to maintain a reasonable balance between defendant and plaintiff work.

If an expert usually acts for the defence then acting occasionally for a plaintiff is likely to improve the quality of his work, because the problem will be looked at from another perspective. The sensible expert will always play devil's advocate, testing his client's facts and arguments, before forming his opinion.

10.3 Compatibility

Litigation involves teamwork and it is a close-knit team of individuals which works together, even if the litigant is a major corporation and the firms of solicitors and accountants retained are some of the largest in the land. Barristers are sole practitioners, and in practice the team will usually consist of:

- the client;
- his solicitor;
- his barrister;
- his expert(s).

The solicitor who is running the case will want to be confident that he is comfortable with the expert (whether or not he agrees with his views) and will want to be reasonably confident that his client will accept what the expert has to say and the way he says it.

If the expert is an essential part of the team then the barrister will also want to be comfortable with the expert and confident about his opinions and expertise.

The solicitor and client and, most particularly, the barrister will also wish to be confident about the way in which the expert is likely to handle himself in court, and the expert may be asked for details of his court appearances and of those for whom he was acting, so that enquiries can be made. Although barristers practice on their own, a great deal of information passes by word of mouth, and not all of it is gossip. An expert would be unwise to try to hide from his new client an earlier bad experience, because the other side will go looking for it.

On the other hand, if an expert has been praised by a judge it is worthwhile trying to find out exactly what the judge said, if the expert was not in court at the time or if the praise was not contained in the judgment. For experts it is certainly not true that all publicity is good publicity, but good publicity is worth remembering.

10.4 Resources

The solicitor will want to know whether the expert has the resources necessary to deal with the case. A large criminal case involving lengthy investigation prior to the drafting of an expert report may need teams of investigators to be available, not only in the UK but abroad, and their availability and cost will be a matter of concern.

10.5 Availability

Availability is a difficult issue, because the solicitor will not normally wish to retain the expert's services from day one of the proceedings until the end (more's the pity).

The expert will have to balance his duties in the litigation with other litigation in which he may be involved and his normal practice work, and will want to be given some idea of the time commitment required of him.

It is, of course, not only the time commitment but the timing of that commitment which is critical, and it is very unlikely that the instructing solicitor will be able to give the expert engaged at the beginning of a piece of litigation any clear idea as to the ultimate timetable.

On the other hand, when the expert is instructed very late he may be asked if he is in a position to produce an expert report within days, if not hours.

If the time available is insufficient to do the job properly then the expert should explain, in writing if necessary, so that the solicitor can apply to the court for an extension of time. Sometimes it happens that the solicitor has had, for a variety of other reasons, all the time the court is prepared to give him and the expert will then have to decide what can be done given the time available. If proper thought can be given and a proper report written in the time available then it is likely that the solicitor (particularly) and his client, and for that matter the court, will be duly grateful, which may be reflected in proper fees for the job in hand and the prospects for future work.

10.6 Identity of other experts

Clients and their solicitors sometimes consider that it is necessary to fight fire with fire – that is, that if there is a 'Big Six' expert acting for the plaintiff, it is necessary to use a 'Big Six' expert for the defence. If Big Six resources are required, then that may be right, but otherwise an expert with the relevant experience and, perhaps, with a good reputation will not be a hindrance or feel inhibited by the expert on the other side or his background.

Fees will have to be agreed, usually based on an hourly rate but, increasingly, competitive tendering is required. While the expert may argue that what the client is getting is a lifetime's experience, which justifies his hourly rate, commercial pressure sometimes makes the client opt for something which promises to be cheaper.

10.7 Using the expert

Although the solicitor and his client will obviously have to decide what they want the expert for before choosing him, they may not go into the detail of how to use him until the choice has been made.

Consideration should be given to appointing an expert as soon as it is clear that some aspect of the case will turn on technical matters. In many cases the need for experts will be obvious:

- personal injury;
- construction;
- professional negligence (including architects, doctors and accountants).

In other cases experts may not be required at all, because the courts have the necessary experience to decide matters for themselves without technical assistance.

Once an expert is engaged it will be inevitable that he will be relied upon, and if he is engaged prior to the commencement of proceedings and those proceedings are commenced in reliance on his advice which turns out to be wrong, then the expert may be liable for the financial consequences.

The code of practice for expert witnesses engaged by solicitors is dealt with elsewhere and included at Appendix 9. As noted above, Lord Woolf proposes that the instructions to the expert should be disclosed as part of the expert's report.

10.8 Without prejudice meetings

The solicitor will want to be comfortable that the expert will be able to conduct himself sensibly and with skill at without prejudice meetings, not least because it is likely that the meetings will be between experts without solicitors present. Meetings are usually held to narrow the issues and with a view to producing a joint report if possible, or at least a statement of what is agreed and what is not agreed. Such meetings serve no useful purpose if the expert is under instruction not to agree anything, but such instructions are wholly unnecessary if the solicitor trusts his own expert, and the expert has the relevant skills and experience.

Chapter 11
Using the solicitor

11.1 Introduction

The instructions to the expert will come from the solicitor and most of the communication, whether oral or in writing, will be with him or at least in his presence.

While meetings may take place between the expert and the client and with other experts and counsel without the presence of the solicitor, the more normal course is that the instructing solicitor will be present. If the solicitor agrees to meetings at which he is not present, he will want, and need, to know what went on and the outcome.

A good working relationship between the solicitor and the expert is therefore vital. The solicitor is free to choose another expert if the relationship is not working, but the same is not true the other way around.

The expert will usually be dealing with a team of solicitors from the instructing firm, including:

- the partner;
- the assistant solicitors;
- trainees.

Much will depend, of course, on the size of the firm and the specialist nature of the practice but, in the authors' experience, the expert's typical involvement with the solicitors will include contact with a number of members of the team.

11.2 The partner

The partner will normally be involved in approving the instructions to the expert, in liaising with the client, and with his insurers if involved, in considering drafts of the expert report, and in most conferences (with junior counsel) and consultations (with QCs).

The partner will also be involved in any settlement negotiations and with the major decisions which have to be taken during the course of the litigation, not least during the course of the trial. It is the partner who may recommend settlement of an action and the terms of that settlement, and it will normally be the partner who seeks instructions from the client and from the insurers and who will arrange to be put in funds.

In smaller firms and in large cases in larger firms the partner may be involved throughout and may, in effect, be the only solicitor with whom the expert has contact.

11.3 The assistant solicitor

In many firms it is assistant solicitors who run cases on a day-to-day basis (supervised by partners), who draft instructions to counsel and who attend interlocutory hearings. It will also be assistant solicitors who attend much of the trial and who have to alert the partner to the need for his presence at key points.

Many assistant solicitors are given great responsibility by their firms and it will be the assistant solicitor who corresponds, on a regular basis, with the expert.

It is therefore extremely important that the expert should have a good working relationship with the assistant solicitor who may, and probably will be, considerably younger than the expert.

The key to a harmonious relationship is for each to respect the other's experience and knowledge and the fact that each is a key part of the team.

Experts who get on with assistant solicitors are likely to be instructed again, and not only by the firm for which they work at that time, because, in the nature of things, assistant solicitors move on taking their experience and their knowledge of the expert's work with them.

In the heat of the battle, particularly in court, it is all too easy for those in the front line, the advocates and the experts, to assume that it is their case and to forget the very important role played by the solicitor.

11.4 Trainee solicitors

Trainee solicitors will usually have law degrees and will be gaining experience in the litigation department.

They will probably be involved in listing discoverable documents, although it will usually be the assistant solicitor or partner who decides what categories of document are relevant and what are not, and what documents are privileged from production.

The expert may be asked to inspect discoverable documents disclosed by the other side, in the company of the trainee solicitor, particularly if the documents are of a technical nature rather than of general interest in the litigation. The expert may need to make arrangements with the trainee for the copying and cataloguing of key documents and may also ask the trainee to bring the significance of certain documents to the attention of his supervisors.

Usually, trainee solicitors are offered employment as assistant solicitors once they have qualified but, once again, they may move on, and a good working relationship with trainees, recognising their desire to improve their skills and knowledge, will assist the expert not only in existing work but in the future.

Experts who use assistants of their own should take care to ensure that they understand the purpose of what they are doing and the roles of the various team members. Some firms of accountants operate litigation support departments where such training takes place as a matter of course. Others draw support from other departments within the firm and training may then be necessary on an ad hoc basis.

11.5 Meetings with counsel

Experts will attend, during the course of litigation, many meetings with counsel attended by solicitors. It will usually be the assistant solicitor, or a trainee, who takes a note of what is said at the conference and the expert should ask for a copy of the note, correcting it where necessary if the note does not properly record the technical aspects of matters discussed and the expert's views and advice.

The expert should also ask to be copied in on all instructions to counsel (to the extent that they are relevant to the work he is doing) and on counsel's opinions, so that the expert has a written note on his file of all material matters relevant to his role, and which can be referred to in finalising his report and before giving evidence.

It is important that the expert understands his client's case, because, although he will not be concerned directly with the legal issues, it will be of assistance for him to know generally the legal basis for the claim being made and, particularly, the legal basis upon which damages might be assessed.

Part 3
Civil proceedings and damages claims

Chapter 12
A High Court action

12.1 Introduction

This chapter provides an overview of a typical High Court action.

The High Court is the forum where most expert accountants will commonly practice. The next chapter looks in more detail at the rules of procedure in both the High Court and county court.

It is important that the accountant acting as an expert should have a general understanding of what is likely to happen between the time when a potential plaintiff first seeks financial redress for loss which he believes he has suffered through, if necessary, to a final ruling in the House of Lords. The accountant may be involved from the beginning to the end.

Litigation is an expensive way of resolving disputes. It can also take a long time.

> ***Example***
>
> An accountant's negligence case which was settled on the eve of the trial in 1996 was concerned with allegations of negligent auditing by two firms of auditors between 1976 and 1986. The sums involved were potentially large (in excess of £50 million) but, in the end and many years after the litigation began, settlement was reached which did no more than reimburse the plaintiffs for the costs they had incurred. The costs ran to many millions of pounds.

Most civil cases settle before trial, and some straightforward cases settle before much cost is incurred. Trials only tend to take place if each side reckons it has at least a 50 per cent chance of success. There is usually a winner or a loser, although sometimes there is what might be regarded as a draw.

> ***Example***
>
> In an accountant's negligence case the plaintiff succeeded in convincing the judge that his accountant had acted in breach of contract and negligently. However, the judge also decided that the breach of contract and negligence did not

cause the loss claimed (although it might have caused some other loss which was not claimed) and the plaintiff therefore received no more than nominal damages for the breach of contract. The accountant had counterclaimed for unpaid fees which exceeded the nominal damages awarded. As a result, the plaintiff had to pay most of the accountant's costs, and his own, even though he had won. In the circumstances, and unsurprisingly, the plaintiff regarded himself as having lost and appealed. There was a cross-appeal by the accountant on liability even though he had 'won' and the Court of Appeal decided the liability issue in favour of the accountant, resulting in more costs being payable by the plaintiff.

It is very important that the accountant, however familiar with the role of an expert witness, should accept that the law is a matter for lawyers and that the accountant should stick to accountancy. That said, what follows is a description of the *players*, the *paperwork* and the *procedures* involved in a typical civil case (perhaps an accountants' negligence case) to be heard in the High Court.

High Court procedure is governed by the Supreme Court Act 1981 and the Rules of the Supreme Court 1965, as amended. There are 115 Orders and under each Order there are rules and sub-rules. In addition, there are practice statements and directions which evolve through the experience of judges at trials and which are, from time to time, incorporated into the rules.

There are three High Court Divisions (Queen's Bench, Chancery and Family) and specialist courts (such as the Official Referees Department, the Companies Court and the Commercial Court) which are sub-divisions of the Queen's Bench and Chancery Divisions. Expert accountants involved in calculating consequential loss, for example in a civil engineering or building dispute, will need to gain some understanding of how Official Referees conduct their cases, and expert accountants acting in the Family Division will likewise need to understand the way in which that Division operates. Generally, however, so far as the accountant is concerned, the procedures in the Divisions are broadly similar.

12.2 The players

There are 10 groups of people who are likely to play a significant part in a civil action such as an accountants' negligence case. They are:

- the plaintiff;
- the defendant;
- third parties;
- solicitors;
- barristers;
- witnesses;

- expert witnesses;
- Masters;
- judges;
- Taxing Masters.

12.2.1 The plaintiff

The potential plaintiff is someone who believes he has suffered a financial loss and that that loss is someone else's fault. He will want to recover all the losses he thinks he has suffered, and may be reluctant to concede that some of his loss is his own fault, or that the loss is no one's fault and just something he has to live with.

The potential plaintiff may well have tried to seek a remedy for himself, and many disputes are resolved between the parties without the involvement of lawyers or any other third parties.

> ***Example***
>
> A company suffers a loss through a fraud by a cashier which it claims should have been discovered by the auditor. The auditor accepts some of the blame and agrees to waive part of his fees to settle the potential claim. In this way the client relationship is maintained and everyone is happy. Agreement is less likely to be reached if the fraud exceeds the fees or if the sums involved are substantial, when it is more likely that solicitors and, particularly, insurers will become involved. The accountant may, under the terms of his policy, have to notify such a circumstance, but may well be permitted to negotiate a settlement, particularly if the result is likely to be that there will be no claim under the insurance policy.

The plaintiff will want to know:

- who he can sue;
- how much he can recover;
- how long it will take;
- what it will cost.

If an individual plaintiff (not a company) has no money, whether as a result of the wrong done him or otherwise, he may be entitled to legal aid (see Chapter 8), because a plaintiff is not generally deprived of his legal remedies for lack of funds to pursue his claim. There are some restrictions on the types of action for which legal aid is available. Alternatively, he may find a solicitor willing to represent him on a conditional fee basis.

In due course, the plaintiff will need to:

(a) assemble the documentary evidence supporting his claim;
(b) disclose all the relevant documents (including those which do not necessarily support his case);
(c) identify witnesses who will provide evidence in support of his case;
(d) attend meetings with lawyers and experts;
(e) prepare and swear a witness statement;
(f) give evidence at a trial.

All of this will be time-consuming and will divert the plaintiff's attention from what he would otherwise be doing. His staff may also be involved and he may seek to recover these internal costs, because, but for the loss he claims he has suffered, he would not have incurred them. Such costs can be claimed (and may be awarded under an order from the court), but it will usually be necessary for detailed time records to be kept showing the hours spent and the nature of the work undertaken, and it may also be necessary for the plaintiff to demonstrate that, but for preparing his case for trial, he would otherwise have been involved in profitable activity.

Much more important, to the plaintiff who is not on legal aid, will be the costs he is incurring in pursuing his action. These costs will include:

- court fees;
- solicitor's fees;
- counsel's fees;
- expert's fees.

At the time of writing there is controversy over a recent increase in court fees. However, as the Lord Chancellor has pointed out in the House of Lords, such costs pale into insignificance compared with the other costs and, for all practical purposes, the services of the courts are provided free to the parties. This is a slightly curious and unexpected advantage of High Court litigation over arbitration and of Alternative Dispute Resolution (ADR) (see Chapter 14) where the additional costs to be contemplated include not only the cost of paying the arbitrator or conciliator but also the costs of hiring premises and incidental costs. Panels of three arbitrators can be very expensive and they usually have discretion about who pays the costs of an award.

In England, in contrast to the position in the USA, the successful litigant recovers his costs, at least in theory. In practice he is unlikely to recover more than, say, 70 per cent of his costs and that is a factor which the plaintiff has to take into account in deciding whether or not to pursue the wrongdoer through the courts. A plaintiff pursuing a claim for £30,000 would be unwise to incur costs of £100,000 in doing so, because, even if he was successful, he would probably end up with nothing.

He might also end up with nothing if the defendant was not worth powder and shot, and the plaintiff will have to form a view very early on as to whether, even if he is successful, he will in fact recover from the wrongdoer.

> ***Example***
>
> A substantial fraud on a company by an employee (even a director) will frequently not result in a civil action by the company against the wrongdoer, because, all too frequently, the proceeds of the fraud have been spent on gambling, loose women and drink or secreted away and/or the wrongdoer may be spending some time as a guest in one of Her Majesty's hotels. The potential plaintiff in this situation will look around for someone else to sue and, all too often, he will decide to take a pot at his auditors (see Chapter 26).

The potential plaintiff will also be told, in due course, about the *vagaries of litigation*. These vagaries mean that a cast-iron copper-bottomed case may not result in victory should the matter come to trial. Even the bravest of lawyers tends not to go beyond indicating an 80 per cent chance of success, and many would stick at about 65 per cent. However, for a case to come to trial *each* side must think they will win, which means, inevitably, that one side's estimate is wrong.

It might be thought that, in a fair world, litigating would not be necessary, because everyone would always own up and settle their differences and debts. In simple cases that sometimes happens (and ought to happen more often), but in other cases the law is complex, the facts are in dispute, and expert opinion can legitimately vary widely.

> ***Example***
>
> His Lordship (Mr Justice Cresswell) said that a court might prefer one body of opinion to another, but that was no basis for a finding of negligence. He added that an expert witness should make it clear in his or her report, if it were the case, that although the expert would have adopted a different approach or practice, that he or she accepted that the approach or practice adopted by the defendant was in accordance with the approach or practice accepted as proper by a responsible body of practitioners skilled in the relevant field. (*Sharpe* v *Southend Health Authority and Another* TLR 9.5.97)

To summarise, the potential plaintiff should:

- identify the wrongdoer;
- ascertain whether he is worth powder and shot;
- estimate his loss;

- seek redress from the wrongdoer;
- seek legal advice;
- act on that legal advice;
- commit himself to a course of action;
- budget for the costs;
- recognise the possibility of failure.

Many potential plaintiffs would be best advised to get on with their lives and to put the loss down to experience. However, the financial consequences may be such that it is appropriate for redress to be sought, and it may not be possible for the potential plaintiff to get on with his life without seeking and obtaining redress.

12.2.2 Defendants

The defendant may not know of any wrong done to the potential plaintiff until a writ is served, perhaps claiming breach of contract or negligence or both.

More commonly, attempts will have been made, as outlined above, by the potential plaintiff to make the defendant aware of the wrong allegedly suffered and of the remedy sought.

If the defendant acknowledges his error then he may wish to settle, although he may be restrained by his insurers from an admission of liability.

Usually, the defendant will at least have some knowledge of the existence of the plaintiff even if he had no contractual relationship with him. If the claim is not for breach of contract then it will be in tort, which is a civil wrong for which the remedy is a common law action for damages or seeking an injunction, specific performance or other remedy. Negligence is a tort actionable by a person suffering damage as a result of the defendant's breach of duty to take care to refrain from injuring him.

As the ICAEW *Members Handbook* puts it (at 1.311):

> 'It would be a defence to an action for negligence to show:
>
> (a) that no duty of care had been owed to the plaintiff in the circumstances; or
> (b) that there had been no negligence; or
> (c) that the negligent act or omission had not been an effective cause of the plaintiff's loss; or
> (d) in the case of actions in tort that no financial loss had been suffered by the plaintiff; or
> (e) the action was statute barred.'

> The fourth defence would not be available to a claim in contract but, as only nominal damages would be recoverable, and in those circumstances it is unlikely that such an action would be brought.'

The scope of damages for breach of contract is usually wider than for negligence and can include consequential loss and non-financial loss – this is a complex area of law with the scope as opposed to the quantum best left to the lawyers.

Whether the defendant would owe a duty in tort to another is a complicated legal matter, but following *Caparo Industries* v *Dickman* [1990] 2 AC 605, a duty of care to a particular third party may be owed where there is:

(a) foreseeability of damage to the third party; and
(b) a relationship of proximity or neighbourhood with that third party; and
(c) a situation where it would be fair, just and reasonable to impose a duty of a given scope.

Example

In an American case decided in 1931 Mr Justice Cardozo said:

> 'If liability for negligence exists, a thoughtless slip or blunder, the failure to detect a theft or forgery beneath the cover of deceptive entries, may expose accountants to a liability in an indeterminate amount for an indeterminate time to an indeterminate class. The hazards of a business conducted on these terms are so extreme as to enkindle doubt whether a flaw may not exist in the implication of a duty that exposes to these consequences.' (*Ultramares Corporation* v *Touche & Co* [1931] 255 NY 170)

It is clear that a person, or partnership, or company, may owe a duty of care to those with whom he or it does not have a contractual relationship, but it will be for the court to decide whether, in the particular circumstances, a duty is owed.

Defendants against whom claims are intimated generally, and wisely, consult solicitors before making admissions or settling claims.

If the defendant is insured, as he usually will be if he is a professional or, for example, a car driver or an employee going about his employer's business, then the terms of the insurance policy will normally require that the insurer be notified of the claim. The terms of the policy will also usually provide that the defendant should act in accordance with the insurer's instructions if he wishes insurance cover to be provided.

The uninsured defendant may be entitled to legal aid depending on his financial circumstances. Because of the wide range of people to whom a duty of care in tort may be owed in a very wide range of circumstances, both legal expenses insurance and public liability cover may well be worthwhile, available and inexpensive.

Provided the defendant has acted reasonably, carefully and cautiously, and with reasonable skill if appropriate, then any loss suffered by the plaintiff will not usually be attributed to him.

Example

As Lord Justice Lopes said in *Re Kingston Cotton Mill Co Limited (No. 2)* [1896] 2 Ch 279:

'It is the duty of an auditor to bring to bear on the work he has to perform that skill, care, and caution which a reasonably competent, careful and cautious auditor would use. What is reasonable skill, care, and caution must depend on the particular circumstances of each case.'

What amounts to standards of reasonable skill and care will move with the times and are more exacting now than they were in 1896 (*Re Thomas Gerrard and Son Ltd* [1967] 2 All ER 525).

In many ways the defendant is in a worse position than the plaintiff. He has no choice about whether to be a defendant or not. He will have to incur costs in defending himself, and his reputation, as well as his pocket, may be at stake. He will not normally be recompensed, even if he is successful, for the time cost and inconvenience of defending the proceedings, and the vagaries of litigation apply equally to the defendant as they do to the plaintiff.

The defendant can seek to join into the proceedings other parties (third parties) whom he considers either wholly or partly to blame for the predicament in which he finds himself. If he loses, it is not too late to seek a contribution from those he regards as having been responsible for the same loss, provided contribution proceedings are brought within two years.

The defendant can make a counterclaim if, for example, he is a professional with unpaid fees, and can seek redress from the court if he considers that he may be able to establish that the complaint made against him is vexatious or frivolous.

To maximise his chances of successfully defending a claim a defendant should:

(a) seek immediate legal advice;
(b) assemble and retain all relevant documentary evidence;
(c) identify and seek the co-operation of potential witnesses;
(d) identify for himself the strengths and weaknesses of his position;
(e) recognise that such proceedings are one of the risks of modern life and that that is what insurance is for (if there is insurance cover).

In the authors' experience the reaction of defendants to claims made varies from righteous, and sometimes justified, indignation to abject terror and guilt. On the one hand there was the accountant who said 'I do not feel negligent therefore I am not negligent'. On the other, there are those who, because their work fell below the highest standard, assume that they were negligent.

In *Lloyd Cheyham & Co.* v *Littlejohn & Co* [1987] BCLC 303, Mr Justice Woolf, as he then was, said:

> 'Mr Cade who was the expert witness for the plaintiff underestimated the extent to which other professional practitioners could responsibly adopt different practices from that which he would adopt.'

He went on:

> 'Furthermore, looking at matters from his own high standards, he failed to appreciate that it was possible to fall below those standards without being negligent.'

Example

Lloyd Cheyham had bought Trec Rentals Limited and Littlejohn had been the auditors. Lloyd Cheyham considered that what they got was not what they had paid for and sued the auditors for negligence. In that particular case the auditors knew that the audited accounts were required by Lloyd Cheyham in relation to the proposed acquisition of Trec and the existence of a duty of care was not argued at the trial. The action failed and the judge concluded that the auditors were extremely conscientious in the work they did for Trec. Mr Justice Woolf added:

'. . . while Mr Anderson [the managing director of Lloyd Cheyham] no doubt believed in the merits of the claim in fact he was placing a wholly unjustified responsibility on the defendants (auditors). He failed to obtain the usual warranties or make the usual enquiries before investing in Trec and then sought to blame his loss on the failure of the defendants (auditors) to provide him with the protection which he did not provide for himself. While it is right that auditors should exercise a duty of care to those who they appreciate will rely on their audited accounts this duty does not mean that a purchaser need not exercise any care to protect himself.'

A defendant may, therefore, it appears, still take comfort from the dictum 'caveat emptor' (let the buyer beware) and any damages awarded against a negligent auditor might, depending on the circumstances, be reduced because of contributory negligence by the plaintiff or others.

12.2.3 Third parties

A third party is a person who is not an original party to the action but from whom the defendant claims a contribution or an indemnity. Once the third party has been joined in the action he will be in much the same position as against the defendant as the defendant is as against the plaintiff, and it will be for the court to decide on the apportionment of blame and of damage, if such apportionment is appropriate.

It is, of course, possible for the dispute to be resolved by agreement between the parties before litigation commences through some form of Alternative Dispute Resolution. The more parties that are involved, however, the more difficult such resolution becomes, because, if litigation is to be avoided, all parties have to agree. If two parties agree but the third will not then litigation may be inevitable and may involve all three parties.

12.2.4 The solicitors

The first solicitor to be consulted will usually be the solicitor contacted by a potential plaintiff. The solicitor will want to understand the nature of the problem and the remedy sought. He will usually do this by discussion with the client and by reference, where appropriate, to contemporary documents.

If the solicitor forms the view that his client has the makings of a case he will advise on how best to proceed. If litigation seems to be potentially an appropriate way of dealing with the problem then the solicitor may well suggest that he should send a 'letter before action' to the defendant setting out his client's complaint and the remedy sought, giving the defendant the opportunity to settle within a set time limit. This is sometimes offered as an alternative to long and potentially costly and disruptive legal proceedings.

It would not be unusual, in such a letter, for the request for recompense to be set at a level below that which the plaintiff would hope to achieve should the claim be litigated, because this would be an additional incentive to the defendant to settle.

In more complex cases specialist advice might be sought from a barrister or from an expert before the 'letter before action' and, usually, before proceedings are issued.

The solicitor has a pivotal role in civil litigation in the High Court and elsewhere. He is the prime contact with the client, from whom he takes instructions, and he gives instructions, with his client's consent, to barristers and to the experts.

The solicitor will agree the basis of his fees with the client and will also normally negotiate fees with barrister's clerks (not with the barrister himself) and with the experts. He will normally be personally responsible for settling barrister's fees whether or not he gets paid himself, and will usually settle the expert's fees having been put in funds to do so by his client, by insurers or by obtaining payment on account from the legal aid fund. Whether the solicitor is responsible for the expert's fees, absent recovery of those fees from other parties, will be a contractual matter between the solicitor and the expert and a matter of conduct, bearing in mind the guidance in the Guide to Professional Conduct.

Before taking on the case, the solicitor will have to check that he has no conflicts of interest, and that he has the relevant resources and experience. The solicitor will also be responsible for ensuring that the case is run in accordance with the rules of procedure and that all the relevant time limits are observed.

One of the key roles of the solicitor will be to advise on, and negotiate, the terms of any settlement which may be reached. A very high proportion of civil actions are settled before trial and, while settlement negotiations are sometimes conducted between the parties directly, it is more usual, in the authors' experience, for negotiations to take place between solicitors, particularly where insurers have an interest on behalf of one party or the other, or both.

Barristers act only on instructions from their client through the solicitor. The experts are instructed by a solicitor and his importance should not be underestimated even in the heat of battle, when it is advocates who are on their feet and the experts in the witness box. Solicitors are also a major source of work, probably the major source of work, for experts, because it will often be the solicitor who recommends an expert to his client, who introduces them and who oversees the relationship between them.

It will also be the solicitor who instructs the expert and it is likely, following Lord Woolf's Final Report to the Lord Chancellor on the Civil Justice System in England and Wales (*Access to Justice*), that expert evidence will not be admissible unless all written instructions (including letters subsequent upon the original instructions), and a note of any oral instructions, are included as an annex to the expert's report.

As Tom Keevil of Simmons & Simmons put it at a recent conference ('Oral and documentary evidence after Woolf', 1 July 1997):

> '. . . the necessity of having clear and precise terms of reference will increase. The precise nature of the work the expert is going to be asked to undertake must be spelt out. Amongst other matters, the terms of engagement should set out:
>
> (a) the nature of the dispute;
> (b) the precise nature of the assignment the expert is expected to undertake and the issue the expert is to address;
> (c) the way in which the expert is to proceed and any assumptions that the expert is to act upon;
> (d) the identity of the party retaining the expert and the basis upon which the expert is to be remunerated, including the hourly rates or rates (and permissible disbursements, such as class of air travel etc) that will be charged for the work product;
> (e) the arrangements for the provision of detailed breakdowns of the time the expert spends on the assignment;
> (f) the timescale within which the expert is expected to produce his or her work product;
> (g) confirmation that the work product will be the expert's own product and if not, what will be the extent of others' input;
> (h) a route by which any tensions that may arise between the expert and the client's advisers can be resolved amicably;
> (i) reporting and work product review procedures;
> (j) a reminder that, ultimately, the expert's report is likely to have to:
> – give details of his qualifications and any written material used in making his report;
> – identify who carried out any test or experience used for the report;
> – identify details of the qualifications of whoever carried out the test or experiment;
> – provide where there is a range of opinion on matters to be dealt with in the report:
> (1) summary of the range of opinion;
> (2) reasons for the expert's opinion;
> – confirm, at the end of the report:
> (1) that the expert understands his duty to the court;
> (2) he or she has complied with that duty;
> (3) the report includes all matters relevant to the issues upon which evidence is to be given;
> (4) the report has detailed any matters which affect its reliability;
> – have attached to it copies of:
> (1) all written instructions given to the experts;
> (2) any supplementary written instructions;
> (3) a note of any oral instructions given to him.'

The precise terms of reference will, of course, be based on the facts and issues and it will usually be sensible for draft terms of reference to be discussed between the expert and the solicitor before they are finalised.

Much of the day-to-day work will, in the authors' experience, be conducted by assistant solicitors who will, in turn, be assisted by trainees. Not all assistant solicitors want or achieve partnership within their firm and it is assistant solicitors who tend to move between firms. A good relationship between assistant solicitors and experts can be of mutual advantage, because the assistant solicitor can introduce his or her new firm to a reliable and experienced expert, and the expert will have the advantage of being able to sell his skills to a new group of solicitors.

12.2.5 Barristers

Osborn's Concise Law Dictionary defines a barrister as follows:

> 'A member of one of the four Inns of Court who has been called to the Bar by his Inn. A barrister intending to practise must have spent twelve months as a pupil. Barristers formerly had the exclusive right of audience in the High Court and superior courts, but this monopoly was removed by the Courts and Legal Services Act 1990 (s.27). The professional conduct of barristers is regulated by the General Council of the Bar of England and Wales.
>
> Barristers' fees at common law are honoraria and no action lies to recover such fees. Under the Courts and Legal Services Act 1990 s.62, they are immune against actions for negligence arising out of their presentation of cases in court (see also the common law position: Rondel & Worsley [1969] I A.C. 191; Saif Ali & Sydney Mitchell & Co. [1980] A.C. 198, HL). Section 62 also gives immunity from related actions for breach of contract. Barristers are now permitted to enter into contracts for the provision of their services, Courts & Legal Services Act 1990, s.61.'

Experienced counsel may be appointed Queen's Counsel (QC) on the recommendation of the Lord Chancellor. A QC is a leader when he is retained to conduct a case in court and leads the '*junior*' instructed to appear with him. Juniors are barristers who are not Queen's Counsel.

Barristers will often be consulted by solicitors about the law likely to apply in particular circumstances and about the conduct of a case generally. It is normally junior barristers who draft the pleadings, who appear on applications and provide submissions to the court, and who act as advocates for the parties under the instructions of the solicitors.

It is common practice for the plaintiff or defendant client to be introduced to the junior barrister at a conference with counsel (or consultation if with Queen's Counsel), which will be attended by the client and the instructing solicitor, and maybe also the expert.

Meetings will occasionally take place between barristers and experts without a solicitor being present and, for example, chartered accountants may now, in certain circumstances, approach a barrister direct rather than through a solicitor. In litigation matters it would be normal for the barrister and expert to meet without the solicitor only with the express consent of the solicitor and for a particular purpose.

Counsel may be instructed orally or in writing to advise on particular aspects of a case and they may give that advice either in writing or at a conference. Counsel may advise on the chances of success and on the best way of advancing their client's cause. They do not have to believe in the client's case, but they cannot advance the case knowing the case being advanced is not true.

In court, counsel will outline his client's case in an opening speech, examine his client's witnesses 'in chief', re-examine after cross-examination by the other side, cross-examine the opposing side's witnesses and make closing submissions. After judgment, counsel will normally draft or advise on the orders required to put the judgment into effect.

Because of their training and experience, counsel have detailed knowledge of the law in their area of specialism and have the resources necessary to research the relevant case law. They are familiar with High Court procedure and will normally advise solicitors and their clients of the best procedure to adopt in furtherance of the case.

Counsel will often offer constructive criticism of the content of experts' reports and will point out any areas where the expert has strayed from his instructions or beyond his area of expertise. Counsel will emphasise throughout that the content of the expert's report is entirely a matter for him, but any sensible expert would take note of points made by counsel unless, unusually, there was any attempt to browbeat the expert into changing his opinions to the advantage of the client.

Chapter 5 deals with the art of advocacy and gives advice to experts on dealing with skilled cross-examination.

Experts may be appointed 'to inquire and report on any question of fact or opinion not consisting of law or of construction'. Experts are only required for the purpose of assisting the court on technical matters. Experts may, therefore, be retained to investigate the facts, to report their findings and, if necessary, to express their opinion on the consequences.

In complicated matters barristers may require assistance from experts in the drafting of sections of pleadings, in dealing with technical matters (such as breaches of auditing and accounting standards), in considering what applications to make and summonses to seek and, particularly, in preparation for trial, in understanding the technical context and consequences of witness evidence, in cross-examining experts for the other side, and in dealing with quantum.

12.2.6 Witnesses

Although cases can be advanced, and defended, by reference to documents and, where appropriate, expert evidence, the general rule is that evidence is given orally by witnesses of fact. The normal course of events is that solicitors will take written statements (sometimes known as proofs) from potential witnesses. These are 'written statements of the oral evidence which the party intends to adduce on any issues of fact to be decided at trial' CRSC Order 38 rule 2A(2)).

It is now normally the practice (and a requirement) for witness statements from all those intended to be called to give evidence at trial to be exchanged simultaneously.

It is the solicitor's job to make sure that the witness statement contains only admissible evidence relating to the issues of fact to be adduced at trial, and the statement should represent the witness's evidence in chief. Following the Civil Evidence Act 1995, hearsay evidence is now admissible in civil proceedings, subject to certain safeguards.

The witness statement should start with the name, address and occupation of the witness and any connection with the parties. It should be expressed in the witness's own words and comment may be made, in court, if it is apparent that the solicitor or counsel had a hand in the wording. The witness statement should follow the chronological sequence of events, with numbered paragraphs, and should be signed.

In *ADT Limited* v *BDO Binder Hamlyn* [1996] BCC 808 (see **3.8**), Mr Justice May said, in his judgment on 6 December 1995:

> 'There is, in my view, some force in the submission that Mr Jermine's written witness statement appears as the product of much assisted fine tuning designed to craft a product which presents the facts most strongly in support of ADT's case in law . . . That said I judged Mr Jermine's oral evidence to be generally quietly impressive and entirely credible . . .'

The above illustrates, perhaps, the recognition by the judiciary that there will inevitably be some 'fine tuning' of witness statements exchanged prior to trial, but all concerned with that fine tuning will recognise that it will not avail them if their witness does not come up to proof in the witness box.

The witness will have, in any event, to sign his witness statement stating that its contents are true to the best of his knowledge and belief and will be examined about it under oath in the witness box.

Experts will normally rely heavily on witness statements for their understanding of the facts upon which their opinion is to be based. A witness who does not come up to proof may well cause the expert to reflect on his opinions if the facts do not turn out to be what he thought they were.

There should be no serious danger of failure to come up to proof if the witness statement is carefully drafted by the solicitor on the instructions of the witness and by reference to contemporary documents including, particularly, contemporaneous notes of conversations and meetings.

Experts will not normally attend meetings at which witness statements are taken, but would be well advised to compare witness statements with the contemporary documentation being relied on, and bring to the attention of the solicitors any anomalies or irrelevant matters.

Judges have to decide on the credibility of witnesses and their decisions as to the facts, where these are disputed, will depend very much on whether the judge forms a favourable view of the witness's evidence.

12.2.7 Expert witnesses

An expert witness is a person with a special skill, technical knowledge or professional qualifications whose opinion is admitted in evidence, contrary to the general rule that opinions are irrelevant. Expert evidence, even if uncontradicted, is not bound to be accepted by the court. Lord Salisbury said in 1877:

> '. . . you should never trust experts . . . They are required to have their strong wine diluted by a very large admixture of insipid common-sense. Many times have I seen the need for this.'

The purpose of expert evidence is to assist the court on technical matters and it follows that the expert must be a person with special skills or qualifications and, importantly, experience, whose opinion will be valued by the court. If the experts disagree, the best that the expert witness can hope for is that his opinion will be preferred to that of the expert for the other side. If the experts agree, then the court will have the benefit of the combined opinion.

The expert should never assume the role of advocate. As Mr Justice Cresswell put it in 'The Ikarian Reefer' (*National Justice Compania Naviera SA* v *Prudential Assurance Co.* [1993] 2 Lloyd's Rep. 68):

'Expert evidence presented to the Court should be, and should be seen to be, the independent product of the expert uninfluenced as to form or content by the exigencies of litigation. . . . An expert witness should provide independent assistance to the court by way of objective, unbiased opinion in relation to matters within his expertise . . . An expert witness in the High Court should never assume the role of an advocate.'

Mr Justice Cresswell went on, in the same case, to outline the requirements of expert reports as follows:

'An expert witness should state the facts or assumptions upon which his opinion is based. He should not omit to consider material facts which could detract from his concluded opinion.

An expert witness should make it clear when a particular question or issue falls outside his expertise.

If an expert's opinion is not properly researched because he considers that insufficient data is available, then this must be stated with an indication that the opinion is no more than a provisional one. In cases where an expert witness who has prepared a report could not assert that the report contained the truth, the whole truth, and nothing but the truth without some qualification, that qualification should be stated in the report . . .

If, after exchange of reports, an expert witness changes his view on a material matter, having read the other side's expert's report or for any other reason, such change of view should be communicated (through legal representatives) to the other side without delay and where appropriate to the Court.

Where expert evidence refers to photographs, plans, calculations, analyses, measurements, survey reports or other similar documents, these must be provided to the opposite party at the same time as the exchange of reports (see 15.5 of the Guide to Commercial Court Practice).'

Lord Woolf expresses his own views in Chapter 13 of *Access to Justice* as follows:

'1. As a general principle, single experts should be used wherever the case (or the issue) is concerned with a substantially established area of knowledge and where it is not necessary for the court directly to sample a range of opinions.

2. Parties and procedural judges should always consider whether a single expert could be appointed in a particular case (or to deal with a particular issue); and, if this is not considered appropriate, indicate why not.

3. Where opposing experts are appointed they should adopt a co-operative approach. Wherever possible this should include a joint investigation and a single report, indicating areas of disagreement which cannot be resolved.

4. Expert evidence should not be admissible unless all written instructions (including letters subsequent upon the original instructions) and a note of any oral instructions are included as an annex to the expert's report.

> 5. The court should have a wide power, which could be exercised before the start of proceedings, to order that an examination or tests should be carried out in relation to any matter in issue, and a report submitted to the court.
>
> 6. Experts' meetings should normally be held in private. When the court directs a meeting, the parties should be able to apply for any special arrangements such as attendance by the parties' legal advisers.
>
> 7. Training courses and published material should provide expert witnesses with a basic understanding of the legal system and their role within it, focusing on the expert's duty to the court, and enable them to present written and oral evidence effectively. Training should not be compulsory.'

The Law Society has published a code of practice for expert witnesses engaged by solicitors, which is reproduced in Appendix 9. The Academy of Experts has produced a model form of experts' report and this is reproduced at Appendix 1.

The detailed requirements of experts in particular circumstances are dealt with in other chapters of this book.

If Lord Woolf's proposals are implemented, and at the time of writing there is good deal of objection to some of them, it seems unlikely that the role of the expert will change, although the circumstances in which experts are used will change.

In his interim report Lord Woolf recommended that:

> 'any expert's report prepared for the purpose of giving evidence to a court should end with a declaration that it includes everything which the expert regards as being relevant to the opinion which he has expressed in his report and that he has drawn to the attention of the court any matter which would affect the validity of that opinion.'

The position at present appears to be that the expert's report should not cover anything outside the pleaded case and that the expert's oath to tell the truth applies only to those matters which he is asked about. In *Derby & Co.* v *Weldon (No.9)* Lord Justice Staughton said:

> 'I do not think that an expert witness, or any other witness, obliges himself to volunteer his views on every issue in the whole case when he takes an oath to tell the whole truth. What he does oblige himself to do is to tell the whole truth about those matters which he is asked about.'

Whether that view will survive the implementation of Lord Woolf's proposals remains to be seen.

12.2.8 Masters

It will be necessary, during the period between the end of pleadings and the trial, for one party or the other to litigation to seek orders or directions from the court. This is usually done by making interlocutory applications to a Master in chambers (that is, not in open court).

Applications are made, having given notice to the other side, so that both parties appear before the Master.

Only two clear days' notice is normally required and the parties, counsel, solicitors and, usually, their responsible representatives, have rights of audience, provided the application is in chambers.

In the High Court applications are made by summons and a Master is assigned to each action when the first summons in the action is issued. This means that the same Master normally hears all other summonses in the action.

There are strict time limits laid down by the court (see **12.6** below), but the time limits are often difficult to meet and it is therefore quite common to seek the consent of the court to extend the time limits.

Time limits can, subject to the discretion of the court, usually be extended by agreement so that, for example, the date for exchange of expert reports can be changed at the behest of one of the parties if the other agrees.

If one party or the other dislikes a Master's ruling, an appeal lies against that ruling to a judge in chambers.

12.2.9 Judges

In civil disputes in the High Court judges normally sit alone without a jury and, having listened to the evidence and arguments on all sides, have to make a judgment. Judgments can run to many hundreds of pages and a typical judgment in an accountant's negligence case might include the following:

(a) a brief outline of the protagonists and of the claim being made;
(b) a summary of the matters which the plaintiffs would have to establish in order to succeed, which might include:

    (i) that the defendants owed the plaintiffs a duty of care (*the duty of care issue*);
    (ii) that the defendants were negligent (*the negligence issue*);

(iii) if the defendants were negligent whether the plaintiffs suffered in consequence (*the causation issue*);
(iv) the amount of loss suffered by the plaintiffs (*the quantum issue*).

The judge might then go on to give details of the names of those from whom he heard evidence, including expert evidence. The judge may express views on the quality of the evidence and, in connection with experts, may say which of the experts gave the evidence which he preferred.

There might then be a recital of the facts, with the judge making a finding of fact where different versions of events have been put to him.

The judge would go on to deal with the issues he had identified, not only, strictly speaking, to the extent necessary to reach a judgment. If, for example, a plaintiff failed on a duty of care issue it would not, on the face of it, be necessary to go on and consider questions of negligence, causation and quantum, but judges do sometimes go on to deal with these.

There may be grounds for an appeal and it is therefore not unusual for judgments to go on to consider the other matters in case an appeal is successful on the issue upon which the judgment is based.

Thus, in a case where there was no dispute about duty of care, and negligence was found, quantum was considered even though the judge found that the plaintiff failed on causation.

Lawyers distinguish between the 'ratio decidendi' of a judgment (literally, the reason for the decision) and 'obiter dicta', the latter being observations on legal issues which do not require final conclusions in order to decide the case. Only the ratio decidendi is to be regarded as setting a precedent.

After a judgment it is usual for there to be a conference with clients, and the losing party may wish to know whether the judgment can be appealed. Final judgments in the High Court can be appealed (in most cases) to the Court of Appeal without leave of the High Court judge and can exceptionally be appealed direct to the House of Lords with leave from both the High Court judge and the House of Lords.

Appeals are normally heard by two or three judges in the Court of Appeal, who will not usually hear further evidence on questions of fact, relying instead on transcripts of evidence in the lower court.

Written judgments are usually given and are confidential until pronounced in court, where they will not normally be read aloud. The expert who thinks it might be interesting to go to the Court of Appeal (or the House of Lords) to hear a judgment pronounced is therefore likely to be disappointed.

While an expert may hope that his opinion will be preferred to that of his opposite number, he also runs the risk of being criticised by the judge, sometimes severely.

In the *ADT* v *Binder Hamlyn* case (see **12.2.6** above) the judge said of one of the expert witnesses:

> 'I record, since it contributed to my general judgement of Mr Bray's evidence, that I judged his evidence here to have been poor to the point of studied evasion.'

In another case, *First National Commercial Bank plc* v *Andrew S Taylor (Commercial) Ltd* [1995] EGCS 200 the judge said:

> 'Both sides called expert witnesses, Mr Wooding on behalf of the plaintiffs, and Mr Shapero on behalf of the defendants . . . I regret to say that I do not find Mr Wooding a satisfactory witness. On occasions it seemed to me that he was more concerned to parry questions than to answer them. I by far prefer the evidence of Mr Shapero, and where there are differences between them I unhesitantly accept the evidence of Mr Shapero in preference to that of Mr Wooding.'

In *Cala Homes (South) Ltd* v *Alfred McAlpine Homes East Ltd (No 2)*, *The Independent*, October 30, 1995 (CS) ChD, Laddie J said:

> 'The Judge is not a rustic who has chosen to play a game of Three Card Trick. He is not fair game. Nor is the truth.'

The expert witness, and for that matter any other witness, should always assume that the matter will come to trial and that, when it does, the witness statement or expert report will be tested by counsel for both sides and that judgment will be pronounced. Judgments, in many cases, are public documents and an expert who is criticised is therefore unlikely to be able to keep that criticism from those who might otherwise instruct him. It is commonplace now to run a 'Lexis' check on an expert's name, with a view to picking up any adverse observations about him.

12.3 The paperwork

This part of this chapter deals with the paperwork commonly seen by experts during the course of litigation and deals with the following:

- writs;
- pleadings;
- discovery;

- witness statements;
- expert reports;
- interrogatories;
- subpoenas;
- affidavits;
- notices to admit;
- trial bundles;
- skeleton arguments;
- judgments;
- orders.

12.3.1 Writs

Writs are used for commencing almost all common law actions, although there are other forms of High Court originating process.

There is one prescribed form of writ and an example is given at Appendix 10.

Writs are issued by the court and time starts running for limitation purposes on the date of issue. The court allocates a case number and endorses each copy of the writ, including the original, one for the court and one for each defendant.

Each defendant must be served with the writ within four months of issue and a writ must be served personally on each defendant, although it can be put through his letterbox or posted to him. Solicitors may accept service on behalf of the defendant.

The writ does not need to contain a fully pleaded statement of claim and may merely contain a concise statement of the nature of the claim and the relief sought.

The defendant has to acknowledge service of the writ on the standard form served with it within 14 days. Failure to acknowledge service within 14 days means that the plaintiff is entitled to enter judgment in default.

A defendant who intends to contest the proceedings must serve a defence and if, a statement of claim is endorsed on the writ, the defence must be served within 14 days after the time for acknowledging service. If a statement of claim is not endorsed on the writ the defence need not be served until 14 days after the statement of claim is served. In practice, time for service of the defence may be extended by agreement between the parties or, if agreement is not reached, by application to a Master.

12.3.2 Pleadings

The questions of fact and law to be decided are set down in formal documents known as pleadings. They are:

- the statement of claim;
- the defence (and counterclaim);
- the reply (and defence to counterclaim);
- further and better particulars.

Technically, the pleadings close with the reply and defence to counterclaim, but in many more complex cases leave of the court will be sought to seek further and better particulars and, indeed, further and better particulars of the further and better particulars.

A defendant may bring a claim against a non-party by issuing a third party notice and, like a writ, a third party notice must be issued by the court. Once served, the third party has the same rights in respect of his defence as the defendant.

Amendments may be made to the pleadings with the consent of the other parties or with the leave of court and, in the early stages of the litigation, in the absence of consent and without the leave of the court, provided the amendment does not change the basis of the claim.

The party wishing to amend may have to pay the costs of the amendment, but leave to amend will rarely be refused even as the time for trial approaches. It may not be too late to amend during the course of the trial.

Example

Towards the end of a trial the judge invited leading counsel for the plaintiff to change the claim for loss after the factual evidence, and the expert witnesses, had been heard. Had the plaintiff's counsel accepted the invitation there would have been vigorous opposition from the defendant on the grounds that the new case being pleaded was not one for which they had prepared or upon which the judge had heard any factual or expert evidence. As it happens, the plaintiff's counsel declined to amend and the judge found that the loss actually claimed was not caused by anything which the defendants did or did not do as pleaded by the plaintiff. It is logical to suppose that, had counsel taken advantage of the judge's invitation, the judge would have allowed the amendment and would have awarded damages to the plaintiff on the amended basis. It would not, on the face of it, be possible to plead any amended case in the Court of Appeal.

The statement of claim

The statement of claim sets out the plaintiff's causes of action and the relief sought. It is the rock upon which the case is built. It is the case which the plaintiff's expert will support and the case which the defendant's expert has to deal with. If the plaintiff's expert cannot support the case, as pleaded in the statement of claim, the usual practice will be to amend the statement of claim to a case which the expert can support. The defendant's expert does not have to deal with the case which the plaintiff could bring if he thought about it. He has to deal with the case as stated in the statement of claim, the further and better particulars, and any subsequent amendments to the pleadings.

The statement of claim has to show the names of the plaintiffs and of the defendants, has to state the material facts in summary form, the particulars of negligence or breach of contract, particulars of the consequences and the remedies sought. Particulars must also be given of the following if they are alleged:

(a) misrepresentation;
(b) fraud, which must be distinctly alleged and not left to be inferred from the facts;
(c) fraudulent intention or malice;
(d) breach of trust or fiduciary duty;
(e) wilful default;
(f) undue influence;
(g) any condition of mind except knowledge; however, if knowledge or absence of it is material, it should be expressly alleged;
(h) negligence;
(i) convictions relied on under the Civil Evidence Act 1968;
(j) special damages;
(k) exemplary damages;
(l) aggravated damages;
(m) provisional damages;
(n) interest.

It is important that the right plaintiff be chosen. In an auditors' negligence case the plaintiff might be the company being audited, or its holding company, or both. Potential plaintiffs might also include directors (if they have had to pay under a guarantee) or shareholders as a class (if they have lost value in their shares).

It is important to consider the contractual relationship between the parties and, if there is no contract, whether a duty of care in tort is likely to be owed by particular defendants to particular plaintiffs. The purchaser of a company may wish to sue the company's auditors if what he acquires is not what he thought, but he will have to establish that the auditors owed him a duty of care, which they may or may not depending on the facts.

It is equally important to identify the right defendants.

> ***Example***
>
> An accountant was alleged negligently to have signed a reference for a client wishing to borrow on a mortgage. The reference was accompanied by a letter on the firm's notepaper, but at the time of the date on the letter the accountant had moved from that firm to a new firm. So far as the plaintiff was concerned, he was holding himself out as being a partner in the old firm. The plaintiff decided to name the individual accountant and his old firm as defendants. The case was settled by the insurers acting for the old firm.

The plaintiff will set out the duties which he alleges the defendant owed him in tort and/or details of the contract. The plaintiff will then set out the alleged negligence and/or breaches of contract in relation to specific facts. The plaintiff will then set out the losses allegedly suffered as a result of the breach of contract or negligence and quantify them. Breaches of contract and negligence may be irritating, but they do not always lead to loss. Obtaining nominal damages for breach of contract is unlikely to be worthwhile.

> ***Example***
>
> A company's auditors failed to spot an error in the stock calculation, with the result that the accounts do not show a true and fair view of the profit for the year. Unless a dividend was paid which would not otherwise have been paid, or management had taken a decision which it would not otherwise have taken, the only consequences are likely to be overpaid or underpaid tax. The accounts can be corrected in the following year and the auditor concerned will normally take a view on his fees, or part of them, if his client has suffered interest on late paid tax which would not otherwise have been suffered. If, however, the stock was wrong not because of error but because of fraud which had continued over a number of years then there might well be a claim from the time that the auditor first ought to have detected the fraud. The auditor is likely, in his defence, to claim contributory negligence by the company through its directors because it is their responsibility to safeguard the company's assets and, where fraud has occurred, they have clearly failed to do so.

The defence (and counterclaim)

Each defendant must file a defence though defendants acting through the same solicitors and counsel with the same defence may serve identical defences. Defendants who serve separate defences may instruct the same or different lawyers, but those serving the same defence must be represented by the same counsel.

The defence must deal with all the allegations in the statement of claim, because unless they are denied or not admitted they will be deemed to have been admitted. For the avoidance of doubt it is normal, in practice, to admit those parts of the claim where it is appropriate to do so. Facts which are known to be true have to be admitted.

The defence must plead specifically any defence which might take the plaintiff by surprise or which raises issues of fact not included in the statement of claim. Limitation, fraud or illegality must also be pleaded as must mitigation, limitation or reduction of damages, and contributory negligence.

If the defendant wishes to make a counterclaim he may do so either in the defence or by starting separate proceedings. In accountants' negligence cases the accountant's professional indemnity policy may provide insurance cover for legal costs in connection with defending proceedings alleging professional negligence. Such policies, however, rarely provide cover for the legal expenses of pursuing claims for fees. In practice, counterclaims for fees are more common than separate actions, and the question of payment of the costs in connection with the counterclaim is a matter for negotiation between insurers and their clients.

The reply (and defence to counterclaim)

There is no obligation on the plaintiff to reply to the defence because the statement of claim and defence are deemed to set out the respective positions of the parties, but a reply may be used to make admissions or to assert an affirmative case in answer to the defence. If a plaintiff only wishes to deny the allegations in the defence, then he does not need to serve a reply as all material facts alleged in the defence are put in issue.

The reply cannot, however, be used to make allegations which are inconsistent with the statement of claim, which can be amended if necessary.

It is necessary to defend any counterclaim, because if the counterclaim is not defended it will be treated as having been admitted.

Further and better particulars

If any party does not fully understand the case pleaded against him, a request for further and better particulars may be served. The numbers in the paragraphs in the pleading are identified and specific requests are made for further particulars of the allegation.

The other side is normally invited to respond to a request for further and better particulars and usually does so by recording each request and the reply.

If voluntary further and better particulars are not given, an order for provision of the particulars may be sought from the court.

There may be requests for further and better particulars of the further and better particulars until each side has adequate knowledge of the other side's case.

Appendices 10 and 11 contain examples of a writ and set of pleadings.

12.3.3 Discovery

Following the close of pleadings, each side has to serve on the other a list of all the documents relevant to the case which are or have been in their possession, custody or power. The list is divided into two schedules of documents which the other side can see (Schedule 1 Part 1), documents a party objects to producing (Schedule 1 Part 2) and documents which cannot be disclosed because they are no longer in the power, possession or control of the party (Schedule 2).

All relevant documents must be disclosed whether or not they advance the party's case, but discovery cannot be used to go on a fishing expedition, so that a plaintiff who does not have the documents necessary for an arguable case cannot obtain them from the other side through discovery.

While it is normally the solicitors who obtain the documents and consider whether they are relevant and/or privileged, advice may well be sought in an accountants' negligence case from an expert on whether particular categories of document are relevant. Advice may also be sought from an expert, once the lists have been exchanged, as to whether the other side is likely to have categories of documents which are relevant but which have not been disclosed.

Arguments about discovery are common and it may, in due course, be necessary for the solicitor or, in some cases, the expert accountant, to swear an affidavit in support of an application to the court for specific discovery of documents believed to exist but which have not been disclosed.

Once lists have been exchanged arrangements are made for the documents to be reviewed by the other side, which is entitled to see the originals. It is common, however, for photocopies to be exchanged, with originals only being inspected if it is not possible to interpret the photocopies properly. Typed versions of manuscript documents which are hard to read may be sought and will be supplied.

In accountants' negligence cases the accountant's working papers will usually be relevant and it may well be sensible for the experts to inspect original files, because the documents can then be seen in context in their original folders and the expert will obtain a better feel for the way the work has been conducted. He will also be better able to compare what the accountant has done with his own experience and his own firm's procedures.

Discovery is very important and may well lead to amendment to the pleadings.

> ***Example***
>
> In an accountants' negligence case, grounds for pleading fraud, as opposed to mere negligence, emerged on discovery. Fraud can only be pleaded where there is evidence to support the allegation and, although in civil litigation the burden of proof remains the balance of probabilities, if fraud is alleged, particularly against a professional person, the burden moves towards the criminal burden which is beyond reasonable doubt. Where fraud can be proved, all the losses which flow can be claimed and there will be no contributory negligence (see *Smith New Court Securities Limited* v *Scrimgeour Vickers (Asset Management) Limited* [1996] 4 All ER 769). The case referred to settled for about 80 per cent of the full value of the claim, although, absent suspicion of deceit, there would have been considerable argument, to say the least of it, regarding contributory negligence.

Lord Woolf proposes, in *Access to Justice*, that what he calls 'standard disclosure' should be limited to two classes of documents:

> '(a) the parties' own documents, which they rely upon in support of their contentions in the proceedings;
>
> (b) adverse documents of which a party is aware and which to a material extent adversely affect his own case or support another party's case.'

Lord Woolf identifies two further classes of documents which the court may exceptionally allow as extra disclosure, which are:

> '(c) documents which do not fall within categories (a) or (b) but are part of the "story" or background, including documents which, though relevant, may not be necessary for the fair disposal of the case;

(d) train of enquiry documents: these are documents which may lead to a train of enquiry enabling a party to advance his own case or damage that of his opponents.'

The authors understand that Lord Woolf's proposals regarding discovery are controversial.

12.3.4 Witness statements

The provisions for compulsory exchange of witness statements are contained in RSC Order 38 rule 2 and CCR Order 20 rule 12A. Witness statements will be taken by the solicitors acting for the parties. They will normally be drafted by solicitors following discussions of the facts to be elicited from the witness. Approaches may be made by solicitors acting for the parties to any potential witness who may be able to assist the party's case, but there is no property in a witness and the same witness might well be aproached by both sides.

'One volunteer is worth ten pressed men' is a maxim best borne in mind, although a witness may be 'pressed' by subpoena.

It is desirable that the expert witness should see the witness statements before they are finalised, not least because he will then be aware of changes as witnesses remember more facts and of the process by which the witness statements may be 'polished'. It is also important that the expert should see all the witness statements as exchanged before he finalises his report, although this may not be possible if the court has ordered the exchange of expert reports before the exchange of witness statements, as sometimes happens.

12.3.5 Expert reports

Where there are issues of an artistic, scientific or technical nature the court may require the assistance of expert opinion from practitioners in the relevant field. In the first instance, the views of the experts for the parties will be set out in expert reports. A model form of report is reproduced at Appendix 1.

The model form is not compulsory (and Lord Woolf does not propose to make it so), but it sets out usefully, in five sections, the matters which are usually relevant to a report:

Section 1 is the introduction, which contains:

(a) the expert's full name, status, specialist field, and details of the party instructing the expert;
(b) an overview of the case;
(c) the specific matters to be addressed in the report;
(d) disclosure of any conflicts of interest.

The curriculum vitae will be an appendix and should be carefully drafted in connection with each case to identify the particular skill and experience required to address the technical issues.

The standing of the expert in his field will be relevant.

> ***Example***
>
> In the *Lloyd Cheyham* case (see **12.2.2**) Mr Justice Woolf said:
>
> 'In addition they [the defendants] called as their expert witness Mr Christopher Swinson, who is a partner in the firm of Binder Hamlyn and is particularly well qualified to give expert evidence since he is the head of that firm's technical services unit which is responsible for setting and monitoring the technical standards of accounting, auditing and other financial report work which the firm undertakes. He is also a member of Council of the Institute of Chartered Accountants and plays an active role in the setting up of European Standards of accountancy practice.'

In another accountants' negligence case the curriculum vitae was used to unsettle the expert.

> ***Example***
>
> Leading counsel's questions and the expert's responses were as follows:
>
> 'Q It is correct that you are a senior partner in one of the largest accounting firms in the world?
> A Yes.
> Q And it is true that over many years you have specialised in share valuation?
> A Yes.
> Q And is it also true that you have valued shares for small corporations, large corporations, the British Government and foreign governments?
> A Yes.
> Q Would it be fair to say Mr Expert that you are one of the leading share valuation experts in the world?
> A I wouldn't put it quite like that.
> R Mr Expert, I am reading from your CV.'

The expert report should always be in the first person and by the person whose opinion is being sought. Where the opinions are those of others which are being adopted by the expert, this should be stated.

The second part of the expert report will deal with the background to the dispute and the issues by reference to contemporary documents and to the witness statements. Where there are disputes as to the facts these should be acknowledged.

The third part of the report will normally deal with technical matters, including the investigation carried out. The fourth part will state the facts upon which the expert's opinion is based and the technical rules, regulations and professional practices which, in the opinion of the expert, are relevant.

Part five will deal with the issues in turn and the expert's opinion on them.

It may be useful for the conclusions to be summarised in the introduction, not least because it sets in context the background, the technical investigation and the technical material referred to in the expert's report.

Where the issues are complex and the opinions lengthy, it may be appropriate to insert an 'executive summary' of the conclusions after the introduction.

Following exchange of expert reports, supplementary reports may be prepared and exchanged either before or after any meetings between experts, which are arranged between the parties or ordered by the court.

The format of supplementary reports will be determined by the issues covered in them. Because they will normally be read in conjunction with the original report there is normally no necessity to repeat anything from the earlier report, except to set the context for the second and subsequent reports.

12.3.6 Interrogatories

The purpose of interrogatories is to obtain information and admissions from the other side in advance of trial.

While interrogatories can be served at any time, and up to two sets can be served without seeking an order from the court, the answers to questions put in interrogatories are normally sought after pleadings have closed and after discovery.

Questions can only be asked about matters relevant to the action and are limited to discovery of facts.

In appropriate circumstances an expert accountant may be asked to assist in drafting interrogatories, which are used to obtain admissions.

A party on whom interrogatories are served without a court order may apply to the court for the interrogatories to be varied or withdrawn and the court can make such orders as it thinks fit.

12.3.7 Subpoenas

Subpoenas can be served on witnesses to compel their attendance at trial. A *subpoena ad testificandum* requires the witness to attend court to give oral evidence and a *subpoena duces tecum* requires a witness to produce specified or described documents at court.

The court has jurisdiction to order a witness to attend in answer to a *subpoena duces tecum* on a notional date well in advance of the trial (*Khanna* v *Lovell White Durrant* [1995] 1 WLR 121). A *subpoena duces tecum* may, for example, be used to force a bank to produce documents which are relevant but are not within the control of the parties, such as bank internal lending records. The drafting of such subpoenas requires care as they will not succeed if drafted so widely as to amount to an application for discovery.

Example

In a case involving an insurance claim by the proprietors of a laundry which had burnt down, documents were subpoenaed from the bank by the defendant insurer in connection with the financial affairs of the plaintiff both before and after the fire. The judge found, partly in the light of the documents disclosed, that the plaintiffs had been dishonest in connection with an earlier application for security for costs, and found that the substantive issues should be adjourned until such security was provided. No such security was provided and the plaintiffs effectively abandoned their case (not least because the judge also found that the plaintiffs had tried to deceive him in a number of other ways).

A *subpoena ad testificandum* is, in the authors' experience, used more rarely, not least because the witness is usually reluctant and those calling him may have no clear idea of what he will say in the witness box.

12.3.8 Notices to admit

Notices to admit are used to establish facts and clarify issues prior to trial.

Because notices to admit narrow the issues to be decided at trial, and save costs and reduce delays, they are favoured by the court. The consequences of making admissions is that the facts admitted are no longer in dispute, although the admissions may be amended or withdrawn on such terms as the court thinks fit. Admissions may not be used in other litigation.

The types of notices to admit are:

- notices to admit facts;
- notices to admit documents;

- notices of non-admission of the authenticity of documents;
- notices to produce documents.

Failure to admit facts which are subsequently proved at trial may result in the costs of that proof being borne by the party who failed to admit the facts, although the trial judge always has a discretion on whether to impose the costs sanction provided in the rules.

Likewise, if a party refuses to admit the authenticity of documents and that authenticity has to be proved at trial costs may be awarded.

The general rule is that the party relying on the contents of a document at trial must produce the original and a notice to produce a document is used to ensure that that original is available.

12.3.9 Trial bundles

Prior to trial, the court requires two trial bundles to be prepared. The first will include the formal documents such as the pleadings, the orders and any legal aid documents. This bundle has to be lodged when setting down the case for trial.

The second bundle will contain:

(a) exchanged witness statements;
(b) disclosed expert reports;
(c) contemporaneous correspondence and other documents considered by the parties to be relevant;
(d) a list of authorities;
(e) a chronology of relevant events.

The plaintiff is responsible for assembling the bundles, although the defendant is required to notify the plaintiff of documents which he wants included in the bundles, in addition to those wanted by the plaintiff.

The rules regarding the form that the bundles take are strict:

(a) the bundle must be contained in a ring-binder or lever arch file;
(b) documents must be arranged in chronological order with the earliest at the top;
(c) the bundle must be paginated consecutively at centre bottom;
(d) documents must be legible and of convenient size;
(e) transcripts must be clearly marked and placed immediately after the original;
(f) the bundle must be properly indexed.

Frequently, a core bundle of the most important documents will be prepared.

An expert to be called at trial should be familiar with the way the trial bundles are organised and should insist on being provided with a copy. He will then be able, when attending court before giving evidence, while giving evidence and while attending court later, to be alert to what is going on and to lay his hands on documents with the same ease as others present.

12.3.10 Skeleton arguments

Skeleton arguments are documents (which should not ordinarily exceed 20 pages of double-spaced A4) outlining each party's case by reference to documents in the trial bundle. The argument will also summarise the law relied on, citing authorities. Such skeleton arguments are now compulsory for High Court trials and they assist judges in preparation for the trial.

They are prepared by counsel, who may consult the expert on the technical arguments where appropriate. They have to be lodged with the court three clear days before the hearing. Copies of the skeleton arguments are sent to opposing counsel and an expert should also seek copies of the skeletons as part of his own preparation for trial.

12.3.11 Judgments and consequential orders

Judgments have been referred to earlier and will not, unless very short and simple, normally be handed down at the end of the trial. Until judgments are drawn up they cannot be enforced.

Orders are drawn up based on the judgment and deal, for example, with costs, any stay of execution of the judgment and with disposal of the third party proceedings and the costs thereof.

12.4 Procedures

The main stages in a negligence action in the High Court are:

- the issue of a writ or other originating process;
- service of the writ;
- service of pleadings;
- discovery;
- directions for preparation of the trial;
- exchange of evidence of fact and opinion;
- listing for trial;
- trial;
- taxing of costs.

12.5 Limitation

Earlier in this chapter an example was given of an extended delay between the cause of action and the trial and, in connection with High Court proceedings, the expert needs to be generally aware of time limits imposed by statute and by the rules. It is therefore worth considering, in connection with the issue of a writ, the time limit within which it has to be issued after the cause of action occurs. Expiry of a limitation period provides a defendant with a complete defence to an action, unless the time limit is subject to extension or exclusion, and, therefore, if an accountant is consulted by a client about the possibility of making a claim, it is important that he should realise that the client should seek immediate legal advice if there is any danger of a limitation period expiring.

Most limitation periods are laid down in the Limitation Act 1980, as supplemented by the Latent Damage Act 1986, and the Foreign Limitation Periods Act 1984.

The table at Figure 12.1 lists the limitation periods from the date when the cause of action accrues most commonly encountered by accountants acting as experts. It is stressed, however, that limitation is a legal issue and that in all cases accountants and their clients should seek legal advice.

Figure 12.1

Class of action	*Limitation period*
Fraudulent breach of trust	None
Recovery of land	12 years (action by Crown 30 years)
Recovery of monies secured by mortgage	12 years
Recovery of a sum due under statute	6 years
Enforcement of a judgment	6 years
Contract	6 years
Recovery of trust, property and breach of trust	6 years
Tort	6 years
Personal injuries claims	3 years
Fatal Accidents Act 1976 claims	3 years
Libel and slander	3 years
Personal injuries or damage to property claims under the Consumer Protection Act	3 years
Contribution under the Civil Liability (Contribution) Act 1978	2 years
Applications for judicial review	3 months (not absolute)

Unfair dismissal under the Employment Protection (Consolidation) Act 1978	3 months
Race/sex discrimination	3 months

In actions in tort for negligence there are two alternative periods of limitation, either the usual six years from accrual of a course of action or, where fact relevant to the course of action are not known at the date of accrual, three years from the 'starting date'. The starting date is the earliest date the plaintiff knew:

(a) that the damage was sufficiently serious to justify commencing proceedings; and
(b) that the damage was attributable to the alleged negligence; and
(c) the defendant's identity.

There is an overriding time limit for bringing proceedings of 15 years.

An expert accountant dealing with an accountants' negligence case may come across these extended time limits where, for example, the accountant's client suffers an ongoing fraud which is not discovered for many years.

Once the writ has been issued there are time limits laid down all the way to trial, although, in most cases, the time limits can be varied by agreement or on application to the court. The main time limits are shown in Figure 12.2.

Figure 12.2

Action	*Time limit*
Service of writ	Within 4 months of issue
Acknowledgement of service of writ	Within 14 days
Service of statement of claim	Within 14 days of acknowledgement of service of writ
Defence (and counterclaim)	28 days after service of writ or 14 days after service of statement of claim, whichever is the later
Reply (and defence to counterclaim)	14 days after service of defence (and counterclaim)
(Close of pleadings)	14 days after service of defence, defence to counterclaim or reply
Exchange of lists of documents	14 days
Inspection of documents	21 days
Exchange of experts' reports	14 weeks
Exchange of witness statements	14 weeks
Setting down	6 months

All the dates after close of pleadings are calculated from the close of pleadings.

12.6 Time limits

It is important that the expert should enquire from time to time as to the time limits, because they vary frequently due to difficulties of one party or the other.

In the authors' view, it is preferable for expert reports to be completed and exchanged after exchange of witness statements, because it will only be after the exchange of witness statements that the experts will be fully aware of the facts upon which their opinions are based (assuming the witnesses come up to proof).

Under Lord Woolf's proposals the court would take much tighter control of the proceedings from beginning to end, with a view to reducing both the time taken and the costs of litigation.

In addition to the formal proceedings as listed above, there will be informal proceedings in that there will be correspondence between solicitors, there may be meetings between solicitors with a view to initiating settlement and there may be informal meetings between experts by agreement between the parties.

Once proceedings have commenced, actions and counterclaims can be discontinued without the leave of the court if written consent is given by all the parties before trial. Leave to discontinue is required in third party and contribution proceedings, and is usually sought by summons to a Master.

If a plaintiff discontinues he usually has to pay the defendant's costs unless agreement is reached between the parties that the action should be discontinued on the basis of each side bearing its own costs (a drop hands settlement).

If a plaintiff seeks to discontinue, then it will normally be easier to obtain a drop hands settlement early in the proceedings than after substantial costs have been run up. If the court has to decide on the question of the basis of discontinuance then it has discretion as to what costs order should be made.

The costs sanction is important and should prevent frivolous claims which put defendants to substantial cost.

At the time of writing it is proposed to extend the circumstances in which solicitors can conduct cases on behalf of plaintiffs on a conditional fee basis – that is, that the solicitor is only paid if the plaintiff wins. The general experience to date appears to be that conditional fee arrangements have not led to frivolous claims being made.

A defendant can take steps to put pressure on a plaintiff and to reduce his own costs. He can:

- apply to strike out or dismiss the plaintiff's claim;
- make a counterclaim;
- apply for security for costs;
- make a payment into court.

12.7 Striking out

If there is inordinate delay in taking a case through to the trial the defendant may apply to the court to have the case dismissed, but he is unlikely to succeed unless he can show that the delay has prejudiced there being a fair trial.

The plaintiff's pleading may also be struck out if:

(a) it discloses no reasonable cause of action;
(b) it is scandalous, frivolous or vexatious;
(c) it is otherwise an abuse of the process of the court.

The court's function is to decide whether the case is so plainly unarguable that there is no point in having a trial, but the court is reluctant to deprive a plaintiff or defendant of the normal procedures. It is possible to seek to strike out part of an action and a counterclaim.

Example

That is what happened in the case of *Deeny* v *Walker*, *Deeny* v *Littlejohn & Co.* [1996] LR 276. Mr Deeny and other underwriting members of Lloyd's of London sought damages from the syndicate auditors of approximately £250 million. The auditors made an application to strike out the proceedings and succeeded to the extent of all but £8 million. The arguments at first instance took several days and the plaintiff's case, in respect of the matters struck out, was regarded by a judge, on appeal, as completely hopeless. The successful application to strike out much of the action saved what would otherwise have been very substantial costs, reduced the claim to well within the defendant's capacity to meet it and probably had a considerable impact on the expectations on Lloyd's Names generally contemplating actions against their professional advisers. In the event, there was a global settlement of proceedings relating to Lloyd's in which auditors, among others, participated.

The argument against striking out applications is that, if they fail, they give the advantage to the other side, because, in effect, a judge has already decided that there is a case to answer. Leave may be granted to cure defects in pleadings by amendment subject to orders as to costs.

12.8 Security for costs

The usual rule is that costs follow the event, which means that who will pay the bulk of the costs of an action will only be determined at the end of the trial when the successful party will generally be entitled to recover costs from the unsuccessful party. If at that stage the defendant wins, it would be unfair in many circumstances were he deprived of his costs because of the impecuniosity of the plaintiff. The plaintiff takes the initiative in the litigation and has to form his own opinion, as previously mentioned, as to whether the defendant is worth powder and shot. The ability to recover costs if he wins will be a factor in deciding whether to pursue a case.

There are five grounds on which security for costs can be ordered in High Court actions against plaintiffs, or against a person in the position of a plaintiff, such as a defendant making a counterclaim. Section 726(1) of the Companies Act 1985 says:

> 'Where in England and Wales a limited company is plaintiff in an action or other legal proceeding, the Court having jurisdiction in the matter may, if it appears by credible testimony that there is reason to believe that the company will be unable to pay the defendant's costs if successful in his defence, require sufficient security to be given for those costs, and may stay all proceedings until the security is given.'

The other grounds are that:

(a) the plaintiff is ordinarily resident outside the jurisdiction;
(b) the plaintiff is a nominal plaintiff who is suing for the benefit of some other person and that there is reason to believe that he will be unable to pay the costs of the defendant if ordered to do so;
(c) the plaintiff's address is not stated in the writ or it is incorrectly stated;
(d) the plaintiff has changed his address during the course of the proceedings with a view to evading the consequences of the litigation.

Security for costs cannot be ordered against a natural person, or partnership, except at the discretion of the court if, having regard to all the circumstances of the case, it is just to do so.

The defendant has to prove that a plaintiff will be unable to pay any costs which may ultimately be awarded in the defendant's favour. Proof that a company is in liquidation is prima facie evidence that it will be unable to pay any costs (unless contrary evidence is given), but otherwise credible testimony is required that a company will not (as opposed to may not) be able to pay the costs awarded.

Assistance from expert accountants may frequently be sought in connection with applications for security, and it will usually be necessary to examine the accounts filed at Companies House to see whether, on the face of it, an application for security of costs might succeed.

Even if a company appears to have insufficient net assets to pay the costs, an application will not succeed if the plaintiff can successfully argue that its impecuniosity arises as a result of the defendant's action, and it may therefore be necessary for the accountant to provide the 'credible testimony' required by the court to demonstrate that any impecuniosity is caused not by the defendant but for the other reasons set out in an affidavit in support of the security for costs application.

The court has discretion as to the amount and form of security to be provided, although it is open to the defendant to argue that a particular form of security offered does not meet the court's requirements. For example, a bond may be offered which is provided by an insurance company which may, because of its own financial position, not be able to or choose not to meet claims.

Defendants are naturally enthusiastic about security for costs applications where plaintiffs are companies, and accountants should be careful to ensure that any affidavit they swear does provide the credible testimony required by the court, not least because the same expert may have to give evidence at the trial in the main action, and if his evidence at an earlier interlocutory hearing was not accepted this may put him at a disadvantage in the main proceedings, by casting doubt on the quality of his opinions.

12.9 Payments into court

A defendant who fears that he may lose at trial may form a different view as to the amount which may be awarded against him to the view of the plaintiff, and can provide himself with some protection in connection with costs if he pays into court what he thinks the claim is worth. If the plaintiff is awarded more than the payment in then he will normally be awarded his costs in addition. If, however, the plaintiff is awarded less than the payment in he will not be awarded the costs beyond the date of the payment in, and he will be ordered to pay the defendant's costs from that date.

The plaintiff has 21 days to accept receipt of notice of payment in. If he accepts the payment in (which will be in respect of his claim plus interest) he will also get his costs.

There will be many cases (and not only those of accountants' professional negligence) where the expert accountant will be consulted regarding the amount of the payment in, because there will be many cases in which the expert has been involved in assessing the quantum of the claim, or at least some aspects of it.

It is important that the accountant should remember that the payment in does have to include interest, and the computation of that interest may well have to be considered on alternative bases. For example, simple interest might be calculated using the judgment rate of interest and compared with interest which would have been earned on deposit, or paid on overdraft. Interest has to be calculated to the date of payment in, so that a judgment which is more than the payment in, merely because of interest accrued between the date of paying in and the date of judgment, will not beat the payment in.

Where there are two or more causes of action a payment in may be made in respect of any or all causes of action.

A payment in may only be withdrawn with the leave of the court. For example, an application to withdraw a payment in might be made in the light of a judicial decision which changed the applicable law, or if the payment in was induced by fraud or if there was a mistake.

A plaintiff may seek to accept a payment in out of time, but he will not normally be allowed to do so if there has been an alteration in the risk, because the payment in is made in the light of the defendant's assessment of the risk at the time of the payment in. If there has been no substantial alteration of the risk then the plaintiff may accept the payment in but may have to pay the defendant's costs from the date of the payment in.

In actions for claims other than debt or damages, it is possible to make a written offer to settle expressed to be 'without prejudice save as to costs'. Such offers are called Calderbank letters (after *Calderbank* v *Calderbank* [1976] Fam 93) and are normally made by letter. Such letters will normally be effective in entitling the offeror to his costs after making the offer, if the offer is at least as favourable to the other party as the eventual order made by the court, and a payment into court could not be made.

During the course of proceedings there may well be without prejudice meetings and correspondence. Such meetings and correspondence may not be referred to in court without the consent of the parties involved.

Negotiations for settlement are normally carried out on a without prejudice basis, because settlements are effectively a compromise, and that is not what trials are about.

12.10 Reference

Rutherford, L. and Bone, S. (1993) *Osborn's Concise Law Dictionary* (8th edn), Sweet & Maxwell.

Chapter 13
Civil court practice – The White Book and the Green Book

13.1 Introduction

The previous chapter set out the way a piece of civil litigation proceeds, from writ to court. A number of procedural matters – such as discovery and costs – were mentioned, and are mentioned further in other chapters in this book. This chapter sets out where the detailed rules for civil procedure can be found, for both the High Court and the county court.

The two principal fora for civil litigation are the High Court and the county court. Each has a set of procedural rules and each rule is accompanied by practice direction notes and case law. For the High Court, these rules are called the Rules of the Supreme Court (RSC), consisting of Orders, subdivided into numbered rules and published with practice notes each year in the Supreme Court Practice, or what is commonly known as 'The White Book'. The county court equivalent are the County Court Rules (CCR) which are published together with practice notes each year in the County Court Practice, or what is known as 'The Green Book'.

The two sets of rules are broadly similar and in most cases identical, although there are a number of important differences. Furthermore, the rules are numbered differently and in some cases the subject matter covered by one RSC may be found in more than one CCR and vice versa. However, in general by s76 County Courts Act 1984:

> 'In any case not expressly provided by or in pursuance of this Act, the general principles of practice in the High Court may be adopted and applied to proceedings in a county court.'

An obvious question to ask is, why on earth two sets of rules? However, one might as well ask why have two types of court for civil proceedings when one, the High Court, routinely deals with large numbers of actions for which the other, the county court, appears better suited. The reason is that the justice system has been unable, to date, to come up with a single system of civil justice due to the complications of a merger of any kind.

However, the Woolf Report, though keeping the formal separation of the two court systems, does recommend a series of rules, the Civil Proceedings Rules, which are common to all civil litigation, and these are currently being developed. Indeed, Draft Civil Proceedings Rules have been published. These and other recommendations of the Report may be put into effect by the end of the century.

Two other matters should be mentioned. First, there is no need for accountants to have anything other than a cursory knowledge of a few of the rules, such as discovery and evidence. However, lawyers are free with their jargon, and the accountant may feel confused by references in a meeting to 'going for an Order 14' (summary judgment), or being asked to prepare an 'Order 23 affidavit' (security for costs). This chapter therefore takes, in most cases, only a superficial look at the rules, although some are considered in more detail, and gives an overview of the structure of the rules.

Second, despite the rules, non-lawyers, including expert accountants, must expect to be surprised by the frequency with which the rules, or their effects in the form of deadlines, are frequently ignored. Often this is by mutual, but unexpressed, consent, between the two sides. The authors have lost count of the number of times they have asked, on being instructed in a case, when the deadline for exchange of expert reports is, and been told it passed months ago, with neither side complying. However, many lawyers appear able unilaterally to flout the rules and get away with it, to the detriment of the other side in what must, on the face of it, be unfair circumstances. One of the authors was once instructed to prepare a reply report to an extremely detailed expert report running to many hundreds of pages and appendices. The author concluded that much of the report was severely deficient because of the use of some fairly basic incorrect accounting assumptions. The other side decided to drop their expert and wished to appoint another to prepare a new report. They applied to the court but permission was refused. They went ahead anyway and instructed a new expert, who produced a report on a completely new basis, some weeks before trial. The effect of this report, adducing much new evidence, was to delay the start of the trial by months, but the report was allowed in, apparently on the basis of the money it had cost to prepare.

Having said that, judges are not really sympathetic to those who flout and/or break the rules and there are costs penalties and, in the county court, the possibility of strike-out.

13.2 The two different types of court

Most accountants will be involved in High Court actions, for the simple reason that the High Court tends to hear the more important and complex civil disputes, and it is in these that expert evidence is often required. The

High Court is divided into three divisions and a number of specialist divisions. The three divisions are:

- Queen's Bench – which can hear any type of common law civil action;
- Family Division – which deals with matrimonial matters; and
- Chancery Division – which hears matters of equity, such as trusts.

The expert accountant, over the course of his career, can expect to be involved in proceedings in each of these divisions.

Two important subdivisions of the Queen's Bench, as far as the accountant is concerned, are the Commercial Court and the Official Referees Department. The former hears particularly specialised and complex commercial cases, the latter hears complex cases such as construction matters. The judges in these two divisions are specialists in these areas. The accountant, on instruction, will know which particular part of the High Court the action will be heard in from the case reference appearing at the top right-hand corner of the first page of each set of pleadings.

The High Court is one court, although it sits in a number of locations. For example, accountants in London, and many outside, will be involved in hearings in the Royal Courts in the Strand. However, the High Court also sits in major towns, such as Winchester, and the cities (district registries).

By contrast, the county court is a series of courts, sitting in towns across the country. Accountants have less experience of this court, although any accountant involved in personal injury work or cases involving accountants' fee disputes will probably come across a county court dispute.

13.3 The jurisdiction of the courts

In distinguishing between an action brought before the High Court and one brought before the county court, the most important consideration is the jurisdiction of the civil court system.

As a general rule the jurisdiction of the High Court is unlimited whilst that of the county courts is in practice restricted. However, there are a number of types of case where the county court has exclusive jurisdiction. The most important of these for the accountant is personal injury claims not exceeding £50,000. The detailed provisions as to jurisdiction are set out in the Green Book in the notes to s15 County Courts Act 1984 and the White Book at 5513.

The restrictions on the county court mean that it cannot hear actions for libel and slander and applications for Mareva injunctions and Anton Piller orders (see s15(2c) and s38 County Courts Act 1984). Further, there is a general presumption set out in s7(4) High Court and County Courts Jurisdiction Order 1991 that where an action has a value greater than £50,000 it shall be tried by the High Court. Also, in equity matters, generally the county court cannot hear cases with a value greater than £30,000 (s23 County Courts Act 1984).

As there is no presumption as to place of trial for claims ranging in value between £25,000 and £50,000 it is possible for relatively small cases to be commenced in the High Court. This often makes little sense, given the large backlog of High Court cases and the fact that the county court could resolve these matters relatively quickly. Not surprisingly, getting rid of this particular problem through case management has been one of the recommendations of the Woolf Report (see **6.2.1**).

13.4 An overview of the two sets of rules

The RSC comprise 115 Orders dealing with all of the various stages of litigation, from commencement of proceedings through conduct of the trial and enforcement. Their structure is shown in Figure 13.1.

Figure 13.1

Preliminary	Orders 1–3
Commencement and progress of proceedings	Orders 4–32
Trial	Orders 33–41
Judgments, Orders, Accounts and Enquiries	Orders 42–44
Enforcement of judgments and Orders	Orders 45–52
Divisional courts, Court of Appeal	Orders 53–61
Costs	Order 62
General and administrative provisions	Orders 63–68
Provisions as to foreign proceedings	Orders 69–74
Special provisions as to particular proceedings	Orders 75–115

The CCR comprise 51 orders and are set out in Figure 13.2.

Figure 13.2

Preliminary	Orders 1–2
Commencement of proceedings	Orders 3–18
Reference to arbitration or European Court	Order 19
Trial	Orders 20–21
Judgments and Orders	Orders 22–24
Enforcement of judgments and Orders	Orders 25–35

Rehearing, setting aside and appeal	Order 37
Costs	Order 38
Administration orders	Order 39
Special provisions as to particular proceedings	Orders 40–49
General and transitional provisions	Orders 50–51

13.5 The detailed rules

This section sets out some of those rules which accountants should be aware of. Reference is made primarily to the RSC, cross-referenced to the relevant rule of the CCR.

13.5.1 Commencement of actions in the High Court

RSC Orders 5 to 11 set out the way in which an action is to be commenced in the High Court. Civil proceedings in the High Court may be begun by writ, originating summons, originating motion or petition.

In practice, the majority are begun by way of one of the first two, and the writ is the most common method of starting an action that the accountant will see. A writ must be used where there is an allegation of fraud (Order 5 rule 2(b)) and where damages are claimed for breach of duty and damages for death, damage to property or personal injury (Order 5 rule 2(c)). An originating summons is used in actions which are likely to be uncontentious with regard to factual evidence or where the principal issue is likely to be the interpretation of law or a document (Order 5 rule 4). Motions are used to commence non-contentious probate actions and judicial reviews. Petitions are used in divorce cases (rule 2.2, Family Proceedings Rules 1991) and for insolvency matters, such as a winding-up petition (s124 Insolvency Act 1986).

When commencing proceedings in the High Court the writ of summons is issued by the plaintiff (i.e., the party bringing the action) having had the summons sealed by the court. The defendant (i.e., the party defending the action) must then respond by way of an acknowledgement of service stating whether or not the action will be defended, before commencing the defence (Order 12 rule 1).

In the county court litigation commences by one of four methods, being a summons (CCR Order 3 rule 3), an originating application (CCR Order 3 rule 4), a petition (CCR Order 3 rule 5) or a request for entry of appeal (CCR Order 3 rule 6). Again, the most common is the first, which is similar to the High Court writ. There are differences in the very first stage of a litigation between the High Court and the county courts. For example, there are differences in the content of the writ of summons and a county court summons. A more marked difference is that within the county court system there is no concept of acknowledgement of service, and the defendant is required to file his defence within 14 days of service of the summons (CCR Order 9). The basic procedure on how to commence litigation is set out under CCR Order 3.

13.5.2 Judgment following service

By RSC Order 13, a plaintiff can apply for judgment where the defendant fails to give notice of any intention to defend. RSC Order 14 deals with what is called summary judgment. A plaintiff can apply for summary judgment where the plaintiff can show that the defendant who has given notice (of intention) to defend has no defence to a claim. By RSC Order 19, a plaintiff can apply for judgment if the defendant fails to serve a defence.

Summary judgment in the county court is covered by CCR Order 9 rule 14, and judgment as a result of failure to serve a defence by CCR Order 9 rule 6. Because of the way in which civil proceedings are originated in the county court, that is, that there is no acknowledgement of service, there is no equivalent of RSC Order 13.

13.5.3 Other actions and third party proceedings

RSC Order 15 deals with the way separate causes of action involving the same parties can be joined and the way a defendant can bring a counterclaim against a plaintiff in the same action. These are designed to remove the need for separate trials. CCR Order 5 deals with joinder and CCR Order 9 deals with counterclaim.

RSC Order 16 concerns third party proceedings, that is, the way a defendant is able to bring into proceedings another party that he wishes to make a claim against in proceedings relating to the matter that is the subject of the proceedings against him, rather than start a separate action. CCR Order 12 deals with third party proceedings.

13.5.4 Pleadings

RSC Order 18 deals with the pleadings in the action, including the form of pleadings, matters which must be pleaded, particulars of pleadings, admissions and denials for claims, defences and counterclaims, and the closure of pleadings. RSC Order 20 is concerned with the amendment of pleadings.

These matters are dealt with in CCR Orders 6, 9 and 15, however, it should be noted that the CCR is by no means as comprehensive as the RSC as far as pleadings are concerned. This is because the county court places less emphasis on pleadings; statements of facts, which disclose a claim in law, and statements of defence, which disclose a genuine dispute, are all that is required. This appears to be to help litigants in person and, where a case in the county courts is complicated, it will probably follow the High Court procedure.

Many accountants are asked to assist with pleadings, either in helping to draft certain aspects of the pleadings, or commenting on the other side's. For example, where there is an allegation of accounting negligence, it is vital that the accountant who is the expert agrees with what is being stated in the pleadings. The pleadings will also contain particulars of damages, which the accountant will have helped to prepare. Furthermore, and this is an extremely important point, the pleadings will effectively set out the areas where the accountant will be giving evidence on behalf of his client. It is therefore worthwhile setting out what the pleadings are and what they contain.

The pleadings are those documents by which each side sets out its case. Therefore, the plaintiff sets out his case in a statement of claim, the defendant files his defence to the statement of claim in a defence, and if he wishes to make a counterclaim against the plaintiff he will prepare a defence and counterclaim (to which, of course, the plaintiff will prepare a defence to the counterclaim). If a defence raises issues to which the other side wishes to plead new facts then a reply will be prepared, otherwise it is assumed that the other side denies the matters in the defence (see RSC Order 18 rule 14(1)).

It should be noted that the reply only deals with new facts. If, for example, a plaintiff wishes to change matters in his statement of claim, having seen the defence, then he will apply to amend his statement of claim.

With leave of the court (Order 18 rule 4), a defendant can serve a further pleading to a reply, called a rejoinder. This is rarely used in practice.

In the county courts the respondent to an originating application may be required to file a type of pleading called an answer (CCR Order 9 rule 18).

RSC Order 18 rule 7 states that facts, not evidence, must be pleaded. Rule 8 lists out those matters which must be specifically pleaded. These are matters where one side alleges that any claim or defence made by the other side is not maintainable, any matters which might take the opposite party by surprise if not pleaded, and any matter which raises issues of fact not arising out of the preceding pleading. There is no equivalent rule in the CCR. Rule 11 states that points of law may be raised. There is no equivalent rule in the CCR.

RSC Order 18 rule 12 requires that pleadings must contain the necessary particulars of any claim, defence or other matter pleaded (CCR Order 9 rule

11). RSC Order 18 rule 13 states that allegations of fact made by a party in the pleadings are admitted by the other side unless 'traversed' (for which, see below). General statements of non-admission are not deemed to be a sufficient traverse (i.e., every allegation of fact made in a statement of claim or counterclaim which is denied must be specifically traversed – Order 18 rule 13(3)). There is no equivalent CCR rule, which means that a defendant can rely on an unpleaded defence or counterclaim in a county court action (but any good pleading would follow the High Court rules).

What all of this means is that pleadings must only deal with material facts in sufficient, but not excessive, detail. The reason for this is so that each side has a thorough understanding of what the other side's case is.

Thus, in an action for accounting negligence, it would not be enough just to state that XYZ & Co audited the accounts negligently. The pleadings would need to set out each material fact on which the plaintiff relies. Thus, the pleadings would state that XYZ & Co are a firm of auditors, that they were retained to audit the financial statement of the plaintiff, and particulars of negligence, etc.

For each matter pleaded in a statement of claim, as noted above, the defence will have to deny the allegation, otherwise it is deemed to be admitted. To deny a fact is called to traverse it, and the defendant does this by saying that he denies it, or that he does not admit it. If the defendant admits a fact, then he will say that he admits it.

The rule stating that facts, not evidence, must be pleaded is often difficult to comply with in practice. The distinction between the two is that a fact is a fact, but evidence is what is to be relied on to prove that fact. Thus, stating that a person is auditor to a company is a fact. Referring to correspondence, such as a letter of engagement or an invoice, to demonstrate that the person was the auditor is pleading evidence.

RSC Order 18 Rule 11 allows a party to raise a point of law in the pleadings, but not to plead law. This is designed to isolate an issue or question of law on the facts as pleaded. Pleading law is held to obscure the facts of the case. Points of law are generally raised in a defence, that is, on the facts as pleaded in the statement of claim a point of law arises which, for example, defeats the claim.

The pleadings are all-important to a case. If a point is not pleaded, then it cannot be raised at trial. This is the reason why the accountant must ensure that the pleadings are complete and drafted widely enough to enable him to give evidence. For example, in a sale and purchase dispute, if the accountant is going to give evidence that stock was overstated, then the pleadings must state that stock was overstated.

In the statement of claim, as well as pleading the facts of the case the plaintiff must plead the relief which he seeks. Of most interest for the accountant will be the damages. It is often not possible to specify the exact amount of damages and therefore an estimate is acceptable. Some pleadings often have various heads of damages, without specific figures under some of the heads (although particulars may be requested by the other side). Furthermore, in some types of case, such as personal injury cases, the claim for special damages is set out in a separate statement to which the pleadings may refer. A claim for interest must be pleaded.

In the defence the defendant, as noted above, will deny or admit the facts of the statement of claim. Within the admissions and denials the defendant will plead those facts which he wishes to rely upon. (An alternative is for the defendant to draft a defence which sets out his side of the facts, and then traverse the facts in the statement of claim by way of what is called a seriatim clause.)

The special position of the defendant's pleading in a county court action has already been noted.

Where any party pleads his case in insufficient detail, the other side can seek further and better particulars of the statement of claim or particulars of claim. These requests do not delay the close of pleadings in a High Court action. Failure to supply these will usually result in the person making the request seeking an order from the court that the particulars are supplied. In practice, what one side is looking for is a full set of facts that the other side intends to rely on at trial. For example, the allegation 'XYZ & Co were appointed to carry out a due diligence . . .' may result in a request for facts supporting this allegation if disputed and insufficiently pleaded. Further and better particulars will not be requested of simple denials in a defence, unless the denial is of a negative allegation, because such a denial may imply an affirmative statement. For example, the denial of an allegation 'XYZ & Co were appointed to carry out a due diligence . . .' will not result in a request for facts to support the denial. However, the denial of an allegation that '. . . XYZ & Co failed to file the necessary election by 30 June 1996 . . .' indicates that the denier did file the election, and he will be asked for particulars of this fact.

These requests are another area where the accountant can expect to have some involvement, in advising his solicitor on requests to make and on replies to give.

Finally, it should be noted that there is a certain amount of overlap between the objects of requests for further and better particulars and interrogatories, for which see **13.5.9** below.

Pleadings are deemed to be closed 14 days after the last pleading has been served (RSC Order 18 rule 20). In theory, this would mean that pleadings could be closed six weeks after the service of the statement of claim. However, see below on directions hearings for the way this is dealt with in practice.

It has been noted above that accountants can have a great deal of involvement in pleadings. Indeed, it is often only after an accountant has reported that one side is able to state the case it will rely on in court. Examples are where a report has been commissioned on loss, or where there is an allegation of negligence. Although possible, most personal injury reports by accountants are not prepared in advance of the issue of a statement of claim. Further, a report by an accountant on an accountant's alleged negligence will only be available after discovery has taken place, and some time after discovery. Pleadings therefore need to be amended.

Amendment to pleadings is dealt with by RSC Order 20 and CCR Order 15. High Court pleadings can be amended once without the leave of the court before the pleadings have been deemed to be closed. In county court cases amendments can generally be made at any time before a pre-trial review. Pleadings can also be amended by mutual agreement between the parties, provided that the parties to the action are not altered, or by seeking leave to amend. Generally, a party will be given leave to amend his pleading other than in specific circumstances, for example at trial or for amendments which are futile. The consequential amendments required to be made to the other side's pleadings will obviously be allowed. Costs of amendments are borne by the person responsible for making the amendment to the pleading, or the amendment which gives rise to the consequential amendment.

An amended statement of claim is called 'the amended statement of claim'. A further amended statement of claim is called 'the re-amended statement of claim' and further amended statement of claim 'the re-re-amended statement of claim'. Words struck out or added are colour-coded red, further amendments green, then violet then yellow (Masters' Practice Direction No 20, White Book 733).

13.5.5 Payment into court

The rules regarding payments into court and Calderbank letters are covered in RSC Order 22 (CCR Order 11). The reasons why payments into court and Calderbank letters are made is to protect one party against the other side's costs. Basically, if a defendant to a personal injury action makes a payment into court of £100,000 to settle the action then, as long as any award at trial is less than or equal to £100,000, the defendant will not be responsible for the costs of the plaintiff from the date of the payment in (i.e., the plaintiff gets his costs as usual up to the date of the payment in, but thereafter he bears his own costs and the defendant's). If the plaintiff accepts the payment in, then this settles the case and he will be entitled to his taxed costs. Thus, a plaintiff who wins an action in such circumstances may find all of his award of damages going to pay his own and the other side's costs.

Calderbank letters perform a similar function where the relief sought is non-monetary (i.e., where a payment into court is not suitable and, for example, an injunction or declaratory relief only is sought). The defendant makes his offer in a letter marked 'without prejudice save as to costs'. Failure to accept leads to the likelihood of the trial judge making similar orders as to costs as above.

The accountant has a role to play in advising on payments into court, although this role can sometimes be rather ambiguous to say the least. If an accountant prepares an expert report in a personal injury case, calculating a quantum of £500,000, what does he say to his solicitors if he is asked to advise on whether to accept a payment in by the other side of £250,000? Or, in the case of a plaintiff's expert who has calculated quantum of £500,000, what does he say if asked to advise on the amount of a payment in?

The accountant in each situation has calculated quantum, he will stand by his report and will defend his calculations in the witness box. If he advises some lower figure, does that mean that he believes that the court will not accept his calculations? If this is the case, then perhaps his calculations are wrong, and should be amended. There are two answers to this. The first is that payments in are tactics in litigation and all the accountant is being asked to consider is how this particular tactic should be employed, bearing in mind that often his calculations are not the only element of the loss being claimed. He is not being told that his figures are wrong. One of the authors was once involved in a personal injury claim where his calculation of lost earnings was zero. This was for the reason that, in his opinion, the earnings from alternative employment were far greater than the earnings which the plaintiff would have earned from the employment he was able to undertake before the injury. However, there were other elements to the claim, such as general damages and medical and retraining expenses. A round sum figure was agreed by the defence, offered to the plaintiff and accepted.

The other answer concerns the basis on which the accountant has prepared his report, that is, factual evidence. Such evidence may or may not be accepted at trial as a result of cross-examination. When advising on payments into court, the accountant is not being asked to act as judge, but he is certainly being asked about those points in his report which have a firm foundation, and those which do not, and to make an assessment of the financial effect of this. The accountant will also be aware that there are legal matters such as remoteness and contributory negligence which may affect the value of a claim, but for which he may not have made allowance in his report.

However, some accountants, perhaps under pressure from solicitors and counsel (and perhaps not) definitely do inflate figures, in the knowledge or hope that a high starting point may lead to a high payment into court. Of course, the corollary is true. In such circumstances it is their role as experts which is ambiguous.

Payments into court include interest but are always exclusive of costs (other than in the case of county court actions for debt) (CCR Order 11 rule 3(4)).

13.5.6 Security for costs

The procedures for security for costs applications, which are covered in detail in Chapter 9, are set out in RSC Order 23 and CCR Order 13 rule 8.

13.5.7 Discovery and inspection

Discovery is the formal process whereby each party to an action discloses the existence of documents which are, or were, in their possession, custody or power and which are relevant. Relevance is based on what is called the 'Peruvian Guano' test (*The Compagnie Financiere et Commerciale du Pacifique* v *The Peruvian Guano Company* (1882) 11 QBD 55), that is, any document which may advance a party's case or damage the other party's or lead the other party to a train of enquiry which may have either of these consequences.

Discovery is a formal procedure, involving each party preparing lists of documents within a fixed period of time after the close of pleadings, and the inspection of those documents after the swapping of lists. This is called general discovery. All relevant documents must be listed and they must be made available for inspection unless privileged. There are also procedures for challenging discovery, such as specific discovery (RSC Order 24 rule 7).

Chapter 27 refers to the very valuable role the accountant can play in specific discovery applications, especially where the disclosure of accounting documents is at issue.

The principles of discovery apply in both the High Court and the county courts. The relevant rules are in RSC Order 24 and CCR Order 14.

13.5.8 Directions

After the close of pleadings, but before an action is set down (High Court) or before a trial date is requested (county court), the action is in what is called the directions stage. Directions are essentially orders of the court for the further preparation of the action. High Court procedure on directions is set out in RSC Order 25 and county court procedure in CCR Order 17.

There are two major differences between the two sets of procedures. In the county courts, the vast majority of cases are subject to what are called automatic directions. In the High Court only certain types of cases are subject to automatic directions. The automatic directions comprise sets of timetables, as shown in Figure 13.3.

Figure 13.3

Direction	*High Court*	*County court*
Serving lists of discovery	14 days from close of pleadings	28 days from close of pleadings
Inspection of documents	7 days after serving lists	7 days after serving list
Service of expert reports	14 weeks after close of pleadings	10 weeks after close of pleadings
Service of factual witness statements	14 weeks after close of pleadings	10 weeks after close of pleadings
Fixing date for trial	6 months after close of pleadings	6 months after close of pleadings

The second major difference concerns the failure to comply with the automatic directions. If no request is made to fix a day for the hearing within 15 months of the close of the pleadings, or within nine months after the expiry of any period fixed by the court for making such a request, then this leads to an automatic strike-out of the action (CCR Order 17 rule 11). There is no such sanction in the High Court.

In the county courts, automatic directions apply to all cases other than those specified in CCR Order 17 rule 11(1), which include summary proceedings and fixed date actions where the time limit for a date for trial is already specified.

In the High Court, the automatic directions only apply to personal injury actions other than Admiralty actions and medical negligence cases (RSC Order 25 rule 8).

In most cases in the High Court, the plaintiff will issue a summons for directions. The hearing of the summons for directions enables the court to review the current preparation of the trial and to give directions for the future course of the action. Pre-trial procedure then proceeds by way of a series of orders for certain things to happen, for example the service of witness statements by a particular date.

It is this aspect of High Court procedure which is likely to make anyone cynical about the whole process of litigation. Despite orders being made, they are often missed or not complied with properly. Non-compliance tends to slow down litigation and obscure issues. The sanctions for non-compliance are often no more than costs directions. However, in some cases, unless an order is complied with the sanctions can be more severe, such as striking out or a refusal by the court to allow certain evidence in.

13.5.9 Interrogatories and admissions

Interrogatories are questions put by one side in an action to the other, relating to matters in question between the two parties. The rules are set out in RSC Order 26 and CCR Order 14. Interrogatories can be served without order on two occasions and afterwards by order of the court (RSC Order 26 rule 3; CCR Order 14 rule 11). Answer to interrogatories is by way of affidavit.

As with further and better particulars, accountants are often heavily involved in the drafting of interrogatories.

Admissions is the process by which one party admits the truth of part or whole of the other party's case. Further, one party will often serve on the other side a notice to admit certain facts or part of the case (RSC Order 27 rule 2; CCR Order 20 rule 2). The purpose of admissions is to cut down the length of time at trial proving facts. The rules on admissions are set out in RSC Order 27 and CCR Order 20. They are generally used in evidence at trial.

13.5.10 Applications in the course of proceedings (interlocutary applications)

One of the purposes of automatic directions is to avoid applications for orders in advance of trial. However, in many cases where automatic directions apply, such applications will be made. The rules for making such applications are set out in RSC Order 32 and CCR Order 13. The procedures are broadly the same and hearings of applications are in chambers either by a Master or a district judge or judges in chambers.

13.5.11 Trial

The procedural rules concerning the trial of an action are shown in Figure 13.4.

Figure 13.4

	High Court	*County court*
Place and mode of trial	RSC Order 33	Covered in CCR Order 4 (venue of bringing proceedings)

Setting down for trial	RSC Order 34	Covered in CCR Order 17 (pre-trial review)
Proceedings at trial	RSC Order 35	
Hearing of action or matter		CCR Order 21
Trials before and enquiries by referees and Masters	RSC Order 36	

The detailed rules under RSC Order 33 allow the court to determine, for example, whether an action is heard by a specialist court, such as a referee, whether assessors are to be present to assist the judge, whether a jury is present and whether there should be separate trials dealing with liability and quantum. Certain of these modes of trial are envisaged in the CCR, such as a jury trial or the use of assessors.

The rules governing the procedure at trial, RSC Order 35 and CCR Order 21, go into considerable detail on matters such as the order of speeches, inspection of places by the court, modes of address, court dress and the use of tape recorders.

13.5.12 Evidence

There are detailed procedural rules concerning evidence. RSC Order 38 is entitled 'Evidence' and sets out the procedure for the examination of witnesses, use of affidavits and the use of expert evidence. The equivalent county court rule is CCR Order 20. Other parts of the White Book deal with specific aspects of evidence, such as Order 39 (evidence by deposition, incorporated in CCR Order 20 rule 13), the use of court-appointed experts in Order 40 (no equivalent CCR) and Order 41 (regarding affidavits, applied to county courts by CCR Order 20 rule 10). The rules concerning admissions, which are part of evidence, are in RSC Order 27, and CCR Order 20 Part 1. The rules regarding expert evidence are set out in Chapter 2.

13.5.13 Costs

Costs are dealt with in the High Court by RSC Order 62, much of which is applied to the county court by CCR Order 38. The main difference between the treatment of costs in the High Court and the county court is in the smaller types of case, where the judgment does not exceed £3,000. In these cases, Scale 1 and the lower scale apply (which regulate the amount of cost allowable for certain items of work). In other cases, costs on Scale 2 apply and are now taxed on the same basis as High Court costs.

13.6 A final word

Even a brief look at the various procedural matters which an accountant will come across in practice is a substantial exercise. The rules themselves, as noted above, are extremely detailed, and there are various subtle differences between the procedures in the two types of court. The civil system will benefit from a unified set of rules, but this is unlikely to happen. However, the Woolf Report recommends a single set of rules applying to those matters common to both courts, and this is discussed in Chapter 6.

Chapter 14
Arbitration and Alternative Dispute Resolution (ADR)

14.1 Introduction

The parties to a dispute may, for a variety of reasons, such as cost, time or confidentiality, choose not to have it resolved through the courts. Instead, they may resort to arbitration. This is a means by which they can resolve the dispute through an arbitrator, who is an independent party appointed by them or on their behalf. The arbitration process is private, unlike a court hearing, and the arbitrator's decision, which is known as 'an award,' is usually final and binding upon the parties.

Alternative Dispute Resolution (ADR) relates broadly to any method of resolving a dispute by agreement, rather than by means of a binding decision imposed on the parties by an arbitrator in an arbitration, or by a judge in litigation. ADR includes mediation, conciliation and executive tribunal.

Accountants could be involved in arbitration, either as expert witnesses or by acting as arbitrators. They could also have a role in ADR, either in advising clients on the process or by acting as mediators, conciliators or experts in expert determinations.

14.2 Arbitration

Arbitration is a contractual process by which a dispute is resolved by an independent person, selected on the basis of expertise, reputation, training and experience as an arbitrator. The arbitrator's power to conduct the arbitration and to give directions to the parties derives principally from the contract under which he is appointed, but also from the law contained in the Arbitration Act 1996. This Act applies to arbitrations which have their seat in England, Wales and Northern Ireland. Under the Arbitration Act 1996, arbitration awards are legally binding upon the parties and under the New York Convention of 1958 they may be enforceable in the courts of other countries.

An arbitrator is usually selected by the parties by agreement or, where they cannot agree, is nominated by an appointing authority. The method of appointing the arbitrator may be specified in the arbitration agreement. Appointing authorities could include the Presidents of the Institute of Chartered Accountants in England and Wales, the Law Society or the Chartered Institute of Arbitrators.

14.2.1 The arbitration process

Arbitrations take place pursuant to an agreement between the parties to refer an existing or future dispute to arbitration. This agreement, which should preferably be in writing, is termed an 'arbitration agreement'. Parties to an agreement often include an arbitration clause specifying that any disputes arising from the agreement will be referred to arbitration.

The Chartered Institute of Arbitrators suggests the following wording for such an arbitration clause:

> 'any dispute arising out of or in connection with this contract shall be referred to and finally resolved by arbitration under the rules of the Chartered Institute of Arbitrators, which rules are deemed to be incorporated by reference into this clause.'

Once the arbitrator has been appointed, he will decide upon the procedure to be adopted in the arbitration in accordance with the wishes of the parties. Alternatively, the procedure may be governed by a set of institutional 'Rules' which the parties agreed upon in advance. The Arbitration Act 1996 also empowers arbitrators sitting in England, Wales or Northern Ireland with procedural powers to conduct the arbitration.

The institutional Rules could cover:

- commencement of arbitration proceedings;
- appointing authority;
- appointment of the arbitrator;
- communications between the parties and the arbitrator;
- arbitration procedure;
- representatives of the parties;
- hearings;
- witnesses;
- deposits and security;
- the award;
- arbitration costs.

Both the format and conduct of the arbitration are flexible and may be decided by the parties. For example, if the dispute is relatively simple, and the sums involved are small, the parties may agree that the arbitration is to be conducted on a 'documents only' basis. This means that both parties will submit their case in writing to the arbitrator, who makes his decision based on the written submissions. On the other hand, if the issues are complex, or the amounts involved are large, a formal hearing would usually be held. This process is similar to a court hearing, with the arbitrator hearing oral evidence from witnesses and considering the submissions of the parties.

In a typical arbitration, following his appointment, the arbitrator will call a preliminary meeting of the parties to agree the most effective procedures for the conduct of the arbitration. The matters to be discussed at the preliminary meeting will depend on the nature of the dispute and the particular circumstances. The agenda could include:

- identification of the issues in dispute;
- whether counsel are to be briefed;
- timetable for points of claim and defence;
- further and better particulars;
- documents and discovery;
- experts and experts' meetings;
- conduct of hearing;
- timetables;
- costs;
- venue for proceedings;
- language for proceedings;
- any other business.

Following the preliminary meeting, the arbitrator will issue directions to the parties, in which he will set out the matters discussed and agreed at the meeting.

It is for the arbitrator to decide all procedural and evidential matters upon which the parties have failed to agree in advance. In any event, the arbitrator remains responsible to ensure that the arbitration is conducted in a manner that will avoid any unnecessary delay and expense.

The procedure generally seeks to avoid reproducing the lengthy procedures of a trial. However, the tribunal is under a duty to ensure that each party is given a 'reasonable opportunity of putting his case and dealing with that of his opponent' (s33(1)(a) Arbitration Act 1996).

14.2.2 Role of the arbitrator

An arbitrator is often selected because of knowledge derived from his primary occupation, but this is not the only consideration. The arbitrator should utilise his knowledge only to the extent that it facilitates his understanding of the issues. This applies to all arbitrators and not only to accountants.

The arbitrator must always act judicially, with complete impartiality and fairness to both parties. He must act in accordance with the law and the rules under which the arbitration is conducted. His role is to consider the evidence put before him and to make a judgment on the issues based on that evidence. An accountant could only act as an arbitrator if he is free from any conflict of interests and has not acted for either party.

The arbitrator will conduct the arbitration subject to the rules applicable to that arbitration. This will include calling meetings of the parties to discuss the conduct of the arbitration, issuing directions to the parties and considering statements of case, or other similar documents setting out both parties' arguments.

The timetable for the arbitration, the number of witnesses and the method of taking evidence will all be decided during meetings with the arbitrator. After the hearing, the arbitrator will give his decision, or award, in writing to the parties. The arbitrator's award will also, unless the parties agree otherwise, include the reasons for arriving at the conclusions.

14.2.3 Comparison of arbitration and litigation

There are a number of differences between arbitration and litigation:

(a) *Confidentiality*. In litigation the hearing is conducted in open court and, therefore, the public and the press may be present. An arbitration, however, is private, the hearing is not open to the public and, unless the parties otherwise agree, the dispute remains a private matter.
(b) *Flexibility and speed*. The manner in which the arbitration is to be conducted can be agreed between the parties and can be adapted to suit their needs and requirements. For example, the dates of meetings and the dates of the hearing will be decided by the arbitrator in consultation with the parties. If the parties want a speedy resolution of the dispute, they can agree on any timetable they choose. This is a major advantage over court proceedings where the parties are always subject to the court's own timetable.
(c) *Finality*. The arbitrator's decision is final and binding upon the parties and can be legally enforced in the courts. Therefore, on conclusion of the arbitration, the dispute is at an end. The right of appeal from an arbitrator's award is limited, whereas there is a general right of appeal on every decision of a High Court or county court judge.
(d) *Business relationship*. Parties often feel that arbitral proceedings are more conducive to the preservation of a business relationship than litigation.
(e) *Expertise*. An arbitrator is often appointed for expertise in a particular field, which may help in understanding the issues in dispute.
(f) *Costs*. Arbitration can result in a more cost-effective resolution of a

dispute than litigation, particularly if the parties agree to a simplified procedure. On the other hand, an arbitration could be more expensive for one or the other party, as the fees of the arbitrator are paid by the parties.

14.2.4 Arbitration Act 1996

The Act applies to all arbitrations commenced after 31 January 1997 and its objective, as set out in the preamble to the Act, is 'to restate and improve the law relating to arbitration . . .'.

It replaces previous Arbitration Acts and its aim is to consolidate English arbitration law into one Act. It applies to all arbitrations which have their seat in England, Wales or Northern Ireland. Certain sections of the Act apply even if the seat of the arbitration is in another jurisdiction, but in such cases the powers of the court are exercised in a limited way.

The objective of the Act is to make the arbitration system in the UK more user-friendly by giving the parties more flexibility to decide how the arbitration should be conducted. The intention is also to make arbitration in the UK more attractive to international participants.

The Act also seeks to reduce the involvement of the courts in the arbitral process and to ensure that the parties are given sufficient autonomy and flexibility to resolve their disputes in a manner which best meets their own needs.

The Act is founded on the following general principles, which are set out in s1 of the Act:

(a) to obtain the fair resolution of disputes by an impartial tribunal without unnecessary delay or expense;
(b) freedom of the parties to agree how their disputes are to be resolved, subject to any safeguards that are necessary in the public interest;
(c) the courts should not intervene, except as set out in the Act.

The general principle that the parties are free to make their own arrangements is embodied in a number of provisions, which allow the parties to make their own arrangements and rules. However, there are a number of mandatory provisions that will apply to all arbitrations, for example:

(a) *Stay of legal proceedings*. Upon an application by a party, the courts will stay any legal proceedings in relation to a dispute which the parties have already agreed to refer to arbitration.

(b) *Liability of parties for fees and expenses of arbitrators.* The parties will be jointly and severally liable to the arbitrators for their fees and expenses.
(c) *Immunity of an arbitrator.* An arbitrator is not liable for errors and omissions in the conduct of an arbitration, unless he is shown to have acted in bad faith. This immunity extends to an employee or agent of the arbitrator.
(d) *General duty of the tribunal.* The duty of the tribunal is to act fairly and impartially between the parties, giving each party a reasonable opportunity of putting its case and dealing with that of its opponent. The tribunal must also adopt procedures suitable for the circumstances of the particular case, avoid unnecessary delay and expense and provide a fair means for the resolution of the matters in dispute.

There are a number of other provisions relating to removal or death of the arbitrator, jurisdiction of the tribunal and various legal and administrative matters.

14.2.5 Accountants in arbitration

Accountants may be involved in any of a number of roles in arbitration. In each role, however, it is necessary to have an understanding of arbitration and the arbitration process.

An accountant in public practice may be called on to advise a client in dispute with another party or to act as an expert witness for a client. A knowledge of arbitration law and practice will help in considering and advising on the various options available for resolution of the dispute. If the accountant is giving expert evidence, a knowledge of the conduct of arbitration proceedings and the requirements of the arbitrator in relation to expert evidence will be essential. The arbitral proceedings may differ significantly from those in litigation and a knowledge of both is required by any accountant involved in a client's dispute.

There are also opportunities for accountants to act as arbitrators. The accountant seeking to become an arbitrator will require certain personal skills, the most important of which is the ability to act with complete impartiality, irrespective of the circumstances. It is also necessary to be able to grasp quickly the issues in dispute and the arguments put forward in order to form a balanced view on the matters to be determined. It is also important to be able to weigh up written and oral evidence in order to reach a conclusion and write an award. Training courses for prospective arbitrators are described later in this chapter.

14.2.6 Arbitration schemes

There are a number of arbitration schemes in operation. Many of these are intended for use in settling disputes, often for small amounts, between subscribers to the schemes and their customers. Some of the schemes provide for disputes to be decided only by reference to written submissions and documentary evidence supplied by the parties.

The arbitration schemes include:

(a) consumer and general schemes:
 - (i) travel industry;
 - (ii) telecommunications;
 - (iii) construction;
 - (iv) professional bodies;
 - (v) financial services;

(b) personal insurance arbitration services – these apply to various member companies, such as insurance companies in disputes with their customers;

(c) commercial schemes – these include organisations such as franchise associations, or industries such as the petroleum industry.

Many arbitration schemes, where the dispute is of a financial nature, will provide an opportunity for an accountant to act as arbitrator.

14.2.7 Expert determination

Expert determination is a variation to the arbitration process. The difference is that, whereas an arbitrator hears evidence and makes a decision based on that evidence, in an expert determination the disputing parties agree that the dispute resolver should use his own knowledge to form a view on the dispute and deliver a decision, which will be binding. In an arbitration, the arbitrator hears evidence and makes a decision based on the evidence alone. The arbitrator's knowledge and experience is used only in interpreting the evidence presented by the parties to the dispute.

In an expert determination, the person appointed to decide the dispute will usually carry out his own investigations and form his own view, taking into account not only the evidence presented by the parties to the dispute. In an expert determination the procedure is usually more informal than in an arbitration. An example of a dispute which could be resolved by way of expert determination is that of a share valuation, where an accountant could be appointed to establish the value after making whatever enquiries he felt necessary.

14.3 Alternative Dispute Resolution (ADR)

14.3.1 Introduction

ADR is any method used to resolve a dispute by agreement between the parties rather than by a decision imposed by a judge or arbitrator. It is actively promoted and encouraged by the courts as an alternative to litigation and arbitration. Because it is quick and cost-effective, parties are encouraged to resolve their disputes by this method. Only if ADR is unsuccessful will the parties proceed to litigation or arbitration. It is likely that the proportion of disputes resolved by ADR will increase as more people become familiar with the process and as the courts encourage parties to utilise it.

ADR can be used during litigation or arbitration as well as before such formal proceedings. The courts encourage ADR by insisting, before the trial date is arranged, that the parties explain what they have already done to try to resolve the dispute.

14.3.2 Types of ADR

Alternative Dispute Resolution includes a number of different methods, for example:

(a) *Conciliation*. The use of an independent and neutral third party to assist the disputing parties in identifying the issues in dispute and in resolving their differences. The conciliation is 'without prejudice' and is non-binding, but the conciliator may deliver an opinion on the merits of the dispute and recommend how it should be settled.

(b) *Mediation*. A voluntary process in which a neutral third party, the mediator, assists the parties to reach a negotiated settlement. The procedure is similar to that of a conciliation, but the mediator who facilitates the negotiation process does not offer his opinion on the merits of the dispute, as the parties are to reach their own solution and settlement. The mediator is not empowered to make a judgment on the issues, but plays an active role in assisting the parties to reach an agreement. Mediation is the most widely used form of ADR and is discussed in more detail below.

(c) *Executive tribunal*. Also known as an executive hearing, or a mini-trial: a voluntary, non-binding settlement procedure which allows the disputing parties to present their case before an executive from each party. This is usually done in the presence of a neutral third party, who facilitates the discussions and assists in assessing the merits of the cases presented. These discussions are usually carried out within a strict timetable and may include an evaluation of the merits of the case or the likely outcome of litigation.

(d) *Expert determination/adjudication*. The use of an independent expert, or adjudicator, appointed by the parties, to give his opinion. This differs from ADR in that the expert's opinion is legally binding upon the parties. It is often an interim process in dispute resolution.

14.3.3 Mediation process

Parties to a dispute may choose to resolve it by mediation rather than by recourse to the courts or arbitration. The mediator will not make a judgment on the merits of the case. Instead, the objective is to assist the parties in reaching their own solution, rather than to impose one on them. The mediator will be someone who is completely neutral and who can be trusted by both parties. He should therefore have no connection with the parties or their advisers and would act as an 'honest broker' in assisting the parties to reach agreement. As the role to be played by the mediator involves a large number of skills, it should only be carried out by one who has had the necessary training.

For a mediation to be successful, the parties must want to reach a settlement. In a typical mediation, each of the parties would prepare for the mediator a written outline, or summary, of their dispute from their point of view. They may submit some key documents as well. The mediator is then able to have some knowledge of the dispute prior to the formal mediation taking place. It is unnecessary for the mediator to have detailed information or documentation, as he is not being called on to adjudicate on the dispute. He needs only to have an understanding of the issues. It is essential, however, that the parties' representatives attending the mediation are sufficiently senior and that they have the authority to settle the dispute. If they do not, the mediation is unlikely to succeed.

The mediation would normally be conducted at a neutral venue where three meeting rooms are available. One room is used for meetings of both parties and the mediator, and each party will also have its own room. It is usually unnecessary to have experts at the mediation, as the details of the merits of the various issues are not being discussed. However, the participants may require the presence of their legal advisers. The mediation will usually start with a joint session with the mediator and both parties. The mediator will make the introductions and invite each party to make a brief presentation on the dispute as they see it. The mediator may ask questions in order to ensure that he has a good understanding of the issues in dispute and the position of both parties.

After the initial presentations, the mediator may have private discussions, or 'caucuses', with each of the parties in a separate room. During a caucus the parties will be encouraged to be open with the mediator, as any disclosures they make are confidential and will not be passed to the other party without their prior agreement.

The mediation process is flexible and will depend on the circumstances in each case. Therefore, there may be a number of caucuses between each party and the mediator and these may be followed by joint sessions in which the mediator summarises the current position to both parties together. He may make comments within the frameworks agreed with him by the parties.

During both the joint discussions and caucuses, the mediator will be using his efforts to narrow the differences between the parties and to reach an agreement that both parties can live with. It is essential to understand that there is no right or wrong answer, nor any winner or loser in a mediation. The objective is merely to reach a settlement on whatever terms are acceptable to the parties.

There is no compulsion upon the parties to reach agreement and they are free to leave the mediation at any time. However, the skills of the mediator will be employed to try to ensure that this does not happen and that an agreement is reached. Once this occurs, the parties may empower the mediator in the presence of the parties to draft a written agreement which, when signed by the parties, will then become binding upon them. If the parties wish to ensure that the agreement they have reached will be enforceable, they could appoint the mediator to act as an arbitrator in order to make a 'consent award', which would be legally enforceable.

On conclusion of the mediation, the mediator would offer to destroy his notes, apart from a copy of any agreement reached. In the event of agreement not being reached, the mediator may not act as an expert in any capacity for either side in any subsequent proceedings. These actions ensure that the mediation is confidential.

It is usually agreed in advance that the discussions between the parties during the mediation will be 'without prejudice' to the parties' rights. This means that things said, or concessions made, in an attempt to reach a settlement cannot be used against the party making such statements or concessions in subsequent legal proceedings. It is usually also expressly provided in the agreement to mediation that the mediator cannot be required to give evidence as a witness or to produce his notes in any litigation or arbitration proceedings.

14.3.4 Comparison of ADR and litigation/arbitration

There are a number of differences between the characteristics of ADR and litigation and arbitration. These include:

(a) *Voluntary*. The mediation process is voluntary and either of the parties may terminate the mediation process at any time for whatever reason.

(b) *Consensual*. The whole process operates with the consent of the parties. No solution or decision can be imposed on them and the mediator merely tries to achieve a settlement to the dispute that both parties can accept. There is no winner or loser as there may be in litigation or arbitration.
(c) *Creative solutions*. The parties may agree to creative solutions in settling their dispute. For example, they may wish to continue their business relationship and part of the resolution of the dispute may be for one party to agree to continue trading with the other, or even for the parties to develop new business possibilities.
(d) *Confidentiality*. The mediation process is confidential.
(e) *Speed and cost*. Mediation can be a cost-effective method of resolving a dispute. The parties can embark on a mediation at any time and, because no evidence is being presented or heard, it is often possible to resolve the dispute by mediation within a day or two. This should be contrasted with arbitration and litigation, which will generally be conducted over many weeks or months. If the mediation is successful, this could result in a significant saving in costs over arbitration or litigation.

14.3.5 Accountants in ADR

There are opportunities for accountants in ADR in much the same way as in arbitration. It is essential for accountants to have an understanding of ADR and the process of dispute resolution so as to be able to advise their clients. In order to be able to participate in either process, accountants must appreciate the essential differences between ADR and litigation and arbitration.

Where an accountant acts as an expert witness, the report produced will be of assistance in establishing liability or in quantifying the damages, but it is unlikely that the accountant would be directly involved in the process of a mediation. There is generally no need for experts of any discipline to attend the proceedings, as the mediator will take no evidence. However, the accountant may be asked to assist a client in preparing for the mediation. This could involve extracting the key financial issues in the case and evaluating both the strengths and weaknesses of the case, within the accountant's area of expertise.

There are also opportunities for accountants to be involved in ADR as mediators. As the number of mediations increases, there is likely to be a greater demand for mediators, particularly those skilled in financial disputes. It is important for an accountant to recognise the essential differences between acting as an expert witness, as an arbitrator or as a mediator. The accountant acting as an expert witness is discussed elsewhere in this book. Where an accountant is acting as an arbitrator he will be considering the evidence impartially and will reach a conclusion in much the same way as a judge would deliver a judgment. An accountant acting as a mediator shares some of the same characteristics as one acting as an arbitrator. These include being professional and acting with integrity and impartiality. Good communication skills are also essential.

The mediator also requires other skills, which differ from those of an arbitrator. Because the mediator cannot impose a solution, it is important to be able to gain and maintain the confidence of the parties. It is also necessary to be able to distinguish clearly between issues that are in dispute and those on which the parties agree. The mediator also must listen to and hear the parties and, at the same time, avoid any value judgments. It is also helpful to be creative in exploring alternative solutions, which could assist in resolving the dispute. The mediator must be able to cope with a process that is physically and mentally draining. A mediation could continue without interruption throughout the day and late into the night. It may not be appropriate to stop the process if discussions are reaching a crucial stage.

The mediator also needs to have sufficient authority in his bearing to control the parties and to diffuse tensions when they threaten to overwhelm the process. Ultimately, the mediator will use his personality to lessen tension and aggression in trying to guide the parties to a solution which is acceptable to them.

There are opportunities for accountants in ADR. However, to become a successful mediator requires the acquisition of particular skills, quite apart from the training that is available for prospective mediators.

14.4 Training

This section sets out the general steps required to undertake training in the areas of arbitration and ADR. There are a number of one-day courses that are offered by many of the companies and organisations that provide accounting and legal seminars. These generally cover topics such as an introduction to, or aspects of, arbitration or ADR. They may assist an accountant in obtaining a general understanding of these areas of expertise.

More detailed courses available for training in arbitration and ADR are set out below.

14.4.1 Arbitration

The Chartered Institute of Arbitrators organises the following courses:

(a) *Associate.* The Institute runs courses which are usually held over a weekend and which conclude with an examination. The topics covered include the Arbitration Act, dispute resolution, powers and duties of the arbitrator, pleadings, meetings, costs and interest, an introduction to the hearing, evidence and writing an award.

(b) *Fellowship*. The courses leading to a fellowship are much more comprehensive and demanding than those for Associature. They are designed to assist candidates to develop a judicial ability. The examinations comprise various papers covering areas of law, including tort, contract, and evidence, the law of arbitration, arbitration practice and procedure, expert witnesses, analysis of evidence leading to the publishing of an award and the writing of an award.

The preparation for the fellowship examinations is by attendance at evening courses, concentrated weekend courses and revision seminars. Once candidates have passed the examinations they are expected to complete a Fellowship Assessment Programme.

The length of the period of study required to complete the Fellowship will depend on the amount of time the candidate is able to devote to it. Typically, it will take one to two years to complete the course.

14.4.2 ADR

Training to become a mediator is offered through organisations such as the Centre for Dispute Resolution (CEDR) and The Academy of Experts. Although the courses may differ, they provide the same broad training for mediation.

The courses include a comparison of methods used for resolving disputes and contrast ADR with litigation and arbitration. They enable the student to obtain a detailed knowledge of the skills required and the process of conducting a mediation. The courses tend to be practical, making use of role-play and case studies. The participants will be expected to take on the roles of claimant, respondent and mediator, using different case studies, in order to obtain practical experience of various mediation situations. At the end of the course, candidates are assessed on their conduct of a mock mediation.

The mediator training takes about five days, which may be spread over a period of time. Once either body has accredited mediators, they would be expected to either conduct mediations to maintain their knowledge or to continue to attend courses by way of continuation training. Both The Academy of Experts and CEDR maintain registers of mediators or 'dispute resolvers'.

14.5 Organisations involved in arbitration and ADR

14.5.1 Arbitration

The Chartered Institute of Arbitrators has the objectives of promoting and facilitating the determination of disputes by arbitration. It is a professional body with a multi-disciplinary membership and maintains a register of arbitrators, a panel of arbitrators and a register of expert witnesses. It sets up and administers small claims arbitration schemes and provides training and education programmes for potential and practising arbitrators.

It also has a special interest group called 'Accountants in Arbitration' to promote accountants as arbitrators. The group also publishes papers on topics of interest to accountants involved in arbitration.

The Chartered Institute of Arbitrators
International Arbitration Centre
24 Angel Gate
City Road
London EC1V 2RS
Tel: 0171 837 4483
Fax: 0171 837 4185

The London Court of International Arbitration provides a service of arbitration, conciliation and mediation for the settlement of international commercial disputes of any nature. The service is available in London as well as in countries throughout the world and under any system of law.

London Court of International Arbitration (LCIA)
Hulton House
6th Floor
161–166 Fleet Street
London EC4A 2DY
Tel: 0171 936 3530
Fax: 0171 936 3533

14.5.2 ADR

The Academy of Experts provides training for expert witnesses and mediators and maintains a directory of expert witnesses and mediators. It also issues *Guidelines for Mediation* which provides a framework for the conduct of mediation and a code of practice for its members.

The Academy of Experts
2 South Square
Gray's Inn
London WC1R 5HP
Tel: 0171 637 0333
Fax: 0171 637 1893

The Centre for Dispute Resolution is an international body in the field of ADR, dispute management and conflict prevention. It campaigns to raise the understanding, profile and use of ADR. It provides training for mediators and users of ADR. It also provides management training and consultancy to encourage better dispute avoidance and dispute management in the business environment.

Centre for Dispute Resolution (CEDR)
7 St Katherine's Way
London E1 9LB
Tel: 0171 481 4441
Fax: 0171 481 4442

ADR Group is a private dispute resolution service. It administers cases and mediation programmes for various groups. It also maintains a pool of mediators.

ADR Group
Equity and Law Building
36–38 Baldwin Street
Bristol BS1 1NR
Tel: 0117 925 2090
Fax: 0117 929 4429

The City Disputes Panel is a financial dispute resolution service set up to work for the benefit of the financial community and its clients. Amongst its fields of activity it lists auditing and accountancy, compliance, corporate finance, financial control, insolvency and investment funds.

City Disputes Panel
5th Floor
3 London Wall Buildings
London EC2M 5PD
Tel: 0171 638 4775
Fax: 0171 638 4776

14.6 Bibliography

14.6.1 Books

Acland, A.F. (1990) *A Sudden Outbreak of Common Sense*, Hutchinson Business Books.

Alexander, L.W.M. *et al.* (1987) *The Architect as Arbitrator*, Royal Institute of British Architects.

Bernstein, R., Tackaberry, J. and Marriott, A.L. (1998) *Handbook of Arbitration Practice*, 3rd edition, Sweet & Maxwell.

Harris, B., Planterose, R. and Tecks, J. (1996) *The Arbitration Act 1996: A Commentary*, Blackwell Science.

Kendall, J. (1996) *Expert Determination*, 2nd edition, FT Law & Tax.

Lemar, C.J. and Chilvers, D.R. (1995) *Litigation Support* (3rd edn), Butterworths.

Mackie, K.J. (ed.) (1991) *A Handbook of Dispute Resolution*, Routledge.

Mackie, K.J., Miles, D. and Marsh, W. (1995) *Commercial Dispute Resolution – An ADR Practice Guide*, Butterworths.

Merkin, R. (1996) *Arbitration Act 1996: An Annotated Guide*, LLP.

Mustill, M.J. and Boyd, S.C. (1989) *The Law & Practice of Commercial Arbitration in England* (2nd edn), Butterworths.

14.6.2 Other publications

Accountants in Arbitration: a New Discovery of an Ancient Discipline, The Chartered Institute of Arbitrators.

Accountants in Arbitration: Share Valuation Disputes – Pitfalls for Accountants, The Chartered Institute of Arbitrators.

Arbitration Act 1996.

Arbitration Rules, The Chartered Institute of Arbitrators.

The Consumer Dispute, The Chartered Institute of Arbitrators.

General Information Handbook, The Chartered Institute of Arbitrators.

The Language of ADR: An International Glossary, The Academy of Experts.

Mediation: Getting Started, The Academy of Experts.

Standard Consumer Arbitration Scheme (1995) The Chartered Institute of Arbitrators.

Wales-Smith, B. (1995) *Resolving Your Dispute by Mediation*, The Academy of Experts.

What is Mediation?, The Academy of Experts.

Chapter 15
Torts and negligence

15.1 Introduction

A tort is the breach of a general duty imposed by the civil law. There are many types of tort, for example negligence – the most common and the tort discussed in this chapter, defamation and deceit – covered in later chapters – and a variety of other actions available where a person, his property or his rights have been injured in some way.

It is important that expert accountants have a general understanding of tort law because the primary remedy in tort is an award of damages. For example, the negligent act of a motorist in accidentally running over a pedestrian is a tort; the loss that the passenger suffers as a result will be remedied by an award of damages.

This chapter looks at the requirements for a tort, the types of defences available – such as contributory negligence – and concepts such as remoteness. The chapter also considers the contrast between an action in tort and the other main area of civil law where the accountant is involved, contract. Damages are considered in Chapter 18.

Where the law has placed a duty on a person, and that person has breached that duty and caused harm, then a tort has been committed. A tort has also been committed if a person's interests have been violated. The person in breach of duty, or breaching another person's interests, is called the 'tortfeasor'. Torts include trespass and deceit, as well as the breach of a statutory duty, such as the duty palced on an employer to provide a safe place for his employees to work.

As a general outline, for a person causing a tort, it is not normally necessary to show that he intended the breach; it is enough that he was negligent or failed to take reasonable care. A defence to an action in tort is that the person in breach did in fact take care.

However, other torts, to be proven, do require a particular state of mind. For example, in an action for malicious falsehood, it is necessary to show that the person making the false statement intended another person harm and acted from a dishonest motive.

15.2 Contract and tort distinguished

Torts occur because the law has imposed on persons generally a duty. By contrast, a contract is an agreement between two or more persons entered into voluntarily. A person in breach of contract, therefore, is in breach of something he has agreed to assume, not that has been imposed on him by civil law. However, the same act or omission by a person which gives rise to a breach of contract may also constitute a tort. For example, a contract exists between an accountant and his client regarding the preparation of tax returns. If the accountant fails to prepare the tax returns correctly, the client may have an action for breach of contract. However, he may also have an action in tort because the law imposes a duty on professionals on the way they carry out work for their clients.

Other distinctions exist. For example, a breach of contract, unlike tort, is not concerned with the state of mind or fault of the parties to the contract, but with whether the parties to the contract have actually fulfilled their side of the bargain. Furthermore, remedies under contract law are primarily concerned with ensuring that a party in breach does what he promised to do; remedies in tort are concerned with compensating a person for his loss.

15.3 Negligence

The tort of negligence is a breach of the legal duty to take care. The duty of care is designed to protect a person from damage to his person, his property or his economic interests. It is important that the expert accountant should understand the tort of negligence because it includes the protection of economic interests. An accountant's involvement in the vast majority of tort actions will be to quantify the extent of harm to the plaintiff's economic interests.

The tort of negligence is a relatively modern invention, and the speech of Lord Atkin in *Donoghue* v *Stevenson* [1932] AC 562 is considered to be the first and classic judicial recognition of the term. This was the famous 'snail in a bottle of ginger beer' case, familiar to all accountants from their conversion course studies. Since then, the courts have found a duty of care to exist in a variety of situations. In *Donoghue* v *Stevenson*, the claim was made by the consumer of the drink, purchased from a retailer, against its manufacturer. The action could not be founded in contract because, despite the existence of contracts between the purchaser and the retailer, and between the retailer and the manufacturer, there was no contract between the parties themselves. However, it was held that a person (in this case the manufacturer) had to take reasonable care to avoid acts or omissions which could be reasonably foreseen as likely to harm persons who ought reasonably to be in contemplation of being harmed, this last aspect being called the 'neighbour' test.

An award of damages in a negligence claim would usually compensate a person for injury to his person or his property and for the financial effects of such injury.

The idea of protecting against pure economic harm – that is, financial loss which is not connected to and does not flow from physical damage to a person or his property – is even younger. Prior to 1963, an action for a loss arising from a misstatement could only be founded in contract. If there was no contract between the parties, there was no action. Thus, in *Candler* v *Crane Christmas & Co.* [1951] 2 KB 164, where the plaintiff had invested money in a company on the basis of inaccurate accounts prepared by the accountant defendants, and had discussed the accounts with the defendants, it was held that the accountants did not owe the plaintiff a duty of care in relation to the preparation of the accounts.

It was not until *Hedley Byrne & Co.* v *Heller & Partners Ltd* [1964] AC 465 extended the tort of negligence by establishing the existence of a duty to give careful advice in certain circumstances, that the causing of economic loss by misstatement became an actionable tort. In this case, the fact that the loss was purely economic did not affect the imposition of liability. The principle upon which liability was established was not the neighbour test, but rather the finding of the existence of a special relationship between the parties, equivalent to that in contract whereby one party owes a duty of care to another. Following that case, plaintiffs have been able to claim damages for pure economic loss even where there was no injury, but only where the loss was as a result of the provision of services, advice or misstatement by the defendant to the plaintiff.

A number of well-known cases involving firms of accountants have considered the law on when a duty of care exists between two persons; these are noted in Chapter 26. However, this is another area of the law of negligence which continues to develop.

To simplify this, for the purposes of an accountant involved in litigation, the principle in English law is that a purely economic loss is not recoverable unless that loss arises from physical injury to a person, or his property or from his reliance on a negligent misstatement or advice or service. However, it is important to appreciate the complexity of the law relating to economic loss.

15.4 Defences

It is important for the accountant to be aware of certain defences available in tort because of the effect they may have on the amount of any quantum award. Having prepared a report on quantum, the accountant may be expected to advise on settlement negotiations. Accountancy is not an exact science, the more so because in attempting to determine loss the accountant is attempting to calculate matters which never occurred. He should, however, know those areas of the claim which are weak and those which are strong, and can assist the solicitors in settlement negotiations.

However, there are other considerations which may have an effect on the quantum claim or on liability overall. The solicitor will certainly have these items in mind when assessing an offer in settlement or when attempting to calculate a payment into court. The accountant involved in these discussions should have an understanding of these matters.

This section therefore looks at contributory negligence, remoteness, new intervening acts and the concept of reasonable care.

15.4.1 Contributory negligence

In many of the cases in which an expert accountant is involved, the issue of contributory negligence will loom large. The accountant will have quantified the amount of damages, but both sides will be aware that, whatever the loss, any award will be reduced if there is found to be contributory negligence on the part of the plaintiff.

Where the defendant is solely responsible for the injury, the plaintiff will be entitled to claim all of his loss. If the injury to a plaintiff is due to his own default alone, he will be unable to establish liability. However, in many cases the injury is due partially to the default of the plaintiff and partially to the defendant's. The amount of the plaintiff's own default is termed his contributory negligence. People must take reasonable care. As Denning LJ stated in *Jones* v *Livox Quarries Ltd* [1952] 2 QB 608:

> 'A person is guilty of contributory negligence whenever he ought reasonably to have foreseen that, if he did not act as a prudent man, he might hurt himself; and in his reckonings, he must take into account the possibility of others being careless.'

Just as the plaintiff is required to prove the negligence of the defendant, the defendant is required to prove the contributory negligence of the plaintiff.

In some types of case such as motor accidents, there are certain 'standard' reductions for contributory negligence, such as the failure to wear a seat belt. However, in many cases the reduction depends on a detailed assessment of the facts which may, in advance of trial, be difficult to estimate with any accuracy.

Finally, in an action for deceit, as noted in Chapter 22, there is no concept of contributory negligence.

15.4.2 Remoteness

A defence to a claim for negligence is that the damage was too remote from the defendant's act for that damage to have been a reasonably foreseeable result of that act. All of us carry out acts which play a part in causing events; however, those events are rarely a natural or an obvious result of those acts.

What the law is trying to establish is whether a particular type of damage was reasonably foreseeable. From this it follows that the defendant may be liable for damage greater in *extent* than that which was reasonably foreseeable, provided the *kind* of damage was forseeable (see *Hughes* v *Lord Advocate* [1963] AC 837; *Vacwell Engineering Co. Ltd* v *BDH Chemicals Ltd* [1971] 1 QB 88). The point to make here is that a defendant can be liable if the damages are greater in extent than was reasonably forseeable, but not if they are different in kind.

The issue of remoteness may completely destroy a claim for damages. Again, it is difficult for the accountant to take the risk of this into account when assessing the level of damages.

The issue of remoteness, particularly as it affects the provisions of professional advice, is very much a live topic for the courts. The issue was considered recently in the *BBL* case (*Banque Bruxelles Lambert SA* v *Eagle Star Insurance Co.* [1997] AC 191). This was one of a series of cases where property lenders had sued valuers over allegedly negligently prepared valuations, on the basis of which the lenders had entered into loan transactions in respect of the properties valued. One of the main points of dispute was whether losses caused by a general fall in the property market were recoverable as damages. In principle, a surveyor would be liable to the extent that his valuation exceeded the true value of the property at the time he carried out the valuation. However, the property crash of the early 1990s exacerbated the losses suffered by property lenders.

The Court of Appeal originally held that losses due to a fall in the market were reasonably foreseeable and therefore recoverable. The House of Lords rejected this approach. The House of Lords' decision was based on a rather subtle distinction between two roles of a valuer. First, a valuer might only be providing information to enable the lender to make a decision. Secondly, however, a valuer might actually advise somebody about a particular course of action. In the former case the valuer's liability to losses is limited to the difference between his valuation and the true valuation (i.e., the valuer is not responsible for all consequences but only for the foreseeable consequences of the information being wrong). In the latter case he is liable to all foreseeable losses, including a fall in the market (i.e., he is responsible for all the foreseeable loss which is a consequence of that course of action being taken).

However, as will be seen in later chapters, the reasonably foreseeable test does not apply in two types of tort. In fatal accident cases the test is whether the defendant has caused harm for which the Fatal Accidents Act 1976 provides damages. In an action for deceit, the defendant is liable for all damage, including that which may not be reasonably foreseen (*Doyle* v *Olby Ironmongers Limited* [1969] 2 QB 158).

15.4.3 New intervening act

A new intervening act is some act which supersedes the defendant's original tort, thereby breaking the chain of causation. New intervening acts include the actions of third parties and the plaintiff himself. In the latter case, such intervening acts may be a form of contributory negligence.

15.4.4 Reasonable care

In many cases, particularly involving an allegation of professional negligence, a defence of reasonable care will be used. Professionals are required to use reasonable skill and care. It can be particularly difficult to assess what is meant by reasonable skill and care in a profession for a number of reasons. The standard varies according to the particular profession, but there is some doubt as to whether the standard of care expected is the standard which a profession should achieve or that which it does achieve in practice. A particular issue is the conflict between best practice and standard practice. Also, the expected standard of care will vary between firms which hold themselves out as specialists in a particular field of a profession and those which do not.

15.5 An example of the difficulties of advising on quantum in a negligence case

In the following example, the difficulties of advising on quantum in a case where defences such as those mentioned in **15.5** above are raised are explored.

Example

X is the auditor to Y. He also prepares the annual tax returns for the directors of Y, who are also its shareholders. The directors of Y meet with X and explain that they have had an offer for Y from a public company and wish to avoid any capital gains tax. X advises the directors that the only sure way of avoiding tax altogether is to emigrate for a six-month period when the shares are sold. They tell him that they do not wish to emigrate. He then says that what they can do is invest the capital gain on the shares in property, but that it has to be certain types of property, and obtain rollover relief. The directors thank him.

The sale of the company proceeds and the directors decide to invest in property. They speak with a local estate agent and ask what will give a good return. He in turn says that development sites which he has on his books could, with planning permission, be very profitable. They purchase a number of sites and then tell X what they have done. X says that he is not sure that these sorts of property are right for rollover relief, but says he will pursue the claim with the Inland Revenue.

The Inland Revenue deny the claim for rollover relief on the basis that the legislation at the time of the sale only permitted the company to obtain the relief. In order to pay the tax on the gain, the directors are forced to sell the properties which, due to a downturn in the market, have lost considerable value. The proceeds of the sale of the properties are just sufficient to pay the tax due and interest on the tax for late payment.

The directors sue X for negligence, claiming the whole of the loss of the value of the properties.

In a case such as this, the actual amount of quantum may be relatively simple to calculate. It is likely to be the total amount of the money lost on selling the properties. However, the decision as to whether any damages should be awarded will be influenced by the following factors:

(a) given that the directors said that they would not be prepared to emigrate, there is on the face of it no way in which they could have avoided the payment of tax altogether;
(b) the tax avoidance method advised by X was wrong and could never have saved tax and therefore the directors would always have found themselves liable to pay the tax;
(c) however, there were other relatively simple tax-saving schemes which could have been recommended, such as taking loan notes or shares in the public company which could have deferred the payment of tax;
(d) X stated that there were only certain types of property which could be available for rollover relief, but the directors did not explore this any further and just purchased what they thought would make a profit;
(e) the directors may have relied on the advice of a third party;
(f) the fall in the property market may have been too remote from X's advice.

The accountant in such a case might, as well as advising on quantum, give expert evidence on the tax aspects of the case. He would then be able to assess the effects of the first three items, the main issue being that of causation. However, item (d) could evidence contributory negligence by the directors, item (e) suggests that there may have been a new intervening act and item (f) raises issues of remoteness. In each of these instances the accountant will need to be advised by his solicitors of the possibility of these defences succeeding before he can advise in settlement negotiations.

Chapter 16
Contract

16.1 Introduction

In contrast to a tort, which is based on the duties one person has to another which are imposed by law, a contract is the voluntary agreement of rights and duties to be assumed between two or more persons. People are free to agree contracts in whatever way they wish, subject only to certain laws relating to contracts which might result in certain provisions or contracts being held to be unenforceable on the grounds of unreasonableness, public policy or illegality. Thus, two parties to a contract can determine the extent of their agreement and the circumstances in which one will be liable to the other for failure to perform his side of the contract, and the financial effects of such failure.

This chapter looks at certain rudimentary aspects of contract law, concentrating on those aspects that the accountant is most likely to meet in practice and, in particular, warranties relating to accounting matters.

Although an accountant may be asked to compute the loss of profits arising from, for example, the failure to supply a piece of equipment, he is much more likely to meet a contractual dispute in company takeovers. This is because purchase and sale contracts normally include a large number of financial clauses which are only capable of interpretation by an accountant, or the effect of which requires an accountant's expert evidence.

The chapter then looks at some common areas of company takeover disputes which the accountant is likely to meet in practice.

16.2 Formation of a contract and the terms of a contract

A contract is formed when one person makes an offer to another person, which that other person accepts while the offer is still open. It is important that both parties intend to be bound by the contract, that the parties have the capacity to enter into the contract (for example they have authority and are not minors) and that some consideration passes under the contract so that each side benefits from the contract.

The terms of a contract include both those express terms which are included within the contract and those terms which will be implied by the court.

Express terms of a contract include those terms which are expressly set out in the contract. Implied terms are terms not expressly included by the parties in the contract but which the court will nevertheless imply as terms of the contract either as a result of statute or because, without those terms, the contract would not be workable, and where the court infers that it is the unexpressed intention of the parties that the term be included in the contract. The most important implied terms which the accountant will see in contract disputes arise from the Sale of Goods Act 1979, for example, terms are implied regarding the quality of goods and title (ss12–15).

16.3 Express terms, breach of contract and remedies for breach

For the purposes of this chapter and looking at the effect of a breach of contract, express terms can be divided into three classes:

- conditions;
- warranties; and
- innominate or intermediate terms.

A condition of a contract is a term which is so fundamental to the contract that its non-performance is a non-performance of the contract itself. In such circumstances, the innocent party can consider himself discharged from the contract and can sue for damages for any loss he has suffered.

Chitty says that a warranty is a term of the contract, the breach of which gives rise to an action for damages, but which does not allow the innocent party to treat himself as discharged from the contract. Warranties are those terms which are collateral to the main purpose of the contract.

Innominate or intermediate terms are a recent invention of the courts, designed to overcome the situation where a breach of a condition gives rise to only a trifling loss, but still allows the injured party to repudiate the contract. The object of the courts is to encourage performance of contracts rather than repudiation. An innominate term is likely to be a term where, if the consequences are serious, then the contract can be repudiated by the innocent party (that is, it may have the effect of a breach of condition), but if in the circumstances the consequences of the breach are only minor, the breach can be remedied with an award of damages and the contract can still proceed (that is, it actually has the effect of a breach of warranty).

16.4 The scope of warranties and breach of warranty claims

Warranties are incorporated into a contract to limit the scope of the general contractual principle of caveat emptor – let the buyer beware. However, there are a number of ways in which a vendor will attempt to limit the scope of the warranties given and therefore put part of the risk of the contract back on the purchaser.

First of all, the warranties will normally be subject to, and limited by, all matters disclosed by the vendor to the purchaser, usually by means of a disclosure letter. However, for the vendor to avoid liability the disclosure letter has to disclose the relevant matter properly. Therefore, if there is a warranty concerning the net asset value of a company being purchased, the mere disclosure of declining profits of the company in question, for example, will not be held to be a disclosure of a lower net asset value than has been warranted.

Opening up the books of a vendor company to a potential purchaser may be sufficient to give the purchaser prior knowledge of certain matters, provided this confirmation can properly be treated as disclosed for the purposes of the contract, meaning that the purchaser will not be able to make a breach of warranty claim.

The contract will often include a restriction on the time limit when the purchaser can make a claim for breach of warranties, generally within two or three years from completion of the contract, thereby shortening the normal six-year limitation period.

Contracts will often include *de minimis* levels below which an individual warranty claim cannot be made and aggregate levels below which a number of warranty claims cannot be made. The contract will normally also include a maximum amount for all claims, usually linked to the value of the contribution to be paid by the purchaser.

A further clause will state that any claim has to be made in a certain way, for example by notice setting out the basis of the claim.

16.5 The accountant's role in investigating breach of warranty claims

Where a contract is litigated, it is almost inevitable that an expert accountant will be brought in to investigate any alleged breaches of warranty.

In order to carry out this role, it is essential that he has a thorough understanding of the following:

(a) those parts of the contract dealing with warranties;
(b) the disclosure letter;
(c) the extent of any due diligence carried out by the purchaser.

Additionally, he may need to see the extent of the vendor's own records, particularly board minutes and internal memoranda.

Although there are as many types of warranty claims as there are warranties, in practice, warranty claims linked to accounting matters fall into one of the following categories:

- compliance of accounts with accounting principles;
- consistency of application of accounting policies;
- true and fair view;
- valuation of stock;
- collectibility of debts;
- net asset value of the company;
- carrying forward expenditure;
- disclosure of contingencies;
- tax warranties;
- projections and forecasts.

16.5.1 Compliance of accounts with accounting principles

There is normally a general warranty in a contract that the accounts have been prepared in accordance with generally accepted accounting principles (GAAP) and the relevant Statements of Standard Accounting Practice (SSAPs). The task of the accountant is to determine whether this is so or not. A company's accounts will disclose its accounting policies and the accountant needs to review these to ensure that they comply with GAAP. However, particularly in small companies these often do not tell the whole story and it is fairly common for a set of accounts to disclose, for example, what the company's policy is on deferred tax and leasing but not on income recognition.

Therefore, the accountant must look at those areas of the accounts which are most capable of manipulation or where there are a variety of possible policies, and determine what policy has been adopted. As an example, if a company receives commission income, the accountant would need to determine whether this is accounted for on a cash basis, a receivable basis or when the company becomes entitled to the commission. The accountant will also need to determine whether there are any circumstances in which a commission could be repaid.

A further risk area is in those accounting policies where judgment is applied – here one is thinking particularly about valuation issues.

As well as determining the non-stated accounting policies, the accountant needs to ensure that the company has complied with the stated accounting policies.

16.5.2 Consistency of application of accounting policies

A further warranty will normally state that accounting policies have been consistently applied. The adjustment of an accounting policy in the year of a sale, for example reducing a general bad debt provision by providing against debts over 120 days rather than 60 days, may make a large difference to the profit shown.

16.5.3 True and fair

Finally, a further general warranty will be that the accounts of the company show a true and fair view. In some cases, the investigation of this may require a re-audit of accounts. Sometimes this warranty does not use the normal term but another term, such as 'true and correct' or 'materially correct'. The investigation of a breach of this warranty is complicated because of the need of the accountant to determine what this warranty actually means and whether it is wider or narrower than true and fair.

In addition to these general warranties, there are a number of specific warranties.

16.5.4 Valuation of stock

Without doubt, stock is one of the most common causes of contract disputes. The reason this is so is because of the range of stock policies which can be used – first in first out, standard cost, etc. – and the judgment which can be applied to valuation of obsolete stock. A further area is in the reversing of old stock provisions.

A particular difficulty for some vendors is that, in the years prior to sale, stock has been reduced to keep profits down in order to pay a low tax bill, but in the year of sale stock is increased, either to show a 'fairer' asset value or because of the immediate beneficial effect on profit in one year.

In any contract dispute, stock should be the accountant's first port of call.

16.5.5 Collectibility of debts

Debts at the time of sale are also capable of being manipulated because of the judgment which is brought to bear on the amount of any bad debt provision.

Having said that, this is a more straightforward area to investigate than stock, so it should be easy to determine whether a debt has been collected or not.

16.5.6 Net asset value of the company

This is probably the second most common area of contract disputes. A company is warranted to have a net asset value of, say, not less than £5 million, but the new owners, when looking at the completion balance sheet, find all sorts of areas where there is underprovision, and overvaluation.

The accountant needs to be careful of a number of matters. First, the contract may often specify different accounting policies to be used in the preparation of the completion accounts. Second, certain areas of the accounts may have a value fixed by the contract. For example, the value of fixed assets may be fixed at a certain level.

Further, completion accounts may be required to be prepared within a limited period of time after the completion of the deal, which means that certain matters, such as the outcome of contingencies or the collectibility of certain debts, cannot be known with absolute precision.

16.5.7 Carrying forward expenditure

In certain instances it is acceptable for a company to carry forward development expenditure or other expenses in its balance sheet. This is often an area where a purchaser may well have carried out due diligence in advance of sale, particularly where the amounts are material.

16.5.8 Disclosure of contingencies

The existence of claims against a company or the outcome of a future event is another rich vein for investigating accountants. The disclosure letter will normally be far more explicit and comprehensive than the accounts of a company in disclosing these matters. In particular, one should consider claims by customers, central government and local authorities and regulators.

16.5.9 Tax warranties

Tax warranties are nowadays written extremely widely, but there is often an extremely wide disclosure of tax matters connected with a company.

Areas where the accountant should concentrate are in reliefs which may be clawed back, assets which have been the subject of rollover relief and the disclosure of all matters to the Inland Revenue or Customs & Excise.

16.5.10 Projections and forecasts

Finally, in the course of negotiations, a vendor may present a purchaser with all manner of projections of sales and forecasts, including estimates of expenditure by customers or calculations of future gross profit levels. There may be a specific warranty in the contract concerning the reliability of these or the bases on which they have been prepared.

Again, many contract disputes arise from the reliability of forecasts, and the accountant may need to carry out a thorough investigation of the commercial assumptions and accounting bases on which these have been prepared.

16.6 Actions of the purchaser

One common defence used by vendors is that the purchaser has effectively brought about the breach of warranty claim himself. For example, there may be a tendency for a purchaser not to bother to collect a debt, knowing that if the debt is not paid he can make a warranty claim.

Further, the reliability of forecasts may be undermined by the actions of the purchaser not fully understanding the nature of the company he has purchased or by not putting adequate resources by way of staff or finance to operate the business, for example.

This aspect of a breach of warranty should not be overlooked by an accountant investigating a breach of warranty.

16.7 Amount of the claim under a breach of warranty

Chapter 18 sets out the basis of calculating damages under breach of contract. However, it is often the contract itself which defines how a loss is to be calculated for a breach of warranty. For example, the contract may stipulate that the extent to which the net asset value of the company falls below a certain level should result in a pound for pound reduction in the consideration.

In many cases, the purchase price paid is based on a multiple of earnings. On the face of it, a reduction in net assets reduces earnings in the year of sale, resulting in a far greater increase in the amount of damages. Having said that, many adjustments to profits may, effectively, be the result of overstatements of profits over a number of years and not in one year. Further, the non-disclosure of a contingency or a contingency which turns into an actual liability post-sale will have a one-off effect on profit.

Working out the amount of loss may therefore not be simple because of this interaction between the net assets acquired and the basis of the consideration.

16.8 Breach of conditions

The above analysis has looked at breaches of warranty. However, in some cases a breach is so serious as to allow the innocent party to terminate the contract. In essence, the approach of the accountant will be the same in investigating breaches of condition as in investigating breaches of warranty.

However, in one particular type of contract dispute, the accountant can be expected to carry out a much more detailed investigation, and this is where fraudulent misrepresentation is alleged. Misrepresentation or deceit is covered in Chapter 22. What the investigating accountant is primarily looking for in such an investigation is inconsistency between what the vendor has told the purchaser and what the vendor knows, and the deliberate suppression of financial information or manipulation of accounting policies.

Chapter 17
Tracing claims – equitable remedies, quasi-contract and restitution

17.1 Introduction

This chapter looks at tracing, which is not a claim per se. However, in order to do so it is necessary to provide an overview of claims in the law of equity and restitution to which tracing often leads. The accountant is most likely to come across these subjects in civil cases where fraud is alleged, and where a plaintiff attempts to trace his property into that held by the defendant.

Claims in relation to misapplied assets are increasingly common in civil litigation. The law allows the original owner to recover his property, through a variety of common law, equitable and restitutionary remedies.

The expert accountant will be involved in tracing normally where fraud is alleged.

17.2 Equitable remedies

Most civil litigation in which the accountant is involved will, ultimately, be about the pursuit of a claim for damages, that is, the quantification of a monetary amount to compensate for a wrong. A person claiming in tort, such as for libel or personal injury, will claim for damages. Furthermore, claims under specific legislation, such as for wrongful dismissal or in matrimonial matters will also normally involve a claim for damages. The accountant has a vital part to play in the quantification of damages, especially where quantification is complex.

However, the relief offered by the law is not limited to damages. There is a branch of the law, equity, which has developed what is called 'equitable relief'. It is not the purpose of this book to describe the development of equity and its relationship to the common law, however, some brief description is necessary to put this chapter into context.

Historically, the way the common law operated was through a number of different causes of action which offered damages as a remedy. Where a person had a possible claim he would try and fit his claim into the available causes of action. If it did not fit, there was no cause of action and therefore no possibility of a case under common law, and if the wrong cause of action was chosen, then the case would fail.

Because the common law offered no remedy in a number of situations, a practice grew up of petitioning the Crown to get relief. This system, which was operated by the Lord Chancellor, eventually through his court termed the Chancery, became the law of equity. Equity was based on a system of fairness, offering remedies where the common law did not. Equitable remedies include claims for specific performance (for example of a contract) and injunctions.

It is over 100 years since equity and the common law operated separately (they were fused by the Judicature Acts 1873 and 1875). Further, the way a common law claim is litigated does not now depend on a limited number of precise causes of action. However, equity still exists as a system of law, and the remedies developed under equity are still called equitable remedies.

17.3 Remedies

The remedies available in equity include the following:

(a) injunctions, that is, an order stopping someone doing something;
(b) specific performance, that is, ordering someone to do something under a contract;
(c) rectification, that is, the correction of a document to reflect the true intentions of the parties to that document;
(d) recission, the setting-aside of a contract;
(e) declaratory relief, for example a declaration that a person is the owner of something;
(f) restitution, the restoration of property.

17.4 Restitution

Restitution is the response to unjust enrichment. Such claims are made in both law and equity. The aim of a restitutionary remedy is to provide redress to a plaintiff where the defendant has been unjustly enriched at his expense.

17.5 The role of the accountant

The accountant's role in these types of claims is primarily the tracing of assets – principally money. However, what these exercises actually involve is the tracing of value through a variety of assets, rather than an actual asset itself, although the two may be indistinguishable. For example, where a director has used his position to profit at his company's expense, the company will have a right to recover property from the director on the basis that he is, for example, the constructive trustee of the company's property. The company may want to trace the original proceeds of his fraud from a sum of money, into stocks and shares, back into money and then into a house. The tracing exercise carried out by the accountant will trace the original value of the sum which the director has received.

This, however, is a relatively straightforward tracing exercise. Many tracing exercises are horrendously complicated and involved, because of the mass of bank accounts and transactions which have been used to hide illicit receipts of money or other property.

Where the accountant has the most to offer in these proceedings is in the interrogation and then presentation of financial information in a form which is readily understandable by lawyers and judges. The reason for this is simple – sets of accounts, the documents most accountants work to produce, are summaries of sometimes millions of transactions in forms which are capable of comprehension in a way that the underlying documentation of itself is not. Accountants have the skills to present financial transactions in comprehensible ways.

The first task facing the accountant is sorting the mass of financial information into some order. Spreadsheets or a database are an obvious means of doing this but in choosing the appropriate medium, it is important to remember that the uses to which this core financial information will be put are likely to change with time, and therefore the database must be flexible enough to accommodate this.

Having input the data it is necessary to carry out two tasks. First of all, the extent of missing information needs to be determined and second, the task of tying up the flows of money through individual accounts must be started; these two tasks are closely related. Sophisticated interrogation techniques can sort transactions by value date in a much more efficient manner than the laborious process of comparing one reconstructed bank statement to another. Further, the identification of 'gaps' in the money flows, and cross-checking back to source documents can indicate the nature of missing bank accounts.

In particularly complex tracing exercises, compiling the financial information will be a gradual process; sometimes the gaps are never filled in, and sometimes the ultimate destination of money is not known. Perhaps it proves impossible to identify a bank account, or money is withdrawn in cash. However, even if the documentation is complete, presenting the information in a digestible format can prove very difficult. It may be that the tracing exercise is required to demonstrate different parts of the claim, for example that money flows passing through a bank account indicate the beneficial ownership of that bank account, and that money ultimately is used to buy an asset.

Money flows represented in diagrammatic form can do a lot to aid the understanding of the tracing exercise and can summarise, like financial statements, large numbers of documents.

These diagrams, when annotated with information concerning evidence on the beneficial ownership of accounts or assets can go a long way to demonstrating fraud, as well as where the property has ultimately ended up.

Tracing diagrams give the reader a picture of financial transactions in a way that listing transactions on a page never can. The use of annotations can help to build that picture and, therefore, the case. What the accountant has achieved is the presentation of the results of an investigation which may involve many thousands of pieces of paper. Even the narrative description of the transactions may be extensive.

To qualify as evidence, these diagrams must be capable of being referenced to the underlying documentation. Because we are dealing with money flows, these will be backed up by appropriate parts of the database showing individual transactions presented in spreadsheet format. The documents supporting individual transactions will be referenced to the database and included on these spreadsheets. Information concerning, for example, the beneficial ownership of accounts or assets may be included on other databases.

Having information organised in this way can make the finding of documents a relatively straightforward procedure, which greatly assists, for example, in explaining these diagrams in oral evidence.

17.6 Tracing principles

There are a number of tracing principles which accountants need to be aware of when carrying out tracing claims.

The first point to be aware of is the timing of transactions. Although it might seem an obvious point, value cannot be traced out of a bank account if the relevant payment out predates the payment in of a sum to be traced. However simple this may sound, in practice it can become extremely complicated when one considers the way in which transactions are entered on to bank statements. For example:

(a) transactions may be entered over a period of time such as a day in alphabetical or numerical order, or at the time they occurred;
(b) an entry date is different to a value date;
(c) items are often entered before they clear.

The tracing rules are far from straightforward and are not easy to apply. Tracing rules exist both at law and in equity, although in practice the equitable tracing rules are more important. At law, the plaintiff has to show that he held, and continues to hold, legal title to the property. In equity, the plaintiff has to show that he held and continues to hold equitable title to the property and that that property has passed through the hands of a fiduciary.

Where a plaintiff is tracing at law, he cannot continue to trace once the money is paid into an account which contains, or which later contains, money from other sources. Equity's rules are more generous and allow the plaintiff to trace into such a 'mixed fund'.

Where the plaintiff is tracing into a mixed fund, further rules are needed in order to determine his share of that fund. First, a distinction has to be drawn between those cases where the plaintiff traces against someone whom he claims is a constructive trustee of the funds received, and those cases in which the person who received the money did so with no knowledge of the misapplication.

Where the plaintiff seeks to trace against a constructive trustee, the order of payments into and out of the bank account into which the plaintiff seeks to trace his funds is irrelevant (*Re Hallett's Estate* (1880) 13 Ch D 696). However, the plaintiff has to look to the mixed fund first in order to satisfy his claim. This means that the plaintiff cannot trace into an overdrawn account and can only trace to the lowest balance on that account between the date when the plaintiff's money was paid in and the date on which the claim is brought (*James Roscoe (Bolton) Limited* v *Winder* [1915] 1 Ch 62).

Where the plaintiff traces against someone whom he cannot show knew the money was his, the general rule is that the parties share rateably – their claims rank *pari passu* (*Ministry of Health* v *Simpson* [1951] AC 251). However, there is one exception to this important rule in the case of tracing money, namely the 'rule in Clayton's Case' ((1816) 1 Mer 572). This provides that, where the mixed fund consists of a current bank account, then payments out of the account are deemed to be made in order of the payments in: first in, first out. This rule leads to some problems in practice.

Where the money to be traced has been used to buy an asset, again a distinction has to be drawn depending on whether the defendant is said to have known that the money was not his (i.e., he is a constructive trustee) or the defendant did not know of the misapplication. If the defendant is a constructive trustee, the court will ask whether it is clear that the plaintiff's money was used to buy the asset. If it was, then the plaintiff can claim the asset, or a charge over it, to the extent of his contribution to the purchase price (*In re Tilley's Will Trusts* [1967] Ch 1179). If the defendant is not said to be a constructive trustee, then the parties should share rateably in the asset purchased (*Re Diplock* [1948] Ch 465).

Tracing can involve some of the most complicated exercises an accountant can be asked to carry out owing to the large number of transactions, the lengths which some defendants will go to to hide or disguise property and the interaction of the various tracing principles.

Chapter 18
Damages

18.1 Introduction

An expert accountant's work is mostly concerned with the computation of damages. Depending on the availability of the information this can be simple or complicated. However, underlying any claim for damages is a complex set of legal considerations, whether the action is in tort or for breach of contract. The chapters on negligence and contract have outlined the circumstances in which damages can be claimed and legal issues, such as remoteness, which limit the claim.

Many claims can only be founded in tort, there being no contract between the parties. However, many claims for breach of contract may give rise to a concurrent claim in tort. This chapter looks at a number of issues. It first of all considers what is meant by damages. It then looks at what an award of damages in tort is attempting to achieve, and the objective of an award of damages for breach of contract. It also considers why a claim which is capable of being founded in contract might be founded instead in tort, or in both tort and contract, and why the courts might not impose concurrent liability on a defendant.

Having set out the legal framework of damages, the chapter then looks at how an accountant should approach any damages claim – this is often primarily an information-gathering exercise.

18.2 Scope of the term 'damages'

Damages are the monetary compensation payable to a successful plaintiff in an action in tort or for breach of contract. An expert accountant's role is, in the majority of cases, the quantification of such damages.

However, the term 'damages' does not include every money claim. It does not include, for example, money payable under the terms of a contract, claims in restitution formerly called quasi-contract and claims under equity and in actions under statutes where the equitable or statutory right to recover is independent of any tort or breach of contract. In the last case, a money claim may include a quantification of earnings by a fraudulent defendant. However, despite the accounting principles in calculating such profits being equivalent to damage quantification, it would be wrong to call such a claim damages.

18.3 General and special damages

There are two different types of damages, the distinction being based on the way a claim is proved. General damages include non-pecuniary damages such as pain and suffering in personal injury cases or loss of reputation in defamation cases. It is difficult, if not impossible, to prove the financial consequences of pain resulting from a motor accident. Indeed, the pain caused and the monetary compensation awarded are, conceptually, quite different. Consequently, the amount of general damages is a question for the judge or jury. The accountant is unlikely to have any involvement in the quantification of general damages, other than including an estimate, as provided by instructing solicitors, in his report to arrive at a total sum for the purpose of settlement negotiations.

By contrast, special damages have to be proved to be recoverable. Special damages are the amount of pecuniary damages suffered as a result of a tort or breach of contract.

The distinction between general and special damages can be highly relevant to a claim, for example, in initiating defamation actions (see Chapter 23) or because of taxation (see Chapter 19).

It is with special damages that the accountant is primarily concerned.

18.4 Other uses of the terms 'general' and 'special' damages

In the classic book on damages, *McGregor on Damages*, Harvey McGregor identifies two further uses of the terms 'general' and 'special' damages. The first concerns liability and relates principally to contract law. General damages are those which are a natural consequence of an action, whereas special damages are those which arise out of particular and special circumstances. In contract, such general damages will always be claimable; however, such special damages are only claimable if the special circumstances have been communicated between the parties (Lord Wright in *Monarch S.S. Co. Ltd* v *Karlshamns Oljefabriker* [1949] AC 196).

The second usage of the terms which McGregor identifies concerns the way in which damages are pleaded. In principle, special damage, if averred in the pleadings, must be proved. General damages must also be averred but the quantification is a jury question. However, the niceties of pleading often blur the distinction. For instance, in personal injury cases loss of future earnings and expenses are general damages in pleading (although the plaintiff must give clear evidence of amount), whereas loss of earnings and expenses incurred between the date of injury and trial must be pleaded as special damage (even though they are ordinary foreseeable consequences).

The accountant should be aware of the various distinctions, but the most common use of these terms is that identified in the previous section.

In his book McGregor does not use the terms 'general' or 'special' because of the ambiguity set out above. Instead, he refers to normal loss and consequential loss. (Normal loss is that which every plaintiff in a situation will suffer, while consequential loss is that loss which is special to the circumstances of the particular plaintiff.) Consequential loss is a far more familiar concept to an accountant than special damage and it is this which the accountant is usually employed to calculate.

18.5 Object of an award of damages in an action in tort

The object of an award of damages was defined by Lord Blackburn in *Livingstone* v *Rawyards Coal Co.* [1880] 5 App.Cas. 25 at 39. Damages were:

> 'that sum of money which will put the party who has been injured, or who has suffered, in the same position as he would have been in if he had not sustained the wrong for which he is now getting his compensation or reparation.'

The award of damages is a once and for all lump sum, as assessed by the court (although by s2(1) Damages Act 1996 the court is empowered to award periodical payments with the parties' consent in personal injury cases). In general, the parties to an action do not normally revisit the court at a later date to determine whether the award is fair. Therefore, if an award is made to an injured plaintiff because of loss of future earning power, but six months after the award a medical procedure is developed which restores the plaintiff to full health, the damages award is not adjusted. It is crucially important for the accountant to understand this when he prepares his report or when he adjusts his calculations in the light of evidence in court. It is possible in personal injury claims to seek a provisional award at trial and to be granted the right to seek further damages at a future date. However, there must be proved to be a chance that at some time in the future the plaintiff will develop a serious condition or suffer serious deterioration as a result of the tort (s32A Supreme Court Act 1981). The normal position, therefore, is that damages are fixed at trial.

Thus, the accountant's quantification of damages is based on the facts known at the time the case is heard. Accountants will, of course, have to make assumptions about what will happen in the future or what might have occurred but for the tort, particularly when working out a future loss claim.

However, such assumptions have to be reasonable and realistic and not based on an over-optimistic or over-pessimistic view of the turn of events.

To take a simple example, where tax rates are applied to a damages award, these should be the tax rates in force at the time of the report or at the date of the hearing or as disclosed by the most recent Budget. The accountant should not make an assumption that tax rates may go up or down in future, or that a particular type of tax such as capital gains tax may be abolished in future.

More complicated examples can be seen in loss of profits claims. If a company has made profits of £100,000 a year for a number of years then, all other things being equal, it will continue to make profits of £100,000 a year in the future. Of course, the accountant will need to determine whether all things will be equal, but he should not conclude on this in an unreasonable way. A speculation that the company's business sector will suffer a recession at some time in the future on the basis that the fortunes of all companies fluctuate over time is just that – a speculation.

18.6 Object of an award of damages in an action for breach of contract

The object of an award of damages in an action for breach of contract is to place the plaintiff in the position in which he would have been had the defendant performed his side of the contract.

To take a simple example, if X enters into a contract with Y to purchase goods and pays for those goods, which Y then fails to deliver, X is entitled to receive the value of those goods. The general position in contract is that the value is that at the time which the contract would have been performed, i.e., on delivery of the goods. Because the plaintiff has a duty to mitigate his loss, in contract he is required to find another buyer/seller once the original contract is breached and, if he has to pay more due to an increase in the market value of the goods between the purchase and the earliest time the action could have been brought to trial, this increase is added as consequential loss. However, whatever the subsequent price movement of the goods, the object is solely to restore X's financial position to what it should have been under the contract.

If X, at the time he entered into the contract, knew of a third party, Z, to whom he could have sold the goods at a profit, the amount of profit he has lost is not (in the absence of special circumstances – see below) claimable from Y, because X would not have any action against Y for this lost profit under his contract with Y.

The important point in contract, therefore, is to look at the terms of the contract.

Under contract law, the courts seek to avoid allowing the plaintiff to make a profit out of the defendant's breach. Therefore, if, given Y's breach, X then went to a third party and purchased the same goods for a higher price, X would be entitled to claim the extra cost which he has suffered. However, if the nearest equivalent goods which X could purchase were of a higher quality, which he was then able to sell to Z at a consequently higher price, the extra profit would be set off against the extra cost of the goods.

An accountant would not be instructed to compute damages in these simple cases. Where an accountant is instructed is, as with claims in tort, in the computation of loss of profits. How is this statement consistent with those comments on profit made in the previous paragraph, that is, that the plaintiff cannot make a profit out of a defendant's breach? The reason is that the parties to a contract are liable based on each of the parties' reasonable contemplation of the likely consequences of a breach of contract, as an implied term of the contract, and if this includes a loss of profits then that is claimable as damages.

Therefore, if one party to a contract, X, supplies defective goods to the other party, Y, and as a result of those defective goods X's own products using those goods are defective, X will be able to recover his losses as a result of those defective goods. These losses will include not just losses on individual contracts where he supplied defective goods to third parties but also the costs of defending any actions against third parties and the loss of repeat business from those third parties. The losses may also include a general loss of custom.

The reason is that it is likely to be held that it was in the reasonable contemplation of the parties that, if defective goods were supplied by Y, then:

(a) X's own goods would be defective;
(b) X would suffer claims from third parties it had supplied with its own defective goods;
(c) those third parties would not place further business with X;
(d) possibly, market knowledge of X's defective goods would lead to a general loss of custom by X.

A further example of a loss of profits claim under contract which accountants will meet frequently in practice is where the delivery of an income-producing asset, such as a piece of machinery, is delayed or where it is defective. It is likely that a court will hold that the deliverer of the machinery knew or ought to have known that the delay in delivering the machinery, or the supply of defective machinery, would result in the user of the machinery suffering a loss of profits.

As well as loss of profits, claims under contract will include the reasonable expenses incurred by the plaintiff in, for example, repairing defective goods or defective machinery, or other remedial action taken by him as a result of his attempts to mitigate his loss.

However, in every case the rule is that the plaintiff is not allowed to profit at the defendant's expense, that is, that he should not receive a greater return than he would have done had the contract been fulfilled. In contract, damages are only there to put the plaintiff in the same position as if the contract had been properly performed.

It was noted above that it is important to look at the terms of the contract when assessing a breach. A further reason for this is that contracts often fix the circumstances in which a claim for damages can be made, and also the amount.

Where a term of a contract seeks to exclude a claim for damages, which may be as a result of excluding liability for a breach, then whether that term is enforceable will depend on whether it is reasonable under the Unfair Contract Terms Act 1977. That Act lists out a number of guidelines setting out what needs to be taken into account to determine whether a term is reasonable, for example the relative bargaining power of the parties. However, certain contracts seek to limit the amount of damages to a fixed sum, and the Act does to a certain extent recognise the need of certain persons to require such terms as a result of, for example, their inability to obtain insurance.

Furthermore, there is a general principle in contract law that if a contract specifies an amount to be paid by a contract-breaker by way of liquidated damages, then that amount is recoverable from the contract-breaker. Liquidated damages rather than penalties exist where the agreed sum is fixed between the parties for a contract breach, where it is a genuine pre-estimate of the damage that could probably arise from a breach of contract (*Clydebank Engineering and Shipbuilding Co.* v *Don Jose Ramos Yzquierdo y Castaneda* [1905] AC 6) (McGregor, p. 329, para 483). Where, however, the amount is found by a court to be a penalty, then the term is unenforceable. The purpose behind this rule is that a liquidated damages clause is supposed to enable one side to recover damages without the difficulty and expense of proving them. The court will find that an amount is liquidated damages if it is a genuine attempt to make a pre-estimate of the likely loss flowing from the breach. If, however, the amount is oppressive, the courts may refuse to implement the intention of the parties. Whether an agreed sum is a penalty or liquidated damages is a question of construction upon the terms of the contract judged at the time of making the contract not at the time of the breach (*Dunlop Pneumatic Tyre Co.* v *New Garage & Motor Co.* [1915] AC 79) (McGregor, p. 320, para 481).

18.7 Contract or tort

In instances where there is a contractual relationship between two parties and there is a breach of that contract, one party may have an action in either contract or tort. Often, the plaintiff will choose to take an action in tort as well as in contract, or in tort alone. However, sometimes contract is the better action to take. The reason is whether, given the circumstances of each case, contract or tort allows the plaintiff to achieve more beneficial rights. Whether the rights are wider depends on each individual contract. As McGregor says at p.552:

> '. . . the scope of the protection afforded to the plaintiff is sometimes wider in tort and sometimes wider in contract, depending on the voluntary factor in contract, varying from agreement to agreement, of the contemplation of the parties.'

A plaintiff may achieve more beneficial rights by suing for a breach of a duty of care. For example, a contract may limit the period of time after discovery of a breach in which a suit can be initiated. An action in tort is limited by the normal limitation periods. Furthermore, the plaintiff may take the view that the contract limits his ability to claim a proper level of damages. Further, many non-pecuniary losses are not claimable because, although reasonably foreseeable (the tort test) they are not reasonably contemplated (the contract test), as held in *Hadley* v *Baxendale* [1854] 9 Ex. 341.

However, sometimes, more beneficial rights may be achieved by suing in contract. This can happen where there are what are called special circumstances. If there are special circumstances which are in the contemplation of both parties to the contract at the time the contract is made, such as that goods are required for a certain specific purpose, any loss arising from the special circumstances will be recoverable. Thus, in contrast to the previous paragraph, what is reasonably and actually contemplated is wider than what was reasonably foreseeable.

18.7.1 Concurrent liability

As noted above, the plaintiff may wish to sue in both tort and contract, or just in tort alone, the tortious liability being based on a set of facts which underlie the contractual relationship. This places on a defendant concurrent liability to the plaintiff under both possible actions. However, a question which the courts have to consider is whether it is right to allow a plaintiff to sue in tort in these circumstances. The reasoning behind this question is as follows. Both parties have defined their relationship, including their rights and duties, within the contract. Is it correct to allow a plaintiff a right which is not provided within the contract?

There are many cases which support the view that it is not right, just as there are many cases which support the view that a contractual relationship does not exclude the rights which exist independent of contract. Whether the court will allow concurrent liability depends on the facts of each case. The court needs to determine whether there is a sufficiently proximate relationship between the two parties such that there is a duty of care. If there is, it then needs to determine whether the contract terms exclude the duty of care. If they do, then there will be no concurrent liability; if they do not, then there will be.

The accountant's role in either an action for damages in tort or for breach of contract is likely to be in computing consequential loss, and the methods he will use will be the same. This aspect is considered next.

18.8 Computation of damages – the object

The object of a computation of damages is to determine, with as much accuracy as possible, the loss which a plaintiff has suffered as a result of the tort or the breach of contract.

> ***Example***
>
> If a machine, in breach of contract, is delivered late and the deliverer is liable for the profits lost as a result of the late delivery, the loss suffered will be the profits which could have been made had the machine been delivered on time. On the basis that mitigation (see **18.14** below) is not an issue, if the machine was three months late and in that time the plaintiff would have sold £100,000 worth of goods in each of those three months, then the loss is the loss of profits on those £300,000 worth of sales. Consequential losses are unlikely to arise where there is a market available in which the buyer can mitigate his loss by buying similar goods for resale. If such a market does not exist, consequential losses are frequent.
>
> However, as a result of his inability to supply a particular customer during that period, that customer may have switched his custom to another supplier. In this situation, the plaintiff may have a permanent loss of profits, that is, the profits it would have expected to earn from sales to that customer after the machine was delivered.

A further example can be seen in a tort.

> ***Example***
>
> If a man is injured by a motor vehicle, for which the driver of the motor vehicle is liable in negligence, then the injured person will have suffered a loss of earnings

for the period of time in which he is unable to work. Again, if his injuries are permanent, meaning that he can never work again, then he will suffer a continuing loss.

In damages calculations, it is standard practice to calculate a plaintiff's earnings to an assumed date of trial and, where relevant, the future loss, that is, the financial damage which will continue to be suffered after trial.

From these two simple examples can be seen the source of the problems which bedevil damages calculations, that is, the uncertainty which results from attempting to compute earnings and profits which would have arisen, but which did not.

It is these problems which are considered next.

18.9 Computation of damages – the problems

Probably the most important part of calculating damages is pulling together all available financial information. The weakest part of an accountant's evidence is likely to be as a result of a lack of information, closely followed by conflicting information. It is in these two areas that skilful cross-examination can draw responses which can be damaging to a client's case on damages. If an accountant has insufficient information on which to base his calculations, then he cannot be certain that his calculations are correct.

18.9.1 Insufficient information

The problems of insufficient information can be seen in the example of the man injured by a motor vehicle. It is assumed that the man earned £50,000 per annum, and as a result of his injuries he has been permanently disabled and is unable to work again. The straightforward way of calculating the man's loss of earnings to trial and after trial is to work on the assumption that the man would have continued to earn £50,000 per annum. An accountant is not needed for that. However, he may have seen his earnings increasing over recent years as a result of promotions. Should one take the potential for future promotions into account? His personnel file or the intentions of his employers may indicate that promotion was due in the future. In that case, the earnings scales used by his employers would need to be referred to. But where does one stop? Can one just assume that the man would have continued to be promoted until he reached the top of his company? Or is it better, by reference to his age, experience, qualifications and those of his peer group, to work on the basis that he would probably have reached a certain level and use this in the calculations? The use of the word 'probably' is important, because of the burden of proof in civil trials. The accountant should work on the basis of his probable earnings rather than his possible earnings.

In addition, the man may have earned a bonus, tied to the level of his employer's profits. To estimate these in the future, one may need to have regard to the level of the company's profits in the future.

In this example, the accountant will obviously be uncertain as to the level of future earnings, even if the information noted in the example is available. However, that information may include, for example, a personnel file or statement from the employer concerning future promotion prospects. Such information may not be available. Alternatively, the employer may only have limited promotion prospects, requiring the man, if he had not suffered the accident, to seek employment elsewhere in order to increase his earnings.

The information drives the calculations and it may be the case that, due to a lack of information, the only calculation that the accountant can prepare with any certainty is the one based on earnings of £50,000 per annum.

This example is based on a man in employment, and these are often the most straightforward calculations to perform. The reason is that the factors which can affect an employed person's earnings are limited, and therefore the amount of information on such factors is limited. Where a man is self-employed, or where one is attempting to assess the profits of a company, there is a far greater range of factors which can affect profits and, therefore, a far wider range of potentially available information.

18.9.2 Conflicting information

It is often the case that, in computing a loss on the basis of certain financial information, an accountant will become aware of other information which conflicts with the way the loss has been calculated. Such information cannot be ignored; at the very least it has to be considered and it may need to be incorporated into the calculations.

To take a simple example, in the case of the machine delivered late, the accountant will review the plaintiff's sales before and after the machine was delivered; such a review may include a review of the sales files of individual customers. The fact that those sales files disclose orders which cannot be met will be an important part of the justification of the quantum calculation. However, it may be that one file indicates that a particular customer was planning to reduce orders anyway. The accountant may need to reduce the level of quantum as a result of this.

The problem which the accountant faces when presented with conflicting information is the weight which he attributes to the individual items of evidence. This is always a matter of judgment. However, it is in this area that an accountant can show that he is truly independent and not just the mouthpiece of his client.

18.9.3 Two specific problem areas – short periods and fluctuating profits

The problems of insufficient information and inconsistency can be seen in two circumstances which all expert accountants will face at some time – short periods of trading and fluctuating profits.

The problem of the short period of trading is seen where damage has been done to a business within a relatively short period after its inception. In this situation, there may only be a few months of trading on which to base a loss of profits calculation. Just because a business has been trading for a short period of time does not mean that it would not have continued in the future, perhaps at higher and higher levels of activity, making greater and greater profits. However, it is often very difficult to prove that this would have been the case.

In such a case the accountant is likely to need large amounts of what can be called indirect information, that is, information on markets, on the likely success of products and on financial requirements. The difficulty in doing this is that the accountant's report on opinion may become an argument because of the large amounts of non-financial information incorporated in the report. The report may not be accounting evidence at all.

Fluctuating profits, especially those demonstrating extreme fluctuations, provide a different problem. The accountant needs to ask what the ongoing maintainable profit level is. Sometimes, the fluctuations can be explained at the turnover level – perhaps because of changes in a client or customer base, or because of seasonality factors. Both of these can be investigated, in the former case by investigation of sales on a client-by-client basis, in the latter by the use of statistical techniques such as moving averages. Often, however, they cannot, and the accountant may be able to do little more than average out the previous years' profits and use this as the basis for loss.

18.10 Averages and ranges

The use of averages was noted in the previous section as something which the accountant is forced to use when he cannot investigate a problem any further, that is, when he has insufficient information to work out the underlying trend of profits. Because the accountant has to use this technique as a result of insufficient or conflicting information, it does not mean that it is an inadequate technique to use. In most circumstances, what the average profit was in the past is likely to indicate what the average profit will be in the future. The technique does not suffer from being inexact but may suffer from being used in the wrong circumstances or improperly applied. Thus, one bumper year in five, where the other four fluctuate only moderately, may lead to an average that is wholly distorted by one year.

The use of ranges also arises from uncertainty. In effect, what the accountant is saying is that it is reasonable to suppose that the loss of profits will be in the range £X to £Y. An accountant computing a loss of profits in this way is not avoiding giving an opinion; what he is doing is setting out where his uncertainties lie and the effect of those uncertainties on his calculations. In many cases, especially where there is conflicting evidence which will only be determined at trial, the accountant must give a range. However, for the greater assistance of the court, the accountant should try to set out the areas of uncertainty which cause the range, and also, where possible, ascribe values to the uncertainties.

18.11 Causation

Although this chapter is concerned, in the main, with the quantification of damages, in many cases involving businesses an inevitable and necessary part of the accountant's investigation of quantum will be the determination of causation of loss, i.e., liability. To give the example of the machine, it was noted above that in investigating sales it may be determined that sales to one customer may have been reduced as a result of lower orders, but that the failure of the machine to be delivered on time was not necessarily the cause of the loss of sales to that one customer.

An investigation of causation takes place side by side with the determination of quantum whenever the accountant investigates the profit trends during the period before the damage and during the period of the loss. The reason this is so is because the accountant must always ask himself whether the matter complained of is what has caused the loss.

In some cases, the question of causation is irrelevant for the accountant, such as in many personal injury cases. However, in other cases, the question is so relevant to the accountant's work that he should consider devoting a separate part of his report to issues concerned with causation.

18.12 Sufficiency of evidence

Having dealt with many of the problems which incomplete or inconsistent financial information causes, this section looks at what information is sufficient for the accountant to prepare his report.

No hard and fast rules can be set out because each case is different. In each case, the accountant should ask himself what other information might exist, and might that information confirm or deny the assumptions which underlie the calculation of quantum. Finally, the accountant should ask, do I have sufficient information to give the opinion in the report?

The information can be considered in a number of categories.

18.12.1 Internal financial information

This comprises the normal accounting information maintained by any business such as ledgers, accounts, tax returns, vouchers, budgets and forecasts and management information.

The accountant is in a good position to know exactly what sort of accounting information a business will maintain and can advise his solicitor accordingly of what should be requested.

18.12.2 Internal non-financial information

This will consist of board minutes, strategic plans, marketing information and production information. It will also include customer files, particularly orders and correspondence, and details concerning employees and quality control.

Enquiries through solicitors may have to be made to determine the extent of this information.

18.12.3 External direct information

External direct information is that held by third parties specifically concerning the business, in their dealings with the business. It may include certain of the working papers of a business's auditors or information held by sources of finance. This information is often the most difficult to come by because it is in the possession of third parties who may be unwilling to disclose it.

However, where internal records have been lost, it may be the only source of reliable financial information. In this regard, one is thinking of the information held by the Inland Revenue, receivers and liquidators or suppliers and customers.

18.12.4 External indirect information

This information comprises, essentially, information on the markets in which the plaintiff operates. This will include information on the company itself or its major suppliers, customers and competitors and information on its sector and wider geographic and macroeconomic data.

Such information may be of little use, may be of partial relevance or may go a long way to supporting or destroying a claim.

18.13 Performing the calculation

The accountant is required to perform a calculation of loss of profits, but which profits? The normal answer is that one looks to calculate the gross profits. This does, of course, assume that the level of overheads is fixed, an assumption which is often not the case. Many overheads do vary with activity (this is an important aspect of mitigation – see **18.14** below). For example, if, as a result of the damage suffered, a business has fewer goods to sell, there is a consequent effect on certain selling expenses as well as on other items such as interest. Some overheads are sunk costs, such as rent and rates. It is of prime importance for the accountant to determine the relationships between the various items in a business's profit and loss account.

Although the calculation of lost profits is the objective, nearly all such calculations are driven by sales projections. Having predicted the sales, one then applies a uniform gross profit and deducts, as noted above, certain overheads. However, the accountant must always be aware of the physical constraints which restrict the ability of any business to achieve a given level of sales. These constraints include the financial, such as the access to funds to generate a certain level of activity, production restrictions and the ease of selling into a market. It seems an obvious point to make but if most businesses had an unlimited ability to expand, then they would; the accountant needs to be aware of the individual restrictions on the business he is investigating.

18.13.1 Loss to date of trial and future loss

It was noted above that there are two parts to a quantum calculation where the loss is continuing. The loss to the date of trial is simply the arithmetical addition of losses in each of the accounting periods from the date of damage to the assumed date of trial. Interest, if awarded, is added later.

However, the future loss is a more involved calculation, because the accountant has to take account of two factors. First, any future loss may be permanent and, second, the future loss has to be discounted to take account of the financial benefit of receiving, in an earlier period, an income stream to be earned in a later period.

Chapter 21 on personal injury and fatal accident claims deals with this issue and introduces the concepts of multiplicands and multipliers. Effectively, what the calculation tries to do is to determine a level of maintainable earnings and calculate the discounted value of such an earnings stream over a period of time. Such an approach is also used in loss of profits claims and applies even where an income stream may be receivable effectively in perpetuity. The accountant has to decide a suitable discount factor to use, and often the starting point is the return on gilts over the period of the future loss, or the return on the longest dated gilts where the loss is permanent.

18.14 Mitigation

Finally, a person having suffered damage as a result of a tort or a breach of contract is under a general duty to take all reasonable steps to mitigate his loss. The person cannot recover damages in respect of a loss which could have been so avoided. Where reasonable steps are taken, then the defendant is liable for the reduced loss. However, losses can be recovered in respect of costs incurred in taking reasonable steps to mitigate any loss, i.e., expenses incurred in minimising loss (for example, medical expenses in personal injury claims, advertising expenditure to counteract the effect of a defendant's infringement of the plaintiff's trade mark).

It is common for expert accountant's reports to deal with the financial effects of mitigation. At the most basic level, in a personal injury case, this may just consist of deducting the plaintiff's earnings from alternative employment. However, in a more complicated breach of contract, for example where an alternative manufacturing process has been used, the quantification of the effects of mitigation can be at least as complicated as the quantum claim.

One particularly difficult aspect of mitigation is the calculation of salary costs incurred. These often comprise management time. The accountant is often faced with an involved exercise attempting to discover from very poor records exactly what has been done.

A further aspect of an investigation of mitigation is the extent to which a plaintiff has continued to incur certain overheads to which he was not committed, and which could have been saved.

These aspects of mitigation again illustrate the importance in any quantum claim of determining how a business operates.

18.15 Calculations on behalf of the defence

This chapter has been written to a great extent from the position of an accountant preparing a quantum claim for the plaintiff, without any specific reference to the work of the accountant instructed by the defence. The reason is that, in many cases, the plaintiff's expert will carry out his work first, the results of which will be served either as a schedule of damages or in a report on the other side. However, the approach taken by the defence accountant is exactly the same as that taken by the plaintiff's accountant. The defendant's accountant is in a different position because the other side will have carried out much of the initial work for him, particularly the pulling together of financial information.

What the accountant for the defence is required to do is to consider the approach adopted by the plaintiff's accountants and critically examine their assumptions and calculations and consider whether they have taken into account all of the information which is, or may be, available.

18.16 Reference

McGregor, H. (1997) *McGregor on Damages* (16th edn), Sweet & Maxwell.

Chapter 19
Taxation of damages

19.1 Introduction

Whenever an accountant investigates a damages claim, either for the plaintiff or for the defendant, he needs to ask himself two questions. Firstly, should the amount of the damages claimed be reduced to take account of taxation and, secondly, if so, what is the tax rate to be applied?

19.2 Gourley

The reason that damages may be reduced by taxation is derived from the basic rule that the object of an award of damages is to put the plaintiff in the position he would have been in if the tort had not occurred or if the contract had been carried out. Thus, the position of a person who has been injured in a motor accident is that he would have earned income on which he would have been taxed. Therefore, the amount of compensation which he should receive should be the amount net of tax.

British Transport Commission v *Gourley* [1956] AC 185 was the first case to reduce an award of damages to take account of tax. The case concerned a negligence action in respect of personal injury. A substantial award was made in respect of past and future loss of income. The reasons for making the reduction were that:

(a) the compensation was in respect of lost income which, had it been received, would have been subject to income tax;
(b) the damages awarded to the plaintiff were capital and would not themselves be subject to tax.

Thus, the court was attempting to ensure that the plaintiff was not over-compensated by the award. (At the time of *Gourley* there was no capital gains tax (CGT) but in any event damages for personal injury are specifically exempted from CGT.)

The House of Lords held that:

> 'A successful plaintiff is entitled to have awarded to him such a sum as will, so far as possible, make good to him the financial loss which he has suffered and will probably suffer as a result of the wrong done to him for which the defendant is responsible.'

In deciding to deduct taxation, the House of Lords was therefore applying the normal principles applying to damages in tort. However, if the damages recoverable would be subject to tax, then *Gourley* is not applied. Thus, in these circumstances, even if the plaintiff makes more money as a result of the damages than he would have done if, say, the tort had not occurred, the court will not reduce the amount the plaintiff receives in damages. This would be the case (as it is in some countries) if damages awards were taxed at a lower rate than trading income.

19.3 Taxation of damages as income

The accountant needs to consider, therefore, whether the damages will be taxed by the Inland Revenue (or any other revenue authority). The general principle to be applied is called the '*Attwoll*' principle, from the case of *London & Thames Haven Oil Wharves Ltd* v *Attwooll* [1967] Ch 772, where Diplock LJ said:

> 'Where, pursuant to a legal right, a trader receives from another person compensation for the trader's failure to receive a sum of money which, if it had been received, would have been credited to the amount of profits (if any) arising in any year from the trade carried on by him at the time when the compensation is so received, the compensation is to be treated for income tax purposes in the same way as that sum of money would have been treated if it had been received instead of the compensation.'

Despite this, the court also held that just because damages are based on a loss of profits does not mean that they will constitute a trading receipt. For example, an award of damages in a personal injury case in respect of the future loss represents a capital receipt not a trading receipt, and the compensation in respect of the future loss is therefore not taxable. Furthermore, the loss of income to the date of trial, which on the face of it does represent a trading receipt, is not put into a taxable category just because of the arbitrary basis of the time the trial is heard.

Whether damages are held to be taxable as income and therefore not subject to a reduction for taxation in their award depends upon whether they can be treated as income as a matter of tax law; a sum can represent a loss of revenue but, nevertheless, that sum can be a capital sum not subject to income tax. However, for example, if there is a continuing business and an element of the profits of this business have been reduced as a result of a tort or a breach of contract, then the receipt of the compensation will usually be taxable in the normal way as a receipt of the trade and *Gourley* will not apply. However, to the extent that the compensation represents a capital sum, then this will not be taxable and *Gourley* will apply.

19.4 General and special damages

The taxation of damages is complicated still further when one considers general and special damages.

In, for example, a personal injury case there will be a claim for general damages, for example pain and suffering, and for special damages, for example loss of income. The general damages are not in respect of any income and are therefore not reduced by taxation; by contrast, the income element of the damages will be reduced under the *Gourley* rule, for the reasons given at **19.3**.

However, this appears to work slightly differently in defamation actions. In *Lewis* v *The Daily Telegraph* [1964] AC 234 the House of Lords held that *Gourley* could apply to general damages for defamation claimed by a company, meaning that the damages are received free of tax. The jury would need to be directed to make an allowance for the taxation. The reason was that a company could not have its feelings hurt, only its pocket and therefore the libel award was in respect of a sum which would have been taxable. This would not apply, of course, to an individual, where an award of general damages is not designed to restore lost income. However, any special damages awarded to the company in a defamation action, that is, for the specific loss of profits as proven, will be taxable under the *Attwooll* principle and not subject to *Gourley*.

Therefore, one is left with the slightly bizarre situation that, in some torts depending on the plaintiff, general damages are not taxable on receipt but not subject to *Gourley* and special damages which are not taxable on receipt are subject to *Gourley*; however, in others general damages would not be taxable on receipt and are subject to *Gourley*, but special damages which will be taxed on receipt, are not subject to *Gourley*!

19.5 Wrongful dismissal claims

Accountants will most often come across the *Gourley* principle in wrongful dismissal claims. When someone has been dismissed, their source of income is no longer present and therefore the damages are not taxable. However, the salary they would have received would have been taxable. *Gourley* therefore applies. Despite this, there are specific provisions which tax golden handshakes and therefore *Gourley* should not apply.

However, what happens is that *Gourley* is applied to the tax-free lump sum which the legislation allows (currently £30,000), but not to the rest, which is taxable in the normal way. The plaintiff gets as compensation the amount he would have received had the defendant paid him on his dismissal but without the benefit of not suffering the tax on the £30,000. The defendant gets the benefit of this, and in respect of the remainder of the damages claim pays over the deducted tax to the Inland Revenue.

An example of the *Gourley* calculation in a wrongful dismissal claim, showing the inconsistencies which arise from this area of the law, is set out at Appendix 13.

19.6 Capital gains tax

The general rule is that capital gains tax is payable on compensation in respect of capital assets which are lost as a result of a tort or a breach of contract. Damages for personal injury, death and defamation, where suffered by an individual, are not subject to capital gains tax by virtue of s51 of the Taxation of Chargeable Gains Act 1992 (but see also Inland Revenue Extra-statutory Concession D33).

However, *Gourley* is expressed in terms of income tax only (capital gains tax did not exist at the time) and appears not to apply.

Two aspects of the incidence of capital gains taxation should be noted. In most cases the plaintiff would not have disposed of his asset and therefore not suffered the tax at the time he does. Additionally, the various reliefs which may be available on the purchase of assets will be lost, and certain other allowances may be clawed back. In these cases, the loss suffered by the plaintiff is somewhat greater than just the loss of the asset, and the accountant should factor these considerations into his computation of damages.

Secondly, in *Zim Properties* v *Procter* [1985] STC 90 it was held that a right of action in negligence (in that case professional negligence) was an asset and that the damages paid were subject to capital gains tax as a capital sum derived from an asset within what is now s22 of the Taxation of Chargeable Gains Act 1992. It was recognised that this principle created a number of anomalies in the charge to capital gains tax. For example, whilst the compensation may relate to an underlying chargeable asset which may have a significant base cost which would shelter a capital gain on the disposal of the asset, there is little base cost in the right to sue. The Inland Revenue attempted to address the anomalies in Extra-statutory Concession D33. In particular, where a right of action, such as a claim for professional negligence, does not arise in respect of loss or damage in connection with a form of property which is an asset for capital gains tax purposes (an underlying asset), any gain accruing on the disposal of a right of action, e.g., by an award of damages by a court, will be exempt from CGT.

19.7 Summary of when to reduce damages to take account of taxation

Figure 19.1

Claim	*Income tax*	*Capital gains tax*
Personal injury – general	Not taxable	Not applicable
Personal injury – special	Apply *Gourley*	Not applicable
Defamation – individual – general	Not taxable	Not applicable
Defamation – individual – special	Apply *Gourley*	Not applicable
Defamation – company – general	Jury directed to take account of tax	Assume that jury has taken into account any taxation as a result of direction
All other claims for pecuniary damages	If compensation will be taxable then do not reduce compensation award for tax	*Gourley* not applicable

19.8 Tax rates to be applied

If the accountant considers that the damages calculation must be reduced to take account of the tax, that is, reduced as a result of *Gourley*, he needs to consider what tax rates to apply. In respect of past loss, he should apply the rates of tax extant in each of the years when a loss is calculated. He should also take account of the personal allowances and other reliefs in those years. The accountant also needs to take account of any other income which the plaintiff enjoys, so that the correct marginal rate of tax is applied to the compensation. The compensation should be taxed as the top slice of the plaintiff's income.

In respect of future loss, the accountant should use the rates ruling at the date of his report, to be updated at the date of the trial. If there has been a Budget announcing new rates, then he should use these.

Chapter 20
Interest

20.1 Introduction

In most civil cases in which the accountant prepares an expert report, there will be a claim for interest on damages. Given his facility with numbers, the accountant will probably be asked to calculate that interest.

Interest is not an award of damages. It is designed to recompense the plaintiff for the time which he has been out of the damages. Therefore, in a claim for the payment of an unpaid invoice, interest at trial will be calculated based on the time interval between when the debt was due and when judgment is given for the payment of the debt.

This chapter deals with how interest is calculated, in particular what rates should be used in the calculation. However, a number of principles should be stated that govern interest claims.

First, a claim for interest must be specifically pleaded, otherwise the court will not award interest. In many simple claims, such as for a debt, the statement of claim will state the amount of interest to the date of issue of the writ, and the amount at which interest continues to accrue on a daily basis. In more complicated claims, for example where damages have to be assessed by the court, or where different sums are claimed from different dates, it is usual just to state that interest is claimed.

Second, interest is, in most cases, awarded at the discretion of the court, not as of right. In a few cases, the court's discretion does not operate, such as where the plaintiff is entitled to interest under the terms of a contract or by statute. The discretion extends to whether to award any interest at all, the rate and the period of time over which interest is calculated. The discretion is given to the court by s35A of the Supreme Court Act 1981 (s69 County Courts Act 1984).

20.2 Interest rates and general categories of claim

It was noted above that interest is generally payable at the discretion of the court, and this includes the particular interest rate to be applied. It is convenient to divide up claims and the rates applicable into three categories, being claims under contract, damages for personal injury and other claims.

20.3 Contract

Under a contract, there may be a provision stating that, in the event of something happening or not happening, interest on an amount will be payable at a particular rate. The most common example is interest on an unpaid contractual debt. Such interest is payable as of right and, in litigation to recover the debt, the claim for interest will be at the rate and for any period specified in the contract (that is, the court has no discretion over the matter). However, it should be borne in mind that for many breaches of contract, there will be no interest provision. The plaintiff will therefore be forced to claim discretionary interest.

There is no double counting of interest on contractual debts by taking the contractual rate of interest and then claiming discretionary interest on top. Subsection 35A(4) of the Supreme Court Act 1981 (s69(4) of the County Courts Act 1984) states that interest under s35A will not be awarded if interest on the debt already runs.

20.4 Personal injury and fatal accident cases

Subsection 35A(2) of the Supreme Court Act 1981 (s69(2) County Courts Act 1984) states that the court is required to award interest where the award of damages is greater than £200, unless there are special reasons to the contrary. There are a number of broad principles which are applied to the calculation of such interest.

First, by *Jefford* v *Gee* [1970] 2 QB 130, interest on special damages (including loss of earnings and specific expenses such as medical expenses) is calculated on the basis of half of the appropriate rate of interest on the whole of the special damages from the date of the injury to judgment. This works on the presumption that the loss will accrue evenly over the period to trial.

Damages for pain and suffering (i.e., non-pecuniary loss) carry interest at 2 per cent per annum from the date of service of the writ to date of judgment, the logic here being that the award is made based on scales extant at the time of the judgment, not by reference to the scales at the time when the accident occurred. Therefore, the pain and suffering award for the same accident on the same day will differ depending on when the trial is. If this is the logic, then it is difficult to see why any interest is awarded on such damages at all. Lord Denning expressed a similar opinion whilst delivering the Court of Appeal's judgment in *Cookson* v *Knowles* [1977] QB 913, basing his reasoning on the impropriety of a plaintiff benefiting from a delay in bringing a case to trial. The House of Lords, however, in *Pickett* v *British Rail Engineering* [1980] AC 136 declined to follow this line of reasoning.

Damages for bereavement in fatal accident claims carry interest at the full rate. The logic here is that because the bereavement award is fixed, it should carry interest at the full rate (*Sharman* v *Sheppard* [1989] CLY 1190).

Damages for future pecuniary loss carry no interest, the logic of which is self-evident. Indeed, such sums will be discounted because they represent money received in advance. However, for non-pecuniary loss there will be compensation as general damages in one lump sum. This is because it is not possible to divide pre- and post-trial deprivation.

The courts will not normally depart from these principles unless there are special reasons to do so. The most obvious reason is that damages do not accrue evenly with time, and heavy expenditure of medical care immediately after an accident should receive interest based on the date of expenditure. This was the situation in *Dexter* v *Courtaulds* [1984] 1 WLR 372. Although in *Dexter* v *Courtaulds* the court did not think it appropriate to depart from the *Jefford* v *Gee* calculation, it was suggested that a plaintiff should specifically plead any special circumstances he wished to rely on to have interest calculated on a different basis. Indeed, given that the principle in *Jefford* v *Gee* appears to have been grounded in expediency of calculation, in the age of spreadsheets there is little to lose and much, perhaps, to gain from applying the full interest rate to the largest items of special damages from the date they were incurred.

Finally, the rate to be used is the 'special account rate', a rate of interest payable on, for example, amounts paid into court. The rate is currently 8 per cent, and has been since February 1993. The full table of rates is set out in Appendix 12.

20.5 Other claims

In all other claims the court has discretion, but it is common practice to make a calculation of the interest in the expert report. Thus, in any claim for loss of profits because of negligence or deceit, or for a claim for breach of warranty, the accountant may be asked to put into his report a calculation of interest.

The simple way to approach the question of on what to calculate interest and for what period is to ask a number of questions.

First, would the plaintiff have had money but for, say, the breach of contract or the negligence? If the plaintiff has lost earnings or has not received the payment of a loan, he has been kept out of the money.

Second, has the plaintiff had to expend more than he would have had to as a result of the matter complained of? For example, if the plaintiff has had to buy more expensive goods as a result of a failure to supply under a contract, or had to pay for remedial work on faulty equipment.

20.6 The interest rate to be applied

Interest is not an award of damages but a payment to the plaintiff for being kept out of the money which ought to have been paid to him. In *London, Chatham and Dover Ry Co.* v *South Eastern Ry Co.* [1893] AC 429 it was held by Lord Herschell that the wrongdoer who is wrongfully withholding money from another ought not to benefit from that money. A problem arises in deciding which rate to use.

There are a number of different interest rates which could be used, and six of them are set out in the notes to the White Book at 6/2/12 (a–f).

20.6.1 Commercial rate

This is the rate which the plaintiff would have had to pay to borrow the money. The White Book indicates that the personal circumstances of the plaintiff may be relevant to some extent and, therefore, a person of high credit rating may receive a lower rate than a person of low credit rating, since the person or corporation of high standing would have been able to borrow money at a lower interest rate (see, for example, *Tate & Lyle Food and Distribution* v *Greater London Council* [1982] 1 WLR 149).

This rate is used in commercial cases. In the commercial court the practice is to award base rate plus 1 per cent, but this is a presumption that can be rebutted on the grounds of unfairness to one party or the other (see *Shearson Lehman* v *Maclaine Watson (No 2)* [1990] 3 All ER 723).

A table of base rates is set out in Appendix 12.

20.6.2 Investment rate

This is the rate at which the money could have been invested by the plaintiff and is usually taken as the rate payable on judgment debts as set out in Appendix 12.

20.6.3 'True' interest rate

This rate disregards the inflation in interest rates, and is reflected in the yield on index-linked gilts. The rate applies where damages are assessed as at the date of trial in depreciated currency. The rise in the value of the currency is offset by the removal of the inflation element in sterling. This method prevents overcompensation of the plaintiff, as would occur if he were awarded interest from the accrual of the cause of action at market rates.

20.6.4 Wilful default rate

In its equitable jurisdiction a much higher rate of interest may be awarded by the court to stop a defendant making a profit from a breach of fiduciary duty.

20.6.5 Foreign interest rates

This is applicable where an award of damages is made in a foreign currency. Interest is usually taken at the rate at which that currency could be borrowed in the country in which the debt should have been paid.

20.6.6 Ordinary interest rate

The White Book states that the judgment rate is only to be used if there is no better indication of which rate is appropriate. Other rates which may be appropriate are the special account rate or the commercial rate, as noted above.

Base rates move more often than the special account rate, which itself moves more often than the judgment rate.

20.7 Compound interest

Subsection 35A(1) of the Supreme Court Act 1981 (s69(1) County Courts Act 1984) refers to simple interest only, effectively denying the court discretion to award compound interest. However, compound interest may be awarded in certain circumstances, for example where there has been fraud or a breach of fiduciary duty. In such cases, the purpose of an award (which may not have been pleaded as interest but as restitution) will be to stop the defendant making any profit from his wrongdoing. Banks will often charge compound interest on unpaid interest (this is often termed default interest) and may attempt to claim compound interest in litigation.

The House of Lords considered the issue of compound interest awards in *Westdeutsche Landesbank Girozentrale* v *Islington Borough Council* [1996] AC 669. The case concerned one of the council swaps disputes, where a local authority had entered into an interest rate swap agreement with a bank which was held to be *ultra vires* the council and therefore void. The issue before the House of Lords was whether the bank could claim compound interest on amounts unpaid.

First of all, it is clear from the case that equity awarded compound interest as a means of stopping a person owing a fiduciary duty and being in breach of that duty from making a profit from his breach. However, could this be extended to non-equitable claims? Lord Goff, dissenting, at p.980 stated that:

> '. . . the equitable jurisdiction to award compound interest may be exercised in the case of personal claims at common law, as it is in equity.'

This was, however, not the view of the majority. Lord Browne-Wilkinson, at p.984 and Lord Slynn at p.1000 both stated that it was common ground that compound interest could not be awarded at common law. Furthermore, Lord Browne-Wilkinson at p.984 stated that:

> 'In the absence of fraud courts of equity have never awarded compound interest except against a trustee or other person owing fiduciary duties who is accountable for profits made from his position . . . The award of compound interest was restricted to cases where the award was in lieu of an account of profits improperly made by the trustee. We were not referred to any case where compound interest had been awarded in the absence of fiduciary accountability for a profit.'

The only way in which this situation will change is through legislation.

20.8 Calculation of interest in expert reports

Accountants are normally asked to calculate interest claims as part of their expert reports. Three problems can be identified in doing this:

(a) interest will be calculated up to an assumed date of trial and, as many accountants are fully aware, that assumption is invariably incorrect;
(b) the final claim awarded by the court may be, and often will be, different from that in the accountant's report;
(c) the interest award, including the rate, is at the discretion of the court.

All of this means that the accountant's calculation of interest is likely to be different to that awarded by the court. Further, a calculation of interest is not strictly a subject for expert accounting evidence. Given this, why should the accountant bother?

There are three very good reasons for the accountant to bother. First, the interest claim is invariably driven by the damages calculations in the expert's report. It is a simple matter to add on to, say, loss of earnings spreadsheets an interest spreadsheet.

Second, interest can often be a very large figure in a claim (sometimes the largest figure, given the speed at which the largest cases progress towards court) and the amount of interest will be an important part of any settlement negotiations. The accountant can factor into his calculations varying rates, periods and items on which interest may be awarded to aid the client.

Finally, although not a subject for expert accounting evidence, in complex claims the accountant is the person best placed to carry out the calculation and then explain it to the court.

Chapter 21
Personal injury and fatal accident

21.1 Introduction

A claim for damages can arise when a person is injured by another. It is usually a claim in tort arising, for example, from another person's negligence. The damages in a personal injury action are to compensate the injured party for losses suffered and for pain and suffering, loss of amenity and future losses. It is the injured party, or a representative on his behalf (if the injured party is a minor or under a mental disability), who will make the claim. The calculation of damages falls under a variety of headings, which are discussed in this chapter.

A fatal accident is one in which a person dies in, or as a result of, the accident. Claims are usually made on behalf of the deceased's estate, or his dependants. Some aspects of the calculation differ from those in a personal injury claim and these will be highlighted later in this chapter.

Accountants are frequently involved in the calculation of damages, but not in matters of liability or in considering who is at fault. The calculation is to establish only pecuniary losses, such as loss of income, and usually not other heads of damage, such as for pain and suffering. This chapter deals with the calculation of pecuniary losses.

Personal injury and fatal accident claims constitute a vast subject, which cannot be dealt with in detail in one chapter. These comments should therefore be considered as an introduction to the subject. Practitioners in this field are recommended to read further into the subject and to familiarise themselves with the relevant cases. A bibliography is included at **21.12.**

21.2 Calculation of damages

21.2.1 General and special damages

The broad headings of compensation in personal injury are general damages and special damages.

General damages are considered by practitioners to compensate the injured person for non-pecuniary losses arising from the accident. These include pain and suffering and loss of amenity. Pain refers to the physical pain resulting from the injury, while suffering relates to a mental state, such as anxiety or fear. Loss of amenity occurs when the injured party has lost or has had reduced the ability to enjoy life as a result of a physical or psychological impediment, such as the inability to participate in a sport due to the loss of a limb.

Special damages are pecuniary losses which flow from the accident. They include loss of earnings and additional expenses incurred by the injured party, such as medical and other expenses from the date of injury to the date of trial.

21.2.2 Principles for the calculation of loss of earnings

The principles for the calculation of damages concerning loss of earnings were considered in the case of *Cookson* v *Knowles* [1979] AC 556. These may be summarised as:

(a) The calculation of a past loss of earnings from the date of the accident to the date of trial can take into account any expected increases in income.

(b) The future loss from the date of trial onwards is based on the earnings level at the date of trial. This implies that no allowance is to be made for factors such as inflation. However, if appropriate, account could be taken of expected increases in earnings.

(c) The future loss is usually to be calculated by applying a multiplier to the annual loss, called the multiplicand. The multiplier can be derived from annuity tables which take into account the number of years from trial to expected retirement, accelerated receipt of the income and average mortality of the population.

In *Mallett* v *McMonagle* [1970] AC 166 it was confirmed that, in assessing damages, it was inevitable that certain estimates would have to be made as to what would have happened in the future. The calculation of the loss of earnings therefore starts with a projection of what the injured person would have earned but for the accident. For example, expected earnings during the year in which the injured person was incapacitated would be established. This is compared to actual earnings, if any, during the period. There would be no ongoing loss of earnings if the person returned to working as before the accident. However, if income on returning to work was affected, for example by missing a promotion, then this ongoing loss of income should be taken into account.

Where an injured person returns to work, but as a result of the injury might, for example, be made redundant in the future, there may still be a loss due to a possible restriction on earnings capacity in the future. This is sometimes referred to as a disadvantage in the labour market or a *Smith* v *Manchester* award, following the case of *Smith* v *Manchester Corporation* [1974] 17 KIR 1 CA.

If there is an ongoing loss, earnings should be projected from the date of the accident until the date of trial. If the date of trial is not known at the time the calculation is made, then it is customary to use a hypothetical future date of trial. A future loss will also be calculated from the notional date of trial until the date of expected retirement.

21.3 Calculation of loss of earnings

The calculation of a loss of earnings will depend on the circumstances in each case. Earnings can include a number of components, the most important of which are:

- salary;
- bonus;
- pension contributions;
- share of profit;
- car allowance;
- medical benefits;
- accommodation and other allowances;
- other financial benefits.

The principle is to establish the total financial loss suffered by the injured party as a direct result of the accident. The calculation therefore includes any loss of salary as well as any benefits that are lost. The determination of projected earnings may be fairly straightforward if the injured person is employed and has had a stable career path. Various occupations, such as the police and teaching, have published pay scales that assist in projecting earnings.

The person's career history will usually require some investigation to establish whether the person would probably have remained in the same job had the accident not occurred. The career prospects and the likelihood of promotions will also require investigation to ascertain the projected levels of earnings over a period of time. Consideration may also need to be given to any past breaks in career or periods of unemployment. This information will be used to establish an overall career pattern and a projection of income.

If the person is self-employed, the projection of income becomes more complex. The business will often need to be reviewed and forecasts made of the levels of profit it would be likely to have achieved in the future. As the loss is to be calculated as a shortfall in profit or income, projections will include both income and expenditure. The loss will be the shortfall in earnings of the injured person had the accident not occurred.

The period for which the loss of earnings is calculated will depend on the circumstances in each case. In general, for personal injury, the period will run from the date of the accident until there is no longer any financial effect directly attributable to it. Where the person is unable to work again, the loss would run until the expected date of retirement. If the person should be able to achieve some residual earnings by, for example, taking another job which may be less demanding, then the calculation will be the projected earnings less those actually achieved. If the injured person has had no earnings at the time the calculation is made, account may still have to be taken of any future expected earnings, reflecting potential residual earnings' capacity.

There are a number of non-accounting factors which may have an impact on the calculation of a loss of earnings. For example, the calculation may indicate that a loss of earnings has occurred, but it must be verified that this is as a result of the injury sustained and not for any other reason. In addition, there may be a question whether the injured person did all they could to minimise their loss. These will usually be addressed by the accountant's instructing solicitors.

21.3.1 Taxation

Once the past and future loss of earnings, including any loss of benefits, has been established, income tax and National Insurance contributions (NIC) should be calculated and deducted to arrive at a loss of earnings after taxation and NIC.

The authority to deduct income tax is set out in *British Transport Commission* v *Gourley* [1956] AC 185. The principle is that earnings will attract income tax and NIC. A person therefore benefits only from the earnings after tax and NIC. When damages are awarded, they are awarded as damages and not as earnings. The successful claimant will not pay tax and NIC on the damages, but would have done so on any earnings on which the damages were based. If tax were not deducted, this would lead to the inequitable situation of a person being better off by recovering damages, rather than being put back in the same position as if the accident had not occurred. Income tax is not deducted for other heads of damage, such as medical costs or pain and suffering.

The method of calculation of taxation and NIC is to establish the amounts that would be payable on the projected earnings to arrive at net earnings after tax. From this is deducted any actual earnings after tax. The result will be a net loss of earnings arising from the accident.

Taxation is calculated on all earnings and benefits that would normally be subject to tax and at the rates that are applicable to the level of earnings. Where a future loss is calculated the taxation and NIC rates and personal allowances will not be known. It is customary, therefore, to use the last known rates. The calculation may be updated as more information becomes available over time.

21.3.2 Interest

The award of interest is usual in personal injury cases, in the absence of special reasons. This was incorporated into guidelines for the calculation of interest in the case of *Jefford* v *Gee* [1970] 2 QB 130 and subsequently in *Cookson* v *Knowles*. The purpose of awarding interest is to compensate the claimant for the late receipt of the income, which is received after the trial, rather than at the time it would have been earned. Section 329 ICTA 1988 exempts from income tax interest on damages awarded by a court in the UK for personal injury or death.

The principles for the calculation of interest on loss of earnings are:

(a) Interest is usually calculated on the past loss from the date of the accident up to the date of judgment. In practice, an accountant will make the calculation up to the first day of trial, as this date is often known.
(b) No interest is calculated on a future loss of earnings after the date of trial, as this part of the loss would not have occurred up to then.
(c) Simple interest is applied.
(d) Interest is added to the net loss after tax. No tax is deducted from the interest itself.

The rate of interest applied is the High Court Special Investment Account. This rate is changed, from time to time, by the Lord Chancellor. The current rate, in effect since 1 February 1993, is 8 per cent per annum. The rate of interest for other damages, such as pain and suffering and loss of amenity, is currently 2 per cent per annum from the date of service of the writ.

It is customary to calculate interest on loss of earnings for the period using one-half of the High Court Special Investment Account rate. There is some authority to use the full rate when the loss is limited in time. Any change of rate during the period needs to be accounted for by establishing the number of days to which each rate applies.

21.3.3 Past and future losses

The past loss is the calculated loss of earnings after tax for the period from the date of the accident to the date of the judgment, together with interest thereon. Where the loss continues beyond the trial, a future loss will be calculated. This is often based on the net loss of income in the year immediately preceding the trial, although there could be exceptions – for example, where there is the likelihood of promotion, redundancy or a significant increase in the earnings of an employed person. The amount of the annual continuing net loss determined at the date of trial is referred to as the multiplicand.

21.4 Multiplier

The multiplier is the number of years of loss of earnings, discounted to account for early receipt of a lump sum. To calculate a future loss it is necessary to multiply the multiplicand by the multiplier. The multiplier should take account of contingencies, early receipt of funds and the rate of return on funds. The medical evidence could also have a bearing on this. The calculation of the multiplier is not an exact science, so it is inevitable that there will be differences in the figures that are applied for various circumstances.

21.4.1 Ogden Tables

A set of tables for multipliers, based on various assumptions, was prepared by the Government Actuary's Department. These tables, known as 'Ogden Tables', are named after Sir Michael Ogden QC, who was chairman of the working party concerned. The tables were revised in 1993 to take into account increased life expectancy and to make allowance for other contingencies. The objective of the tables is to assist in the computation of a capital sum which, when invested, will provide funds for future costs of care and loss of earnings of the injured person.

The tables set out multipliers for a range of ages and rates of return on funds invested. For example, the multiplier for loss of earnings to pension age of 65 for a male aged 34 at date of trial will be 16.2, whilst the multiplier will be 14.7 if the person is 39 at the date of trial. These examples of multipliers are based on a rate of return of 4.5 per cent.

In the past, the Ogden Tables were not acceptable as evidence in court until they had been proved by an actuary. Cases such as *Hunt* v *Severs* [1994] 2 AC 350 attacked the use of actuarial tables. However, s10 Civil Evidence Act 1995 provides for the admissibility of actuarial tables as evidence, without their accuracy having to be proved in each case. This provision is not yet in force but, once it is, it will no longer be necessary to call expert evidence to prove the accuracy of the tables.

21.4.2 Rate of return

The Ogden Tables set out multipliers based on rates of return varying from 1.5 per cent to 5.0 per cent. There has been much debate on the appropriate rate of return and whether this should be based on risk-free investments, such as index-linked government stocks. The Court of Appeal in the cases of *Page* v *Sheerness Steel Co plc*, *Thomas* v *Brighton Health Authority* and *Wells* v *Wells* [1997] 1 All ER 673 held that a claimant should not be in a better position than an ordinary investor who is able to invest in a range of different ways. The Court of Appeal stated that the rate of return should be 4.5 per cent and not 3 per cent, which had been allowed in a number of cases at first instance. These cases have been taken to the House of Lords and a decision is pending.

Section 1 of the Damages Act 1996 makes provision for the Lord Chancellor to determine the rate of return. If he exercises this authority this will cease to be an issue for argument. The multiplier could then be read off the Ogden Tables, although the court is not obliged to follow the tables.

21.5 Deductions

Once the loss of earnings for past and future loss has been calculated, it is necessary to account for certain deductions. The deduction for actual earnings should have already been made in the calculation of loss of earnings.

The injured party may have received various benefits as a result of the injury. Each of these needs to be considered to establish whether it is to be set off against the claim. The Social Security (Recovery of Benefits) Act 1997 sets out the benefits and their treatment. There are a number of transitional provisions which should be noted. In general, if the case is settled after 6 October 1997 the provisions of the Act will apply.

The Act provides that damages arising from an accident or injury may not be affected by any benefits which the injured party has received or is likely to receive. The person who makes the compensation payment, i.e., the defendant, is liable to repay an amount equal to the total amount of recoverable benefits to the Secretary of State for Social Security.

Where an injured person receives compensation for past loss of earnings, the following benefits, if received, are to be repaid to the Government by the defendant:

- disability working allowance;
- disablement pension;
- incapacity benefit;
- income support;
- invalidity pension and allowance;
- jobseeker's allowance;
- reduced earnings allowance;
- severe disablement allowance;

- sickness benefit;
- statutory sick pay;
- unemployability supplement;
- unemployment benefit.

21.6 Pension losses

The loss of pension or the reduction in pension rights is usually a head of claim for future loss. There are a number of approaches to calculating pension losses. The loss is determined by comparing the benefit that the injured person would have received at normal pensionable age but for the accident and the pension receivable at that date as a result of the accident.

21.6.1 Pension schemes

The two broad categories of pension scheme, defined benefit and defined contribution, can be summarised as follows:

Defined benefit schemes

The benefits payable on retirement are defined by the scheme and this determines how the scheme is funded. The pension benefit depends on the number of years that the employee has worked for the company and the final salary at retirement. These are also known as occupational pension schemes. The calculation of the pension loss is fairly straightforward in that one need only project the final salary and determine the number of years of service.

Defined contribution schemes

The benefits payable under a scheme are determined by the amount of the contributions paid into the scheme until the date of expected retirement. These are also known as 'money purchase' schemes. The employer usually makes contributions to the fund, as does the employee. The contributions can usually be established without difficulty, but the overall rate of return achieved by the investment house used is unknown and therefore the eventual benefit cannot be determined with accuracy. In calculating a loss of pension, caution should be exercised in using the rates of return used by the Personal Investment Authority. These could be 6 per cent, 9 per cent or 12 per cent. However, these are only illustrative rates and may not be representative of rates of return expected in the future.

21.6.2 Imponderables

The Court of Appeal has held that in calculating pension loss, various 'imponderables' should be taken into account. These include voluntary wastage, redundancy, dismissal, supervening ill health, disablement or death before age 65, with death being the major discount. A further discount is to take account of accelerated receipt of the pension loss. These principles were set out in the case of *Auty* v *National Coal Board* [1985] 1 WLR 784. The Court of Appeal considered various cases and the discount was broadly 1 per cent for each year from the date of trial to the date of intended retirement.

With the admissibility of the Ogden Tables it is unclear how the deduction to account for 'imponderables' will be taken into account. The tables allow for the risk of mortality, but not for other factors. It is likely that each case will be assessed on its own merits, depending on individual circumstances.

21.6.3 Set-off of benefits

In *Parry* v *Cleaver* [1970] AC 1 it was stated that early receipt of pension benefits through ill health or disability could be set-off against the loss of pension benefit from the date of normal pensionable retirement. However, pension benefits could not be set off against a loss of earnings. There was no guidance on the treatment of the early receipt of lump sum benefits. This was clarified with the decision in *Longden* v *British Coal Corporation* [1995] ICR 957; *The Times*, April 14, 1995, where it was held that the early receipt of a disability pension before retirement age should not be deducted from the loss of pension benefit. There appears to be some inconsistency in the application of this judgment in practice.

21.7 Structured settlements

Damages for personal injury are usually awarded in a lump sum. An alternative is to set up, with the consent of the parties, a financial structure for the payment of the damages. The defendant pays an initial smaller lump sum and purchases an annuity to fund periodic payments to the plaintiff. This offers advantages to both the plaintiff and defendant, particularly if the settlement is large. For the plaintiff, funds will be received regularly and will be linked to life expectancy. There is, therefore, more likelihood that the cash will last for the plaintiff's lifetime and will not be dissipated through overspending or poor investment. For the defendant, payment can be spread over the plaintiff's lifetime and may not have to be paid in a lump sum.

The receipt of an annual amount in the form of a structured settlement is tax-free to the recipient, provided the structure is set up as specified in s329AA of the Finance Act 1995. This means that the calculation of special damages is unaffected in that the net loss of earnings after taxation is computed. In practice, the structure is set up only after the damages have been agreed. The payments, in the form of an annuity, will usually take into account the injured party's life expectancy and will be index-linked. There are likely to be some guarantees on minimum payments. Any initial costs, such as alterations to a home for a disabled person, or modifications to a motor car, will be taken into account in setting up the structure.

21.8 Fatal accidents

Claims for fatal accidents may be brought under two Acts:

- Law Reform (Miscellaneous Provisions) Act 1934;
- Fatal Accidents Act 1976.

The application of the Acts in the calculation of damages in fatal accidents is discussed in the following sections.

21.8.1 Law Reform (Miscellaneous Provisions) Act 1934

This Act allows an action brought by an injured person prior to death to be continued for the benefit of the estate. A claim for financial loss would be brought for the period from the date of accident until the date of death. From death to the end of the claim period, the claim would be brought under the Fatal Accidents Act 1976.

21.8.2 Fatal Accidents Act 1976

The Act creates a right of action for death caused by a wrongful act, neglect or default. The cause of action is one which would have entitled the injured person to bring an action for damages, had death not ensued. So, the person who would have been liable had death not ensued remains liable, notwithstanding the death. The action can be brought for the benefit of the dependants of the deceased.

The Act also stipulates that:

(a) if damages are payable to a widow, they should not take into account her remarriage or prospects of remarriage;
(b) benefits that have accrued or will accrue to any person from the estate or otherwise as a result of the death should be ignored; and
(c) there is no statutory limit on the amount of damages, but they must be awarded for only financial loss and bereavement.

21.8.3 Dependency damages

Where, for example, a husband is killed in an accident, his wife and children lose the benefit of his income on which they were dependent. In calculating the financial loss, the income that would have been expended on the husband for his personal needs and his living expenses needs to be taken into account.

The loss is the calculated loss of income after taxation less the deceased's personal expenses. It takes into account only the personal expenses of the deceased and not any joint or household costs.

Instead of attempting a detailed calculation of the costs and expenses that were incurred by the deceased for his own benefit, a simpler method is applied by using a dependency percentage. This was established in *Harris* v *Empress Motors Ltd* [1984] 1 WLR 212. The net income is established and a percentage is deducted to account for the expenditure which would have been spent exclusively on the deceased for his own benefit. This dependency percentage may vary according to the family circumstances, such as the number and ages of children.

For example, where there is a husband and wife, the dependency percentage could be 2/3, representing one-third of the expenditure for the husband, for the wife and for their joint needs. Where there are children, the dependency percentage could be 3/4 because there may be less income available for the deceased's personal use. The dependency percentage could change during the period of the claim when, for example, children reach ages after which they are no longer dependent.

There is an exception to the practice of establishing a dependency percentage where the wife of the deceased has been earning a substantial sum herself, or had a significant private income prior to her husband's death. This was addressed in *Coward* v *Comex Houlder Diving Ltd* (unreported, see Kemp & Kemp, volume 1, paragraph 21–003/2). As it is likely that such a couple were pooling their joint earnings, the calculation starts with the joint income. From this a percentage of, say, 33.33 per cent is deducted, as is the wife's income, to arrive at the loss of dependency.

The dependency percentage is usually based on the circumstances of each case. It is established with reference to past cases and will be a matter for instructing solicitors or counsel.

The calculation of financial loss in a fatal claim is similar to that for loss of earnings described earlier in this chapter. The net loss of earnings after taxation and NIC is reduced by the dependency percentage. The calculation is made for each year from the date of the accident, or from when earnings were affected, until the date of trial. To this past loss interest is added. The last period before the date of trial is usually the basis for the multiplicand.

The multiplier is established by reference to the deceased's age at the date of death, taking into account the deceased's expectation of working life at that time. This may be contrasted with a personal injury claim where the multiplier is determined at the date of trial. The multiplier, less the number of years from date of death to date of trial, is applied to the multiplicand to calculate a lump sum, at date of trial, to account for earnings to date of retirement. To this will be added a pension loss, as set out earlier in this chapter.

There may also be a services dependency to be included in the claim. This could relate to tasks which the deceased performed, which may have to be paid for following death. These include items such as decorating or gardening and are not subject to a reduction for dependency.

21.9 Self-employed persons

Where the injured person is self-employed, a number of considerations apply which are absent in calculations involving a salaried employee. These are in addition to the obvious difficulty of projecting earnings where there may be little or no basis for a projection due to fluctuations in income and in the prospects for the business.

21.9.1 Partnership share

The plaintiff must be able to show that the injuries sustained gave rise to a financial loss. The loss suffered is that of the plaintiff and of no other person or company. In the case of an injured person who is in partnership, the loss would be limited to that person's share of the lost partnership profits.

This principle applies even when the partnership is between husband and wife, whether established for convenience or for taxation considerations. If there is a partnership agreement, the share of profit attributable to the injured person is likely to be set out in it. Where there is no agreement, the courts may apportion profits equally between the partners.

The division of profits between partners for tax purposes may not be the appropriate allocation for a claim. In *Kent* v *British Railways Board* [1995] PIQR Q42, a husband and wife were in partnership but did not have a partnership agreement. The court ignored the sharing of profits for taxation purposes and, in the absence of a partnership agreement, referred to the Partnership Act 1890, where it is stated that partners are entitled to share equally in profits and losses.

21.9.2 Market value of services

In a business where a husband and wife work together, the wife may be paid a salary in excess of the market rate. This could occur in a partnership where they share profits equally, but where the wife devotes little time to the business.

In *Malyon* v *Plummer* [1964] 1 QB 330 the court considered that, in assessing dependency under the Fatal Accidents Act, it had to adopt a realistic approach. It would assess a true loss and would look behind any arrangement between the partners. This would involve an assessment of the market value of the services provided by the wife to be deducted from the dependency.

21.9.3 Accounting for income

When calculating the loss of profit of a self-employed person who has been injured, an accountant may find that not all income has been included in the books of account. This raises issues of how the claim should be calculated, as well as ethical considerations.

The matter should be referred to the instructing solicitor for advice. Often, the person's own accountant will become involved and the person may choose to declare the income for VAT and income tax and face any penalties that might arise. If the person is not prepared to rectify the situation, the expert accountant needs to consider the ethics of the situation. It is clear that the report cannot be prepared on the basis of false accounts if the expert accountant knows these to be false.

If the accountant who prepared the accounts was unaware that the accounts were incorrect and he prepared them in good faith, the expert accountant has a duty to inform him that the accounts are incorrect, giving him the relevant information. On the other hand, if it is clear that the accountant knowingly prepared fraudulent accounts, the expert accountant has a duty to inform the ICAEW or other relevant body. There is no obligation on the expert accountant to inform the Inland Revenue.

21.10 Role of the expert accountant

The obvious role of the expert accountant in personal injury claims is in the calculation of pecuniary losses. This is usually in the calculation of loss of earnings and pension, although there are other losses such as a reduction in the value of a business or a loss of opportunity that may need to be addressed.

The accountant must document his calculations and conclusions by accumulating the necessary support for them. Any opinion expressed is likely to be challenged by an opposing expert accountant and will have to stand up to scrutiny and possible cross-examination.

The work of the expert accountant is limited to his expertise in the calculation of damages. It is unlikely that he would become involved in issues of liability and apportionment of liability between various parties. The accountant is also unlikely to be involved in general damages for pain and suffering and other losses such as a handicap on the job market. It is essential for the accountant involved in a personal injury claim to keep within his area of expertise.

21.10.1 Other experts

The accountant will often come into contact with other experts. Their opinions could form the basis of the calculations made by the accountant, or add further support for these. For example:

(a) *Medical.* These could be physicians, orthopaedic surgeons, psychiatrists or any other medical practitioner consulted as a result of the accident. A medical opinion could indicate the severity of the injuries and the period for which the injured person is likely to be off work. Also, if the effect of the injuries is to continue, the medical evidence could indicate what the injured person would be capable of doing in the future.

(b) *Employment consultants.* They could be retained to consider the job market at the time and to advise on the possible career options of the person, taking into account the injuries.

(c) *Technical and industry experts.* They could advise on the prospects for the industry in which the injured person works, or the impact on the injured person's business.

21.10.2 'Without prejudice' meetings

It is often helpful for the expert accountant to attend without prejudice meetings with the opposing accountant. The limits of these meetings are often set out by instructing solicitors, but the objective is to narrow the issues in dispute, wherever possible. This should ensure that the court hearing, as far as quantum is concerned, focuses on the relevant matters. This can have the advantages of shortening the hearing and limiting cross-examination to the areas in dispute.

Even when two accountants appear to have vastly differing views on quantum, it is still possible to find areas of common ground. For example, it should be possible to agree the figures which have been extracted from available source records. The calculations, including the computation of tax and NIC, should also be able to be agreed. This will leave only areas of principle or opinion on which the accountants may not agree.

It is useful for the accountants to prepare a note of the areas agreed and those on which they cannot agree. This will help the parties to focus on the areas of difference, rather than on all matters affecting quantum.

21.11 Conclusion

Personal injury is an area of litigation where accountants are used to calculate a pecuniary loss. It is a field which changes frequently and it is essential for the practitioner to keep up to date to ensure that the calculations are based on current law and practice. It is also a field in which accountants must be aware of the limits of their own expertise.

21.12 Bibliography

21.12.1 Books

Goldrein, I.S. and de Haas, M.R. (1997) *Butterworths Personal Injury Litigation Service*, Butterworths.

Goldrein, I.S. and de Haas, M.R. (1997) *Structured Settlements – A Practice Guide* (2nd edn), Butterworths.

Holding, F. J. (1997) *Essential Quantum Cases*, Butterworths.

Kemp, D. (1995) *Damages for Personal Injury and Death*, FT Law & Tax.

Kemp, D. (1997) *Kemp & Kemp: The Quantum of Damages*, Sweet & Maxwell.

McGregor, H. (1997) *McGregor on Damages* (16th edn), Sweet & Maxwell.

Munkman, J. (1996) *Damages for Personal Injuries and Death* (10th edn), Butterworths.

Nelson-Jones, R. and Burton, F. (1995) *Medical Negligence Case Law* (2nd edn), Butterworths.

Ogden, M. (1994) *Actuarial Tables for Injury and Fatal Accident Cases*, HMSO.

Ward, G. and Evans, A. (1994) *Pensions – Your way through the maze*, Accountancy Books.

21.12.2 Other publications

Association of Personal Injury Lawyers *Journal of Personal Injury Litigation*, Sweet & Maxwell.

Gordon, J. (ed.) *Kemp & Kemp Quantum Newsletter*, Sweet & Maxwell.

Finch, J. (ed.) *The Personal and Medical Injuries Law Letter*, Monitor Press.

Nelson-Jones, R. *Butterworths Personal Injury Litigation Service – Special Damages Statistics*, Butterworths.

Chapter 22
The tort of deceit

22.1 Introduction

Accountants who never practise in criminal cases may still come across proceedings where fraud is alleged. These will be in certain cases under the Insolvency Act, where restitution is sought or where a person is sued for the tort of deceit. An allegation of deceit is equivalent to allegation of fraud by a defendant, and the word fraudulent is often used instead.

The basis of an allegation of deceit is that the defendant knowingly made a false representation of fact, intending it to be relied upon, and that the plaintiff, in relying on the false representation, suffered loss as a result.

Despite the allegation of fraud, the burden of proof is based on the normal civil standard of the balance of probabilities. However, it has been held that to prove fraud, the probability must be high, and that:

> '. . . the more serious the allegation the higher the degree of probability that is required.' (*Hornal* v *Neuberger Products Ltd* [1957] 1 QB 247)

Furthermore, it is generally more difficult to show that a person who has made a statement that is wrong has made it, not negligently, but knowing it to be wrong.

Therefore, the allegation of fraud is not made lightly. However, in contract disputes it is a common allegation. This chapter discusses the requirements for an action in deceit, and the role of the accountant in such actions.

22.2 Why allege fraud?

Following the purchase of a company, the purchaser claims that he was induced to enter into the contract as a result of misstatements by the vendor. The purchaser may already have an action against the vendor for negligent misrepresentation; why should he plead fraudulent misrepresentation? The burden of proof must be higher because any statement, although demonstrably wrong, need not necessarily have been made fraudulently.

There are four main reasons.

22.2.1 Pressure on the defendant

There is no doubt that an allegation of fraud against a person is a serious allegation. If proven, fraud could damage any person's future career. This, of itself, may encourage settlement on more favourable terms. (On the other hand, the difficulty in proving fraud may not.) Alternatively, it could hinder settlement as a company would not wish to be seen as admitting fraud. Even though most settlement agreements are on the basis of 'denial of liability', the 'smoke' is there.

Furthermore, many professional people such as directors are insured for civil litigation. An allegation of fraud may well invalidate their insurance cover in those proceedings (although if not proven, the cover will be restored). This is again double-edged: if the defendant has no assets other than insurance, he will not want the policy 'avoided'.

Tactically, alleging fraud can be a valuable weapon.

22.2.2 Limitation

Section 32(1) of the Limitation Act 1980 states that the period of limitation on a action based on fraud by the defendant does not start until the fraud has been discovered or could reasonably have been discovered by the plaintiff.

Because of limitation, some actions may only be possible if fraud is alleged and distinctly proved.

22.2.3 Damages

Damages in tort are designed to put the person in the position in which he would have been had the tortious action not taken place, subject to questions of remoteness of damages. However, where an action for fraud is proven, the plaintiff will be entitled to recover all damages directly flowing from the fraudulent inducement, whether or not such damage is reasonably foreseeable, unless it is caused by the plaintiff behaving completely without prudence or common sense (however, see *East* v *Maurer* [1991] 1 WLR 461). This extends the amount of consequential losses, for example lost profits, that may be claimed in an action for fraud compared with an action for negligence.

There is no contributory negligence in an action for fraud. Therefore, the court will not consider whether the plaintiff should have been able to discover the falsity of a statement by, for example, undertaking a due diligence examination which he did not carry out or which he carried out negligently. Furthermore, the fact that goods sold are worth the price paid will not necessarily prevent damage arising. As well as there being no reduction of damages for contributory negligence, this also removes a defence from the defendant.

22.2.4 Duty of care

As every accountant knows, one of the main elements of an action for audit negligence is the necessity to show a duty of care between an auditor and a person relying on a statement made negligently by an auditor. In the *Hedley Byrne* case it was held that a duty of care existed where there was a special relationship:

> '. . . not limited to contractual relationships or to relationships of fiduciary duty, but also include relationships which . . . are "equivalent to contract".' (*Hedley Byrne & Co.* v *Heller & Partners Ltd* [1964] AC 465).

In an action for deceit, there is no need to show the existence of a 'special relationship'. Therefore, where there is an allegation of misstatement, it may only be possible to pursue an action where there is an allegation of fraudulent misrepresentation, rather than negligent misrepresentation.

22.3 The elements of the tort of deceit

The elements of the tort of deceit are as follows. The defendant knowingly made a false representation of fact knowing it to be untrue or having no belief in its truth or being reckless as to its truth, intended it to be relied upon, and the plaintiff, in relying on the false representation, suffered loss as a result.

Each of these elements is considered below in relation to false warranties in a purchase and sale agreement.

22.4 False representation of fact

The representation must be false and must be of a past or existing fact. Thus, the seller of a company tells the buyer of the company that the stock owned by the company is valued at cost. If it is valued at selling price, the statement is false.

The statement of an opinion that is false can be held to be the statement of a false fact, where the opinion is not honestly held. This is because the person making the statement represents that he holds that opinion honestly. (This is, of course, moving into the territory of the next element of deceit.) Thus, if the seller says that, in his opinion, the stock will sell for at least cost price, this may be held to be a false statement of fact where the stock is obsolete. An alternative way of looking at this is that the seller is making an implied statement that he knows of facts which justify his opinion.

Many statements mix fact and opinion. For example, a statement that stock is held at the lower of cost and net realisable value combines a statement of fact, that this is indeed the way that stock has been valued, and opinion, that is, concerning the opinion involved in assessing net realisable value.

The representation of fact does not include non-disclosure or silence. However, it does include partial disclosure and deliberate concealment implied by conduct. A partial disclosure is as much a false statement as if it were misstated altogether. This distinction can be seen as follows. Where the seller makes no representation concerning the stock whatsoever, and the stock is unsaleable, there is no misrepresentation.

If a defendant does not acquire knowledge of the falsity of the statement until after it has been made but before the plaintiff has acted on it, he is bound to communicate the truth and will be answerable in damages if he does not. Therefore, representations can be said to be continuing.

22.5 Knowingly – the state of the defendant's mind

The leading case is *Derry* v *Peek* [1889] 14 AC 337. Lord Herschell said:

> '. . . fraud is proved when it is shown that a false representation has been made (1) knowingly, or (2) without belief in its truth, or (3) recklessly, careless whether it be true or false . . . To prevent a false statement being fraudulent, there must, I think, always be an honest belief in its truth.'

Two important points in this judgment give constructive knowledge of the falsity of a statement to a defendant. First, a false representation can be made even though the maker of the statement does not know of the falsity of the statement. He will be equally responsible if he has no belief in its truth and does not care whether it is true or not. Second, where the defendant makes a statement which he does not believe to be true, he will be responsible although he may not know that the statement is false.

Someone who makes a representation regarding the net realisable value of stock will not be making a fraudulent misrepresentation if his opinion is honestly held, despite being reached negligently. On the other hand, making such a statement without having carried out any enquiry whatsoever will be.

For obvious reasons, claims for fraudulent misrepresentation will normally include an alternative claim under s2(1) Misrepresentation Act 1967. The burden on the plaintiff for proving knowledge is shifted to the defendant by s2(1). This reads as follows:

> 'Where a person has entered into a contract after a misrepresentation has been made to him by another party thereto and as a result thereof he has suffered loss, then, if the person making the misrepresentation would be liable to damages in respect thereof had the misrepresentation been made fraudulently, that person shall be so liable notwithstanding that the misrepresentation was not made fraudulently, unless he proves that he had reasonable ground to believe and did believe up to the time the contract was made that the facts represented were true.'

The other aspects of deceit (set out above) apply to a claim under this section. In particular the rules concerning damages were interpreted by the Court of Appeal in *Royscot Trust* v *Rogerson* [1991] 2 QB 297 to mean that damages under this subsection should be assessed on the same basis as in an action for fraud. According to *Clerk and Lindsell on Torts*, 'the deceit rules on remoteness apply – the defendant will be liable for losses even though they were not reasonably foreseeable'.

22.6 Representation must be intended to be acted upon by plaintiff

This includes statements made to a class of persons or to the plaintiff's agent. Therefore, the statement need not be made to the plaintiff directly.

22.7 Reliance

Reliance in this context means causation, that is, just because the statement was false and the plaintiff suffered damage does not mean that the falsity of the statement caused the loss. However, partial reliance by the plaintiff on the misrepresentation will not help the defendant. If the plaintiff's mind was partly influenced by the defendant's misstatements, the defendant will not be any less liable because the plaintiff was also partly influenced by a mistake of his own (*Clerk and Lindsell on Torts*). Therefore, the materiality of the representation to the overall transaction is irrelevant. Furthermore, the carelessness of the plaintiff in not discovering the falsity of the statement is no defence, because contributory negligence is inapplicable.

Therefore, a false statement concerning the valuation of stock along with a number of other statements which are not false will still entitle the plaintiff to recover his total loss. Further, his failure during a due diligence exercise (or even the failure to carry out a due diligence exercise) to discover the falsity of the statement will be of no assistance to the defendant in his case.

22.8 Loss

The pecuniary loss to be calculated is, as stated above, based on a tortious not contractual measure. Therefore, the loss is calculated on the basis that the misrepresentation had not been made (other than in a no-transaction case, for which see below). The whole subject of the losses claimable under deceit was considered by the House of Lords in *Smith New Court Securities Limited* v *Scrimgeour Vickers (Asset Management) Limited* [1996] 3 WLR 1051 HL.

That case involved the fraudulent inducement of the plaintiff to purchase shares in Ferranti owned by Scrimgeour Vickers. The plaintiff was led to believe that it was in competition to buy the shares with two other companies which had made bids. It paid 82.5p per share. If it had not held this belief, it would have offered 78p per share. However, at this level, the sellers would have rejected the bid. Therefore, without the misrepresentation, there would never have been a transaction. The difference between the two prices in overall terms was £1 million.

Unknown to either party was the fact that there had been a massive fraud at Ferranti. When this became known, the share price plummeted, which led to the plaintiff losing £11 million on its disposal of the shares.

In a purchase and sale agreement the level of loss had always been taken to be the difference between the price paid for the business or company and its market value at the time the agreement was entered into. Damages assessed on this basis, therefore, would have been £1 million, being the difference between the cost of the shares at 82.5p and what the cost would have been at 78p. However, the House of Lords ruled that the loss was the actual realised loss of £11 million. In allowing this larger loss, the court determined that the value does not have to be assessed at the date of purchase if a later date better compensates the plaintiff. Two circumstances were identified where this would be the case. First, where the misrepresentation continues after the purchase whereby the plaintiff keeps the asset and, second, where the plaintiff is 'locked in' to the asset he has acquired. Of course, assessment at a date later than the date of purchase means that later intervening acts which may break the chain of causation may need to be brought in. Such acts would include the fraud taking place after the purchase or a general fall in the market.

The method of calculating damages in tort is to place the plaintiff in the position he would have been in had the tortious act not been made. This is to be contrasted with the assessment of damages under contract law where the object is to put the plaintiff in the position he would have been in had the representation been true. In contract, this means that the plaintiff can claim damages for loss of bargain, that is, the prospective gains which the plaintiff would have expected to receive, were it not for the misrepresentation.

On the face of it, therefore, a plaintiff is better suing in contract than in tort because the losses claimable will be higher. The plaintiff suing in tort can only claim for what he has physically lost from his pocket. However, many representations do not form part of the contract, and therefore the plaintiff only has a remedy in tort if one of these is false. Many of the representations made prior to entering into a contract do not become terms of the contract. If these representations are false, the plaintiff has no remedy for breach of contract, his only remedy being in tort for misrepresentation. Furthermore, in tort, losses include consequential losses and, given that the action is for fraud, as noted above, these do not need to be reasonably foreseen by the defendant. Thus, if the plaintiff has suffered lost profits as a consequence of the deceit, then these will be claimable.

Finally, there are certain types of fraudulent misrepresentation cases where the loss is calculated on the contract. It was noted in the *Smith New Court* case above that without the misrepresentation, the plaintiff would have made a lower offer, but that offer would have been rejected by the sellers, and therefore the deal would not have proceeded. Such cases are called no-transaction cases. In no-transaction cases the measure of damages is not based on losses arising from the misrepresentation, but from the contract itself.

22.9 The role of the expert in actions for deceit

The expert's role in assessing damages in cases of deceit may be relatively minor. Unless there are consequential losses, such as lost profits, the schedule of damages will comprise the price paid under the contract. Where the purchase has involved buying a company which is on a far less stable financial footing than has been represented, then the damages may also include finance injected by the plaintiff to keep the company afloat. Further, the accountant may have to calculate the value of the company at the time of the contract (or at the time the loss is realised in a *Smith New Court*-type case).

Where the expert accountant is extensively used is in helping to prove or disprove the allegations of misrepresentation. The most common misrepresentations are likely to concern the financial status, profitability and accounts of the company to be purchased.

There are two areas where the accountant will carry out investigations.

First, the expert will be expected to look at the financial representations made to the plaintiff and to consider them in the wider context of all financial information available to the plaintiffs. Thus, in the sale of a company transaction, if the vendors write to the purchasers during negotiations confirming the health of the company while at the same time writing to the Inland Revenue stating that tax outstanding will be reduced by large current year losses, this will be evidence of deceit. Not all cases will be this simple, but the principle holds.

Second, the accountant will look at the representations with regard to accounting policies and the way in which items in the accounts have been accounted for. One of the most common areas of dispute in takeovers is the treatment of stock. It has to be said, unfortunately, that stock is an extremely easy item to manipulate. Stock provisions can be reversed without justification, different bases of valuing stock can be used and the concept of net realisable value forgotten. However, the issues arising in stock – compliance with GAAP and consistency – apply to all items in the accounts. It is in this area that the accountant's evidence can be of greatest value.

22.10 Reference

Brazier, M. (ed.) (1995) *Clerk and Lindsell on Torts*, Sweet & Maxwell.

Chapter 23
Defamation

23.1 Introduction

The making of a defamatory statement is a tort, giving the wronged person a right of action against the defamer. To quote a well-known book (by Carter-Ruck) on libel and slander:

> 'The law of England recognises in every man the right to have the estimation in which he stands in the opinion of others unaffected by false and defamatory statements and imputations in whatever form they may be published or conveyed.'

The accountant's role in defamation cases is in the quantification of special damages.

This chapter gives an overview of the law of defamation, discusses the difference between special and general damages, and looks at how the expert accountant plays a part in a defamation case.

23.2 The law of defamation

There are two main types of defamation:

- libel;
- slander.

There is also a related action for injurious falsehoods.

Carter-Ruck says:

> 'A defamatory statement is one which tends to lower a person in the estimation of right-thinking people generally, or which causes him to be shunned or which exposes him to hatred, ridicule or contempt or which discredits him in his profession or trade.'

If the defamatory statement is made in permanent form, such as in print, rather than transient, then the action will be for libel. Additionally, words broadcast by wireless telegraphy for general reception are treated as being made in permanent form by s1 of the Defamation Act 1952, as are words, pictures and gestures, by s4 of the Theatres Act 1968, and words in any cable or broadcast television or radio programme by s166 of the Broadcasting Act 1990. A non-permanent form, such as a speech, is slander.

In all cases, the statement has to be made to a third party, that is, published, and it must touch the reputation of the person.

The principal difference in the way libel and slander are litigated is that, in a libel, it is presumed that damage has been caused, and therefore there will be a right of action against the person making the statement. Such defamatory statements are what is termed actionable *per se*. In an action for slander, for there to be a right of action against the person making the statement, some damage must be proved to have arisen from the slander. By damage, it is meant actual pecuniary loss, or special damage. These types of action are termed actions on the case. (Having said that, there are four types of slander which are actionable *per se*, that is, no pecuniary loss need be proved. These are imputations of the commission of criminal offences punishable by imprisonment, having certain contagious diseases, unchastity in a woman, and the disparagement of a person in an office, profession, calling, trade or business held or carried on by him at the time of the publication.)

Normally included within discussions on libel and slander is the analogous (and often alternative) class of proceedings called injurious falsehoods. Actions for injurious falsehoods are not necessarily defamatory, that is, they do not reflect upon the reputation. Injurious falsehoods are a further type of action where special damage must be proved (subject to certain statutory exceptions). There are three different types of injurious falsehood (none of which needs to be defamatory).

Slander of title relates to a false statement about someone's title to real or personal property. Slander of goods is the disparagement of a person's goods. Clearly, these do not necessarily reflect on the reputation of a person.

The third type of injurious falsehood is malicious falsehood, that is, a statement which is false but not defamatory, but which is published maliciously. Indeed, in all actions for injurious falsehood, it has to be proved that the statement was made with express malice. The classic example of this is to say that someone has retired when he has not. The statement is not defamatory, that is, it does not lower a person's reputation. However, it is false, and as a result that person may lose custom. If made maliciously then that person has an action for malicious falsehood.

It was stated above that, for an action for injurious falsehood to succeed, the plaintiff must prove special damages, subject to certain statutory exceptions.

The statutory exceptions are provided by s3(1) of the Defamation Act 1952. This provides that statements which are calculated to cause financial loss are actionable if they are published in written or other permanent form (that is, akin to a libel), or if the statements are calculated to cause financial loss in respect of any office, profession, calling, trade or business held by the plaintiff or carried on by him at the time of publication (that is, akin to one of the four exceptions which makes slander actionable *per se*).

The law of defamation and injurious falsehood is notoriously complicated, even at the early stage of what particular branch of the law a false statement falls into. The above can be summarised, as in Figure 23.1.

Figure 23.1

Action	*Defamatory?*	*False?*	*Malicious?*	*Special damages to be proved?*	*Form of publication*
Slander	Yes	Yes	No	Yes, subject to four exceptions	Transitory
Libel	Yes	Yes	No	No	Permanent
Slander of title	No	Yes	Yes	Yes, subject to s3(1)	Transitory, but if permanent then actionable *per se*
Slander of goods	No	Yes	Yes	Yes, subject to s3(1)	Transitory, but if permanent then actionable *per se*
Malicious falsehood	No	Yes	Yes	Yes, subject to s3(1)	Transitory, but if permanent then actionable *per se*

As well as individuals, corporations and companies can sue for defamation as can a firm in respect of the publication of defamatory matters which affect its business or trading reputation.

The main defences to a defamation action are absolute privilege, qualified privilege, unintentional defamation, justification (that is, the truth) and fair comment.

Furthermore, the Defamation Act 1996 introduced other defences including an extension of the defence of innocent dissemination to persons who are not authors, editors or publishers of the statement complained of, who have taken reasonable care as to its publication and did not know that they caused or contributed to a defamatory statement (s1). This defence is therefore available, in certain circumstances, to processors or operators of communications systems such as Internet providers.

The 1996 Act will also update the defences of qualified and absolute privilege. Absolute privilege, which traditionally applied to UK court and parliamentary proceedings, now extends to reporting the proceedings of the European Court of Justice and European Court of Human Rights and certain international criminal tribunals.

Qualified privilege, which applied to matters such as reports of parliamentary and judicial proceedings, is extended to reports of legislatures, courts and government bodies around the world.

23.3 The two different types of damages

Damages which may be awarded in defamation cases are either special or general damages.

23.3.1 Special damages

The importance has already been noted of proving a pecuniary loss in order to bring certain types of defamation action, that is, slander (subject to the statutory exceptions) and injurious falsehoods (subject to the statutory exceptions). In such cases the damages recoverable will be special damages. The main type of special damage recoverable is business loss, that is, a loss of contract, employment or profits. This will include loss of a customer or loss of a client, provided it can be proved that this was caused by the publication. Furthermore, a general loss of customers, clients or trade if the defamation is reasonably likely to have caused the loss will form part of a claim for special damages (Carter-Ruck, p. 204).

It should be noted that special damages are claimable in respect of defamatory statements actionable *per se*, but again these must be pleaded.

23.3.2 Remoteness of special damages

Because business losses are invariably the result of a third party or parties undertaking some act, it is often argued that this action is a new intervening act, relieving the defendant of liability. Furthermore, many slanders are repeated by third parties, and an individual hearing a slander from such third parties rather than the defendant may as a result refuse to deal with the plaintiff.

In these cases, whether the damage is too remote depends on whether the new intervening act is something which might have been reasonably contemplated by the defendant. (Of course, where the defendant intended this very course of action then the intended consequences would not be too remote.) There is therefore a distinction between the third party's act which is not wrongful in the sense of giving rise to an action for damages by the plaintiff against the third party. Even a situation where the plaintiff has a right of action against a third party as a result of, for example, a wrongful dismissal, will not relieve the defendant from liability. The defendant would remain liable where, if the slander had been true, the third party's dismissal of the plaintiff would not have been wrongful.

The repetition may be a new intervening act, but this depends on whether the repetition was intended by the defendant or a natural and probable consequence of the publication in the first place. In the case of *Slipper* v *BBC* [1991] 1 QB 283 an action was brought by a policeman who had attempted to bring back the Great Train Robber, Ronnie Biggs, from Brazil. A BBC programme told of this attempt and was shown in preview to various journalists before being broadcast. The journalists previewed the programme and national newspapers reviewed it, repeating matters in the broadcast. Slipper sued the BBC for both the broadcast and preview, and claimed additional damages for repetition of the defamation in the newspapers. In refusing to allow a strike-out of this part of the claim, the Court of Appeal in effect allowed the plaintiff to recover from the original publisher of a libel the repetition by others where the repetition was a natural and probable or reasonably foreseeable consequence of the original publication.

There is of course a contradiction in this, whereby a claim for special damages may be based on a falling-off of trade, which is, as noted above, recoverable, but such falling-off is the result of the repeating of the slander within a large group of the plaintiff's customers.

With the reduction in general damages (see below), it is becoming more important to claim special damages to make an action viable.

23.3.3 General damages

General damages comprise injury to reputation, to feelings and to health. General damages (other than exemplary damages) do not have to be pleaded, but the plaintiff will usually raise evidence to support his claim. The court is free to form its own estimate of the injury done. This means that a jury decides the amount, although they are now given some guidance by the judge in respect of an award of exemplary damages.

General damages fall into a number of categories. Contemptuous damages, normally the award of 'the smallest coin in the realm', are awarded when the action should never have been brought. Nominal damages, of a few pounds, are awarded when the harm is slight to the plaintiff's reputation or feelings or where the plaintiff is only trying to clear his name. Compensatory damages are those designed to compensate for the harm done, that is, 'to vindicate the plaintiff's reputation and to compensate the plaintiff for injury to his feelings' (Carter-Ruck, p. 194).

Aggravated damages are awarded in addition to compensatory damages where the defendant has, for example, continued to make the defamatory statement, or by the way his defence is conducted. Finally, exemplary damages, which must be specifically pleaded, are to a certain extent a penal award against a defendant and are awarded in addition to compensatory and aggravated damages.

23.3.4 The decreasing importance of general damages

Juries have traditionally had the only say in the determination of general damages at the trial of first instance. Indeed, the practice was that neither counsel nor the judge could suggest an appropriate award. This was increasingly seen as a weakness in the legal system because of the tendency of juries to make extremely high awards. Such awards were criticised as being overgenerous, particularly when compared with the awards in personal injury cases. The legal system was seen by many to be at fault if it could award £1 million to a well-known public figure for libel, but a lesser sum to someone who, for example, had lost a limb in an industrial accident.

Although awards could be reduced on appeal, some of the general damages awarded by juries were truly frightening. In this latter category there is the £1.5 million awarded to Lord Aldington (*Lord Aldington* v *Count Tolstoy* [1989] *The Times*, 1 December, *The Guardian*, 1 December). In the former category, the Court of Appeal reduced the £600,000 award made to the wife of the Yorkshire Ripper against *Private Eye* to £60,000 in 1991 (*Sutcliffe* v *Pressdram* [1991] 1 QB 153 CA), and cut the £350,000 damages (of which £75,000 was compensatory and £275,000 was exemplary) awarded to Elton John against Mirror Group Newspapers in 1995 to £75,000 (being £25,000 compensatory and £50,000 exemplary) (*John* v *MGN* [1997] QB 586.

As a result of the *Elton John* case, that has all changed. In future, juries could be advised of the comparison of awards in libel cases and other cases. In particular, counsel can address the jury on the size of an award and the judge can suggest a figure or a range, and consider the awards made in personal injury litigation.

The expectation is that general damages awards will fall in future. However, at the same time special damages may well become of increasing importance. Having said that, these have to be proved and that is where the expert accountant comes in.

23.4 Involvement of the expert accountant

The expert accountant's role in a defamation case is the quantification of special damages.

As noted above, the ability to prove a pecuniary loss is essential in the proof of certain types of defamation. The pleadings must therefore include the particular instances of loss and, where they are not so pleaded, the plaintiff cannot try to prove them at trial.

Where they are pleaded they must be proved by evidence of specific losses. Where the defamation action is an action *per se* and special damages are claimed then, as noted above, these must also be specifically pleaded.

However, where:

> '. . . the facts do not admit of particularising specific instances of loss, then the courts are prepared to accept a generalised statement of special damage in pleading and general evidence of special damage in proof.' (McGregor, para 1887, p.1222)

Thus, the accountant will carry out a loss of profit calculation either by reference to individual lost items of income, such as a lost contract, or by reference to a general fall-off in trade, or by reference to both, the former supporting the latter.

The total destruction of a business by a libel may give rise to a claim in respect of future income streams, goodwill and loss of shareholder value.

The special tax treatment of defamation damages, as set out in Chapter 19, should be referred to.

The customary method of quantifying special damages is as set out in Chapter 18 on damages.

23.5 References

Carter-Ruck, P.F. and Starte, H. (1997) *Carter-Ruck on Libel and Slander* (5th edn), Butterworths.

McGregor, H. (1997) *McGregor on Damages* (16th edn), Sweet & Maxwell.

Chapter 24
Divorce

24.1 Introduction

Although it is not yet in force (and may not be until the year 2000), it is appropriate to commence this chapter with a quote from the Family Law Act 1996 because it provides a framework for current thinking. Only Part IV of the Act, which deals with the occupation of family homes and domestic violence is now in force.

> 'The court and any person, in exercising functions under or in consequence of Parts II and III . . . [those parts dealing with divorce and separation, and legal aid for mediation in family matters] . . . shall have regard to the following general principles–
>
> (a) that the institution of marriage is to be supported;
> (b) that the parties to a marriage which may have broken down are to be encouraged to take all practicable steps, whether by marriage counselling or otherwise, to save the marriage;
> (c) that a marriage which has irretrievably broken down and is being brought to an end should be brought to an end–
>   (i) with minimum distress to the parties and the children affected;
>   (ii) with questions dealt with in a manner designed to promote as good a continuing relationship between the parties and any children affected as is possible in the circumstances; and
>   (iii) without costs being unreasonably incurred in connection with the procedures to be followed in bringing the marriage to an end; and
> (d) that any risk to one of the parties to a marriage, and to any children, of violence from the other party, so far as reasonably practicable, be removed or diminished.'

The principal source of law on financial provision and property adjustment remains Part II of the Matrimonial Causes Act 1973 as amended, particularly by the Matrimonial and Family Proceedings Act 1984 and s166 of the Pensions Act 1995.

While accountants, and experts, may be keen to earn fees out of divorce they should remember the need to minimise costs.

The accountant involved professionally in divorce proceedings, whether as an expert or otherwise, should always remember that his costs, and the related legal costs, come out of the family pot, and that excessive costs can make an otherwise fair arrangement meaningless. There have, for example, been cases where the legal and other costs have ended up being greater than the family assets.

That said, there will be aspects of divorce upon which the advice of accountants may be sought. The most common aspects are:

(a) the valuation of family businesses or shares in family and unquoted companies;
(b) the taxation consequences of divorce;
(c) the establishment of family assets;
(d) quantifying reasonable requirements.

The expert accountant more used to proceedings in the Queen's Bench or Chancery Divisions of the High Court may be surprised at the relative informality of the Family Division. Only rarely will claims for ancillary relief (which relate to financial provision between the parties) be heard before a High Court judge in the form of a trial, and even then it is not customary for wigs and gowns to be worn, either by the judge or by counsel. Also, in contrast to hearings in the Chancery and Queen's Bench Divisions, the only persons who may attend such trials are the parties, their legal advisers and expert accountants where appropriate. Hearings are essentially in private and confidential.

Section 25 of the 1973 Matrimonial Causes Act, as amended by the 1984 Act and the Pensions Act 1995, requires the court, in dealing with financial provision and property adjustment in connection with divorce, to have regard firstly to the welfare of any children under 18 and then to the following:

> '(a) the income, earning capacity, property and other financial resources which each of the parties to the marriage has or is likely to have in the foreseeable future, including, in the case of earning capacity, any increase in that capacity which it would in the opinion of the court be reasonable to expect a party to the marriage to take steps to acquire;
> (b) the financial needs, obligations and responsibilities which each of the parties to the marriage has or is likely to have in the foreseeable future;
> (c) the standard of living enjoyed by the family before the breakdown of the marriage;
> (d) the age of each party to the marriage and the duration of the marriage;
> (e) any physical or mental disability of either of the parties to the marriage;
> (f) the contributions which each of the parties has made, or is likely in the foreseeable future to make, to the welfare of the family, including any contribution by looking after the home or caring for the family;
> (g) the conduct of each of the parties, if that conduct is such that it would in the opinion of the courts be inequitable to disregard it;
> (h) in the case of proceedings for divorce or nullity of marriage, the value to each of the parties to the marriage of any benefit which, by reason of the dissolution or annulment of the marriage, that party will lose the chance of acquiring.'

Section 25c of the Pensions Act 1995 amended Section 25 of the Family Law Act 1973 and, if divorce proceedings began on or after 1 July 1996, the court may now order the trustees or managers of a pension scheme to pay part of the pension and/or any lump sum directly to the divorced party, and the pension thus becomes earmarked. Although s16 of the Family Law Act 1996 establishes the concept of pension splitting, as opposed to earmarking, it is not in force and so the law does not yet give the courts the powers that are necessary to split pensions at the time of the divorce proceedings.

Before going on to consider the ways in which the expert accountant can assist in connection with the financial aspects of divorce, it is worth reiterating the importance of costs. It was the disproportionate level of costs in *Evans* v *Evans* [1990] 2 All ER 147 which led to the court laying down general guidelines to be followed in the preparation of substantial ancillary relief cases. The guidelines laid down by Mrs Justice Booth are as follows:

> '1 Affidavit evidence should be confined to relevant facts and should not be prolix or diffuse. Each party should normally file one substantive Affidavit dealing with the matters to which the court should have regard under Section 25 of the Matrimonial Causes Act 1973 [as substituted by Section 3 of the Matrimonial and Family Proceedings Act 1984] . . . and matters which are material to the application. If any further Affidavit is necessary it should be confined to such matters as answering any serious allegation made by the other party, dealing with any serious issue raised or setting out any material change of circumstances.
>
> 2 Inquiries made under Rule 77 of the Matrimonial Causes Rules 1977 SI 1977/344 should, as far as possible, be contained in one comprehensive questionnaire and should not be made piecemeal at different times.
>
> 3 Wherever possible valuations of properties should be obtained from a valuer jointly instructed by both parties. Where each party instructs a valuer then reports should be exchanged and the valuers should meet in an attempt to resolve any differences between them or otherwise to narrow the issues.
>
> 4 While it may be necessary to obtain a broad assessment of the value of a shareholding in a private company it is inappropriate to undertake an expensive and meaningless exercise to achieve a precise valuation of a private company which will not be sold [see *P* v *P* [1989] 2 FLR 241].
>
> 5 All professional witnesses should be careful to avoid a partisan approach and should maintain proper professional standards.
>
> 6 Care should be taken in deciding what evidence, other than professional evidence, should be adduced and emotive issues which are not material to the case should be avoided. Where Affidavit evidence is filed the deponents must be available for cross-examination on notice from the other side.
>
> 7 Solicitors on both sides should together prepare bundles of documents for use at the hearing and should reach agreement as to what should be included and what excluded: duplication of documents should always be avoided.

8 A chronology of material facts should be agreed and made available to the court.

9 In a substantial case it may be desirable to have a pre-trial review to explore the possibility of settlement and to define the issues and to ensure readiness for hearing if a settlement cannot be reached.

10 Solicitors and Counsel keep their clients informed of the costs at all stages of the proceedings and, where appropriate, should ensure that they understand the implications of the legal aid charge: the court will require an estimate of the approximate amount of the costs on each side before it can make a lump sum award: see Practice Direction [Divorce Registry: Lump Sum Award] [1982] 2 All ER 800.

11 The desirability of reaching a settlement should be borne in mind throughout the proceedings. While it is necessary for the legal advisers to have sufficient knowledge of the financial situation of both parties before advising their client on a proposed settlement, the necessity to make further enquiries must always be balanced by a consideration of what they are realistically likely to achieve and the increased costs which are likely to be incurred by making them.'

24.2 The valuation of businesses and private companies

Business and share valuation is one of the skills which many accountants in general practice have, and it is a skill which may be required of an expert accountant in divorce proceedings.

The valuations required are not valuations for tax purposes, although there may be a tax consequence to any transfer of assets (see **24.3.2** below). The valuation is also not a valuation under the terms of the Articles of Association of a company which may be required under shareholder pre-emption rights, although if there is an actual transfer of shares it will have to be in accordance with the Articles of Association.

The court will not normally require the business or company from which one of the parties to the marriage derives his or her income to be sold to make financial provision for the other. This is based on case law rather than statute.

Example

In a recent case the wife had a significant minority shareholding in a family company which had been very profitable and which had accumulated very substantial assets. The valuation accepted by the court was based on the prospect of future dividends, taking into account current profitability, rather than any valuation based on past profitability or dividend performance. The net asset value was effectively ignored because there was no realistic prospect of a sale.

The husband was in business on his own account and, consistently, the valuation of his business was based on a realistic assessment of its future earning capacity, taking into account the evidence given to the court as to that by the husband's accountant.

In *B* v *B* [1989] 1 FLR 119, Mr Justice Lincoln held that a detailed valuation of the husband's business was irrelevant where the business was not to be sold. The following is a summary of the case by Rakusen, Hunt and Bridge.

'The parties were married for 21 years and had three children. Upon the separation of the parties the wife retained care and control of the children. The wife applied in ancillary proceedings for a lump sum and periodical payments. The husband earned a substantial income from his architectural practice. In the course of the ancillary proceedings approximately £50,000 was spent by the parties in detailed and widely divergent valuations of that practice by various accountants. The husband and his business partner also owned properties in the partnership name, and there was disagreement between the parties over the value of the equity available to the husband in respect of these. The main capital asset of the parties was the matrimonial home, which was valued at £342,225 and the parties agreed that it should be sold.

Lincoln J held that, in a case where there was no question of the business being sold, it was meaningless and irrelevant to embark upon detailed and widely divergent valuations of the husband's assets. The important matter was to establish the ability of the husband to meet the wife's reasonable needs. In order to do that, s25 of the Matrimonial Causes Act 1973 enjoined the court to take into account the husband's resources. This involved the court in a general, and not a detailed, consideration of his sources of income and capital. Upon the facts the proper order was that the matrimonial home be sold, with a lump sum of £275,000 to be paid to the wife from the proceeds and the balance to the husband. Any interest held by the wife in the partnership properties would be transferred to the husband. The husband would pay periodical payments of £10,500 per annum to the wife and £2,600 to each of the children.'

In a trading business or company usual valuation principles will be followed, almost always based on maintainable future earnings. Guidance may be given to the valuer by recent earnings and the trend thereof, taking into account the fact that earnings may have to be adjusted for excessive directors' remuneration, benefits, etc.

The valuer should also bear in mind that the multiples applicable to the valuation of private companies, which have every prospect of remaining such, are generally not the multipliers to be found by reference to quoted price–earnings ratios. If there is any indication that a company may have grown sufficiently to be floated then that factor should, of course, be taken into account, both in the valuation and in identifying the sources from which cash might be made available to make a payment from one spouse to the other. However, where the possibility of a flotation is remote and the particular shareholder is uninfluential, the prospect of flotation would normally be disregarded.

In some cases the business or company may have substantial property assets from which either a trading income or rents are derived. The court will take into account both the value of the assets and the capacity of the owner to borrow against them in assessing proper financial provision between the parties.

24.3 Tax

The taxation consequences of divorce have to be taken into account by the parties and, if necessary, by the court, in any financial settlement. Accountants may be asked about the tax consequences of particular transactions, but the general rules are clear and well known to solicitors specialising in divorce and to the courts, so it would normally be unusual for expert accountancy advice to be required regarding tax.

24.3.1 Income tax

Payments of alimony and maintenance falling due after 14 March 1988, and made other than under an obligation which existed at that date, do not have tax deducted at source and are not income, for tax purposes, of the recipient. Tax relief to the payer on the payments is limited to the amount of the married couple's allowance for the year (currently £1,830 at 15 per cent) and therefore can be ignored for practical purposes in all but the smallest cases.

24.3.2 Capital gains tax

The general position is that while a couple are living together as husband and wife they can make disposals of property to each other without incurring any liability to capital gains tax. They are treated as transferring the assets on a no gain/no loss basis (s58(1) Taxation of Chargeable Gains Act 1992).

In practice, in the year of separation transfers between spouses are also treated on a no gain/no loss basis. After that period there may be capital gains tax consequences to transfers and, for example, if shares have to be sold to generate cash then the normal capital gains tax consequences follow.

In most cases a transfer of an interest in the family home will have no capital gains tax consequences because of the exemption applicable to houses occupied as the sole or main residence. However, where two properties are involved it is important to establish which of those is the principal private residence and the tax consequences, should the second home be transferred as part of the divorce settlement.

The potential liability to capital gains tax should also be taken into account on assets transferred in the year of separation, even though there is no tax payable on the transfer, because for capital gains tax purposes the transfer between husband and wife is ignored, and the cost of acquisition to the spouse acquiring the property will be the cost to the other spouse rather than the value at the date of transfer.

Example

A second home with a value of £100,000 is transferred between husband and wife in the year of separation. The house had been purchased for £20,000 in 1982 and is subsequently sold, after the transfer between spouses, for £100,000. There would be a capital gains tax liability on the then owner of the property (assuming the owner was liable to capital gains tax) on the difference between the £100,000 and the cost of £20,000 adjusted only for inflation, the costs of disposal and any improvements.

In assessing the capital value of the family's assets, this potential liability to capital gains tax should be taken into account.

24.3.3 Inheritance tax

The Inheritance (Provision for Family and Dependants) Act 1975 enables certain people to make an application for financial provision from the deceased's estate whether or not the deceased had made a will. Former wives, or husbands who have not remarried, and children of the deceased are categories of people who may apply.

If an order is made under the Act where a marriage has not been dissolved the disposition is exempt (within limits) from inheritance tax (s18 Inheritance Tax Act 1984), but tax may be payable where the marriage has been dissolved because s18 applies to spouses only. Under s18, the amount must not exceed £55,000 where the transferee is domiciled outside the UK immediately before the transfer is made.

If the dispute is resolved without proceedings under the Act then it is usually possible to avoid the inheritance tax problem provided agreement is reached within two years of death.

24.4 Family assets

The expert accountant may become involved in identifying and valuing the family assets, but it is more likely, in substantial cases, that this work would be carried out by the spouse's own accountants. It has been known for one spouse to try to defeat the other's legitimate financial expectations by transferring assets or hiding them. Where substantial sums are involved, experienced forensic accountants may have to conduct an asset-tracing exercise with a view to establishing the existence and value of the assets and their location. The court can make an order restraining the disposal of assets, or transfer of assets out of the jurisdiction, or set aside such dispositions, where their intention was to defeat a claim for financial relief (see s37(2) of the Matrimonial Causes Act 1973).

The evidence of assets which the court will consider will be contained in affidavits from the respective spouses, and what is contained in the affidavits may well be based on the answers to a questionnaire prepared under Rule 2.63 of the Family Proceedings Rules 1991. The accountant may be in a position to assist the parties in the preparation of a questionnaire tailored to the family's circumstances, but the parties and their advisers would do well to remember the court's views on costs, and the power of the courts to order costs to be paid by one party or the other, particularly in circumstances where excessive costs could be avoided.

24.5 Reasonable requirements

The accountant, whether an expert or otherwise, may be in a position to assist the parties, and thus the court, in assessing the reasonable requirements of the parties – that is, the outgoings as opposed to the income. Consultation with an accountant may, in any event, be required to ascertain the net income of the parties after tax and appropriate allowances.

24.6 Summary

Much of the financial information necessary for divorce proceedings will be readily available to the parties, quite often from the accountant previously acting for both.

It will sometimes be necessary for family property to be valued and one valuer will normally be appointed.

Substantial arguments can arise over the value of private businesses and limited companies and it is here that the accountant, and particularly the expert accountant familiar with divorce procedure, may be involved. It is important, however, that he should remember what has been emphasised throughout this chapter, which is that any costs incurred reduce the family assets, and what the court requires is that costs should be kept to a minimum so that the assets available for distribution between the parties are maximised.

24.7 Reference

Rakusen, M., Hunt, D.P. and Bridge, A.J. (1989) *Distribution of Matrimonial Assets on Divorce*, Butterworths.

Chapter 25
Employment disputes

25.1 Introduction

An accountant acting as expert may become involved in various aspects of employment disputes. Most commonly he will be involved in the financial consequences of dismissal. This chapter therefore deals with:

- basic concepts;
- remedies;
- the role of the expert accountant;
- taxation consequences.

25.2 Basic concepts

25.2.1 Dismissal

An employee is treated as dismissed if:

(a) the contract under which he is employed is terminated by the employer with or without notice;
(b) a fixed-term contract expires without being renewed under the same contract;
(c) an employee terminates the contract with or without notice and is entitled to do so because of the employer's conduct.

25.2.2 Constructive dismissal

A termination of employment which occurs under (c) at **25.2.1** above and which is effected by the employee in response to a serious breach of contract by the employer constitutes constructive dismissal.

25.2.3 Wrongful dismissal (breach of contract)

This will occur when an employee's employment is terminated without the period of notice specified in the contract or the minimum period of notice prescribed in the Employment Rights Act 1996 (one week for every year of continuous service up to a maximum of 12 weeks), whichever is the greater. The reason for the dismissal and the procedure used are not normally relevant; the focus is on the amount of notice received. A contract may provide for a payment to be made in lieu of notice and, provided that such a payment is made on termination, the dismissal will not in those circumstances be wrongful even though the employee has not received the prescribed period of notice. An employer may be able to justify the summary dismissal of an employee without notice or pay in lieu if he can show that the employee has been guilty of behaviour incompatible with his continued employment in that position. Any acts of fraud or dishonesty would be examples, although exceptionally poor performance may be sufficient.

25.2.4 Unfair dismissal

A dismissal will be 'unfair' either:

(a) if it is not effected for one of the potentially fair reasons listed in the Employment Rights Act; or
(b) there is a potentially fair reason but the employer has not acted reasonably in treating that reason as a reason for dismissal.

The potentially fair reasons are as follows:

(i) the capability or qualifications of the employee for the particular type of work;
(ii) the conduct of the employee;
(iii) the fact that the employee was redundant;
(iv) the fact that the continuation of the employee to work in the particular position would contravene a statutory duty or enactment;
(v) 'some other substantial reason' justifying dismissal (not defined but commonly embracing business reorganisations).

The focus in assessing the fairness of a dismissal is on the reason, the procedure and whether dismissal was a reasonable step for the employer to take. An unfair dismissal need not be a wrongful dismissal; conversely, a wrongful dismissal need not be an unfair dismissal (although it usually will be).

25.3 Remedies

An employee who has been wrongfully dismissed can seek damages in the High Court or in the county court within six years of the termination of employment. Alternatively, a claim may be made in the industrial tribunal in respect of claims of up to £25,000, although here the claim must be brought within three months of termination. The award of damages is designed to put the employee in the position he would have been in had the contract been performed according to its terms. This involves calculating what the employee would have earned net of tax during the notice period. The principles of calculation and tax are dealt with below.

An employee who claims to be unfairly dismissed has a right to make a complaint to an industrial tribunal within three months from termination of employment, provided that (in most cases) he has at least two years' continuous employment.

If the claim is successful, the industrial tribunal may exceptionally make an order for reinstatement or re-engagement but will usually award compensation. This will usually consist of:

(a) a basic award (calculated according to a statutory formula relating to age, length of service and a maximum 'week's pay' and subject to a maximum presently of £6,300);
(b) a compensatory award (an amount designed to reflect the loss (after tax) to the employee caused by the dismissal and subject to a maximum presently of £11,300); and exceptionally
(c) an additional award where the employer refuses to comply with a reinstatement or re-engagement order.

Interest is payable on awards if not paid within 42 days.

25.4 The role of the expert accountant

An expert accountant may be retained to:

(a) carry out an investigation prior to dismissal;
(b) report and give evidence on the skills expected of an employee (particularly as a director, secretary or accountant);
(c) report and give evidence on the extent to which the employer's or the employee's conduct fell below that required by the contract in question;
(d) calculate loss;
(e) calculate the tax consequences of dismissal.

25.5 Investigations prior to dismissal

An employer may wish to dismiss an employee because of suspected misconduct or poor performance. Usually, the emphasis will be on justifying summary dismissal (thereby disentitling the employee to compensation) and demonstrating the required degree of culpability. However, regard should also be had to the possibility of an unfair dismissal claim where the emphasis will be on showing to a tribunal that a fair procedure was adopted. In cases involving misconduct this will involve ensuring that:

(a) the employer conducts a full investigation of the allegations;
(b) the employee knows the case against him;

(c) the employer gives proper consideration to the employee's defence;
(d) the employer has a reasonable and honest belief in the employee's guilt; and
(e) dismissal is an appropriate sanction.

An accountant with experience of fraud investigations may be engaged for the following reasons:

(a) to establish the nature of the dishonesty;
(b) to ascertain the extent;
(c) to determine whether others are involved;
(d) to advise on preventative measures;
(e) to attend or conduct interviews with the employee concerned;
(f) to trace the proceeds of the dishonesty;
(g) to give evidence at an industrial tribunal or in civil or criminal proceedings;
(h) to identify whether recovery might be made from others (including, particularly, the auditors).

25.6 Evidence as to skills expected

Where he is qualified to do so, an expert accountant might be retained by either the employer or the employee to advise and, if necessary, give evidence on the skills expected in a particular role and in particular circumstances.

Example

A company secretary was summarily dismissed, *inter alia*, for breach of fiduciary duty, including being party to the execution of his own employment contract, on terms which members of the board and the shareholders regarded as unreasonable and excessive. There were complaints about the employee's conduct in connection with his secretarial duties and, particularly, in connection with his acceptance of certain instructions from the managing director (who was also dismissed) without reference to other members of the board. The expert accountant was retained by the employee, who claimed damages for wrongful dismissal (and compensation for unfair dismissal), to advise on the quantum of loss suffered and also on whether the conduct complained of was sufficiently culpable to justify summary dismissal.

25.7 Calculation of loss

In some cases the loss suffered by an employee dismissed in breach of contract will be simple to calculate. However, where the notice periods are lengthy the calculation can be complicated. The calculation involves a number of steps:

(a) Aggregate the value of cash and non-cash benefits to which the employee is entitled during the notice period. Calculations of some cash benefits can be complex, particularly pension loss.
(b) Make a deduction in respect of:
  (i) the tax and National Insurance payable on those emoluments;
  (ii) accelerated receipt; and
  (iii) the amount (net of tax) that the employee earned from alternative employment during the notice period (or, if greater, the amount he should have earned had he acted reasonably in seeking alternative employment).

To the extent that the amount resulting from the application of (a) and (b) above exceeds £30,000, gross up the excess at the employee's marginal rate of tax.

It is not uncommon, following the sale of a private company, for former directors and shareholders to be retained by the new owners and for them to be paid a salary which contains an element relating to profits earned after the sale. In these cases further difficulties can arise in quantifying the amount of the salary for the purposes of the damages claim.

While the contract of employment may try to define precisely how profits are to be calculated, there will often be room for dispute (and legitimate differences of opinion) as to the profits which will form the basis for the remuneration. While the parties maintain a working relationship, such disputes can usually be resolved by negotiation, but following dismissal disputes may arise which may result in litigation.

Example

The former chairman of a private company was retained in an advisory capacity for a period of three years following the sale for remuneration, on the basis that he would work a fixed number of hours per week. He was also entitled to a (reduced) share of the profits.

He was constructively dismissed and claimed:

(a) for additional hours worked in excess of his contractual hours, on a quantum meruit basis;

(b) for the recovery of deductions allegedly wrongly made from his remuneration;

(c) for a share of profits based on his estimate of the profits which would have been shown in the audited accounts (as defined in the agreement), but for adjustments which were allegedly made and which had not been contemplated by the agreement. The audited accounts complained of contained management charges from the new holding company, a charge for interest on inter-company indebtedness, and accountancy and audit fees which were regarded as excessive and caused by the dispute.

The chairman retained an expert accountant to advise him on the merits and quantification of his claim.

25.8 Taxation consequences

Special considerations apply to the taxation of damages arising out of employment contracts, not least because the general principles of Schedule E may apply.

Section 19 ICTA 1988 imposes a tax charge under Schedule E in respect of any office or employment on emoluments therefrom under one of three cases.

Part V of the Act contains provisions relating to the Schedule E charge and s131 defines emoluments as including all salaries, fees, wages, perquisites and profits whatsoever. If, therefore, a payment to an employee or former employee arises out of the employment then it is potentially liable to tax under Schedule E. However, s19 will only normally apply where any payment upon termination includes compensation for work actually done or includes a sum which the employer is contractually bound to pay. Otherwise, the special provisions of s148, relating to payments on retirement or removal from office or employment, will apply subject to the exemptions contained in s188.

It is therefore important to establish the nature of any compensation or damages payable. If the contract provides for compensation for loss of office if terminated then the general PAYE rules will apply and the special s148 scheme will not. This applies to payments in lieu of notice where these are made pursuant to a contractual provision, even if the employer has a discretion whether or not to apply it.

25.9 The special scheme

Section 148 charges to tax under Schedule E any payment made to the holder or past holder of any office or employment, or to his executors or administrators, whether made by the person under whom he holds or held the office or employment, or by any other person. Section 148(2) reads:

> 'This section applies to any payment (not otherwise chargeable to tax) which is made, whether in pursuance of any legal obligation or not, either directly or indirectly in consideration or in consequence of, or otherwise in connection with, the termination of the holding of the office or employment or any change in its functions or emoluments, including any payment in commutation of annual or periodical payments (whether chargeable to tax or not) which would otherwise have been so made.'

The exemptions from tax contained in s188 apply only to payments chargeable under s148 and do not apply to payments chargeable under the general provisions. If, therefore, compensation is paid for work actually done (as in the above example) the £30,000 exemption provided in s188(4) will not apply. The £30,000 exemption has not changed since 1988.

Any benefits which are not chargeable under the normal rules will also be chargeable to tax by reason of s148(3), as any valuable consideration other than money is treated as a payment of money equal to the value of that consideration at the date when it is given. This means that in assessing the tax consequences of a termination payment it is important to take into account the value of any benefits provided, such as the continued use of a car.

25.10 Costs

It is important for the employee or ex-employee contemplating litigation against his former employer and seeking compensation to appreciate that tax relief may not be available for the costs incurred. Neither s19 nor s148 contains any provision for tax relief on costs (in connection with the latter see *Warnett* v *Jones* [1980] STC 131).

However, where the former employer agrees to reimburse certain costs, there is an Extra-statutory Concession (A81) which says that no charge will be imposed on such payments if they are made:

(a) direct to the former employee's solicitor; and
(b) in full or partial discharge of the solicitor's bill of costs incurred by the employee only in connection with the termination of his employment; and
(c) under a specific term in the settlement agreement providing for that payment.

The concession does not apply to accountancy costs or other professional fees, but the concession does apply to legal costs when payment is made by the employer in accordance with a court order. It is therefore important that, either in settlement negotiations or in seeking an order from the court, provision should be made for legal costs as part of the agreed compensation.

Because of the general charge to tax under s19 on contractual rights to compensation, care is needed in reaching any agreement prior to the termination of employment as to any payment of compensation, although the Revenue are likely to treat the payment as falling within s148 if it is done as part of the process of termination.

There may be tax advantages, and therefore increased prospects of settlement without litigation, if consideration is given to:

(a) payments into approved retirement benefit schemes;
(b) payments for assistance in outplacement.

There will also be a cash flow advantage to the employee if any compensation is paid after the employee leaves and after form P45 is issued, because the rate of tax then deducted by the employer is at the basic rate of income tax.

25.11 Conclusion

The expert accountant asked to advise in connection with employment disputes needs a basic understanding of certain employment law concepts, a general understanding of how damages are calculated and, particularly, of the special tax consequences outlined at **25.8** above, including the position regarding costs.

Chapter 26
Accountants' professional negligence

26.1 Introduction

The role of the expert accountant in cases of accountants' professional negligence is not necessarily limited to quantification of loss, although it may be. While the definition of the standard of care required has not changed to any appreciable extent since 1896, the work required to meet the standard has changed. Accountants will frequently be accused of failing to meet that standard and the court will normally be prepared to listen to expert evidence from accountants:

(a) as to what the standard was at the time of the alleged failure; and
(b) whether, in the opinion of the expert, the accused failed to meet the standard.

It is not for the expert to say or decide whether or not the accused was negligent, in breach of contract or guilty of some criminal offence.

The expert accountant in accountants' professional negligence cases may be concerned with liability, with causation, reliance and the quantum of damages. He may also be asked, in court or otherwise, about contributory negligence, failure to mitigate and the liability of third parties for the same damage.

Because it is possible that the expert accountant's opinion will be sought in all these areas, it is necessary for the accountant who wishes to act as expert to have a general understanding of all of these issues. He can then advise if instructed or volunteer opinions if it seems to him, from his general understanding of the facts and the allegations, that others in the team may have inadvertently failed to consider some relevant factor. (This is a contentious issue and it is important that the accountant should not stray beyond his areas of expertise, particularly in reports which he may write which will be disclosed and answered for in court.) There have been instances where judges have expressed the view that they did not need the opinions of experts in reaching conclusions and giving judgment. In one such case, it gave the expert some satisfaction to see that the judgment largely mirrored the opinions expressed by the expert in his report.

This chapter, therefore, deals with the legal framework within which accountants operate and the role of the expert in accountants' negligence cases, before going on to look at such cases from the plaintiff's perspective and the areas in which, from experience, accountants and auditors are most at risk of being accused of acting negligently or, *in extremis*, fraudulently.

Finally, suggestions are made which are intended to heighten the awareness of the users of accountants' services as to the limitations of their work and some hints for accountants on how to avoid being sued or prosecuted.

26.2 The legal framework

The accountant is expected to exercise reasonable skill and care in carrying out his responsibilities, whether they are statutory, contractual or under a common law duty of care.

What amounts to reasonable skill and care will depend on the responsibilities undertaken and the circumstances. See also the more recent decision in *Bolam* v *Friern Hospital Management Committee* [1957] 1 WLR 582.

In *Re Kingston Cotton Mill Company* (*No 2*) [1896] Ch 279, Lopes LJ said:

> 'It is the duty of an auditor to bring to bear on the work he has to perform that skill, care, and caution which a reasonably competent, careful and cautious auditor would use. What is reasonable skill, care, and caution must depend on the particular circumstances of each case.'

Mr Justice Laddie gave judgment on 24 March 1998 in *Bank of Credit and Commerce International (Overseas) Limited and Others* v *Price Waterhouse and Others*. The judgment followed an application by some of the defendants to strike out various parts of the claim under the provisions of Order 18 rule 19. The judgment contains a useful summary of the law as it applies in accountants' negligence cases and emphasises the importance of identifying the scope of the duty by reference to the kind of damage from which the adviser must take care to hold the advisee harmless. It deals with remoteness and causation, and in this connection it also deals with the scope of the duties of auditors. At paragraph 57 Mr Justice Laddie says:

> 'The auditor is employed by the company to exercise his professional skill and judgment for the purpose of giving the shareholders an independent report on the reliability of the company's accounts. In the course of the professional life of an average auditor he will carry out audits for numerous clients involved in widely differing businesses. The skill he offers and for which he is paid is the skill in looking at the company's accounts and the underlying information on which they are or should be based and telling the shareholders whether the accounts give a true and fair view of the company's financial position. He is not in possession of facts nor qualified to express a view as to how the business should be run, in the sense of what investments to make, what business to undertake, what prices to

> charge, what lines of credit to extend and so on. Not only does he not normally have the necessary expertise but those are areas in respect of which his advice is not sought. When the company engages an auditor, it is not seeking his help in steering the management into making better management decisions. There are others who hold themselves out as able to give that sort of assistance.'

It was argued, for the plaintiffs, that the auditors owed a duty to protect them from general trading losses in the future, or generally to safeguard the assets of the company. Mr Justice Laddie rejected theses contentions saying they were contrary to established authority, and that the duty to safeguard the assets rests with the directors. The Judge also said that the established authorities do not say that the auditors' duty of care extends to protecting the client against general trading losses in the future. Auditors may, of course, and frequently do, take on responsibilities in addition to their strict statutory responsibilities and the extent of their duties will ultimately be a matter for the court to decide on the facts.

It would not be unreasonable to substitute the word accountant for the word auditor in appropriate circumstances.

The standard is therefore the standard of the reasonably competent, careful and cautious accountant doing that work, i.e., the standard is determined by reference to members of the profession. It is for the court to decide what standard accountants ought to achieve, but expert evidence on what accountants ordinarily achieve may assist the court in reaching its decision. If the accountant professes some special skill (such as in share valuation) then his work may be tested against the work of the ordinary accountant professing such special skills.

The accountant may have a statutory responsibility to his client (for example, as auditor to a limited company) and will frequently have a co-existing contractual relationship whether or not the contract is reduced to writing. An accountant may, and usually will, be liable to his client for negligence in tort as well as in contract.

The appendix to section 1.311 of the ICAEW *Members Handbook* (Managing the professional liability of accountants) says that:

> 'It would be a defence to an action for negligence to show:
>
> (a) that no duty of care had been owed to the plaintiff in the circumstances; or
> (b) that there had been no negligence; or
> (c) that the negligent act or omission had not been an effective cause of the plaintiff's loss; or
> (d) in the case of actions in tort that no financial loss had been suffered by the plaintiff; or
> (e) that the action was statute-barred.'

The appendix points out that, although the defence at (d) would not be available to a claim in contract, only nominal damages would be recoverable if there was no loss and that it is therefore unlikely that an action would be brought for breach of contract where no loss had arisen.

It is obviously reasonable that an accountant should act with appropriate skill and care when carrying out his statutory and contractual duties, and should be liable to his client if the client suffers foreseeable loss if the accountant's work falls below the requisite standard and causes that loss. It is less obviously reasonable that third parties should be able to look to an accountant for recompense for loss arising as a result of reliance by those third parties on his work.

26.2.1 Liability to third parties

While there is no general duty to third parties, so that, for example, an investor who buys shares in a quoted company on the stock market relying, in part, on the contents of the published accounts, as a general rule cannot sue the auditor if the accounts subsequently turn out to be wrong (see for example, *Caparo Industries* v *Dickman* [1990] 2 AC 605; *Morgan Crucible & Co. Plc* v *Hill Samuel & Co. Ltd* [1991] Ch 295; and *Galoo Limited* v *Bright Grahame Murray* [1994] 1 WLR 1360), a duty may be owed to third parties in certain, and not unduly restricted, circumstances.

While many of the accountants' negligence cases which come to court are actions between accountants and their clients, those which tend to send most shivers down the spines of accountants are the reported cases where it turns out that an accountant owes a duty to a third party.

This book is not the place to go into the history of duties owed by accountants (and other professionals) to third parties, but following *Caparo* it is likely that a duty of care to a particular third party may be owed by accountants where there are all three of the following:

(a) foreseeability of damage to the third party;
(b) a relationship of proximity or neighbourhood with that third party;
(c) circumstances in which it would be fair, just and reasonable to impose a duty of a given scope on the accountants.

The test in *James McNaughton Paper Group Limited* v *Hickson Anderson & Company* CA [1991] 2 QB 113 should be noted:

- the purpose for which a statement was made;
- the purpose for which the statement was communicated;
- the relationship between adviser, the advisee or any relevant third party;

- the size of any class to which the advisee belonged;
- the state of knowledge of the adviser;
- reliance by the advisee.

The recent cases support the concept that the plaintiff will need to establish that there was an 'assumption of responsibility' and that it was fair, just and reasonable in the circumstances to impose a duty of care (see the Court of Appeal decision in *Peach Publishing Limited* v *Slater*).

Lord Bridge in *Caparo* said that:

> 'The concepts of proximity and fairness . . . are not susceptible of any such precise definition as would be necessary to give them utility as practical tests, but amount in effect to little more than convenient labels to attach to the features of different specific situations which, on a detailed examination of all the circumstances, the law recognises pragmatically as giving rise to a duty of care of a given scope.'

More recent cases suggest that the plaintiff has to establish that there was an 'assumption of responsibility' and that it would be fair, just and reasonable to impose a duty of care. The 'assumption of responsibility' test was referred to in *Hedley Byrne & Co.* v *Heller & Partners Ltd* [1964] AC 465, was later doubted but has now been restored (see *Henderson* v *Merrett Syndicates Ltd* [1995] 2 AC 145 and *White* v *Jones* [1995] 2 AC 207).

In *Bank of Credit and Commerce International (Overseas) Limited and Others* v *Price Waterhouse and Others (*Court of Appeal 13 February 1998) it was stated that three separate, but parallel, paths should be followed in the search for a principle or test.

The first of these paths was referred to in Sir Brian Neill's judgment as being 'the threefold' test set out in *Smith* v *Eric S Bush* [1990] 1 AC 831 and followed in *Caparo.* The second path referred to in the judgment was the 'assumption of responsibility' test referred to in *Henderson* (see above) and the third path referred to was the 'incremental approach' suggested in the Australian case of *Sutherlandshire Council* v *Heyman* [1984–5] 157 CLR 424.

Sir Brian Neill said that it might be useful to look at any new set of facts by using each of the three approaches in turn. The judgment goes on (at paragraph 7.20):

> 'The threefold test and the assumption of responsibility test indicate the criteria which have to be satisfied if liability is to attach. But the authorities also provide some guidance as to the factors which are to be taken into account in deciding whether these criteria are met. These factors will include:
>
> (a) The precise relationship between (to use convenient terms) the adviser and the advisee. This may be a general relationship or a special relationship

which has come into existence for the purpose of a particular transaction. But in my opinion Counsel for Overseas was correct when he submitted that there may be an important difference between the cases where the adviser and the advisee are dealing at arm's length and cases where they are acting "on the same side of the fence".

(b) The precise circumstances in which the advice or information or other material came into existence. Any contract or other relationship with a third party will be relevant.

(c) The precise circumstances in which the advice or information or other material was communicated to the advisees and for what purpose or purposes, and whether the communication was made by the adviser or by a third party. It will be necessary to consider the purpose or purposes of the communication both as seen by the adviser and as seen by the advisees, and the degree of reliance which the adviser intended or should reasonably have anticipated would be placed on its accuracy by the advised, and the reliance in fact placed on it.

(d) The presence or absence of other advisers on whom the advisee would or could rely. This factor is analogous to the likelihood of intermediate examination in product liability cases.

(e) The opportunity, if any, given to the adviser to issue a disclaimer.'

In the light of the above, it is clearer than ever that whether a duty is owed, and the extent of that duty, will depend on the facts of the case, but, as the professional guidance referred to above points out, it will be prudent to assume that a duty will exist:

(a) if the accountant knows of the existence of the third party;
(b) if it can be reasonably expected that the third party will receive and rely on the accountant's work;
(c) for a particular transaction or purpose; and
(d) where damage will be caused if the work has been done negligently.

Lord Oliver's judgment in *Caparo* says that the necessary relationship between an adviser and advisee may typically be held to exist where:

'1 the advice is required for a purpose, whether particularly specified or generally described, which is made known either actually or inferentially, to the adviser at the time when the advice is given;

2 the adviser knows, either actually or inferentially that his advice will be communicated to the advisee, either specifically or as a member of an ascertainable class, in order that it should be used by the advisee for that purpose;

3 it is known either actually or inferentially, that the advice so communicated is likely to be acted upon by the advisee for that purpose without independent inquiry; and

4 it is so acted upon by the advisee to his detriment.'

The conditions are not conclusive or exclusive.

The ICAEW guidance goes on:

> 'The danger of a duty being imposed will be increased where that third party has no other source of advice and where the purpose of the accountant's work is to induce the third party to take the particular action that he has taken.'

A recent case which has highlighted the possibility of a duty to a third party is *ADT Ltd* v *BDO Binder Hamlyn* [1996] BCC 808. Mr Justice May gave judgment on 6 December 1995 and awarded damages to ADT of £65 million. Interest was awarded on the damages and Binders had to pay ADT's costs. It was estimated that Binders would have to find something in the region of £100 million, which was thought to be well outside Binders' insurance cover. Binders appealed but, before the appeal, agreement was reached between the parties. The agreement is thought to have cost BDO and its insurers at least £50 million, even though this was under half the original damages.

Because the case has been settled, no one will ever know whether the appeal would have been successful, but a brief outline of what happened may assist readers in forming their own opinions.

BDO Binder Hamlyn were the joint auditors of Britannia Security Group (BSG) and the secondary auditor of the main subsidiary, Britannia Security Systems Plc. McCabe & Ford, a much smaller firm, were the sole auditors of Britannia Security systems Limited, a BSG subsidiary which contributed 70 per cent of profits. BSG published their statutory accounts for the year 30 June 1990 and Binders and McCabe & Ford signed the audit certificate on 20 October 1989. In February 1990 ADT made an agreed bid for the entire issue share capital of Britannia Securities Group Plc. ADT had previously owned some shares. Prior to the bid:

(a) Mr Bishop (Binder's audit partner) was asked by BSG to attend a meeting with ADT at short notice;
(b) all those who attended the meeting on 5 January 1990 knew that for ADT it was the 'final hurdle' before they committed themselves to the bid and expected that the hurdle would be cleared without difficulty, and to that extent regarded the meeting as a formality. It was, nevertheless, a serious business meeting;
(c) Mr Jermine asked Mr Bishop if he 'stood by the 1989 accounts' and Mr Bishop said that he did; Mr Jermine said that he was not sure why the Chairman of ADT (Mr Ashcroft) wanted the meeting and did not know what he was trying to achieve by asking whether Mr Bishop stood by the published accounts on the 30 June 1989;
(d) the question whether Mr Bishop stood by the accounts was asked only once, and then quickly in a manner and tone which expected the answer 'yes' as a matter of course. It was a near certainty that Mr Bishop would give that answer. A note of the answer was not made. It was asked as one of a number of general questions relating to the accounts;

(d) Mr Bishop was aware during the meeting (as indicated by his note) that ADT had been relying and were continuing to rely upon the BSG 1989 accounts;

(d) Mr Ashcroft agreed while giving evidence that auditors would be likely to stand by their accounts unless there was a relevant subsequent event which made them change their mind, and that all that could be expected from asking them whether they stood by the accounts was to discover whether there was any such event.

As the judge put it:

> 'In these proceedings ADT claim enormous damages from Binders arising out of their acquisition of BSG. ADT's summary case is that Binders, in the person of their audit partner Mr Bishop, assumed responsibility to them at a meeting on 5.1.90 by restating to ADT, in the person of their director Mr Jermine, that the 1989 accounts which Binders had audited showed a true and fair view of the state of affairs of BSG. ADT say that those accounts did not in fact show a true and fair view of the state of affairs of BSG; that this arose from Binders' negligence; and that by reason of Binders' negligent breach of duty they have suffered loss. ADT say that had Mr Bishop not said what he did on 5.1.90 they would not have acquired BSG at all or at least not on the terms which they did. They claim as damages the difference between the price which they paid and what they claim to have been the true worth of the group. Binders now admit that they were in certain respects negligent in relation to the 1989 BSG audit, but they deny that they assumed any responsibility to ADT on 5.1.90. They also dispute ADT's quantification of their damages.'

The judge went on to state that the issues which he had to determine were whether Binders assumed any responsibility to ADT on 5 January 1990, whether ADT relied on what they were told on 5 January 1990, the extent to which Binders were negligent and damages.

BSG's year end ran to 30 June, and the audit report on the accounts for the year ended 30 June 1989 was signed on 20 October 1989.

On 5 October 1989 Mr Ashcroft, the Chairman and CEO of ADT, met Sir Peter Lane (now Lord Lane), the senior partner of Binders, at a trustees' meeting of a charity. Mr Ashcroft's written evidence was that:

> 'After the meeting I took Sir Peter Lane outside and told him very specifically that ADT was considering making a bid for BSG and that, in doing so, ADT would place considerable reliance on the audit certificate of his firm.'

Neither Mr Ashcroft nor Lord Lane made any note of the conversation, although Lord Lane did tell the audit partner, Mr Bishop, about it.

Mr Ashcroft instructed Mr Jermine, a director of ADT, to obtain direct confirmation from Binders that they stood by their audit report and in due course a meeting was arranged which took place at Binders' offices on 5 January 1990. It was attended by Mr Bishop, Mr Jermine and Mr Watters and Mr Record of BSG.

Mr Jermine's written evidence about the meeting included:

> 'While I cannot now recall the precise words that I used, at the outset of the meeting, I explained to Mr Bishop that before ADT would make an offer for BSG, my chairman, Michael Ashcroft, had asked me to obtain confirmation of various matters directly from Binder Hamlyn. I made it clear to Mr Bishop that if I received such confirmation then it was likely that the offer would be made very shortly . . . I have no doubt that Mr Bishop was aware by reason of what I had told him that if his answers were qualified or negative then it was unlikely that the deal would proceed. Mr Bishop showed no surprise at what I said to him. I assumed from his demeanour this was because he had been told in advance of the purpose of the meeting by Mr Record.
>
> I asked Mr Bishop for confirmation that the audited accounts showed a true and fair view of the company's financial position as at 30 June 1989. Although I cannot now recall the precise words used by Mr Bishop he told me that he confirmed that he stood by the accounts of 30 June 1989 in that they did show a true and fair view of the company's financial position at that date, and that he had no reason to consider changing his mind . . . I asked him whether he was aware of anything that had affected BSG's financial position in the time since the accounts had been signed and he said that he knew of nothing which had happened since then to cause him to have any second thoughts about the accuracy of the accounts. He said that he had no reason now to seek to change the audit report. He said that as far as he was aware BSG's financial position had not altered in any material respect.
>
> I also asked Mr Bishop for confirmation that there was nothing of which he was aware that ADT, as a potential acquirer of the company, should know about the financial position of BSG which was not reflected in the audited accounts. He gave that confirmation.
>
> . . . To conclude the meeting I asked Mr Bishop to reconfirm that he was generally happy with the accounts; that the balance sheet genuinely reflected the value of the business; that the accounts were broadly true and fair; and that nothing had come to light since the accounts had been finalised which caused him to challenge that view or have any concern. Mr Bishop gave the confirmation sought without qualification.'

Mr Justice May stated in his judgment that he preferred Mr Jermine's oral evidence to his written statement but rejected the suggestion that Mr Jermine had asked the question of whether Mr Bishop stood by the accounts twice.

It turned out that Mr Bishop had done no relevant work for BSG and knew nothing of the progress of the bid between October 1989 and 5 January 1990. Mr Bishop made brief notes during the meeting and dictated an attendance note which was typed and dated 9 January 1990. The judgment goes on:

'Mr Bishop was asked to attend the meeting by a telephone call from Mr Record that morning. He did not receive any written instructions or an agenda for the meeting. He met Mr Record and Mr Watters before Mr Jermine arrived so that they could put him in the picture. Mr Bishop said that he had discounted the significance of the fact that in October 1989 it had been said that ADT would rely on the BSG accounts. Mr Record explained that Mr Jermine was likely to ask questions about the 1989 BSG group accounts. The meeting was the "final hurdle" for ADT. His file note records that if they were satisfied with the outcome of the meeting, they would proceed to do a deal with BSG, hopefully to be announced on 8.1.90. Mr Bishop was unconvincingly reluctant to accept that this was to be taken as accurate of what he understood, but I am satisfied that it was . . .

Mr Bishop's note records:

> "During the session with John, I could not help thinking back to Sir Peter's words following his meeting with Michael Ashcroft where I believe that Michael indicated that he would be relying on the audit report for Britannia's accounts to June 1989."

He copied the note to Sir Peter Lane among others. Mr Bishop did not accept that this showed that he was fully aware that reliance would be placed on what he said. He was entirely satisfied that he had not assumed at the meeting any responsibility to ADT.'

The judge found that all those who attended the meeting knew that it was the final hurdle for ADT before they committed themselves to the bid and that, although the meeting was friendly and informal, it was a serious business meeting.

He went on to consider the question of duty of care and in doing so referred to *Caparo, Henderson & Merrett*, *Hedley Byrne* and *Candler* v *Crane Christmas & Co.* [1951] 2 KB 164, among others.

The judge concluded that he had to answer two questions:

'Whether the defendants are fairly to be taken to have assumed responsibility when Mr Bishop was – to make the point – bounced into answering questions for which he had inadequate notice or time for preparation and where the potential additional liability he would assume was enormous.

Whether the defendants are fairly to be taken to have assumed responsibility for the professional competence of their published opinions on accounts, when the work which led to those opinions was in the past and was done in circumstances where the extent of their responsibility was limited to that defined in *Caparo*.'

The judgment goes on:

'In my judgement, the answer in this case to both these questions is yes. I start from the proposition that all the ingredients which I have identified were present. I explicitly guard against the heresy [*Anns* v *Merton London Borough Council* [1977]

> 2 WLR at 1024] of finding a duty of care unless it can be negative. For all that the crucial questions were short and Mr Bishop had a short time only to consider immediate answers, he was plainly not being asked to redo all the audit work in his mind. Rather he was being asked the simple question whether the BSG accounts were accounts which ADT could rely on. This was by its nature a serious business meeting. Mr Bishop did not have to say yes. He could have declined to answer. He could have given a disclaimer. He could have said that, if ADT were to rely on his answers, he would need to take advice. He could have said words to the effect "Yes, I do stand by the accounts but this was a difficult audit because . . .". Rather than doing any of these he undertook to answer the question posed [see Lord Brown Wilkinson in *White* v *Jones* [1995] 2 WLR 187 at 212B] and gave an unqualified favourable answer.
>
> I see the force in human and commercial terms of what Hoffman J said in *Morgan Crucible* at p.294 and take account of the fact that the Court of Appeal acknowledged that such matters may be potentially relevant. I am not, however, persuaded that the size of potential liability and commercial problems over insurance are by themselves reasons for saying that responsibility was not in law assumed when, apart from these considerations, it was. It is well recognised that these matters can be guarded against by a *Hedley Byrne* disclaimer. If for commercial reasons those who give advice do not want to give disclaimers or otherwise limit their liability, then I see no reason why they should not have to live with the consequences.'

The judge found that Binders had assumed responsibility to ADT, that ADT did rely on what Mr Bishop said and was entitled to rely on what he said, because his answers played a real and substantial part in their decision to proceed.

The judge found that the auditors had certified accounts whose profits did not show a true and fair view. In the event, the judge concluded, having heard evidence including expert evidence on behalf of both parties, that it was likely that a fully informed purchaser would have concluded that maintainable profits might be in the region of £42.5 million per annum rather than (the £96 million) shown by the 1989 accounts and that the true value of BSG was £40 million. ADT had paid £115 million (so the judge awarded ADT £65 million).

Any losses made by the acquired company following its acquisition were not considered in the ADT case, but they were considered by the Court of Appeal in *Galoo Limited* v *Bright Grahame Murray* [1994] 1 WLR 1360.

In 1987 Hillsdown Holdings acquired Galoo, of which Bright Grahame Murray were and remained the auditors, at a price based on the profits shown by the 1986 accounts. In 1991 Hillsdown discovered that Galoo's stock had been fraudulently overstated in the 1986 accounts and, to an increasing extent, in the 1987, 1988 and 1989 audited accounts and in the draft accounts for 1990. Although the initial price paid was only some £1.5 million, by the time the fraud was discovered Hillsdown had lent Galoo some

£20 million which had been lost. Galoo claimed that if the auditors had spotted the fraud they would not have suffered the losses they did, but the Court of Appeal found that the losses were caused by bad trading and not by anything which the auditors did or did not do, even though the losses would not have been suffered if the auditors had discovered the fraud back in 1986.

Hillsdown continued to pursue Bright Grahame Murray for recovery of the acquisition price, even though its own accountants had carried out an investigation, but that case settled before trial. BGM had joined the investigating accountants in the action and, although there was a trial of the third party action, there was no judgment because settlement was reached after the end of the trial but before judgment. Such settlements are sometimes reached because, based on the way the evidence has emerged at trial (and sometimes on indications of the judge's thinking), neither side can be confident of the outcome, and settlement on agreed terms is better for both sides than the risk of losing. In terms of costs, however, it is clearly better to compromise early rather than late.

Mr Justice May, in his *Binders'* judgment, referred in passing to the first instance decision in *Peach Publishing Limited* v *Slater & Co* (which was subsequently revised on appeal) and the judgment of Mr Justice Rimer on 12 April 1995, which was then unreported ([1995] BCC 751). Mr Justice May said:

> 'The defendants submit that the ordinary case where a defendant intends that a plaintiff should rely on his work is the case where, rather than simply responding neutrally to an enquiry, he uses or authorises the use of his work as an instrument of persuasion. It is submitted that this was the critical factor which made it arguable that there was a duty of care *Morgan Crucible* v *Hill Samuel Bank* [1991] Ch 259, 362–3 and led Rimer J to conclude that there was such a duty in Peach Publishing Limited v Slater & Co [Rimer J, 12.4.95, unreported]. Such a factor may no doubt be critical in particular cases, but I do not consider that it is a necessary ingredient in every case that the giver of the information or advice should assume a role of positive persuasion . . .'

Mr Justice Rimer's decision was appealed by both parties because, although he found that the defendant owed the plaintiff a duty of care, he also found that the plaintiff had not suffered any loss as a result of anything the defendant did or did not do.

It had been alleged that, during negotiations by Peach to purchase a company (ASA) of which Slater & Co were the auditors, Mr Slater had made a negligent misrepresentation to Peach in connection with the management accounts of ASA.

The Court of Appeal allowed the appeal on duty of care and emphasised that the question was not whether Slater & Co had assumed legal responsibility for the representation, but whether they had assumed responsibility *to Peach* for the substantial accuracy of the management accounts. The court emphasised that both the vendor and the purchaser had their own advisers, including solicitors and accountants, and that Peach's representative was both professionally qualified and an experienced businesswoman. Morritt LJ said:

> 'The maxim "Caveat Emptor" remains as applicable in such a transaction as ever; one party does not just rely on what he is told by the opposite party or his adviser.'

Whether or not there is a duty of care is, of course, a legal issue based on the facts with which the expert accountant will not be directly involved. However, the accountant with the experience necessary to deal with the breach of contract or negligence aspects of a case will be familiar, again through experience, with the *expectations* as to the use to which their work is likely to be put. Whether that use gives rise to a legal duty of care will be a matter of law.

Example

The auditors of limited companies are frequently asked, by their clients, to send a copy of the accounts to the company's bankers. This will usually be because the terms and conditions of bank facilities include the provision of the annual audited accounts. Mere knowledge that the accounts will be seen by the bank, even if they are sent to the bank by the auditor, will not normally mean that a duty is owed by the auditor to the bank should the bank act or refrain from acting in reliance on those accounts and thereby suffer loss. However, if the bank required the accounts for some specific purpose, which was made known to the auditor by the bank, then the position might be quite different. What the auditor should do is take note of the advice from the ICAEW in TR 846–91 and make quite clear the basis upon which the accounts are sent to the bank and the limits on their suitability for any purpose other than the statutory purpose defined in the Companies Acts.

26.2.2 The standard of care required

In many cases duty of care will not be an issue, because there is either a statutory basis for the relationship or a contractual basis. A duty of care to a third party may be acknowledged (as it was effectively in the *Littlejohn* case referred to earlier at **12.2.2**).

What then has to be considered is whether there was any breach of statutory duty or contract or negligence. There may, and usually will, be co-existing statutory contractual and tortious duties.

Once again, it is for the court to decide on whether there has been a breach of statutory duty or a breach of contract, or negligence, but the court may seek guidance, through expert evidence, on what reasonably competent, careful and cautious accountants normally do in particular circumstances.

The court may be referred, by the expert or otherwise, to guidance given by the ICAEW or other accountants' professional bodies as to the work required to meet professional standards.

Example

In a typical auditors' negligence case reference will be made to auditing standards. Auditors are required to comply with Statements of Auditing Standards (SASs). SASs contain basic principles and essential procedures which are indicated in bold type and with which auditors are required to comply. SASs also include explanatory and other material which, rather than being prescriptive, is designed to assist auditors in interpreting and applying auditing standards. Until May 1993, when the first SAS was published, there were only two auditing standards which were supported by auditing guidelines. The auditors' operational standard had the merit of simplicity and had stood the test of time, having been issued in April 1980. There were six paragraphs and it was against the requirements of these paragraphs that the auditors' work was, in effect, judged. The paragraphs read as follows:

Planning, controlling and recording

The auditor should adequately plan, control and record his work.

Accounting systems

The auditor should ascertain the enterprise's system of recording and processing transactions and assess its adequacy as a basis for the preparation of financial statements.

Audit evidence

The auditor should obtain relevant and reliable audit evidence sufficient to enable him to draw reasonable conclusions therefrom.

Internal controls

If the auditor wishes to place reliance on any internal controls, he should ascertain and evaluate those controls and perform compliance tests on their operation.

Review of financial statements

The auditor should carry out such a review of the financial statements as is sufficient, in conjunction with the conclusions drawn from the other audit evidence obtained, to give him a reasonable basis for his opinion on the financial statements.

The accounts being audited will themselves have to comply with accounting standards and with the relevant provisions of the Companies Acts which now incorporate much of what is in accounting standards. Statements of Standard Accounting Practice are not necessarily definitive, but as Woolf J said in *Lloyd Cheyham & Co. Limited* v *Littlejohn & Co.* [1986] 2 PN 154:

> 'While they are not conclusive, so that a departure from their terms necessarily involves a breach of the duty of care, and they are not, as the explanatory foreword makes clear, rigid rules, they are very strong evidence as to what is the proper standard which should be adopted and unless there is some justification, a departure from this will be regarded as constituting a breach of duty.'

The Companies Act 1985, as modified by s19 of the 1989 Act, now gives statutory authority to accounting standards.

Where auditing and accounting standards exist, or there is other guidance from the appropriate professional body, the expert would be unwise to argue that the general standard of accountants doing that work is lower (or higher) than the standard laid down in the guidance. Where there is no specific guidance relevant to the facts in issue, then the expert clearly has more freedom to rely on his own experience, but the authors have seen experts get into serious difficulties in trying to argue that the standard to be applied in their particular case is lower than that to be applied generally. The authors have also seen propositions in expert reports and heard evidence from the witness box that the standards promulgated by the ICAEW are lower than the standard which the expert would apply and that it is the expert's standard which should be applied to the facts of the case.

While it is true that failure to apply an accounting standard which has not found universal favour may not in itself be evidence of negligence, a failure to comply with the auditors' operational standard in circumstances where the standard clearly applied would be strong evidence of a failure to meet the appropriate professional standard.

It is sometimes argued that a higher standard applies to larger firms than smaller ones, and the converse, which is that lower standards apply to small firms, particularly sole practitioners, than to large firms with their much larger resources. Those arguments are unlikely to find favour with the court principally because an accountant should not undertake work which he is not competent to perform (see, for example, the third fundamental principle in the ICAEW Guide to professional ethics which reads:

> 'A member should not accept or perform work which he or she is not competent to undertake unless he obtains such advice and assistance as will enable him competently to carry out the work.')

Small firms will not be able to undertake some of the work undertaken by the larger firms, but the work that they do has to comply with the appropriate professional standard. Large firms will take on larger work and the skills required will be those applicable to that larger work. Expert evidence of the appropriate professional standard will be from accountants experienced in that work which will usually mean that the evidence will be from an accountant in or with experience of the courts or a larger firm. That does not mean, in the authors' view, that the standard required is higher – just that the accountant has to demonstrate that he has complied with the professional standard and applied it appropriately to the work in hand.

26.2.3 Manuals

Many firms prepare their own audit and other manuals both for use internally and, sometimes, for use by other firms if the manual is published. Such manuals can, of course, be used against the authors and their firm if, in a particular instance, the firm has failed to comply with its own procedures and a client has suffered a loss as a result. It is sometimes argued that firms should not be judged by the standards in their own manuals, because the manuals may be setting down best practice rather than merely being designed to enable the firm to comply with standards set by, for example, the Auditing Practices Board (APB). If a firm was appointed because of its high standards as set down in its manuals (or perhaps in its advertising), then it risks being judged by those higher standards.

While the standard is the standard for accountants generally, a firm or expert arguing that the manual set a higher standard would have to demonstrate:

(a) that the manual did indeed set such a higher standard; and
(b) the extent to which the work could fall below that standard without being in breach of standards generally.

The authors have considered a number of manuals published by firms and have yet to see any indication of the extent to which the firm believes the standards set in the manual exceed the minimum standard, and, for practical purposes, it would be sensible for any firm, and any expert, to assume that compliance with a firm's manual was necessary to demonstrate compliance with standards generally. In any particular circumstances departure from a manual, or a standard, might be justified and demonstrable, but that is another issue.

Because the standard is the general standard of accountants doing that work, it follows that if the work is very specialised then the standard may be that of the specialist. Tax advice and share valuations might, for example, be areas of an accountant's work where a specialist standard was required and would be applied, but that would not necessarily be the case.

In *Whiteoak* v *Walker* [1988] 4 BCC 122 the court decided on the facts that the expertise required of an auditor valuing shares under the terms of the pre-emption rights in a company's Articles of Association was the standard of the auditor who sometimes did that work rather than that of the specialist valuer. The judge took the view that if the members of the company had wanted a specialist valuer to value the shares then that is what the Articles would have provided. The plaintiff in that case retained a specialist share valuation expert, who expressed the view that there were very few accountants who were properly qualified to value shares. The defendant's expert was an auditor who sometimes valued shares in circumstances similar to those in the case, and his evidence was preferred. However, each case will turn on its facts and a duty to act to a specialist standard may apply.

It is likely that, in tax cases, a similar approach would be taken by the court. General practitioners, particularly those in practice on their own, provide general tax advice to their clients as a matter of course. If the advice they are required to give is outside their experience or expertise then they should, and usually do, seek specialist tax advice from other firms or specialist tax services. If a general practitioner gives tax advice within his area of competence, and is alleged to have given wrong advice, then on the face of it the appropriate expert would be a general practitioner with experience of the sort of tax advice given by the practitioner, rather than a tax expert.

If that is right then it follows that an accountant can act as an expert on, say, share valuation or taxation work without himself being a specialist in either of those fields, provided he has the relevant experience within his own practice. Very specialised experts tend to be very expensive and in many circumstances it will not be necessary for any of the parties to go to that expense.

26.2.4 Causation and loss

A plaintiff, whether suing in contract or tort, has to prove his loss. If there is no loss then there is in practice no claim. For a loss to be recoverable then, in contract, the general rule is that:

> 'A type or kind of loss is not too remote a consequence of a breach of contract if, at the time of contracting (and on the assumption that the parties actually foresaw the breach in question), it was within their reasonable contemplation as a not unlikely result of the breach.' (*Chitty on Contracts*, at 26–023)

> ***Example***
>
> An auditor fails to spot a fraud which has caused his client loss. If the fraud occurred before the auditor first had the chance to spot it then the only loss for which the auditor could be responsible if he subsequently failed to spot it would be the lost opportunity, if there was one, to recover the loss after it had occurred. The 'lost opportunity' would be quite different to a claim for the original loss.

Questions of remoteness, foreseeability and *novus actus interveniens* (a break in the chain of causation) are legal matters but, as a practical matter, the accountant and the expert accountant would normally consider:

(a) whether the plaintiff has suffered any loss;
(b) whether the loss arises from anything which the accountant did or did not do;
(c) the amount of the loss;
(d) whether others contributed to the loss;
(e) whether the plaintiff, had he acted differently, could reasonably have reduced his loss.

The plaintiff, and his expert accountant, will likewise have to consider these issues and will probably (but not necessarily) have considered them prior to the issue of proceedings.

26.3 The role of the expert

The role of the expert is to provide technical assistance to the court, but in the first instance the role will be to provide technical assistance to the parties to the dispute.

The lay client, and his solicitor, may have unrealistic expectations of what an audit is for and what can be achieved by it. They may forget, for example, that under the provisions of the Companies Acts it is the directors who are responsible for safeguarding a company's assets. It follows that if those assets go missing then the primary responsibility for that will usually be that of the directors. If the auditor fails to spot that the assets are missing then he may or may not be in breach of his statutory duties, in breach of contract and negligent, depending on whether it was reasonable in all the circumstances to expect him to discover that the assets were missing. Even then, he may not be liable for any loss arising unless his failure was the cause of further losses which would not have occurred had the auditor carried out his duties competently.

Expert evidence may well be of assistance to the court on the question of contributory negligence by directors (and others), because the expert will be aware of the responsibilities of directors to safeguard assets, of the ways in which assets are customarily safeguarded (by having adequate systems, controls and management) and of weakness in those systems, etc. which may give rise to loss.

In *Daniels & Others* v *AWA Limited* 16 ACSR 607, an Australian case, the court allowed a 33.33 per cent deduction for contributory negligence, even though the auditors, who knew of inadequacies in the system, had failed to warn the board of them.

In a New Zealand case (*Dairy Containers Limited* v *Auditor General* [1995] 2 NZLR 30), the court found that the directors had been negligent in failing to monitor and control the activities of three senior executives who had defrauded Dairy Containers of NZ$11 million. The auditors were found negligent but damages were reduced by 50 per cent because of the directors' negligence.

While auditors can take some comfort from these decisions, 50 per cent of NZ$11 million is a lot of money and a 50 per cent contribution is probably as high as the courts will go.

The expert will rely primarily on his experience, because he has to be an expert in doing properly what the defendant is alleged to have done badly.

The expert has to be wary of acceptance of 'common practice', as this does not necessarily meet the appropriate professional standard just because it is common.

Example

Loans by companies to directors are commonplace, even though they are illegal (with limited exceptions) under s330 of the Companies Act 1985. The Companies Act itself acknowledges that such loans are commonplace, to the extent that provision is made in the Act for disclosure of particulars of the loans if made. Accountants and auditors do not always explain properly to their clients both the illegality of the loans and the taxation consequences. While such loans may be commonplace, and failure properly to disclose them in the accounts may be equally commonplace, that would probably not be a valid defence to a claim from a client who said that he relied on his accountant in ensuring that he complied with his obligations not only under the Companies Act but also to the Inland Revenue.

The expert accountant, in accountants' professional negligence cases, will thus need to have experience, in real life, of situations similar to those in which the defendant accountant finds himself. He will have to know what the relevant standards are and how they are applied in practice.

He will normally be asked to advise first on liability, whether he is instructed by the plaintiff or the defendant. He may well also be asked to deal with the question of loss and, particularly, the quantification of loss. He may have to consider whether the plaintiff could have mitigated his loss and the extent to which the plaintiff himself, or other parties, are responsible for the loss (given that the legal framework will be set by the lawyers).

26.4 The plaintiff's perspective

The plaintiff, in accountants' negligence cases, will claim that he has relied on the accountant, usually for some particular purpose, that the accountant has let him down and that as a result he has suffered a loss. In that, he will not be in any different position to any other plaintiff against any other defendant.

As in any other case, whether the plaintiff can recover his loss will depend on whether he can establish a duty of care, that the accountant was in breach of that duty and that as a result a loss has been suffered.

The plaintiff will also have to consider his own position and the position of any others who might be to blame for the loss which has been suffered, which is recoverable from the accountant.

Quite often, the potential plaintiff will seek the advice of another accountant or may be offered that advice casually in the light of some adverse comment on the competence of the accountant. Accountants in practice are always on the lookout for new work and one way of obtaining new work is to be unkind about one's opponents. Accountants now recognise that those they previously described as their professional colleagues are their competitors.

Sometimes new accountants are appointed because the old accountants' level of fees, or the manner of rendering them, is unacceptable, and new accountants usually do things differently to old. That does not necessarily mean that the new way is better than the old (or that it will be cheaper) but potential plaintiffs should, in the authors' experience, be wary of listening too closely to advice from new accountants that the old ones were negligent. That is not to say that the new accountant should not give his client the opportunity of making an informed decision as to whether to pursue the former accountant.

Sensible potential plaintiffs will seek legal advice and will have their new accountants' opinions tested, sooner rather than later, by reference to an independent expert.

Example

A businessman sued his former accountant claiming to have been inadequately advised about the benefits of rollover relief in deferring capital gains tax. After tax he received £700,000 rather than the £1.1 million worth of assets which his company would have owned had the company 'rolled over' its gain.

The businessman spent much of the net proceeds in pursuing the accountant and lost at first instance and in the Court of Appeal. If he had invested the net proceeds of £700,000 in stock market securities, he might, as it happens, now have assets worth in excess of £2 million. He could not have made such stock exchange investments or made any use of the net proceeds other than on qualifying assets had he been 'properly' advised about rollover relief, and followed that advice.

There may, of course, be plaintiffs who have suffered a real injustice and lost substantial sums of money due to indefensible negligence. In such cases it should be possible to obtain recompense (if the defendant has adequate insurance) without recourse to the courts, although it may be necessary to issue proceedings to speed up the process of settlement.

One factor which potential plaintiffs against accountants should take into account, and frequently do but for the wrong reasons, is the fact that they assume that accountants are insured. Plaintiffs tend to assume that accountants are worth suing because they are insured and forget the other side of that coin, which is that insurers will generally not pay unrealistic sums to settle claims. Insurers tend to use experienced lawyers and experts and will generally support arguable defences, not only in the interests of their assured but in the interests of assureds generally – in the accounting profession and in other professions.

In the authors' experience this is so even where the plaintiff is legally aided and, even if the defendant accountant wins, he will not recover his costs. Insurers do take a commercial view and will sometimes settle cases which are worth a fight, but it would be an unwise plaintiff who assumed that insurers would always settle.

Accountants may not in fact be insured at all. There is no statutory requirement that they should be and no statutory requirement that an accountant in public practice should be a member of a recognised professional body. This position is unlike that of solicitors, who are not only required to have professional indemnity insurance but also have a compensation fund to cover uninsured losses. There is, to the authors' knowledge, no such compensation fund available to clients of uninsured accountants.

Members of the ICAEW are obliged to carry professional indemnity insurance and the regulations regarding this are contained in the *Members Handbook*. At the time of writing the minimum limits of indemnity are contained in Regulations 13 to 16, which read as follows:

> '13 Subject to Regulations 14–16 the annual Minimum Limit of Indemnity shall be £1 million for any one claim and in all.
>
> 14 Where the Firm's Gross Fee Income is less than £400,000, the annual Minimum Limit of Indemnity shall be a sum equal to two and a half times its Gross Fee Income subject to a minimum of:
>
> (a) in the case of a sole practitioner, £50,000;
> (b) in any other case £100,000.
>
> 15 The annual Minimum Limit of Indemnity required under Regulations 13–14 may be met in whole or in part through the self-insured excess permitted under Regulation 16.
>
> 16 The self-insured excess applicable in the annual aggregate to Qualifying Insurance shall not exceed £20,000 in the case of a sole practitioner or £20,000 multiplied by the number of Principals in any other case save that the self-insured excess of a Corporate Practice shall not exceed the higher of:
>
> (a) £20,000; and
> (b) the sum of such amounts, not exceeding £20,000 for any one Principal, as are accepted by the Principals or any of them as legally binding personal obligations.
>
> The Principals of each of the constituent Firms of a Compound Firm shall, for the purpose of this Regulation, be treated as the Principals of a single Firm.'

The potential plaintiff needs to be aware of the minimum levels of indemnity and to make enquiries of his professional advisers as to the likely levels of professional indemnity cover available. Even the largest firms do not have unlimited cover, because such cover is not available in the market.

A plaintiff should think carefully before pleading the tort of deceit against an insured accountant, particularly if the accountant is a sole practitioner. If fraud is proved (or likely to be proved) then the insurers may be entitled to deny cover. The 'Institute Special Conditions' in ICAEW-approved PII policies are intended to protect innocent partners in accountancy practices from undisclosed dishonesty of a partner, so that insurance cover will continue to protect the innocent partners (who do, of course, have joint and several liability with the 'guilty' partner). A sole practitioner will not be covered for the consequences of his own fraud. In the case of partnerships there is some doubt as to whether the special conditions are effective in all the circumstances in which the partners may hope they are effective. Full particulars of an allegation of fraud have to be pleaded in the statement of claim and counsel have a professional duty to consider the evidence before drafting such a pleading. In practice, fraud is more difficult to prove but, if it can be proved, then all the losses which flow can be recovered (*Doyle* v *Olby Ironmongers Limited* [1969] 2 QB 158) and a plea of contributory negligence may be of no avail (see *Smith New Court Securities Limited* v *Scrimgeour Vickers (Asset Management) Limited* [1997] AC 254.

Smith New Court does in fact suggest that causation, remoteness and limitation are limiting factors, but that all reasonable foreseeable losses will flow.

Establishing such loss will be of no avail if the accountant turns out to be uninsured, which could well be the case if the accountant is a sole practitioner, unless he has substantial assets.

A claim in negligence or for breach of contract may not alert the insurers to the possibility of fraud and the assured accountant is hardly likely to plead fraud in mitigation.

Once again, the potential plaintiff should be advised to take experienced legal and expert accountancy advice on what is a complex subject.

The potential plaintiff should also be aware, although it should be obvious, that specialist lawyers and expert accountants make a living out of litigation and the potential plaintiff should, therefore, insist on realistic estimates of:

- the costs involved;
- the time-frame;
- the amount of his time which will be involved;
- the chances of success.

The potential plaintiff should insist on revisiting these questions at regular intervals during the litigation and should be prepared from the outset to call a halt to proceedings, if it becomes clear that the game is not worth the candle. Arthur Hugh Clough wrote, in 1854, 'It is better to have fought and lost, than never to have fought at all'. A potential plaintiff will have to decide whether those words apply to him.

A plaintiff who starts an action and then discontinues after service of the writ will probably have to pay the costs of both parties. Caveat emptor (of professional services).

26.5 Areas of risk

Accountants in professional practice provide a wide range of services and as a result of providing these services the accountant may find himself being sued. The accountant may also provide advice or his opinion informally and for no reward to those whom he does not regard as his clients and he may stand the risk of being sued if the advice is acted upon and gives rise to a loss.

An analysis of some of the cases in which the authors have been involved as experts reveals the following broad categories of work which have given rise to claims:

- audits;
- unaudited accounts;
- cash flow projections;
- share valuations;
- income and corporation tax;
- capital gains tax;
- value added tax;
- references;
- purchase and sale of businesses;
- investment advice;
- fee disputes;
- failure to comply with statutes;
- statutory reporting.

Another way of looking at the problems is to analyse them by the type of conduct which gives rise to claims and, again based on the authors' experience, claims arise most frequently because of:

(a) fraud;
(b) delay;
(c) lack of awareness (of standards, law and practice);
(d) lack of application (of appropriate standards);
(e) failure to advise properly on the consequences of a particular course of action.

26.5.1 Audits

Failure to discover fraud is a frequent cause of action against auditors, particularly fraud by management (or part of it).

> ***Example***
>
> The finance director of a travel company extended credit over a long period to a customer who promised to pay but failed to do so. There was no element of personal gain but, because of embarrassment at failing to do his job properly, the director eventually manipulated the management figures and annual accounts (to disguise the mounting debt from the managing director) and gave false explanations to the auditors when asked to explain why the debt had not been paid. Even though there was no personal gain the director concerned was prosecuted and the auditors were sued, principally for not bringing to the attention of the managing director the fact of the debt, and the fact that it was unusually large and appeared not to have been paid since the balance sheet date. By the time the fraud was discovered by the managing director the debt had increased fourfold and the auditor was sued for the difference between the debt at the time it should have been brought to the attention of the company and the amount of the eventual debt. The auditors claimed that it was sufficient to obtain an explanation from the company through its finance director, but in the particular circumstances the claim was settled for close to the amount claimed, not least because any substantial debt in a travel agency warrants special attention because, as any user of a travel agency knows, you have to pay for your holiday before you travel.

> ***Example***
>
> The stock at the company's year end was inflated over many years deliberately by management, including the managing director (the major shareholder) and the finance director. The stock included in the accounts was based on a physical count at each year end, but the finance director fraudulently added substantial quantities of stock before the final stock sheets were evaluated and presented to the auditors for audit.
>
> Although the auditors had attended the physical stocktaking, they had arguably not complied with the ICAEW guidance on attendance at stocktaking and, in particular, had arguably not taken adequate steps to ensure that the final stock sheets presented to them for audit were the same as those prepared at the time of the physical count.

26.5.2 Unaudited accounts

It might be thought that unaudited accounts would be unlikely to give rise to claims, but it was unaudited accounts which were the subject of the claim by Peach against Slater & Co (see **26.2**), and unaudited accounts are sometimes presented to bankers in support of requests for renewal of or increased bank facilities. Even though such accounts may be based on the books and records of the client and explanations given by him, if the accounts are prepared carelessly without, for example, proper provision for bad debts and liabilities, then claims may arise.

26.5.3 Cash flow projections

Cash flow forecasts and profit projections may be prepared, or checked, by accountants on behalf of their clients. If the accounting policies adopted are not appropriate and if the assumptions are not reasonable, with the result that the actual results are very different to the forecast, the accountant may be vulnerable. That may be so even if the forecasts are not part of any formal documentation, but are submitted to a third party who intends to rely on them.

> ***Example***
>
> Cash flow forecasts were prepared and submitted to bankers in connection with an application for further facilities. The cash flow forecasts assumed that debtors would pay in 60 days when experience showed that, in practice, the average delay in payment was 120 days. The accountant was sued by the bank which relied on the figures in making additional facilities available to the client. The case was settled on the basis that it was likely that, but for its reliance on the negligently prepared figures, the bank would not have provided the additional facilities and would not have lost the sums advanced.

26.5.4 Share valuations

The valuation of shares in private companies is commonly carried out by accountants:

- when there is dispute between shareholders;
- on the death of a shareholder;
- for capital gains tax purposes;
- with a view to a sale of a business;
- in connection with divorce proceedings.

It might be thought that because valuation is an art and not a science that accountants might rarely be sued over share valuations, but that is far from the case. As Mr Justice Jacob put it in *Platform Home Loans Limited* v *Oyston Shipways Limited and Others* [1996] 49 EG 112 (which was not a share valuation case):

> 'It was in my judgment negligent just to conjure a figure out of the air. Valuation is an art and not a science but it is not astrology . . .'

> ***Example***
>
> The auditor had valued 50 per cent of the shares in a company at some £66,000 for the purposes of their acquisition by the other 50 per cent shareholder from the estate of the deceased shareholder. The executors, having taken advice, argued that the shares were worth over £800,000. A difference of this size meant that, in the absence of an obvious error on either part, a compromise was unlikely to be reached and, unusually, two experts on share valuation were retained by each side. The conventional wisdom is that each side should only have one expert on a particular topic and this case proved the point, because, after two days of cross-examination of the plaintiff's second, and more illustrious, expert, the court was told by him that the only negligent accountant involved was the other expert retained by the plaintiff, at which point the case was settled on the defendant's terms.

26.5.5 Income and corporation tax

Many cases involving income and corporation tax are settled without the assistance of experts, or at least after only the initial involvement of experts, because many tax claims arise because of missed deadlines. If, for example, an Inland Revenue time limit is missed, resulting in a loss of loss relief or in a liability to tax which could otherwise have been avoided, then any claim arising is likely to be settled promptly to minimise costs and interest.

Accountants and auditors will also be vulnerable to attack where they fail adequately to explain to their clients the consequences of the client's own actions. A typical example is directors' loans. Loans to directors are illegal under the Companies Acts (except in very restricted circumstances) and give rise to tax consequences not only on the company but on the director. If the existence of a director's loan is not properly disclosed in the accounts, as required by s232, and is corrected by the accountant at the end of the year by means of voting a director's bonus or a dividend, then the Inland Revenue are likely to seek not only the tax due but interest and penalties.

> ***Example***
>
> An accountant faced with the tax consequences of substantial loans to directors suggested that the loan position could be corrected by the transfer into the company of certain assets held privately by the directors. He failed to advise the directors on the tax consequences for the directors of the transfers into the company, and compounded his problems by suggesting to his clients that the transfers be backdated. When it was suggested to him that the backdating was not appropriate, the accountant said that it was common practice. That accountant is no longer in practice.

It is not uncommon for directors to argue that they did not know that:

(a) loans to directors were illegal;
(b) if such loans were made the company would have to pay the equivalent of advance corporation tax, which could only be recovered when the loan was repaid;
(c) they would have a personal liability to income tax on the benefits of the loan;
(d) interest is payable on tax paid late;
(e) penalties may be applied both to the company and the individual if the loan is not properly disclosed on a timely basis.

The tax treatment and consequences obviously follow the original transaction and a claim for tax paid, interest and penalties will only succeed if there was an alternative way of achieving the same objective without the same or similar tax consequences, or if it can be argued that the transaction would not have taken place at all had the directors known the true position. The general position on tax paid late is that, if the tax was payable in any event, any claim for interest will be limited to the excess of the interest paid to the Revenue over the benefit from the use of the money in the meantime. There may be some claim, even though Inland Revenue interest rates are based on overdraft rates, because no tax relief is available on interest paid to the Inland Revenue.

Coulthard v *Neville Russell* (NLP 2971117205 CA 27.11.97) related to another form of loan which turned out to be illegal and which resulted in the directors being disqualified. The loans were financial assistance prohibited under s151 Companies Act 1985, and the directors sued for loss of reputation and the costs of defending the disqualification proceedings, claiming that the auditors had wrongly advised them. The Court of Appeal considered that it was possible, depending on the facts, for an auditor to be expected to inform directors how they, as auditors, would regard the treatment of an item in the accounts, even though the auditors were not specifically engaged to advise the directors and had no statutory duty to do so.

In the case of financial assistance in breach of s151, the auditors would have to know the directors' intentions – accounting treatment after the event would not, on the face of it, affect legality one way or the other.

26.5.6 Capital gains tax

Clients frequently seek advice from their accountants as to the likely tax consequences of a sale of their business or company. If the tax consequences are worse than the client is led to expect then the client is likely to feel aggrieved and may sue, even if the tax payable is a natural consequence of the actual transaction carried out.

Example

A company was sold for £1.1 million and the capital gains tax otherwise payable was deferred by the vendor taking loan notes in the plc purchaser rather than cash. The loan notes could only be redeemed annually on 31 March. The accountant had obtained clearance from the Inland Revenue for the transaction on the basis that the loan notes would not be redeemed before 31 March 1989, although, in accordance with the documentation, the loan notes could in fact be redeemed on 31 March 1988, which is what the vendors wanted to do in the light of their concerns about the soundness of the purchaser. They were dissuaded from redeeming the loan notes at the first opportunity and, by the time the second opportunity arose a year later, the loan notes were worthless. The vendors sued for the value of the consideration lost on the basis that they could have taken cash, and that the tax consequences on an earlier redemption of the loan notes were not such as to justify the accountant's advice that they should not be redeemed.

Example

The client had the opportunity to sell either the shares in his company or the business. Most of the value was attributable to goodwill and the whole of the proceeds were gains for capital gains tax purposes. The client had expressed a desire to 'cash in his chips' because he needed cash for various personal purposes and he was concerned about the political climate. He sold the shares and paid his capital gains tax, but subsequently claimed that, if he had been properly advised, he would have caused his company to sell its business and reinvest the proceeds in assets which qualified for rollover relief. At the trial he admitted, for the first time, that he had been advised generally about rollover relief, but the judge found that the advice he had been given was not the definitive advice to which he was entitled. The judge found, however:

'It absolutely is not the duty of an accountant to give a client a 90 page analysis of every possible tax avoidance scheme whether he wants it or not. I was interested, but certainly not wholly disposed to agree, with what the expert for the plaintiff said in the witness box about the degree to which an accountant should try and over-persuade a client about whether he should become an ex-patriate. My own view in practice at the Bar was that there was no amount of tax which would justify over-persuading someone to take themselves off abroad if they did not want to. There have been more marriages broken by too much to drink and not enough to do in Jersey! Anyway, it was interesting to hear his views on the subject.'

The judge found, however, that the plaintiff would not have caused his company to reinvest the whole of the proceeds in qualifying assets, which is what was claimed, and the claim therefore failed on causation. The Court of Appeal found for the defendants on liability and concluded that the plaintiff had had the advice he needed to make an informed decision (*Lowes* v *Clark Whitehill* [1997], unreported, judgment 97).

> ***Example***
>
> A client was determined to make a tax-free sale of a piece of land. He was told that:
>
> (a) he would have to demonstrate that he owned the land beneficially;
> (b) he would have to show that he was not trading in land;
> (c) if the sale was by conditional contract the condition had to be such as to have the sale treated for capital gains tax purposes as being not before the date upon which the condition was satisfied;
> (d) at the date of sale he was not resident and not ordinarily resident in the UK.
>
> He later claimed that trying to meet the last two conditions meant that he lost the opportunity of the sale, and claimed the difference between what he maintained would have been the sale proceeds and the value of the land in question after the fall in values caused by the recession.
>
> The facts were such as to make the tax scheme unlikely to be effective and the claim settled on a commercial basis not least because the facts caused difficulties for both parties to the action.

26.5.7 Value added tax

The auditors of public companies may not generally assist their clients with bookkeeping and accounting, but many auditors of private companies and unincorporated businesses assist with the bookkeeping and preparation of accounts as a matter of routine and some offer, as an additional service, to prepare returns required by the Inland Revenue and Customs & Excise.

Auditors generally have an obligation to ensure that the balance sheets of companies which they audit show a true and fair view and this normally entails consideration of whether the Inland Revenue and Customs & Excise regulations have been complied with, at least to the extent of being able to demonstrate that no material errors have occurred.

Failure to consider the VAT position properly can give rise to claims.

> ***Example***
>
> The accountants assisted with the writing-up of the books and prepared quarterly VAT returns. They also acted as auditors to the company. Part of the company's turnover was standard-rated, but some was claimed to be exempt and the quarterly returns were completed on this basis. Visits from Customs & Excise did not reveal any problems. After a period of years it was recognised that restrictions on exemption applied and that VAT at the standard rate had been due

all along. Something over £500,000 had to be paid to Customs & Excise and the accountant was sued as a consequence, on the basis that VAT could and would have been charged to and recovered from customers had the company known the true position.

26.5.8 References

The proprietors of unincorporated businesses and directors of limited companies frequently ask their accountants for references in connection with application for loans either for business purposes or for the purchase of private residences. Such references are normally given and, usually, no charge is made to the client. Such references can have unfortunate financial consequences for the accountant, unless they are given after due consideration, carefully and honestly.

An ICAEW technical release (TR846–91) gives an example of a reference which might be given and which might reasonably be expected to minimise the risk (see Figure 26.1).

Figure 26.1

Accountant's reference

TO [Name of Lender]

[Name of Client]

Our above client has approached us for a reference in connection with the proposed loan by you of £..................... [repayable by monthly instalments of £................ over .... years].

We have acted in connection with our client's [personal, business, corporate tax] affairs since ....

Our client's income as declared to the Inland Revenue as at 5 April 199.. amounted to £.................... [to be adapted as appropriate for borrowers who are not individuals].

[Income/profits for previous years and identification of those agreed with the Inland Revenue may be added].

While we have no reason to suppose that our client would be likely to enter into a commitment such as that proposed which he [it] did not expect to be able to fulfil, we can make no assessment of our client's continuing income or future outgoings.

TR846 is in fact guidance for those seeking references *from* accountants rather than guidance *to* accountants, and there is no guidance for accountants in the ICAEW manual about references.

Example

The consequences of one reference were considered by the Court of Appeal in *First Interstate Bank of California* v *Cohen Arnold & Co* (*The Times,* 11 December 1995). The plaintiff was a US bank and (over a number of years) it had financed property transactions entered into by a Mr Gross, who was a client of Cohen Arnold, a firm of chartered accountants. Substantial profits were made on the earlier transactions and the judge found that over the years the bank had got to know Mr Gross and Mr Barnett of Cohen Arnold and, further, that Mr Barnett positively induced the bank to believe that Mr Gross was a man of great financial substance.

In November 1987 a loan was made to a single venture company with Mr Gross as the guarantor, and originally the loan was to be for 12 months. It was extended and modified and by the summer of 1990 it stood at £4.8 million. Interest had been paid, but the loan was due for repayment on 30 June 1990 when a further extension was requested.

The judge found that during the discussions regarding the extension Mr Barnett again represented that Mr Gross was a man of wealth. On 22 June 1990 Mr Barnett wrote to the bank as follows:

'Re Mr Milton Gross

I understand from Joanne Barnett that the bank requires a statement of assets and liabilities for the above-mentioned client.

However, when we are dealing with a client of such substance, who probably controls between 30 and 40 property investment companies, it would be virtually impossible to produce such a statement.

However I would inform you that, in our considered opinion, the net worth of Mr Gross is in excess of £45m. In addition, together with his wife, Mr Gross is the beneficiary under certain trusts and settlements set up by his father-in-law, Mr Sighismond-Berger, and the estimated value of these interests is in excess of £25m.

I am sure the above is satisfactory for your purposes, however, if you require any further information, please do not hesitate to contact me.'

The judgment in the Court of Appeal went on.

At the trial it was admitted by the defendants that that letter was mistaken, Mr Gross having been personally the owner of assets worth no more than

£57,000 at that time. It was also admitted by the defendants that they owed a duty of care to the bank when writing the letter, of which duty they were in breach.

That meant that there was no investigation at the trial of how the letter came to be written or how the earlier representations as to Mr Gross's wealth came to be made by Mr Barnett, who did not give evidence. Mr Justice Jacob, as he was well entitled to, clearly took a serious view of the matter, which he thought might well be one for Mr Barnett's professional body.

During the trial the defendants conceded that the bank, in granting the extension, had relied to a material extent on Mr Barnett's letter of 22 June. The judge had to consider, firstly, how long the bank had continued to rely on the letter and, secondly, what would have happened if the bank had known the true position on 22 June and so had not relied on it. The judge found that the bank placed significant reliance on the letter until at least 17 August, which was when Mr Barnett wrote to the bank setting out details of Mr Gross's assets, which came to a total of £57,000.

The property was ultimately sold in lots between October 1990 and June 1992 for £1.4 million. The judge found that the property would have sold for £3 million in September 1990 if the bank had not relied on Cohen Arnold's letter, and judgment was entered for £1,944,126.24. The Court of Appeal found that the judge had failed to evaluate the chances of the property being sold at the figure of £3 million. The Court of Appeal found that the chances were 2:1 that the sale would have taken place and reduced the £3 million likely proceeds in September to £2 million. Judgment was entered for £2 million subject to the £1.4 million actually received and making adjustments for interest.

Example

An accountant wrote the following letter to a potential lender:

21 April 1989

A Building Society

Dear Sirs

Our client is a director of Smith Limited, Jones Limited and Another Limited and he has advised us that his remuneration for the current year from these sources, together with one new source will be £165,000. This figure consists of both salary and bonuses, the latter being based on the companies' projected profits. You will appreciate that, as the figures rely upon future profits, we accept no responsibility for the projected income amount.

Yours faithfully

Seven months later the following letter was filed with the Registrar of Companies:

24 April 1989

For the attention of the Company Secretary

Dear Sir

I, the auditor hereby tender my resignation as auditor to Another Limited, effective from 24 April 1989.

In accordance with the provisions of Section 390(2) of the Companies Act 1985, I hereby state that the reason for my resignation is the Company's decision not to accept my professional advice. I have advised that, in my opinion, the Company cannot support further borrowing but, notwithstanding this, a Director has taken on large personal borrowings which have to be serviced by the Company and associated Companies. Having regard to the trading profitability to date and the Company's existing borrowings, it is my professional opinion that the Companies will be unable to service the total borrowings, thus putting the Company's future at risk.

Yours faithfully

Some time later the borrower defaulted on the loan and the lender claimed against the accountant saying that, had it not received the reference it did, it would not have lent.

The lender noted that the two letters were dated three days apart and asked for an explanation. Before the question was answered the case settled, perhaps because of the lender's difficulty in establishing reliance or reasonable reliance on the earlier letter.

26.5.9 Purchase and sales of businesses

This is perhaps the greatest area of risk for the auditor of the company being sold. Quite apart from the tax risks referred to above, there will be the risk of the purchaser not receiving all that he has paid for. Claims can be very substantial, not least because of the 'multiplier' effect of the price frequently being based on a multiple of profits.

If, to take a simplified example, the price is based on 11 times the net profits shown by the last accounts, and the profits shown by those accounts are £800,000, then the price will be £8.8 million. If the accounts should have shown a profit of only, say, £680,000, the purchaser will have overpaid by £2.2 million and he may seek to recover that, if not from the vendors then from the auditors, if he can establish that they owed him a duty of care.

The auditor may also be sued by the vendor if he has to pay under a warranty which he claims he would not have given had he been properly advised by his accountant.

What happens will, of course, depend on the facts in every case. Auditors do not have increased responsibilities merely because they are aware that their client company is being sold – their duties remain those given to them under the Companies Acts or their terms of engagement, but a wise auditor should take particular care to ensure that his own procedures and appropriate professional standards are followed and that the accounts being audited comply with the relevant accounting standards.

26.5.10 Investment advice

The ability of accountants to give investment advice is now, in certain circumstances, covered by the requirements of the Financial Services Act 1986, e.g., s3. In other circumstances it may not be, but that will not mean that an accountant can give investment advice with impunity.

Example

An accountant agreed to assist his client with raising finance for the first of a chain of entertainment complexes. It was alleged that the accountant had indicated that, because of his experience, he did not anticipate any difficulty in raising some £20 million. On the basis of that assurance the investor claimed that he made preparations to trade, became a director and shareholder, employed staff and acquired, on lease, the first premises. In the event no substantial funds were raised, the company went into liquidation, and the investor sued the accountant for recovery of his losses including the loans and a substantial call for unpaid capital. The client and the accountant had fallen for a number of advance fee frauds (substantial funds are said to be available and fees are payable in advance before the funds are advanced – the fraudsters then disappear with the fees), and no funds had been raised. The case settled on the fourth day of trial with no order as to costs. The plaintiff was legally aided.

Example

Mr Keith Fawkes-Underwood was a bookseller and antique dealer for close on 40 years. From 1 January 1985 to 31 December 1994 he was a Name at Lloyd's of London. He lost money at Lloyd's in the years of account 1989 to 1992 inclusive and sought to recover those losses from his accountants, who had acted for him from August 1987 until July 1994. Mr Fawkes-Underwood increased his participation in Lloyd's between 1985 and 1988 and the judge found that he had a very dangerous syndicate list even for someone seeking an average spread.

The case was about the extent of the defendant's retainer and Mr Hamilton, the accountant, accepted that he had agreed to assist Mr Fawkes-Underwood with understanding and interpreting his letters from his members' agents. At the beginning of August 1988 Mr Hamilton submitted bills for work to date, including general advice and assistance concerning Lloyd's underwriting activities including examining paperwork, telephoning underwriting agents and letters of explanation. After recounting his understanding of what had happened, the judge went on.

'Findings of fact

The key witnesses were Mr Fawkes-Underwood and Mr Hamilton. I have significant reservations about the reliability of both of them. On the totality of the evidence, documentary and oral, my findings of fact in relation to the years of account 1989 to 1992 inclusive are as follows:

1 Mr Fawkes-Underwood did not have much understanding of Lloyd's and this was apparent to Mr Hamilton.
2 Mr Hamilton did claim to be au fait with Lloyd's.
3 He did not in terms approve any syndicate list.
4 He did not say that he could not give advice on syndicate selection.
5 His letter dated 23 December 1988 and its enclosures were not relied upon by Mr Fawkes-Underwood in making the choice of syndicates for 1989, because he did not have them before he finalised that choice.
6 Mr Hamilton was supplied with the syndicate reports and lists each year, and not merely for filing.
7 Mr Fawkes-Underwood relied not only upon his members' agents but also to a material extent upon the absence of advice by Mr Hamilton querying the appropriateness of his portfolio.
8 A consideration by Mr Hamilton of what was appropriate for Mr Fawkes-Underwood would have led to a realisation that high risk syndicates were inappropriate.

Conclusion on scope of retainer

The defendants held themselves out as able to and agreed to and did advise him generally and in a variety of respects on his Lloyd's involvement without specific exclusion of choice of syndicates. The syndicates were, however, at the very heart of their client's investment. In my judgement, review of choice of syndicates at the appropriate times and advice upon them was within the confines of the retainer.

The standard of performance

I do not consider that it is appropriate to equate the defendants' duties, and in particular the standard of reasonable skill and care to be exercised, either with those of accountants in general, ie accountants who do not profess themselves to be au fait with Lloyd's, or with Members' Agents, who are inside the market and for whom there is no substitute.

I consider that it was the defendants' duty to identify which syndicates were high risk on the information available to them and to advise Mr Fawkes-Underwood not to allow himself to be placed on such syndicates.

The information available to them included the syndicate reports and the Lloyd's "League Tables" published by Chatset Limited. These together make looking at individual syndicates a relatively straightforward exercise . . .

Breach

In my judgment the defendants were in breach of duty by failing to advise Mr Fawkes-Underwood each Autumn that he should not allow himself to be on the syndicates identified in the Amended Statement of Claim.

Causation

In my judgment the breach caused loss to Mr Fawkes-Underwood. He relied on the advice given by the defendants to a material extent. The chain of causation was not broken by other advice given to him . . .

Quantum

. . . Judgment will [therefore] be for £668,620 plus interest subject to any further argument on calculation of loss.'

There was no letter of engagement and the judge accepted that there was no such thing as a general retainer. He had to decide the extent of the duties requested and undertaken. The implication of the judgment is that in the absence of specific exclusion an accountant's duties may be wider than he thinks.

It is understood that the judgment is the subject of an appeal.

26.5.11 Fee disputes

Clients do not always pay their accountants the fees the latter think are due and, all too often, fee disputes end in litigation, with the accountants suing for fees and being met, somewhat unexpectedly, with a counterclaim. Many accountants think that the counterclaims are spurious and made merely with a view to avoiding or delaying liability to pay sums properly due. While that may sometimes be the case, the fact of the counterclaim will have to be notified to insurers, and the counterclaim will have to be dealt with on its merits. Sometimes counterclaims can dwarf claims for fees.

There is often pressure on individual partners in accounting firms to recover fees from their clients. If the partner fails to recover fees then the decision on whether or not to sue may be taken out of his hands. In the authors' experience, accountants should consider carefully before suing for fees and it will usually be the case that negotiation or the fee dispute resolution procedure offered by the ICAEW will be preferable.

There is no point in suing for fees if the client cannot pay. If he can pay but will not then there is a dispute, and it is important for the accountant to ascertain the nature and extent of the dispute before starting the litigation process. It will usually be possible to come to some agreement as to a reduction in the fees or phased payment programme. If the agreement reached is not kept to then it may be appropriate to sue based on that agreement, but again there will be no point if the client's financial circumstances are such that he cannot keep to the agreement he made.

Accountants' professional indemnity policies will not provide legal expenses insurance cover for pursuing fees (unless special terms are arranged and special premiums paid) and, in the event of a counterclaim, to the extent that the PI insurers pay the legal expenses in connection with the counterclaim and the fee action, it will be necessary for accountants to agree with their underwriters who is to pay what.

26.5.12 Breaches of statutory requirements

Sometimes, companies are struck off the Register for failing to file documents, including accounts. If the striking-off arises because of a failure by an accountant to file documents then the accountant may be sued for the consequential losses.

> ***Example***
>
> An accountant had agreed to be responsible for making all necessary returns to the Registrar of Companies. Accounts could not be filed because they had not been formally approved by the directors or audited. The accountant failed to respond to letters from the Registrar indicating that the company would be struck off. All that he needed to do, but did not, was to write to the Registrar explaining that the company was still in business but that the accounts could not be filed and the reasons therefor. The company owned premises which could not be disposed of once it was struck off and it was necessary for the company to be restored to the Register. It was also claimed that negotiations for sale of the business had foundered once the potential purchaser realised that the company he was seeking to acquire did not exist. A claim was made for the consequential loss as being the reasonably foreseeable result of the company being struck off.

> **Example**
>
> An accountant was asked to advise on whether the payment of certain dividends would be legal. He advised that the dividends would be legal without taking the steps required by s263 Companies Act to demonstrate that the company had distributable reserves. The company subsequently went into insolvent liquidation and the liquidator sued the shareholders for the return of the dividends which it claimed had been paid illegally. The shareholders, in turn, sued the accountant on the basis that, had the appropriate steps been taken as required by the Companies Acts, the distributions would in fact have been legal.

> **Example**
>
> For commercial reasons the directors of a private company wished it to become a plc. They sought the advice of their accountant and, on the basis of that advice, increased the company's share capital to £50,000 25 per cent paid (the minimum paid up share capital for a plc). The company subsequently went into insolvent liquidation and the liquidator sought from the shareholders the 75 per cent unpaid share capital. The shareholders counterclaimed against the accountants arguing that they had never been made aware of the possibility that the balance of the capital might be called.

26.5.13 Statutory reporting

Accountants are frequently asked to report under the terms of statutes other than the Companies Act 1985 (e.g., s39 Banking Act 1987, Financial Services Act 1986, Lloyd's Act 1982) and if the reports are not justified by the circumstances in which they are given and a loss arises, then they may be sued. They may also be sued for losses arising as a consequence of not reporting on a timely basis.

> **Example**
>
> An accountant undertook to report to the Law Society under the provisions of the Accountant's Report Rules but failed to make the necessary report within the time limit of six months from the end of the financial year. As a result, the solicitor could not renew his practising certificate and did not do so. He was struck off the roll and sued his accountants for his loss of future earnings.
>
> In another case involving reporting under the Accountant's Report Rules, the accountant reported that the rules had been complied with when he ought to have been aware that they had not, having treated significant failures to operate the client account properly as trivial mistakes of bookkeeping, which

they clearly were not. Three out of four partners in the solicitors' firm sued the accountants claiming that, had they reported correctly, the fourth partner would have been prevented from committing frauds on the firm's clients exceeding £3 million.

26.6 Prevention is better than cure

This chapter has dealt at some length with things that can go wrong and areas in which accountants being sued may require assistance from experts. Litigation is a very expensive process for the accountant to be involved in as defendant. It can also have a serious effect on the defendant's health and it is rumoured that more than one accountant has committed suicide as a result of being sued for professional negligence.

The chances of being sued may be lessened by:

(a) awareness of applicable standards;
(b) application of applicable standards;
(c) recording the work agreed to be done (the engagement letter);
(d) recording the work actually done;
(e) taking and retaining notes of meetings and telephone conversations;
(f) maintaining a detailed diary and adequate accounting records;
(g) recruiting and retaining appropriately qualified staff;
(h) adequately training and supervising staff;
(i) keeping up to date;
(j) acting carefully and honestly.

Even if all these things are done something may go wrong, but that is what insurance is for. If his house burnt down, an accountant would not think twice about making a claim. Claims on professional indemnity policies are no different, except that it may be more difficult for the accountant to identify:

(a) whether he has fallen below the appropriate professional standard;
(b) whether any failure has caused a loss;
(c) if there is a loss, the extent of that loss;
(d) whether others are to blame.

Professional indemnity insurers retain experienced solicitors and expert accountants to help their clients resolve these issues and the insured accountant should have no hesitation in taking advantage of that experience.

26.7 Reference

Guest, A. G. (1994) *Chitty on Contracts* (27th edn), Sweet & Maxwell.

Chapter 27
Affidavits in respect of security for costs and other applications

27.1 Introduction

During civil proceedings there are a number of applications which either party can make. Such applications are held in front of a Master or a judge in chambers or before a judge in open court, and the merits of the application are argued by each side (or one side if it is *ex parte*). Such applications are often backed up by affidavit evidence, that is, a sworn statement. Most affidavits are sworn by the parties to the action or their solicitors. However, there are a number of areas where the solicitor may instruct an accountant to prepare an affidavit to support the application. The accountant may not necessarily be an expert in the case when it goes to trial; indeed, the case itself may not require an expert. However, he is performing the role of an expert and needs to approach the preparation of such affidavits with all of the normal care and consideration he would give to an expert report.

The accountant swearing such an affidavit will generally not be examined in court, but there is provision for cross-examination on affidavits in RSC Order 38 rule 3. However, his affidavit will be disclosed in advance to the other side (unless the application is *ex parte*) and the other side are likely to involve their own accountant to scrutinise his work. Of course, he may ultimately give evidence in the case as an expert witness. Any matters in his affidavit on which he could be subject to criticism will no doubt be brought up in his cross-examination at trial.

The most common defect which the authors have noted in affidavit evidence prepared by accountants is partiality, probably because of a subconscious expectation that the swearer is unlikely to be called to account. However, the general principles for all written evidence hold true – a good point can be ruined by trying to improve weaker points and 'stepping into the arena' can lead to all the evidence being discounted.

The most common application where an accountant may be called to give evidence is an application for security for costs. The accountant may also be asked to give affidavits in respect of discovery applications and *ex parte* applications such as Mareva and Anton Piller injunctions. Each of these is considered in this chapter.

27.2 Security for costs applications

An application for security for costs is made by a defendant against a plaintiff in an action to force the plaintiff to pay money into court in advance of trial to cover the defendant's costs in the event that the plaintiff is unsuccessful at trial. Not all plaintiffs can be the subject of a successful application, but the application is designed to give some measure of protection against a potentially impecunious plaintiff or a plaintiff resident outside of Europe.

Order 23 of the Rules of the Supreme Court sets out the situations in which the court will grant an application by the defendant to an action or other proceeding in the High Court for an order for security for costs.

Rules 1 to 3 of Order 23 read as follows:

> '(1) Where, on the application of a defendant to an action or other proceeding in the High Court, it appears to the Court–
> (a) that the plaintiff is ordinarily resident outside of the jurisdiction, or
> (b) that the plaintiff (not being a plaintiff who is suing in a representative capacity) is a nominal plaintiff who is suing for the benefit of some other person and that there is reason to believe that he will be unable to pay the costs of the defendant if ordered to do so, or
> (c) subject to paragraph (2) that the plaintiff's address is not stated in the writ or other originating process or is incorrectly stated therein, or
> (d) that the plaintiff has changed his address during the course of the proceedings with a view to evading the consequences of the litigation,
> then if, having regard to all the circumstances of the case, the Court thinks it just to do so, it may order the plaintiff to give such security for the defendant's costs of the action or other proceeding as it thinks just.
>
> (2) The Court shall not require a plaintiff to give security by reason only of paragraph (1)(c) if he satisfies the Court that the failure to state his address or the mis-statement thereof was made innocently and without intention to deceive.
>
> (3) The references in the foregoing paragraphs to a plaintiff and a defendant shall be construed as references to the person (howsoever described on the record) who is in the position of plaintiff or defendant, as the case may be, in the proceeding in question, including a proceeding on a counterclaim.'

The most common applications are in respect of incorporated plaintiffs. In such circumstances s726(1) of the Companies Act 1985 provides that:

> 'Where in England and Wales a limited company is plaintiff in an action or other legal proceeding, the Court having jurisdiction in the matter may, if it appears by credible testimony that there is reason to believe that the company will be unable to pay the defendant's costs if successful in his defence, require sufficient security to be given for those costs, and may stay all proceedings until the security is given.'

These rules are primarily designed to protect a defendant in an action brought by a plaintiff who cannot pay costs or could evade costs if unsuccessful. Someone who is ordinarily resident outside Europe and therefore could avoid any judgment or keep his assets beyond the reach of the English courts could evade a costs order. An English company could be placed into liquidation if unsuccessful in the litigation. However, for non-incorporated UK residents, other than those suing on behalf of someone else, or where there is evidence of an attempt to conceal an address, there will be no order. Thus, even though an individual has no money whatsoever, a defendant cannot force him to abandon his action by getting an order for money to be paid into court. If he could, then many actions would not start for the simple reason that many plaintiffs are legally aided. It should be noted that an action is possible against a legally aided person, though unlikely in practice.

It should also be noted that the application is made against a person who is in the position of a plaintiff, which will include a defendant bringing a counterclaim which is more than merely defensive. This rule also means that a third party to proceedings cannot issue an application against a plaintiff because the plaintiff is not in the position of a plaintiff *vis-à-vis* the third party.

Because the rule provides discretion, the courts will not always grant an application against a plaintiff and only will if an order would be just in all the circumstances (RSC Order 23 rule 1).

The court will take into account all of the circumstances of the case, including:

(a) whether the claim is bona fide or a sham;
(b) whether the plaintiff has a reasonably good prospect of success;
(c) any admissions by the defendant that money is due;
(d) whether there is a payment into court or an open offer by the defendant;
(e) whether the plaintiff's lack of money is as a result of the conduct of the defendant;
(f) whether the application is being used to stifle a genuine claim.

In the last instance, allowing a defendant in such circumstances to have genuine proceedings stifled for want of providing adequate security would operate against the interests of justice. However, if the plaintiff is unsuccessful, the defendant will probably be unable to recover any costs. The court will take into account the following additional factors when assessing how to use its discretion:

(a) whether the plaintiff is using its impecuniosity to put pressure on the defendant;

(b) the plaintiff's prospects of success;
(c) whether the plaintiff would be forced to abandon the claim (and it is up to the plaintiff to show this).

Where a defendant in a security for costs application is successful, the plaintiff will be required to give such security as the court feels fit, normally by making a payment into court. Whilst rule 2 of Order 23 provides that 'the security shall be given in such manner, at such time, and on such terms (if any) as the Court may direct', payment into court is by far the most common direction, although in certain restricted circumstances security may be by way of bond. The amount of the security may be the costs requested by the defendant or some lesser amount as directed by the court.

The costs requested by the defendant will usually be supported in affidavit evidence by a bill of costs. These normally set out three sets of costs:

- those already incurred to the date of the application;
- those to trial; and
- those to completion of trial.

Alternatively, requests for security can be made at an early stage in the proceedings to cover the costs up to directions hearings, and at a later stage to cover the costs of preparing for trial and the trial itself.

Where the plaintiff who is the subject of a successful application for security for costs is unable to provide that security, he will normally be ordered to give security within a limited time, failing which his action will normally be dismissed.

In making an application for security for costs against a limited company, it should be noted that the defendant must demonstrate that the company 'will not', not 'may not', be able to pay the defendant's costs. Unless the company is in liquidation, the application:

> '. . . must be supported by an affidavit which credibly and reasonably shows the inability of the company to pay the costs of the successful defendant.' (RSC Order 23 rules 1–3, Note 14)

It should also be appreciated that the assessment of the ability of a company to pay is at the date the application is made, although evidence of future expectations may be admitted.

Security for costs applications are taken very seriously by the court. Furthermore, the burden on the defendant is high in that he must show inability to pay, rather than possible inability to pay. The court places a great deal of weight on the sworn evidence of accountants, and this is considered next.

27.3 The role of the accountant in security for costs applications

The accountant for the defence will normally be requested by his instructing solicitor first to advise on the merits of an application. This involves the accountant considering whether, on the basis of the financial information presented, the application is likely to be successful. In many situations, the accountant will be able to determine, even from a brief review of the papers, that an application is unlikely to succeed. In other cases, it is apparent that the application will succeed; some situations require further more detailed work before a view on the merits of the proposed action can be reached.

If there is a good case, the accountant will carry out a detailed review of the papers and then prepare an affidavit setting out his views on the ability of the plaintiff to pay. The accountant for the plaintiff will prepare an affidavit reply to any affidavit submitted by the defence. Given that the plaintiff's accountant will have access to all of the plaintiff's financial information, his investigation may be able to be more in depth.

27.4 A simple example

The following is a simple example of the financial information which may be presented to an accountant.

Example

During the course of proceedings, an accountant is provided with the audited financial statements of the plaintiff. It is assumed that the financial statements are current and properly reflect the current financial circumstances of the plaintiff company. The accountant is asked to provide an affidavit to support an application for security for costs of £75,000.

The financial statements of the plaintiff company show the following:

Profit and loss account	*£'000*
Turnover	500
Costs	(600)
Loss	(100)
Balance sheet	
Fixed assets	100
Current assets (cash £10,000)	1,650
Total assets	1,750

Current liabilities	1,650
Net assets	100
Share capital	50
P&l b/fwd	150
Loss for year	(100)
Reserves	100

The audit report makes no reference to the going concern status of the company. Is then the plaintiff company able to meet the defendant's costs in respect of the action?

There must be grave doubts as to whether the company will be able to meet the amount of costs. Whilst the balance sheet shows positive net assets of £100,000, current liabilities match current assets. Even on the basis that all assets could be realised in full for cash, the company would have to dispose of some of its fixed assets to raise further monies to pay the costs or to take out a bank loan secured on the assets. With only £10,000 in cash and no evidence of refinancing it is clear that, at the date of the balance sheet, the company does not have sufficient resources to meet any costs order. Therefore, the prospective trading of the company becomes crucial. In the absence of any other evidence, the current year losses indicate future losses. Clearly, further evidence would be required for the plaintiff to satisfy the court that it could pay.

However, what is the accountant to make of this evidence? For most accountants, there is so little information as to make it very difficult for an accountant to form an opinion either way. The order asks for credible testimony. Is it reasonable for a defendant's accountant to say that, on the basis of so little information, the plaintiff cannot pay? The accountant for the defendant may conclude that the information he has seen indicates that the plaintiff cannot pay, but without further and up-to-date financial information it is impossible to say at the current time. The accountant for the plaintiff will no doubt insist on seeing more up-to-date financial information.

This makes the point that these affidavits are never simple. There is always a large amount of financial information unavailable and, given time constraints, little opportunity to obtain it. Furthermore, there is often no good reason why a plaintiff should disclose missing financial information, but the court can be invited to draw its own conclusions from a refusal to provide up-to-date figures.

27.5 More complex financial information

Financial information is never as simple or incomplete as in the example at **27.4** above. The accountant, for whichever side, is more likely to be presented with a mass of information, much of it out of date, some of it conflicting and all of it incomplete. The accountant for the defendant, normally having first bite, is going to be in the position where the only financial information to which he has access will be the filed accounts of the company (which may be modified). The accountant for the plaintiff is likely to be able to get access to more complete and up-to-date financial information from the plaintiff himself, often requiring a reply affidavit from the defendant.

Whichever side the accountant is instructed by, he should have regard to the checklist of questions shown in Figure 27.1.

Figure 27.1

Audited accounts

(a) How old are these?
(b) Is the company late in filing its accounts?
(c) Are the accounts qualified, particularly with regard to going concern?
(d) Are the accounting policies reasonable and in accordance with GAAP?

Management accounts

(a) How recent are these?
(b) Do they make sense when compared with trading as shown by the audited accounts?
(c) Are expenses, stock or levels of gross profit prima facie accurate or have they been prepared using notional amounts or percentages?

Budgets

(a) Has the basis of preparation been disclosed?
(b) Does the basis on which these have been prepared look reasonable?
(c) Do they make sense when compared to management accounts and audited accounts?

Trading history and trading prospects

(a) Is there a trend in the profits or losses which allows one to predict what future trading levels are likely to be?
(b) Is anything known of the company's trade which would bring into doubt its future trading prospects, for example a particular sector or evidence of trade becoming dormant?

Cash position

(a) What is the company's cash position, and is this sufficient to pay the costs?
(b) Do the company's accounts disclose an increasing or decreasing level of cash resources?
(c) What bank facilities are disclosed by the accounts and what bank support is disclosed?
(d) What are the terms of long-term loans?

Assets

(a) To what extent is the company's asset position dependent on fixed assets, which may not be available to meet the defendant's costs without disposal, which may damage the business, or refinancing?
(b) Are there intangible assets which may have a doubtful realisable value?
(c) Are there any debtors due after more than one year?
(d) Are there any indications of bad debts, such as an aged debtor analysis?
(e) Are any of the assets charged?
(f) Is stock surplus to the requirements of the business or obsolete?

Liabilities

(a) Are current liabilities greater than current assets?
(b) What are the terms of long-term liabilities?
(c) Are there any contingent liabilities?

Groups

(a) What are the relationships with group companies, who may not be in the action?
(b) To what extent are assets intra-group assets, the repayment of which may be in doubt?
(c) To what extent are liabilities intra-group liabilities, the repayment of which may be deferred?
(d) Is cash available from other parts of the group?
(e) Does the company support other parts of the group?

An accountant's investigation and reasoning may need to run to many pages of affidavit in order to express an opinion.

27.6 Discovery applications

Order 24 rule 1(1) reads as follows:

> 'After the close of pleadings in an action begun by writ there shall, subject to and in accordance with the provisions of this Order, be discovery by the parties to the

> action of the documents which are or have been in their possession, custody or power relating to matters in question in the action.'

Books have been written about what documents are, and are not, discoverable. Essentially, discoverable documents are those which are relevant and which allow one party to advance his case or harm the other side's case, or lead to either of those two consequences. The most innocuous-looking document may be discoverable, and the fact that a piece of paper is headed up 'addressee only, strictly private and confidential' makes no difference to its discoverability. Documents which are not relevant are not discoverable. Privileged documents, for example documents from a solicitor to his client concerning the matter in hand, are discoverable and must be listed. However, they are privileged from production for inspection by the other side.

In a commercial action of any size, discovery is likely to be an onerous and time-consuming process. Not surprisingly, a party to an action will be loath to spend vast sums finding and indexing documents. Furthermore, one key document may be extremely damaging to a party's case. However, solicitors and their clients are under a duty to the court to comply with Order 24.

It is a fact of life that some parties do not provide full discovery. This may be through design, but is often due to a failure to understand the relevance rule or through inattention. Accountancy, more than most things in life, has developed processes to produce truly vast amounts of documents, and it is probably not surprising that full discovery is often inadvertently not made. Additionally, solicitors may not appreciate that accounting documents exist which are or could be of relevance.

Order 24 rule 7 gives the court the power to order a party to swear an affidavit stating whether or not he has a particular document or class of documents in his possession. Such an order will be made on the basis of an application by the other side, such application being supported by an affidavit. Such an affidavit sets out the deponent's belief that the other side has, or had, the document or class of documents, and the reasons for it or their relevance.

Clearly, the accountant can have an important role in such applications. First, he should be instructed to review the other side's list of discovery to identify any relevant documents which may be missing. Second, he may write to the solicitor setting out the reasons he believes such documents are held by the other side and their relevance. The solicitor may exhibit this letter to his own affidavit or, alternatively, the accountant himself might swear an affidavit.

This aspect of an accountant's role should not be underestimated, either by accountants or solicitors. The accountant, from his auditing experience, will have a great deal of knowledge of the sorts of files which businesses maintain and the type of information which they contain. It is sometimes the forgotten files which have information of fundamental importance to a case.

27.7 Mareva injunctions

An application for a Mareva injunction is an example of what is called an *ex parte* application, that is, it is heard in the absence of the other side. The basic objective of a person applying for a Mareva is to stop an individual disposing of assets which the applicant says are his. The most common object of a Mareva is to stop the defendant removing assets from the jurisdiction of the court hearing the action so that the judgment will not be enforced against them. If the applicant is successful, he will obtain an injunction against a named party which reads as follows:

> 'NOTICE TO THE DEFENDANT
>
> (1) This order prohibits you from dealing with your assets up to the amount stated. The Order is subject to the exceptions at the end of the order. You should read it all carefully. You are advised to consult a solicitor as soon as possible. You have a right to ask the court to vary or discharge this order.
>
> (2) If you disobey this order you will be guilty of contempt of court and may be [sent to prison or] fined or your assets may be seized.'

The Mareva is most commonly used where fraud has taken place. For the sufferer of a fraud, the normal civil and criminal remedies can be completely inappropriate for his basic desire, that is, to protect and then recover the defrauded assets. Once the fraudster becomes aware that his fraud has been discovered, he will want to dispose of the assets as quickly as possible. Armed with the Mareva, the applicant can get his interim relief within a very short period of time, without the knowledge of the defendant, thereby protecting the assets before they disappear.

It is important to realise that the successful applicant does not gain a charge over the assets, nor does he recover them. However, he stops custodians of those assets using them in any way. This, together with the costs of defending subsequent actions and the possibility of being in contempt for breaching the Mareva can be enough to bring the defendant to the table and an early settlement.

The Mareva injunction also orders the defendant to make full disclosure of all of his assets.

Mareva applications need to be supported by affidavit evidence. The accountant often has an important role to play in putting together the evidence because of the need to consider and interpret financial information. In particular, the accountant may be requested to trace assets or to put together a report showing evidence of fraud by, say, an officer of a company.

Because of the serious effects of a Mareva, there are a number of safeguards for defendants, one of the most important being the undertaking which the applicant must give to compensate the defendant for any loss he has suffered as a result of the Mareva, which in the opinion of the court he should not have suffered because the Mareva injunction should not have been made. This undertaking, which is given to the court, not to the defendant, is called the cross-undertaking in damages. Therefore, if the defendant's business fails as a result of a Mareva which should not have been granted, the applicant will have to make good the loss. Accountants will therefore find themselves required to prepare the usual business interruption reports to assess the quantum of the loss.

27.8 Anton Piller orders

The Mareva injunction is a legal device enabling the individual obtaining it to protect assets held by the respondent or third parties. By contrast, an Anton Piller order seeks to protect specific documents and materials by allowing the entry and search of premises and seizure of the documents the order concerns. Paragraph 1 of the order reads as follows:

> 'This order orders you to allow the persons mentioned below to enter the premises described in the order and to search for, examine and remove or copy the articles specified in the order . . . The order also requires you to hand over any of the articles which are under your control and to provide information to the plaintiff's solicitors, and prohibits you from doing certain acts. You should read the terms of the order very carefully. You are advised to consult a solicitor as soon as possible.'

Failure to comply with the order is a contempt of court and can result in the defendant being sent to prison, fined or having his assets seized. As with the Mareva, the application is made *ex parte*.

To obtain an Anton Piller, the court has to be satisfied that there is an extremely strong prima facie case, very serious potential or actual damage for the applicant and clear evidence that the defendant has incriminating 'documents or things' which have a real possibility of being destroyed. This standard of proof is much higher than that required for a Mareva injunction.

However, the order does not allow for a general seizure of documents – the purpose of the order is to allow taking and copying of specific material for the current action, not a fishing expedition for documents which may be of use to commence an action. Furthermore, it does not allow the plaintiff to obtain documents which would be subject to legal privilege. The plaintiff has to set out the grounds on which his case is founded, which means the precise allegations and the precise facts. Like the Mareva, there is a duty on the plaintiff to make full and frank disclosure of the facts to the court. In addition, the plaintiff is required to give to the court an undertaking to pay damages should the defendant suffer loss and should the court be of the opinion that compensation is due.

The accountant's role in Anton Piller applications will be in identifying documents of a financial nature which have gone missing or in identifying the use of such documents. Additionally, of course, he will be involved in assessing any damages due as a result of the cross-undertaking.

27.9 Affidavit preparation and swearing

The accountant will see a sufficiently large number of affidavits to give him a thorough understanding of what an affidavit should look like and how it should read. Order 41 of the White Book sets out formally what is required, as follows:

(a) title of the case (but it is sufficient so far as multiple parties are concerned to name the first and refer to the others as 'and others');
(b) expressed in the first person;
(c) address (in the case of a deponent acting in a business or professional capacity, such as an accountant, he may state alternatively his business address, the position he holds and the name of his firm), occupation and, if employed by a party to the action, this must be stated (in the case of an accountant, he will state that he is instructed by the solicitors for defendant or plaintiff);
(d) bound in book form with all pages consecutively numbered;
(e) divided into numbered paragraphs, each dealing with a distinct portion of the subject;
(f) dates and numbers to be expressed in figures, not words;
(g) signed by the deponent and completed and the jurat must be signed by the person before whom it is sworn;
(h) erasures or corrections to be initialled.

There is also a practice direction in Order 41 requiring on the first page and the backsheet:

(a) the name of the party on whose behalf the affidavit is filed;
(b) the initial and surname of the deponent;
(c) the number of the affidavit, that is, whether it is the deponent's first or second, etc. affidavit in the action;
(d) the number of each exhibit to the affidavit; and
(e) the date on which the affidavit is sworn.

Many affidavits sacrifice a free and open writing style for tortuous and cumbersome legalese. Whether or not solicitors enjoy writing and reading this sort of language, the accountant should avoid it at all costs. Not only does it make for a boring affidavit, it also gives the impression that someone has drafted the affidavit for the accountant. However, there are some legal formulae which are unavoidable. Where an accountant refers to a document he will need to write 'The 1996 accounts are now produced and shown to me marked "GMac1"', the initials being the deponent's own. Where an accountant relies on hearsay evidence (which he should keep to the absolute bare minimum), he will need to write 'I am informed by Mr Smith, the managing director, and truly believe, that these budgets will be produced on 14 July'.

Other than the above requirements, the accountant should draft the affidavit in whatever way he feels conveys best and most persuasively the evidence he is attempting to give. The accountant is therefore free to break up the affidavit into sections with appropriate headings, to provide introductions, summaries and conclusions, to quote from documents and in general to set out in full his reasoning.

Having prepared his affidavit, the accountant will send it to his solicitors to be 'engrossed', which means no more than having the document retyped on heavy paper, bound with tape and covering sheets provided for each of the exhibits.

The accountant will then swear the affidavit in front of a solicitor. By RSC Order 41 rule 8 that solicitor cannot be the solicitor of the party on whose behalf the affidavit is being prepared, nor one of his partners or employees. It is also acceptable for affidavits to be affirmed.

Finally, the accountant will pay the person before whom he swears the affidavit the fee for the swear (normally £5) and a fee for each exhibit (normally £2).

Part 4
Insolvency, fraud and criminal proceedings

Chapter 28
Criminal procedure

28.1 Introduction

This chapter sets out the rules for criminal procedure, from the initiation of criminal proceedings to verdict. Emphasis is placed on the role of the expert in criminal proceedings. Expert accountants are only likely to be involved in cases which are tried in the Crown Court and to a large extent procedures in magistrates' courts are therefore ignored, other than in respect of committal proceedings.

28.2 Types of offences and mode of trial

Criminal offences fall into three types as regards mode of trial. Indictable offences are serious offences such as murder, rape and robbery. Such offences are tried in the Crown Court before a judge and jury. Summary offences are less serious offences, such as most road traffic offences, failure to pay for a television licence and common assault. Assaulting a police officer in the execution of his duty is a summary offence. Summary offences are tried in a magistrates' court.

Between these two types of offences are those of medium gravity, called offences which are triable either way, that is, either triable in the Crown Court or in the magistrates' court. Such offences include unlawful wounding, criminal damage involving a loss of greater than £5,000 and many offences under the Theft Acts.

At common law, all offences are indictable offences, but there are very few remaining common law offences. Most offences are those created by statute and the legislation will define the offence as being either triable on indictment only, triable summarily only or triable either way. The statute creating an offence triable either way will specify the maximum punishment for an offence if the trial of that offence takes place in the Crown Court or in the magistrates' court. Alternatively, s17 of and Schedule 1 to the Magistrates Court Act 1980 lists out offences which are triable either way. If an offence is a summary offence, the statute creating the offence will specify the maximum punishment on summary conviction, and will not refer to a second greater penalty for offenders convicted on indictment.

The ultimate effect of a summary trial is in the punishment on conviction.

Magistrates are limited in the sentences they can give, being a maximum of six months imprisonment and/or a fine of £5,000 for one offence triable either way, and 12 months imprisonment and/or a fine of up to £5,000 per offence for two or more either-way offences. The Crown Court is unrestricted in imposing terms of imprisonment or fines, save as laid down by statute. For example, false accounting is an offence by s17(1) of the Theft Act 1968. The offence is triable either way, and on indictment the maximum term of imprisonment is seven years.

As will be seen in **28.6.1** below, all criminal proceedings commence in the magistrates' court. A summary offence will stay there for trial, and an indictable offence will be transferred or committed to the Crown Court for trial. The location of trial for an offence which is triable either way depends on the magistrates and the accused. If both magistrates and the accused agree, the trial will be held in the magistrates' court. However, either has the option to have the trial heard in the Crown Court. The consideration for the magistrates is primarily one of sentence. The magistrates will consider, *inter alia*, whether, on conviction, they will be able to pass an adequate sentence, given the alleged offences. Having said that, after conviction, magistrates are empowered to commit an individual for sentence in the Crown Court if they consider that, having regard to the seriousness of the case, their own powers of punishment are too limited. The accused will be aware that, if convicted in the Crown Court, his sentence may be greater, but will balance that with the thought that he has a better chance of an acquittal by a jury.

28.3 The Crown Court

The Crown Court is part of the Supreme Court and has jurisdiction over trials on indictment and sentencing of offenders committed for sentencing by the magistrates' court and appeals from the magistrates' court. The judges who sit in Crown Courts are either High Court judges, circuit judges or recorders. High Court judges are those who can hear civil cases in the High Court, and in the Crown Court will hear the most serious criminal cases. There are about 20 High Court judges sitting in the Crown Court.

Circuit judges, of whom there are about 400, sit mainly in the Crown Court, but also sit in the county court and hear civil cases. Recorders are part-time judges. Together with the circuit judges, they hear most Crown Court cases. In addition to these judges, there are appointments for fixed periods of time of deputy circuit judges and assistant recorders. Finally, magistrates sit as judges of the Crown Court for certain types of hearing. This is always with a High Court judge, circuit judge or recorder.

The Crown Court sits at various locations, being major towns and cities in England and Wales, grouped into six regional circuits. Each circuit is presided over by a High Court judge. There are three types of Crown Court. The first tier locations have facilities for both High Court and Crown Court trials. The second tier locations do not hear civil trials but have a High Court judge sitting on a regular basis. The third tier locations have no High Court judge.

28.4 Magistrates' courts

Magistrates' courts try the vast majority of criminal cases in England and Wales. They also have other functions such as hearing committal proceedings, granting licences and dealing with certain aspects of civil proceedings such as maintenance orders in divorce proceedings.

The magistrates' courts are divided into commission areas, which follow county borders, other than in London where there are six commission areas. Each commission area is divided into a number of petty sessional divisions, each of which has a magistrates' court.

There are two types of magistrate. The vast majority are the 30,000 lay magistrates, assisted by qualified clerks who advise the magistrates on points of law. Two magistrates are required to hear a summary trial.

Stipendiary magistrates, of whom there are about 100, are barristers or solicitors, paid a salary for their work, who can try cases on their own (except when sitting in the juvenile court).

28.5 Initiating a prosecution

The first step in criminal proceedings is the initiation of a prosecution.

Prosecutions can be undertaken by anyone in England and Wales. In practice, most are initiated by the police. Where the police have arrested an individual on suspicion of what is called an arrestable offence, that is, an offence where the sentence is fixed by law or which carries maximum term of imprisonment of five years or more on conviction, plus others which are defined by statute as being arrestable, and have sufficient evidence for a conviction, they will charge the suspect by writing down the offence on a charge sheet. This sheet is sent to the court and the person charged will be kept in custody or bailed to appear in court at a later date.

The alternative to charging, which is open to any person, is to lay before a magistrate an 'information' or document which sets out the offence and the name of the suspect. The magistrate will then issue a summons to the accused to appear in court at a later date to answer the allegations made in the information. The police will also use this means of initiating a prosecution for less serious offences and prosecutions against corporate bodies. Indeed, for offences which are not arrestable, this is the means of initiating the prosecution.

As noted above, most prosecutions are initiated by the police. However, about a quarter are started by other bodies and it is these prosecutions that the accountant is most likely to meet in practice. These bodies include the Inland Revenue, Customs & Excise, the DTI and the Serious Fraud Office (SFO).

Where the police have initiated the prosecution, the continuation of proceedings will, in general, be handed over to the Crown Prosecution Service (CPS). The CPS Crown Prosecutors will be responsible for conducting proceedings in the magistrates' court, preparing the case for trial and briefing counsel as agents for the CPS. Bodies such as the DTI and the Inland Revenue will continue with the prosecution of an offence once they have initiated it.

28.6 Committal proceedings and transfer to the Crown Court

28.6.1 Committal proceedings

As noted above, an accountant is only likely to be involved in trials heard in the Crown Court, that is, on indictment. However, the prosecution of such offences will nearly always commence in the magistrates' court by way of committal proceedings.

Committal proceedings involve the magistrates' court deciding whether there is a case to answer against the accused and, if so satisfied, then committing the accused for trial at the Crown Court. In the past, this consisted of the magistrates hearing the oral evidence against the accused and the defence cross-examining witnesses. Effectively, the committal proceedings were a rehearsal of the prosecution's evidence to be heard at the ultimate trial. Changes were introduced by s2 of the Criminal Justice Act 1967, as amended by s102 of the Magistrates Courts Act 1980, whereby written statements became admissible as evidence for committal proceedings where both prosecution and defence agreed. The written statement was read out in court and was unchallenged, for the purposes of the committal proceedings alone, by the defence.

At the end of any oral evidence and the reading of the written statements, the defence could make a submission that there was no case to answer. If the court was satisfied that, on the basis of these statements, there was a case to answer, then the accused would be committed for trial. Bearing in mind that they were not ruling on the guilt or innocence of the accused, but merely whether the evidence disclosed at least a prima facie case, the burden of proof was low and most cases were committed for trial.

Section 6(2) of the Magistrates Courts Act 1980 provides a system whereby the need for the prosecution to prove a prima facie case is dispensed with if the defence accepts that such a case exists. In these circumstances the case will be committed to the Crown Court without any legal argument and the committal is therefore little more than an administrative exercise. This type of committal is known as the 'quick' or 'new style' committal.

Committal proceedings were due to be replaced by 'transfer' provisions for cases where the accused was only charged with an indictable offence or where the Crown Court had been chosen as the most appropriate venue. These changes were introduced by s44 of the Criminal Justice and Public Order Act 1994; however, new procedures were never brought into force and s44 was later repealed by s44 of the Criminal Procedure and Investigations Act 1996. The result is that most cases for trial in the Crown Court are still subject to committal proceedings.

It is now no longer possible for magistrates to hear oral evidence from witnesses. Their consideration of the evidence is confined to the statements and documents tendered by the prosecution. The defence is unable to present any oral or documentary evidence.

28.6.2 Transfer to the Crown Court

By s4 of the Criminal Justice Act 1987, in cases of serious fraud certain 'designated authorities' are able to give a notice of transfer which bypasses the committal stage, allowing the accused to be committed for trial without approval of a magistrates' court. The designated authorities are the Director of Public Prosecutions, the Director of the SFO, the Commissioners of Inland Revenue and Customs & Excise and the Secretary of State.

The notice of transfer is given if:

> '(a) a person has been charged with an indictable offence; and
> (b) in the opinion of an authority designated by subsection (2) below or of one of such an authority's officers acting on the authority's behalf the evidence of the offence charged–
>   (i) would be sufficient for the person charged to be committed for trial, and
>   (ii) reveals a case of fraud of such seriousness or complexity that it is appropriate that the management of the case should without delay be taken over by the Crown Court;'

Again, this is to save the time of preparing for and attending at committal proceedings.

28.7 Pre-trial

28.7.1 The indictment

Between committal or transfer and trial, there are a number of procedural matters to be undertaken.

First, there is the indictment. This is the formal document listing the charges against the accused on which he is arraigned at the commencement of a trial on indictment. The indictment sets out the Crown Court where the case will be held, the name of the accused, the counts on which the accused is charged, brief particulars of each offence and the signature of an officer of the Crown Court.

The indictment may list one or more persons charged with the offences in the indictment.

28.7.2 Preparatory hearings

The first formal involvement of the Crown Court will be at a preparatory or plea and directions hearing.

The majority of cases are committed to the Crown Court and, at the time of committal, the magistrates will specify a first date for the defendant to attend the Crown Court for a 'plea and directions hearing'. The purpose of such hearings is for the defendant to enter his plea and for the Crown Court to ensure that all necessary steps have been taken in preparation for trial and to fix a trial timetable.

For those cases that have been 'transferred' to the Crown Court, the Crown Court's first involvement will be by way of a preparatory hearing rather than a plea and directions hearing. An application for a preparatory hearing can be made to the Crown Court either by the prosecution or the defence. The judge himself can order a preparatory hearing. In practice, the prosecution makes the application for the preparatory hearing at the time of transfer. Section 7(1) of the Criminal Justice Act 1987 sets out the reasons for ordering a hearing as being:

> '(a) identifying issues which are likely to be material to the verdict of the jury;
> (b) assisting their comprehension of any such issues;
> (c) expediting the proceedings before the jury; or
> (d) assisting the judge's management of the trial.'

The preparatory hearing is the start of the trial. At this hearing the accused will be arraigned, that is, asked whether he pleads guilty or not guilty to the charges. The remainder of the hearing is to ensure that both sides will be properly prepared for trial, to fix a date for the trial and for each side to get rulings from the judge on matters of law. Once the case has been allocated to a particular judge, it is normally the case that he will be involved in the preparatory hearing and the trial itself.

In practice, and particularly in complex trials, there are likely to be a number of hearings up to the trial itself to assist the court in the management of the case.

Of particular interest to the accountant will be the following:

- the prosecution case statement;
- the defence case statement;
- admissions;
- skeleton arguments;
- orders in respect of expert evidence and the presentation of evidence;
- date of trial and other deadlines.

28.7.3 Prosecution case statement

In the more serious/complex fraud cases where there has been a 'transfer' rather than a committal, s9(4)(a) of the Criminal Justice Act 1987 states that a judge may order the prosecution to provide to the court and the defendant a statement ('the case statement') which sets out:

> '(i) the principal facts of the prosecution case;
> (ii) the witnesses who will speak to those facts;
> (iii) any exhibits relevant to those facts;
> (iv) any proposition of law on which the prosecution proposes to rely; and
> (v) the consequences in relation to any of the counts in the indictment that appear to the prosecution to flow from the matters stated in pursuance of sub-paragraphs (i) to (iv) above.'

For the accountant instructed by the prosecution, this will involve a summary of the evidence in his witness statement and the documents referred to by him. The prosecution case statement is often made available shortly after transfer. For the accountant instructed by the defence, the case statement often gives the first intelligible overview of the case against his client.

When a case has been committed to the Crown Court, the prosecution's primary duty under s3(1) of the Criminal Procedure and Investigations Act 1996 is to disclose to the accused all material in the prosecution's possession which has not previously been disclosed and which, in the prosecutor's opinion, might undermine the case for the prosecution, or to give the accused a written statement that there is no such material.

28.7.4 Defence case statement

In the serious/complex fraud cases that have been transferred rather than committed, s9(5)(i) of the Criminal Justice Act 1987 also allows the judge to order each defendant to serve a statement in writing setting out his defence and the principal matters on which he takes issue with the prosecution, after the serving of the prosecution case statement. The idea behind this is to shorten and simplify the eventual trial, and is similar to the exchange of pleadings in a civil case.

However, it goes against the ingrained attitude of many defence lawyers to disclose their hand in advance of trial. Additionally, the defence does not have to reveal evidence which it intends to adduce at trial, other than expert evidence (see **2.6**).

Therefore, the section only requires the general terms of the nature of the defence and the principal matters at issue. This can include just a general denial of the charges, and there is little that the courts can do to sanction non-compliance with the spirit of the ideas behind case statement legislation.

In practical terms, it can sometimes be difficult for the defence to put together a full case statement. This is often the case where an accountant has been instructed to review a mass of documentation, and part of the defence may rely on the accountant's findings.

In those cases where there has been a committal, the accused is obliged under s5(5) of the Criminal Procedure and Investigations Act 1996 to provide the court and the prosecutor with a 'defence statement' once the prosecution have complied with their duty to disclose relevant material. The defence statement must:

(a) set out in general terms the nature of the accused's defence;
(b) indicate the matters on which the defendant takes issue with the prosecution;
(c) set out in respect of each such matter the reason why the defendant takes issue with the prosecution; and
(d) provide details of any alibi that is to be relied upon by the defence.

Once the accused has given this defence statement the prosecutor is then obliged under s7 of the Act to disclose any prosecution material which has not previously been disclosed and might be reasonably expected to assist the accused's defence as disclosed by the defence statement, or to give the accused a written statement that there is no such material.

28.7.5 Admissions

In cases where there has been a transfer rather than a committal, s9(4) and (5) of the Criminal Justice Act 1987 enables the judge to order both prosecution and defence to try to reach agreement on admissions. The prosecution is ordered to give to the court and the defence a notice of documents, the truth of which ought to be admitted, and other matters which ought to be agreed. The defence is ordered to give to the court and the prosecution notice stating which documents and other matters in the notice are agreed, the extent of agreement, which are not agreed, and the reasons for non-agreement.

As with case statements, the defence does not always comply with its obligations, and again there is little that the court can do to try to ensure compliance. However, agreeing admissions is a valuable method of reducing documentary evidence or the length of oral evidence called to adduce such documents.

Where accountants are involved it should be possible for agreement to be reached on purely factual matters such as documents or summaries of documents. The difficulty arises where accounting information is interpreted and agreement is effectively being invited in respect of opinion evidence which the defence may wish to test in cross-examination. Indeed, the accountant for either side should ensure that the proposed facts to be admitted are just facts and not facts with a prejudicial gloss put on them. If the defendant's accountant feels that what is being proposed is prejudicial and the prejudicial element cannot be removed, he should strongly advise his solicitor not to accept.

This happens most often where the prosecution chooses to analyse and present factual accounting information in a particular way, such information being capable of analysis and presentation in a variety of ways. It also happens where the prosecution selects certain accounting information for agreement and chooses not to rely on other information.

In the former case, an example would be the presentation of a cash flow statement in such a way that emphasises, for example, payments to directors. An alternative presentation would be the presentation in FRS 1 format or in normal management accounting format. The underlying financial information is factually correct; however, the presentation in one format is not a 'fact'.

In the latter case, an example would be a schedule showing unpaid creditors in an insolvency. Factually, these creditors were unpaid. However, the complete picture would list out the creditors which had been paid. In such a case, acceptance may be justifiable, but the accountant should explain what evidence should be presented by the defence to complete the picture.

28.7.6 Skeleton arguments

At the pre-trial hearing it is normal for arrangements to be made to exchange the skeleton arguments which will form the basis of the opening speeches.

28.7.7 Orders in respect of expert evidence and the presentation of evidence

As set out in Chapter 2, each side has to give advance notice of expert evidence otherwise it will not be allowed to adduce such evidence at trial. The judge can make orders concerning the timing for submission of expert evidence in advance of trial. It should be borne in mind that this need not be a full expert witness report, but must set out the opinion and the facts on which the expert will base his opinion.

The judge can also make recommendations for meetings of experts to agree matters or narrow the areas of disagreement. This is similar to a meeting of experts in a civil trial, but is rarely asked for. The comments concerning the showing of the defence's hand, noted above, are relevant to any agreement by the defence to such a meeting, let alone to any agreements arising from such a meeting. The defence view is that it is up to the prosecution to prove its case, and there is no reason why the defence should make its job any easier. The prosecution and the court will try to agree those areas where there really is no dispute or to identify areas where there is a lack of understanding by either side.

The judge can order the prosecution to prepare its evidence in a way that helps comprehension by the jury and to supply it in that form to the court and the defendant. Given the disorganised state in which the prosecution sometimes presents its case, particularly in fraud trials, it is surprising that this power is not used more often. A valuable role that the accountant instructed for the defence can carry out is to identify where the prosecution's accounting evidence is badly prepared or confusing and advise his solicitor.

Given what has been said in the preceding paragraph, a by-product of a defence expert's work can often be an explanation to the prosecution of what their accounting case is!

28.7.8 Date of trial and other deadlines

At the pre-trial hearing the date of trial is fixed, and other deadlines such as the last date for submission of evidence or case statements are set. Such matters are set by the judge after hearing arguments from counsel and it is particularly important that the accountant for the defence advises his lawyers of matters which may have a bearing on, for example, the ability of the defence to be ready for trial. Obtaining documents from third parties, the length of time taken to review unused material and delays in the granting of legal aid prior authorities are all matters which will cause problems in preparation. If necessary, the accountant should be prepared to go to preparatory hearings to make an oral statement on matters affecting his work.

28.7.9 Notice of further evidence

The prosecution is not allowed to ambush the defence with new or additional evidence at trial. It is often the case that between indictment and trial new evidence comes to light. This is particularly the case in fraud trials where difficulties are met in obtaining evidence, such as from third parties like banks. The admissibility of further evidence is covered by s9 of the Criminal Justice Act 1967, which basically provides that such evidence must be in a form similar to s102 statements. If the defence objects to the statement within seven of service days then the witness must be called to give evidence.

28.8 The trial

After the swearing of the jury, the clerk of the court will read out the charges to the jury and prosecuting counsel opens his case. This is limited to an overview of the case, being the charges against the defendant, the evidence the prosecution intends to call and how this evidence will show, beyond reasonable doubt, that the accused is guilty of the charges. After the opening, the prosecution will call its oral witnesses one by one, examine them in chief and offer them for cross-examination, and read out written statements as agreed with the defence or as allowed by the court.

After the prosecution has finished its own evidence, the defence can make a submission of no case to answer, that is, the judge is asked to decide whether the jury, properly directed, could not properly convict on the basis of the prosecution's evidence. The hearing of this submission is made in the absence of the jury. If the judge agrees with the submission, then he recalls the jury and directs them to find the accused not guilty on each of the counts where he has found no case to answer. If the submission fails, then the defence presents its case on those counts for which the defence has accepted or the judge has ruled that there remains a case to answer.

Where the defence calls only evidence from the accused and character witnesses, there is no opening speech. Where the defence calls other evidence, then the defence can outline its own case and criticise the prosecution's evidence.

Following any opening speech, the defence calls its first witness.

28.8.1 Oral evidence in criminal trials

In general, evidence in criminal trials is oral. There are a number of exceptions to this, for example where s9 statements are not in dispute or witnesses cannot physically attend court for certain reasons.

However, expert accountants will invariably have to attend court and give oral evidence, including evidence in chief. This is somewhat different to civil trials where the expert accountant's report will have been read by the judge before he gives evidence, and often his evidence in chief will be extremely limited. In a criminal trial, whatever evidence it is intended an expert should give in chief will be given orally, despite the report having been served on the other side.

Having said that, a great deal of expert accounting evidence will consist of original documents and analysis produced for the purpose of the proceedings. It is normal for schedules produced by the accountant to be copied, passed to the judge and jury, and for the accountant to give his evidence on those schedules. Those schedules then become exhibits in the trial.

The defence does not need to call the defendant to give evidence, nor indeed any witness. However, the defendant must give evidence before the other defence witnesses unless the judge gives leave to do otherwise. Witnesses for whichever side (other than experts, see below) are forbidden from attending court until they have given evidence. This prevents witnesses from altering their evidence to tie in with the evidence of witnesses who have gone before. This logic requires that the defendant gives his evidence in advance of his own witnesses.

The expert witness is normally allowed to attend court all the way through the proceedings. The reasons are explored in Chapter 2 but can be summed up by stating that, because so much expert evidence is based on facts, which may be disputed or may change from what has been said in witness statements, it is right that the expert should hear the facts on which his expert opinion will rely. For example, if a fact on which he has relied is in some way modified or withdrawn in oral evidence, the expert will need to be aware of this in order to amend his opinion, if necessary.

In general, the defence does not have to give advance notice of the evidence which it intends to call. The defence does not, therefore, have to show its hand and can spring a witness on the prosecution by surprise (compare with civil proceedings where trial by ambush is heavily curtailed). However, the defence does have to give advance notice of two types of evidence – expert evidence. Where the expert is called, his work will have been subject to the scrutiny of the prosecution and his cross-examination will be far more thoroughly prepared than that of the other witnesses.

The prosecution has to disclose all relevant evidence, including that on which it chooses not to rely (what is called 'unused material') in advance. The Criminal Procedure and Investigations Act 1996 defines relevant material as being material which, in the prosecutor's opinion, might either undermine the case for the prosecution or be reasonably expected to assist the accused's defence.

Following the defence evidence, prosecuting counsel may make his closing speech, the defence may do the same, the judge sums up and the jury retires to consider its verdict.

Chapter 29
Company directors' disqualification

29.1 Introduction

The courts have had powers to disqualify persons from being directors of companies since the 1929 Companies Act. Successive Companies Acts and insolvency legislation have increased these powers. In 1986 an Act was passed, the Company Directors Disqualification Act 1986 (CDDA), which provided a comprehensive set of sanctions which the courts could apply against directors.

This chapter sets out the provisions of the CDDA of relevance to accountants involved as experts in disqualification proceedings, looks at the *Carecraft* procedure, and discusses the evidence which accountants may be expected to give.

29.2 The CDDA

By s1 of the CDDA the court is empowered to make an order under s6 disqualifying a person from being a director, liquidator or administrator, or receiver or manager of a company without the leave of the court. Subsection 1(1)(d) extends the disqualification by stating that the court may make an order that a person shall not (without leave of the court):

> '. . . in any way, whether directly or indirectly, be concerned or take part in the promotion, formation or management of a company . . .'

The CDDA sets out various circumstances in which a disqualification order may be made and the maximum periods of disqualification for each circumstance. Section 6 also sets out a minimum period of disqualification. The relevant sections are as shown in Figure 29.1.

Figure 29.1

CDDA section	*Reason for disqualification*	*Maximum period*
2	On conviction of an indictable offence in connection with promotion, formation, management or liquidation of a company, or with the receivership or management of its property.	5 years in magistrates' court, otherwise 15 years

3	For persistent breaches of companies' legislation (at least three convictions or default orders within the last five years), that is, for failing to file accounts, etc. with the Registrar of Companies.	5 years
4	Disqualification for fraud in a winding-up, either for fraudulent trading under s458 of the Companies Act 1985 or any other fraud.	15 years
5	Disqualification on summary conviction, where there have been at least three default orders in five years for failing to file accounts, etc. with the Registrar of Companies.	5 years
6	Disqualification where a person has been a director of a company which has become insolvent and where his conduct makes him unfit to be involved in the management of a company.	15 years (minimum 2 years)
8	Disqualification after investigation of a company (for example, under s437 of the Companies Act 1985) where his conduct makes him unfit to be a director.	15 years
10	Participation in wrongful trading, where under s213 or s214 of the Insolvency Act 1986 a person is made liable to make a contribution to a company's assets.	15 years

(The difference between s3 and s5 is that s3 requires a separate application to the court, whereas under s5 the court can make the disqualification order at the same time as it makes the conviction for the offence.)

It can be seen from the above that, in certain cases, a disqualification order may be made at the same time as other proceedings. In other cases – s3, s4, s6 and s8 – disqualification is as a result of an express application. (Section 10 can be applied in either manner.)

The accountant will become involved in CDDA proceedings arising out of an express application, and usually in respect of a s6 application. There is no role for an accountant in a s3 application, and in s8 or s10 proceedings he will probably have a wider role acting in Companies Act or Insolvency Act proceedings.

29.3 Period of disqualification

There are three bracketed periods of disqualification which the court will apply, as set out in *Re Sevenoaks Stationers (Retail) Ltd* [1990] BCC 765 CA (concerning s6 CDDA 1986):

(a) 10–15 years, for the most serious cases, and for second time disqualifications;
(b) 6–10 years, for serious cases which did not deserve the maximum sentence;
(c) 2–10 years, for relatively not very serious cases.

What is serious will depend on the individual case. Additionally, the court may take into account various mitigating factors. These issues are considered at **29.7** below, where the role of the expert accountant is discussed.

29.4 Section 6

Section 6 reads as follows:

> '6. Duty of court to disqualify unfit directors of insolvent companies
>
> (1) The court shall make a disqualification order against a person in any case where, on an application under this section, it is satisfied–
>
> (a) that he is or has been a director of a company which has at any time become insolvent (whether while he was a director or subsequently), and
> (b) that his conduct as a director of that company (either taken alone or taken together with his conduct as a director of any other company or companies) makes him unfit to be concerned in the management of a company.
>
> (2) For the purposes of this section and the next, a company becomes insolvent if–
>
> (a) the company goes into liquidation at a time when its assets are insufficient for the payment of its debts and other liabilities and the expenses of the winding up,
> (b) an administration order is made in relation to the company, or
> (c) an administrative receiver of the company is appointed;
>
> and references to a person's conduct as a director of any company or companies include, where that company or any of those companies has become insolvent, that person's conduct in relation to any matter connected with or arising out of the insolvency of that company.
>
> (3) . . . and in both sections "director" includes a shadow director . . .'

Section 7 deals with applications to the court under s6 and reads as follows:

> '7. Applications to court under s 6; reporting provisions
>
> (1) If it appears to the Secretary of State that it is expedient in the public interest that a disqualification order under section 6 should be made against any person, an application for the making of such an order against that person may be made–
>
> (a) by the Secretary of State, or
> (b) . . . in the case of a person who is or has been a director of a company which is being wound up by the court . . ., by the official receiver . . .
>
> (3) If it appears to the office-holder responsible under this section, that is to say–
>
> (a) . . . the official receiver,
> (b) . . . the liquidator,
> (c) . . . the administrator, or
> (d) in the case of a company of which there is an administrative receiver, that receiver,
>
> that the conditions mentioned in section 6(1) are satisfied as respects a person who is or has been a director of that company, the office-holder shall forthwith report the matter to the Secretary of State.'

Under s7(2) applications must be made within two years of the date of the company becoming insolvent.

29.5 'Unfit to be concerned in the management of a company'

Section 9 of the CDDA is entitled 'Matters for determining unfitness of directors'. This directs the court to have regard to Part I of Schedule 1 to the CDDA and, where the company has become insolvent, to Part II.

Part I of Schedule 1 reads as follows:

> '1. Any misfeasance or breach of any fiduciary or other duty by the director in relation to the company.
>
> 2. Any misapplication or retention by the director of, or any conduct by the director giving rise to an obligation to account for, any money or other property of the company.
>
> 3. The extent of the director's responsibility for the company entering into any transaction liable to be set aside under Part XVI of the Insolvency Act (provisions against debt avoidance).
>
> 4. The extent of the director's responsibility for any failure by the company to comply with any of the following provisions of the Companies Act [those

referred to in s4 of Schedule 1 Part I including accounting records, registers of members and officers, annual returns, duty to register charges].

5. The extent of the director's responsibility for any failure by the directors of the company to comply with–

   (a) . . . (duty to prepare annual accounts)
   (b) . . . (approval and signature of accounts).'

Part II of Schedule 1 reads as follows:

'6. The extent of the director's responsibility for the causes of the company becoming insolvent.

7. The extent of the director's responsibility for any failure by the company to supply any goods or services which have been paid for (in whole or in part).

8. The extent of the director's responsibility for the company entering into any transaction or giving any preference, being a transaction or preference–

   (a) liable to be set aside under section 127 or sections 238 to 240 of the Insolvency Act [1986] . . .

9. The extent of the director's responsibility for any failure by the directors of the company to comply with section 98 of the Insolvency Act (duty to call creditors' meeting in creditors' voluntary winding up).

10. Any failure by the director to comply with any obligation imposed on him by . . . the Insolvency Act . . .'

(Section 127 of the Insolvency Act 1986 makes void transfers of a company's property after the commencement of a winding-up by the court. Sections 238 to 240 deal with transactions at an undervalue and preferences within two years prior to the onset of insolvency in cases involving connected persons (not employees), or six months in other cases.)

29.6 *Carecraft* orders

It is clear from the above that the defence of a CDDA application under s6 or s8 may be very expensive and time-consuming. The courts have, however, developed a summary procedure for the respondent in a CDDA effectively to enter into settlement negotiations with the Secretary of State to agree to a certain period of disqualification and, where the parties have agreed facts, getting rid of the need for a full hearing. This procedure was developed in the case *Re Carecraft Construction Co Ltd* [1994] 1 WLR 172. However, the procedure is not as straightforward as a normal civil settlement.

First, the power of the Secretary of State to compromise proceedings is extremely limited. Ferris J stated that:

'The Secretary of State has no general power to compromise a claim for a disqualification order which he continues to regard as being expedient in the public interest.'

An order under the CDDA is designed to protect the public, not through the disqualification order itself, but as a result of the criminal sanctions which apply to breaching the order. Furthermore, whether a director is unfit is a matter for the court, not the Secretary of State; the court has to consider any of the matters which determine unfitness. Finally, it is up to the court to determine the length of any disqualification.

In order to deal with these issues, the *Carecraft* procedure involves putting together a statement of agreed facts and a bracketed disqualification period to the court.

On a without prejudice basis and for the purpose of summary procedure, the respondent sets out the agreed facts, those facts which he will dispute and, based on those agreed facts, the disqualification bracket which should apply. If acceptable to the applicant the document will be put before the court.

The position of the court is intriguing. First, it has to be satisfied that, on the admissions, the conduct of the director is sufficient to make him unfit. However, it also has to be satisfied that the facts in respect of which the admissions have been made are based on evidence. This means seeing, for example, the affidavit evidence of the company's liquidator. However, the court also has to look at the disputed evidence and if it feels, on the basis of the admissions and the disputed evidence even if proven, that unfitness may not be found by a full court hearing, then the court will direct a full hearing.

On the other hand, if the court disagrees with the proposed disqualification bracket because the undisputed evidence or the disputed evidence might warrant a more serious disqualification bracket, then again a full hearing will be directed.

The court must therefore fully appraise the disputed evidence and consider its potential impact which, if substantial, will be suitable for a full hearing.

If the matter does go to a full hearing then the admissions and agreements made for the purposes of the *Carecraft* procedure cannot be used in that full hearing.

It should be noted that admissions for the purposes of a *Carecraft* order cannot be used against a respondent in any other proceedings. This is particularly important for directors who are being pursued by, for example, liquidators to make a contribution in respect of wrongful trading.

29.7 The role of the expert accountant – factors which will merit a disqualification

29.7.1 Insolvency

One of the most common grounds for a disqualification is insolvent trading. The role of the expert accountant is primarily that of investigating whether the company was insolvent, and continued to trade.

Whether a company is insolvent, or the date that a company became insolvent, or when the directors of a company should have realised it was insolvent are all issues on which an accountant can be expected to give expert evidence. However, there are a number of judgments which indicate that insolvency is not enough, and the expert accountant needs to bear these in mind when carrying out his investigation.

In *Re CU Fittings Ltd* [1989] BCLC 556, Hoffman J said:

> 'It may be that in January [1984], or even earlier, a dispassionate mind would have reached the conclusion that the company was doomed. But directors immersed in the day-to-day task of trying to keep their business afloat cannot be expected to have wholly dispassionate minds.'

In *Re McNulty's Interchange Ltd & Another* [1988] 4 BCC 533, Browne-Wilkinson VC said:

> 'It may be that wrong commercial decisions were taken. But I deplore the suggestion that a director who makes what in retrospect appears to be a commercial misjudgment is in some way acting in a manner which is culpable so as to justify disqualification . . .'

Finally, one should never forget the famous 'clouds and sunshine' judgment of Buckley J in *Re White and Osmond (Parkstone) Ltd* (unreported) (not a CDDA case):

> 'In my judgement there is nothing wrong in the fact that directors incur credit at a time when, to their knowledge, the company is not able to meet all its liabilities as they fall due. What is manifestly wrong is if directors allow a company to incur credit at a time when the business is being carried on in such circumstances that it is clear that the company will never be able to satisfy its creditors. However, there is nothing to say that directors who genuinely believe that the clouds will roll away and the sunshine of prosperity will shine upon them again and disperse the fog of their depression are not entitled to incur credit to help them get over the bad time.'

Many companies will suffer problems, even severe problems – that does not of itself mean that the directors are carrying on in such a way as to merit a disqualification. Something more is needed.

In *Re Lo-Line Electric Motors Ltd & Others* [1988] 4 BCC 415, Browne-Wilkinson VC said:

> 'Ordinary commercial misjudgment is in itself not sufficient to justify disqualification. In the normal case, the conduct complained of must display a lack of commercial probity although I have no doubt that in an extreme case of gross negligence or total incompetence disqualification could be appropriate.'

The accountant should be aware of two matters which come out of the above cases:

(a) a serious breach of commercial practice or complete incompetence is necessary;
(b) the actual knowledge of the directors must be determined.

29.7.2 Other matters

The accountant should also be aware of other areas meriting his investigation, as follows:

(a) the selection of those creditors for payment who are the most pressing;
(b) financing further trading out of money owed to existing creditors;
(c) phoenixism;
(d) excessive remuneration;
(e) failure to file accounts or keep proper books or records.

Expert accountants should be aware that, whether they cover the matter in their report or not, there is a strong possibility that they will be asked questions on the sufficiency of accounting records. After all, the court will have to hand someone who, as a result of his profession, should know how useful a particular set of records is.

29.8 The role of the expert accountant – mitigating factors

The court will take into account a number of mitigating factors when deciding a period of disqualification. The accountant can be expected to investigate the following:

(a) loss of own money;
(b) honesty and absence of personal gain;
(c) reliance on professional advice;
(d) actions to relieve the situation;
(e) extent to which the individual was involved in day-to-day management.

In respect of the reliance on professional advice and involvement, these mitigating factors are not designed to allow a company director to say that the finances of the company are the responsibility of another person – as a director he is responsible. However, as was said in *Re Douglas Construction Services Ltd & Another* [1988] BCLC 397 by Harman J:

> 'He [the respondent] was advised, but he was advised by people on whom any reasonable man could properly expect to be able to rely. He did not evade his responsibilities and shuffle off the matter. He acted, in my view, in a sensible way in getting in financial men who ought to have been able . . . to help him properly . . .
>
> Of course he is responsible as a director. Every director of a company is responsible for all its affairs, and nobody assuming the office of director can say, "I am not responsible for part of the company's affairs", but the question is: has that responsibility been operated in such a way as to render the individual unfit to be a director in the future.'

These statements again emphasise the need for the accountant to look at the whole picture and especially the individual knowledge of the director.

Chapter 30
Insolvency

30.1 Introduction

The purpose of this chapter is to discuss the definitions of insolvency and to set out the problems of investigating and assessing insolvency.

Accountants involved in criminal (and civil) trials will often be asked for their opinion on various aspects of insolvency. Insolvency issues will be found in cases alleging fraudulent trading, wrongful trading and conspiracy to defraud. Issues of solvency and insolvency will also be found in disqualification proceedings, in contract disputes and in auditors' negligence actions. However, it is in criminal trials that insolvency issues will be encountered most often, and this chapter looks primarily at the role of the accountant in criminal proceedings. Having said that, the matters raised are relevant to all proceedings where an allegation of insolvency is raised.

Expert accountants do not need to be licensed insolvency practitioners in order to give expert evidence in these cases; solvency and insolvency are concepts which most accountants will have to consider in their professional careers. However, the investigation of possible solvency can be an extremely difficult issue because of the need to investigate what, at any one time, accounting records disclose, what transactions could be expected to occur and what information was available to, say, a director, or what should have been available.

30.2 The standard definition of insolvency

The standard definition of insolvency is an inability to pay debts, that is, a cash flow test. By s122 of the Insolvency Act 1986 the court may wind up a company if, *inter alia*, it is unable to pay its debts.

Section 123 of the Insolvency Act 1986 sets out the definition of an inability to pay debts, as follows:

> '(1) A company is deemed unable to pay its debts–
>
> (a) if a creditor (by assignment or otherwise) to whom the company is indebted in a sum exceeding £750 then due has served on the company, by leaving it at the company's registered office, a written demand (in

the prescribed form) requiring the company to pay the sum so due and the company has for 3 weeks thereafter neglected to pay the sum or to secure or compound for it to the reasonable satisfaction of the creditor, or

(b) if, in England and Wales, execution or other process issued on a judgment, decree or order of any court in favour of a creditor of the company is returned unsatisfied in whole or in part, or
(c) [position in Scotland]
(d) [position in Northern Ireland]
(e) it is proved to the satisfaction of the court that the company is unable to pay its debts as they fall due.

(2) A company is also deemed unable to pay its debts if it is proved to the satisfaction of the court that the value of the company's assets is less than the amount of its liabilities, taking into account its contingent and prospective liabilities.'

It should be realised that the above is not a definition of insolvency. Indeed, there is no statutory definition of insolvency. One has to infer that the court has the power to wind up an insolvent company, and that a prima facie indication of insolvency is the inability of a company to pay its debts. The Insolvency Act then gives a number of circumstances when a company will be deemed to be unable to pay its debts.

The first four circumstances set out in s123 deal with the statutory demand and the non-payment of a judgment debt. For the purposes of any criminal proceedings these, of themselves, have little relevance. It is possible for a company to be solvent for all practical purposes and yet fail to make the necessary response under s123(1)(a) through negligence or inattention. For the purposes of criminal trials, what a successful statutory demand or an unsatisfied judgment debt may do is provide an indication of insolvency, and that indication may be outweighed by other matters, such as meeting all other debts.

Subsection (1)(e) is what would commonly be regarded, as noted above, as the standard definition.

Subsection (2) is much more problematical. Many companies have balance sheets where assets are exceeded by liabilities, even excluding contingent liabilities. They may have financial problems (then again they may not) but have no problems in being able to pay their debts. A simple example would be a company with a loan repayable some time, say 10 years, in the future, but with a healthy current cash flow from which to meet current expenses, including interest.

A further problem is what the Act means by assets and liabilities. Accounts are normally drawn up on a going concern basis. The balance sheet of any company drawn up on a break-up basis may look very different indeed. Many assets may have little immediate realisable value.

As with subsections (1)(a) to (d), all that the circumstances envisaged in subsection (2) can provide is an indication of insolvency.

Bearing in mind that ss122 and 123 are concerned with the circumstances in which a company can be wound up by the court, for the purposes of criminal proceedings it is submitted that the most important test for insolvency is the standard definition, that is, an inability to pay debts as and when they fall due.

Byblos Bank v *Al-Khudhairy* [1987] BCLC 232 (a case decided under the equivalent section in the Companies Act 1948) provides some guidance on what the court will take into account in these matters.

Nicholls LJ held the following:

(a) if a debt presently payable is not paid due to lack of means, that will normally suffice to prove that the company is unable to pay its debts;
(b) in determining whether a company was able to pay its debts it was not correct to take into account assets which it would hope or expect to acquire in the future without a right to acquire such assets;
(c) although the Act focuses attention on the present position of a company so far as its assets are concerned, it looks towards both current creditors and those which are contingent or prospective.

Nicholls LJ (at 247) gave an example of the last two points.

> 'Take the simple, if extreme, case of a company whose liabilities consist of an obligation to repay a loan of £100,000 one year hence, and whose only assets are worth £10,000. It is obvious that, taking into account its future liabilities, such a company does not have the present capacity to pay its debts and as such it "is" unable to pay its debts. Even if all its assets were realised it would still be unable to pay its debts, viz, in this example, to meet its liabilities when they became due. It might be that, if the company continued to trade, during the year it would acquire the means to discharge its liabilities before they became presently payable at the end of the year. But in my view para (d) [the relevant part of the legislation then in force] is focusing attention on the present position of a company. I can see no justification for importing into the paragraph, from the requirement to take into account prospective and future liabilities, any obligation or entitlement to treat the assets of a company as being, at the material date, other than they truly are.'

However, he then went on to say:

> 'Of course a company's prospects of acquiring further assets before it will be called upon to meet future liabilities will be very relevant when the court is exercising its discretion: for example, regarding the making of a winding-up order . . .'

Many companies do rely on their ability to trade out of difficulties. However, the test as set out above would not help the company which is insolvent, but which expects its trade to generate further funds to wipe out any deficit.

Indeed, another case, *Cornhill Insurance plc* v *Improvement Services Ltd & Others* [1986] 2 BCC 942 gives an even more stringent test. In that case the large insurance company Cornhill was the subject of a winding-up order. The petitioner of the winding-up said that Cornhill was insolvent under s518(1)(e) of the Companies Act 1985 (now replaced by s123 of the Insolvency Act 1986), because it had not paid a debt of £1,154. The debt was undisputed, Cornhill could no doubt pay it but the judge said that it had chosen not to do so, and it was held that, in these circumstances, a winding-up petition could be validly presented.

In a later case, *Taylor's Industrial Flooring* v *M & H Plant Hire* (*Manchester*) [1990] BCC 44, it was held that if there was a dispute, the reason for non-payment had to be substantial. It was not enough for a thoroughly bad reason to be put forward, no matter if it was put forward honestly.

That case was heard before the Court of Appeal, appealing a judgment of Scott J. Referring to s123(1)(e) Scott J said at 46:

> 'In my judgment, something more must be proved than simply that the company has not paid a debt. In some cases the circumstances surrounding the non-payment may justify the inference that the debtor is unable to pay its debts as they fall due. A series of dishonoured cheques might justify that inference. But in the present case a reason for non-payment has been put forward. The reason may not be a very good one, but unless it is not being put forward honestly, I do not see why an inference of inability to pay should be drawn from the fact of non-payment.'

The Court of Appeal overturned this, restated Harman's judgment in *Cornhill*, and as to non-payment, Dillon LJ at 51 held that the test was whether there was a substantial ground of defence.

A question raised earlier on in this section concerned what was meant by assets and noted that the balance sheet of a company can have a very different look if prepared on a break-up as opposed to a going concern basis. One issue in particular is whether intangible assets such as goodwill have a value which can be taken into account.

In the *Byblos Bank* case, the alleged date of insolvency of the company was 3 June 1985, and on that date the receiver had prepared a statement of affairs. It was this statement of affairs which the court had used to determine whether the company was insolvent, implying that the court had relied on a break-up basis for determining solvency. Furthermore, an objection had been raised that the statement of affairs did not take account of goodwill. However, the court said (Nicholls LJ at 246):

> '... there was no realistic hope of being able to establish before this court that as at 3 June 1985 the value of goodwill could have been as high as £1.15m so as to cancel out the estimated deficiency as regards creditors ...'

Therefore, it would seem that intangibles can be included, subject to there being evidence that they do have a value. On a break-up basis, this is often difficult to achieve.

30.3 Other definitions of insolvency

Insolvency is referred to in other parts of the insolvency and companies legislation.

30.3.1 Statutory declarations

Where it is proposed to wind up a company voluntarily, by s89(1) of the Insolvency Act the directors of that company may, at a meeting of directors:

> '... make a statutory declaration to the effect that they have made a full enquiry into the company's affairs and that, having done so, they have formed the opinion that the company will be able to pay its debts in full, together with interest at the official rate, ... within such period, not exceeding 12 months from the commencement of the winding up ...'

This declaration is termed the statutory declaration of insolvency and making the declaration without having reasonable grounds is an offence under s89(4) carrying imprisonment or a fine or both.

There are similar declarations in the Companies Acts.

Section 156 of the Companies Act 1985 concerns the statutory declaration to be made where financial assistance is proposed to be given under s155 of the Companies Act 1985 (i.e., financial assistance given by the company to a person who is acquiring shares in that same company). Subsections 156(2) to (4) state the following:

> '(2) The declaration shall state that the directors have formed the opinion, as regards the company's initial situation immediately following the date on which the assistance is proposed to be given, that there will be no ground on which it could then be found to be unable to pay its debts; and either–
>
> (a) if it is intended to commence the winding up of the company within 12 months of that date, that the company will be able to pay its

debts in full within 12 months of the commencement of the winding up, or

(b) in any other case, that the company will be able to pay its debts as they fall due during the year immediately following that date.

(3) In forming their opinion for the purposes of subsection (2), the directors shall take into account the same liabilities (including contingent and prospective liabilities) as would be relevant under [section 122 of the Insolvency Act] (winding up by the court) to the question whether the company is unable to pay its debts.

(4) The directors' statutory declaration shall have annexed to it a report addressed to them by the company's auditors stating that–

(a) they have enquired into the state of affairs of the company, and
(b) they are not aware of anything to indicate that the opinion expressed by the directors in the declaration as to any of the matters mentioned in subsection (2) of this section is unreasonable in all the circumstances.'

Section 173 of the Companies Act 1985 deals with the conditions to be met by a private company wishing to redeem or purchase its own shares out of capital. One of the two conditions is the making of a statutory declaration and subsections (3) and (4) state the following:

'(3) The company's directors must make a statutory declaration . . . stating that, having made full enquiry into the affairs and prospects of the company, they have formed the opinion–

(a) as regards its initial situation immediately following the date on which the payment out of capital is proposed to be made, that there will be no grounds on which the company could then be found unable to pay its debts, and
(b) as regards its prospects for the year immediately following that date, that, having regard to their intentions with respect to the management of the company's business during that year and to the amount and character of the financial resources which will in their view be available to the company during that year, the company will be able to carry on business as a going concern (and will accordingly be able to pay its debts as they fall due) throughout that year.

(4) In forming their opinion for the purposes of subsection (3)(a), the directors shall take into account the same liabilities (including contingent and prospective liabilities) as would be relevant under [section 122 of the Insolvency Act] (winding up by the court) to the question whether a company is unable to pay its debts.'

Subsection (5) deals with the issue of an audit report and whether the declaration by the directors is reasonable.

30.3.2 Wrongful trading

Section 214 of the Insolvency Act 1986 concerns the liability of directors where a company goes into insolvent liquidation. Insolvent liquidation is defined by subsection (6) as follows:

> '(6) For the purposes of this section a company goes into insolvent liquidation at a time when its assets are insufficient for the payment of debts and other liabilities and the expenses of the winding-up.'

30.3.3 Directors' disqualification

Section 6(2) of the Company Directors Disqualification Act 1986 states the following:

> '(2) For the purposes of this section and the next, a company becomes insolvent if–
>
> (a) the company goes into liquidation at a time when its assets are insufficient for the payment of its debts and other liabilities and expenses of the winding up,
> (b) an administration order is made in relation to the company, or
> (c) an administrative receiver of the company is appointed . . .'

30.4 What is insolvency?

It will be clear from the above that there are two extreme points of insolvency. The most severe is the position of the company in insolvent liquidation, as defined by s214(6) of the Insolvency Act 1986. The accountant should be aware of the strictness of the test under s123 as set out in *Byblos* and *Cornhill* above. At the other end of the scale is the presumption of solvency if a company is a going concern 'and therefore able to pay its debts as they fall due' (s173(3)(b) Companies Act 1985).

The going concern/non-going concern boundary is likely to be the issue with which the expert accountant is concerned. The reason for this is that issues of insolvency in criminal trials are tied up with the conduct, whether reasonable and whether honest, of directors. A company may be a going concern at a particular date and yet, if wound up on that date, would go into insolvent liquidation. A director may not necessarily be acting unreasonably if he continues to allow the company to trade when it cannot pay its debts. These issues are explored in more detail in Chapter 31 on fraud. However, one should remember the judgment by Buckley J in *Re White and Osmond (Parkstone) Ltd*:

> 'In my judgement there is nothing wrong in the fact that directors incur credit at a time when, to their knowledge, the company is not able to meet all its liabilities as they fall due. What is manifestly wrong is if directors allow a company to incur

> credit at a time when the business is being carried on in such circumstances that it is clear that the company will never be able to satisfy its creditors.'

A further issue arises on the balance sheet test. What basis for valuing assets and liabilities does the accountant use? How does one take into account prospective or contingent liabilities? What about future trading?

The accountant is normally likely to be asked his opinion on the date when a company became insolvent and the period of insolvency. The date a company ceased to be a going concern will be all-important; the date a company would have been likely to go into insolvent liquidation may be of little relevance.

The next section deals with the investigation of insolvency and the difficulties likely to be faced.

30.5 Investigation of insolvency

In almost every case where an accountant is being asked to consider insolvency, the company concerned will have gone into insolvent liquidation. The only exception is likely to be where an insolvent company has been represented as being solvent, and has subsequently returned to solvency.

30.5.1 Documents and other evidence likely to be available

The problem facing the accountant will be to try to determine the date of insolvency. In an ideal world, all of the books and records of the company will be obtained and the accountant will be able, with some degree of accuracy, to estimate when the company was no longer able to operate as a going concern and when it was no longer able to pay its debts as and when they fell due. Investigators are rarely presented with a full set of books in these circumstances. It is more often the case that records are missing or incomplete, making the accountant's job much more difficult. However, a consideration of the ideal position will give guidance on how to proceed when less than ideal circumstances are met.

In addition to this information, there may be evidence which is produced as a result of an investigation into insolvency. Whether or when the accountant gets this depends on when he becomes involved in the proceedings.

The accountant may be instructed by a government agency, such as the Department of Trade and Industry, to carry out the investigation as part of the process of trying to determine whether a prosecution should be undertaken. At this stage there may be little information outside the books and records of the company other than the report of the liquidator.

However, the accountant may be instructed by the defence once charges have been made, and the further evidence may include witness statements from creditors, liquidators, DTI officials such as the Official Receiver and an accountant's report commissioned by the prosecution, either from an internal accountant employed by the prosecuting authority such as the Crown Prosecution Service or the Serious Fraud Office, or from an external accountant in public practice. An indictment, case statement and defendant's proof of evidence will also be available.

These two different types of evidence are considered separately, although their investigation will probably take place side by side.

30.6 The company's books and records

The accountant's first task is to make a list of what information is available.

The accountant must then gain some understanding of the business of the company, in particular where it gets its income and how long it takes to convert this into cash. There are likely to be large differences between the insolvency considerations applying to companies with few customers and those with many. The accountant also needs to understand the cost base of the company and, again, its payment terms.

The accountant will then have to consider the major obligations and contracts which the company has entered into and liabilities and contingencies which may not appear in the accounting records. These may be the terms of loans with lenders, contracts to supply goods or services or to pay for goods and services. They will also include legal claims and other disputes.

The accountant will then have to find out what are the major assets and liabilities, as disclosed by the last accounts or management accounts.

Finally, the accountant should review correspondence in key areas of the business. These will always include correspondence from directors and with any bought ledger departments, and may include other areas such as sales or personnel.

At this stage the accountant will have formed an impression of the way the company is run and what are likely to be the risk areas for the insolvency of the company and his analysis of the company's financial affairs in order to determine insolvency can start.

It may be the case that the insolvency is the result of a single event, for example, the cancellation of a major contract, the insolvency of a major debtor or the withdrawal of bank facilities. The accountant may therefore be able to state that, on such-and-such a day, such-and-such an occurrence caused the insolvency. The company was solvent before and was insolvent afterwards. More often, the cause of insolvency is a build-up of various factors. Even the withdrawal of bank finance, although an event in itself manifestly demonstrating insolvency, may occur when the company has been insolvent for some time.

This last point should never be overlooked – banks will withdraw finance when they cannot see any prospect of their exposure reducing. If a bank has not withdrawn facilities it does not mean that the position for creditors as a whole has some prospect of improving.

The most common analyses will be graphical analyses of figures describing certain aspects of the company's financial health. For example, the accountant may graph over time the following information:

(a) cleared daily bank balance with a note on overdraft limit;
(b) daily book bank balance;
(c) changes in outstanding creditors at the end of each week or month, broken down by trade and expense creditors, Crown creditors and lenders;
(d) new credit taken on each month;
(e) cash received as against cash paid each week or each month;
(f) purchases;
(g) sales;
(h) net assets.

The accountant may produce some or all of these graphs; he may design others. Which analyses he actually produces will depend on the circumstances of the case. Additionally, he may produce spreadsheet analyses showing the following:

- purchases and payments by individual creditor;
- occurrence of bounced cheques;
- sales by individual customer.

None of these analyses, of themselves, may be sufficient to demonstrate the point of insolvency. However, a number together may give a picture which indicates the period over which insolvency occurred, on the basis of the accounting records. The accountant may be able to conclude in the following terms:

> 'Based on the above analyses, and in the absence of any other matters, by such-and-such a date, the company was insolvent.'

The other matters referred to above will often be the area of greatest dispute in a trial where insolvency is alleged, for these refer to the directors' expectations about future events. These events will almost certainly refer to an increase in business and the ability to fend off or negotiate with creditors. The evidence supporting such expectations often comes, primarily, from the directors themselves in their proofs of evidence. As such, the investigation of these matters is dealt with in the next section.

30.7 Other documents

Vast amounts of documents are produced in the run-up to a criminal trial. Depending at which stage the accountant is instructed, he will be able to get access to some or all of these, and they may help him in his investigation of the date of insolvency. The accountant should review the following documents for the reasons stated in Figure 30.1.

Figure 30.1

Document	*Significance*
Indictment	Sets out the offences with which the defendant is charged. The indictment will note the alleged period of insolvency.
Case statement	Sets out the case against the defendant in more detail. In support of each charge, the case statement will give details of the witnesses on which the prosecution will rely and significant documents.
Prosecution witness statements	These will consist of those witness statements referred to in the case statement, together with documents referred to in the witness statement. It is through the calling of such witnesses that their statements and the documents are introduced as evidence. These documents will include primary material, such as invoices or accounting records, and secondary material such as analyses of creditors. The witnesses may be factual, such as creditors or the liquidator, or opinion, such as an accountant instructed by the Crown.

Unused material	This will consist of all of the material on which the Crown chooses not to rely for the purposes of the prosecution. The unused material is likely to consist of large amounts of the company's accounting records.
Interviews with directors under compulsion and under caution	Various people are authorised to interview officers and others connected with a company. The transcripts of such interviews may give information on the circumstances of the insolvency.
Defendant's proof of evidence	The defendant's answer to the charges and explanation of the circumstances set out in the case statement.
Defence witness statements	These will consist of those witness statements together with documents referred to in the witness statement on which the defence chooses to rely.

Regardless of the stage of his instruction, the accountant's first port of call is likely to be the liquidator of a company, who will often be a prosecution witness in the case. The accountant should obtain a copy of the statement of affairs and the report to creditors on the reasons for the insolvency. As well as providing valuable information on the business and the reasons for failure, the returns filed by the liquidator will give details of the largest creditors, the involvement of lenders, the nature of any security and whether the Crown, as represented by Customs & Excise and the Inland Revenue, is owed money. In many cases, the liquidator is likely to be the Official Receiver.

Directors and other persons can be interviewed by certain authorised persons under various statutory powers. However, replies to questioning may be admissible in evidence and may give evidence of insolvency.

Chapter 31
Fraud

31.1 Introduction

Fraud is an area of criminal law in which the expert accountant is likely to be involved, although there is no offence of 'fraud' *per se*. However, fraud can be pleaded in civil cases as fraudulent misrepresentation. The tort of deceit has already been considered in Chapter 22. There are also certain civil remedies which can be taken against individuals under the insolvency legislation for actions which are fraudulent, as discussed in Chapter 30.

This chapter is principally concerned with considering what criminal fraud is. It also considers some of the difficulties in proving fraud and looks at two offences involving fraud – conspiracy to defraud and fraudulent trading. Finally, the role of the accountant is discussed.

Fraud trials cover a number of other offences, such as cheating. These offences are considered separately in Chapter 32, although many of the comments made in this chapter are pertinent to their prosecution.

31.2 Characteristics of fraud

There is no legal definition of fraud, notwithstanding that the word is used extensively in litigation. Fraud is not a legal term and therefore has, in courts, its ordinary meaning. There is no all-embracing offence of fraud. Thus, it is not itself a criminal offence to commit fraud upon a person (although the act may be a criminal offence, such as theft). However, the words 'defraud' and 'fraudulently' are used in both common law and statutory offences, with the result that certain acts of fraud are offences.

31.2.1 Dishonesty

A key element in any fraud is dishonesty. The legal authorities seem to accept that fraud and dishonesty amount to the same thing. Viscount Dilhorne said in *Scott* v *Metropolitan Police Commissioner* [1975] AC 819:

> 'I have not the temerity to attempt an exhaustive definition of the meaning of "defraud". As I have said, words take colour from the context in which they are used, but the words "fraudulently" and "defraud" must ordinarily have a very similar meaning. If, as I think, and as the Criminal Law Revision Committee appears to have thought, "fraudulently" means "dishonestly", then "to defraud"

> ordinarily means, in my opinion, to deprive a person dishonestly of something which is his or of something to which he is or would or might but for the perpetration of the fraud be entitled.'

The Criminal Law Revision Committee referred to is that which presented to the Home Office its Eighth Report entitled *Theft and Related Offences*, Cmnd 2977 (1966), where, at paragraph 39 it is stated:

> '"Dishonestly" seems to us a better word than "fraudulently". The question "Was this dishonest?" is easier for a jury to answer than the question "Was this fraudulent?". "Dishonesty" is something which laymen may easily recognise when they see it, whereas "fraud" may seem to involve technicalities which have to be explained by a lawyer.'

Whether a person has been dishonest is a question of fact, either for a jury or the magistrates. It is not something that expert accountants give evidence on. The test for the jury is laid down in *R* v *Ghosh* [1982] QB 1053 per Lord Lane CJ:

> 'In determining whether the prosecution has proved that the defendant was acting dishonestly, a jury must first of all decide whether according to the ordinary standards of reasonable and honest people what was done was dishonest.'

This was distinguished by *R* v *Holden* [1991] Crim. LR 478 CA. The reasonableness of a defendant's belief was irrelevant to the question of dishonesty. The question was whether the defendant has the necessary honest belief, reasonably or not. The issue of the reasonableness of the belief is only relevant in considering whether the accused had an honest belief (although this case concerned s2(1)(a) Theft Act 1968).

Dishonesty requires a particular mental state, that is, a person must either be intentionally dishonest or his conduct must be such that, if he was not intentionally dishonest, he closed his mind to matters which would have told him his conduct was dishonest. In *Ghosh*, Lord Lane continued:

> 'If it was dishonest by those standards, then the jury must consider whether the defendant himself must have realised that what he was doing was by those standards dishonest. In most cases, where the actions are obviously dishonest by ordinary standards, there will be no doubt about it. It will be obvious that the defendant himself knew that he was acting dishonestly. It is dishonest for a defendant to act in a way which he knows ordinary people consider to be dishonest, even if he asserts or genuinely believes that he is morally justified in acting as he did.'

This last aspect, non-intentional dishonesty, is particularly important in fraud trials in which expert accountants become involved, because of the importance of showing whether certain circumstances, for example insolvency, should have been obvious to an individual. (Or, alternatively, that a person's belief that circumstances were not as bad is reasonable, thereby raising a reasonable doubt as to that person's alleged dishonesty.) The director charged with fraudulent trading may not be intentionally dishonest. However, where he takes on new credit in circumstances where it is obvious that the company is never going to be able to repay that credit, then he is likely to be found to be dishonest.

However, the dishonesty test goes even further than this, because of the statement that it is dishonest 'to act in a way which he knows ordinary people consider to be dishonest'.

The director who raises money in circumstances where he does not disclose all relevant information may think that he has done nothing wrong; however, if he knows that most other people would think he was wrong in not disclosing such information, then he is dishonest. Basically, a person is not allowed to be the one to determine his own moral standards.

31.2.2 Real moral blame and whether there are two types of dishonesty

In *Re Patrick and Lyon Limited* [1933] Ch 786, Maugham J said:

> 'I will express the opinion that the words "defraud" and "fraudulent purpose", where they appear in the section in question, are words which connote actual dishonesty involving, according to current notions of trading among commercial men, real moral blame. No judge, I think, has ever been willing to define "fraud", and I am attempting no definition. I am merely stating what, in my opinion, must be one of the elements of the word as used in this section.'

Real moral blame appears to be equivalent to a special type of dishonesty, that is, dishonesty in business. This passage was considered in *R* v *Lockwood* [1986] Crim.LR 244. The Court of Appeal was asked to consider a number of submissions on behalf of the appellant, one of which was that there was one standard of dishonesty for criminal cases in general and a separate and more restricted standard of dishonesty for cases involving commercial fraud. The court was not prepared to accept this proposition and held that the definition of dishonesty used in criminal cases was of general application and therefore *R* v *Ghosh* was applied.

Just because many businessmen over the years have hoodwinked banks into lending them money on the basis of false information, have gone on to prosper and have never been prosecuted does not mean that an offence has not been committed, and a defendant cannot rely on the non-prosecuted activities of others for his defence. The fact that many people exceed the speed limit but few are caught is hardly a defence for those who are.

31.2.3 Deception

A key element of any fraud is deception, although this is not essential. However, it is difficult to see how, in a case involving fraud, there cannot be a deception.

> ***Example***
>
> Consider an insolvent company. A director raises money from a bank, hiding the insolvency by not disclosing the parlous position. The act of hiding deceives the bank into thinking that the company's position is different – i.e., solvent. If, however, the director discloses the complete insolvent position and the bank, with knowledge of this, advances money, where is the fraud? There is none, of course.

In the *Scott* case, referred to at **31.2.1** above, the defendant had been convicted of conspiracy to defraud where he had encouraged cinema staff to 'temporarily abstract' films so that he could make illicit copies. The argument was that he had not defrauded the cinema owners because he had never intended to deceive them in that his conduct was never intended to come to their attention.

The House of Lords in that case held that deceit was not an 'essential' ingredient of fraud:

> 'One must not confuse the object of a conspiracy with the means by which it is intended to be carried out.'

Clearly, there was deceit in this case, but by the employees of the cinema not the defendant. Taking the circumstances of *Scott* into account, one can say that deceit can be an intrinsic part of a fraud; however, not every person involved in the commission of the fraud need necessarily have been deceitful.

The issue of deceit is important for accountants in fraud cases because of their investigations into whether information, such as insolvency, has been withheld or suppressed.

31.2.4 Gain, loss and risk

Fraud involves somebody trying to gain something – or does it? Most fraud cases seem to involve a person dishonestly attempting to get some sort of economic advantage, even if it is only putting off the evil day when the receiver appears. But what of the situation where a person carries out a dishonest action with no intent that that action should involve any benefit for himself.

In the *Scott* case, what was it that the cinema owners had lost? Lord Diplock stated that it was:

> '. . . some property or right, corporeal or incorporeal, to which he is or would or might become entitled . . .'

This is very wide, but the courts have since widened it even further.

In *Wai Yu-tsang* v *R* [1991] 4 All ER 664, the defendant had submitted at his trial that his concealment, with others, of dishonoured cheques which gave a false impression of his employer bank's balances was in the best interests of the bank. Although at first this might look ridiculous, he said that he was trying to prevent a run on the bank. Lord Goff stated:

> '. . . it is enough . . . that . . . the conspirators have dishonestly agreed to bring about a state of affairs which they realise will or may deceive the victim into so acting, or failing to act, that he will suffer economic loss or his economic interests will be put at risk. It is however important in such a case . . . to distinguish a conspirator's intention (or immediate purpose) dishonestly to bring about such a state of affairs from his motive (or underlying purpose). The latter may be benign to the extent that he does not wish the victim or potential victim to suffer harm; but the mere fact that it is benign will not of itself prevent the agreement from constituting a conspiracy to defraud. Of course, if the conspirators were not acting dishonestly, there will have been no conspiracy to defraud . . .'

Lord Goff also stated of an intent to defraud:

> 'In broad terms, it means simply an intention to practise a fraud on another, or an intention to act to the prejudice of another man's right.'

Effectively, the court extended the thing potentially to be lost from 'property and rights' to 'interests'. Furthermore, even if there was no loss, it was sufficient if the 'interest' was put at risk. In this case, the fraud was on not just the bank but its existing and potential shareholders, creditors and depositors.

However, the courts have put a limit on what can be put at risk. In *Adams* v *R* [1995] 2 Cr.App.R 295 (a Privy Council case), the defendant, deputy chairman of a company called EHL, had been involved in setting up an offshore structure (called the 'Yeoman Loop') for the purpose of receiving two sums of money (the 'H' fee and the 'retreat' fee) and subsequent payments from other transactions. The appellant acknowledged that the Yeoman Loop was deliberately set up with the intention that ownership of the structure should be anonymous and incapable of being detected. Although it was not known what the 'H' fee was, from whom it came, why it was paid or to whom it was payable, the judge concluded that despite the suspicions that surrounded it, he could not make an affirmative finding that the 'H' fee itself was fraudulent. The sums acquired from the Yeoman Loop were used, *inter alia*, to purchase shares in companies which were subsequently sold to EHL for a profit or for shares in EHL. EHL had attempted to find out whether it had any interest in the sale of the shares. Two lower courts held that Adams, as deputy chairman of EHL, could be convicted of conspiracy to defraud the company, since a company is entitled to recover from directors secret profits made by them at the company's expense. It would therefore follow that any dishonest agreement by directors to impede a company in the exercise of its right of recovery would constitute a conspiracy to defraud. The Court of Appeal stated:

> 'Whoever took part in the agreement to use the Loop for them must be seen as intending to practise a fraud on at least the other directors of Equiticorp and its auditors, by making it difficult for them to conduct legitimate inquiries into the source of the moneys concerned to ascertain whether the Equiticorp group had any interest in them.'

The Privy Council disagreed. Lord Jauncey referred to the criticism by counsel for the appellant of the passage in the judgment of the Court of Appeal relating to count 1 that:

> 'This statement was . . . in far too broad terms and would allow A to be convicted of defrauding B of moneys in which B had no interest whatsoever merely because A's actions made it more difficult for B to ascertain whether or not he had any interest therein.'

Lord Jauncey stated:

> 'A person is not prejudiced if he is hindered in inquiring into the source of moneys in which he has no interest. He can only suffer prejudice in relation to some right or interest which he possesses.'

There were frauds in this case, i.e., the appellant was a party to the use of the Yeoman Loop in the case of four out of the five transactions for the purpose of dishonest concealment of information (for which the appellant had his conviction confirmed). However, the inability, due to concealment, to conduct enquiries into money which did not belong to the bank, and did not amount to a right or interest which could be prejudiced, was not one of them.

31.3 Fraud

In fraud trials, the issues in dispute normally concern transactions of a type which are, in normal business life, completely acceptable (that is, their execution does not involve any dishonesty). The expert accountant is in court, generally, to give evidence on certain factors which may or may not be indicative of dishonesty. However, fraudulent conduct is a subset of generally dishonest conduct, which takes place within the specific area of commerce. The courts have refused over the years to attempt a legal definition of fraud, and this book is not going to take any alternative temeritous course.

However, the accountant should understand the nature of fraud and its limits, so that when he carries out his work he is aware of the conduct that fraud trials are attempting to penalise. An accountant can think of fraud in the following terms:

> Fraud is the dishonest obtaining of a benefit by a person from another person, or the dishonest exposing by one person of another person to risk or possible risk, in circumstances where, but for the dishonesty, the obtaining of the benefit or the exposure to the risk would be lawful.

This focuses on the key element of fraud – dishonesty and the rights which are being infringed.

Thus, obtaining credit from a bank is, prima facie, lawful. The credit is a benefit to a person and a risk to the bank. Where that credit is obtained dishonestly, it is fraud. The accountant's role will be to consider those circumstances, such as overwhelming evidence of insolvency, which would support, or not support, a finding by the jury of any dishonesty.

31.4 The difficulty in proving fraud

31.4.1 Dishonesty

As will be clear from the above, the difficulty in proving fraud is proving dishonesty.

In *Re William C. Leitch Brothers Limited* [1932] 2 Ch 71 Maugham J said:

> '. . . if a company continues to carry on business and to incur debts at a time when there is to the knowledge of the directors no reasonable prospect of the creditors ever receiving payment of those debts, it is, in general, a proper inference that the company is carrying on business with intent to defraud . . .'

This indicates that actual knowledge is required to be proven before a fraud charge can stick.

Consider the following, taken from the 'clouds and sunshine' judgment of Buckley J in *Re White and Osmond (Parkstone) Ltd* [30 June 1960] (unreported):

> 'In my judgement there is nothing wrong in the fact that directors incur credit at a time when, to their knowledge, the company is not able to meet all its liabilities as they fall due. What is manifestly wrong is if directors allow a company to incur credit at a time when the business is being carried on in such circumstances that it is clear that the company will never be able to satisfy its creditors. However, there is nothing to say that directors who genuinely believe that the clouds will roll away and the sunshine of prosperity will shine upon them again and disperse the

> fog of their depression are not entitled to incur credit to help them get over the bad time.'

At first sight, this judgment appears to be a rogues' charter for delinquent directors. What director is not going to say that he genuinely believed that the company would get over its bad time?

This case was considered in *R* v *Grantham* [1984] 3 All ER 166. Lord Chief Justice Lane stated:

> 'We have been fortunate enough to run to earth a transcript of the whole of that judgement. The judge eventually decided in favour of the trader on the basis that, although he might have been guilty of insufficient care and supervision of his business, he could not be said (in the words of Maugham J.) to have been guilty of real moral blame so as to justify the judge in saying that he ought to be liable for the debts of the company without limit. In other words he acquitted the trader of dishonesty, an essential ingredient to liability. Insofar as Buckley J. was saying that it is never dishonest or fraudulent for directors to incur credit at a time when, to their knowledge, the company is not able to meet all its liabilities as they fall due, we would respectfully disagree.'

In the *Grantham* case the Court of Appeal was being asked to overturn a conviction for fraudulent trading based in part on the direction of the trial judge as to what the jury needed to be satisfied of in order to convict. The appellant's case was that the judge should have directed the jury that it was for the prosecution to prove that the appellant knew at the time at which the debts were incurred that there was no reasonable prospect of the creditors ever receiving payment of their debts.

The direction by the trial judge complained of was as follows:

> 'Members of the jury, if a man honestly believes when he obtains credit that although funds are not immediately available he will be able to pay them when the debt becomes due or within a short time thereafter, no doubt you would say that is not dishonest and there is no intent to defraud, but if he obtains or helps to obtain credit or further credit when he knows there is no good reason for thinking funds will become available to pay the debt when it becomes due or shortly thereafter then, though it is entirely a matter for you this question of dishonesty, you might well think that is dishonest and there is intent to defraud.'

The Court of Appeal found these directions in accordance with the law.

However, what of the person who takes on credit at a time when he knows that he will not be able to pay his debts when they become due, or shortly thereafter, but who honestly believes that he will be able to pay them at some time in the future, perhaps the near future, but certainly not shortly after they become due? The point is really about the expectations of the creditors. A person incurring credit will normally know that his creditors expect payment on the due date or within a reasonable period afterwards. He would not expect his creditors to advance him credit if they knew that, although he would be able to pay their debts, it would not be for a period of six months.

The fraud is not necessarily the non-payment of debts; it is the dishonest suppression of the person's intention of when he intends to pay those debts.

Where fraud, or dishonest conduct, becomes very difficult to prove is where the director has certain expectations of his creditors' attitude towards non-payment. Creditors may set a due date for payment, but have regularly not pressed for payment or have been prepared to accept partial payment. On the other hand, taking credit from suppliers who have, in the past, refused to supply goods without assurances of payment on the due date, or the discharge of outstanding balances, will be evidence, where a company cannot pay, of dishonesty by a director.

31.4.2 Offence charged

Part of the difficulty with proving fraud lies with the offences charged. Many frauds are extremely complicated. The victim or potential victim may be difficult to identify and the property or the right or interest which is put at risk equally difficult to identify. Individual transactions may be the subject of an indictment, but the overall fraudulent intent of a scheme may be lost by this particularisation. Non-fraud offences are prosecuted by proving each item of the offence. To do this takes a large amount of court time with, perhaps, different offences alleged for different parts of the scheme.

Finally, many frauds are not suitable subjects for prosecution as a different offence like theft. Theft is the dishonest appropriation of property belonging to another, but it is usually the case involving fraud that the victim has parted with his property willingly, thereby consenting to any appropriation.

31.5 Criminal offences specifically mentioning fraud

31.5.1 Fraudulent trading

Section 458 of the Companies Act 1985 reads as follows:

> 'If any business of a company is carried on with intent to defraud creditors of the company or creditors of any other person, or for any fraudulent purpose, every person who was knowingly a party to the carrying on of the business in that manner is liable . . .'

On indictment, the maximum punishment is seven years' imprisonment.

This is, on the face of it, an extremely wide offence. It covers not only creditors of the company but creditors of any other person. It also extends to any fraudulent purpose carried out by the company. It should also be noted that, unlike fraudulent trading under s213 of the Insolvency Act 1986, there is no need for the company to have been wound up.

In *R* v *Kemp* [1988] QB 645 the Court of Appeal was asked to determine whether fraudulent purpose included an attempt to defraud customers. In the first trial, the court had heard how the defendant had induced businesses to believe that they had ordered more office supplies than had in fact been ordered. At the trial, the defence made a submission of no case to answer on the basis that none of those defrauded were creditors of the company. This submission failed, but the trial judge asked the Court of Appeal to consider whether s458 Companies Act 1985 (amending s332 Companies Act 1948) imposed criminal liability if the fraudulent purpose was to defraud customers, rather than creditors.

The Court of Appeal found that the words 'for any fraudulent purpose' could not be wider, there was no ambiguity and no way of limiting them. It obviously included potential creditors (and this included the customers as they could have taken legal action to become creditors in respect of payment for the non-ordered supplies). The court held that, as a matter of law, the words had to refer to customers as potential creditors. That was the narrowest possible meaning and the alternative was to ignore the words altogether, which was impermissible.

This section seems, therefore, to create a general offence of fraud, as long as that offence is carried out through a company. It should be noted that there is no similar offence of fraud perpetrated through the medium of a partnership, or by a sole trader.

However, it is normally the defrauding of creditors, that is, taking on new credit without any prospect of being able to repay it, for which this section is likely to be used. There are other offences, such as deception, which could be used against directors undertaking other fraudulent activities. One matter which is often raised in fraud trials is the preference of one creditor over another. However, the payment of one genuine debt is not a fraud on the others. Furthermore, if the directors of a company prefer a creditor in which they have a financial interest, this is not, apparently, fraud. *Re Sarflax Ltd* [1979] 1 All ER 529 involved a case where the directors of an insolvent company had paid off the debt owed to its holding company. The case was actually an application by the directors for the allegation of fraudulent trading to be struck out as disclosing no cause of action. The judge agreed. Oliver J stated:

> 'What is alleged here . . . is the bare fact of preference . . . that that, per se, constitutes fraud within the meaning of the section is not one which is, in my judgement, arguable with any prospect of success.'

This does seem very surprising. In the *Grantham* case (see **31.4.1**), it was referred to by Lord Lane:

> 'In the present case however there was great deal more than the bare fact of preferring one creditor to another as was the case in Re Sarflax Ltd.'

The implication is that preferment is not enough. However, in the *Sarflax* case it appears that the preference was the only allegation that was made against the directors. Obviously, any preferment of one creditor over another would result in a deficit to that other. It was perfectly legal to pay creditors when a company was insolvent (otherwise there would have to be a moratorium on all payments) and this included related companies.

This indicates that preference will be a matter which goes to the conduct of the directors along with any other relevant matters. Certainly, in the *Sarflax* case, the company had ceased trading and had entered into voluntary liquidation and had stopped taking on further credit.

It is enough for a conviction for fraudulent trading that only one transaction is fraudulent. In *R* v *Lockwood* referred to at **31.2.2** above, the trial judge had said to the jury:

> 'You have heard of many transactions, the evidence of many suppliers. One transaction, if it was carried out dishonestly with intent to defraud a creditor, can constitute the offence of carrying on business with intent to defraud creditors.'

31.5.2 Conspiracy to defraud

Conspiracy to commit an unlawful act is a common law offence. It is therefore an offence for two or more persons to conspire to defraud a third person. The offence is triable on indictment and, by statute, carries a maximum prison sentence of 10 years.

The state of mind is important in conspiracy because to conspire requires intention. Therefore, to succeed in a conspiracy to defraud trial, the prosecution must prove that the co-conspirators have agreed to act dishonestly and therefore agreed to practise a fraud upon another person. It does not matter whether the offence is actually carried out or not.

Clearly, this aspect of the offence must make it more difficult to prove than other offences alleging fraud. In such cases, a lesser mental state than intention is required.

It is, of course, necessary to have more than one person in a common law conspiracy to defraud. In *R* v *Lockwood*, referred to at **31.2.2** above, the original trial had involved two counts against two persons – the first of fraudulent trading and the second of conspiracy to defraud. The trial judge's direction read in part as follows (as set out in the judgment of Stephen Brown LJ):

> 'If you find both defendants guilty on Count 1 [fraudulent trading] then go on to consider Count 2 [conspiracy]. If you find both the defendants not guilty on Count 1, then find them not guilty on Count 2 also. If you should find one defendant guilty on Count 1, and the other defendant not guilty on Count 1, then find them both not guilty on Count 2, because if that is your finding in relation to Count 1 it will mean that you are not satisfied that there is any sort of common purpose between the defendants. You are not satisfied that there was an agreement between them, and, as I have already told you, in the conspiracy charge it is the agreement which is the object of the charge.'

This is not to say that all co-conspirators have to be charged on indictment. Indeed, it is possible to have a single defendant charged with conspiracy, for example, when the co-conspirators are 'unknown' or outside of the jurisdiction.

31.6 The accountant in fraud trials

Accountants are appointed as experts by both sides in criminal fraud trials. Their primary role is often investigative, in terms of analysing financial information and preparing schedules or charts of the analysis.

It is not the accountant's role to conclude on the honesty or dishonesty of a person. However, the result of an expert's findings may be that the jury, on the basis of that and other evidence, concludes that the defendant is guilty or not guilty of dishonesty. A simple example concerns insolvency. An expert's opinion that, by a certain date, a company was insolvent may be used, in part, by the jury to make a finding of dishonesty. The jury may view that particular piece of evidence as crucial to their findings. On the other hand, the jury may consider that there is ample evidence elsewhere on which to convict and the accountant's evidence is merely confirmatory.

It was noted in Chapter 2 that much accounting evidence in criminal trials was factual evidence, being either evidence of fact for which the observation, comprehension and description requires expertise, or evidence of fact which does not require expertise for its observation, comprehension and description but is a necessary preliminary to the giving of other evidence by the expert.

With these two matters in mind – that the accountant is not giving an opinion on the honesty of the defendant and that much of his evidence may be factual – the work the accountant carries out in criminal trials can be discussed.

31.6.1 Investigation

Much of the accountant's work will be investigating financial records. For the accountant employed by the prosecution there will be a mass of information to sort out and analyse before any view can be taken of the case. For the accountant involved with the defence, he may have a similar task if the prosecution have not employed an accountant and he will certainly spend many hours looking through unused material (material not relied on by the prosecution).

Much of this work is a process of reconstruction. It is almost certainly the case in fraud trials that financial information is incomplete, even if this is limited to accounts not having been drawn up or drawn up incorrectly. Often, the underlying financial records are missing in part as well.

The results of this work, produced in tabular, accounting or graphical form, may be used as exhibits in the case, displaying certain aspects of a company's financial history. These matters are often used to demonstrate the solvency or otherwise of a company (see Chapter 30).

31.6.2 Confirmation

The accountant for either side will be expected to confirm (or otherwise) financial documents produced by the other side. This will either be for the specific purposes of agreeing schedules (see Chapter 28) or for the purposes of the cross-examination of the other side's witnesses. Such documents may not necessarily have been produced by another accountant. Police officers, officials from Customs & Excise, officials from the Inland Revenue or lawyers acting on behalf of the prosecution may all have prepared documents as a result of their own investigations as part of the prosecution's decision-making process.

31.6.3 Interpretation

The interpretation of the accounting and other financial information is opinion work by the accountant. This may be his opinion on the solvency or otherwise of a company. However, it may also be an interpretation of a set of circumstances which the prosecution have used to justify the case against the defendant. For example, the prosecution may have interpreted a series of transactions between a director and a company whereby a director acquires a charge over the assets of a company as indicative of dishonesty. The accountant employed for the defence may see these transactions in a different light and may, for example, be able to demonstrate that the transactions were commercially and legally justifiable, individually and when taken together.

This last aspect is particularly important. Even only moderately complicated financial transactions can be confusing to a member of a jury. Either side in a criminal case has the potential to 'blind with science' or confuse. The prosecution could leave a jury with the belief that, because a transaction is so complicated and involved, for example offshore trusts, it must be dishonest. The defence could leave the jury with the impression that the same transaction is just normal business practice and therefore not dishonest.

Therefore, as well as interpreting financial transactions, the accountant also has the job of explaining them and their context to the jury.

31.6.4 Explaining

Members of a jury cannot be expected to have more than a very basic knowledge of company accounts. The sort of knowledge which can be imputed to a judge or barrister cannot be imputed to a jury. For example, the terms 'FRS' or 'GAAP', while understandable by the legal profession (perhaps by saying what the acronyms stand for!) are going to confuse the jury, and yet these terms form two of the most important bases for the way financial statements are put together.

The accountant should always be ready, therefore, to explain to the jury exactly how a set of accounts is constructed, the books and records which companies maintain and any other financial terms which may be relevant to a case, such as preference or debenture.

31.6.5 Reasonableness

Defendants in criminal fraud trials will invariably give in their evidence, either in their written proof or in their oral evidence, an explanation of their behaviour. The accountant's work, for either side, can include an analysis of the reasonableness of those explanations, having regard to the financial information.

31.6.6 Documents

Finally, the accountant can give invaluable advice on the documents which should be available in a criminal trial. This can include directing the solicitors for the defence as to the types of documents which should be available in the unused, or the types of documents which should be in the unused but which are not. He can also advise on the documents which could be available from third parties but which have not been obtained by the prosecution.

When working for the prosecution the accountant can advise, similarly, on the documents which should be sought.

Chapter 32
Other types of offences

32.1 Introduction

This chapter sets out the other types of criminal offences which the accountant is likely to meet in practice.

32.2 VAT and Revenue frauds

There are a number of offences concerned with fraud on the public revenue, normally involving Customs & Excise or the Inland Revenue.

32.2.1 Cheating

The common law offence of cheating was abolished by s32(1) of the Theft Act 1968 except as regards offences relating to the public revenue. Cheating appears to be very similar, if not the same, as an offence involving fraud, and therefore is another arm in prosecuting fraud. Unlike conspiracy to defraud, it can be carried out by one person; unlike fraudulent trading, it need not be carried out through a company. However, it is narrower than those two offences in the sense that it is only available where the public purse is put at risk.

Subject to demonstrating fraudulent conduct and intention, a vast range of action or inaction can amount to cheating. For example, a person may be guilty of cheating as a result of failure to register for VAT, failure to submit VAT returns, failure to submit VAT returns correctly completed or a failure to pay VAT across to Customs & Excise. If a person acts dishonestly to the possible detriment of public revenue, then they can be charged with this offence.

32.2.2 VAT frauds

Section 72 of the Value Added Tax Act 1994 creates a large number of offences. The basic offence, that of a person 'being knowingly concerned in, or in the taking of steps with a view to, the fraudulent evasion of VAT by him or any other person', is triable either way and on indictment is punishable with an unlimited fine and/or imprisonment of up to seven years. The rest of the section deals with matters such as the production of false documents and making false statements.

32.2.3 Inland Revenue frauds

By contrast, there is no wide-ranging set of offences for Inland Revenue frauds similar to s72 for VAT. There are specific frauds, such as under ss559 to 567 of the Income and Corporation Taxes Act 1988 for subcontractor frauds, or under s20BB of the Taxes Management Act 1970 for falsification, concealment or destruction of documents relevant to assessing any tax liability. However, these offences carry penalties of two years' or less imprisonment and many other offences are not covered specifically at all by the legislation.

Therefore, in the case of a serious fraud on the Revenue, it is more likely to be charged as an offence of cheating under the Theft Act or as an offence of false accounting (or conspiracy to defraud).

The accountant is most likely to come across frauds against the Crown where a company has gone into liquidation owing Customs and the Revenue substantial amounts of tax in circumstances which would justify a conspiracy or fraudulent trading charge. Such cases will be brought by Customs or the Revenue.

The considerations for the accountant are broadly similar to those set out in the previous chapter.

32.3 Theft Act offences

There are a large number of offences under the Theft Acts.

32.3.1 Theft

Subsection 1(1) of the Theft Act 1968 reads as follows:

> 'A person is guilty of theft if he dishonestly appropriates property belonging to another with the intention of permanently depriving the other of it; and "thief" and "steal" shall be construed accordingly.'

The offence is triable either way, and on indictment a conviction carries a maximum sentence of seven years' imprisonment.

Despite what seems a relatively simple definition, this offence is often inappropriate in fraud cases. First of all, although by s4(1) Theft Act 1968 property includes intangible property and this includes rights, there are doubts as to whether this includes knowledge. Furthermore, money taken from a person's bank account which is already overdrawn is not always the property of that person.

Appropriation is not straightforward either. Using a creditor's money which has been lent to you is not appropriation because that money does not belong to that other person. This is why a failure to account for VAT due is not theft. The money received as output tax from debtors is not the property of Customs & Excise.

Finally, fraudsters do not always intend to deprive someone permanently of their property. The rolls of film in the *Scott* case (*Scott* v *Metropolitan Police Commissioner* [1975] AC 819 – see **31.2.1**) were only ever intended to be taken temporarily.

These legal matters can often be fatal to obtaining a successful prosecution for theft in a fraud trial. In the *Barlow Clowes* trial, where the main charges were theft, one of the legal issues was whether the relationship between the defendant and the investors was one of debtor and creditor or trustee and beneficiary. As noted above, a relationship of debtor and creditor is fatal for a charge of theft. The doubt arose from the agreements entered into between the defendant and the investors. Although theft has been charged in many successful high profile trials, these doubts often limit its use.

32.3.2 Deception

There are a number of offences of deception under the Theft Acts. The legal definition is from Buckley J in *Re London and Globe Finance Corporation Ltd* [1903] 1 Ch 728:

> 'To deceive is . . . to induce a man to believe that a thing is true which is false.'

Section 15 of the Theft Act sets out the basic offence of obtaining property by deception and also provides a statutory definition of deception for the purposes of statutory offences (s15(4)). Subsection 15(1) reads as follows:

> 'A person who by any deception dishonestly obtains property belonging to another, with the intention of permanently depriving the other of it, shall on conviction on indictment be liable to imprisonment for a term not exceeding ten years.'

The offence is triable either way, but certain serious offences, for example breach of trust or high value, will often mean that an offence of deception is tried on indictment.

The offence includes obtaining property for another, and the deception can be of fact or law including a deception as to the present intentions of the person using the deception or any other person.

The related deception offences are set out in Figure 32.1.

Figure 32.1

Theft Act 1968

Section 16 Obtaining a pecuniary advantage by deception, the pecuniary advantage being defined as borrowing by way of overdraft, taking out a policy of insurance or annuity contract (or obtaining an improvement in the terms on which he is allowed to do so) or the opportunity to earn remuneration or greater remuneration in an office or employment or to win money by betting.

Section 20 Procuring the execution of a valuable security by deception, applying to such things as cheques, CHAPS orders, share certificates or an irrevocable letter of credit. The statute specifies that the offence takes place when a person is dishonest and acts with a view to gain for himself, or another or with intent to cause loss to another.

Section 18 makes it an offence for company officers to have consented or connived in offences under ss15 and 16, s17 (false accounting, see **32.4** below). Section 5(1) Theft Act 1978 extends the liability of company officers for offences by the company to ss1 and 2 Theft Act 1978 (see below).

Theft Act 1978

Section 1 Obtaining services by deception, that is, obtaining services where the other party is induced to confer a benefit by doing some act, or causing or permitting some act to be done, on the understanding that the benefit has been or will be paid for.

Section 2 Evasion of liability by deception, that is, dishonestly securing the remission of the whole or any part of any existing liability to make a payment, whether his own liability or another's; or with intent to make permanent default in whole or in part on any existing liability to make payment or with intent to let another do so, dishonestly induces the creditor or any person claiming payment on behalf of the creditor to wait for or forgo payment; or, dishonestly obtaining any exemption from or abatement of liability to make a payment.

Deception as a description of fraudulent behaviour appears apposite, and therefore the statutory offences of deception should be appropriate for charging fraud. However, as with the offence of theft there are many difficulties. Fraudulent trading invariably involves taking on credit in circumstances where there is no reasonable prospect of payment. However, charging a person with taking on credit from an individual would involve proving first of all that the defendant had made a promise to pay, and at the same time had an intention not to pay. The demonstrable hope by a person that he will be able to pay is inconsistent with showing that he intended not to pay. A further possible issue is the belief of the person allegedly being deceived. When taking on credit, there is commonly no representation as to when payment will be made, merely an expectation that payment will be made within the normal credit terms or a reasonable time. Another issue arises when the deception is perpetrated not on a person, but a computer – how can a computer be deceived, given that it does not think? It is likely that fraud involving a computer can be charged as a different offence, e.g., conspiracy to defraud, theft or false accounting.

The concepts of gain and loss in s15 may not be capable of being extended to the sorts of rights which were discussed in the previous section on fraud.

These somewhat philosophical questions can often make deception a difficult charge to prove in fraud trials.

32.4 False accounting

Section 17 of the Theft Act 1968 provides that:

> '(1) Where a person dishonestly, with a view to gain for himself or another or with intent to cause loss to another,–
>
> (a) destroys, defaces, conceals or falsifies any account or any record or document made or required for any accounting purpose; or
> (b) in furnishing information for any purpose produces or makes use of any account, or any such record or document as aforesaid, which to his knowledge is or may be misleading, false or deceptive in a material particular;
>
> he shall, on conviction on indictment, be liable to imprisonment for a term not exceeding seven years.
>
> (2) For purposes of this section a person who makes or concurs in making in an account or other document an entry which is or may be misleading, false or deceptive in a material particular, or who omits or concurs in omitting a material particular from an account or other document, is to be treated as falsifying the account or document.'

False accounting is triable either way.

False accounting is a very powerful weapon against fraudulent behaviour. Despite its obvious overlaps with theft (and indeed, theft of property in commerce is often achieved and concealed by false accounting) in fraud cases it has an extremely wide reach. It does not, for instance, suffer from the same conceptual problems outlined above.

Not only does the charge extend to accounting documents; it includes documents made or required for an accounting purpose. *The Attorney-General's Reference (No 1 of 1980)* [1981] 1 WLR 34 held that a loan proposal form fell into this latter category, even though the document was made for some other purpose but was required for accounting purposes. Accountants will be familiar with the very large number of business documents which have the potential to fall into this class. Furthermore, the document need only be falsified in part, and that part need not be required for an accounting purpose (as long as the document as a whole is so required). All sorts of documents could be, in part, required for accounting purposes, for example board minutes, personnel records, even a diary (for the purpose of compiling a timesheet). This section therefore has a very wide ambit.

False accounting covers falsification, defacement, destruction and concealment. However, it also includes making a document misleading, a term which is of special interest to accountants. A person can take accounting records, which are in no way false, and construct a set of accounts or other financial summary, which is in no way false other than in being misleading. Therefore, a set of accounts which does not contain the terms of a loan may be misleading. If these were sent to a bank for the purposes of raising an overdraft the bank may very well be misled. If knowledge of the terms of the loan were material to the bank's decision then the bank would be misled. This is where the term 'material particular' comes in, although of course the material particular does not have to be connected to the accounting purpose. Of course, this covers not just the accountancy information which might be supplied to a bank. However, it should be noted that it is still necessary to be 'dishonest' and if there is a reasonable body of opinion that says it is a normal practice, then the defence may succeed in showing it is not dishonest. The standard of whether it is dishonest may, or rather should, be what ordinary people would think and whether the defendant realised they would think that.

False accounting by omission also takes place where a document, such as a voucher, is not filled in or a transaction is ignored. In *R* v *Shama* [1990] 1 WLR 661, a telephone operator committed the offence of false accounting by connecting a call without filling in a 'charge ticket', with the result that the subscriber was not charged for the call. Even were this not the case, a person responsible for filling out vouchers would be concurring in the falsification of a further document, that is, the accounting summary of those vouchers.

False accounting is a charge commonly used by prosecutors because it is very specific and it is, or should be, relatively easy to show that a document is other than it should be.

32.5 Specific charges versus general charges

This chapter has looked at a number of charges which deal with specific instances of fraud. A charge will be proved if the prosecution can demonstrate a specific instance of, for example, theft or of false accounting. The offences dealt with in the previous chapter were what can be described as offences of general criminality. Thus, fraudulent trading may cover a number of dishonest transactions. Such offences are termed continuing, that is, they consist of a number of acts committed over a period of time (although the offences of both conspiracy and fraudulent trading can be committed if there is just one transaction).

Over the years, prosecutions have been commenced on the basis of a large number of separate counts of, say, theft, but for reasons such as case management, the prosecution has been forced to withdraw many of the charges and rely, at trial, on a limited number of specimen counts. The difficulty with this is that specimen counts and the evidence available to adduce those counts may not give the court a true flavour of what has happened during a period of fraudulent activity. The evidence in respect of the dropped counts is simply not admissible in the trial of the specimen counts. It may also be difficult to show, where there is more than one defendant, which defendant committed each individual offence.

Therefore, on the face of it, choosing continuing offences as a basis of prosecution should ensure that more evidence is heard, because evidence of all relevant conduct will be admissible, giving a higher likelihood of conviction

Having said that, a charge of conspiracy may be difficult to prove if there are more than two defendants because of the need to find an agreement between, say, four people. Of course, there may be a number of separate conspiracies between discrete groups of people, rather than a general conspiracy between all the defendants. Furthermore, the courts have tended to show disfavour to conspiracy charges if a more specific charge could be brought. Of course, conspiracy and specific charges could be brought in the same indictment, but this too is discouraged by the courts.

Charging fraudulent trading provides less of these problems, but there is still the obvious issue that fraudulent trading could be made up of a whole series of individual transactions which could be prosecuted successfully using a number of specific charges.

These issues face any prosecutor trying to decide how to prosecute suspected fraud and provide another example of why fraud is difficult to prove. The accountant, employed by whichever side, should be aware of the framework within which prosecutors work when carrying out his work. His work must be directed to the offences in the indictment when he is preparing work which may form the basis of the prosecutor's decision-making process.

Chapter 33
Fraudulent trading and wrongful trading under the Insolvency Act

33.1 Introduction

The Insolvency Act 1986 creates two principal methods of penalising directors and officers of a company who are found to be at fault when that company is wound up. The first of these is fraudulent trading and the second wrongful trading. The bulk of this chapter is concerned with these two matters because of the likely involvement of expert accountants in proceedings for fraudulent and wrongful trading. The effect of a successful action is the application of a financial penalty against a director or officer.

There is a third possibility, which provides a summary remedy against what are called 'delinquent' persons involved in the running of a company. Under s212 of the Insolvency Act 1986 a person who is or has been an officer, liquidator or person involved in the management of the company who has misapplied, retained or become accountable for the property of a company, or been guilty of misfeasance or breach of duty, can, on the application of the liquidator, be compelled to restore the property and make a contribution to the company's assets. However, the accountant is most likely to be called upon in fraudulent and wrongful trading cases.

33.2 Fraudulent trading

Section 213 of the Insolvency Act 1986 reads as follows:

> '(1) If in the course of the winding up of a company it appears that any business of the company has been carried on with intent to defraud creditors of the company or creditors of any other person, or for any fraudulent purpose, the following has effect.
>
> (2) The court, on the application of the liquidator may declare that any persons who were knowingly parties to the carrying on of the business in the manner above-mentioned are liable to make such contributions (if any) to the company's assets as the court thinks proper.'

First of all, it should be noted that fraudulent trading under s213 is not a criminal offence – it merely imposes civil financial liability. However, it is inevitable that there is a large amount of overlap between matters which will fall under this section and a prosecution under s458 of the Companies Act 1985, not least because of the similarity of the wording.

Where an individual is subject to a successful action under s213, he will be required to make a contribution to the company's assets from the date when the company should have ceased trading and not taken on any further credit. This is discussed further below. An order made against a wrongdoer under s213 may include a punitive, as well as a compensatory, element (*Re Cyona Distributors Limited* [1967] Ch 889). This section applies to any winding-up, not just an insolvent winding-up, and unlike wrongful trading (see below) it applies to any person.

The major problem with fraudulent trading applications is the same as that in a fraudulent trading prosecution and that is the need to prove dishonest intent. Reference is made to Chapter 31 on criminal fraud which discusses the issues at length. Despite not being dishonest (or because of the difficulty in proving dishonesty), there are occasions when a person's conduct is so unreasonable that the law should demand some sort of recompense by that person to the company. For this reason, the 1986 Act brought in the concept of wrongful trading. Cases dealing with the concept of fraud are set out in Chapter 31.

33.3 Wrongful trading

Section 214 of the Insolvency Act 1986 reads as follows:

> '(1) Subject to subsection (3) below, if in the course of the winding up of a company it appears that subsection (2) of this section applies in relation to a person who is or has been a director of a company, the court, on the application of the liquidator, may declare that that person is to be liable to make such contribution (if any) to the company's assets as the court thinks proper.
>
> (2) This section applies in relation to a person if–
>
> (a) the company has gone into insolvent liquidation,
> (b) at some time before the commencement of the winding up of the company, that person knew or ought to have concluded that there was no reasonable prospect that the company would avoid going into insolvent liquidation, and
> (c) that person was a director of the company at that time . . .
>
> (3) The court shall not make a declaration under this section with respect to any person if it is satisfied that after the condition specified in subsection (2)(b) was first satisfied in relation to him that person took every step with a view to minimising the potential loss to the company's creditors as (assuming him to have known that there was no reasonable prospect that the company would avoid going into insolvent liquidation) he ought to have taken.

(4) For the purposes of subsections (2) and (3), the facts which a director of a company ought to know or ascertain, the conclusions which he ought to reach and the steps which he ought to take are those which would be known or ascertained, or reached or taken, by a reasonably diligent person having both–

(a) the general knowledge, skill and experience that may reasonably be expected of a person carrying out the same functions as are carried out by that director in relation to the company, and
(b) the general knowledge, skill and experience that that director has . . .'

Unlike a successful action for fraudulent trading (as noted above at **33.2**), these provisions are primarily compensatory in nature (as opposed to being compensatory and penal) and apply only to directors (and shadow directors) and only where there is an insolvent liquidation. The standard placed on directors is that of persons in similar positions and on that director's actual skill. Directors will attempt to demonstrate that they carried out their duties properly, according to the general expected standard as well as one based on their own abilities. Therefore, the position of, say, a non-executive director is likely to be very different from that of a full-time executive director, particularly one of great business experience or with professional qualifications.

In wrongful trading cases, directors are likely to be found liable if a company continues trading past a date when an insolvent liquidation is apparent. The issue of the determination of the date of insolvency is dealt with in Chapter 30 – the area where an accountant can expect to become involved.

There are a number of reported cases dealing with establishing liability and determining the amount of any contribution.

In *Re Produce Marketing Consortium Ltd* [1989] 1 WLR 745, the liquidator took action against the directors of a fruit importing agency. Although solvent in 1980, there was a general drift towards insolvency and by 1984 assets substantially exceeded liabilities. The draft annual accounts for September 1985 and September 1986 were produced in January 1987 and showed the company was insolvent and could only continue with bank support. The bank renewed facilities, but at a lower level, and this decrease was financed out of increased liability to the company's main shipper. The company continued trading until October 1987.

It was held that the directors should have realised that there was no reasonable prospect of the company avoiding going into insolvent liquidation by July 1986. This was the date that the September 1985 accounts should have been filed. Even though these accounts were not available until January 1987, the directors had an intimate knowledge of the business and should have known that turnover had fallen. Thus, the 'ought to have known' and the 'ought to have ascertained' tests were applied.

The amount of the contribution the directors were ordered to make was £75,000. Knox J stated that:

> 'Prima facie the appropriate amount that a director is declared to be liable to contribute is the amount by which the company's assets can be discerned to have been depleted by the director's conduct . . .'

The judge found that the deterioration between July 1986 and October 1987 was not easy to quantify from the books. However, he accepted the liquidator's estimate of £92,000.

Re DKG Contractors Ltd [1990] BCC 903 concerned a groundworks contractor. In this case (which also involved actions under s212 and for a preference under s239 of the Insolvency Act 1986), the company was in financial difficulty in early 1988. From February 1988 there were unpaid invoices and later judgments against the company by a number of its creditors. John Weeks QC said:

> 'It is admitted that Mrs Gibbons [one of the directors] was aware of pressing creditors in April and Mr Knight's [a bailiff] first visit to her occurred in May. In April, Mr Gibbons (the other director) himself became aware of a supplier refusing to make further deliveries to the company and consequently had a row with his wife . . . In my judgment, the warning signs were such that by the end of April the directors should have instituted some form of financial control. If they had done, they would, in my judgment, have concluded that there was no reasonable prospect of avoiding liquidation.'

The directors were therefore held liable for the trade debts incurred on or after 1 May 1988.

Re Purpoint Ltd [1991] BCC 121 concerned a printing company which had been formed in February 1986 to take over the business and assets of another company which had failed. The respondent admitted that the new company was unable to pay its debts as and when they fell due after December 1986. In May 1987 the company's accountant informed the directors of their liabilities for the debts of the company should it continue to trade insolvently. Trading ceased in November 1987 and the company went into liquidation in May 1988.

In dealing with the s214 liability, the judge found that the latest date when there was no reasonable prospect was May 1987, when the advice was given by the accountants. However, what was the earliest date? Vinelott J said:

> 'I have felt some doubt whether a reasonably prudent director would have allowed the company to commence trading at all. It had no capital base. Its only assets were purchased by bank borrowing or acquired by hire purchase. And its working capital was contributed by a loan . . . The business it inherited . . . proved

unprofitable . . . However, I do not think it would be right to conclude that Mr Meredith [the respondent] ought to have known that the company was doomed to end up in an insolvent winding up from the moment it started to trade. That would, I think, impose too high a test. Mr Meredith believed that his connections in the advertising and publicity field would enable him to introduce new business and the failure of the old company . . . had been due to . . . an inability to attract custom. I cannot say that that was a belief that could not have been entertained by a reasonable and prudent director conscious of his duty to persons to whom the company would incur liabilities in the ordinary course of carrying out its business.'

However, the judge found that it should have been plain that the company could not avoid an insolvent liquidation by the end of 1986. Furthermore, it owed large amounts to the Crown and had no prospect of trading at a profit to pay them off quickly. However, it was impossible to ascertain the liabilities at the end of 1986 because of the total failure to keep proper accounting records. The application was therefore stood over until the figures could be agreed.

Re Sherborne Associates Ltd [1995] BCC 40 concerned an application by a liquidator under s214 for a contribution from three non-executive directors. The three directors resigned in December 1988 and the company went into liquidation in February 1989. The liquidator contended that the directors should have concluded there was no reasonable prospect by January 1988. It was clear from board minutes that the company was in a very serious position in January 1988. His Honour Judge Jack QC said:

'I should always keep in mind . . . the following. First, there is always the danger of hindsight, the danger of assuming that what has in fact happened was always bound to happen and was apparent.'

One of the directors stated that, at the board meetings, forecasts indicated profits and that the board was satisfied that the company could be pulled around. The judge continued:

'The outcome is that I am not satisfied that in January 1998 Mr Squire [one of the directors, who was the non-executive Chairman] ought to have concluded that there was no reasonable prospect that Sherborne would avoid going into insolvent liquidation. I am not satisfied that he was not entitled to conclude that there was a prospect for the company achieving the turnaround into profit, which was a reasonable rather than a fanciful prospect. It did not need to make the forecast profit to . . . survive, something better than even would probably have done.'

The application having failed against the non-executive Chairman, it also failed against the other two respondents. However, the judge did consider, in part, what would have happened had the case against Mr Squire succeeded:

'. . . I would have had to consider the difficult question of the extent to which, in such circumstances, they were entitled to say they looked to and relied on Mr Squire. I do accept that these two non-executive directors were entitled to place reliance on the highly experienced chairman who had far the greater involvement with the company and the figures. In particular it was he who had the discussions with the executive directors between the two January board meetings. In my view, where in circumstances such as here, one director seeks to rely on another, the other director's view or conclusion is a matter to be taken into account with the other matters which the director should be taking into account as required by s. 214(4).'

These cases indicate the important areas where the accountant will be required to carry out work. First, he should determine the date of insolvency of the company. If acting for the respondent, he will need to assess the reasonableness of the matters on which the liquidator seeks to rely as indicating insolvency. As can be seen in the *Sherborne* case, this is not an easy matter. The availability of, for example, projections and the discussion of projections at board meetings, may be matters which push the date of insolvency into the future. This underlines the importance of considering all of the papers in the case.

The accountant will also need to make a calculation of the liabilities at this date in order to calculate the likely amount of the contribution, if any.

Finally, he should consider the involvement of individual respondents in the decision-making process of the company, weighing up the seemingly conflicting demands of 'ought to' against the reliance on others, as contemplated in *Sherborne*.

33.4 Misfeasance

Finally, the summary remedy available against directors and officers under s212 of the Insolvency Act 1986 should be mentioned. Subsections 1 and 2 read as follows:

'(1) This section applies if in the course of the winding up of a company it appears that a person who–

(a) is or has been an officer of the company,
(b) has acted as liquidator, administrator or administrative receiver of the company, or
(c) not being a person falling within paragraph (a) or (b), is or has been concerned, or has taken part, in the promotion, formation or management of the company,

has misapplied or retained, or become accountable for, any money or other property of the company, or been guilty of any misfeasance or breach of any fiduciary or other duty in relation to the company.

(2) The reference in subsection (1) to any misfeasance or breach of any fiduciary or other duty in relation to the company includes, in the case of a person who has acted as liquidator or administrator of the company, any misfeasance or breach of

> any fiduciary or other duty in connection with the carrying out of his functions as liquidator or administrator of the company.'

The remedy available is as follows, under subsection (3):

> '(3) The court may, on the application of the official receiver or the liquidator, or of any creditor or contributory, examine into the conduct of the person falling within subsection (1) and compel him–
>
> (a) to repay, restore or account for the money or property or any part of it, with interest at such rate as the court thinks just, or
> (b) to contribute such sum to the company's assets by way of compensation in respect of the misfeasance or breach of fiduciary or other duty as the court thinks just.'

It should be noted that this procedure is open to creditors as well as liquidators and the Official Receiver. Furthermore, this procedure is simpler than taking an action against, say, directors by way of a writ. The misfeasance procedure is used where there has been, for example, the sale of assets at an undervalue, a fraudulent preference, secret profits by or improper payments to directors.

Part 5
Regulatory matters

Chapter 34
Regulatory matters and disciplinary proceedings

'In an inquisitorial Inquiry, the questioning of the witnesses by the Inquiry is not an examination in chief, nor is it a cross-examination. Hearsay evidence may be sought. Opinions, whether or not expert, may be sought. Questions to which the questioner does not know the answer will frequently be asked – and, indeed, will be asked *because* the questioner does not know the answer. The techniques of questioning witnesses in adversarial litigation can be set aside. The questioning process is, or should be, a part of a thorough investigation to determine the truth. It is not a process designed either to promote or to demolish a "case".' (Sir Richard Scott's Chancery Bar Association Spring Lecture 1995)

34.1 Introduction

The above quote from Sir Richard Scott's lecture, which was entitled 'Procedure at Inquiries – the duty to be fair', was in the context of his own enquiry into the Arms to Iraq affair, which was a very unusual inquiry. The quote highlights some of the potential differences between the litigation process referred to elsewhere in this book and the proceedings at inquiries, particularly those under the provisions of the Companies Act 1985, the Financial Services Act 1986, the Insolvency Act 1986 and the Insurance Companies Act 1982.

This chapter deals with inspections and investigations under the above Acts and with the proceedings, whether civil, criminal or regulatory, which may follow. Particular reference will be made to the disciplinary procedures available to the Institute of Chartered Accountants in England and Wales, the Institute of Chartered Accountants of Scotland and the Chartered Association of Certified Accountants, who are all participants in the Joint Disciplinary Scheme (see **34.10**). Other professional bodies, such as the Law Society and the Royal Institution of Chartered Surveyors, have similar disciplinary procedures in which an accountant is only likely to be involved where there is the possibility of financial irregularity and the extent of such irregularity has to be established. Opinion evidence might be sought from accountants acting as experts where, for example, there were allegations of breaches of the Solicitors' Accounts Rules. Whether or not such rules have been complied with is within the province of accountants acting under the provisions of the Accountant's Report Rules.

34.2 Inspections and departmental inquiries

> 'The immediate purpose of most investigations is to find out what has happened or is happening when there are grounds to suggest some irregularity in the conduct of a company, business or individual in order to provide the Secretary of State with the information needed to decide what is to be done . . . The ultimate purpose of any investigation is to provide information on which to take some action if the facts discovered in the course of the investigation warrant it.' (Paragraph 9, Investigation Handbook, HMSO 1990)

The Investigation Handbook is required reading for those conducting inspections and investigations and for anyone who is called as a witness.

34.3 Powers of the Secretary of State to initiate an inspection or investigation

Section 431(1) Companies Act 1985 says:

> 'The Secretary of State may appoint one or more competent inspectors to investigate the affairs of a company and to report on them in such manner as he may direct.'

Under s432 the Secretary of State has to appoint one or more competent Inspectors to investigate the affairs of a company and report on them in such manner as he directs, if the court by order declares that its affairs ought to be so investigated. In other limited circumstances, the Secretary of State has a discretion whether to appoint Inspectors (see s431).

Section 432(2) says:

> 'The Secretary of State may make such an appointment (under Section 432(1)) if it appears to him that there are circumstances suggesting:
>
> (a) that the company's affairs are being or have been conducted with intent to defraud its creditors or the creditors of any other person, or otherwise for a fraudulent or unlawful purpose, or in a manner which is unfairly prejudicial to some part of its members, or
> (b) that any actual or proposed act or omission of the company (including an act or omission on its behalf) is or would be so prejudicial, or that the company was formed for any fraudulent or unlawful purpose, or
> (c) that persons concerned with the company's formation or the management of its affairs have in connection therewith been guilty of fraud, misfeasance or other misconduct towards it or towards its members, or
> (d) that the company's members have not been given all the information with respect to its affairs which they might reasonably expect.'

When Inspectors are appointed under s431 or s432, directors and agents of the company have a duty to produce to the inspectors all documents relating to the company, to attend before the inspectors when required to do so, and to give the Inspectors all assistance necessary in connection with their investigation which they are reasonably able to give. The Inspectors have power to require directors or agents and any other person who is or may be in possession of information to produce to them any documents, save for those subject to legal professional privilege or, in certain cases, subject to an obligation of confidence as a result of a client relationship to attend before them, and otherwise to give them every assistance. The term 'agents' includes, particularly, bankers, solicitors and auditors (see s434(4)).

The Inspectors have the power to examine any person on oath and any answer given by a person to a question put to him during an investigation, under ss431 to 433, may be used in evidence against him.

Section 442 gives the Secretary of State power to appoint inspectors to investigate the ownership of companies, and s94 of the Financial Services Act 1986 gives the Secretary of State power to appoint Inspectors to investigate the affairs of any authorised unit trust schemes, recognised schemes relating to activities carried on in the UK and collective investment schemes.

Investigations under the above sections lead to a report which may be published and such investigations are announced when they are set up. It is the general practice of the Secretary of State to publish reports by Inspectors under ss431, 432, 442 and 446 (investigation of share dealings) if they relate to the affairs of a public company. The Investigation Handbook goes on:

> 'Reports by inspectors relating to private companies are not normally published unless they raise issues of general public interest. However, if it appears to the Secretary of State that matters have come to light in the course of an inspection which suggest that a criminal offence has been committed, and those matters have been referred to the appropriate prosecuting authority, he may direct the inspectors to take no further steps or take only such further steps as are specified in the direction. If the Secretary of State makes such a direction the inspectors will only make a final report if the Secretary of State directs them to do so, or they were appointed by court order.'

If Inspectors are appointed to investigate the affairs of a large public company, it is customary for two inspectors to be appointed, 'one of whom is a senior partner of a firm of accountants and the other is a Queen's Counsel or a leading solicitor'. Appointments under these sections are comparatively rare and the best way of finding out what happens at such enquiries is to read the published reports, which are available from HMSO.

There are two aspects of such investigations which should be borne in mind when reading the reports and which are relevant to investigations under other statutory provisions. These are the duty to be fair and confidentiality.

34.4 The duty to be fair

Under the heading 'Fairness to Witnesses' the Investigation Handbook says at paras 41 and 42:

> '41. Inspectors have a general duty to behave in a fair way, both in their personal conduct, and by giving witnesses a reasonable opportunity to seek legal advice.
>
> 42. If inspectors are minded to conclude that a person has contravened the Act then they should put to him the substance of the evidence against him and give him an opportunity to respond, either at an interview (or further interview) or in writing if he so wishes.'

The proceedings are inquisitorial and are undertaken to establish facts and to make them available.

The Investigation Handbook contains, in Appendices E and F, the full text of the judgments of the Court of Appeal in *Re Pergamon Press Limited* [1970] 3 All ER 535–546 and *Maxwell* v *Department of Trade and Industry and Others* [1974] 2 All ER 122.

In the first case the Court of Appeal held:

> '(i) Although the proceedings before the inspectors were only administrative, and not judicial or quasi judicial, yet the characteristics of the proceedings required the inspectors to act fairly, in that if they were disposed to condemn or criticise anyone in a report they must first give him a fair opportunity to correct or contradict the allegation, for which purpose an outline of the charge would usually suffice.
>
> (ii) Save for the requirement to act fairly, the inspectors should not be subject to any set rules of procedure and should be free to act at their own discretion; accordingly, as the inspectors had shown that they intended to act fairly and had given every assurance that could reasonably be required, the directors' refusal to give evidence was unjustified.'

The second case arose because Robert Maxwell was criticised in the interim report of the Inspectors in the first case (he was at the time chairman and chief executive of Pergamon Press). The report was very critical of Robert Maxwell, who brought an action against the Inspectors and the DTI claiming a declaration that the Inspectors had acted in breach of the rules of natural justice in that, having formulated their tentative criticism of him, they had failed to give him an opportunity of answering those criticisms before signing their report and, further, that they had failed to put to the plaintiff all relevant statements made by other witnesses or in documents which were prejudicial to him so as to give him an opportunity of answering them.

The Court of Appeal held that Robert Maxwell was not entitled to the relief sought because:

'(i) A clear distinction was to be drawn between an inquiry based on a charge or accusation and one such as that on which the inspectors had been engaged in which they were asked to establish what had happened and, in the course of so doing, to form certain views or conclusions. Having heard the evidence and reached their conclusions the inspectors were under no obligation to put to a witness such of those conclusions as might be critical of him. All that was necessary was that the inspectors should put to the witness the points that they propose to consider when he first came to give evidence. Once the inspectors had heard the evidence they were entitled to come to the final conclusions which would be embodied in their report. The inspectors had conducted the inquiry fairly; the fact that certain matters of detail had not been put to the plaintiff when he was giving evidence was not a ground for impugning the report.

(ii) Even if the inspectors had failed to observe the rules of natural justice the bare declaration sought by the plaintiff was one that the court would only make in exceptional circumstances and was not appropriate in the instant case.'

The above conclusions are dealt with in some detail here, because they have consequences for the way in which DTI investigations are conducted.

Sir Richard Scott highlighted, in the lecture referred to above, the tension between the requirement of fairness and the need for efficiency. He said:

> 'It is not, I think, an oversimplification to say that the objects to be served by procedures, for Inquiries as for litigation generally, are likely to be threefold; first, the need to be fair and to be seen to be fair to those whose interests, reputations or fortunes may be adversely affected by the proceedings; second, the need for the proceedings to be conducted with efficiency and as much expedition as is practicable; third, the need for the cost of the proceedings to be kept within reasonable bounds. While the second and third of these desiderata should never be allowed to submerge the need to be fair, nonetheless there is inevitable tension between, on the one hand, the requirement of fairness and, on the other, the need for an efficient process. This tension is apparent in the very familiar procedural rules that govern civil litigation. It is unfair to give judgment against a litigant without allowing his case to be heard. But a judgment in default of defence will not always be set aside at the instance of a defaulting defendant who, late in the day, wants to defend. The circumstances of the case, and the need to maintain an efficient and expeditious system of justice will sometimes lead to the refusal of an application to set aside a judgment obtained in default of appearance or in default of defence. The right to cross-examine and the right to make submissions to the Court can, at the discretion of the trial judge, be subjected to time limits. I mention these examples in order to make the point that some of the fundamental procedures that fairness to litigants in civil litigation may be thought to require may, in the interests of efficiency and expedition, sometimes have to be curtailed. As I have said there is a tension and balance between the need to be fair and the need to be expeditious that is well understood in ordinary civil litigation.'

There is now a process known as 'Maxwellisation' whereby, when Inspectors propose to criticise individuals in their report, they provide details of those circumstances to the person criticised and give that person the opportunity to make representations on why the proposals are unfair. The Inspectors will take account of such representation when finalising their criticisms, although these criticisms may remain unchanged. Similar Maxwellisation procedures are now common in disciplinary proceedings, for example, in proceedings contemplated by the Joint Disciplinary Scheme.

34.5 Confidentiality

DTI enquiries and inspections, under the provisions referred to above, are normally conducted in private (as, by definition, are the confidential enquiries referred to below). The evidence of witnesses, however, will not necessarily remain confidential. The Investigation Handbook puts it thus:

> 'Inspectors may tell witnesses that they are conducting their enquiry on a confidential basis but it would be wrong to lead witnesses to think that any evidence which they give will remain completely confidential. Inspectors may themselves wish to put such evidence to other witnesses or to refer to it in their report in a manner which identifies the witness who gave it. Furthermore witnesses may find themselves asked to give evidence in court if criminal proceedings follow the inspection. Moreover, information obtained by the Inspectors may be disclosed for the purposes specified in s180 of the Act, for example to regulatory bodies to assist them to perform their functions. Any discussion with a witness about whether or not his evidence might be disclosed to third parties should be recorded in the transcript. No assurances should be given to witnesses about the confidentiality of their evidence without consulting the Department first.'

The auditor of a public company which is the subject of a s432 inspection may be asked to give evidence to the Inspectors. Such an auditor may, and usually will, be accompanied by his solicitor and by counsel, particularly if there is any suggestion that the audit may ultimately be criticised. Civil or criminal proceedings may follow and, as mentioned above, what is said to the Inspectors may be used in evidence and transcripts may also be made available to regulatory bodies carrying out their own enquiries, for the purpose of disciplinary proceedings against an accountant or auditor relating to the exercise of his professional duties.

On 17 December 1996, the European Court of Human Rights held (by 16 votes to 4) that Ernest Saunders' (of Guinness) right not to incriminate himself under Article 6 of the Convention for the Protection of Human Rights had been violated because transcripts of interviews with DTI Inspectors, appointed under ss432 and 442 Companies Act 1985, were read out to the jury during his criminal trial.

However, the court refused to speculate on whether he would have been acquitted if the transcripts had not been used, rejected his compensation claim of £4.6 million, and awarded him costs of £75,000, reduced from the £340,000 for which he asked.

Notwithstanding that Britain was one of the first signatories of the European Convention in 1953, it has not incorporated the convention into British law, although the present Government while in opposition promised to do so.

What follows is a transcript of the preliminaries to the examination of an auditor by Inspectors appointed under s432.

Example

Inspector	Good morning, gentlemen. My name is (Leading Counsel) and on my left sits (Senior Accountant), and we two are appointed to be Inspectors into the affairs of (a public company plc). Our secretary who sits on our far left should have supplied you with a minute of our appointments.
Auditor	Yes he has. Thank you.
Inspector	On my right is (Junior Counsel) who is assisting us in our investigations. You will also observe that we have a shorthand writer present, and during the course of the whole of our proceedings the shorthand writer will take a note of what transpires between us. In due course we will supply you with a copy of the transcript of today's proceedings, and we invite you, when you receive that transcript, to make such amendments by way of extension or correction as you feel fit. So that at the end of it we shall have the totality of what you can tell us on the matters that we raise. So please feel free to submit any further comments that you wish to once you have that transcript.
Auditor	Will that be within the next few weeks?
Inspector	I can't tell you what the timescale will be. It is partially when the transcript comes to us, which is dependent upon the demands on the shorthand writer's time, but it will be as soon as we reasonably can. We asked you if you will treat the proceedings between us as confidential and not disclose them to other parties, save, of course, your legal advisers. We, for our part, will try and treat your evidence as confidential, but we can use it for the purpose of our enquiry as we see fit, and we may also refer to what you tell us in any report that we come to write, so that to that extent it may be published. Hereafter the transcript of your evidence may be available to others who are entitled to access to it, and we can have no control over what use those others may be entitled to make of that transcript, but as far as we can we will treat it as confidential.
Auditor	If I could ask one question: It is almost certain I shall be asked by my partners about today's interview. Do I take it that I am not at liberty to discuss that with them?

Inspector	In the broadest sense yes, you may, but in the narrow sense there may be questions that we shall want to pursue independently with some of your partners, and we would not like the detail of what we are discussing with you to be disclosed to those others.
Auditor	Right.
Inspector	Now we notice that today you have counsel and your solicitor attending, and may we take it for this moment that you are acting together, gentlemen, for this partner or for the firm?
Counsel:	It is for the firm.
Inspector	If at any stage the scope or the ambit of your representation either enlarges or reduces for any reason, perhaps you would let us know.
Counsel:	Indeed.
Inspector	Thank you very much. I think without more ado we will ask you to take the oath please.
Auditor	I swear by Almighty God that the evidence that I shall give to this enquiry will be the truth, the whole truth and nothing but the truth . . .

34.5.1 Confidentiality and privilege

The accountant acting as expert is bound, as in any other engagement, to comply with the code of conduct of his professional body. There are the usual professional obligations of confidentiality regarding client's affairs, but, by their very nature, reports prepared by experts on behalf of clients are written to be disclosed to others and it is, therefore, appropriate to consider the question of defamation and the related question of privilege.

Osborn's Concise Law Dictionary defines privilege as:

> 'An exceptional right, immunity or exemption belonging to a person by virtue of his office or status, eg the immunity from arrest of diplomats and Members of Parliament.'

A statement made in the course of judicial proceedings enjoys absolute privilege, which means that no action can be taken in the light of it even if it is made maliciously. Absolute privilege also applies in quasi-judicial proceedings (such as disciplinary proceedings) and to statements contained in documents made in judicial or quasi-judicial proceedings.

Privilege extends not only to everything in the course of proceedings by judges, counsel, witnesses and parties, including documents put in as evidence, but also to everything which is done from the commencement of proceedings onwards.

34.6 Investigations under s447 Companies Act 1985 and s177 Financial Services Act 1986

Section 447 gives the Secretary of State, if he thinks there is good reason to do so, power to authorise an officer of his or any other competent person, to require the company to produce to him forthwith any documents which he may specify. The person appointed has power to require production of those documents from any person who appears to him to be in possession of them without prejudice to any lien on the documents.

The power given by s447 includes the power to take copies of the documents or extracts from them and to require the person in possession of the documents, or any other person who is or was an officer or employee of the company in question, to provide an explanation of any of them.

Section 177 of the Financial Services Act 1986 gives the Secretary of State power to appoint one or more competent inspectors to carry out such investigations as are requisite to establish whether or not there may have been a contravention of the Company Securities (Insider Dealing) Act 1985.

Until 1989 enquiries under s447 were carried out by the DTI itself. Investigations under s177 have normally been carried out by investigators from the private sector, usually senior accountants in practice, although not necessarily only from one of the larger firms. Since 1989 (when the law was changed) investigations under s447 have increasingly been conducted by accountants in practice, although the DTI still conducts most s447 investigations itself.

There is no statutory definition of the 'good reason' referred to in s447, but, according to the Investigation Handbook, it is taken by the DTI to include grounds for suspicion of fraud, misfeasance, misconduct, conduct unfairly prejudicial to shareholders or a failure to supply shareholders with information they may reasonably expect.

Appendix B to the Investigation Handbook is the notes published by the DTI for the guidance of Inspectors appointed under the Companies Act 1985 and Appendix C is notes for the guidance of Inspectors appointed under s177 Financial Services Act 1986, and Inspectors under both sections would be well advised to take heed of that advice. These appendices are reproduced as Appendices 14 and 15 respectively to this book.

Because confidentiality, in connection with inspections and investigations under the Companies Acts and the Financial Services Acts, is a term of art rather than science, what is said to investigators or Inspectors may come to the knowledge of other parties involved in other proceedings, sometimes notoriously, such as in connection with the prosecution of Ernest Saunders, referred to earlier, and sometimes less obviously as in connection with civil or disciplinary proceedings. Any accountant called to give evidence to Inspectors or investigations, or for that matter to the Serious Fraud Office using its powers under s2 of the Criminal Justice Act 1987, should assume that his evidence may be available to others and, while giving evidence which is the truth, the whole truth and nothing but the truth in answer to questions which are put to him, should not volunteer information for which he is not asked and should confine himself to answering the questions put to him. He should take advantage of the opportunity given to him to consider the transcripts of his evidence, with his legal advisers, and to amend or supplement the transcript if the answer given does not appear, on reflection, to be a fair reflection of what the accountant said in evidence or believed to be true.

What the accountant says to the Inspectors may be relevant not only in actions directly involving the accountant but in criminal or civil proceedings involving others. For example, following a DTI investigation or enquiry, directors of a company may be the subject of criminal proceedings and/or civil proceedings, and the evidence of the auditor in those proceedings may be required. The accountant may be cross-examined in those proceedings by counsel who is well aware of what the accountant said to the Inspectors or investigators at the Companies Act inquiry. What the accountant says in the proceedings against the directors may, in turn, be used in any proceedings against him or his firm, and any accountant asked to attend to give evidence to investigators or Inspectors should ensure that he is well prepared in the light, not only of the likely questions from the Inspectors, but also in the light of the possibility of later criminal or civil proceedings.

Accountants' professional indemnity policies customarily provide cover for legal costs incurred in relation to disciplinary and quasi-judicial proceedings and, if the policy requires notification of circumstances which may lead to claims, the accountant asked to give evidence to DTI Inspectors or investigators would be well advised to inform his insurers if it is possible that the accountant's conduct will be criticised in any way.

34.7 Finally, some statistics

Accountancy Books published, in April 1997, the results of a research study by Peter Boys, a lecturer in accounting at Canterbury Business School. The research study was prepared for the Auditing Practices Board and was entitled *Raising Auditing Standards: The Impact of DTI Inspectors' Reports 1971–1995*.

Between 1948 and 1995 a total of 119 DTI Inspectors' reports were published. From 1966 to 1976 eight such reports were published in each year and there were nine such reports in 1981. Since 1981 the peak year has been 1993, in which six reports were published. Appendix B to the research study provides details, for each year, of the companies reported on, the authors of the report, the section or sections under which the report was required, the length of the report, the date of appointment of the Inspectors, date of completion of the report, and date of publication. The length of the reports appears to have varied from one page (a report in 1959) to 664 pages in the case of the report on Pergamon and Robert Maxwell published in 1973.

The delay between appointment of Inspectors and the publication of their report seems to be lengthening. Inspectors were appointed to investigate the affairs of James Ferguson Holdings plc and Barlow Clowes Gilt Managers Limited in the summer of 1988. Their report was not completed until March 1995 and was published in July of that year. Delays of three, four or five years between the date of appointment and publication are not uncommon, but it is rare for there to be any significant delay between completion of the report and its publication; the delay being a matter of months rather than years, except in the case of the report on Alexander Howden Holdings plc which appears to have been completed by June 1987 and was not published until August 1990.

The Guinness scandal was in 1986, Ernest Saunders' trial was held in 1990 and the DTI report was finally published in November 1997. Publication was deferred because criminal proceedings were taken in order to avoid the possibility of prejudice to such proceedings.

Applications are sometimes made to defer regulatory proceedings because of actual or potential civil proceedings, and such a deferral was achieved by Price Waterhouse in connection with an enquiry by the Joint Disciplinary Scheme into its role as auditors of BCCI. However, no deferral was granted to Coopers & Lybrand in connection with an enquiry into their role in connection with Maxwell. The court was to carry out a balancing exercise, weighing the public interest in the prompt and efficient operation of the regulatory scheme and the risk of serious prejudice to the defendant in the other proceedings. The established position seems to be that it is only in wholly exceptional circumstances that the courts will prevent regulatory bodies from carrying out their proper function. An adverse finding by a regulatory body might well have an impact on the result of civil proceedings, but it is considered that those who breach their profession's standards must accept the consequences of their actions. Were it to be otherwise, self-regulation might well be replaced by statutory supervision.

Peter Boys explains the objective of his research study in his introduction as follows:

> 'The purpose of this research study was to review the published reports of Department of Trade and Industry inspectors extracting comments of relevance to auditing. These comments were then summarised, firstly to analyse and categorise the types of issues raised, secondly to examine the positive action taken by the auditing profession and to a lesser extent by the legislature in addressing them, and finally to highlight areas where further action may be necessary.'

The study makes excellent reading and deals in turn with:

- deception of auditors;
- professional ethics;
  - independence;
  - changes in professional appointment;
- responsibilities;
  - general responsibilities;
  - joint audits;
  - other auditors;
- planning, controlling and recording;
  - planning and control;
  - working papers and audit programmes;
- evidence;
  - internal control;
  - opening balances;
  - fixed assets;
  - stock and work in progress;
  - investments;
  - bank reports for audit purposes;
  - inter-company balances;
  - long-term liabilities;
  - creditors;
  - provisions;
  - sales;
  - expenses;
  - lease and hire purchase transactions;
  - related party transactions;
  - illegal payments;
  - post balance sheet review;
  - management accounts;
  - minutes;
- reporting;
  - information and explanations;
  - proper books of account;
  - compliance with Companies Acts;
  - transactions with directors;
  - truth and fairness;
  - wording of reports;

  - going concern;
  - ultra vires transactions;
  - illegal acts;
  - notes to financial statements;
  - communication between auditors and regulators;
  - reports to management;
- specific industries;
  - Lloyd's underwriters;
  - leasing;
  - building society;
- auditors' additional roles;
  - reporting accountants;
  - auditors acting as registrars;
- summary and conclusion;
  - summary findings;
  - further considerations on auditing standards;
  - conclusion.

The study ends on a positive note with two quotations from the Inspector's report. In *Re Saint Piran Ltd* [1981] 1 WLR 1300:

> 'Much of the documentary evidence on which this chapter of our report is based was obtained only because of the diligence of the auditors, Ernst & Whinney, in carrying out their audit of the 1979 accounts (para 19.47).
>
> . . . The auditors, Ernst & Whinney, demonstrated themselves to have been acutely aware at all times of the need for the board to act with proper care and with due regard for the interests of all of the shareholders. In our view they did all that could reasonably be expected of them in difficult circumstances and with often incomplete or inaccurate information (para 19.59).'

It is, of course, not only accountants acting as auditors who may be criticised in DTI reports (whether published or not).

It has been argued that accountants acting as experts have themselves, when their evidence has been accepted by the court, raised the standards to be expected of the ordinary accountant doing that work, and experts have been criticised for that, in that, it is said, life is made more difficult for the rest of the profession.

If what is said is true and the standards are raised, that must, on the face of it, be for the benefit both of the general public and for the esteem in which the profession is regarded, unless the cost of compliance with the standard outweighs the benefit.

The fact that the vast majority of accountants and auditors meet the required standard nearly all the time suggests that the costs do not yet outweigh the benefits.

Although only one DTI Inspector's report was published in 1995, there were 411 investigations under the Companies Acts and under s44 of the Insurance Companies Act 1982. Of these investigations the vast majority (389) were under s447. Twenty-seven of those investigations were undertaken by investigators from accountancy firms. Fifty per cent of the complaints giving rise to investigations came from the public.

34.8 Conclusion

While few accountants can expect to be asked to act as Inspectors under s432 Companies Act 1985, there will be a greater number who are asked to carry out investigations under s447 Companies Act 1985 or s177 Financial Services Act 1986. There will be an even greater number who have to deal with the consequences of such investigations on behalf of their client accountants.

34.9 Disciplinary proceedings

Members of the participating bodies are potentially subject to the disciplinary proceedings which, in the case of the ICAEW, are set out in the *Members Handbook*.

Firms of accountants have a duty to investigate complaints (section 1.112 of the *Members Handbook*) and have a duty to report misconduct (section 1.113). Paragraph 6(b) of Schedule 2 to the Bye-laws provides that:

> 'It shall be the duty of every *member* where it is in the public interest to do so to report to the *Secretary and Chief Executive* any facts or matters indicating that a *member* and/or *firm* or *student* may have become liable to disciplinary action. In determining whether it is in the public interest to report such facts or matters regard shall be had to such guidance as the *Council* shall from time to time give.'

The *Handbook* gives examples of circumstances in which it is deemed to be in the public interest that a member's conduct should be considered by the Investigation Committee. The circumstances are wherever a member or student has or may have:

(a) committed any offence involving dishonesty, fraud or cheating;
(b) committed an imprisonable offence under the Company Securities (Insider Dealing) Act 1985, the Insolvency Act 1986, the Company Directors Disqualification Act 1986, the Financial Services Act 1986, the Companies Acts 1985 and 1989 or any comparable piece of legislation in the corporate or financial services spheres;

(c) been convicted of any offence for which he has received a custodial sentence, whether suspended or not;
(d) as a member or employee of a firm authorised by the Institute for investment business been responsible for a serious breach of the Institute's Investment Business Regulations;
(e) as a member or employee of a firm registered by the Institute as an auditor, been responsible for a serious breach of the Institute's Audit Regulations;
(f) as an insolvency practitioner licensed by the Institute, committed a serious breach of the Insolvency Act or Rules;
(g) been responsible for a serious breach of the Institute's Client Money Regulations;
(h) performed his professional work or the duties of his employment in a grossly incompetent manner;
(i) committed a serious breach of faith in a professional respect;
(j) committed a serious financial irregularity.

The normal practice is for complaints which do not give rise to or include questions of public concern to be referred, after investigation by the Investigation Committee, to the Disciplinary Committee. If the complaint gives rise to matters of public concern it will, after investigation by the Investigation Committee, be dealt with in accordance with the Joint Disciplinary Scheme (JDS).

Accountants may be involved in JDS disciplinary matters in four capacities:

(a) as a member of investigation or disciplinary committees, or as a member of a Joint Disciplinary Tribunal;
(b) as the subject of disciplinary proceedings;
(c) as a witness of fact in connection with proceedings against other accountants;
(d) as an expert witness either for the defendant accountant or the body bringing the complaint (either the Investigation Committee in the case of complaints referred to the Disciplinary Committee or the Executive Counsel in the case of complaints to the Joint Disciplinary Scheme).

In practice, firms or individual accountants criticised in published DTI reports can expect their conduct to be investigated under the provisions of the Joint Disciplinary Scheme. Other complaints will initially be investigated by officials at the Institute, who will advise the Investigation Committee on whether there is, prima facie, a case to answer.

Expert accountants may well be retained to advise solicitors acting for accountants under enquiry, even if the accountant is confident that there is not even a prima facie case against him. The initial assumption of those at the Institute charged with investigating complaints appears to be that the complaint is justified, and this can lead to friction between a member against whom a complaint is preferred and the Institute, which the member expects to provide support against unwarranted complaints.

The reality is, in the authors' experience, that the member should expect the Institute officials to act as devil's advocates and he should, therefore, expect to have to justify his actions in some detail. It is, however, worth spending the time, and if necessary the money, to deal properly, and with appropriate external and impartial advice, with enquiries from the Institute following complaints. If such enquiries are dealt with properly and fully then, even if the complaint is referred to the Investigation Committee, it may well be that the committee will decide, based on the evidence put forward to the officials, that there is no case to answer, which will mean that no complaint will have to be dealt with by the Disciplinary Committee.

34.10 The Joint Disciplinary Scheme

Section 1.106 of the *Members Handbook* gives details of the Joint Disciplinary Scheme. Paragraph 4 says that the objectives of the scheme are:

> 'to promote the highest possible standards of professional and business conduct, efficiency and competence:
>
> (a) by Members in the performance of their professional or business activities (including duties as a director, servant, partner or employee of any organisation); and
> (b) by Member Firms in the provision of the services which they offer to the public.'

It should be noted that complaints can be made against individuals and firms so that, in the case of an audit which is the subject of adverse criticism in a DTI Inspector's report, disciplinary proceedings under the JDS rules may be taken against the audit partner as an individual, against any other member involved (such as an audit manager or qualified assistant) and/or against the firm.

Under the terms of the JDS it is the Executive Counsel, a legally qualified officer appointed by the Executive Committee, who enquires into the complaint and who has power to engage solicitors and/or counsel and members or member firms to carry out detailed investigations.

Such investigations normally result in a draft report which will, if it criticises the conduct of a member or member firm, be disclosed, as a draft, to those under investigation before any complaint is laid before a tribunal.

This procedure is adopted in the interests of fairness, and the reporting accountants will take account, to the extent they consider necessary, of representations made in connection with their draft.

If there are grounds for criticism, in that the Executive Counsel is of the opinion that there are grounds upon which a Joint Disciplinary Tribunal could make an adverse finding concerning the professional or business conduct, efficiency or competence of a member or member firm, then the Executive Counsel will deliver to the Executive Committee a formal complaint, specifying the manner in which he alleges that the conduct or quality of the work fell below that to be expected, to the Executive Committee with a request that a Joint Disciplinary Tribunal be appointed.

Before the formal complaint is laid, the Executive Counsel has to give the member or member firm an opportunity of making written representations to him and a member may admit in writing that there are grounds for an adverse finding. Such admissions may have an impact on the costs which the member or the member firm has to pay.

At any tribunal hearing the Executive Counsel acts as complainant and the member under enquiry has a reasonable opportunity to lead evidence in his defence, to hear the evidence against him, to cross-examine witnesses called by the Executive Counsel and to make representations orally or in writing to the Joint Disciplinary Tribunal. However, the rules of evidence adopted by the courts of England and Wales or Scotland do not apply.

The order of the proceedings for the hearing of a complaint is normally as set out in paragraph 23 of the Joint Disciplinary Scheme Regulations, which reads as follows:

> 'The order of the proceedings for the hearing of a complaint shall, unless the Joint Disciplinary Tribunal otherwise directs, be as follows:
>
> (a) submissions by or on behalf of the Executive Counsel;
> (b) hearing of any witnesses called by the Executive Counsel, followed by cross-examination of such witnesses by the Member/Member Firm concerned;
> (c) submissions by the Member/Member Firm concerned;
> (d) hearing of any witnesses called on behalf of the Member/Member Firm concerned, followed by cross-examination of such witnesses on behalf of the Executive Counsel;
> (e) closing submissions by or on behalf of the Executive Counsel;
> (f) closing submissions by the Member/Member Firm concerned.
>
> A Representative may act on behalf of a Member or Member Firm under this Regulation.
>
> The Tribunal may permit a witness to be recalled.'

It can be seen that the procedure at the tribunal is comparable to civil proceedings, with the exception that the rules of evidence do not apply. So far as the expert accountant is concerned, he should expect his report to be admitted as evidence and to face cross-examination upon it, and the advice in this book regarding expert reports and the giving of evidence will apply to such disciplinary proceedings.

34.11 Other disciplinary proceedings

An accountant involved in investigations into the financial aspects of disciplinary proceedings brought by other professional bodies, such as the Law Society and the RICS, should take steps to ensure that he understands the regulations which are the subject of the proceedings and his role in them. He should assume, absent instructions to the contrary, that his duties and obligations to the tribunal are similar to the duties which he owes to the court in the circumstances outlined in this book. (For an outline of the disciplinary procedures of the Law Society see *Solicitors Accounts* (MacGregor, 1993), and of the RICS see *Surveyors, Architects and Estate Agents – An Industry Accounting and Auditing Guide* (MacGregor, 1996), both published by Accountancy Books.)

34.12 Financial regulation

In October 1997 the new Financial Services Authority (FSA) was launched following a report from the SIB to the Chancellor at the end of July 1997.

The new super authority will incorporate the former functions of nine regulatory bodies which are:

1 The Building Societies Commission;
2 The Friendly Societies Commission;
3 The Insurance Directorate of the DTI;
4 The Investment Management Regulatory Organisation (IMRO);
5 The Personal Investment Authority (PIA);
6 The Registry of Friendly Societies;
7 The Securities and Futures Authority (SFA);
8 The Securities and Investments Board (SIB);
9 The Supervision and Surveillance Division of the Bank of England.

The FSA has inherited a fully functional regulatory system, and the functions of the existing SROs will be formally transferred to the FSA. Statutory objectives will be set out in legislation.

It is intended that the new body will provide better regulation, but it remains to be seen whether it will be effective in preventing or detecting financial irregularity more quickly.

Appendices

Appendix 1
Academy of Experts model form of expert's report

Introduction

In 1989 the Lord Chancellor approved the formation of the Judicial Committee consisting of seven senior Judges representing the English, Scottish and Northern Irish Benches, since when it has rendered invaluable assistance in the promotion and improvement of standards.

The Model Form of Expert's Report has been prepared by The Judicial Committee to further assist Experts and their clients by indicating a format that the Judiciary would find of assistance. In other words a 'judge friendly' format. It must be remembered that the form is for a Model rather than a Standard.

The Judicial Committee members are:

The Rt Hon The Lord Slynn of Hadley PC
President of The British Academy of Experts
Chairman of the Committee

The Rt Hon Lord Justice Neill
Court of Appeal

The Rt Hon Lord Justice Saville
Court of Appeal

The Rt Hon Lord Justice MacDermott
Supreme Court of Judicature Northern Ireland

The Hon Lord Prosser
Court of Session Scotland

The Hon Mr Justice Garland
Queens Bench Division

His Honour Judge Bowsher QC
Official Referees Court

Julian Cohen
Secretary to the Committee
(Masons Solicitors)

1. Why a model form?

1.1 Some senior judges have expressed concern at the length of many experts reports and at the tendency to mix matters of fact and opinion.

1.2 The Judicial Committee of the Academy has commented that the hallmarks of a good report include:

(a) A stand-alone, concise, user-friendly format, expressed in the first person singular by the person whose opinion has been given or who adopts as his own the opinion of others.
(b) Text which is arranged in short sentences and paragraphs.
(c) Judicious use of appendices
(d) Matters of fact being kept separate from matters of opinion. Conclusions should be given in the final section of the report before appendices. They should be cross referenced to the text which supports the Conclusions.

1.3 Each opinion expressed in the report must be the opinion of the writer whether it was formed by the writer or formed by others and adopted by the writer as his own.

1.4 The following must be identified separately and distinguished:

(a) facts which the writer is asked to assume;
(b) facts which the writer observed for himself eg the results of experiments, investigations, etc, carried out by the writer himself;
(c) facts which others, acting on behalf of the writer, observed, identifying the persons concerned;
(d) opinions of others upon which the writer relies in forming his own opinion.

1.5 The model form of report has been developed with these comments in mind and with the aim of assisting both experts and those instructing to address the relevant issues in the most direct way. The model is intended as a guideline only. There may be valid reasons for departing from it and/or introducing additional sections.

2. The scheme of the model form of report

The Model Form is written in 5 distinct sections with suggested headings: notes are given.

The Front Sheet – the *first visible sheet* should contain the items of keypoint information indicated by the model and should not be obscured by a cover. The first report prepared for disclosure should be entitled 'Report' and not 'First Report'.

The Contents Page – may be omitted altogether in the case of a short report of say seven pages or less.

Section 1 Introduction – deals with all the formal matters and chronology. The text is largely standard. Most of the material is transferred to appendices.

Section 2 The Background to the Dispute and the Issues

This section of the report will normally include:

(a) a list of the people who will be referred to in the report with a short uncontroversial description of their role.
(b) the assumed or given factual background of the case.
(c) the issues, set out clearly and numbered, which the expert will address.

No opinion is expressed in this section.

Section 3 Description of the Technical Investigation or Enquiry – this section is, again, factual only. The description should be given in itemised paragraphs with sub-headings.

Section 4 The Facts on which the Expert's Opinion is based – distinguishing those facts which he was told from those he observed for himself.

Section 5 The Expert's Conclusions – with opinion and reasons in full on each issue in turn, set out clearly and numbered. In this section, there should only be such repetition of fact as is necessary for the exposition of the opinion.

Signing Block – the report must be signed by the writer and dated at the end of the Conclusions.

Appendices – each Appendix should be provided with a front sheet of the type indicated in the model.

Headers – each continuation page of a section should be provided with a header on the left hand side showing the number and short title of the section and a header at the right hand side with the information suggested by the model.

Presentation – the practice is growing of the Court directing that a copy of experts' reports be made available on disc to the judge or official referee. Where practicable, therefore, reports should be typed in double spacing and prepared on or readily transferable to Wordperfect 5.1. The report should be presented on A4 paper, already hole punched for use in a standard lever arch binder and in a format that can be copied readily on a photocopier with automatic feed.

3. Evaluation of the expert witness

The following passage taken from the dicta of Stuart-Smith LJ in **Loveday v Renton [1990]** 1 Med LR 177 at 125 provides a clear description of the processes which the Court has to undertake in order to evaluate the Expert witness, the soundness of his opinion and the weight to be attached to it.

> '. . . This involves an examination of the reasons given for his opinions and the extent to which they are supported by the evidence. The Judge also has to decide what weight to attach to a witness's opinion by examining the internal consistency and logic of his evidence; the care with which he has considered the subject and presented his evidence; his precision and accuracy of thought as demonstrated by his answers; how he responds to searching and informed cross-examination and in particular the extent to which a witness faces up to and accepts the logic of a proposition put in cross-examination or is prepared to concede points that are seen to be correct; the extent to which a witness has conceived an opinion and is reluctant to re-examine it in the light of later evidence, or demonstrates a flexibility of mind which may involve changing or modifying opinions previously held; whether or not a witness is biased or lacks independence . . .'

[SHORT TITLE OF ACTION]

[DRAFT]

REPORT OF

[EXPERT'S NAME]

DATED

[ ]

Specialist Field	:	[State title of specialism]
Assisted By	:	[State names of assistants]
On behalf of	:	[State party's name]
On instructions of	:	[State name and business of those instructing)
Subject Matter	:	[State briefly the nature of the dispute and the date when it arose]
Inspection Date(s)	:	[Give the dates or period of all inspections]

[Name Address and Occupation of the writer's
Firm (if any) and telephone, fax, DX and reference]

(1.00 Introduction)

Report of :
Specialist Field :
On behalf of :

CONTENTS

[Change or omit as appropriate]

(1.00 Introduction)

Report of :
Specialist Field :
On behalf of :

REPORT

1.00 INTRODUCTION

1.01 Formal Details

[Note 1 – state (as applicable) your full name. Give your status (eg., partner of), the name of your firm, the nature of its business and its address.]

[Note 2 – state your own specialist field; there is provision later on for you to deal with qualifications, experience etc.]

[Note 3 – state on behalf of whom you were instructed and the name, address and business of those instructing you.]

1.02 Synopsis

[Note 1 – Set out concisely the general nature of the dispute eg. 'In this case, Ambridge Cricket Club alleges faulty design and erection of a new cricket pavilion. The main areas of complaint relate to the roof and verandah. I am advising the engineers. There are also complaints against the architects.]

1.03 Instructions

[Note 1 – State briefly what you have been asked to do eg. 'to identify the issues within my specialist field that arise in this case, to make a technical investigation and to express my opinion with full reasons on each issue'.]

1.04 Disclosure of Interests

[Note 1 – State any actual or potential conflict of interests that you may have, for example a connection with any of the parties or witnesses or advisers which might be thought to influence the opinions expressed in the report.]

[Note 2 – State (if it is so) that you have no such connection with any of the parties, witnesses or advisers involved in the case.]

1.05 **Appendix 1** – contains details of my experience, qualifications, appointments and specialist field(s) [together with those of ( ) who has/have assisted me in (state the areas of assistance).]

[Note 1 – every person who has been involved in the investigation or enquiry and who has formed opinions on which the writer of the report is relying must be identified here and their details provided at Appendix 1.]

1.06 **Appendix 2** – contains a list of some of the documents I have considered together with copies of only those documents which I regard as essential for the understanding of my report.

[Note 1 – every effort should be made to limit the number of documents which are added to the report.]

[Note 2 – where documents are bulky they should be listed shortly by reference to bundles and not individually.]

1.07 **Appendix 3** – contains a list of the texts and published material to which I have referred in this report. I have included some copies or extracts for ease of reference.

1.08 **Appendix 4** – contains a list and copies of the [photographs, drawings, laboratory reports, schedules etc.] which [name of assistant and/or] I have prepared for the purposes of this report.

1.09 **Appendix 5** – contains [a full chronology].

1.10 **Appendix 6** – contains [etc. as/if applicable].

(<u>2.00</u> <u>Background / Issues</u>)

Report of :
Specialist Field :
On behalf of :

2.00 THE BACKGROUND TO THE DISPUTE AND THE ISSUES

2.01 The Relevant Parties

[Note 1 – set out briefly in short itemised paragraphs the names of those to whom you will refer in this report, together with a short, uncontroversial statement of their role in the relevant events.]

[Note 2 – Please avoid acronyms. For example, the firm name Smith Jones Brown & Co Limited may better be shortened to 'Smith' than 'SJBCL'.]

2.02 The Assumed Facts

[Note 1 – set out in short itemised paragraphs a background narrative of the facts you have been asked to assume.]

[Note 2 – bear in mind that a full chronology, if appropriate, will be provided at Appendix 5.]

2.03 The Issues to be addressed

[Note 1 – identify, in short itemised paragraphs, each of the allegations and issues that you will, in turn, address. Say where in the case papers it arises and which party has raised it.]

[Note 2 – where practicable, keep the list of issues raised by one party separate from those raised by any other party.]

[Note 3 – this part of the report is factual only; no opinion should be expressed here.]

(3.00 Investigation)

Report of :
Specialist Field :
On behalf of :

3.00 THE TECHNICAL INVESTIGATION [ENQUIRY]

[Note 1 – give in short itemised paragraphs the date(s), and time(s) of day you attended to investigate the factual position. State where you went, what you saw and did and who assisted you, who else was present and what you found.]

[Note 2 – it is desirable to avoid reporting second or third hand hearsay; this is not, however, an inflexible rule. There may be occasions when reliable hearsay should be reported. State in each case the name of the person who relayed the hearsay.]

[Note 3 – experiments, detailed surveys, measurements, audits etc. should be briefly described. The full report should appear as an Appendix.]

[Note 4 – this section of the report is factual only; no opinion should be expressed.]

(4.00 Factual Basis)

Report of :
Specialist Field :
On behalf of :

4.00 THE FACTS ON WHICH THE EXPERT'S OPINION IS BASED

[Note 1 – Identify separately and distinguish between:

a) Facts which the writer has been asked to assume;
b) Facts which the writer observed for himself eg. the results of experiments, investigations etc. carried out by the writer himself;
c) Facts which others, acting on behalf of the writer, observed (and identify the persons concerned);
d) The opinions of others upon which the writer relies in forming his own opinion.]

[Note 2 – refer as convenient to any rules, regulations or other documentary guidance which you consider to be relevant. Where essential, these should be copied at Appendix 3.]

(5.00 Conclusions)

Report of :
Specialist Field :
On behalf of :

5.00 CONCLUSIONS

5.01 [Set out the first issue and your opinion on that issue with reasons in full.]

[Note 1 – if practicable provide a sub-heading for each of the issues.]

[Note 2 – provide cross references to the text or any published material which supports the Conclusions.]

[Note 3 – only refer to matters of fact so far as may be necessary to the understanding of the opinion.]

5.02 [Continue to set out each issue in turn with opinion and full reasons following the notes given above.]

Signature...

Name in full......................................Date ....

Report of :
Specialist Field :
On behalf of :

APPENDIX 1

CONTENTS

1. [ ]

2. [ ]

3. [ ]

4. [ ]

Appendix 2
Academy of Experts model terms of engagement

Introduction

1. An Expert enters into a contractual relationship to provide services for a fee to his/her Appointor. In any such contract it is important that both sides are aware of the responsibilities that they have. Though there will be similarities between appointments each case is a unique appointment.

2. It is important therefore that the responsibilities of each party are clearly set out in a letter of engagement. This letter of engagement should be drafted by the Expert and should be acknowledged by a signature from the Appointor to indicate their approval of the terms.

3. The drafting of such a letter is in itself a worthwhile exercise as it assists in the planning of the assignment. It makes the expert focus on the responsibilities of the parties involved. It also clearly defines the position as to costs. If there are additional costs incurred because the Appointor has not performed as originally set out in the terms of engagement then the engagement letter will assist in recovering such costs.

4. Each letter of engagement will be unique and must be tailored to the individual matter in which the Expert is instructed. The Model Terms of Engagement are intended to provide assistance to members of the Academy in drafting their letters of engagement. It is not envisaged that all of the paragraphs within the Model Terms of Engagement necessarily be included in each and every letter of engagement. Members should be selective in taking paragraphs or parts of paragraphs and use them in their tailored letters of engagement. For example, paragraph 5. refers to the rights of ownership over certain items. In some instances this will not apply and so there will be no need for such a clause to be inserted in any letter of engagement.

5. Without a formal letter of engagement it is difficult to prove fees which may be in dispute. A formal letter of engagement can resolve situations as regards such fees and costs.

Model terms of engagement for the employment of experts on behalf of a party involved in a dispute before any court of law or at arbitration or any other tribunal

1.0 Recital of Appointment – The Appointor has appointed the Expert to provide advice and services in accordance with these Terms of Engagement.

2.0 Definitions – Unless the context otherwise requires:

2.1 **'The Appointor'** means the lawyer, insurer, Government department, local authority, firm, or other body or persons instructing the Expert.

2.2 **'The Expert'** means the person appointed hereunder to render expert advice and services, including the giving of evidence, but not formal advocacy.

2.3 **'The Client'** means the person(s), Government department, local authority, firm or company to whom the Expert has been instructed to provide such advice and services

2.4 **'Fees'** means (in the absence of written agreement to the contrary) the reasonable charges of the Expert based on the Expert's normal hourly rate for work of the type instructed. A daily rate shall be applied to any day or part of any day of a hearing, including preparatory work and waiting time. Unless otherwise agreed, time spent travelling may be charged at the full hourly rate. Value Added Tax or the equivalent tax will be charged where applicable.

2.5 **'Disbursements'** means all reasonable expenses necessarily incurred in rendering expert advice and services, including the giving of evidence. By way of example, they include the costs of relevant photography, video recordings, computer software, reproduction of drawings and diagrams, printing and duplicating, the cost of obtaining published documents including those withdrawn, as well as all appropriate out of pocket expenses including car mileage, first class rail travel, business class air fares, reasonable refreshments and four star hotel accommodation where an overnight stay is necessary. Value Added Tax or the equivalent tax will be charged where applicable.

2.6 **References** to the masculine gender shall be deemed to include the feminine.

3.0 The Appointor – The Appointor will:

3.1 Provide full instructions in writing supported by legible copies of all relevant documents.

3.2 Deal promptly with every reasonable request by the Expert for authority, information and documents.

3.3 Not alter or permit others to alter the reports of the Expert.

3.4 Ascertain the availability of the Expert for every hearing, meeting or other appointment at which the Expert's attendance will or may be required and give the Expert immediate written notification together with adequate notice.

3.5 **In Legal Aid cases:**

(a) inform the Expert at the outset if the case is or is expected to be legally aided;

(b) provide the Expert with sufficient details of the case and promptly answer any queries that will enable the Expert to prepare any requited estimate of charges;

(c) not require the Expert to provide any services before the grant of authority by the Legal Aid Board for his fees and disbursements;

(d) apply to the Legal Aid Board for prior approval of the Expert's anticipated fees and promptly inform the Expert accurately of the outcome of the application;

(e) apply as above for additional fees required by any further work not originally authorised;

(f) make timely application to the Legal Aid Board or to the Court for interim and final payments for the Expert's fees and disbursements as invoiced and promptly remit to the Expert all such payments upon receipt;

(g) use his best endeavours to ensure that the Expert's fees and disbursements are recovered in full by way of the Legal Aid Fund and in the case of the Crown Court from the Lord Chancellor's Department;

(h) so advise the Expert if he is a Legal Aid Franchisee with devolved powers in the relevant category of work and ensure prompt remittance of interim and final payments as invoiced;

(i) use his best endeavours to ensure that the Expert's fees and disbursements are promptly remitted in full in the event of termination or suspension of a Franchise Agreement or of a Legal Aid Certificate. Where a taxation of costs is necessary it will be applied for, pursued or defended (as applicable) in a timely manner.

3.6 In privately funded cases ensure that he is at all times in funds to discharge and promptly discharge the fees and disbursements of the Expert.

3.7 Unless otherwise agreed, pay in full the Expert's fees and disbursements irrespective of the outcome of any taxation of costs.

4.0 The Expert – The Expert will:

4.1 Undertake only those parts of a case in respect of which the Expert considers that he has adequate qualifications and experience.

4.2 Use reasonable skill and care in the performance of the instructions received.

4.3 Act with objectivity and independence with regard to his instructions and, in the event of a conflict between his duties to the Client and to the Court or Tribunal, will hold his duties to the Court or Tribunal paramount.

4.4 Promptly notify the Appointor of any matter including a conflict of interest or lack of suitable qualifications and experience which could disqualify the Expert or render it undesirable for him to have continued involvement in the case.

4.5 Endeavour to make himself available for all hearings, meetings and other appointments of which he has received adequate written notice.

4.6 Not without good cause discharge himself from the appointment as Expert.

4.7 Preserve confidentiality save as expressly or by necessary implication authorised to the contrary.

4.8 Not negotiate with an opposing party or adviser unless specifically instructed by the Appointor so to do. For avoidance of doubt this clause does not apply to any Order of a Court or Tribunal.

4.9 Attend such Meetings of Experts as Ordered by the Court or Tribunal or as required by the Appointor. At any such Meeting adhere strictly to the terms of reference set down in writing.

4.10 Provide all relevant information to allow the Appointor to defend the Expert's fees or disbursements at any taxation of costs.

4.11 Promptly respond to any complaint of the Appointor and within a reasonable time provide a statement of explanation or a means of rectification.

5.0 Intellectual Property Rights – The intellectual property rights of all original work created by the Expert shall remain vested in the Expert unless otherwise agreed in writing. The Expert asserts all his Moral Rights.

6.0 Fees and Disbursements

6.1 The Expert may present invoices at such intervals as he considers fit. Payment of each invoice is due on presentation, subject to any written waiver or indulgence granted by the Expert.

Note: The Judicial Committee's Guidelines make a) payment upon a contingency fee basis unacceptable and b) the placing of pressure upon the Expert by the Appointor to provide extended credit terms or any other arrangement for inclusion in the Appointor's approved list of Experts improper, as they compromise the Expert's independence and impartiality.

6.2 For the avoidance of doubt, in the following circumstances the Expert shall be entitled to charge fees on such basis as he considers appropriate:

(a) where the Expert's time has been reserved by subpoena or otherwise for a specific hearing, meeting or other engagement, or

(b) where specific instructions have been given to the Expert for an inspection/examination and report,

and where, due to settlement of the dispute or any other reason not being the default of the Expert, the reservation of time has been cancelled and/or instructions have been withdrawn.

6.3 The Appointor and the Client shall be jointly and severally liable for payment of the Expert's fees and disbursements.

6.4 The Expert shall at his discretion be entitled to invoice and recover interest at 1.5% per month on all unpaid invoices after 30 days. The full amount of his administrative, legal and other costs of recovering unpaid invoices is chargeable.

7.0 Disputes

7.1 In the event of a dispute over the amount of the Expert's fees such sum as is not disputed shall be paid forthwith irrespective of any set off or counter-claim which may be alleged.

7.2 Any dispute arising between the Appointor or the Client and the Expert shall be referred to Mediation in accordance with The Academy of Experts' Mediation Guidelines. Upon the application of any party the Faculty of Mediation of The Academy of Experts will appoint a Mediator.

7.3 Any dispute or difference not resolved by Mediation as in 2 above within 30 days of the appointment of the Mediator shall be referred to a single arbitrator who, if not agreed upon by the parties within 14 days thereafter, shall be appointed upon the application of either party by the President of the Chartered Institute of Arbitrators.

Appendix 3
Academy of Experts code of practice

Code of practice

1. Experts shall not do anything in the course of practising as an Expert, in any manner which compromises or impairs or is likely to compromise or impair any of the following:

   (a) the Expert's independence or integrity;
   (b) a person's freedom to instruct any Expert of his or her choice;
   (c) the Expert's duty to act in the best interests of the client;
   (d) the good repute of the Expert or of Experts generally;
   (e) the Expert's proper standard of work;
   (f) the Expert's duty to the Court.

2. An Expert who is retained or employed in any action, suit or other contentious proceeding shall not enter into any arrangement to receive a contingency fee in respect of that proceeding.

3. An Expert should not accept instructions in any matter where there is an actual or potential conflict of interests. Notwithstanding this rule if full disclosure is made in writing the Expert may in appropriate cases accept instructions when the client specifically acknowledges the disclosure.

4. An Expert shall for the protection of his clients maintain with a reputable insurer proper insurances for an adequate indemnity.

5. Experts shall not publicise their practices in any manner which may reasonably be regarded as being in bad taste. Publicity must not be inaccurate or misleading in any way.

6. The Academy's plaque may only be used on firm's stationery when all Principals of that firm are Members of the Academy. Individual members, who are also members of a firm or company may use the Academy plaque on their personal stationery provided no references to the firm or company is made.

Appendix 4
Academy of Experts guidance notes on contingency fees

Guidance note on contingency fees issued by the Judicial Committee

The Rt Hon The Lord Slynn of Hadley PC, The Rt Hon Lord Justice Neill, The Rt Hon Lord Justice Saville, The Rt Hon Lord Justice MacDermott, The Hon Lord Johnson, The Hon Mr Justice Garland, His Honour Judge Bowsher QC.

It has come to Judicial Committee's attention that there is increasing pressure for Expert Witnesses involved in litigation to be paid on a contingency fee basis. This causes the Judicial Committee concern.

It is clearly established law that Expert Witnesses in adversarial proceedings must give the court, or tribunal, their independent, objective and unbiased opinions on the aspects of the case that come within their expertise. The Expert Witness is not an advocate employed on behalf of a party.

An Expert Witness' written report and oral evidence must genuinely reflect his independent opinion. An Expert must not mislead a court or tribunal by placing undue emphasis on points that favour his client, whilst omitting or understating legitimate points that he believes go against his client.

The Judicial Committee considers that any form of contingency fee arrangement for Expert Witnesses is incompatible with the Experts' duty of independence and impartiality. A contingency fee means that the Expert Witness has a direct financial interest in the outcome of the case. Such a direct financial interest must increase the pressures on Expert Witnesses to give evidence that favours their client. Even if an Expert Witness resists this pressure, his independence may still be compromised. An Expert Witness must not only be independent, but must be seen to be independent.

The Judicial Committee considers that a contingency fee arrangement, in this context, is any arrangement that leads to the Expert Witness having a financial interest in the outcome of the particular case. Examples of such an agreement include:

- an agreement that the Expert Witness will be paid a percentage of any damages recovered by his client;

- an agreement that the Expert witness will be paid a basic fee together with a bonus if his client wins; and
- an agreement that the Expert Witness will be paid a percentage of his fee in advance, but will not bill the client for the rest of the fee if the client loses.

The Judicial Committee also understands that solicitors sometimes place undue pressure on Expert Witnesses. For example, there are instances when a solicitor has indicated to an Expert that if he agrees to the solicitor's terms, he will be placed on the firm's approved list of Experts. The clear implication being that the Expert will then receive further referral work from the solicitor. The Judicial Committee considers that this practice is objectionable and does compromise the Expert's independence and impartiality. If an Expert feels that a solicitor has attempted to exert improper pressure on him or her, the Expert should report the matter to the Academy.

Council at its meeting on 14th June, 1995 adopted the Guidelines.

Appendix 5
ICAEW statement 1.204

Conflicts of Interest

(Revised 1 September 1997)

This Statement applies only to practising members, affiliates and where appropriate, employees of practising firms.

Introductory note

1.0 This Statement deals with two types of conflicts of interest: conflicts between the interests of a firm and a client, and conflicting interests of different clients. (Members' attention is drawn to **1.203**, 'Corporate Finance Advice' for the particular circumstances arising from certain Corporate Finance activities.)

Situations frequently arise which are perceived by the clients to be a conflict of interest but which, in reality, are no more than concerns about confidentiality of information which is a separate issue: members are referred to **1.205**, 'Confidentiality'.

Firms should have in place procedures to enable them to identify whether any conflicts exist and to take all reasonable steps to determine whether any conflicts are likely to arise in regard to new assignments and to existing clients.

Firms should consider recording the safeguards adopted to address any conflicts which have been identified.

[For general guidance on the application of safeguards to threats members are referred to **1.201** 'Integrity, Objectivity and Independence'.]

(In cases of Investment Business advice please refer to Chapter 3 of the Investment Business Regulations.)

Section A – Conflict between a firm's interests and those of its client

2.0 A self-interest threat to a firm's objectivity will arise where there is or is likely to be a conflict of interest between a firm and its client.

2.1 A test is whether the perception of a reasonable observer at the time would be that the objectivity of the firm is likely to be impaired. The firm should be able to satisfy itself and its client that any conflict can be managed with appropriate safeguards.

Safeguards

2.2 Safeguards will include:

(a) disclosure of the circumstances of the conflict;
(b) advising the client that, in the particular circumstances, he may wish to seek alternative independent advice;
(c) obtaining the informed consent of the client to act.

Disengagement

2.3 Where effective safeguards are not available the firm should refuse or discontinue the particular assignment.

2.4 In such circumstances disengagement should take place as speedily as possible.

Conflicts of interest arising from receipt of commission or other benefits from a third party

3.0 A self-interest threat will arise where any benefit is or is likely to be received by a firm, or anyone in it, or by an associate of the firm, from a third party for the introduction of a client or as a result of advice given to a client.

Safeguards

3.1 Safeguards will include:

(a) disclosure of a commission or other benefit

Where a member becomes aware that any commission, fee or other benefit may be received by the firm or anyone in it or by an associate of the firm for the introduction of a client to a third party, or as a result of advice given to a client, the firm should disclose to the client in writing:

(i) that commission or benefit will result or is likely to result, and
(ii) when the fact is known, that such commission or benefit will be received, and
(iii) as early as possible, its amount and terms.

(b) disclosure of an association

In making any recommendation for the use of the services of a third party, any relevant connection between that third party and the firm should be disclosed to the client.

(c) obtaining the informed consent of the client to act

Members are reminded that where a fiduciary relationship exists at the time between a member and a client, the member is legally bound to account to the client for any commission, fee or other benefit received from a third party. The Institute is advised that the effect is that a member will require the informed consent of the client if the member is to retain the commission, fee or other benefit or any part of it. If members are in doubt as to whether the circumstances give rise to a fiduciary relationship, they are recommended to seek appropriate legal advice.

(More information as to the legal considerations involved is given in Section **1.314**, 'Accounting for commission'.)

Section B – conflicting interests of different clients

4.0 A self-interest threat will arise or be seen to arise where the interests of two or more clients are in conflict.

4.1 There is, however, nothing improper in a firm having two clients whose interests are in conflict with each other.

4.2 In such a case the activities of the firm should be so managed as to avoid the work of the firm on behalf of one client adversely affecting that on behalf of another.

4.3 Where a firm believes that the situation may be managed, sufficient disclosure (see paragraph 4.6 below) should be made to the clients or potential clients concerned together with details of any proposed safeguards to preserve confidentiality and manage conflict.

Safeguards

4.4 Safeguards should include:

(a) the use of different partners and teams of staff for different engagements, each having separate internal reporting lines;
(b) standing instructions and all other steps necessary to prevent the transfer of confidential information between different teams and sections within the firm;

(c) regular review of the situation by a senior partner or compliance partner not personally involved with either client;
(d) advising all the relevant clients that, in the particular circumstances, they may wish to seek alternative independent advice; and
(e) obtaining informed consent to act from all the clients concerned.

Disengagement

4.5 Where the acceptance or continuance of an engagement would, even with safeguards, prejudice the interests of any of the clients involved, the engagement should not be accepted or continued, or one of the assignments should be discontinued.

4.6 Where adequate disclosure (see paragraph 4.3 above) is not possible by reason of constraints of confidentiality the firm should disengage from the relevant assignment/s.

4.7 In such circumstances disengagement should take place as speedily as possible.

Sole practitioners and small firms

4.8 Any decision on the part of a sole practitioner should take account of the fact that the safeguards at (a) to (c) of paragraph 4.4 above will not be available to him or her. Similar considerations could apply to a small firm where the number of partners is insufficient to spread the work as indicated in 4.4 (a) and (c) above. (Members are referred to paragraph 3.7 of Statement **1.201**, 'Integrity, Objectivity and Independence' with regard to possible consultation procedures available to members.)

Appendix 6
Two standard letters of engagement

Private and Confidential

FAO Mr Smith [Date]
ABC Solicitors
1 New Town [Our ref]
Somewhere

Dear John

Case name

Further to your recent telephone conversation this letter sets forth our arrangements for the litigation support services to be provided to you in connection with

[May include a section outlining our understanding of the case]

Phase I

1 [Details of the work to be performed, may be more than one phase to the assignment]

Phase II

2 We will prepare a report in a form suitable for introduction to the Court setting out details of our findings.

Phase III

3 We will be available to provide expert testimony or other assistance at the trial stage, if required, with regard to our findings.

Fees

4 The charges for this type of work, like those of most accountants, are based upon time spent on the matter by our Partners and Staff. We will allocate, as far as it is practicable to do so, tasks to Partners or Staff at an appropriate level having regard to:

- The skill, specialised knowledge and responsibility required of the staff handling the matter.
- The complexities and the difficulty or novelty of the questions involved in the matter.
- The place and circumstances in which the business involved is transacted, for example, if special expedition is required or if an unusual amount of documentation needs to be considered.

5 Each individual, including the Partners, has an hourly charge-out rate being the selling price of an hour of his or her time. Specific hourly rates for differing levels of our personnel are as follows:

Partner	[ ]
Manager	[ ]
Assistant Manager	[ ]
Supervisor	[ ]
Senior	[ ]
Staff	[ ]

6 The above rates are the rates prevailing at the date of this letter. It is practice to review our rates regularly and the rates quoted are subject to increase following such reviews. For the purpose of charging time to this assignment the rates prevailing at the time the work was carried out will be the rates used in calculating our fees.

7 As well as this firm's charges, disbursements such as Counsel's fees if incurred, travelling expenses and overnight accommodation will be added to the bill, as will VAT where appropriate.

8 We estimate that the cost of carrying out Phase I of the assignment, excluding disbursements and VAT, will be £[ ].

9 Please note that the basis of charging fees is not contingent upon the outcome of any action in the Courts or the question of any values or damages relating to the action.

10 Litigation can be a protracted business, sometimes taking months to conclude, and our staff and overhead costs involved in financing a client's litigation affairs become prohibitive. Consequently, it is our standard practice to render regular interim bills where appropriate. We find this system assists both our clients, in spreading the costs more smoothly

over the period involved, and us, in ensuring that we cover our overheads on a consistent basis.

11 The Courts usually make an award of costs in favour of the successful party in litigation. However, you should note that costs so awarded are based on Court scales consistent with the circumstances of the case, which will not necessarily be the same amount as the firm's charges.

Complaints

12 If at any time you would like to discuss with us how our service to you could be improved, or if you are dissatisfied with any aspect of the service you are receiving, please let us know by contacting myself or the firm's senior partner.

We undertake to look into any complaint carefully and promptly. In the event that you are not satisfied with the resolution of any complaint you may raise with us, then you have the right to report the matter to the Institute of Chartered Accountants in England and Wales.

Agreement in Terms

13 In the event of any dispute arising in respect of or relating to the services to be provided in accordance with this letter or any additional services to be provided by us, such dispute shall be determined by the exclusive jurisdiction of the English Courts.

We shall be grateful if you will confirm in writing your agreement to the terms of this letter. Once it has been agreed, the letter will remain effective until it is replaced.

Please let us know if there is anything else with which we can assist at this stage or anything we can explain further whether in relation to what we have said in this letter or otherwise.

If this letter correctly expresses your understanding of the basis of our engagement please indicate your agreement by signing the enclosed copy of this letter and returning it to us as authorisation to proceed with Phases I and II of this engagement.

Yours sincerely

XYZ Accountants

Accepted by:

Date:

Private and Confidential

FAO Mr Smith [Date]
ABC Solicitors
1 New Town [Our ref]
Somewhere

Dear John

Case name

Further to your recent telephone conversation, this letter sets forth our arrangements for the litigation support services to be provided to you in connection with

[May include a section outlining our understanding of the case]

We understand that you require a quotation for submission to the Legal Aid Board for preparing a report on whether assessing [the loss and damages, if any, suffered by the Plaintiff as a result of the Defendant's alleged negligence].

Phase I

1 [Details of the work to be performed, may be more than one phase to the assignment]

Phase II

2 We will prepare a report in a form suitable for introduction to the Court setting out details of our findings.

Phase III

3 We will be available to provide expert testimony or other assistance at the trial stage, if required, with regard to our findings.

Fees

4 The charges for this type of work, like those of most accountants, are based upon time spent on the matter by our Partners and Staff. We will allocate, as far as it is practicable to do so, tasks to Partners or Staff at an appropriate level having regard to:

- The skill, specialised knowledge and responsibility required of the staff handling the matter.

- The complexities and the difficulty or novelty of the questions involved in the matter.
- The place and circumstances in which the business involved is transacted, for example, if special expedition is required or if an unusual amount of documentation needs to be considered.

5 Each individual, including the Partners, has an hourly charge-out rate being the selling price of an hour of his or her time. Specific hourly rates for differing levels of our personnel are as follows:

Partner	[ ]
Manager	[ ]
Assistant Manager	[ ]
Supervisor	[ ]
Senior	[ ]
Staff	[ ]

6 The above rates are the rates prevailing at the date of this letter. It is practice to review our rates regularly and the rates quoted are subject to increase following such reviews. For the purpose of charging time to this assignment the rates prevailing at the time the work was carried out will be the rates used in calculating our fees.

7 As well as this firm's charges, disbursements such as Counsel's fees if incurred, travelling expenses and overnight accommodation will be added to the bill, as will VAT where appropriate.

8 We estimate that the cost of carrying out Phase I of the assignment, excluding disbursements and VAT, will be £[ ].

9 Please note that the basis of charging fees is not contingent upon the outcome of any action in the Courts or the question of any values or damages relating to the action.

10 [You will need to give a detailed breakdown of the estimated fees and include the following paragraph below the analysis.]

11 We understand that the [Plaintiff/Defendant] is legally aided. We will not commence any work on this matter until you have received prior authorisation from the Legal Aid Board for costs plus VAT.

12 Litigation can be a protracted business, sometimes taking months to conclude, and our staff and overhead costs involved in financing a client's litigation affairs become prohibitive. Consequently, it is our standard practice to render regular interim bills where appropriate. We find this system assists both our clients, in spreading the costs more smoothly over the period involved, and us, in ensuring that we cover our overheads on a consistent basis.

13 The Courts usually make an award of costs in favour of the successful party in litigation. However, you should note that costs so awarded are based on Court scales consistent with the circumstances of the case, which will not necessarily be the same amount as the firm's charges.

Complaints

14 If at any time you would like to discuss with us how our service to you could be improved, or if you are dissatisfied with any aspect of the service you are receiving, please let us know by contacting myself or the firm's senior partner.

We undertake to look into any complaint carefully and promptly. In the event that you are not satisfied with the resolution of any complaint you may raise with us, then you have the right to report the matter to the Institute of Chartered Accountants in England and Wales.

Agreement in Terms

15 In the event of any dispute arising in respect of or relating to the services to be provided in accordance with this letter or any additional services to be provided by us, dispute shall be determined by the exclusive jurisdiction of the English Courts.

We shall be grateful if you will confirm in writing your agreement to the terms of this letter. Once it has been agreed, the letter will remain effective until it is replaced.

Please let us know if there is anything else with which we can assist at this stage or anything we can explain further whether in relation to what we have said in this letter or otherwise.

If this letter correctly expresses your understanding of the basis of our engagement, please forward to the Legal Aid Board for prior authority in respect of our fees. Once authority has been obtained please notify us, indicate your agreement by signing the enclosed copy of this letter and returning it to us as authorisation to proceed with Phases I and II of this engagement and a copy of the authorisation.

Yours sincerely

XYZ Accountants

Accepted by:

Date:

Appendix 7
Legal Aid Board forms CLA 31 and APP 6

Appendix 7
Legal Aid Board forms CLA 31 and APP 6

PAGE 1

Application for prior authority

(Civil Legal Aid Certificates, Including Magistrates' Court Proceedings)

CLA 31

LEGAL AID BOARD LEGAL AID ACT 1988

If the authority is required urgently, please write "URGENT" in this box [ ]

Hearing date: ____ / ____ / ____

You can use this form for up to 2 applications for authority under the same reference.

Assisted person's details

Legal aid reference: ____________________

Assisted person's full name: ____________________

Current address: ____________________

____________________ Postcode: ____________

Solicitor's details

Name of firm & address or DX: ____________________

____________________ Postcode: ____________

Ref: ____________ Tel No: ____________

1. I request the following: *(tick one box)*

☐ Authority Regulation 59 (Counsel) (c26) or ☐ Authority Regulation 61 (Expert etc) (c27)

Wording suggested:

(including in relation to counsel the combination you are seeking e.g. leader alone, leader plus junior, two counsel; and whether you are seeking authority to brief or to instruct - see the Notes for Guidance in the current Legal Aid Handbook)

Reason for request:

(Continue on page 2 and on a separate sheet if necessary. You must submit any relevant documents, e.g. written estimates (if available))

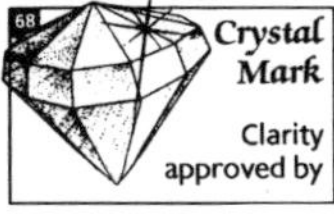

Please complete the following pages

PAGE 2

Reason for request: *(continued from page 1)*

(Continue on a separate sheet if necessary. You must submit any relevant documents, e.g. written estimates (if available)

Have previous applications for authority been made which are the same as or similar to this one?

☐ Yes ☐ No

If yes, give the date of authority or refusal: ______ / ______ / ______

If there are Children Act proceedings where leave of court is required, has leave been obtained?

(If not, your application is likely to be refused) ☐ Yes ☐ No ☐ Not relevant

Has any blood test including DNA tests been directed by the court?

☐ Yes ☐ No

If not, have both parties agreed to be bound by the result?

☐ Yes ☐ No

Total authority *(before apportionment if appropriate)* £ ______________

Maximum authority you are seeking £ ______________

(after apportionment,by this we mean e.g. the net cost of an expert's report shared with other parties, if appropriate)

Hourly rates on which the maximum is based £ ______________ /hour (preparation)

£ ______________ /hour (travel)

Travel expenses *(if relevant)* £ ______________

and daily rate *(if expert to give evidence)* £ ______________ /day

Type or status of expert: ______________

Name and address of expert: ______________

____

______________ Postcode: ______________

Have alternative quotes been obtained? ☐ Yes ☐ No

If 'yes', what were the amounts quoted? ______________

If 'no', state why not ______________

Please complete the following for non-matrimonial or non-family cases only

Please provide a current estimate of your final costs, including disbursements and counsel's fees. Your estimate will need to take account of your view of likely settlement:

☐ Less than £1,500 ☐ £1,500 - £2,500 ☐ Over £2,500

If 'over £2,500' please give an approximate amount

£ ______________

What is the likely value of the claim? £ ______________

For Area Office use only

Decision date: ______ / ______ / ______ ☐ G 10 Granted ☐ R 10 Refused ☐ RF 1 Referred

Document type and standard wordings required:

Reason for referral:

Initials:

Please complete the following page if applying for a second authority, or sign page 4.

PAGE 3

2. I also request the following: *(tick one box)*

☐ Authority Regulation 59 (Counsel) (c26) or ☐ Authority Regulation 61 (Expert etc) (c27)

Wording suggested:

(including in relation to counsel the combination you are seeking e.g. leader alone, leader plus junior, two counsel; and whether you are seeking authority to brief or to instruct - see the Notes for Guidance in the current Legal Aid Handbook)

Reason for request:

(Continue on a separate sheet if necessary. You must submit any relevant documents, e.g. written estimates (if available))

Please complete the following page

PAGE 4

Have previous applications for authority been made which are the same as or similar to this one?

☐ Yes ☐ No

If yes, give the date of authority or refusal: ______/______/______

If there are Children Act proceedings where leave of court is required, has leave been obtained?

(If not, your application is likely to be refused) ☐ Yes ☐ No ☐ Not relevant

Has any blood test including DNA tests been directed by the court?

☐ Yes ☐ No

If not, have both parties agreed to be bound by the result?

☐ Yes ☐ No

Total authority
(before apportionment if appropriate) £ ______________

Maximum authority you are seeking £ ______________

(after apportionment,by this we mean e.g. the net cost of an expert's report shared with other parties, if appropriate)

Hourly rates on which the maximum is based £ ______________ /hour (preparation)

£ ______________ /hour (travel)

Travel expenses *(if relevant)* £ ______________

and daily rate *(if expert to give evidence)* £ ______________ /day

Type or status of expert: ______________

Name and address of expert: ______________

____

______________ Postcode: ______________

Have alternative quotes been obtained? ☐ Yes ☐ No

If 'yes', what were the amounts quoted? ______________

If 'no', state why not ______________

Please complete the following for non-matrimonial or non-family cases only

Please provide a current estimate of your final costs, including disbursements and counsel's fees. Your estimate will need to take account of your view of likely settlement:

☐ Less than £1,500 ☐ £1,500 - £2,500 ☐ Over £2,500

If 'over £2,500' please give an approximate amount

£ ______________

What is the likely value of the claim? £ ______________

For Area Office use only

Decision date: ______/______/______ ☐ G 10 Granted ☐ R 10 Refused ☐ RF 1 Referred

Document type and standard wordings required:

Reason for referral:

Initials:

For the solicitor to complete

I apply for the authority or authorities above. I certify that the nominated solicitor holds a current practising certificate and will not act or delegate the conduct of this matter under the legal aid certificate while not certificated.

Signed by or on behalf of the nominated solicitor: ______________ **Date:** ______/______/______

July 1994

Application for amendment or prior authority in civil cases **APP6**

Please complete in block capitals

Urgent? ☐ If so please explain why on page 3. Devolved power exercised? ☐

Your client's details

Legal aid case reference number: ____________________

Title: __________ Initials: __________ Surname: ____________________

Surname at birth: ____________________ Date of birth: ___/___/___
(if different)

Current acting solicitor's details

Legal aid supplier number: ☐☐☐☐☐☐☐☐ ☐☐☐☐☐☐☐☐

Name of firm: ____________________

Phone: ____________________

Name of acting solicitor: ____________________

➤ *The acting solicitor must have a valid practising certificate. The Board cannot pay for any work done during any period in which the acting solicitor does not have a practising certificate.*

Solicitor's reference: ____________________

Contact name for enquiries: ____________________

Type of application

- ☐ A change to the proceeding(s)
- *☐ A change to the scope limitation
- *☐ A change to the costs condition / limitation
- ☐ A change of solicitor
- ☐ A change to the other party details
- ☐ To correct a mistake
- ☐ Prior authority to incur expenditure
- ☐ Authority to instruct counsel

➤ *Those application types marked * can be granted by a franchisee where the devolved power is available to the franchisee and in accordance with the guidance provided.*

If granted under devolved powers:

Tell us the date you amended the certificate: ___/___/___

If the amendment is to an emergency certificate, tell us the date you granted emergency legal aid to your client: ___/___/___

Tell us the wording code(s) you used and provide a brief description of the amendment and, if applicable, tell us the revised cost limitation:

Page 1

Costs and merits

Which of the following best describes the prospects of achieving the outcome your client wants:

☐ A Very good (80%+) ☐ B Good (60-80%) ☐ C Average (50-60%) ☐ D Below average

Profit costs to date: £ ____________ Disbursements to date: £ ____________

Estimate your likely financial costs, assuming the case goes to trial, including disbursements.

☐ Less than £1,500 ☐ £1,500 - £2,500 ☐ £2,500 - £5,000

☐ £5,000 - £7,500 ☐ £7,500 - £10,000 ☐ Over £10,000

If over £10,000 please give an approximate amount: £ ________:____

Likely value of claim: £ ____________

If the matter does not have a monetary value what are the issues currently at stake?

If the other party has been granted legal aid, what is the legal aid case reference number?

Are you still satisfied that the other party has the means to pay and, if so, why?

If you are acting for any other clients in respect of the same matter, please give the legal aid reference number(s) or details and explain how their position has been considered in relation to the current request(s):

The other party

Title: ____________ Initials: ____________ Surname: ____________

First name: ____________

Address: ____________

Town: ____________

County: ____________ Postcode: ____________

Page 2

Amendment/authority requested

➤ *Please say what is being asked for. For a change of solicitor give detailed reasons and if appropriate indicate whether a complaint has been made using the firm's complaints procedure.*

Current situation report and reasons for request

➤ *Please give a summary of work done and justify your request in all cases.*

New acting solicitor's details

➤ *Complete if change of solicitor requested.*

Legal aid supplier number: ____________ ____________

Name of firm: ____________________

Phone: ____________________

Name of new acting solicitor: ____________________

➤ *The acting solicitor must have a valid practising certificate. The Board cannot pay for any work done during any period in which the acting solicitor does not have a practising certificate.*

Solicitor's reference: ____________________

Contact name for enquiries: ____________________

Page 3

Prior authority details

➤ *Complete if prior authority requested.*

Name of expert: ______________________

Company name: ______________________

Address: ______________________

Town: ______________________

County: ______________ Postcode: ______________

Phone: ______________ Type/status of expert: ______________

Total authority: £ ____ : ____ Maximum authority: £ ____ : ____
(before apportionment, if appropriate) *(after apportionment, if appropriate)*

Preparation: £ ____ : ____ Preparation-hourly rate: £ ____ : ____

Cost of travel time: £ ____ : ____ Travel - hourly rate: £ ____ : ____

Daily rate: £ ____ : ____
(if expert to give evidence)

How many alternative quotes have been obtained? ______________

What were the amounts quoted? ______________

Why have you chosen the quote you have? ______________

If these are Children Act proceedings where the leave of court is required, has leave been obtained? ☐ Yes ☐ No

Counsel's details

Authority is requested to: ☐ instruct ☐ brief

Type: ☐ leader alone ☐ leader plus junior ☐ two counsel ☐ junior (Magistrates' Court proceedings only)

Enclosures

➤ *Only copies should be sent.*

☐ counsel's opinion ☐ witness statements ☐ expert report(s) ☐ pleadings
☐ photographs/ plans ☐ other, give details: ______________

Certification

I certify that the information provided is correct.

Signed: ______________________ Date: ____ / ____ / ____
(A Solicitor or a Fellow of the Institute of Legal Executives)

Name: ______________________

V.3 April 1998 **Page 4**

Appendix 8
Legal Aid Board forms CRIM 10 and APP 7

Application for prior authority for expenditure in criminal proceedings

➤ **Please read the notes overleaf before completing this form in block capitals.**

CRIM 10

LEGAL AID BOARD LEGAL AID ACT 1988

Legal Aid Order number (please copy this from the order) LA

Has this application been granted over the telephone? ☐ YES ☐ NO

App Type 02

Defendant's details

Surname: *Mr/Mrs/Miss/Ms* ______ First Names: ______

Address: ______

Date of birth: __/__/__ Occupation: ______

Solicitor's details

Name of Solicitor: ______ Initials: ______ Title: ______

Name & Address of firm: ______

Legal Aid account no: ______ Reference: ______ DX No: ______

Tel No: ______ Fax No: ______

Court/charge details

Court Name:

Nature of charges (including statute and section):

Likely plea:

Date of next hearing:

Purpose of next hearing:

Give the full reasons for the application and state clearly the purpose of the authority sought; in the case of a medical report indicate whether as to fitness to plead and/or plea and/or disposal:

Give a brief summary of the prosecution case. You may attach the advance disclosure or extracts:

Give a summary of the defence or mitigation. Attach your client's statement and details of any previous convictions, if available in either case:

Type of Expenditure e.g. medical report

Details of Charging Rates per hour
(Do not include VAT) Please read the notes overleaf

Preparation

Travel (do not include travelling expenses)

Total authority you are seeking

Name and address of expert or other person you want to instruct:

Type of expertise and qualifications:

Only applicable to medical reports: Consultant: ☐ NO ☐ YES

Are there any other defendants who would benefit from the expenditure and with whom there is no conflict of interest?
☐ NO ☐ YES: What consideration has been given to a joint instruction?

Have alternative quotes been obtained?
☐ NO ☐ YES: What were the amounts quoted?

Specific information required

1. Court attendance fees of expert witnesses cannot be authorised - these are payable from Central Funds in the absence of a court direction to the contrary. Solicitors should consider what fee is likely to be allowed (if necessary, by asking the court) so that instructions are not given to an expert whose full court attendance fee is unlikely to be allowed by the court. The costs of medical reports ordered by the court to assist in sentencing are also payable from Central Funds and will not be authorised.
2. In Intoximeter or excess alcohol cases, include the reading or blood level, the nature or amount of alcohol consumed before and after driving with the times of consumption and the times of the test. In "hip flask" cases, also give details of any corroborative evidence.
3. The absence of alternative quotes will not, in itself, lead to a refusal to incur expenditure.
4. Check that the application has been sent to the appropriate area office and that a legal aid order is held which covers the proceedings. The Board will deal with applications on the basis of the information sent by the solicitor and an Area Committee only has jurisdiction where it is the correct Area Committee and there is the appropriate legal aid cover.
5. Send applications to the Area Office in whose area the court is situated. A covering letter is not needed but you can continue on a separate sheet of paper if necessary.

For area office use only

COURT CODE: DATE:

DECISION:

RF2	Request further information	
G10	Granted - Delegated	
G12	Granted - Committee	
R21	Refused - Committee	

CL4	Out of Time	
W10	Withdrawn	
CL5	No Jurisdiction	

DOCUMENT CODES AND STANDARD WORDINGS CODES REQUIRED:

SUMMARY FOR COMMITTEE:

Application for amendment or prior authority in criminal cases

APP7

Please complete in block capitals

Your client's details

Legal aid order number: ______________________ Date of order: ___/___/___

Title: ______________________ Initials: ______________________

Surname: ______________________

First name: ______________________

Surname at birth: ______________________
(if different)

Date of birth: ___/___/___

National insurance number: [| | | | | | | |]

Sex: ☐ Male ☐ Female

Marital status: ☐ Single ☐ Married ☐ Cohabiting

☐ Separated ☐ Divorced ☐ Widowed

Place of birth: ______________________ Job: ______________________
(town)

Current address: ______________________

Town: ______________________

County: ______________________ Postcode: ______________________

Current acting solicitor's details

Legal aid supplier number: [| | | | | | |] [| | | | | | |]

Name of firm: ______________________

Phone: ______________________

Name of acting solicitor: ______________________

➤ *The acting solicitor must have a valid practising certificate. The Board cannot pay for any work done during any period in which the acting solicitor does not have a practising certificate.*

Solicitor's reference: ______________________

Contact name for enquiries: ______________________

Page 1

Type of application

➤ *The Magistrates' Court notice of refusal must be attached where appropriate*

☐ Prior authority ☐ Change solicitor ☐ To assign counsel

☐ To instruct QC without junior ☐ To withdraw legal aid order

Case details

Main offence: ______________________ Date of offence: ___/___/___

Likely plea: ☐ Guilty ☐ Not Guilty ☐ Mixed plea

Date of next hearing: ___/___/___ Name of Court: ______________________

Purpose of next hearing: ______________________

Details of application

➤ *For prior authority applications complete page 3.*

Please give details of and reasons for the application:

Page 2

Prior authority details

Tell us what authority you are seeking and why it is required. If you wish to obtain a medical report, state whether as to fitness to plead and/or plea and/or disposal:

Give a brief summary of the prosecution case. You may attach the copy advance disclosure or extracts:

Give a summary of the defence or mitigation. Attach a copy of your client's statement and details of any previous convictions, if available in either case:

Type of expenditure: *(e.g. medical report)* ______________________

Name of expert: ______________________

Company name: ______________________

Address: ______________________

Town: ______________________

County: ______________ Postcode: ______________

Phone: ______________ Type/status: ______________

Total authority: £ ______ : ____ *(before apportionment, if appropriate)*

Preparation: £ ______ : ____ Preparation-hourly rate: £ ______ : ____

Cost of travel time: £ ______ : ____ Travel - hourly rate: £ ______ : ____

How many alternative quotes have been obtained? ______________

What were the amounts quoted? ______________

If there are any other defendants who would benefit from the expenditure and with whom there is no conflict of interest, what consideration has been given to a joint instruction?

Name(s) of other defendant(s): ______________________

Page 3

New acting solicitor's details

➤ *Complete if change of solicitor requested.*

Legal aid supplier number: ⎣⎦⎣⎦

Name of firm: ______

Phone: ______

Name of new acting solicitor: ______

➤ *The acting solicitor must have a valid practising certificate. The Board cannot pay for any work done during any period in which the acting solicitor does not have a practising certificate.*

Solicitor's reference: ______

Contact name for enquiries: ______

Enclosures

➤ *Only copies should be sent.*

- ☐ Magistrates' Court notice of refusal
- ☐ Legal Aid Order and any subsequent amendments
- ☐ Advance disclosure
- ☐ Client's statement
- ☐ Other ➤ *Give details*

______

Certification

I certify that the information provided is correct.

Signed: ______ Date: ___/___/___

(A Solicitor or a Fellow of the Institute of Legal Executives)

Name: ______

Appendix 9
Law Society code of practice for expert witnesses engaged by solicitors

Acceptance of instructions

1. Experts should ensure that they receive clear instructions from the solicitor (in writing unless this is not practical). Experts should be aware that on occasions they may be instructed jointly by more than one party/solicitor, or be invited to answer specific questions raised by a party, other than the one by whom they have been primarily instructed. They should answer those questions promptly and impartially.

2. Instructions should be accepted only in matters where the expert:

   (a) has the knowledge, experience, academic qualifications or professional training appropriate for the assignment;
   (b) has the resources to complete the matter within the time scales and to the standard required for the assignment.

3. Experts should not accept instructions if they are not able to prepare a report within a reasonable time, having regard to the timetable of the case. In any event, a time scale for the production of the report should be agreed. Where the agreed time scale cannot be met, notice of the delay should be given as soon as possible.

4. Experts should make clear to solicitors what can and cannot be expected on completion of the assignment and in particular, as soon as possible after being instructed, they should identify any aspects of a commission with which they are unfamiliar, or are not competent to deal with, or on which they require or would like further information or guidance.

5. If any part of the assignment is to be undertaken by parties other than the individual instructed, then:

   (a) prior agreement must be obtained from the instructing solicitors;
   (b) the names of the individuals to be engaged and details of their experience and qualifications must be given.

6. Where a firm has been instructed, the names of the individuals to be

assigned to the project and details of their experience and qualifications must be given on request.

Terms of business

7. Experts should provide Terms of Business for agreement with the instructing solicitors prior to the acceptance of any instructions. These should include:

   (a) daily or hourly rates of the experts to be engaged on the assignment or alternatively an agreed reasonable fee for the project or for the services;
   (b) treatment of travelling time;
   (c) likely expenses or disbursements;
   (d) provision for preferred timing of payment, including any special provisions where the case is legally aided or the fees are to be paid by a third party.
   (e) contingency provision for payment of a specified reasonable fee in the event of late notice of cancellation of a court hearing, when the expert is likely to incur irrecoverable losses.

8. Experts should not accept payment for services contingent upon the nature of the evidence or the outcome of the case.

Professional conduct

9. Experts must comply with the Code of Conduct of any professional body of which they are a member.

Confidentiality

10. The identity of the client or any information about the client acquired in the course of the commission shall not be disclosed except where consent has been obtained from the client or where there is a legal duty to disclose.

Independence

11. Experts will disclose to solicitors at the start of each project any personal or financial or other significant circumstances which might influence work for the client in any way not stated or implied in the instructions, in particular:

    (a) any directorship or controlling interest in any business in competition with the client;

(b) any financial or other interest in goods or services (including software) under dispute;
(c) any personal relationship with any individual involved in the matter;
(d) the existence but not the name of any other client of the expert with competing interests.

12. Any actual or potential conflict of interest must be reported to the solicitor as soon as it arises or becomes apparent and the assignment must be terminated.

Investigation

13. Experts should consider whether there is a need to see the client, visit a site etc and, if so, agree the practical arrangements with the solicitor in advance.

14. In the case of medical reports, the following considerations apply:

(a) if the doctor has treated the patient before, ensure that the patient's consent has been obtained to the release of the information contained in the notes and that such consent is informed consent;
(b) if the doctor has not treated the patient before, ensure that the patient's consent is obtained to the examination and to the disclosure of their records to the doctor; and, where practicable, consent of the other doctors involved in the care of the patient should be obtained before releasing information held by them.

Preparation of the report

15. The report should cover:

(a) basic information such as names and dates;
(b) the source of the instructions and the purpose of the report;
(c) the history of the matter;
(d) the methodology used in investigation;
(e) the documents referred to in the preparation of the report and/or any evidence upon which the report is based;
(f) facts ascertained;
(g) inferences drawn from the facts, with reasoning;
(h) the conclusions, cross-referenced to the main text;
(i) summary of the expert's qualifications and experience.

16. Matters of fact and opinion should be clearly distinguished. An expert should not express an opinion in a report on any matter outside the

scope of his or her competence. Plain English should be used and any technical terms explained in the text or a glossary.

17. Copies of any original material prepared by the expert for the case, and upon which he relies, should be annexed to the report. Copies of other reference or technical material referred to should be readily accessible to be produced when required.

18. Experts should be aware that any documents referred to in a report disclosed in proceedings may be subject to discovery. Experts should, therefore, find out from the solicitor to which documents provided with the instructions reference should not be made, usually on grounds of privilege.

19. Experts should also be aware that they may be invited by the solicitor to amend or expand a report for the purposes of completeness, clarity, readability, or to ensure factual accuracy or consistency, but not to change, withdraw or omit statements of fact or opinion which are relevant to the issues in the case.

20. The expert's report for the court should be dated and signed by the individual(s) who will if required give evidence in support of it.

21. If new evidence comes to light subsequent to disclosure of the expert's report to the other party or the court, which leads the expert to modify his or her opinion, the expert should promptly advise the solicitor.

Meetings of experts

22. Experts should be aware that they may be instructed by the court, or invited by the parties/solicitors to discuss or meet with other parties' experts, with a view to reaching agreement on the whole or aspects of the expert evidence, or narrowing the areas of disagreement. In these circumstances, experts should ensure that the following are prepared:

    (i) an agenda for the meeting;
    (ii) a note of the main points of agreement/disagreement reached at the meeting, agreed jointly with the other experts, if at all possible. Agreements between experts should be limited to technical issues: legal liability is not a matter for an expert to decide.

Availability for court and attendance at trial

23. An expert should be aware that when agreeing to prepare a report for court, he or she may be called to give oral evidence. The expert should

take all reasonable steps to ensure he or she will be available to attend court if and when required, but should be aware that the solicitor may need to serve a subpoena in the event of real difficulty.

24. When giving evidence at court, the role of an expert is to assist the court, and remain independent of the parties. Experts should give evidence in an objective and unbiased way, and confine that evidence to matters within their competence relevant to issues in dispute.

Complaints procedure

25. Experts should provide a procedure for resolving complaints by solicitors, including the following:

(a) at the start of the assignment, the expert must give the solicitor/client the name of the person to contact in the event that they are dissatisfied with the service provided;
(b) in the event of a complaint being made, the expert should tell the solicitor what the procedure will be for resolving the complaint, and give them the names and addresses of any professional or trade bodies of which the firm or the individuals assigned to the commission are members;
(c) in the event of allegations relating to an expert's failure to adhere to the above Code of Practice or any breach of their contract with the instructing solicitors, the Law Society and FT Law & Tax reserve the right to exclude such an expert from any future edition of the Directory of Expert Witnesses.

Reference to the Directory

26. An expert listed in the Directory may describe themselves as so listed and use the term 'checked', but may not refer to this listing as a qualification or describe themselves as approved, accredited, or recommended by the Law Society or by FT Law & Tax.

Appendix 10
Example of a writ

COURT FEES ONLY

Writ indorsed with Statement of Claim [Unliquidated Demand] (O. 6, r. 1)

IN THE HIGH COURT OF JUSTICE **1995 .— .—No.**

Queen's Bench Division

[District Registry]

Between

(1) Plaintiffs
(2)

AND

(formerly) (a firm)

Defendant

(1) Insert name.

To the Defendant ([1]) , Chartered Accountants

(2) Insert address.

of ([2])

This Writ of Summons has been issued against you by the above-named Plaintiff in respect of the claim set out on the back.

Within 14 days after the service of this Writ on you, counting the day of service, you must either satisfy the claim or return to the Court Office mentioned below the accompanying **Acknowledgment of Service** stating therein whether you intend to contest these proceedings.

If you fail to satisfy the claim or to return the Acknowledgment within the time stated, or if you return the Acknowledgment without stating therein an intention to contest the proceedings, the Plaintiffs may proceed with the action and judgment may be entered against you forthwith without further notice.

(3) Complete and delete as necessary.

Issued from the ([3])
[District Registry] of the High Court
this day of 19

NOTE:—This Writ may not be served later than 4 calendar months *(or, if leave is required to effect service out of the jurisdiction, 6 months)* beginning with that date unless renewed by order of the Court.

Statement of Claim

The Plaintiff's claim is for loss suffered as a result of the negligence of the Defendant and/or breach of contract as the Plaintiffs Accountant between 1987 and 1990 and interest thereon pursuant to Section 35A of the Supreme Court Act 1981.

(Signed)

---

(1) If this Writ was issued out of a District Registry, this indorsement as to place where the cause of action arose should be completed.
(2) Delete as necessary.
(3) Insert name of place.
(4) For phraseology of this indorsement where the Plaintiff sues in person, see *Supreme Court Practice*, Vol. 2, para. 1.

([1])

([4]) **This Writ** was issued by

of

[Agent for

of]

Solicitor for the said Plaintiffs whose address ([2]) [is] [are]

Solicitor's Reference Tel. No:

Appendix 11
Example set of pleadings

199 W No.

IN THE HIGH COURT OF JUSTICE

QUEEN'S BENCH DIVISION

DISTRICT REGISTRY

Writ issued the 4th day of July 199

BETWEEN

LIMITED Plaintiff

and

& COMPANY (A FIRM) Defendant

AMENDED STATEMENT OF CLAIM

1. The Plaintiff is and was at all material times a Company carrying on business as from premises at High Street,

2. The Defendant was at all material times a firm of Chartered Accountants, practising at   , London, and held themselves out as skilled, competent auditors and accountants.

3. By an agreement made on a date between June 1985 and October 1986 the Defendant was retained and ~~employed~~ engaged by the Plaintiff to provide statutory audit and accountancy services (including but not limited to the preparation of the annual balance sheet and profit and loss accounts) in each of the financial years from 1985/6 up to and including 1991/2.

4. The Defendant, by its servants and agents well knew at all material times that the Plaintiff required and relied upon the accuracy and legality of the said accounts, inter alia, for the purposes of submission to the Inland Revenue.

5. It was an implied term of the said agreement that the Defendant would exercise all reasonable skill and care, diligence and competence in the exercise of the said retainer.

6. Further and in the alternative, the Defendant owed a duty of care at common law to exercise such skill, care and competence as Accountants in the discharge of its said retainer.

7. Without prejudice to the generality of the aforesaid implied term and/or duty the Plaintiff will contend that the Defendant was under a duty to take reasonable care to:

   7.1 adequately plan the audit work at each and every stage of its progress;

   7.2 assess the overall design of the Plaintiff's accounting system and the adequacy of the accounting records from which the financial statements were to be prepared;

   7.3 in the light of the above assessment, determine what audit tests ought to be carried out and execute the same in order to provide sufficient and adequate audit evidence as to the completeness, accuracy and validity of the information contained in the accounting records and/or in the financial statements provided by the Plaintiff's servants and agents and/or as to whether internal control procedures were being applied as prescribed;

   7.4 assess the accounting capabilities, the reliability and trustworthiness of and/or the quality of information provided by the

Plaintiff's servants and agents and in particular by a Mr. (who at all material times was the Plaintiff's Managing Director) upon whom the Defendant relied exclusively or overly for financial information as to the state of the Plaintiff;

7.5 report to all of the Directors upon any weaknesses in the Plaintiff's accounting system and suggest any improvements that might be made and/or upon any fraud and suspicion of fraud which arose;

7.6 prepare adequate audit working papers containing, inter alia, the following:

7.6.1 audit planning information;

7.6.2 the Defendant's assessment of the Plaintiff's accounting system and its review and evaluation of the Plaintiff's internal controls;

7.6.3 details of the audit work executed;

7.6.4 a summary of significant points affecting the financial statements and the audit reports, indicating how those points were dealt with;

7.7 ensure that its servants and agents conducted all audit work to an acceptable standard.

8. In purported performance of the said retainer the Defendant purported to act as the Plaintiff's auditors and accountants in the said financial years.

9. In breach of the said implied term and/or duty the Defendant failed to exercise reasonable skill and care, diligence and competence in the discharge of the said retainer.

PARTICULARS

(a) failed to conduct any or any proper adequate or sufficient review of the Plaintiff's accounting system in time or at all;

(b) failed to identify, properly or at all in time or at all, any problem areas in the said accounting system;

(c) failed to conduct any or any proper audit procedures and/or tests to assess and/or verify the Plaintiff's own records and/or accounts;

(d) failed to assess, properly or at all in time or at all, the reliability, accuracy and trustworthiness of the information about the Plaintiff's financial position supplied by the said Mr. and/or other employees of the Plaintiff;

(e) failed to determine, in time or at all, that Mr. was providing misleading, inaccurate and/or dishonest financial statements regarding the state of the Plaintiff;

(f) relied exclusively and/or overly on financial information supplied by the said Mr. as to the state of the Plaintiff's finances without testing the same;

(g) failed to prepare any or any adequate audit file in time or at all;

(h) failed to respond adequately or at all in time or at all to queries raised by the Defendant's own servants and agents;

(i) failed to audit all material items;

(j) incorrectly caused permitted or suffered a batch of invoices dated August 19 but processed in September 19 , to be redated to September 19 . The Defendant treated and/or authorized and/or advised the Plaintiff that it was acceptable and/or permissible to treat invoices raised and sent out in August 19 but not posted in the Plaintiff's books by the 31st August as work in progress rather than sales and thereby removing the profit element of such invoices from the Plaintiff's profit for the year ended 31 August 19 . The said profit element totalled £54,050. Thereafter, the same were redated to September 19 in accordance with the wishes of Mr . Further, in addition to the above incorrect treatment of the invoices as work in progress, the Defendant's method of calculation of the value of the supposed work in progress was both incorrect and unsubstantiated;

(k) failed to provide any or any adequate response to and/or co-operate with the Inland Revenue, its servants and agents in dealing with the inquiries made, inter alia, as to the Plaintiff's work in progress figures at 31st August 19 ;

(l) failed to detect by means of proper audit tests, audit work or howsoever and/or to respond appropriately upon the discovery of problems, discrepancies and/or irregularities throughout the said retainer, inter alia, relating to:

(i) Work in Progress

The calculation of work in progress was inaccurate in respect of each of the said financial years. The job costing report was not reliable. It failed to interact with the Sage accounting system and was not updated properly and/or consistently. When jobs were invoiced out the costing reports were not updated properly and/or consistently. Further, and in the alternative, not all of the costs were entered.

(ii) Petty Cash

Mr. maintained total control over the Plaintiff's petty cash. Cash differences arose in the Plaintiff's expenses where vouchers to support the same fell short of total petty cash expenditure. Petty cash figures were supplied to the Defendant by Mr. with no independent audit work. A significant quantity of petty cash was used to purchase alcohol and for corporate entertainment. All such expenditure was charged to the customer, the description on the invoices being disguised. A substantial proportion of the cash difference is attributable to payments made to freelance workers from petty cash.

(iii) The use of Company Credit Cards

In January 19 the Plaintiff introduced the use of Company credit cards. Mr. used his card for a substantial volume of private expenditure in the financial years from 19 to 19 without the knowledge and/or permission of his fellow Directors.

(iv) The use of Company Cheques

Company cheques were used by Mr. for non-Company business without the knowledge and/or permission of his fellow Directors.

(v) The operation of the PAYE Scheme for 19   onwards

Various payments were made which should have been subject to PAYE Income Tax, National Insurance contributions and/or entered on to form P11D.

The Plaintiff will provide full particulars in relation to each of the above areas upon discovery and/or exchange of experts' reports herein.

The Plaintiff will contend that the Defendant should have been put on alert by the above and made further investigations, conducted further audit tests, modified or adopted the Plaintiff's accounting procedures and/or the Defendant's audit procedures and/or reported the same to all of the Plaintiff's Directors.

10. By reason of the aforesaid breaches the Plaintiff will be exposed to penalties and/or interest payments imposed by the Inland Revenue in relation to late and/or non-payment of Corporation Tax, Income Tax and/or National Insurance contributions.

11. Further and in the alternative, by reason of the aforesaid breaches and in particular the breaches particularised in Paragraph 9(j), hereof, in about May 19   the Inland Revenue commenced a major investigation into the Plaintiff's accounts and/or affairs. The costs of co-operating with the said investigation will have to be borne by the Plaintiff. The Defendant failed to inform any of the Plaintiff's Directors (apart from the said Mr.   ) of the commencement of the said investigation.

12. Further and in the further alternative, had the Plaintiff's Directors (other than Mr.   ) become aware of the aforesaid accounting irregularities, problems and inconsistencies and/or of the said Inland Revenue investigation, the said Mr.   would have been dismissed at some time prior to the commencement of the financial year commencing the 1st September 19   . In the subsequent period Mr.   used Company credit cards to make unauthorised expenditure of £5,300.17 in the financial year 19   and £3,300.74 in the following financial year. Further unauthorised expenditure was made in the said period by means of Company cheques and/or petty cash withdrawals. Full particulars will be provided upon discovery and/or exchange of experts' reports herein.

13. In the premises, the Plaintiff has suffered loss and damage.

PARTICULARS

(i)	Costs of co-operating with the Inland Revenue inquiry	£23,000.00
(ii)	Interest of £9,514.95 and penalties of £18,372.51 imposed by the Inland Revenue	£27,887.46
(iii)	Such sums obtained by from the Plaintiff Company used for personal expenditure which cannot be recovered from Mr.	£38,529.75
(iv)	Disruption to the Plaintiff's business and/or management costs	£56,000.00
(v)	Loss of profit (net of expenses) suffered by the Plaintiff	£178,000.00

14. Further, the Plaintiff claims interest on all sums due pursuant to Section 35A of the Supreme Court Act at such rate and for such period as this Court shall deem just.

AND the Plaintiff claims:

(1) Damages.

(2) The aforesaid interest pursuant to Section 35A of the Supreme Court Act 1981.

Served this day of 19 by

Solicitors

for the Plaintiff.

Amended pursuant to the Order of District Judge Griffiths dated August 19 .

199 W. No.

IN THE HIGH COURT OF JUSTICE

QUEEN'S BENCH DIVISION

DISTRICT REGISTRY

BETWEEN:

LIMITED

Plaintiff

– and –

& CO. (A Firm)

Defendants

AMENDED DEFENCE

1. Save that it is averred that the Plaintiff carries on business from Road, London, (the address pleaded in paragraph 1 of the Statement of Claim being the Plaintiff's registered office), paragraphs 1 and 2 of the Amended Statement of Claim are admitted.

2. At all times material to this action:

   (a) Messrs. , and were directors and shareholders of the Plaintiff; and

   (b) their respective shareholdings were in the proportions 49 : 26 : 25 of an issued share capital of 100 shares of £1 each.

3. Save that:

   (a) no admissions are made:

      (i) as to the date or manner in which the Defendants were first retained; or

      (ii) as to the extent of the accountancy services which the Defendants agreed to provide; and

   (b) it is denied:

      (i) that the Defendants were 'employed' by the Plaintiff at all;

      (ii) that the Defendants were engaged or had any involvement with the 199 /199 accounts;

paragraphs 3 and 8 of the Amended Statement of Claim are admitted.

4. Save that it is admitted that the Defendants knew that the accounts would be submitted to the Inland Revenue, paragraph 4 of the Amended Statement of Claim is denied.

5. Paragraphs 5 and 6 of the Amended Statement of Claim are admitted.

6. As to paragraph 7 of the Amended Statement of Claim:

   (a) sub-paragraphs 7.1, 7.2 and 7.3 thereof are not admitted; the Defendants' responsibilities were as provided for in the Companies Act 1985.

   (b) sub-paragraph 7.4 is denied. The Defendants were under no express or implied obligation to assess the accounting capabilities, reliability or trustworthiness or quality of information provided by the Plaintiff's servants or agents. The Defendants' task as auditors was to examine the accounting records of the Plaintiff and to comment upon the same. It is further denied that the Defendants relied exclusively or overly upon Mr. as alleged or at all. The Defendants carried out their own audit testing and went back to the prime records of the Plaintiff (where available) rather than rely on the Plaintiff's computer system;

   (c) sub-paragraph 7.5 is denied. The Defendants were under no express or implied obligations to report on weaknesses in the Plaintiff's accounting system. The Defendants' obligation was to carry out a proper audit (as they did) and to draw any matters that they came across to the Plaintiff's attention. The Defendants did in fact warn the Plaintiff about the quality of their book-keeping in respect of the 19 /19 accounts and qualified the accounts in respect of the 199 /199 accounts;

(d) sub-paragraph 7.6 is denied. The Defendants' obligation was to carry out an audit and to express an opinion on the financial statements, not to prepare particular audit working papers.

7. It is denied that the Defendants acted in breach of the terms of their retainer or in breach of duty whether as alleged in paragraph 9 of the Amended Statement of Claim or at all. Without prejudice to the generality of the foregoing denial, the Defendant pleads further to the individual allegations as follows:

(a) the allegations set out in sub-paragraphs (a) to (i) and (k) are general and wholly unparticularised allegations which the Plaintiff should either particularise properly or withdraw. If and when the same are properly particularised, the Defendants reserve the right to plead to the same. The Defendants qualified each of their reports to the Directors, stating, for example in respect of 19 /19 :

> '. . . We have not obtained all the information and explanations that we consider necessary for the purpose of our audit and we were unable to satisfy ourselves as to the completeness and accuracy of the accounting records'.

So far as the remaining particulars provided by the Plaintiff:

(i) the Defendants did carry out audit tests including the examination of primary records; work in progress and profit margins;

(ii) the Defendants did not circularise debtors as it was their experience that responses were generally insufficient and inconclusive;

(iii) Audit Guidelines 3.203 does not exist; Audit Guidelines 3.2.203 makes no reference to 'accurate results';

(iv) expenses claimed by way of company credit cards were paid by company cheques countersigned by one of the directors other than Mr. ;

(v) the Defendants received assurances from Mr. as director and reported the same to the Plaintiff each year;

(vi) the Defendants did carry out sufficient tests to form the (qualified) opinion;

(vii) the Defendants' audit files were adequate, being opened at the planning stage and maintained throughout the audit;

(viii) the Defendants addressed and dealt with all queries promptly and appropriately;

(ix) the investigations of petty cash and work in progress were part of the audit process which led to the qualifications of the audit report;

(b) in respect of allegation (j):

(i) on going through the Plaintiff's records for the year to 31st August 19 , the Defendants discovered the existence of some copy sales invoices with dates in August 19 which did not otherwise feature in the Plaintiff's records at all;

(ii) the Defendants asked about these invoices who informed them:

(1) that the copy invoices were wrongly dated and had not been sent out in August at all

(2) that the invoices had in fact been sent out after the year end prior to the Defendants' audit;

(3) that he did not consider it necessary to account for the invoices in the year to 31st August 19 at all;

(iii) on the basis that the invoices were wrongly dated (which the Defendants had no reason to doubt especially as the same were not included in the Plaintiff's records) the Defendants advised the Plaintiff (through Mr.) that it was necessary to account for the work represented by the invoices as work in progress as at 31st August 19 and they were so treated in the accounts;

(iv) it is accordingly denied that the Defendants:

(1) gave the advice and/or treatment or authorisation alleged in sub-paragraph (j);

(2) that any act or advice of the Defendant caused either Mr. or the Plaintiff to undertake a fraud or attempted fraud upon the Inland Revenue;

(3) gave advice which was, on the facts presented to them, in any way incorrect;

(v) the effect of this sub-paragraph is to allege that the Defendants participated in a fraud upon the Inland Revenue. The Plaintiff has failed to give any adequate or proper particulars sufficient to justify such a pleading of the Defendants' alleged advice. Unless such particulars are provided promptly, the Defendants reserve the right to strike out this paragraph as being frivolous and/or vexatious and/or an abuse of the process of the Court; <u>The particulars now provided are inconsistent with the Amended Statement of Claim in that:</u>

<u>(a)</u> <u>the Amended Statement of claim alleges that Mr. caused the re-dating of the invoices after advice from the Defendants' advisers;</u>

<u>(b)</u> <u>this case is disavowed in the Particulars;</u>

(c) as to sub-paragraph (1):

(i) it is denied that the Defendants were negligent as alleged or at all;

(ii) the job costing report was produced by the Plaintiff and not by the Defendants;

(iii) the Defendants did not use the same but went back to the basic records of the Plaintiff;

(iv) no admissions are made as to whether Mr. maintained total control over the petty cash as alleged or at all;

(v) no admissions are made as to the statements made in sub-paragraph (ii) , (iii) , (iv) and (v);

(vi) if the facts and matters there set out are established it is denied that the Defendants were at fault in failing to discover the same when, on the Plaintiff's own case, Mr. was, apparently, able to deceive his fellow directors;

(d) it is averred that all letters and reports written to the Plaintiff were addressed to the Plaintiff's directors and not to Mr. alone.

8. Save that it is denied that any act or omission of the Defendant caused the Plaintiff to suffer the loss and damage alleged or any loss and damage, paragraphs 10, 11 and 12 of the Amended Statement of Claim are not admitted. On the Plaintiff's own case it appears that the loss and damage was caused by the defaults of Mr. and not by any act or omission of the Defendants.

8A. Further and in any event:

(a) it is denied that the Plaintiff is entitled to recover interest imposed by the Inland Revenue as the Plaintiff received a benefit for the same;

(b) it is denied that the Plaintiff is entitled to recover both disruption to its business and loss of profit;

(c) it is denied that any such loss of profit was reasonably foreseeable to the Defendant;

(d) it is averred that the disruption caused by the dismissal of the Plaintiff's Managing Director would have been equivalent to or greater than the disruption caused by the need to co-operate with the Inland Revenue enquiries.

9. Save that it is denied that any act or omission of the Defendant has caused the Plaintiff to suffer the alleged or any loss and damage, paragraph 13 of the Amended Statement of Claim is denied.

10. Further or alternatively, in the event that the Defendants would otherwise be found to be liable to the Plaintiff, it is averred that any loss or damage which the Plaintiff may prove to have suffered was wholly caused:

(a) by the pleaded failures and defaults of Mr. ; and/or

(b) by the failure of the other directors of the Plaintiff to set up proper controls and arrangements and/or to monitor Mr. in the manner alleged in the Re-Amended Statement of Claim;

11. Further or in the further alternative it is averred that any loss and damage which the Plaintiff may prove to have suffered was caused or contributed to by its own negligence in that it is vicariously liable for the defaults of its directors as pleaded in paragraph 10 above.

11A. Further and in any event it is averred that the Plaintiff has failed to mitigate any loss which it may prove to have suffered by issuing proceedings against Mr. in respect of the defaults alleged in the Amended Statement of Claim.

12. It is denied that the Plaintiff is entitled to the interest alleged in paragraph 14 of the Amended Statement of Claim or to any interest.

13. Save as specifically admitted or otherwise pleaded to, each and every allegation in the Amended Statement of Claim is denied as if separately set out and traversed seriatim.

SERVED this day of November 199 by ,

, London EC , Solicitors for the Defendants

PARTICULARS

(i)	Costs of co-operating with the Inland Revenue inquiry	£23,000.00
(ii)	Interest of £9,514.95 and penalties of £18.372.51 imposed by the Inland Revenue	£27,887.46
(iii)	Such sums obtained by from the Plaintiff Company used for personal expenditure which cannot be recovered from Mr.	£38,529.75
(iv)	Disruption to the Plaintiff's business and/or management costs	£56,000.00
(v)	Loss of profit (net of expenses) suffered by the Plaintiff	£178,000.00

14. Further, the Plaintiff claims interest on all sums due pursuant to Section 35A of the Supreme Court Act at such rate and for such period as this Court shall deem just.

AND the Plaintiff claims:

(1) Damages.

(2) The aforesaid interest pursuant to Section 35A of the Supreme Court Act 1981.

Served this day of 199 by

Solicitors for the Plaintiff.

Appendix 12
Interest rates

Bank base rates

Date	Rate
06.01.86	12.50
19.03.86	11.50
08.04.86	11.25
09.04.86	11.00
24.04.86	10.50
27.05.86	10.00
14.10.86	11.00
10.03.87	10.50
10.03.87	10.00
29.04.87	9.50
11.05.87	9.00
07.08.87	10.00
26.10.87	9.50
05.11.87	9.00
04.12.87	8.50
02.02.88	9.00
17.03.88	8.50
11.04.88	8.00
18.05.88	7.50
03.06.88	8.00
06.06.88	8.25
07.06.88	8.50
22.06.88	9.00
29.06.88	9.50
05.07.88	10.00
19.07.88	10.50
08.08.88	10.75
09.08.88	11.00
25.08.88	11.50
26.08.88	12.00
25.11.88	13.00

Date	Rate
24.05.89	14.00
05.10.89	15.00
08.10.90	14.00
13.02.91	13.50
27.02.91	13.00
25.03.91	12.50
12.04.91	12.00
24.05.91	11.50
12.07.91	11.00
04.09.91	10.50
05.05.92	10.00
16.09.92	12.00
17.09.92	10.00
22.09.92	9.00
16.10.92	8.00
13.11.92	7.00
26.01.93	6.00
23.11.93	5.50
08.02.94	5.25
12.09.94	5.75
07.12.94	6.25
02.02.95	6.75
13.12.95	6.50
18.01.96	6.25
08.03.96	6.00

Special account rate

From	%
01.08.86	11.50
01.01.87	12.25
01.04.87	11.75
01.11.87	11.25
01.12.87	11.00
01.05.88	9.50
01.08.88	11.00
01.11.88	12.25
01.01.89	13.00
01.11.89	14.25
01.04.91	12.00
01.10.91	10.25
01.02.93	8.00

Rate payable on judgment debts

From	%
16.04.85	15.00
01.04.93	8.00

Appendix 13
Example Gourley calculation

The leading case on the application of the Gourley principle is *Shove* v *Downs Surgical plc* [1984] 1 All ER 7. The following example is taken from Graham Chase's *Tax Treatment of Compensation and Damages* (Butterworths 1994).

Marie had her employment contract wrongfully terminated on 1 January 1993. The contract was for a fixed term, with three years to run at the date of termination. The terms of that contract provided as follows:

1 an annual salary of £50,000;

2 contribution of £2,000 per annum towards Marie's personal pension plan;

3 provision for health care, at a cost of £300 per annum;

4 company car, taxable on the income tax scale rates as a benefit equal to £2,770 per annum so far as the car is concerned and £630 so far as fuel is concerned. The aggregate benefit of that car and petrol to Marie based on AA figures is in the sum of £5,000 per annum.

The first stage in the calculation is to establish the net loss to Marie. This is achieved by ascertaining the yearly tax cost, deducting that from her total yearly remuneration and multiplying the result by the unexpired term of her contract for three years. The result (assuming tax rates and bands for 1992/93 to remain in force) is as follows:

	£
Salary	50,000
Car	2,770
Health care	300
Petrol	630
	53,700
Less:	
Personal allowance	(3,445)
Taxable remuneration	50,255

Tax on £50,255:

£0 to £2,000 @ 20% =	400
£2,000 to £23,700 @ 25% =	5,425
£23,700 to £50,255 @ 40% =	10,622
National Insurance (21,060 – 2,807 @ 9%) =	1,643
Total tax cost	18,090

Net yearly benefit:

Salary	50,000
Car and petrol (value)	5,000
Pension contribution	2,000
Health care	300
Less: tax	(18,090)
Net benefit	39,210

Net loss over three years. £39,210 × 3 = £117,630

The second stage in the calculation is to take the net loss and reduce this by reference to (i) mitigation and (ii) discount for early receipt. This will of course depend on whether Marie has good prospects for obtaining other employment and the expected salary thereon as to item (i), and prevailing interest rates as to item (ii).

For the purposes of this example, it is assumed that the second stage of the calculation produces a figure of £78,867 after deducting (i) the sum of £30,000 on account of mitigation and (ii) £8,763 on account of accelerated receipt at the rate of 10%. Any reduction on account of early receipt should be made after taking mitigation into account.

The third stage in the calculation is to 'gross up' the net loss of £78,867 in order to arrive at the amount which should be paid to Marie so as to leave her with that amount net of tax. The termination of Marie's employment occurred late in the 1993/94 tax year. Any receipt is subject to tax at the higher rate of 40%, being Marie's marginal rate of tax:

	£
Amount to be grossed up:	78,867
Less: tax-free amount	(30,000)
Amount to be grossed up	48,867

Calculation to gross up £48,867:

$$\frac{48{,}867}{60} \times 100 = 81{,}445$$

The gross payment is therefore:

Tax-free amount	30,000
Amount subject to tax at 40%	81,445
Total amount due	111,445

Appendix 14
Investigation Handbook Appendix B – Notes for the guidance of inspectors appointed under the Companies Act 1985

Introduction

1 Inspectors appointed by the Secretary of State under the Companies Act 1985 are invested with statutory duties and powers and the responsibility for the conduct of the investigation is theirs alone. The following notes have been prepared by the Department of Trade and Industry for the guidance of such inspectors. It is, however, impossible to be definitive about every situation which inspectors may encounter during the course of an investigation, accordingly inspectors are encouraged to refer to the Department for advice if at any time they are in doubt.

2 Powers to appoint inspectors are conferred on the Secretary of State by sections 431, 432, 442 and 446. The Secretary of State does not disclose to a company the reasons for the appointment of inspectors and the courts have decided that he is under no legal obligation to do so (see Norwest Holst Ltd v Secretary of State for Trade and Others (1978) 3 WLR 73). Additionally inspectors appointed under section 94 of the Financial Services Act 1986 exercise powers similar to those of inspectors appointed under the Companies Act 1985.

Purpose of investigations

3 The primary purpose of an investigation by inspectors under the Companies Act 1985 is to establish the facts where prima facie some irregularity may have occurred and to report those facts to the Secretary of State. In the words of Buckley LJ in Re Pergamon Press Ltd (1970) 3 All ER 535 referring specifically to an inspection under section 165 of the Companies Act 1948 (now section 432 of the Companies Act 1985) 'the function of an inspector appointed under section 165 . . . is an inquisitorial function. His duty is to investigate the affairs of the company and to report on them to the Board of Trade. It is not a judicial function.'

4 A report may serve a number of purposes including the following:

– it may be made available to the Director of Public Prosecutions, the Serious

Fraud Office and other prosecuting authorities for the purpose of considering whether criminal proceedings should be brought; or

- it may be published so as to provide investors, employees and creditors with information about the way in which the body under investigation has been run. In some instances such information may alert affected parties to the possibility of instituting civil proceedings and may, for example, be used by a contributory to support a petition for the winding-up of the company (eg Re St Piran Ltd (1981) 3 All ER 270). Reports of inspectors are admissible in any legal proceedings as evidence of the opinion of the inspectors in relation to any matter contained in the report (section 441 as amended by the Companies Act 1989); or
- it may enable the Secretary of State to present a petition to wind-up a company (section 124A of the Insolvency Act 1986); to bring civil proceedings in the name of any company (section 438); or to petition the court for an order under section 460 (power of the court to grant relief where a company's affairs have been conducted in a manner unfairly prejudicial to its members); or
- it may form the basis for applications to the court under section 8 of the Company Directors Disqualification Act 1986 for disqualification orders against past or present directors or shadow directors (and under section 6 of that Act in respect of unfit directors of insolvent companies); or
- it may be disclosed to the Treasury, the Bank of England, the Securities and Investments Board or self regulating organisations; for use for regulatory and investigatory purposes under the Companies Act 1985, the Banking Act 1987, the Financial Services Act 1986, the Insolvency Act 1986 and other legislation. A report may also be disclosed for use by professional bodies for the purposes of disciplinary proceedings in relation to a member. The persons to whom and the circumstances in which the Secretary of State can disclose reports and information obtained by inspectors are set out in section 451A and section 449 of the Companies Act 1985; or
- a published report provides the press and general public with information and so may form a basis for public discussion and action by Government or professional bodies on aspects of company law and administration which the facts may show to be in need of improvement or reform.

The Companies Act 1989 (section 55) amended section 432 so that inspectors may now be appointed on terms that any report they make is not for publication (section 432(2A)).

Timescale

5 The Secretary of State attaches great importance to the timely completion of investigations. Inspectors are appointed on the understanding that they are able and prepared to give the inspection top priority and as much time as it proves to require. Additionally the inspector providing administrative support, often an accountant, should make available the resources required for completion of investigations as quickly and cost effectively as possible. Within a short time of the appointment, the Department will agree with inspectors a provisional timetable for the inspection and for the submission of a final report and any interim report that may be considered necessary or desirable. Regular meetings are held with all inspectors to monitor progress and inspectors are made aware of the necessity to complete their investigations as quickly and effectively as possible. It is important that any departures from this timetable are agreed with the Department as and when necessary. The length of time between the date of appointment and submission of the inspectors' report can affect the ability to take action or the utility of subsequent actions by the Department or others, and it is preferable that minor issues should be ignored if they would unduly prolong the enquiries and submission of a report. Inspectors are asked to bear in mind the importance of ensuring that there is no unnecessary delay in the institution of any prosecution or regulatory proceedings and should therefore where appropriate provide relevant information to the Department as provided for by section 437 (1A) without delay.

Conduct of inspections

6 The initial direction and thrust of an enquiry will be indicated to the inspectors by the terms of their appointment and information passed to them by the Department on appointment. This will include any information on the basis of which the Secretary of State has reached his decision to make the appointment and any other relevant information which he has. Inspectors should bear in mind that the information which is passed to them may include information which has been given to the Department in confidence by, for example, an informant who may still be in the employ of the company. It may, therefore, be necessary to conceal the source of the information during the enquiry so as to avoid any breach of confidence or to protect an informant against retaliatory action. It may be possible at an early stage in the enquiry to get the same information from the books and papers of the company so that the inspectors can ask witnesses questions about the relevant matter without revealing the original source of the information. In other circumstances it may be appropriate to include the informant among the first witnesses examined on oath so that he can defend his disclosure as compulsory.

7 Inspectors should discuss with the Department beforehand any proposed interview with an informant. So far as possible the inspectors should avoid identifying an informant as such in the transcript of his formal interview. It is advisable to discuss this point before the interview with the informant. Neither the informant's identity nor any information which might enable others to identify him should be disclosed to anyone else without prior discussions with the Department.

8 Inspectors are free to conduct their investigations in any way which seems to be appropriate. As a general rule all witnesses should be examined on oath and may attend for interview with their legal advisers if they wish. The circumstances of the matter will determine whether it is better to study the documentary evidence before interviewing witnesses or to interview some or all witnesses immediately. In many instances it will be financial issues that have focused attention on the company's affairs, and experience suggests that inspectors find it helpful to start by examining generally the company's financial records and other company documents. Such an examination is generally carried out by the staff of the accountant inspector (if applicable) who can extract from the company's documents information in them that may be of value to the inspectors. Such work may call for the employment of more staff than are needed for later stages of the inspection. The information obtained by such a process provides a firm basis for the examination of witnesses and may speed up the inspection. In some cases further documentation has been discovered after witnesses have been seen and this has made it necessary to recall them.

9 Inspectors will find it worthwhile to consider carefully the sequence in which witnesses are to be called so as to build up a picture of the company's affairs in a way that reduces the need to recall witnesses and enables the evidence of some of them to be taken into account or employed in examining others. However, for a variety of reasons, for example absence abroad or illness, it may be impossible to see the witnesses in the order planned or possible to do so only at the cost of delaying unreasonably the completion of the inspection.

10 Inspectors may wish to make enquiries informally of witnesses before they are formally examined. Such informal interviews may be of assistance in clarifying the issues in the enquiry, or the ways in which witnesses may be able to help the inspectors. In such circumstances a witness may be interviewed informally by one only of the inspectors, or by the Secretary. It is, however, unwise for an informal interview of this kind to take place either with a person who may wish not to tell the truth, to tell less than the whole truth, or to change his story later. If there is doubt, then a witness should be interviewed formally on oath, with a shorthand writer present.

11 Some appointments of inspectors are consequential on preliminary enquiries conducted by investigators appointed under section 447 to inspect a company's documents. The information obtained by those investigators under that section may not be published or disclosed except as permitted by section 449. Unlawful disclosure is a criminal offence. Inspectors appointed under sections 431, 432, 442 and 446 are 'competent authorities' within the meaning of section 449 so that information obtained under section 447 can properly be communicated to them; by virtue of section 449(1)(c) inspectors may disclose such information for the purpose of enabling or assisting them to discharge their functions. For example it may be disclosed to witnesses for the purpose of their examination. It should be noted that any person appointed or authorised to exercise any power under section 94, 106 or 177 of the Financial Services Act 1986 and any officer or servant of such a person is also a competent authority for section 449 purposes.

Procedure

(a) Obtaining books, records, documents and other information

12 By virtue of section 434(1) all past and present officers and agents of the company are under a duty 'to produce to the inspectors all documents of or relating to the company', 'to attend before the inspectors when required to do so' and 'otherwise to give to the inspectors all assistance in connection with the investigation which they are reasonably able to give'. Agents include the company's bankers, solicitors and auditors (section 434(4)). Section 434(2) enables the inspectors to require anyone (including those covered by section 434(1)) whom the inspectors consider have or may have any information relating to a matter which they believe to be relevant to the investigation to produce documents, attend before them and otherwise to assist them with the investigation. Section 443 applies section 434 to the particular circumstances of an investigation under section 442. Section 446(3) makes analogous provision for investigations under section 446. By section 434(6) 'documents' includes information recorded in any form, and in relation to information recorded otherwise than in legible form, the power to require its production includes power to require the production of a copy of the information in legible form. Banks do not have to disclose information or produce documents in respect of which they owe an obligation of confidence unless the person to whom the obligation of confidence is owed is the company under investigation or consents to the disclosure or production or the Secretary of State authorises the inspectors to require the information for production.

13 Any refusal to comply with the requirements of the inspectors may be certified by the inspectors to the court, which after enquiring into the case, may punish the offender as if he were in contempt of court (section 436(2)). This provision applies also to investigations under sections 442 and 446 – see sections 443(1) and 446(3) respectively. If the inspectors are considering certifying a witness they are asked to raise the matter with the Department. It is the practice to instruct the Treasury Solicitor on their behalf.

14 Inspectors appointed under section 442 who experience difficulty in finding out relevant facts about any shares should be aware that the Department may be able to help them under section 445. That section empowers the

Secretary of State to impose restrictions on the relevant shares, for example on their transfer, the exercise of voting rights; and the payment of dividends. Where inspectors are considering a request to the Secretary of State to invoke such powers they should discuss the matter with the Department without delay. They should not wait for the preparation of a report.

15 A person cannot be required to disclose to inspectors or produce to them any document if he would be entitled to refuse to do so on grounds of legal professional privilege in civil proceedings in the High Court or in the Court of Session (section 452). A lawyer, however, is not entitled to refuse to disclose the name and address of his client, but except in this respect the usual rules relating to legal professional privilege apply. The privilege is the privilege of the client and not of the lawyer and may be waived by the client but not by the lawyer.

(b) Enquiries outside Great Britain

16 The Department has reached agreement on the exchange of information with regulators in some countries, and further agreements are under negotiation. Close links are maintained with regulators in a number of other countries, but there is no standard method for seeking assistance. Consequently if inspectors wish to obtain evidence or information from a person overseas – including by correspondence – they should consult Investigations Division before making any attempt (whether formal or informal) to do so. Similarly if inspectors consider that it would be desirable for interviews to take place with witnesses overseas, they should consult Investigations Division on the procedures to be followed. Overseas regulators will need to be consulted in advance, and their own procedures will need to be followed. For example, in many countries foreign inspectors may not be allowed to examine witnesses directly; in others, the local regulator may require to be represented, and there may be variations in how such examination can be recorded.

(c) Examination of witnesses

17 A witness should be given reasonable notice that he is required to attend upon the inspectors for examination. Depending on the urgency of the investigation reasonable notice might vary between a day and two weeks. A witness should be given a copy of the inspectors' minute of appointment, either beforehand or on arrival for interview. While it is not always easy to anticipate the line which an enquiry will take, and inspectors may on occasions want the reaction of a witness to unexpected questions, they may find their enquiries will be facilitated if a witness is given advance notice in general terms of the matters on which he is to be examined, together with particulars of any documents which the inspectors require him to produce or propose to refer to while examining him. In some cases it may be worthwhile to ask witnesses for a brief written statement about the matters on which they are to be questioned.

18 It is expected that persons under an obligation to attend before the inspectors when required to do so under section 434 will meet the cost of so attending. Where a person is unable to meet the costs of attendance the Department should be consulted.

19 Some witnesses attend accompanied by their legal advisers. When inspectors become aware that legal advisers are acting for a witness they should ask the legal advisers to identify all the clients for whom they are acting in relation to the enquiry and to advise them of any changes. It is desirable for this information to be recorded at the beginning of the transcript of the examination of the client (or clients) of the legal advisers. There can, of course, be no question of a barrister or solicitor who accompanies a witness answering the inspectors' questions on behalf of the witness. Legal advisers attending before the inspectors may, on occasion, be able to assist by intervening on such matters as the clarity of a question or on the implications of non compliance with the inspectors' requirements. They should be given an opportunity to question their clients if they wish to do so and to make representations. There can be no question of the Department paying the costs incurred by a witness who chooses to bring his legal advisers with him. Witnesses or their advisers have no right to cross-examine other witnesses who have given evidence or to see transcripts of evidence of other witnesses.

20 Inspectors may find that legal advisers represent more than one client attending before them. In some instances, this may be advantageous and ease the burden of the inspectors, but the inspectors may sometimes feel that they should ask the legal advisers to consider whether their representation of different clients involves a conflict of interest. In exceptional instances inspectors may feel that the investigation would be prejudiced if the same legal adviser were to act for more than one client. Particular care may be needed where a legal adviser is adviser to the employer of a witness as well as to the witness himself. In some such cases the inspectors may consider that the risk of prejudice would be removed if a particular legal representative were to give an undertaking not to use the information from one interview in advising another witness who is also his client. In other instances inspectors may feel that the risk of prejudice is such that they should tell the legal adviser and his clients that one or more of the clients should seek separate legal representation.

21 Section 434(5) of the Companies Act 1985 provides that an answer given by a person to a question put to him in exercise of powers conferred on inspectors by Section 434 may be used in evidence against him. The fact that the answer to a question may incriminate the witness does not preclude the inspectors from putting the question to him, but the inspectors cannot properly try to insist that a witness give them an answer to a question which he refuses to answer. That would be a 'wrongful assumption of power' (see Lord Upjohn in McClelland, Pope and Langley v Howard and Another (HL) (Noted [1968] 1 All ER 569). Lord Upjohn went on to say 'section 167(3) (of the Companies Act 1948 – subsequently amended and now section 436(2) and (3) of the Companies Act 1985) makes it plain that a witness may refuse to answer questions, and, if he does so, the question whether he did so properly is a matter for the court, if the inspectors so refer the matter, and not for the inspectors.'

22 Inspectors may tell witnesses that they are conducting their enquiry in private but it would be wrong to lead witnesses to think that any evidence they give will remain completely confidential. Inspectors may themselves wish to put such evidence to other witnesses or to refer to it in their report in a manner which identifies the witness who gave it. Furthermore there are a wide variety of circumstances in which transcripts and documents can be released, while witnesses may find themselves asked to give evidence in court if criminal proceedings follow the inspection. Circumstances in which documents can be released include release to regulatory bodies and to prosecuting authorities to assist in the prosecution of offences. Any discussion with a witness about whether or not his evidence might be disclosed to third parties should be recorded in the transcript. Inspectors should not give a witness any assurance about confidentiality without consulting the Department.

23 Where there is more than one inspector both should, if possible, be present when any witness is examined. Inspectors should engage a firm of official shorthand writers to provide a transcript of all formal interviews. The transcript should record:

- who was present;
- the times at which the interview began and finished;
- the times when any break in the interview began and finished, and whether refreshments were served in any such break.

Normally there should be a short break for refreshment at intervals of about two hours.

24 A witness should be supplied with a copy of his own examination at an appropriate time during the course of the enquiry unless in a particular case there are compelling reasons, such as fears about confidentiality, for withholding it altogether. The inspectors should consider whether it is appropriate to obtain an undertaking from the witness (and his legal representative if any) regarding confidentiality of the transcript. If inspectors decide to seek such an undertaking then the Department will advise on the wording.

25 It is a matter for the inspectors' discretion at what stage in the enquiry they provide transcripts to witnesses and whether there is good reason for holding back some part of the transcript either until later into the enquiry or altogether. Inspectors will often find it helpful to have witnesses review their transcripts for accuracy at some stage in the enquiry. However, they may wish not to disclose transcripts at a particular time until other witnesses have been examined.

26 Witnesses should particularly be warned of the danger of disseminating transcripts which include statements that might form the basis of an action against him for defamation. If the inspectors are in any doubt they should consult the Department.

Use of evidence obtained

27 The general policy of the Department is to treat transcripts which come into its possession as confidential. They can, however, be released in certain circumstances, for example:

- they may be released to the Director of Public Prosecutions, the Serious Fraud Office and other prosecuting authorities and the police where it is thought this will assist the investigation and prosecution of crime and the answers given by a witness, whether or not on oath, may be admissible evidence against him in criminal proceedings; or
- statements in transcripts may be used in evidence in proceedings on an application for a disqualification order under the Company Directors Disqualification Act 1986 and in civil proceedings brought in the name of a company by the Secretary of State pursuant to section 438; or
- although there is no gateway in the Companies Act 1985 for transcripts or other information obtained in enquiries to be disclosed to liquidators of companies investigated, in the past such material has been provided to the liquidator for the purposes of civil proceedings as a result of an application by him to the court under what is now section 236 of the Insolvency Act 1986; or
- in accordance with section 451A, information may be disclosed to a competent authority listed in section 449(3) or in any circumstance in which or for any purpose for which disclosure is permitted under section 449. Competent authorities include the Treasury and the Bank of England.

28 Disclosure is discretionary and the Department may impose preconditions for release by it of transcripts and/or excise passages which it considers it would not be in the public interest to disclose.

Investigation of the affairs of related companies

29 Section 433(1) empowers inspectors appointed under section 431 or section 432 to investigate the affairs of any related subsidiary company or the holding company (as defined in section 736 which is prospectively amended by section 144 of the Companies Act 1989 which is not yet in force) of a company subject to an inspection. It is to be noted that the powers of inspection under section 433 may only be exercised where the inspectors think it necessary for the purposes of the investigation for which they have been appointed. Section 433(1) provides that for inspections under section 431 or section 432 the inspectors shall report on the results of their investigation of related companies in so far as they think they are relevant to the investigation of the company whose affairs they were appointed to investigate. The powers under section 433(1) extend to any past and present subsidiary and holding company.

30 It is suggested that the powers under section 433(1) may not be exercisable to explore, for example, misfeasance in an acquired subsidiary prior to its acquisition except in so far as the nondisclosure of the misfeasance affected the terms of acquisition or the misfeasance has consequences which could not have been foreseen and which form part of the subsidiary's affairs after acquisition. Where inspectors become aware of matters which they consider merit investigation and it may be questionable whether they can be investigated under section 433(1), they should approach the Department about the possibility of a specific appointment under sections 431, 432 or 442, in relation to the company in question.

Department of Trade and Industry assistance

31 Inspectors have a distinct statutory position and are independent of the Department, which does not involve itself with the day-to-day conduct of the inspection. The Department is, however, ready to assist inspectors by facilitating access to public records and in such other ways as the circumstances of a particular case may permit. In particular the Department will assist inspectors to obtain technical or professional assistance, where necessary. The Department will introduce inspectors to those officers of public bodies such as the Bank of England, The Securities Association, the Securities and Investments Board and the Panel on Takeovers and Mergers, or to those officials of other government departments who may be able to help them.

32 The Department needs to keep itself informed of the progress of investigations, and for this purpose it will arrange regular discussions with inspectors and invite a brief informal progress report in advance of such discussion. Inspectors are encouraged to discuss the progress of their investigation with the Department at any time and to raise any matters on which they feel that the Department could provide guidance or assistance.

33 If an inspection involves an enquiry into the affairs of a life assurance office, inspectors will be advised about possible advantages of discussing with the Government Actuary's Department the position and function of the appointed actuary.

Treatment of witnesses

34 Inspectors are not called upon to conduct a trial of those associated with the company, but to ascertain the facts and to make them available. For this reason, and because there is no appeal against the validity of any criticisms made by inspectors, it is most important that inspectors should exercise restraint in the manner and the extent of their criticisms – particularly of individuals – and should make criticisms only to the extent necessary for a proper appreciation of their report. As explained in paragraph 50 below, inspectors are invited to inform the Secretary of State separately (other than in their report) of matters which in their view require further action against individuals.

35 Nevertheless, inspectors must inevitably be critical on occasions in reports which may be published of the conduct of individuals (eg they may have to decide which of conflicting accounts of particular occurrences they accept) and in some instances criticism may be called for in order to refute unwarranted suspicions that an individual's conduct was even more reprehensible (eg they may wish to say that someone was negligent but not dishonest). Inspectors may need to point the finger of criticism in order to demonstrate how particular events occurred and must, if their report is to have value, state their findings on the evidence and their opinions on the matters referred to them 'with courage and frankness, keeping nothing back' per Denning MR, in Maxwell v Department of Trade and Industry and Others [1974] 2 All ER 122. Inspectors should avoid superfluous epithets and the eye catching phrase which is likely to lead to unbalanced comments, and to limit remarks about conduct to conduct in the company's affairs.

36 The decision of the Court of Appeal in Re Pergamon Press Ltd [1970] 3 All ER 535 and Maxwell v Department of Trade and Industry and Others [1974] 2 All ER 122 involved consideration as to how company inspections should be conducted. The full text of these judgments is at Appendices E and F. In the view of the Department the broad effect of these judgments is as follows:

– although the proceedings are only administrative, inspectors must act fairly, in that if they are disposed to condemn or criticise anyone in a report

they must first give him a fair opportunity to correct or contradict the evidence against him;
- inspectors do not have to put all the evidence against him to the person concerned in precise detail; it suffices to indicate the substance of the evidence on which the criticism would be based;
- save for the requirement to act fairly, the inspectors are not subject to any set rules of procedure and are free to act at their own discretion.

37 Inspectors have in the past taken steps over and above those they are required by law to take in order to satisfy witnesses that they have been treated fairly. This has caused considerable delay in concluding enquiries. Inspectors are requested to balance carefully the need to act fairly to witnesses with the need to complete their report in a reasonable time so that the result of their enquiries become available for use by the Department and others as soon as possible.

38 The inspectors will discharge their duty to treat a witness fairly if they give him notice of the evidence on which their intended criticisms are based in terms which are sufficient to enable him to know what is being said against him and to enable him to give such explanations as he may wish. Inspectors are not bound to put to a witness all the statements which have been made by other witnesses which may be prejudicial to him. Nor are they bound to name such witnesses, identify sources of information or provide the witness with transcripts of evidence adverse to him. Their duty is to put to him points of substance so as to give him a chance to explain the relevant evidence which is prejudicial to him.

39 In the Maxwell case Lawton LJ said: 'In my judgement [inspectors] are no more bound to tell a witness likely to be criticised in their report what they have in mind to say about him than has a judge sitting alone who has to decide which two conflicting witnesses is telling the truth. The judge must ensure that the witness whose credibility is suspected has a fair opportunity of correcting or contradicting the substance of what other witnesses have said or are expected to say which is in conflict with his testimony. Inspectors should do the same but I can see no reason why they should do any more.'

40 Inspectors are not obliged to give a witness more than one opportunity to respond to evidence which is prejudicial to him or to possible criticisms. Nor are they required to enter into prolonged correspondence with witnesses or their advisers about the terms of criticisms nor to negotiate with them over the text of their report. Indeed it may be inadvisable to send witnesses extracts from a draft report for if the inspectors subsequently wish to change a draft on which a witness had commented they may feel obliged to send him the revised draft for further comments. However, if inspectors feel it would be helpful, or in the light of new evidence, to seek further views from witnesses in respect of revised criticisms then they may do so.

41 The sort of approach that might be adopted is as follows:

- where inspectors at the time when they examine a witness already have evidence which they feel may prompt them to criticise him, and it is convenient to do so, they should consider putting the substance of evidence and their intended criticisms to the witness during his examination. If they decide to put provisional criticisms or conclusions to the witness then they should do so separately from their examination of the witness as to the facts; possibly at the end of the interview;
- once the inspectors have prepared a first draft of their report they may think it appropriate, even though they have put to the witness at interview the substance of the evidence against him, to write to the witness setting out the intended criticisms with notice of the evidence on which they are based giving him a fixed period of, for example, 21 days to respond;
- where the inspectors consider it appropriate in fairness to the witness to do so, a statement or representation by a witness in response to proposed criticism may be included in the report either wholly or in part whether in the text or as an Appendix. In deciding whether to include such material in their report, inspectors should bear in mind the qualified privilege which it enjoys and that the inclusion of irrelevant or defamatory matter which might inhibit the Department from publishing the report must be avoided;
- witnesses to whom draft passages of a report are submitted should be warned that they are expected to treat them as confidential; and that as they only reflect the provisional views of the inspectors it does not necessarily follow that the passages will appear in their report; and of the implications of unwarranted publication. It may be desirable to seek an undertaking as to confidentiality from a witness and his advisers before disclosing extracts from a draft report;
- the fact that a witness has been charged with a criminal offence does not absolve the inspectors from their duty to give him a fair opportunity to deal with the substance of material evidence given by other witnesses which is adverse to him.

42 The above guidance on treatment of witnesses sets out the position in a case where a report may be published. In other cases a report of an investigation cannot be published but may, nevertheless, be disclosed to bodies or persons other than the Department under the provisions of the legislation under which the investigation has taken place. Although such investigators have a duty to be fair, the implications of that duty are different in the different circumstances.

Transmission of information to the Secretary of State

43 Under section 437(1A) inspectors appointed under section 431 or 432 may at any time, and if the Secretary of State so directs them shall, inform him of any matters coming to their knowledge as a result of their investigations. Such matters do not include judgments, evaluations or opinions formed by the inspectors in the course of their investigations. The Secretary of State can be given this information without the necessity of the inspectors making a formal interim report. This means that in suitable cases the Secretary of State may pass information to the Serious Fraud Office or police for enquiries with a view to prosecution or information may be disclosed for regulatory, investigatory or disciplinary purposes (see also sections 451A and 449).

44 In particular the Department asks inspectors to use their power under section 437(1A) to advise it promptly of any matter which comes to light during the course of an inspection which suggests that an offence has been committed or that consideration may need to be given to regulatory or disciplinary action or that information may need to be disclosed to other investigators or to a competent authority (see section 449). Inspectors are reminded that proceedings for an offence under the Companies Act 1985 which is triable only summarily cannot be instituted more than three years after it has been committed (section 731).

45 When giving information under section 437(1A), inspectors should not devote effort to preparing a formal interim report unless asked to do so. The Department is ready at all times to discuss with inspectors the operation of section 437(1A) the nature of the information required and the format in which such information should be presented.

46 Where serious offences come to light, it is desirable that Serious Fraud Office and police enquiries should proceed as rapidly as possible and inspectors are asked to do all they can towards this end. There are two ways in which inspectors can facilitate any consequential proceedings. The first is by keeping a full record of all original and copy documents obtained in the course of their enquiries. The second is that under section 434(5), an answer given by a person to a question to him under that section can be used in evidence against him. The preparation of any proceedings for prosecution based upon the work of inspectors is much eased if inspectors ensure that where a document is put to a witness in the course of his examination, the transcript of evidence clearly identifies the relevant document by, for example, an exhibit number. In that way anyone reading the transcript may immediately know the document which is being referred to and it may be conclusively identified. Where the document is short, it may be more convenient to attach a copy of it to the transcript. The Department places great importance on the evidencing of the provenance of documents which may be required in criminal proceedings. Inspectors will be informed by the Department at the beginning of their enquiries of the procedures which should be adopted.

47 Under section 437(1B) where it appears to the Secretary of State that matters have come to light in the course of the inspectors' investigation which suggest that a criminal offence has been committed, and those matters have been referred to the appropriate prosecuting authority, he may direct the inspectors to take no further steps in the investigation or only such further steps as are specified in the direction. In such cases the inspectors will only make a final report if they were appointed under section 432(1) (appointment in pursuance of an order of the court) or the Secretary of State directs them to do so. Inspectors can themselves be called upon to give evidence in proceedings and can be cross examined.

Preparation of the report

48 Inspectors embark on the preparation of a report after a period of close familiarity with the affairs of the company or other matters under investigation. Some reports can be expected to attract public interest and considerable press coverage, especially if well known public figures are involved or the company is one with which the public has much dealing. Inspectors are asked to bear in mind that some who read the report may have no prior knowledge of the company or the matters under investigation and that it may be difficult for such readers to appreciate the importance and relevance of particular parts of the report. It may sometimes be helpful to start with a very brief history of the company under inspection down to the time of the appointment, a general picture of the group structure, if the company is a subsidiary or has subsidiaries, and a synopsis of the matters dealt with in the report.

49 As to the particular issues covered by the report, it is suggested that inspectors should consider:

- how far issues which they have considered may be ignored, being irrelevant to the affairs of the company or to the subject matter of the investigation;
- how deeply specific issues should be dealt with. Some may merit no more than passing mention, eg where the investigation revealed that the matter in question gave no cause for concern or was unimportant;
- how best to set out the facts discovered by the inspectors in order to indicate whether any offences may have been committed or to indicate conclusions on wider matters. However, inspectors should avoid using eye catching language or commenting on any behaviour of witnesses which is not directly relevant to the matters to be investigated.

50 Inspectors should consider whether to include a summary of the findings and if so, how the summary should be drafted. Experience has shown that where a summary is included, the press sometimes consider only this part of the report and, on occasions reproduce all or parts of it verbatim. Consequently, accuracy and attention to balance are particularly important in the drafting of a summary. It is also suggested that it is inadvisable to include findings that particular individuals have committed particular offences if only because a jury may subsequently acquit the person and even the bare recital of facts could be prejudicial in certain circumstances and might necessitate consideration of whether publication of a report should be deferred. A preferable alternative is for the inspectors to inform the Secretary of State (otherwise than in their report) of any matters coming to their knowledge as a result of their investigations which they believed were relevant to further action against individuals.

51 The preceding comments assume that the inspectors are minded to make only one report. By section 437(1) inspectors are empowered, and required if so directed by the Secretary of State, to make an interim report or reports. Cases in which it may be appropriate to consider an interim report, include:

- where it appears to the inspectors that there is a need to take urgent action on their report. Examples would be the presentation of a petition by the Secretary of State in accordance with section 124(4) of the Insolvency Act 1986 or the institution of civil proceedings under section 438 of the Companies Act 1985 or disqualification proceedings under section 8 of the Company Directors Disqualification Act 1986;
- cases involving matters of major public interest where there is urgent public demand for information;
- cases where the investigation is likely to be unavoidably lengthy;
- cases where key witnesses are not immediately available and are unlikely to be available in the foreseeable future;
- cases where the enquiry naturally divides itself in some way and it is convenient to split up the report;
- cases where litigation over issues relevant to the enquiry makes it desirable to defer further action;
- cases where criminal proceedings are pending against witnesses.

52 In such cases the interim report should be made on the basis of the evidence which the inspectors have been able to obtain and the substance of which has been put to witnesses whom they propose to criticise in the light of that evidence. Further evidence may emerge, for example in a criminal trial, to cause the inspectors to come to a different conclusion. It is important, therefore, that in their interim report inspectors should expressly state that they reserve the right to revise their conclusions in the light of any further evidence. Subsequently the inspectors should make a final report which in appropriate cases may replace the interim report. Once inspectors deliver their final report their statutory powers and duties as inspectors cease. Their assistance may however continue to be needed in relation to any follow up action.

Recovery of costs

53 Inspectors are reminded of the provisions of section 439(6), regarding recommendations about the recovery of expenses of the investigation where inspectors are not appointed on the Secretary of State's own motion.

Publication of report

54 When inspectors have prepared a draft of their interim or final report, they are invited to submit it to the Department. The object of this procedure is not for the Department to influence the substance of the report, but to facilitate the discussion of whether the report is in a form suitable for publication and whether it contains material which might inhibit the Department from publication.

55 The normal practice is for the Department to publish reports submitted to it under section 437 in respect of public companies as being matters of public interest, but not to publish reports in respect of private companies unless there is a particular public interest in them. Publication may, however, be deferred if there is a possibility that criminal proceedings may be taken, in order to avoid the possibility of prejudice to such proceedings. Additionally, by section 432(2A), inspectors may be appointed on terms that any report they make is not for publication.

56 Except when inspectors are appointed on the basis that their report is not to be published, the Secretary of State may, whether or not a report is published, if he thinks fit forward a copy of it to the company's registered office and furnish a copy on request and on payment of the prescribed fee to any member of the company or other body corporate which is the subject of the report and certain other persons including any person whose conduct is referred to in the report and the applicants for the investigation if the inspectors were appointed under section 431 or 442(3) (see section 437(3)). If the Secretary of State is of the opinion that there is good reason for not divulging any part of a report of an investigation under section 442 he may publish or disclose the report under section 437(3) (or both) with the omission of that part.

Publicity

57 Inspectors may be approached by the press from time to time for information about the progress of enquiries. It is not the Department's practice to comment on the progress of investigations. Any approach by the press to the inspectors should be referred to the Department's Press Office at 1 Victoria Street, London SW1H 0ET. Investigations Division in consultation with the Press Office and, if necessary, the inspectors, will consider whether there are exceptional circumstances which justify a departure from the usual practice.

Appendix 15 Investigation Handbook Appendix C – Notes for the guidance of inspectors appointed under section 177 of the Financial Services Act 1986

Introduction

1 The Secretary of State may appoint one or more inspectors under section 177(1) of the Financial Services Act 1986 (the FSA) if it appears to him that there are circumstances suggesting that there may have been a contravention of the Company Securities (Insider Dealing) Act 1985 (the Act). Such inspectors have the statutory duties and powers which are set out in sections 177 (as amended by section 74 of the Companies Act 1989) and 178 of the FSA. Their main duty is to carry out such investigations as are requisite to establish whether or not any such contravention has occurred and to report the results of their investigations to the Secretary of State. They have the powers in section 177(3) to require co-operation from any person who they consider may be able to give information concerning any such contravention.

2 These notes have been prepared by the Department of Trade and Industry for the guidance of such inspectors. However the circumstances of inspections vary, and it is impossible to offer guidance about every situation which inspectors may encounter.

3 The Department cannot fetter the discretion of inspectors with respect to how they carry out their enquiries and these notes are not intended to give that impression. Inspectors are masters of their own procedure. The responsibility for the conduct of the investigation is theirs. However they must act fairly and reasonably. Inspectors are encouraged to refer to the Department for advice if they are in doubt, and are particularly asked to consult the Department in the circumstances where these notes specifically recommend that they should.

4 The Secretary of State may, whether at the outset or later, limit the period during which the inspectors are to carry out their investigation, or confine it to particular matters. After appointment he may extend any limit on the period of the enquiries. In addition the Secretary of State may direct the inspectors to take no further steps in the investigation, or only such further

steps as he directs. If he gives such a direction, then the inspectors submit a final report only if he so requires.

5 The FSA does not specify how many inspectors there should be in a particular case. Normally there are two, one of whom is a lawyer, and these notes are written on that basis.

General points

6 The minute of appointment is drafted in the light of the facts which constitute the 'circumstances suggesting that there may have been a contravention' in the particular case.

7 Inspectors are not obliged to investigate everything which is within the terms of the minute of appointment. They should concentrate their attention on the possible contraventions suggested by the documents which were the basis for their appointment, and supplied to them by the Department, together with any other promising lines of enquiry which emerge from their investigations.

8 Inspectors are appointed on the understanding that they are able and willing to give the inspection top priority, and as much time as it proves to require. They should complete their investigations as quickly and cost effectively as possible. The inspector responsible for providing administrative support (often an accountant) should make available the resources that are required to enable this to be done.

9 Inspectors will be asked to agree, on or soon after their appointment, a target date for the completion of their report, and should ensure that there is no delay in its submission, together with supporting documents. This is particularly important where their report is likely to result in the institution of criminal proceedings, or where its contents are likely to require other follow up action.

10 If during their investigation inspectors come to believe that the Department should consider:

- appointing them (or others) to investigate suspected contraventions of the Act not covered by their minute of appointment;
- authorising enquiries under other powers (for example under sections 432, 442, or 447 of the Companies Act 1985 as amended by the Companies Act 1989);
- informing the police, or regulatory or enforcement authorities, whether in the UK or abroad, of matters which have come to their attention;
- taking any other enforcement action;

they should consult the Department as soon as possible.

11 Inspectors are encouraged to keep the Department informed of the progress, direction and likely cost of the investigation, to discuss progress with the Department at any time, and to raise with the Department any matters on which they feel that the Department could provide guidance or assistance. Regular meetings are held with all inspectors to monitor progress.

12 The Department does not involve itself with the day-to-day conduct of the inspection, but is ready to assist inspectors by facilitating access to public records and in such other ways as the circumstances of a particular case may permit.

13 Inspectors should feel free to discuss problems concerning the interpretation of the Act or of the FSA, including any relating to the exercise of their powers, with the Department which may have had to consider a similar problem in a different case.

Publicity

14 The appointment of inspectors under section 177 FSA is not normally announced or acknowledged. However such announcement or acknowledgement may take place in a particular case if it is in the public interest, for example if public servants are thought to be involved, or if there has already been publicity for an investigation and it is judged that it would be less damaging to the individuals or organisations concerned and appropriate in the circumstances if the existence of an investigation were acknowledged. The main reason for this policy is to avoid unnecessary public criticism of the people or firms concerned when in fact no wrong doing may be found.

15 If information about an unannounced inspection is disclosed, and the Department is asked whether an investigation is taking place, it will normally neither confirm nor deny that inspectors have been appointed or that an investigation is being made. If inspectors are approached by the Press with questions about an investigation, then whether or not it has been announced they should decline to comment and alert Investigations Division or, if the approach is made outside normal working hours, the DTI duty officer on 071-215 4657. Any claim by the Press that they have received clearance from the Department to speak to the inspectors should be checked with the Department.

16 If an announcement is to be made then its terms and timing will be discussed with the inspectors. The content will be kept to the minimum and no answers given to questions about the details and source of the evidence.

Role of the Secretary

17 Inspectors are asked to appoint a Secretary to provide administrative support. Such a Secretary is an officer or servant of the inspectors (see section 179(3)(i) of the FSA – which concerns disclosure of information) but has no specific statutory status. The Secretary should, however, be of sufficient status and competence to ensure that the investigation proceeds quickly and efficiently.

Conduct of the investigation

18 Inspectors should ask for original documents to be produced by the person having custody of them, and should retain them or copies of them. If the same inspectors are appointed under other powers as well as under section 177 FSA – eg under section 442 of the Companies Act – they, when seeking information or co-operation, should make it clear which powers they are exercising.

19 As a general rule all witnesses should be interviewed on oath. The circumstances of the matter under investigation will determine whether it is better to study the documentary evidence before interviewing witnesses or to interview some or all witnesses immediately. Generally the former course is preferable as it enables the inspectors to ask more precise questions. Normally it is advisable to see those able to give background information first and the suspect last. Inspectors should consider carefully the order in which witnesses are seen with a view to reducing the need to recall any of them, and in order to enable the evidence of some of them to be taken into account or employed when examining others. However for a variety of reasons, for example absence abroad or illness, it may be impossible to see the witnesses in the order planned, or it may be possible to do so only at the cost of delaying unreasonably the completion of the inspection.

20 The information given to inspectors at the start of their investigation may include information which had been provided in confidence by an informant. The source of any such information should be concealed in order to avoid breaching confidence and to protect the informant from possible retaliatory action. It might be possible to obtain the same information from a different source so that inspectors can question witnesses without revealing the original source. In other circumstances it might be appropriate to include the informant among the first witnesses examined on oath so that he can defend his disclosure as compulsory.

21 Inspectors should discuss with the Department beforehand any proposed interview with an informant. So far as possible the inspectors should avoid identifying an informant as such in the transcript of his formal interview. It is advisable to discuss this point before the interview with the informant. Neither the informant's identity nor any information which might enable others to identify him should be disclosed to anyone else without prior discussion with the Department.

22 Inspectors may wish to make enquiries informally of witnesses before they are formally examined. Such informal interviews may be of assistance in clarifying the issues in the enquiry, or the ways in which witnesses may be able to help the inspectors. In such circumstances a witness may be interviewed informally by one only of the inspectors, or by the Secretary. It is, however, unwise for an informal interview of this kind to take place with a person who either is a suspect, or who may wish either not to tell the truth, or to tell less than the whole truth, or to change his story later. If there is doubt, then a witness should be interviewed formally on oath, with a shorthand writer present.

Formal interviews

23 A witness should be given reasonable notice that he is required to attend upon the inspectors for examination. Depending upon the urgency of the investigation reasonable notice might vary between a day and two weeks. A witness should be given a copy of the inspectors' minute of appointment, either beforehand or upon arrival for interview.

24 A witness should also be told that he is entitled to seek legal advice, and that he may, if he wishes, be accompanied at the interview by his legal advisers. When inspectors become aware that legal advisers are acting for a witness they should ask the legal advisers to identify all the clients for whom they are acting in relation to the enquiry and to advise them of any changes. It is desirable for this information to be recorded at the beginning of the transcript of the examination of the client (or clients) of the legal advisers.

25 It is not always easy to foresee the direction which an enquiry may take, and on occasions inspectors may wish to obtain the reaction of a witness to unexpected questions. But it may often be helpful to give a witness advance notice in general terms of the matter on which the inspectors expect to examine him, together with particulars of any documents which the inspectors will require him to produce, or to which they propose to refer while examining him. There is, however, no obligation to do this. Some inspectors have also found it worthwhile to ask witnesses for a brief written statement about the matters on which they are to be questioned.

26 Inspectors should engage a firm of shorthand writers to provide a transcript of all formal interviews. The transcript should record:

- who was present;
- the times at which the interview began and finished;
- the times when any break in the interview began and finished, and whether refreshments were served in any such break.

Normally there should be a short break for refreshment at intervals of about two hours.

27 Both inspectors should be present at formal interviews. Inspectors have found that it is normally preferable not to conduct such interviews on the witness' own premises.

28 Section 177(6) of the FSA provides that a statement made by a person in compliance with a requirement imposed by virtue of section 177 may be used in evidence against him. The fact that the answer to a question may incriminate the witness does not preclude the inspectors from putting the question to him, but the inspectors cannot properly try to insist that a witness give them an answer to a question which he refuses to answer. That would be a 'wrongful assumption of power' (see Lord Upjohn in McClelland, Pope and Langley v Howard (HL) (noted [1968] 1 All ER 569). Lord Upjohn went on to say 'section 167(3) [of the Companies Act 1948 – subsequently amended and now section 436(2) and (3) of the Companies Act 1985, which is similar to section 178(1) and (2) of the FSA] makes it plain that a witness may refuse to answer questions, and if he does so, the question whether he did so properly is a matter for the court, if the inspectors so refer the matter, and not for the inspectors'.

29 In the case Re an Inquiry under the Company Securities (Insider Dealing) Act 1985 [1988] 1 All ER 203) the House of Lords held that the protection of a journalist's source was not a reasonable excuse if a response by the journalist to the inspectors' question was necessary or 'really needed' for the purpose of the inquiry of the inspectors, the aim of which was the prevention of crime.

30 If a witness has been charged in respect of a particular matter inspectors should not question him further about that matter. They may, however, question him about other matters.

31 Inspectors may find that legal advisers represent more than one client attending before them. In some instances this may be advantageous and ease the burden of the inspectors, but the inspectors may sometimes feel that they should ask the legal advisers to consider whether their representation of different clients involves a conflict of interest. In exceptional instances inspectors may feel that the investigation would be prejudiced if the same legal adviser were to act for more than one client. Particular care may be needed where a legal adviser is adviser to the employer of a witness as well as to the witness himself. In some such cases the inspectors may consider that the risk of prejudice would be removed if a particular legal representative were to give an undertaking not to use the information from one interview in advising another witness who is also his client. In other instances inspectors may feel that the risk of prejudice is such that they should tell the legal adviser and his clients that one or more of the clients should seek separate legal representation.

32 There can be no question of a barrister or solicitor who accompanies a witness answering the inspectors' questions on behalf of the witness. Legal advisers attending with a witness may, however, be able to assist by intervening on such matters as the clarity of a question or the implications of non-compliance with the inspectors' requirements. They should be given an opportunity to question their clients if they wish to do so, and to make representations. However witnesses or their advisers have no right to cross examine other witnesses, or to see the transcripts of evidence of other witnesses.

33 At the end of an interview the legal adviser may be invited to comment, or to make written representations, or he may be asked to make enquiries or to provide information about the witness on lines indicated by the inspectors.

34 Inspectors should be cautious about allowing any other representation, or observers, at interviews, unless they feel that it would assist their investigation.

33 Inspectors should explain the restrictions on the disclosure of information in section 179 of the FSA (see paragraph 38 below) to all witnesses, legal advisers and observers, and satisfy themselves, before consenting to the attendance at an interview of anyone other than a witness, that he will not pass on information in breach of that section.

Legal professional privilege

36 A person cannot be required to disclose to inspectors any information or produce to them any document if he would be entitled to refuse to do so on grounds of legal professional privilege in civil proceedings in the High Court or in the Court of Session. The usual rules relating to legal professional privilege apply: the privilege is the privilege of the client and not of the lawyer, and may be waived by the client but not by the lawyer.

Obtaining information from banks

37 Inspectors may not require a person to disclose information, or to produce a document, in respect of which he owes a duty of confidence by virtue of carrying on the business of banking unless either the person to whom the obligation is owed consents or the Secretary of State authorises the inspectors' requirement. Any request to the Secretary of State for such authorisation should be made in a letter signed by both inspectors. If the Secretary of State agrees to such a request, the inspectors will be sent a letter granting authorisation that may be produced to the bank in support of the requirement from the inspectors.

Confidentiality of information obtained

38 Information obtained by inspectors (or by their officers or servants) for the purposes of, or in the discharge of, their functions is restricted information for the purposes of section 179 of the FSA. The effect is that such information, insofar as it relates to the business or other affairs of any person, must not be disclosed without the consent of the person who provided the information and, if different, of the person to whom it relates, except as permitted by virtue of section 179 or section 180 of the FSA. This prohibition applies both in respect of disclosure by the inspectors themselves, or by any of their officers or servants, or by anyone who obtains the information directly or indirectly from them. Thus it applies to anyone who is interviewed or consulted in the course of the investigation.

39 Breach of the prohibition on disclosure contained in section 179 is a criminal offence. However other provisions, mainly in section 180, ensure that such disclosure is not an offence if it is for specified purposes. Inspectors will often need to disclose information by virtue of section 180(1)(p) – to assist them to discharge their functions. It may also be proper by virtue of section 180(1)(c) for them to disclose information to another inspector or investigator. Where inspectors are minded to disclose information otherwise than to facilitate their own enquiries or to the Department, they should consult the Department before doing so.

40 Inspectors may tell witnesses that they are conducting their enquiry on a confidential basis, but it would be wrong to lead witnesses to think that any evidence which they give will remain completely confidential. Inspectors may themselves wish to put such evidence to other witnesses, or to refer to it in their report in a manner which identifies the witness who gave it. Furthermore, witnesses may find themselves asked to give evidence in court if criminal proceedings follow the inspection. Moreover, information obtained by the inspectors may be disclosed for the purposes specified in section 180 of the Act, for example to regulatory bodies to assist them to perform their functions. Any discussion with a witness about whether or not his evidence might be disclosed to third parties should be recorded in the transcript. No assurances should be given to witnesses about the confidentiality of their evidence without consulting the Department first.

Fairness to witnesses

41 Inspectors have a general duty to behave in a fair way, both in their personal conduct, and by giving witnesses a reasonable opportunity to seek legal advice.

42 If inspectors are minded to conclude that a person has contravened the Act then they should put to him the substance of the evidence against him and give him an opportunity to respond, either at an interview (or further interview) or in writing if he so wishes.

Costs

43 The Department will not meet the expenses of witnesses required to attend before inspectors, except in exceptional circumstances. If inspectors have it in mind to pay any such expenses then the Department should be consulted before they agree to do so. The Department will not pay the costs incurred by a witness of obtaining legal advice, or of bringing his legal advisers with him, and this should be made clear to witnesses.

44 Inspectors should not normally offer to pay for information – eg copies of bank statements in cases where they could issue a requirement under section 177(3) for someone to provide it. If they consider that, exceptionally, payment should be made in such a case they should consult the Department before agreeing to make it.

Release of transcripts of evidence

45 A witness should be supplied with a copy of his own examination at an appropriate time during the course of the enquiry unless in particular circumstances there are compelling reasons, such as fears about confidentiality, for withholding it altogether. It is a matter for the inspectors' discretion at what stage in the enquiry they provide transcripts to witnesses and whether there is good reason for holding back some part of a transcript, either until later into the enquiry or altogether.

46 If a transcript is released, then the witness should be warned about the effect of disclosing restricted information contrary to section 179 of the FSA, and also about the risk of disclosing a transcript if it includes statements that might form the basis of an action against him for defamation.

47 If inspectors are minded to release a transcript to a witness, it may be advisable to wait until all the oral evidence has been taken, especially if there is a likelihood of collusion, or a likelihood that witnesses will be recalled. On the other hand it may help the inspectors if witnesses can comment on any inaccuracy or gaps in their evidence before the inspectors draft their report. Sight of a transcript may also assist the witness to take legal advice.

48 Inspectors should consider whether it is necessary to seek appropriate undertakings as to confidentiality from a witness or from his legal adviser before releasing a transcript. If inspectors decide to seek such an undertaking then the Department will advise on the wording.

Enquiries outside Great Britain

49 The powers of inspectors apply in Northern Ireland by virtue of section 209 of the FSA. The Department has reached agreement on the exchange of information with regulators in some countries, and further agreements are under negotiation. Close links are maintained with regulators in a number of other countries, but there is no standard method for seeking assistance. Consequently if inspectors wish to obtain evidence or information from a person outside the United Kingdom they should consult Investigations Division before making any attempt (whether formal or informal) to do so. Similarly if inspectors consider that it would be desirable for interviews to take place with witnesses overseas, they should consult Investigations Division on the procedures to be followed. Overseas regulators will need to be consulted in advance, and their own procedures will need to be followed. For example, in many countries foreign inspectors may not be allowed to take evidence directly; in others, the local regulator may require to be represented; and there may be variations in how evidence can be recorded.

Certification to the court for failure to co-operate with inspectors

50 If a person fails to comply with a requirement to produce documents, to attend before the inspectors, or to give all assistance that he is reasonably able to give, or if he refuses to answer questions put to him by inspectors, they may certify that fact in writing to the court.

51 The court may enquire into the case and if it is satisfied the alleged offender did not have a reasonable excuse may punish him as if he had been in contempt of court or direct that the Secretary of State may exercise his powers under section 178 of the FSA. These powers include the cancellation of an authorisation to carry on an investment business, disqualification from becoming authorised to carry on an investment business and various restrictions on the activities of an authorised investment business including conducting business with an unauthorised person who is the subject of a direction.

52 Inspectors are requested to inform the Department as soon as the possibility of such certification arises, and before they take any formal steps to do so. It is the practice in such circumstances for the Treasury Solicitor to be instructed to act on behalf of the inspectors.

The report

53 It is helpful if inspectors show a draft of the report to the Department. The purpose is to help to make the report as useful as possible to those who have to decide on any further action.

54 The report should set out the facts discovered by the inspectors in order to establish whether or not there has been a contravention of the Act. Advice on whether or not these facts constitute all the ingredients of an offence should be given in a separate communication to the Department. All relevant parts of the Act should of course be considered in this context.

55 Inspectors should avoid using extravagant language or commenting on any behaviour of witnesses which is not relevant to the matter they have been asked to investigate. If it appears to them there are other matters which should be investigated, they should report them separately to the Department as soon as possible (see paragraph 10 above). Where criticism of individuals is contemplated it is suggested that inspectors inform the individual of the criticism intended and the evidence for it with a fixed period of, for example, 21 days for response.

56 In some circumstances inspectors may wish to be directed to make a written interim report to the Secretary of State. The Department should be consulted on the format and content of any such report.

57 Inspectors cease to have the powers and duties conferred on them by the FSA when they have submitted their final report. However, the inspectors and the Secretary may need to liaise subsequently with the Department, particularly where follow up action is to be taken by the Department.

Glossary

Authors' note: This glossary is of words commonly used by lawyers some of which may not be familiar to accountants. For more legal definitions see *Osborn's Concise Law Dictionary* (Sweet & Maxwell).

a fortiori – the more so (literally with stronger reason)

ad idem – of the same mind

adjudication – a process, usually in relation to construction disputes, in which a third party resolves disputes as they arise, without resort to arbitration or litigation

affidavit – a written statement by a deponent which is voluntarily signed and sworn to or affirmed

allegation – a statement or charge as yet unproved

***Anton Piller* order** – an order from the High Court for the seizure and preservation of documents relating to an action

arbitration – the resolution of disputes by an arbitrator

aver – to allege

bona fide – in good faith, honestly, without fraud, collusion or participation in wrongdoing

brief – the instructions by a solicitor to a barrister to attend at a trial or hearing

burden (and standard of proof) – the plaintiff (civil) or prosecutor (criminal) must prove his case – on a balance of probabilities, in civil, and beyond reasonable doubt, in criminal

Calderbank letter – a 'without prejudice' letter offering to settle litigation which may state that it may be brought to the attention of the court in connection with costs. It is only effective where payment in is not appropriate

causation – did the wrongdoer's 'offence' cause the loss claimed?

chambers – counsel's offices

Chancery Division – a division of the High Court

Commercial Court – part of the Queen's Bench Division of the High Court: the judge may act as arbitrator or umpire

conciliation – the use of a neutral third party to overcome a deadlock, commence a dialogue or facilitate difficult negotiations. A conciliator may recommend how the dispute should be settled if the parties cannot reach agreement during the conciliation process

conference – a meeting with junior counsel usually in chambers

consultation – a meeting with leading counsel

contract – an agreement enforceable by law

contributory negligence – damages recoverable by a plaintiff may be reduced to the extent which the court thinks just and equitable to take account of the plaintiff's share of responsibility

counsel – a barrister

counterclaim – may be made by a defendant against the plaintiff or any other person who is liable together with the plaintiff. A counterclaim must be separately pleaded and the plaintiff must serve a defence (ordinarily) within 14 days of service

court expert – an independent expert witness (rarely) appointed by the court to enquire into and report on any question of fact or opinion

cross-examination – questions to a witness called by the other party to an action which may include leading questions

damages –
- exemplary (and/or punitive) – enhanced damages reflecting particularly outrageous conduct (and/or to punish such conduct)
- general – unquantified loss
- liquidated – quantified loss
- special – must be pleaded and proven
- remoteness – the damage must be reasonably foreseeable

de bene esse – in effect 'for what it's worth'; frequently used to dignify otherwise inadmissable/unprovable allegations. Beware!

de facto – in fact

de jure – by legal right

defence – a defendant's formal response to a statement of claim; should deny, admit or 'not admit' (i.e., put the plaintiff to proof) in, re all material allegations in the statement of claim

defendant – a person against whom an action is brought; or a person charged with a criminal offence

discontinuance – when the plaintiff voluntarily stops an action. He has to pay the defendant's costs. A defendant who discontinues a counterclaim will have to pay the plaintiff's costs

discovery – the process of disclosure by the parties to an action of all documents (whether helpful or not to the disclosing party's case) in their possession, custody or power relating to the action

ex post facto – retrospectively

examination in chief – questions to a witness on oath – by the party calling him (cf., 'cross-examination')

expert determination – the use of a neutral expert who considers the submissions of the parties and gives a legally binding decision

false accounting – see ss17–20 Theft Act 1968

Family Division – a division of the High Court

first after fixture – the time when the trial will take place if the preceding fixture is not effective

fixture – a case allocated a fixed date for a trial

floater – a case allocated only an approximate trial date/time

foreseeability – the test of reasonable foreseeability (of damage) is applied in determining liability in tort

further and better particulars – the details of a claim or defence which are necessary for the other side to understand the case it has to meet

hearing – the arbitration equivalent of a trial, during which the arbitrator hears evidence and the submissions of both parties to the dispute

inspection of documents – examination (and copying) of documents disclosed by the other party to an action on discovery

inter alia – among other things

inter alios – among other persons

interlocutory hearing – a hearing prior to the trial, usually concerning procedural matters

interrogatories – written questions, to be answered on affidavit

ipso facto – by that very fact

judgment – the reasoned decision of the court

judge in chambers – hears interlocutory appeals from masters in QBD and some original jurisdiction (e.g., re mareva and Anton Piller injunctions)

junior – a barrister who is not Queen's Counsel

leader – Queen's Counsel

mareva injunction – an interlocutory order preventing a defendant from disposing of his assets (beyond a specified limit) such as practically to render judgment unenforceable

Master – the judicial official who deals with most interlocutory hearings

mediation – the most widely used form of ADR, in which an independent third party mediator assists the parties in the resolution of their dispute but does not advise them of his own opinion on the issues or merits of the dispute

mens rea – a guilty mind (*mens rea* is a prerequisite in most criminal cases)

mitigation –
(a) civil: the obligation to take reasonable steps to reduce damages. The party who has been wronged generally has a duty to mitigate damage
(b) criminal: factors mitigating criminal culpability

mutatis mutandis – the necessary changes being made

negligence – a tort actionable by a person suffering damage as a result of the defendant's breach of duty to take care to refrain from injuring him

non sequitur – it does not follow

notice to admit – any party, within 14 days after a case has been set down for trial, can call upon the other party to admit any material fact or document, on pain of paying the costs of proof

novus actus interveniens – a breach in the chain of causation due to the intervention of a third person or cause

obiter dictum – an observation by a judge on a legal matter not requiring a decision and thus not binding as a precedent (cf., *ratio decidendi*)

Official Referee – a judge specialising in construction and technical disputes

order for directions – the directions of a court for the preparation of a civil trial

Order 14 – the High Court rule pursuant to which a plaintiff may claim summary (pre-trial) judgment where a defendant has no arguable defence

pari passu – equally

payment in – a payment by a defendant into court in satisfaction of a claim. Notice must be given to the plaintiff, who risks paying the defendent's subsequent costs if he:
(a) does not accept it; and
(b) recovers judgment for a lesser sum

per se – by or in itself

plaintiff – the claimant in High Court/county court proceedings

pleadings – the documents served by the parties to litigation setting out the questions of fact and law to be decided

precedent – a previous decision of a court cited as binding authority

proof of evidence – a (usually signed) statement of evidence to be given in court by a witness

QC – Queen's Counsel appointed on the recommendation of the Lord Chancellor

quantum meruit – the worth of the work done or service performed where no agreed price

Queen's Bench Division (QBD) – a division of the High Court

ratio decidendi – the judge's/court's reasons for deciding a relevant issue – may be cited as authority or precedent

re-examination – examination of a witness after cross-examination confined to matters arising out of the cross-examination

Registrar – in the county court, performs functions similar to a Master

Reply – a pleading in response to a defence

res ipsa loquitur – the thing speaks for itself (ie., 'it's obvious')

respondent – a person against whom a claim is made in an arbitration

security for costs – a defendant may apply to the court for the plaintiff to provide security for his costs in certain circumstances

settlement –
(1) – the resolution of a dispute at any time before judgment
(2) – the cause of many professional negligence claims against surveyors

Silk – Queen's Counsel

specific discovery – the disclosure of (a) specific document(s) at the request of the other party

stare decisis – the principle whereby previous court decisions are binding

statement of claim – a pleading stating the facts of the plaintiff's case and the remedy he seeks

statute-barred – a claim which cannot be pursued because it is out of time (usually six years, three in the case of personal injuries). No such limitation applies to criminal proceedings

stay of proceedings – the suspending of proceedings, preventing a claimant from bringing or continuing an action in court

subpoena
– ***ad testificandum*** – a writ issued to compel a witness to attend and give evidence
– ***ad duces tecum*** – a writ issued to compel a witness to attend and give evidence and to bring specific documents with him

summons for directions – a summons in High Court proceedings to deal with interlocutory matters in connection with the preparation of a civil trial

third party – a person who is not an original party to the action but from whom the defendant claims a contribution or an indemnity

Taxing Master – a Master who carries out taxation of costs in all cases in the Chancery and Queen's Bench Divisions

third party notice – a notice by a defendant joining a third party in an action and seeking contribution or indemnity

tort – a civil wrong for which the remedy is a common law action for damages

trial bundles – agreed documents to be produced at trial by all parties

tribunal – a body appointed to adjudicate or arbitrate on a disputed matter, which could consist of one or more arbitrators

volenti non fit injuria – a defence in civil proceedings: 'the plaintiff brought it upon himself'

White Book, The – contains the Rules of the Supreme Court and notes thereon

without prejudice – proposals made with a view to settlement and which are not later to be admitted as evidence if unaccepted (save, possibly, as to costs)

witness – a person who makes a sworn (or affirmed) statement to a court on a question of fact

writ of summons – a document issued in the High Court at the request of the plaintiff instituting proceedings and giving the defendant notice of the claim against him

Index

Entries in this index are referenced to paragraph number.